AN ETHIC FOR SURVIVAL

AN ETHIC
FOR SURVIVAL

Adlai Stevenson Speaks
On International Affairs
1936-1965

✸

EDITED WITH INTRODUCTION AND COMMENTARY BY

Michael H. Prosser

Assisted by Lawrence H. Sherlick

William Morrow & Company, Inc.

<small>NEW YORK 1969</small>

To my son, Louis Mark Prosser, that he may come to understand why "it is no wonder that this is the anxious age and that we want an ethic—an ethic for survival" and may come to contribute to this "ethic" as expressed in the life of Adlai E. Stevenson, of whom President John F. Kennedy wrote: "Governor Stevenson raised the level of our national political dialogue. As our representative in the United Nations, he has similarly raised the level of the international political dialogue."

Editor's Preface

SINCE Adlai Stevenson's death on July 14, 1965, more than a dozen books have attested to his continuing reputation as a national and international statesman. His dedication to the advancement of moral principles as a politician and as a diplomat served as the dominant factor in his public life. To him, foreign affairs were always "the most important consideration for the American people." Mrs. Franklin D. Roosevelt called him "Mr. United Nations" and went on to say, "Indeed, our friend, Adlai, has done more to make the United Nations an effective instrument for the development of human rights and world peace than any other living American." Wallace Irwin, Jr., Stevenson's former adviser, has stressed his importance to the world community by stating: "If there had been no United Nations, Stevenson would have created it."

Although as Richard Murphy writes, "The man's best biography is his speeches," no work so portraying him through his public statements has appeared since his death. This volume, then, seeks to fill that void by offering a coherent view of his concerns in the area of international affairs through his speeches from 1936 to 1965. The book was conceived during the summer of 1962, when I spent much time at the United States Mission and at the United Nations in New York and at the Department of State in Washington, D.C., collecting and studying documents relating to Stevenson's speeches on international affairs for my doctoral study. At that time, Ambassador Stevenson provided me with the opportunity to photocopy the bulk of his unpublished volumes of speeches from 1936 to 1961 entitled: "Foreign Affairs Speeches of Adlai E. Stevenson." He also gave me the United States Mission press releases of his addresses and statements from 1961 to 1962. Later, the Mission provided me with the remainder of these releases from 1962 until the time of Ambassador Stevenson's death. While dis-

7

cussing the concept of my proposed edition with him briefly in 1963, Stevenson informed me that an edition of his speeches, *Looking Outward*, was forthcoming. He encouraged me to continue my interest in preparing a more comprehensive volume of his foreign affairs speeches based on the materials he had given me.

In December, 1964, I wrote Mr. Stevenson that I planned to be in New York on December 11 and would like to present him a copy of my completed doctoral dissertation analyzing his speeches in the United Nations. Receiving no reply, I appeared at the United States Mission on the appointed day to find the United Nations engulfed in several of the crises about which Stevenson had written in the introduction to *Looking Outward*. Che Guevara of Cuba was speaking in the General Assembly and was being picketed outside the United Nations; the Congo crisis was being hotly debated in the Security Council, with charges of American aggression being made; and the Foreign Minister of Indonesia was conferring with Secretary of State Rusk at the United States Mission concerning Indonesia's intention to withdraw from the United Nations. After chiding me for selecting the most difficult day perhaps in the United Nations' history, the receptionist called Stevenson's office and told me to wait: "Something might happen." Shortly after, the Prime Minister of Indonesia came down to the lobby and held a press conference, a few feet from me. After he left, Ambassador Stevenson, followed by his Protocol Officer Miss Rosemary Spencer, came into the lobby. Seeing me, Miss Spencer called: "Mr. Prosser, follow me." And follow I did—through a cordon of police—to the Ambassador's waiting limousine. With the wailing of a police escort's sirens we drove across the street to the United Nations as I presented my "autographed" copy of the dissertation to him. His graciousness seemed to suggest that my gift was more important to him at that moment than the crisis soon to face him in the Security Council. As his guest at that meeting, I felt deeply honored to see the dissertation accompany him to the Council table. Fortunately, for all of us there that day, the mortar that some disgruntled Cubans hurled across the East River toward the United Nations missed the Security Council windows and made only a tremendous splash.

Later I learned, much to my chagrin, that the printer had misspelled part of the title on the bound dissertation which I had given to Ambassador Stevenson, making him "Adeli" instead of Adlai. He probably would have been amused by that mistake since he was never, as Herbert Muller writes, "a solemn ass."

On April 14, 1965, Stevenson wrote me:

Dear Mr. Prosser:

Last weekend I looked again at your thesis on my speeches at the United Nations. And again I was overwhelmed with the enormous research you put into it. I am moved, therefore, to send this further word of thanks for telling Stevenson so much about Stevenson's speeches! I hope the time will come soon when I can examine it more carefully, and doubtless profit from your analysis.

And I also look forward to seeing you again when you are in the city.

With so many thanks, and great esteem,

Cordially yours,
(signed) Adlai E. Stevenson

The title of this volume suggests itself from Stevenson's own phrasing in an address at a dinner held in his honor and celebrating the creation of the Stevenson Foundation in the Herbert Lehman Institute of Ethics at the Jewish Theological Seminary of America. Because of his lifetime search for such an ethic, Stevenson's statement is pertinent: "War is no longer rational, we say, yet the response to our mistrust of one another is more lethal weapons. And then to loudly proclaim that we never plan to use them. It is no wonder that this is the anxious age and that we want an ethic— an ethic for survival."

In this volume I have included a representative sampling of the hundreds of Stevenson's speeches on foreign affairs—many of which demonstrate his search for an ethic for survival. The omission of some of his most significant addresses or of his thoughtful consideration of certain critical issues is accountable largely to lack of available space and to an attempt to avoid needless repetition of already published materials. Naturally, some speeches are of such importance that they must be duplicated. Among the fifty speeches and statements that I have chosen, I have maintained absolute fidelity both in exactness to and in completeness of the original Stevenson text, whether found in his unpublished works or in the United States Mission press releases. I have given speeches their titles based on the texts except where titles already exist. Because readers may be interested in the entire development of his thoughts on foreign affairs, I have listed in Appendix C every speech that, to my knowledge, he gave on international affairs. I have also provided, in Appendix B, special treatment for one speech, "A Privilege Abused: 100 Soviet Vetoes," so that readers may see his problems in delivery when the Soviet ambassador sought to destroy the speech's effectiveness and Stevenson was forced to alter the speech considerably as he sat at the Security Council table. I have included, too, the United Nations Memorial tributes to Stevenson. But the best tribute to his memory is of course his own speeches.

While editorial judgments, and thus their responsibility, are entirely mine, my debt of gratitude is naturally large. Ambassador Stevenson's encouragement and provision of essential materials is obviously the single most important factor in preparing such an edition. His son, Adlai III, has also been encouraging. Ambassador Arthur Goldberg has provided me with Stevenson's United States Mission press releases from 1963 until his death. Miss Elinor Green, formerly Public Affairs Officer at the Mission, coordinated my research there during the summer of 1962. Miss Rosemary Spencer, Stevenson's Protocol Officer, and Wallace Irwin, Jr., the former Director of Public Services at the Mission and one of Stevenson's speech writers, were both most helpful. Arnold Michaelis, Producer of "Adlai Stevenson Reports," provided me with verbatim transcripts of these programs. Pierre Fuerst, Director of the United Nations Archives, provided verbatim transcripts of the United Nations proceedings for days on which Stevenson spoke there. Michael Moynahan, the Public Affairs Officer of the Department of State's Bureau of International Organization Affairs, assisted me with my interviews in Washington. Mrs. Franklin D. Roosevelt and Clark Eichelberger, Executive Secretary of the American Association for the United Nations, both gave me generous assistance.

The University of Illinois Research Board, through a grant to

Professor Halbert E. Gulley, made possible my travel, research, and collection of documents in New York City and Washington, D.C., during the summer of 1962. Thanks are due to Professor Gulley, now of Colorado State University, Professor Karl R. Wallace of the University of Illinois, Professor Ray Nadeau of Purdue University, Professor Carroll C. Arnold of Pennsylvania State University, Professor Alfred H. Marks of the State University of New York at New Paltz, and Professor Jane Blankenship of the University of Massachusetts for their long-term encouragement. I am particularly grateful to Professors Stanley D. Travis and Ernest C. Thompson, Jr., and the staff of the Department of Speech Communication at the State University of New York at Buffalo for providing research assistance and typing. Thanks are due to James Landis of William Morrow & Company for his editorial assistance. And thanks, too, to my typist Jeanne M. Getman. I am grateful to my colleagues and students for their candid criticism.

Lawrence H. Sherlick, my research assistant, has shared more than any other single person both my excitement and frustrations in the actual preparation of the manuscript. For him, my thanks are inadequate. Although I am responsible for the selection of materials used in my introduction and footnotes, he has spent several hundred hours researching obscure quotes and persons so that they could be cited properly. He has also updated my bibliography and has assisted me in preparing the index. Through his efforts in my behalf, he has developed his own interest in future research, and has come to know better than most undergraduates do the facilities of the University's Lockwood Library, and its staff—to whom I also offer considerable gratitude.

Finally, my special gratitude is due to my wife, Carol Hogle Prosser, often a straw widow because of Stevenson; to my daughter, Michelle Ann, born while I was writing the first draft of my introduction to the dissertation; to my son, Leo Michael, born while I was writing the final draft of my introduction to the dissertation; and to my son, Louis Mark, born not long after the dissertation was finished, and all too often since fatherless because of Stevenson.

I am reminded of the story Stevenson used to tell of the pregnant lady who sat in the front row during one of his campaign speeches shouting, "Adlai's the man!" Indeed he is, and I am proud to have a small part in helping to continue the Stevenson tradition.

MICHAEL H. PROSSER
February 5, 1968
Adlai Stevenson's Birthday
Buffalo, New York

Contents

Introduction by Michael H. Prosser

ADLAI E. STEVENSON has been extolled frequently as a man of high ethical values. Secretary of State Dean Rusk said in his eulogy at the United Nations: "We sent you our best." Stuart Gerry Brown called him "The Conscience of the Country." Alden Whitman wrote: "The essence of Stevenson's example was that he demonstrated that moral values are relevant to politics. . . . His clear moral insight guided him through the ambiguities and indirections of diplomacy." In his earlier biography, Kenneth Davis said that he was a "prophet in his own country," and in his later biography, he referred to Stevenson's public life as "The Politics of Honor." Herbert J. Muller's book is entitled *Adlai Stevenson: A Study of Values*. Stevenson was variously called: "Man of Honor —Man of Peace," "A Gold Nugget," and "Citizen of the World."

Obviously, Stevenson also had his detractors. His own poignant reference to himself at Oxford University as the "Champion of Lost Causes" reminds us of the sign with which someone struck him in Dallas: "Adlai, Who Elected You?" He pondered whether Truman's "Give 'Em Hell" campaign in 1952 had largely accounted for his overwhelming defeat and whether Truman's switch to Harriman in 1956 had not made his nomination much more difficult to achieve. The bitter Kefauver-Stevenson primary fights in 1956 included Kefauver's expressed surprise that Stevenson would allow "scurrilous attacks" by his campaigners, and Stevenson's charges against Kefauver that his remarks were "distortions," "abuse," and "misrepresentations." In his 1960 nominating speech, Senator Eugene McCarthy reminded the delegates: "He has stood off the guerrilla attacks of his enemies and the sniping attacks of those who should have been his friends." Kennedy referred to him as "my official liar" during the Bay of Pigs crisis. Stevenson's obligation to support Kennedy and Johnson "this side short of treason or madness," the White House "leaks"

17

that made his position on the Cuban missile crisis look foolish if not treasonous, and Johnson's abrupt reversal of decisions on the Dominican Republic that he had made in Stevenson's presence profoundly disturbed him and constantly challenged his sense of ethics. Such problems caused Irving Howe to call the final phase of Stevenson's life "these last sad years" and Eric Sevareid to write about "The Final Troubled Hours of Adlai Stevenson." While it now seems certain that Stevenson would have resigned at the end of 1965, his own sense of patriotic ethics prevented him, I believe, from a protest-resignation that would discredit our national leaders in a time of crisis. If there was a tragic flaw in Stevenson, as several writers suggest, it stemmed from his conscious, and sometimes painful, search for an ethic for survival.

Personally, I prefer to view him basically as a man of joy, as expressed by his constant optimism and usual good humor, with his appropriate sense of balance for serious events as they affected man's relations with man. Much of his search for an ethic is reflected in his public addresses and statements from 1936 to his death, especially when he discussed his overriding interest—international affairs. Although many of his nearly 650 speeches and statements on foreign affairs are routine, many more than the fifty speeches included in this volume are timeless and enduring. His issues were often as universal as man's most fundamental needs: survival of the human race, war and peace, national and international morality, human rights, freedom, the self-determination of peoples, peaceful coexistence, and a uniting world. I have found him rarely self-righteous, although at times he does become indignant, in responding to the Republicans at home or the Communists abroad. A major characteristic of Stevenson's speeches in the United Nations, distinguishing him from other American diplomats, is his frequent digression from a specific issue to its implications for world peace or for the member nations of the world organization. This certain almost prophetic quality, noticeable also in many of his earlier speeches, will make his addresses an important contribution to American and international thought long after his death. He was capable not only of giving timeless speeches, as suggested by his own statement that to be immortal a speech need not be eternal. He also could give immediately timely speeches. His self-deprecating humor made him quip: "Eggheads of the world unite, lest we lose our yolks." His rapier-swift attacks against errant Republicans caused Eisenhower to remark when Stevenson was about to appear on television to concede the 1956 election: "I haven't listened to that fellow yet, and I don't intend to start now." In the United Nations, while he preferred not to answer the Soviets in the same hammer-blow style used by Ambassador Lodge, his "I am prepared to wait for your answer until Hell freezes over" statement to Russian diplomat Zorin in 1962 demonstrates his ability to offer sharp and pointed retorts to reach the focal point of an issue.

An ethical problem that I wish to discuss in this essay faced Stevenson increasingly as he became more famous and overworked. This was the writing of his own speeches. Ernest G. Bormann writes: "In contemporary history only a few statesmen, such as Churchill, Wilson, and Theodore Roosevelt, have had enough faith in their rhetorical skill to withstand, for the most part, the pressure of using ghost-writers. Indeed, so common is the practice today, that the first question a critic of contemporary public address ought to ask himself when he contemplates a research project is the same question the cynical contemporary audience probably asked when they heard the speech, namely, 'I wonder who wrote that for him?' "[1] Stevenson's own dislike of using ghost-writers from early in his public career is expressed by Debs Myers and Ralph Martin:

One reason he insists on writing his own speeches—it's a personal challenge he insists on meeting. Somehow, he seems constitutionally unable to stand on a rostrum and deliver effectively the words someone prepares for him. On occasions when he was terribly pressed for time, he has tried this. It doesn't come off, because it's just not a part of the Stevenson makeup. With him a speech isn't just words—it means something. And Stevenson doesn't want anyone, even his best friends, putting words in his mouth. "When it comes to expressing an idea," he once said, "I have only two bosses—my conscience and my wrist watch."[2]

It seems patently clear to me that Stevenson did write his early speeches—perhaps most of them up to the 1952 campaign. Among the photographic copies that I have of his original unpublished foreign-affairs speeches, alterations in his own handwriting are evident in most of his speeches from his first address in 1936 to his

Crusade for Freedom Luncheon Address on September 19, 1951.
In a speech to the William Allen White Committee in Chicago on
December 16, 1940, he made thirty-one alterations in a two-page
manuscript. Most of the changes were minor—often including
indications of emphasis which he wished to make at various parts of
the speech. In the longer Crusade for Freedom Address, Stevenson
made thirty-six hand-written alterations—again most being minor
stress marks—but several indicating the addition or subtraction of a
dozen words or more. Since Stevenson gave relatively few speeches
on international affairs during his period as Governor of Illinois, he
probably spent more time in preparing them, and his ideas stemmed
from his experiences in helping to create the United Nations and
from his attitudes toward Soviet-American relations. As a relatively inexperienced administrator, no doubt he called upon his
staff in writing his speeches and messages on domestic affairs.
Hermon Dunlap Smith writes that Lloyd Lewis drafted Stevenson's 1948 election victory speech. Probably he assisted him with
others.[3] Still, his biographers relate that because Stevenson felt
himself a failure as a husband, he was determined to prove himself
successful as Governor. For this reason, he spent many extra hours
reading reports and preparing messages and speeches.

During Stevenson's campaign for President, John Steinbeck pondered: "Does Stevenson write his own speeches? I don't know, but
as a writer I know that only one man writes those speeches. There
may be people working on ideas and organization and so forth, but
I am sure that either Stevenson writes every word of the speeches
or some other one man writes every word of them. Individuality is
in every line. I don't think it could be imitated."[4] George Ball
quotes Stevenson as saying during the early summer of 1952: "If I
do have to run, I must run on my own, with no one telling me
what to do or say. I'm going to be myself, and the poor unfortunate electorate will have to take me for what I am. Every word I
write or speak during the campaign must be mine. It must bear my
own imprimatur."[5]

An article in the September 26, 1952, issue of the *U.S. News and
World Report* entitled "Stevenson's Ghost Writers" agrees that
during the campaign "Mostly, the addresses are the Governor's
own product. Often he writes a speech himself from the first draft

onward. Always the final version is his own. . . . Associates say
that the process reflects a man never quite satisfied with what he is
about to say, hoping always to make it a little better." The article
indicates that two groups of men assisted him in writing his
speeches. The first group consisted of "big-name writers, all old
friends, all skilled in political polemics": Samuel I. Rosenman, a
speech writer for Roosevelt and Truman, who provided attacks
against the Republicans; Robert E. Sherwood, the poet and playwright, who offered considerable phraseology; Archibald Mac-
Leish, the poet; and Bernard De Voto, a specialist on the American
West, who was consulted for speeches in the West. The historian
Arthur M. Schlesinger, Jr., served as the link between these four
isolated writers, and the small research staff that he headed for
Stevenson in Springfield. Stevenson's regular staff included: David
E. Bell, a specialist on economics, taxes, and budgets; Willard
Wirtz, an authority on labor-management questions; T. Don
Hyndman, who had assisted Stevenson with his research on a
variety of earlier issues; Robert W. Tufts, his foreign-policy adviser; and Stevenson's top-policy adviser, Carl McGowan.[6] Mc-
Gowan also assisted Stevenson in writing his acceptance speech at
the Nominating Convention in 1952.[7] Despite this aid, evidence
still suggests that during the campaign, the large part of the speech
writing was Stevenson's. Ball writes: "Adlai's insistence upon
working on his speeches to the last minute has become part of the
legend. We used to tell him that 'he would rather write than be
President.' On more than one occasion he completely missed press
coverage by withholding his speeches for further polishing until
after it was too late to make the morning newspapers."[8]

William Attwood was assigned by *Look* to accompany Stevenson on his 1953 world travels to assure the editors that the Governor's eight commissioned articles would reach them on time and in
the correct form. He suggests that no one concerned had any idea
what a nerve-racking experience it would be to get the right words
from Stevenson on time. "I doubt if I ever wrote a paragraph for
Stevenson that he did not manage to make his own by penciling in
some fresh sentence or phrase in his neat but not always legible
script. He had such pride of authorship, such an affection for the
right (for him) sentence, that he inwardly—and sometimes out-

wardly—winced at the mention of anyone being his speech writer; with those of us so described he could be brusque, impatient and argumentative during the agony of editing. It was as if he resented never having the time to do all of his writing himself."[9] Attwood recalls that when he and Stevenson sat down to write the first installment, he soon realized that "the graceful travelogue I was reading would neither grip *Look*'s readers nor boost its circulation. With some trepidation—this was after all a *Stevenson* manuscript, the first I'd ever seen—I began editing, cutting and sharpening the copy . . . until we grudgingly compromised on a final version that reached the cable office with only hours to spare. . . . My wife . . . said later that getting out one of these articles was like childbirth—except that it took longer and happened more often."[10] Almost all of Stevenson's later commissioned articles for a popular magazine were contracted with *Look*, and Attwood continued as his editorial collaborator.

The Governor made 80 Congressional campaign speeches from coast to coast in 1954, more than 150 speeches between November 1955 and the Democratic Convention in 1956, and during the 1956 campaign he gave 242 speeches.[11] Arthur Schlesinger, Jr., and Seymour Harris comment on the writing of his speeches for the 1956 campaign:

Stevenson himself was an unusually skilled writer—better than anyone on his staff. He had long experience in speech writing, including ghost-writing for Secretary of the Navy Frank Knox during the war. . . . As much as possible, he has always written his own speeches. However, no one—not even Alexandre Dumas—could write the number of speeches a modern presidential candidate has to give and at the same time do all the other things a presidential candidate is supposed to do. Nonetheless—as the newspapermen who traveled with Stevenson can testify—he worked intensively over all his speeches, even at times when he might have been better occupied talking with local politicians or making public appearances.[12]

For almost two years before the 1956 campaign, Stevenson and his "hard-core" advisers, including Thomas Finletter, J. K. Galbraith, George W. Ball, Seymour E. Harris, Arthur Schlesinger, Jr., and Willard Wirtz, met to discuss and prepare position papers on almost every conceivable issue. A member of the inner group would present a brief paper on the issue about which a specialist would comment. After an active discussion, in which Stevenson was centrally involved, the position paper was prepared for an issue book, which included the background of the issue, Republican and Democratic positions and records on the issue, Stevenson's past and present position, and recommended methods of treating it. Russel Windes states that "for all of Stevenson's protestations, the burden of preparing and delivering almost 250 speeches in an eight-week period forced him to assemble a speech-writing staff in both campaigns."[13]

Fortunately, through the issue books, the writers had Stevenson's precise views and his quoted statements on all the issues. Wirtz served as the head of the speech staff and Schlesinger, aided considerably by John Bartlow Martin, headed the editorial group. Possibly 100 other persons contributed to his 1956 speeches. In New York City, John Fischer and Charles Bolte headed their own volunteer speech staff of fifty writers who sent Stevenson materials and speeches either at their own initiative or by request from Wirtz or Schlesinger.[14] Although Schlesinger, Martin, or Tufts would initiate the first draft for many speeches, and Wirtz was in charge of rewrites, Stevenson himself would rework the speech line by line, making enough alterations to satisfy himself that the speech "might work out." In examining fifteen reading manuscripts used by Stevenson in the 1956 campaign, Windes discovered 976 alterations that the Governor had made personally. In three of these speeches he made about 125 changes in each speech. Windes asks: "Did Stevenson's speech staff run the campaign or did Stevenson? Whatever may be the case with other candidates, one may well conclude that a speech by Stevenson was a speech of Stevenson."[15]

Mary McGrory writes about Stevenson's twenty-four line statement that he made as he finished his three-week tour with the State Department in 1957: "He had penciled in thirteen corrections and amendments and a whole last paragraph. Like all perfectionists, he was subject to second thoughts, and he took as much time as he could to scrounge for just one word more."[16] William Benton, who accompanied Stevenson on his 1960 Latin-American trip, comments: "I heard him give at least sixty extemporaneous speeches. And he repeated himself only once. . . . When I asked him why he didn't use a good speech a second time, why he didn't repeat himself, he laughed gently, 'Because I can't remember what I said yesterday.' "[17]

William Attwood had sent Stevenson one unsolicited speech during the 1956 campaign, which may have prompted the Governor to invite him to assist him in preparing speech material for the 1960 campaign just in case he should receive the nomination. Attwood writes that Stevenson's backers, George Ball, Tom Finletter, and Senator Monroney hoped that he would develop his first major spring speech in 1960, the Founder's Day Address at the University of Virginia, as a sharp attack against the Republicans. Thereby he would kick off the 1960 campaign as the Democrat's chief spokesman. Attwood comments: "A draft of the speech, written by Professor Julian Boyd, the nation's foremost authority on Jefferson, was a literary and historical gem but lacked any political punch. My revision added plenty of punch, but we didn't know whether Stevenson, then vacationing in the West Indies, would be willing to deliver it before an academic audience."[18] Stevenson, Schlesinger, and Attwood spent long hours hammering out a draft that would satisfy the Governor and his academic audience without sparing Nixon.

During the 1960 Democratic Convention, Attwood wrote a draft for Senator McCarthy's speech nominating Stevenson and then began Stevenson's speech introducing Kennedy to the Convention. Schlesinger completed this address with almost no disagreement by Stevenson. In my own reading of his 1960 campaign speeches for Kennedy, I noticed considerable repetition among speeches and materials from his earlier ones. Attwood, Bill Blair, and Willard Wirtz wrote a few basic speeches for him to deliver, but as Attwood suggests, Stevenson still felt that he was short-changing his audience when he failed to add new material at each rally, even though it received only local publicity. In preparation for a rally in Sacramento, his writers wrote a speech for him that attacked every wild and reckless statement Nixon had ever made. Attwood adds: "Stevenson, who detested Nixon as much as any man in public life, liked it well enough to make only a few changes. . . . Outside, some reporters stopped him. 'Governor,' said a voice in the dark, 'since when have you become Jack Kennedy's hatchet man?' And that was the last time he delivered *that* speech."[19]

When Stevenson assumed his duties as Ambassador Extraordinary and Plenipotentiary, Permanent Representative to the United Nations, and a member of President Kennedy's Cabinet, he received an official staff of more than 100 persons who were specifically assigned to assist him in:

Representing the United States in meetings of United Nations councils, commissions and other bodies; Negotiating and consulting . . . other national delegations in order to find common ground with them and thus to gain majority votes for resolutions which the United States can support; Reporting to Washington on all these activities, especially on the views and intentions of other delegations; Making recommendations to Washington to help in the making of United States policy decisions involving the United Nations.[20]

Since he could not acquaint himself with the details of the more than 1,600 meetings held annually in the United Nations, he was directly aided by Ambassadors Francis T. P. Plimpton, his former law partner, and Charles Yost, a career diplomat, as his Deputy Representatives, and by a number of other officials. Miss Elinor Green called Plimpton and Yost Stevenson's "alter egos" because of their intimate participation in his work and their ability to substitute for him in many functions.[21] The State Department often sent as many as seventy liaison officers and advisers to assist the delegation. When the General Assembly was in session, Stevenson attended from five to twenty meetings weekly at the United Nations. "Those infernal meetings," as I once heard Stevenson call them, were tedious even when there was no speech to make. The wide range of issues discussed in the Plenary Session, its First Committee, and the Security Council forced him and his delegation to acquaint themselves thoroughly with a variety of American and foreign documents crossing his desk daily.

Stevenson's heavy speaking schedule in the United Nations was coupled with his extensive speaking engagements to non-United Nations audiences. Wallace Irwin, Stevenson's speech writer for most of his speeches given outside of the United Nations, suggested that he received 100 first-class invitations for every one which he accepted. Since he normally cast about fifty key votes each session, he was "busy making decisions, or preparing to make decisions, or explaining why he made these decisions. He has found decision-making a most back-breaking part of public life."[22] Stevenson reflected in *Looking Outward*:

The crises are incessant; so is the travel back and forth between New York and Washington; the cables and reports from every quarter of the globe come in daily torrents; so does the mail; the conferences and meetings and politicking are unending; so are the speeches that have to be written, the visitors that have to be seen, and the luncheons, receptions and dinners that have to be attended. And they say I have diplomatic immunity! Add to this the everlasting combat with the Russians and you may understand why there are times when I yearn for the peace and quiet of a political campaign and a rally in Madison Square Garden![23]

Despite the fact that Stevenson "worried and worried over his speeches [at the United Nations],"[24] his dependence upon speech writers increased sharply in his post there. Miss Elinor Green suggested to me: "Stevenson doesn't write any of his own speeches. A speech for United Nations delivery is simply called 'the government speech' and generally can be given by Stevenson or one of his deputies."[25] Wallace Irwin told me: "I consider it a great pity that a man like Stevenson doesn't have time to shape his own ideas. He considers it one of his major disappointments at the United Nations."[26] Michael Moynahan, Public Affairs Officer in the State Department's Bureau of International Affairs, whose office helped prepare or edit all of Stevenson's statements in the United Nations, indicated to me that Stevenson had written totally only three or four of his speeches during his early tenure at the United Nations. He believed that these included most of his 1961 and 1962 statements to the Economic and Social Council in Geneva, given when Stevenson had some time for thoughtful reflection, a speech to the Princeton Club in May, 1961, and a speech to members of the Italian Society for International Organizations in Rome during that summer. Moynahan also thought that Stevenson might have composed most of his address at the Seattle World's Fair in 1962.[27] Irwin himself claimed authorship for this speech except for a segment which Stevenson added on the development of international law.

During Stevenson's first years at his United Nations post, Irwin drafted most of his speeches to non-United Nations audiences plus Stevenson's speeches in the United Nations when he spoke about the Chinese representation question. Often these speeches were prepared by pulling Stevenson statements out of his earlier addresses. He named Stevenson's four major writers at the Mission as Clayton Fritchey, his former Director of Public Relations, Richard Pederson, the Senior Adviser on Political Affairs, Thomas Bartlett and Christopher Thorin, both advisers on Political and Security Affairs. Additionally, Ambassadors Plimpton and Yost occasionally assisted in drafting speeches.[28] At the Department of State, members of a concerned bureau would submit early drafts or later revisions of speeches which Stevenson was to give in the United Nations. For example, the Bureau of Chinese Affairs assisted Irwin in drafting the speeches on the Chinese representation question, and Robert White traveled from Washington to assist in drafting some of Stevenson's speeches on the 1961 Cuban complaint.

As a national political speaker, Stevenson's own desire to serve as a reasoned critic and molder of ideas was often in conflict with his inadequate time to prepare his messages. Now at the United Nations, there were still other priorities. Speechmaking is not the essence of statecraft: it is only a necessary adjunct. On Stevenson's first ABC "Adlai Stevenson Reports" program, his guest, Dean Rusk, commented: "It is not correct to think that the United Nations is a place where debates go on and that negotiations occur somewhere else in some other framework. I dare say that Governor Stevenson spends far more of his time in negotiations—with other delegates than with debates on the floor of the United Nations. These two processes are complementary. . . ." Stevenson responded: "I once said the real business of Congress is conducted in the cloakrooms and much of the business of the United Nations is conducted in the corridors."[29] Sydney D. Bailey, author of *The General Assembly of the United Nations*, writes that the public nature of the United Nations debate tends to expose rather than reconcile differences between nations, as speeches there rarely are given to convince diplomatic opponents by reasoned argument,[30] but to convince third parties, or to appeal to peoples over the heads of their governments, or to win the approval of the public opinion at home, or to ensure that a special point of view is on record.[31] Before agreeing to accept the United Nations post, Stevenson had pondered: "I don't want to be a lawyer arguing a case whether he believes in it or not. I'm not interested in explaining or defending a policy; I want to be involved in the making of that policy."[32] Still, at the United Nations, by the very nature of his position, he became "a puppet speaker speaking to a shadow audience."[33]

Although Robert T. Oliver has called the United Nations commitment to decide issues by open parliamentary methods "the most futile of all diplomatic speech,"[34] the American appeal to public opinion at home and abroad or to official government policy was often reflected in Stevenson's speeches in the United Nations. Thus, a great number of specialists, both at the Mission and at the State Department, *had* to be involved in them. To suggest that Stevenson's speeches were written by committee does not imply his detachment either from the speeches or the issues. In a crisis, such as the Indian attack against Goa in 1961, Stevenson did not receive the hastily written first draft until delivery time. As he was reading the first page to the Council, later pages were being transmitted from Washington to the Mission by telephone, typed at the Mission, and delivered by courier to Stevenson at the Security Council.[35] Still, as in most other speeches in which he was involved in various stages of preparation, he was consulting with his own staff and the principals in the dispute for long hours before the actual speech was given. His preparation of the speech condemning the Soviet misuse of the veto, with the actual problems which he encountered during the speech, is demonstrated in Appendix B. He had to extemporize hundreds of brief responses in exercising his right of reply to charges made by other delegations or in explaining the American vote on a variety of issues. To be cogent, he had to involve himself in the issue at every stage of its development.

An example of the progression of a statement through varied channels before its actual delivery can be seen in the address on the colonialism question. In March of 1961, Stevenson's speech on the Angolan question had implied an apparent change in American

policy toward Africa. Because of certain basic disagreements between Stevenson and his advisers at the Mission and the State Department staff, this speech had been altered by members of several
bureaus, by the Under-Secretaries of State, and by Kennedy's
advisers at the White House. To emphasize further a real policy
change, Stevenson decided that he should give a significant speech
on the colonialism question during the General Debate in the
autumn of 1962. He wanted it to pinpoint the Kennedy policy
toward Africa for years to come.

Stevenson drew up an outline of points he wished covered.
Sydney Hyman, a political scientist from Johns Hopkins University, prepared the initial draft based on Stevenson's outline. Michael Moynahan, who received it for editing, called it brilliant, but
simply not a policy speech. Nevertheless, it was the best draft
available. It was sent to the varied State Department bureaus: those
dealing with African affairs, Western European affairs, and Soviet
affairs. In each of the bureaus it was altered extensively. Finally, it
was returned to the Mission.[36] There, Clayton Fritchey and Wallace Irwin revised it further, attempting to bring it back in line
with what Stevenson had originally requested, without changing
the policy statements inserted in Washington. Stevenson also made
numerous revisions. However, eventually he felt that the speech
had been so weakened by the various State Department Bureaus
that it was now an unacceptable manuscript and no longer reflected his point of view. He gave it to the Mission's fourth-
ranking diplomat, Jonathan Bingham, to deliver. Bingham's presentation of the speech in place of Stevenson, poor attendance by
the African delegations, and scanty press publicity caused his
advisers to label it "an abysmal failure" instead of the diplomatic
triumph that Stevenson had wanted for the Administration.[37]

Apart from his ability to pass off a distasteful speech to one of
his deputies, Stevenson apparently was forced on certain occasions,
such as during the debates on Chinese representation, Vietnam, and
the Dominican Republic, to defend Administration policies with
which he disagreed. As I have indicated, I believe that his sense of
ethics compelled him to defend these policies this side "short of
treason or madness" and precluded his resigning in protest. But,
what of the ethics of having so many of his speeches written for

him, especially at the United Nations, and since he so much disliked ghost-writers? Is a volume relevant that includes some or many "committee speeches" attributed to Stevenson? Ernest G. Bormann, very possibly speaking of Stevenson, writes:

If the audience is to know a candidate through what he speaks and writes, then he must be honest with them and present himself as he really is. When he reads a speech that reveals to his audience a quiet humor, an urbane worldliness, subtle and incisive intellectual equipment, then he should be that kind of man. If his collaborators, one a man of quiet humor, another an urbane worldly man, and the third a man of subtle and incisive intellectual equipment, are responsible for the "image" revealed in the speech, and if the speaker has different qualities and intellectual fiber, the speech is a deceit and it can be labeled as ghostwritten and condemned as unethical.[38]

Just as a variety of authors have defended Stevenson's position in this matter concerning his 1952 and 1956 speeches, his Deputy Representative at the United Nations, Francis T. P. Plimpton, writes:

All of this means that Stevenson's speeches in the UN (locally called statements or interventions) were conglomerates of State Department drafts, USUN and AES objections (sometimes substantive and always stylistic) and redrafts, occasional White House arbitrations of those objections, and eventual hard-fought cease-fires and compromises.

No matter how confused the exact parentage of Stevenson's UN speeches may have been, they invariably bore his stamp of clarity and vividness (often added in the last post-department clearance minute), and they most certainly reached what was for the UN unprecedented heights of reasoned intelligence—just as did his 1952 and 1956 presidential campaign speeches for the United States.[39]

A key premise in Stevenson's speeches in the United Nations was his personal commitment to "make the United Nations successful, to make this great experiment in international collaboration fulfill the dreams of its founders that one day reason would rule and mankind would be liberated from the everlasting scourge of war."[40] Again and again, he would ask: "But what of the implications for the United Nations? Shall the United Nations survive?" In his speeches on the Congo situation Stevenson expressed his intense pride in the United Nations as "the last best hope of us all," "the only elements that stand foursquare against civil and tribal war," and "the only assurance for all of us of peace in the years to come." In his speeches on the Cuban complaint, he remarked: "Each such encroachment on the freedom of these people is a threat to the freedom of all peoples." Such a statement was reminiscent of his speeches in the 1950's about Eastern Europe. Speaking on disarmament, he commented: "For man must escape—not in wishful dreams, but in hard reality. We must escape from this spiral of fear, from the outmoded illusion that lasting security for peoples can be found by balancing out the wildly destructive power in the hands of their governments."[41] These assumptions about the universal brotherhood and interdependence of man, underlying nearly all of his speeches in the United Nations, can be found in similar ways in his speeches of 1956, 1952, 1946, and 1940. Over and over, his biographers, associates, and friends have emphasized that Stevenson was the same man of quiet humor, urbane worldliness, and subtle and incisive intelligence when he died that he had been ten, twenty, and thirty years before.

There is considerable evidence to demonstrate that Stevenson's use of the universal themes of freedom and human survival was unique among the American diplomats at the United Nations. Wallace Irwin pointed to this conclusion when he said to me:

Stevenson has a public personality widely known and that personality constantly reflects itself in the United Nations. Some things which he might often say in a philosophical vein about the United Nations might not be suitable for an ambassador like Lodge or a career diplomat like Yost. When I wrote for Lodge, he was quite different. Lodge was more blunt and clipt, and less given to Stevenson's subtle analytical reasoning which often takes him far afield from the specific issue. Stevenson's viewpoint is more rhetorically sweeping with a wider scope in his thought-range.[42]

Michael Moynahan concurred with this judgment, saying:

The Stevenson ideas are more complicated, more subtle, more far-reaching, than Lodge's ideas. Distinguished writers would find writing for Lodge boring because of his hammer-blow expression of ideas which was right to the point, and writing for Stevenson challenging because of the breadth of ideas which he might include in a single speech. While

Stevenson cannot always mould his own significant ideas into words, he has done the next best thing. He has changed and remoulded the men who frame his ideas.[43]

Several important points seem obvious. For the main part, Stevenson's views about man's relationships with man remained constant throughout his public life. He disliked war as much in 1965 as he did in 1940. His pleas for peace, with honor, were as eloquent in his last speeches as in his first. His ideas about specifics matured, sometimes changed, and occasionally appeared compromised. His dislike for using ghost-writers was passionately intense. Nevertheless, more important priorities compelled him to accept their services at varying points in his career. At the United Nations, he was not always Adlai Stevenson, but more often the symbol of the United States. He had to accept and present "the government speech" with which he could not always agree. Still, by and large, it was Stevenson who listened, who read dispatches, who conducted "corridor diplomacy," who philosophized about the fate of the world organization which he had helped create. It was Stevenson who continued to stamp his own character and imprimatur on what he said and what he wrote. Did his speech writers package him as a quietly humorous, urbane, and intelligent leader? No. These qualities sprang from his own character. Was he an ethical speaker? To be sure. He was, as his citation from Oxford University stated: "amid the strains and stresses of national and international politics, the champion of humanism in word and deed, and himself the source."

Stevenson wrote in *Looking Outward:* "The crises are incessant. . . . It is all worthwhile? Of course it is—if peace is worthwhile. . . . We have constantly to carry on, or rebegin, the work of building the institutions and the practices of a non-violent world, keeping in mind, beyond the setbacks and disappointments, our own vision of a peaceful future for men."[44] Beyond the fact that he had to rely upon speech writers at varied times for specifics, this was his own message. Stevenson was his own man and this statement is characteristic of his own humanism and his lifelong search for an ethic—an ethic for survival.

The Reciprocal Trade Agreement

OCTOBER 23, 1936

✡

Adlai E. Stevenson served as a member of Roosevelt's Agricultural Administration in 1933, and in 1934 as the Assistant General Council for the Alcohol Control Administration. After leaving Washington in 1935, he became a member of the prestigious Chicago law firm of Cutting, Moore, and Sidley. A leader in the Chicago Council on Foreign Relations and in New Deal projects, Stevenson gave a number of speeches for Roosevelt's 1936 Presidential campaign. The speech given at Carleton College, October 23, 1936, received national attention because of his comments on the Reciprocal Trade Agreement sponsored by Roosevelt. Only the conclusion remains.

BUT before I conclude I must advert to one reason why I would feel obliged to vote against Mr. Landon,[1] even if the evidence for Mr. Roosevelt, which I have clumsily reviewed, were less convincing. I am afraid the Republican party has learned little and has again fallen victim to an ancient error; an error acutely distressing to many Republican sympathizers. They are advocating a policy of aloofness, isolation and narrow nationalism. They would abrogate the reciprocal trade agreements:[2] they would make tariffs more prohibitive of foreign trade than ever before. It was the loss of our foreign markets for agricultural surpluses that occasioned the demand for crop control and a planned economy for agriculture. It is the loss of foreign markets for industry that is responsible in large measure for persisting unemployment. But if we don't buy we can't sell, and the best antidote for regimentation and discontent is wholesome international commerce. The reciprocal trade agreements sponsored by President Roosevelt are the first thaw in a

33

frozen world. That way lies hope and peace. The other leads to another economic suicide behind a Smoot-Hawley tariff wall.[3]

In conclusion, let me remind you that conservatives in critical moments are sometimes disturbingly shortsighted. In France they fought a pacific German republic, and got Hitler. In Russia they fought Kerensky and got Lenin.[4] In a world of violence and conflict between extremists, it is not easy to see life steadily and see it whole. But there is a middle road and we are on it. I hope we stay there.

I Am a Zionist!

JANUARY 31, 1940

✡

On January 29, 1940, President of the World Zionist Organization Dr. Chaim Weizmann—who had been responsible for bringing about Britain's Balfour Declaration in 1917 favoring the establishment in Palestine of a national Jewish homeland—addressed the Chicago Council on Foreign Relations. As an active leader in the Council, Stevenson heard Weizmann's speech and two days later spoke at the Zionist Mass Meeting in Chicago. As would be the case in many of his later speeches, Stevenson here coupled humor with seriousness of purpose. Nevertheless, looking back at his early speeches, Stevenson recalled, "I was scared to death when I spoke. I still am for that matter."[5]

I MUST confess at the outset that I hardly know why I am here, and I suspect that before I have finished my brief remarks, you will wish I wasn't here. I am not a Zionist and I am not distinguished in any way, but I am a practicing lawyer in Cook County and when your friend and my friend, Judge Harry Fisher,[6] suggests that I do something, I generally find it convenient to do it with alacrity! Moreover, I must admit that to have a part in this meeting is the most flattering thing that ever happened to me. Though, if I had foreseen my terror at this moment, Judge Fisher would have had to lock me up for contempt of court before I could get across the state line!

I said I was not a Zionist. I am a Gentile and what is worse, I am a Scotch Presbyterian—on my father's side. But on my mother's side I am a Unitarian. I shall never forget a conversation between my devout and aggressive grandparents. The Unitarian said acidly that the Scotch Presbyterians kept the Ten Commandments and

35

everything else they could lay their hands on. The Scotch Presbyterian replied that he had made some study of the Unitarian faith and would be obliged if the Unitarian could enlighten him as to how it differed essentially from the Jewish! So I guess I cannot claim to be a religious purebred.

But I don't see why the Jews are so exclusive about their Zionism and in so far as it represents the aspiration for a national home, I am a Zionist; and you will have to accept me, gentlemen, even if you do not like to be adulterated with crossbred Protestants!

I said that to be here tonight was the most flattering thing that ever happened to me. I do not need to tell you why. Like everyone that has followed world events since the last war, I have known something of Dr. Weizmann and his heroic work. Day before yesterday I saw and heard him for the first time at the Council on Foreign Relations—I saw and heard a great man! And for a moment I lost his words and thought of the quality of great leadership —of enduring greatness. I thought of an indomitable will to gain a great objective—not by hate, not by bigotry, not by ignorance, enslavement, brutality and blood, but by compromise and peace. Here, I thought, is no conqueror; here is a creator! Here is the imperishable quality of great historical leadership.

And just then I emerged from my reverie to marvel again at his tolerant understanding. With the humble, earthy good humor of many great men, he complained not of his adversaries, not of the Arabs and the British, but of the type of Jew who, as he put it, is delighted to get a seat in a crowded street car and even more delighted that you haven't got one! And then I lapsed into another reverie and thought of the afternoon in May last spring when I slipped into the galleries of the House of Commons to find the place packed, hushed, and tense. The Colonial Secretary [Malcolm MacDonald] was presenting the White Paper on Palestine and gently but firmly reclaiming the seat in the crowded street car of the world which Lord Balfour [author of the Balfour Declaration] had promised the Jews twenty-odd years ago.[7] I stayed until Parliament adjourned and I went back the next day and the next and I heard the plan attacked and damned from every quarter of the House; I heard an eloquent, courageous and moving appeal for the

Arabs, and I heard the name of Dr. Weizmann mentioned by
everyone with something more than respect! And I never envied a
man his job less than Malcolm MacDonald, the Colonial Secretary.
Britain in that conflict of interest reminded me of that charming
line in *The Beggar's Opera* when the girl, beset by two suitors,
laments: "How happy I would be t'were either dear charmer
away"—or more appropriately to our scheme of things, how
nations, like politicians, sometimes find too many promises embar-
rassing. But I felt, as an ignorant, inexperienced outsider, that the
heart of Britain was not perfidious, that for manifest reasons everything had not been said in the House of Commons and that with
the world rushing to the crisis the Moslem East must be tranquil.

What was the crisis in May is now the war which is gradually
creeping over Europe. Things must get worse before they get
better and it may well be, as many have foreseen, that before the
fury has spent itself, the fire of hate and fear and intolerance will
engulf the Catholics and other groups as well as the Jews. Perhaps
even we here in America are in for a period which will test our
restraint and fidelity to our ancient ideals of tolerance and civil
liberty on which the precious democratic tradition rests. At least
one detects unpleasantly familiar symptoms—the restless unemployed, growing anti-Semitism, red scares, intolerance and a quick-
ening nationalist feeling—all in the name of Americanism.

But I cannot help but feel that the civilization of our times is
destined to survive the present challenge; that the basis for this
wave of oppression, bitterness and bloodshed is insufficient to support it long enough to wreck our world. A demoniac ambition for
world mastery sustained by a loyalty which is bred of falsehood
and force cannot, I believe, ultimately prevail. You remember the
old wisecrack—that God gave Germany three gifts: intelligence,
honesty and national socialism, provided that they could not use
more than two of them at the same time!

So, as long as prophecy is free and I am not running for public
office, I foresee that the garden the Jews have wrested from the
wasted sands of Palestine must and will flourish; and in large part
because inscrutable Providence has given them a great leader in this
dreadful hour of trial. And perhaps some time when the Hebrew

scholars and scribes of latter days continue the chronicle of their imperishable race, they will find an illumined page for the man who, after 2,000 years of troubled wandering, led them back to their promised land—led them back with an example and an ancient admonition: "To do justice and to love kindness and to walk humbly with thy God."

No American Wants War!

JULY 14, 1940

✿

At the 1940 Democratic National Convention, Stevenson wrote the Party's plank on foreign affairs, which follows. His statement on July 14, "Our soldiers shall fight only for our defense and not in Europe," won wide acceptance from Party leaders. While he became very active in his efforts to assist the British in winning the war, none of his preserved prewar speeches actually advocated that the Americans themselves should enter it. Nonetheless, the Chicago Tribune *frequently denounced Stevenson as a "warmonger."*

THE Democratic party reaffirms its faith in the principles of individual freedom, equal justice and the dignity of man on which our nation was founded and has endured the envy of the world. We believe that peace is the only assurance of the preservation of these principles. We pledge ourselves anew, therefore, to furtherance of the Democratic party's traditional and constant effort to prevent war and to organize peace by cooperation with all nations similarly disposed; we applaud and reaffirm our faith in the good-neighbor policy in our international relations.

We believe that influences in the world which exalt force and deny the validity of the democratic principles, on which our government and our way of life depend, endanger not only the liberties of free peoples, but also the standard of living and the prosperity of the American people. We must, therefore, and we do, recognize that in a world so constituted preparedness is the path to peace. Mindful of the sacrifices by all the people which such a program entails, we dedicate ourselves to the immediate organization and building of an invincible defense on land and sea

39

and in the air—a defense adequate not only for our own territory but also to discharge if necessary our historical responsibilities.

We believe that no American *wants* war; we believe that the Democratic party expresses a unanimous national sentiment in declaring unequivocally, as we do, that our armed forces shall not be used for aggression anywhere, and that our soldiers shall fight only for our defense and not in Europe.

We recognize that qualified opinion may differ as to our true defense; we recognize that the freedom, security and prosperity of our people is closely associated with the fortunes of those nations that are fighting for their survival. Moreover, it has not been the historical role of the United States to view with indifference the tyrannical subjugation and suppression of freedom. Hence we believe that it is compatible with our traditions and in our manifest national interest to extend to Great Britain in this hour of peril to her democracy and to ours all possible material aid and comfort.

Finally, we believe it is the part of forthright leadership not to minimize the menace to our country, our civil liberties and the economic order on which our civilization rests in the triumph of aggressive force. What lies ahead is obscure. America must meet it with unity, conviction and courage!

Aid to Britain Will Keep America Out of War

OCTOBER 4, 1940

✡

In the winter of 1939–1940, Stevenson and other Council on Foreign Relations members joined in forming a national organization called the Committee to Defend America by Aiding the Allies, also named the William Allen White Committee for its founder, the editor of the Emporia (Kansas) Gazette. Stevenson gave two important speeches late in 1940 on this subject, the one below to the League of Women Voters in Chicago on October 4, and another to the Chicago William Allen White Committee, which he headed, on December 16. Stuart Gerry Brown writes that because of his increased pleas for American aid to Britain and France "the isolationists became abusive. The Chicago Tribune *began to carry editorial attacks on Stevenson personally. He was a 'warmonger,' a 'bloodthirsty Anglophile,' etc. His Committee, said the McCormick paper and the broadside literature of the America First Committee, was selling the United States down the river in the interests of a foreign power."[8] Stevenson's speech to the League was an eloquent argument for "all possible aid short of war—and, if you will, even at the risk of war."*

I APOLOGIZE for using a hastily prepared manuscript—but the League of Women Voters does not have a good reputation among careless, extemporaneous ad-libbers.[9]

Much as I dislike to contradict the omniscient *Chicago Tribune* or Mr. Judson,[10] I must, at the outset, challenge the constant imputation of a dishonest motive to the Committee to Defend America by Aiding the Allies. It is *not* trying to get us into war by the back door, the front door or even the cellar door. Although 17

41

per cent of the people favor immediate participation in the war, the White Committee does not. On the contrary it confidently believes that aid to Britain is best calculated to keep us out of war. It believes, in short, that the best way, the only way, to keep America out of war is to keep the war out of America—be it military or economic war.[11]

I am going to tell you as briefly and simply as I can why I favor all possible aid to Britain short of war; why, according to the most recent poll, a majority of all Americans support the principal objective of the Committee to Defend America by Aiding the Allies— all possible aid short of war—and, if you will, even at the risk of war.

Why do I believe in this program; why do both candidates for the Presidency;[12] why does almost every scholar with distinguished qualifications in the field of international relations who has publicly expressed an opinion; and why do more than *half* the American people favor this program?

The answer is that they believe:

1. That Hitler is a menace to the United States;
2. That Britain is resisting that menace; and—
3. That, therefore, in helping Britain the United States is helping itself.

These propositions seem simple and self-evident, but you have just heard a contrary point of view expressed by another American whose motives are certainly as good as mine and who, like many other citizens of unimpeachable patriotism, believe that our mutual purpose of preserving our institutions and economy intact as long as possible can best be served by either no aid to Britain whatever, or no aid except private aid. To determine which of these two points of view is correct one must examine the assumptions underlying them.

We think that Hitler is a menace to us. The record is clear. You can *never* believe Hitler when he says anything reassuring; but his record for fulfillment of what we thought were fantastic, chauvinistic threats is fearful! A world revolution started in 1914 and is still going on. Its objective is *world domination,* and there is no secret about it. The superior race heresy did not start with the Versailles Treaty.[13] It has been going on for three generations. In

1868 Professor Lasson,[14] of the University of Berlin, said that the state could reach the full fruition of its destiny only through the destruction of other states. In 1895 a German wrote: "Germans alone will govern. . . . Let no man say every people has a right to existence. They may live only as long as they do not stand in the way of a mightier one. If they stand in our way to spare them would be folly." Bismarck labeled the Monroe Doctrine as an international impertinence.[15] A member of the German Center party,[16] in 1897, said that the task of the new German navy would be to *end* the Monroe Doctrine. Thereafter, surveys were made of the American coastline and much was written about the prospects for successful invasion. In 1900 von Schlieffen,[17] of whom you have heard so much, was indignant not because the von Edelsheim plan for conquest of the United States was *prepared* but because it was *published*.[18] The Kaiser told King Edward that the German navy was aimed not at England but at the United States. Early in this century Theodore Roosevelt, writing to Senator Lodge, said that Germany was "the only power which may be a menace to us in anything like the immediate future."[19] It serves no purpose to multiply quotations. As recently as 1938 the *New York Times* published a report of a survey made by German engineers, naval and air officers of Anticosti Island at the mouth of the Gulf of St. Lawrence.

But let us see what the dictators have said more recently. Mussolini has frequently expressed his contempt for democracy. His favorite metaphor is something about Fascism trampling on the putrid corpse of individual freedom; and more recently, speaking of the aims of the Axis, he said that the pluto-democracies must and should be destroyed. Which democracy was and is the most "pluto"?

Rauschning quotes Hitler as saying:

The present government of the United States . . . is the last disgusting death-rattle of a corrupt and outworn system which is a blot on the history of this people. Since the Civil War . . . the Americans have been in a condition of political and popular decay.

We shall soon have storm troopers in America. We shall train our youth. We shall have men which degenerate Yankeedom will not be able to challenge. National Socialism is destined to liberate the American people from their ruling clique and give them back the means of becoming a great nation.

I shall undertake this task simultaneously with the restoration of Germany to her leading position in America. . . . The German component of the American people will be the source of its political and mental resurrection.

I guarantee that at the right moment a new America will exist as our strongest supporter when we are ready to take the stride into overseas space. We have the means of awakening this nation in good time. There will be no new Wilson arising to stir up America against us.[20]

And Hitler *wrote* these words, of dreadful and prophetic accuracy, in *Mein Kampf:* "Each country will imagine that it alone will escape. I shall not even need to destroy them one by one. Selfishness and lack of foresight will prevent each fighting until it is too late."[21] Rauschning adds,

In the Nationalist Socialist view the political situation in America is unstable and can be developed into an outright revolution; to do this is both a tactic aim of National Socialists, in order to hold America aloof from Europe, and a political one, in order to bring both North and South America into the new order. National Socialism is preparing to occupy the key possessions for colonial domination; for domination of the great sea routes, and for domination of America and the Pacific.[22]

Yes, I believe Hitler *is* a menace, though perhaps the destroyer trade for British bases in the Atlantic has, at least in part, forestalled this last mentioned intention.[23] And I remind you that the isolationists in and out of Congress opposed the destroyer deal— including, I believe, General Johnson,[24] the first radio sponsor for Mr. Judson's America First Committee. In this connection I must add that it is now abundantly clear that if the Embargo Act had not been repealed last November,[25] six months after the President asked for it, Britain might have been defeated already. The isolationists vigorously opposed *that* also.

But perhaps the *Tribune* is right and I am just a "cookie-pusher," a "warmonger," and a "professional bleeding heart" to believe any of these boastful things that the dictators say. But I do believe them. I do believe that if Britain and her navy fall, somewhere, sometime, we cannot escape a frontal impact with the triumphant National Socialists.[26] I do not think that the centrifugal dynamism of dictatorship *can* stop, even if it wanted to. *I do not think there are any limits to Hitler's ambition short of world conquest, just as there were no limits to the ambitions of Napoleon, Caesar, and Alexander. I do not think a world that has obliterated time and space can exist half slave and half free.* I do not think that tyranny in four-fifths of the world and freedom in one-fifth can endure.

But you will say these are mere surmises, and General Wood and others have confidently assured us that the British fleet cannot be destroyed,[27] though in the same breath they seem to admit the possibility because they propose an impregnable defense for America and endorse the appropriation of more than $12 billion in a single session of Congress to commence militarization of this country and the building of a two-ocean navy; which can only be necessary if Britain *is* defeated. Some of us who never shared the pathetic faith in the Maginot Line feel the same about the British navy.[28] We do not think it will surrender, but we *cannot* be sure. We know that Britain confronts a mighty drive on Suez, on Haifa, and the Near East oil fields and on Gibraltar. The Mediterranean may be closed. The battle of Britain is not yet over. With Europe and North Africa consolidated Britain may yet be defeated, and how can we be sure that the British fleet will not follow the French. Threats of brutal reprisal and extermination of the families of soldiers and sailors is an ancient device. It has worked before. It may work again. If the opportunity comes no one can seriously believe that humane considerations will deter the author of concentration camps, pogroms and Polish slavery from trying it.

In short, with the multiple lessons of the past so fresh, we must not let overconfidence and complacency suddenly confront us with the horrifying spectacle of a Nazi Britain. A year ago few of us foresaw a Nazi France. I'm sure Mr. Judson didn't. Responsible men are constantly reminding us in General MacArthur's tragic words, "too little and too late"; that if we don't help Britain enough we may have to *fight* Britain, as well as Germany, Italy and Japan.

Another assumption that deserves scrutiny is that even if Britain falls we are in no danger of attack, that German difficulty with the English Channel multiplied 100 times is the short answer; that when this phase is over Germany will be exhausted, her allies even more so, and all this talk of possible invasion is "fantastic hysteria" —to borrow General Wood's words and "impossible" in Mr. Judson's. If it is fantastic hysteria, then it is even more fantastic to be spending $12 billion to merely *commence* preparation for the defense of this continent and this hemisphere against such an attack. There is something tragically inconsistent about all this.

But the paradox is easily explained; for *if* Britain falls the Axis' naval power will at once outclass us, and if the British fleet falls into their hands—as the French navy has in part, and would have in whole had it not been for Britain's decisive action—they will outclass us 2 to 1, and in addition to that they will have naval shipbuilding facilities exceeding ours from 5 to 8 times! Will they stand by like good sportsmen and give us the necessary five years to double our naval strength? *Of course* a successful invasion requires bases but the answer to bases is sea power, and there is, as I have said, a real possibility of predominant Axis sea power if the British navy is surrendered or even destroyed. But, notwithstanding, the isolationists say, to use General Wood's words, "There is absolutely *no* danger of an invasion of the United States even if Germany is completely victorious."[29]

I am disposed to agree that an immediate invasion of our continental area is quite unlikely. But how about South America and our outposts where we would be as far from home as they are? It is only 1600 miles from Africa to the bulge of Brazil; it is 3400 miles from the United States. And General Wood also says, "I would unhesitatingly throw everything we have into a war to defend the North American continent and part, if not all, of the South American continent." Now consider this problem of hemisphere defense a moment. With our fleet divided in the Atlantic and the Pacific, with Japan pressing from the west and superior naval forces from the east, with the Panama Canal threatened from both sides, and perhaps from Nazi air fields in Latin America; with no absolute certainty that Canada will not follow the mother country into the Nazi orbit; with no certainty that Hitler cannot do what Napoleon III did in Mexico and do it better;[30] with no certainty that there will be time to get ready to defend *ourselves*, let alone the Monroe Doctrine, I cannot share their confidence that military danger can be dismissed. Two million Americans crossed the same ocean in 1918; perhaps Germans and Italians can cross it too. At all events we are, with almost undivided national approval, preparing feverishly against that very possibility. And every day that Britain holds out on the island and in the Mediterranean gives us that much more time to get ready. Furthermore, I have yet to hear any military expert say that partial defense of South America is practical. Maybe it is, but when the time comes I suspect that we will try to defend all or none of it. Let us not forget, moreover, that the coastline of this hemisphere is 43,000 miles; that there are some 3 million Germans in Brazil, Uruguay, the Argentine;[31] that the cultural affinities of South America are European; that the percentage of literacy is not high; and that the mass of the people share but little of our heritage of individual liberty and democracy.

But let us adopt the assumption that there is *no* military threat to this hemisphere. The export trade of South America outside the United States was one and a quarter billion dollars in 1937 and vital to the economy of Chile, Argentina, Uruguay and Brazil. If the British blockade is broken and these countries want to trade with Hitler's Europe, as they must, what are we going to do? If we permit it, have you any doubt that Nazi political control will follow Nazi economic control attained by the barter system? Suppose we decide that we will have to wage economic war to defend the Monroe Doctrine which we have considered essential to our security for 100 years. How can we do it? We can buy up their export surpluses. That will cost us about a billion a year, which can be added to our own foreign-trade loss outside the American continent of three-quarters of a billion. What will our farmers say about buying all this wheat?[32] If this war ends in a stalemate with the domination of all Europe, Hitler will still lack four essential raw materials—petroleum, grain, cotton and copper. But if he subjugates the Near East, the petroleum shortage is eliminated; if the Axis squeezes Britain out of the Mediterranean and takes Africa, the copper shortage is eliminated. Africa and a reluctant Russia will in time fill the grain and cotton shortages. With this prospect do you doubt for a moment that South America, producing surpluses that we can't use and won't buy, will not be begging to trade with Europe? Of course she will, and probably we will, too!

And that brings me to the most important reason for supporting Britain. Have the dictators still another weapon? I think so. I refer to the dislocations and *readjustments that we will suffer in this country as the result of a Hitler victory*. If the Nazi system is a menace to our way of life, it is a menace after, as well as before, the killing stops in Europe. *So what will our military expenditures have to be? Possibly one-quarter of our national income*. Will we be economically blockaded? Will we have to ration strategic materials like rubber and tin? Will Germany reverse the tables and will we be forced to develop substitutes at great cost and inconvenience? Will conscription become permanent? After 150 years of blessed peace will we become an armed camp like Europe? What happens to our civil liberties? Much is being written and said on that score and it is not reassuring. I have already suggested some of the problems that will arise in preventing Nazi economic penetration in South America. Walther Funk, the Reichsminister of Economics,[33] tells us that Germany will organize the economy of all Europe on a continental monopoly basis, and insolently adds that it will not deal with any other unit similarly organized. How can our individual competitive system compete economically with totalitarian Europe on one side and totalitarian Asia on the other? What happens to the little independent [owner] in a chain store town? Will we be able to sell outside Canada and the Caribbean precisely what the masters want us to and no more? After their temporary deficiencies are satisfied *we* will still have to get many important raw materials from the totalitarian monopolists. On whose terms—theirs or ours? To wage economic war against not merely government but continental monopoly will we have to adopt similar controls? Will all our foreign trade inevitably pass under government control, or perhaps, "pass out"? What happens to the standard of living as foreign-trade contracts and more and more production goes not into goods, but arms? What has happened to the standard of living in Germany in the seven years of her great effort for guns instead of butter? And how will we make our arms pay dividends as she has? How do we finance coincident arms expansion and trade contraction? How much debt can we stand before inflation and repudiation begin?—And when in this process will we begin to hear demands for "a strong man"? When will people begin to ask, "Can't we get along with this new order in Europe, in Asia?" When will someone suggest a halt to the defense spending? And will others say, "No, we can't play with Hitler and survive"? In a two-party system will one inevitably become the party of appeasement? Where then is our unity, our faith in the American way of life, our passion for freedom, truth and justice?

Pragmatism is central to our philosophy: we believe in what works. The derogation of values which has characterized the age of applied science and industrial society has established performance as the criterion. The values of American life have, I'm afraid, only a modified appeal to many people in various groups: pragmatic industry, cynical youth, those to whom property outranks principle, and, conversely, the unemployed. Combine the prestige of Nazi technique, and how many of these people will conclude that Nazi society cannot be so bad after all?

Frankly, if Britain falls, it is the development of this tolerant attitude nourished by economic pressures and the Fifth Column from within (and one can detect signs of it already),[34] that concerns me most.

I think this is the most critical moment in our history. I think we are witnessing a death-struggle for control of the Western world, a death-struggle between our traditions and pagan traditions never disciplined by the Roman Empire in the West or Christendom in the East. It is only as we believe the Western tradition worth preserving, *at any price*, that we will as a nation have the counter-dynamic required to meet and defend the Nazi outthrust if Britain falls. Division, cupidity and treachery are Hitler's deadliest weapons. He has said so! He may be right. We cannot be sure that the economic and social controls which must follow British collapse will not themselves ultimately betray us. We cannot be sure that in trying to save freedom we will not embrace slavery, either in or out of war.

I have attempted to suggest the shape of things to come and why Britain plays a strategic role in our defense, both military and economic—why if Britain falls we face incalculable dangers from within and without—why there is everything to gain and little to lose by helping Britain to stop Hitler now! I have said nothing

about our racial and lingual heritage, our common traditions, our
100 years of peace and prosperity and unarmed security, thanks to
the British navy. Nor have I mentioned the moral effect of American aid on the British Dominions against the day when we may
desperately need friends. I have in short said why, in America's self-
interest alone, we should help Britain; why, if you will, we should
defend America to the last Englishman!

And now in conclusion let me read you some prophetic words of
Winston Churchill to the House of Commons on February 22,
1938—seven months before Munich: "I predict the day will come
when at some point or other, on some issue or other, we will have
to make a stand, and I pray God that when that day comes we will
not find that through an unwise policy we are left to make that
stand alone!"[35] We too can pray God that through an unwise
policy we may not be left to suffer or to fight, alone![36]

Mr. Judson's argument is that aid to Britain will surely involve
us in the war and that involvement is to be avoided irrespective of
the consequences of Nazi victory. He makes a distinction, evidently, between aid to Britain by our *government* and aid by our
private industries. Later I will comment on the implication of a
Nazi victory—which Mr. Judson didn't mention at all. But at the
outset I want to refer to this involvement of business and government as contrasted to private aid. Now if it is in our national
interest to give *private* aid, why isn't it in our national interest to
give *government* aid? And if it is *not* in our national interest for the
government to send materials, then it is *not* in our national interests
to permit private industry to do so. There is an artificial line here
that makes no sense to me. Either stopping Hitler at the English
Channel is or is not good for us. (I've yet to hear anyone but a pro-
German say it would be good for us if Britain was destroyed.) If it
is good for us to stop Hitler now, then our only consideration
should be what kind and how much aid can we afford to sell—not
where does the aid come from, government or private manufac-
turers.

*The question is simply, what is the cheapest, surest way to avoid
the incalculable effects of a hostile totalitarian world.* In short,
what is our best defense? The answer is clear—let Britain do it, or
keep *her* fighting *our* enemy as long as possible so we can get

ready—for we know not what. That means materials, wherever they may come from; government armories or private factories. But to say that arms from one source is fine and another is bad seems to me about on a par with Col. Lindbergh's proposal last fall, that we embargo *off*ensive arms and sell *def*ensive arms.[37]

But evidently the real reason for this curious distinction is that arms from government supplies are more likely to involve us in war than arms from private sources, because that is not unneutral. This danger of involvement in the war seems to me the real reason advanced for not helping Britain. Of course, I think the surest way to keep America out of war is to keep the war out of America, and that if we don't help Britain to stop Hitler now we are sure to become involved later alone and against greater aggregate forces.

But aside from that, I can't understand why aiding Britain will inevitably involve us in the war if we don't want to be in it. It takes two to make a war and I doubt if Germany will sink an American ship and risk the chance of adding our navy and air force to Britain's already formidable defenses. Japan is the better possibility and my guess is that she will wait until Britain falls and we have to withdraw from the Pacific before she does much more poaching.

Or is the reasoning that by aiding Britain we will make Hitler angry and he will mistreat us later in reprisal? Surely everyone knows that Hitler makes war when and where he pleases without regard to previous provocations, *or appeasements*.

The United Nations: Collaboration
Based on National Self-Interest

JUNE 28, 1945

✿

In 1940, President Roosevelt invited Colonel Frank Knox, active with Stevenson in the Council on Foreign Relations and the William Allen White Committee, to become Secretary of the Navy. In May, 1941, Knox asked Stevenson to join him in Washington as his Assistant. Stuart Gerry Brown writes, "Stevenson responded with enthusiastic dedication. He could not, of course, have known it, but his career as a statesman was about to begin."[38] Stevenson traveled to war plants and naval yards in the United States, accompanied Knox on a visit through the whole Pacific theatre of war in 1942, and headed Roosevelt's commission to plan the economic support and postwar revival of Italy in 1943. Although he later disliked having campaign speeches ghosted for himself, Stevenson "wrote most of Knox's public speeches and prepared the Secretary's testimony for him when he was called before committees of the Congress."[39] After Knox's death in 1944, Roosevelt sent Stevenson on an Air Force mission to London and the European theatre of war.

In February, 1945, Stevenson was appointed to assist Secretary of State Stettinius in the preliminary stages of founding the United Nations. Stevenson later wrote that this period was "the most exacting, interesting and in many ways most important interval of my life. After almost four years of preoccupation with war, the satisfaction of having a part in the organized search for the conditions and mechanics of peace completed my circle."[40] He gave many speeches in the Midwest and in England, detailing the events

*surrounding the creation of the United Nations. This first pre-
served speech after 1940 was given to the Chicago Bar Association
on June 28, 1945, two days after he had returned from handling
the American delegation's public relations at the San Francisco
Conference, where the Charter was ratified by representatives of
fifty signatory nations on June 26.*

MR. CHAIRMAN,

I had the good fortune to sit with the American representatives
at the Big Five Meetings in San Francisco where I heard for the
first time Lord Halifax's familiar figure of speech—he said one day,
"Mr. Chairman, I am more than a little impressed with what just
fell from Monsieur Paul-Boncour."[41]

And I, Mr. Chairman, am more than a little impressed with what
just fell from you. Perhaps "depressed" would be better, because I
have neither the talents and qualifications which you suggested,
nor have I the thoughtful, well-prepared speech which this historic
Conference and this distinguished gathering of my fellows at the
Chicago Bar deserve.

Rather I have recorded hastily some desultory thoughts which I
hoped may be of some slight interest to you as background, if you
please, for the Senate's consideration of the Charter of the United
Nations which commenced with Senator Connally's speech this
afternoon,[42] and which will continue with hearings before the
Senate Foreign Relations Committee next week, and thence to
debate on the floor, without interruption we hope.

Speaking of the Senate Foreign Relations Committee, you will
be amused by a fragment of conversation I heard at a party one
night when a French delegate asked Sol Bloom, a member of our
delegation and chairman of the House Foreign Affairs Committee, why in the Senate it was called the Foreign Relations
Committee and in the House it was called the Foreign Affairs Committee. Congressman Bloom replied that it was because the Senate
was too old to have affairs. I'll admit it's an old joke, but I'm not
sure whether the Frenchman laughed or marveled at the sophisticated delicacy of our parliamentary practices.

My primary job was to try to keep the American working press assigned to cover the American delegation informed accurately, promptly, and as fully as possible, consistent with the best interviews of our negotiations and the conduct of the business of the Conference. I was, of course, in constant trouble, with complaints of indiscretion on the one hand and too much discretion on the other. I don't know yet whether my office was a positive menace or not—but certainly when I arrived a couple of weeks after the Conference started, the situation was deplorable both for the press and for the delegates. The delegates were heavily outnumbered and the newspapermen, without other sources of information, pursued them like a cloud of mosquitoes. My wife, who was with me for a few days of that early frenzy, summarized the situation very neatly I thought in [her] verse entitled "San Francisco."[43]

There were, as you know, 50 nations represented at San Francisco by 285 delegates and some 1,450 advisers and technical staff. The accredited representatives of the press, radio, and newsreels numbered 2,600. The office of the Secretary-General included more than 1,000. In all, almost 10,000 people were involved on a full-time basis. The average daily output of printed or mimeographed material by the International Secretariat was 500,000 pages with a high for any one day of 1,700,000. The press filed an average of 150,000 words a day. The *New York Post* printed and sold a daily San Francisco edition, and the *New York Times* published a wire-photo edition, and distributed *gratis* 3,000 copies daily at a cost to the *Times* of about 50¢ a copy. It was a remarkable demonstration of future possibilities in newspaper making.

The Conference was divided into four commissions: one on General Provisions, one on the General Assembly, one on the Security Council, and one on Judicial Organizations. The commissions, in turn, were divided into committees. For example, Commission III on the Security Council had committees on:
 Structure and Procedures,
 Peaceful Settlement,
 Enforcement Arrangements, and
 Regional Agreements—
and, of course, there were many subcommittees of the various committees. The Conference in Plenary Session was the top body, and the Conference was managed by a Steering Committee com-

prising the heads of each delegation, of which the Secretary of State [Stettinius] was chairman. He was also chairman of the Executive Committee of the Steering Committee, which included the chiefs of fourteen delegations and was the working managing body.

The work of debate and drafting was done in the committees and their subcommittees. They reported their work to the commissions for approval, and from the commissions the approved articles went to a Coordinating Committee to coordinate the document as a whole, and thence to the Plenary Session for final approval.

There were interminable debates about procedure and the jurisdiction of various committees and, if you are impressed with the ponderous magnitude of the whole thing, let me ask you also to reflect on the fact that every word spoken in a meeting had to be translated into at least one other language, and frequently two—every English word into French, and every French word into English; and every Spanish or Russian word into both English and French. But translation has its compensations and I suspect many a hot word cooled while the interpreter droned on.

Some of the interpreters were remarkable! (Stories about interpreters—Kaminka and Luchar.)[44]

This, then, was the setting in which fifty nations of different colors, creeds, and cultures met to write a charter for a world organization. The *reason* they met was because in a period of thirty years some 40 million human beings have been killed by the oldest and worst plague we know. The *purpose* for which they met was to write a constitution for an organization through which the nations of the world might work together in their common hope for peace.

Amid the confusion, the babel of tongues, and the complexity of it all, a cynic could well say that the remarkable thing was not that they wrote a better charter than anyone had a right to expect, but that they succeeded in writing a charter at all! They succeeded because it was the common and equal determination of all those who participated in its labors that the Conference *must* reach agreement; that a charter *must* be written—not *a* charter, but the best possible charter on which all could agree.

There was no cynicism, no complacency, and no resignation. The principal delegates knew too well the temper of their peoples; they knew too well the horrors of war; and they knew the meaning for every one of them of that endless, stately procession of ships in and out the Golden Gate. The atmosphere was urgent—patient, but urgent. But they didn't look at the clock at San Francisco, and they *did* look, and looked hard, at every clause and every word. They brought in over 100 amendments to the Dunbarton Oaks proposals,[45] and they discussed, debated, revised, and compromised—and slowly, painfully wrote a document which is at once a declaration of peace by the United Nations and an instrument by which that declaration can take practical effect. They didn't merely ratify what the Big Powers proposed; they performed a great task of creation, and produced a document immeasurably better than the Dunbarton Oaks proposals.

It was an achievement about which history will have much to say, and perhaps it could only have been done in the course of a great war by a generation which has suffered frightfully, and by nations many of whom have lost the best of two succeeding generations.

As a *declaration*, it constitutes a binding agreement by the signatory nations to work together for peaceful ends and to adhere to certain standards of international morality. As a *constitution*, it creates four principal social instruments by which these ends may be achieved in practice and these standards maintained.

What are these instruments?

—a police force continually in operation and continually vigilant;
—a forum in which to discuss, to let the light in, to ventilate;
—a court whose decisions are binding on the parties and all member states;
—and an institute to apply to social and economic problems the knowledge and experience of the world.

These are the fundamental instruments to which free men are accustomed—instruments in the use of which we have become experienced over many generations—instruments which have behind them the impetus and momentum of the long history of democratic institutions.

The preamble, the statement of purposes, and principles of the organization are, I think, clear and as strong as they can be made. But what about these tools to effectuate the purposes, to give them life, vitality, and endurance? Are they adequate? You can say with reason, and it is going to be said in the next few weeks by people who really want a better charter, and, in part, by people who really don't want any charter, that the purposes and principles are fine, but that these instruments, these tools, are incomplete and inadequate and can't do the job. It is going to be said that the Security Council has no weapons of its own; that it can use only what forces the member nations agree to give it. It is going to be said that the General Assembly is only a debating society which can't legislate. It will be said that the World Court can't compel member states to accept its jurisdiction. It may even be said that the Trusteeship system is a fraud because no state is compelled to place any territory under the system.

And all of these things are true! But, before anyone writes it off as a futility, let him always think, first, whether he would have it any other way as to his own country; second, even if he would, what would he think of the chances of ratification; and, finally, whether he would rather not make a start by transplanting into the international world instruments of proven social values, subject to *whatever* limitations, which have behind them a demonstrated usefulness and a historical momentum which mean far more than the precise legal terms by which they are established in their new position.

Take the Economic and Social Council—what can it do? It can initiate studies, make reports and recommendations with respect to international economic, social, cultural, educational, health, and related matters. It can make recommendations for the purpose of promoting respect for and observance of human rights and fundamental freedoms for all, and it can draft conventions and call international conferences. I submit that, if you have an agency operating in a field as close to the lives and direct interests of human beings throughout the world as these fields of interest are and you authorize that agency to make reports and recommendations, call conferences, and draft conventions, you can come out at the far end with a whole body of world opinion and you have something that can roll right up a mountain.

Much was said about the veto—about the necessity for unanimity among the five big powers in taking enforcement action. Many felt that the unanimity requirement would be modified, but *beyond the point of discussion of disputes,* it was recognized that decisions and actions by the Security Council could well lead to major political consequences. In view of their primary responsibility, the permanent members felt they could not be expected, in the present condition of the world, to assume the obligation to act in so serious a matter as the maintenance of international peace and security in consequence of a decision in which they had not concurred.

But even the requirement of unanimity among the permanent members for enforcement action does not invest them with any new rights, and the formula proposed for taking action in the Security Council by a majority of seven, including the permanent members, makes the operation of the Council *less* subject to obstruction than under the League of Nations Council which required complete unanimity of all its members, whether permanent or not.[46]

The League [of Nations] broke up because the great powers were not united, and history may say that the attention directed to the veto at San Francisco was less important than the unanimity of the large powers. Like the great medieval Pope who declared that he was the servant of the servants of God, so the major powers must be the first servants of the common society, for San Francisco was a great effort to tie up the shattered bits of international order under the leadership of the *major* powers in an association of all powers.

In other respects the new Charter marks a long advance from the League.

1. When ratified, it will command the support of all the powers which the League did not.
2. It successfully marries regional arrangements with world organization. The Pan-American security system and the Act of Chapultepec,[47] for example, finds its proper place, not as a substitute but as a buttress of the main edifice.
3. The arrangements for military contingents and for strategic plan-

ning and the disposition of forces are an important advance over the League.

4. The Trusteeship chapter is a landmark in the treatment of dependent territories. They are a sacred trust and the members are bound to protect the peoples from exploitation and to develop self-government and free political institutions.

5. Likewise, the Social and Economic Council sets up a great target and at the same time protects us from interference in our domestic affairs.

But the San Francisco Charter is not only a long advance from the League of Nations, it is also a much more flexible and democratic document than the Dunbarton Oaks proposals—thanks in large measure to the leadership of the American delegation and the very aggressive participation of some of the smaller states—and most of all to the fact that the Big Five were able to compromise and reach agreement on *all major issues*.

I don't have the time, nor have you the patience, to listen to a detailed discussion of some of the major problems on which we had to work out laboriously a common position, like the question of the veto or discussion and consideration of disputes in the Security Council, on which the Soviet Union finally acquiesced in the interest of harmony after a prolonged deadlock. But I do want to point out what I am sure you all knew—that the *disagreements* made the news, not the much wider area of *agreement*.

The Great Powers did not spend their time during these past two months discussing the things on which they *agreed* (like the Dunbarton Oaks proposals themselves, or the twenty-odd four-power amendments which they proposed at the outset). They spent the time discussing the area of *disagreement*, and most of the news reports dealt with the negotiations on these disagreements, thereby creating the impression of endless contention. The result—in spite of the fact that agreement was reached over a vast area and on most everything of importance, in spite of the fact that the Russians and ourselves agreed in this conference far, far more often than we disagreed—the result seems to be, in some quarters at least, dark forebodings, fear, and a widespread feeling that the conference has merely proved how difficult it is going to be for the United States, Great Britain, and France to work with Russia.

It *is* difficult to work with the Russians. I am told it always has been—back to the days of Nicholas I [Czar, 1825–1855], 100 years ago. Their representatives do not have the same latitude ours do. Negotiations have to be interrupted constantly for them to consult their government. You can argue for hours and they don't budge (more often than not because they can't). They are suspicious of the Western states which intervened during the Revolution, which haven't been so cordial until recently, which did little to save the League or stop Germany's rearmament or Mussolini's aggressions, and which have detested and feared their political philosophy. And there are doubtless Russians who dislike and fear capitalism just as we dislike and fear communism; perhaps they even fear the great American democratic tradition which has now emerged from a successful war as the most powerful moral and intellectual force of our time.

And let us not forget that, after a few tentative unsuccessful probings between the wars, it is only now that Russia is emerging from a long isolation because they, like we, know that in the modern world isolation is not strength but weakness.

Russia (and these are personal opinions) will attempt to surround her borders with friendly governments as a defense against the world of capitalism whose motives and power still worry and frighten her. They made it quite clear at San Francisco that they are not going to abandon and weaken those primary alliances, and they want a minimum of outside interference in this zone. But beyond lies the world and, like ourselves, they see in this new organization an instrument through which they can watch and take part in world politics and decisions which might adversely affect their interests. This can be the great information center, *the assay office of world opinion.* Here they can watch trends, help impede anti-Soviet developments, and work with the rest of the world toward conditions that will help them restore and develop their shattered, backward country for which peace and our cooperation is the first essential.

I don't think it requires any blind, slaphappy optimism to conclude that the earnestness with which the Russians approached Dunbarton Oaks and San Francisco is the measure of their sincerity and self-interest in creating and supporting the United Nations organization. But I have no illusions that there will be many years of difficulties, misgivings, and even contentions, which only patience, firmness, and organized reason in the forum of the world can resolve.

Meanwhile, the Charter has been written—a better, more liberal and flexible charter than seemed possible a few months ago—but it is only paper and no better and no worse than the will and intentions of its five major members. Everything depends on the active participation, pacific intentions, and good faith of the Big Five, and particularly the United States, Russia, and Britain. Everything we hope for depends on their collaboration in peace as in war; and I risk the estimate that in the United Nations Organization that collaboration is based on the most solid of all foundations—national self-interest.

UNO Gets Under Way

MARCH 22, 1946

✿

Stevenson's skill in public relations at San Francisco led to his appointment as a delegate to the U.N.'s Preparatory Commission, convening in London in November, 1946. As a delegate to the preliminary Executive Committee meeting there in September, he replaced Stettinius as the American delegation leader and chairman of the executive committee when the Secretary of State grew ill and returned to the United States. Not long after the Preparatory Commission began its work, Stevenson addressed the British-American Forces Dining Club at Nuffield House in London, November 13, 1945. His dominant theme, repeated in many of his United Nations addresses of the 1960's, was "We must choose to live together, or, we must choose not to live" and "Let us begin the world again—together." At the end of the First General Assembly of the United Nations in London, as the senior adviser to the American delegation, he spoke briefly on the British radio, February 15, 1946, expressing American gratitude for the Assembly's choice of the United States as the permanent headquarters for the United Nations. Because he had maintained a neutral position on the site selection, the Chicago Tribune *earlier charged, "It is easy to understand why he does not want the international capital in America. He and his kind profess an interest in foreign affairs only because they wish to get away from America and associate with foreigners, to whom they pay fawning obeisance."[48]*

Stevenson's first speech after returning to the United States, which he gave to the Commercial Club of Chicago, March 9, 1946, is lost. Its title, "Building the UNO," and the speech printed here—which Stevenson himself titled and which he presented to his old friends at the Chicago Council on Foreign Relations on March 22, 1946—suggest that both speeches treated similarly the initial progress of the international organization. In this speech he referred to "the birth of this extraordinary infant"—the United Nations—and to the "tough baby" who surprised the "more cynical midwives" when it "stood up and trudged off the stage amid a chorus of cheers." These remarks call to mind Stevenson's Intro-duction to his Looking Outward: Years of Crisis at the United Nations, *which he published in 1963: "I was one of the jubilant midwives at its birth at San Francisco and one of its anxious nurses during its infancy in London and New York. . . . At a dinner in London during those early days we all made little speeches express-ing satisfaction with 'our baby's' progress. The Soviet Delegate's brief and acid contribution was: 'When does baby get teeth?' "*[49]

I HAVE been away from Chicago for almost five years in govern-ment service—for the last year in the State Department working on the United Nations, and for the last six months masquerading as a diplomat in London as United States Minister and Delegate to the Preparatory Commission, and then as senior adviser to the United States Delegation to the First General Assembly. That should at once disqualify me from speaking here because, like the surgeon, I probably know more about the insides of the patient than I know about the patient.[50] I've been lost among the trees—or perhaps "viscera" would preserve the unhappy metaphor—so long that I've probably lost my perspective. And I have found it difficult to winnow the chaff in which I've been engulfed and find anything worthwhile to tell you that hasn't been far better reported in the press.

You remember the steps that brought the infant to birth in London last month; that brought to birth in the dawn of peace a hope conceived on the darkest days of the war:

First, the Atlantic Charter of Roosevelt and Churchill in August, 1941.[51]

Second, the United Nations declaration of January, 1942, when twenty-six nations united not only to win the war but to prevent further war.[52]

Third, the Moscow Declaration of November, 1943, calling for the establishment at the earliest possible date of an organization for the maintenance of peace and security.[53]

Fourth, the Dunbarton Oaks proposals of October, 1944.

Fifth, the San Francisco conference, and at long last the Charter of the United Nations.

Sixth, the Executive Committee of fourteen nations which met in London from the end of August to the end of October of last year and hung the flesh on the bare bones of the Charter. I presided over the last two weeks of those memorable battles which fixed in broad outline the organizational character of the United Nations for many years to come; and I should like publicly to acknowledge my gratitude to the distinguished delegates who served on that committee for the forbearance and charity with which they treated an inexperienced chairman during those trying days and nights.

Seventh, the Preparatory Commission of fifty nations (Costa Rica was absent) which met in London from the end of November to the end of December and redebated, refined, ratified and in some cases revised the organizational work of the Executive Committee.

Those are the bare prenatal facts. And coincident with this development a series of United Nations conferences has resulted in a group of specialized agencies to deal with specific aspects of the world's needs: Relief and Rehabilitation, Food and Agriculture, the International Bank and the Monetary Fund, Civil Aviation, and Educational, Scientific, and Cultural Cooperation.

Finally came the First General Assembly of the United Nations, which officially solemnized the birth of this extraordinary infant, washed, clothed and baptized it painstakingly and tenderly, and then soundly whipped it with about everything within reach! But the baby was tough and, somewhat to the surprise of the more cynical midwives, it stood up and trudged off the stage amid a chorus of cheers—from a world that has staked everything on its survival.

It was conceived in the din of battle when the peace-loving nations of the world were fighting for their very existence, and it was born and equipped for its mighty mission amid all the stresses and strains which have been the aftermath of this elemental struggle.

It is safe to say that each of these successive steps was in large measure due to the initiative and leadership of the United States. I am confident that when the history of the development and organization of the United Nations is written—whether it ultimately succeeds or fails—we will feel that as a nation we have expiated the sins of failure to support and further the effort to organize the world for peace after the last war. What the future has in store I do not know, whether America will have the courage, the will, the wisdom to meet its destiny, to answer the world's prayers, I do not know. But I do know that this time no one will charge us with failure to do our part and more at every step and in every detail to build the complicated machinery of peace and progress well and quickly. And for my part I am profoundly grateful to the President, to the Secretary of State [James F. Byrnes], and to Mr. Stettinius for the opportunity to share in the development of this grand design.

But it was by no means the United States alone which built the UNO. Britain's participation has been as keen and continuous from the start. The Soviet Union joined in the Moscow Declaration and participated actively and painstakingly in the formulation of the Dunbarton Oaks proposals along with China. At San Francisco and in the subsequent preparatory work in London the middle and many of the smaller states left their enduring impress on the work. The extraordinarily competent and experienced representatives of many of these states, like the Netherlands, Australia, Canada and Mexico, were as zealous as the great powers and often contributed disproportionately to the thoughtfulness of the debates and the quality of the work.

Although some vigorous conflicts of view developed in the Executive Committee phase and the Soviet Delegation, supported by Yugoslavia and Czechoslovakia, was stubbornly uncompromising on a few questions to which they attached major importance, they yielded on many others.

At the conclusion of the Executive Committee's work, I said, "We have had our disagreements in this Committee, just as we had them at San Francisco. But on 90 per cent of our report, including most of the important points, we have agreed unanimously. We shall continue to have our differences. The more we extend the area of *collaboration*, the greater number of differences we have to compose. That's inevitable."

On the whole the Executive Committee was a phenomenal success. It started with a blank sheet of paper the end of August and in two months of tireless work produced complete blueprints and specifications for the United Nations. What I said then about the area of agreement was literally true, but of course what made the news were the fights, the disputes, the small area of disagreement.

In this connection I should like to add that the United States took the position, vigorously supported by the British and others, that as a general rule meetings of the United Nations and all of its subsidiary bodies should be open to the press and the public and that in the exceptional case where private meetings are deemed necessary the decisions should be made in public. This view prevailed and is written into the basic rules of each of the organizations.

To one who believes that mutual confidence is the cornerstone of peace the importance of this principle cannot be exaggerated—for in the last analysis public opinion is the sovereign of us all.

After the Executive Committee phase we allowed a month to intervene for study of its report by the other nations, and then the Preparatory Commission of all the United Nations met on November 24. Its work was divided among eight committees on which each country was represented. The organization of the Preparatory Commission was preceded by the Big Five meetings to see if we could agree on slates of officers and committee chairmen. In London the British were never very keen about Big-Three or Big-Five consultations and agreements, preferring the hazards of open contest and perhaps feeling that Russian intransigence would diminish in public. The Russians on the other hand doubtless felt that some prearrangement was the best way of insuring a fair share of the honors and critical posts for the Soviet Union and Eastern Europe in view of the inferior number of votes they could count upon. The smaller states, or most of them, were expecting leadership from the great powers and looking largely to the United States to get the thing properly organized with the least waste of precious time and with the best reconciliation on the one hand of

the Russian preoccupation with adequate representation and on the
other hand the British and Dominion insistence on personal competence irrespective of country.

I spent a great deal of my time and energy throughout those six
months in tedious and trying negotiations that bore little apparent
relation to the substance of our work. I appreciate that there has
been considerable discussion and not all of it favorable about the so-
called political activities of the United States. But to those of you
who are not familiar with international conferences I cannot exaggerate the incredible expenditure of time on procedure, the sometimes ludicrous complications that develop, and the vital importance of strong, alert and experienced presiding officers.

Nor, on the other hand, can I exaggerate the importance many
attach to suitable recognition of their countries, both for prestige
and practical advantage. And there are always the self-seekers who
want something that sounds important at their foreign office or in
the newspapers back home. We felt, therefore, both to speed up
the work all along the line, to avoid unnecessary friction and
jealousy, and to reconcile as many conflicting interests as possible
that it was worthwhile trying to get the Preparatory Commission
and later the First Assembly organized as efficiently and fairly as
possible.

Patterns and precedents and balances of representations among
the three broad groups—Russia, Britain, and the United States—
are now established. Many people from all over the world have
become better acquainted and in the future, with minor adjustments from time to time, elections and organizations should take
place easily and with but little prearrangement. This time there
were some sixty positions, excluding the fifteen members of the
World Court, to fill with nations or individuals in the General Assembly. This was the start, and the competition for posts and
positions was lively, and also a wholesome evidence of the vitality
of the organization and the interest and importance that the nations
attach to it. Hereafter there will be much fewer offices to fill.

I am not going to belabor you with a recitation of the month's
work of the Preparatory Commission. Its pace was as relentless as
that of the Executive Committee. It was serious and humorless,
enlivened only by incessant cocktail parties and luncheons to

which many of the delegates, including the host himself frequently, could not come because of conflicting committee meetings. I am sure they are a remedial curse of international conferences.

The exertions of the British government to accommodate the conference, the delegates and their staffs in shattered London has never gone unnoticed. It was a remarkable achievement and was duplicated again on a much larger scale for the General Assembly.

The Preparatory Commission was fortunate in the choice of Dr. Zuleta-Angel of Colombia as its President—a forceful, self-confident and experienced man, theretofore virtually unknown in international gatherings.

The Commission resolved some of the conflicts that had carried over from the Executive Committee—and developed several new ones! Perhaps the most vigorous debate related to the location of the permanent headquarters. The position of the United States was one of complete neutrality; we were not seeking the headquarters, but if a majority favored the United States it would be welcome. It was not an easy position to maintain, what with pressure from the proponents of the United States for some indication that we really wanted it, and on the other side pressure of all kinds to vote for Europe and all sorts of inspired stories and rumors that we really didn't want it. Then there were formal invitations from sixty American localities; not to mention representatives of some sixteen cities who came to London to invite the United Nations to come everywhere, from San Francisco to Miami, and finally a Congressional resolution of invitation.

China, Russia, Australia and most of Latin America favored the United States and a new start in the New World. Britain, France, the Dominions, Western Europe and the Arab states fought for Europe and the establishment of the clinic near the patients. The prolonged debate in the Committee was conducted with the utmost candor and vigor, and my perilous posture on the fence became increasingly painful as the fever mounted.

It is well to remember that many saw in this issue the migration of the center of gravity in world affairs to the New World after 2,000 [years] in Europe. Others saw in it the removal of the greatest obstacle to the expansion of Soviet influence over Europe.

Others saw the only hope for the organization in the free and democratic atmosphere of America. Many mentioned in their speeches the importance of American public opinion. There was a general, if not unanimous, feeling that the closer the world's problems were to the American people the better they would understand them and in that understanding was the world's best hope.

When the vote was finally taken and the decision made, I said to the Preparatory Commission and now that I am home I would like to say it again and again: "You have not only conferred a great honor upon the United States, but have entrusted to our government and people a heavy responsibility for the success of the United Nations. Your decision will require from the government and people of the United States an extra measure of that loyalty and devotion to the purposes of the United Nations Charter which is an obligation that rests upon us all."

I hope we can remind ourselves as time goes on that in spite of the antics of some residents of a New York suburb, these people are coming to our shores because our government, our Congress, and our people from coast to coast said they would be welcome; that we have assumed a great responsibility and have a great opportunity to demonstrate to the leaders of the world what our system is and why it has produced incomparable results. I hope we can do it with a dignity, restraint and tolerance befitting a great people whose renown, respect and influence has few historical counterparts.

I don't know what to say about the General Assembly. You know in general what it did. Its five weeks of day and night deliberations were widely reported. It met in thirty-three public plenary sessions under the presidency of the very competent M. Spaak, Foreign Minister of Belgium, and two or more of its nine committees were in session all the time. It called into being the Security Council, the Military Staff Committee, the Economic and Social Council, the International Court of Justice. It elected Trygve Lie, Foreign Minister of Norway, Secretary-General, and did a multitude of other things to complete and formalize the organization of the United Nations.

It has been our intention from the early days of the Executive Committee that this first General Assembly should be primarily organizational and that urgent matters of substance could be handled better after careful preparation at the next General Assembly. However, before the Assembly was even organized it was confronted with several broad problems such as the food crisis, the international control of atomic energy, trade and employment, health and refugees; also, specific political problems such as Spain, Iran and other cases presented to the Security Council. But these unexpectedly hard tests proved how imperatively urgent it was to establish the United Nations as a going concern at the earliest possible moment.

I will make no attempt to review the work of the Assembly. Let me say only that it was dispatched in the committees and the plenary sessions with a resolution, a refreshing frankness and a sober earnestness that augurs well for the future of the most serious of mankind's undertakings.

Canada's withdrawal as a candidate for the Security Council in favor of Australia which was being supported by many of the smaller powers although Canada had the support of the great powers, and New Zealand's withdrawal in favor of Yugoslavia to break a deadlock in the elections for the Economic and Social Council were fine gestures of harmony.

I was also impressed with the atmosphere of relentless realism of the Assembly in contrast to the boundless optimism of the League's birth which was widely proclaimed as the omnipotent organ of universal and perpetual peace. Woodrow Wilson reached a height rarely equaled by mortal man at Paris, but there were no such great figures at London—nor any great generation of Frenchmen like Briand and Clemenceau.[54] It was a striking contrast and, rightly read, perhaps a heartening one. There were no illusions, no slap-happy optimism and no melancholy pessimism; just sober restraint and prayerful anxiety to build well and wisely and enduringly.

The men of London were not happy men released at last from the bondage of war. They had seen too much. They knew too much. They were still at war with suffering, hunger, disease, devastation, political and economic chaos. There was an undertone of terrible urgency. They knew they would be judged harshly; that the peoples of the world were groping among the ruins for something new, something that would work. They knew that what

they were constructing was only a spade; that it was not self-oper-
ating, but that without the spade, without the machinery, there
would be no organized concentration of human aim and effort, of
human will. And I suspect they didn't forget Kant's grim prophecy
that "the world would be the graveyard of the human race."[55]

It was sober business. Looking back across this historic year it
has all been sober, intense business. Less than a year ago we had
nothing but some tentative proposals for an organization and the
war was still going full blast in Europe and Asia. And now the
United Nations is a going concern. The machinery is complete in
almost every detail. It has had a trial spin, a severe road test, and it
worked far better than we had any right to expect.

In retrospect some things stand out that are worth passing mention. First, the healthy independence of the smaller states. The
Russian bloc, including Poland, Yugoslavia and Czechoslovakia, to
be sure, acted as a unit generally. The Latin-American states and
the United States generally saw alike on major issues and matters of
concern to the Western Hemisphere. But the Latins, though conscious of the strategic importance of their twenty votes and of
maintaining their solidarity, did not hesitate to vote their own convictions and split off in different directions on many issues. For
example, for several reasons we supported only three Latin-American judges for the Court. The Latins were dissatisfied and made
some arrangement of their own and elected four and almost
elected five judges.

Western Europe and the Dominions generally went along with
British positions, but by no means always, and Australia in particular more often than not was in the opposite camp—a role initiated
by Dr. Evatt at San Francisco.

The principal preoccupations of the Arab League were, of
course, the Palestine issue and anticolonialism. But in other respects
they were not always a unit.

Throughout it all many of the smaller powers, with the exception of the Russian bloc, have repeatedly and vigorously manifested their independence, have not been afraid to line up one way
or the other, and have invariably accepted adverse decisions in
good spirit. To me the virile independence of the lesser powers, led
by Australia, has been important and encouraging evidence of the

vitality of the organization. Perhaps it has even begun to persuade the Russians that Latin America is not under the thumb of the United States. And after Australia's performance no one any longer hears the old refrain of "six votes for England"!

Many governments find it difficult to furnish sufficient qualified people for these conferences and to man adequately the many committees, commissions and specialized agencies, with the result that many delegations are seriously overworked. We, as in everything else, are far better off in this respect than anyone else. Even the British representatives carry back-breaking loads. I will never cease to marvel at Andrei Gromyko, Soviet Ambassador to the U.S. and my opposite number, and the load he has carried—not just management of his always difficult assignments, but of continuous personal participation in the work in all fields and at all levels.

It is well to remember that for thirty years the Russians have had little contact with the outside world; that this generation has been educated and trained at home for the most part. There are few of an older generation experienced in Western ways to call upon. They can't, like the French, call upon distinguished old men like Paul-Boncour and Léon Blum,[56] to pinch-hit where younger men are not available. Considering their background, their education, their insecurity, the iron discipline, the limited authority, the mistrust, the secrecy, the conflicts of philosophy and their sense of Slav or Soviet mission on earth, it is not so hard to understand why they are so uncompromising, so determined, so tireless, so blunt and so very difficult—nor why we have a long hard job of learning to understand and get along with one another.

Another thing worth passing mention is the matter of Trusteeships under the Charter for the former League of Nations mandates. The Soviet has all along been building up a position as the champion of freedom for the oppressed, dependent, exploited peoples of the world. They took a very active and stubborn interest in the Trusteeship provisions of the Charter at San Francisco. At the last moment in the Executive Committee they refused to accept proposals for formulation of Trusteeship agreements to which everyone had agreed. And in the Preparatory Commission they fought for a strongly worded recommendation calling on the mandatory powers to deliver up their territories promptly, evidently on the assumption that they would stall. But then in the Assembly the nations holding the mandates deflated the whole question by promptly *volunteering* to place their territories under the Trusteeship system.

One more thing: There has been some discussion of the merits and demerits of blunt speech in public which was brought to dramatic focus in the Security Council. Some say it has been a good thing, some disagree and say public arguments of this kind fix positions from which it is awkward for nations to retreat; that if this sort of thing goes on in the Security Council it will only increase tensions and aggravate hostility; that it has devalued the coinage of diplomacy.

In the opinion of the *London Times:*

The trouble lies in the fact that both parties, while sincerely desiring friendship, indulge in words and action which excite the suspicions of the other and are treated by the other as provocative. The only remedy immediately available would be to reduce the occasions of public controversy and to multiply those of direct confidential discussion between leaders of both countries.

M. Spaak was quoted in the press as saying:

The debates in the Security Council have created an entirely new technique and atmosphere of diplomacy. The completely frank public debate of international issues, followed by a vote, followed by general acceptance of the majority decision—nothing like this has ever happened before; certainly not at Geneva. It sets an entirely new precedent. I think it is to the good. The public exposition of their theses by great nations implies the admission that they need the approval of public world opinion. . . . To take recourse to public opinion in diplomacy introduces a new factor that makes for peace.

On balance I think it was generally agreed that the startling candor and vigor of the debates in the Security Council was wholesome—that a new era of open diplomacy has commenced—that the prestige of the United Nations as the town meeting of the world has been established sooner, if more violently, than anyone expected.

This has been a tiresome recitation. I have not mentioned the debates in the Security Council and the dramatic exchanges between Bevin and Vishinsky.[57] I know what you want to hear about is Russia, and not the dry recollections of a machinist about the machine he helped to build.

It is a temptation to say something sensational or make some positive proposals. Everyone is doing it. And each edition of the papers produces a new crop of Russian experts. It seems to me a good time to keep still.

The Security Council meets again on Monday in New York and things will unfold there, at least a little. Meanwhile it may be well to take a more historical and less hysterical view of things, as someone has said.

So with that excuse I'll venture to say only a few things you already know—at the risk of a sharp reduction in the large fee you were doubtless going to give me!

Our list of grievances against Russia is long and getting longer every day—troops in Iran, pressure on Turkey, agitation among the Kurds, stripping of Manchuria and Korea, infiltration in the Middle East, claims in the Mediterranean, domination of Eastern Europe and at the same time violent protest against a Western bloc, delays and intransigence in the peace-treaty negotiations, espionage in Canada, incessant propaganda attacks against Great Britain, and so on.

Why does she do these things? Why does she treat her allies of yesterday this way? Can there be no peace—except on her terms?

Perhaps we should try to look at things the way she does, at her list of grievances against Britain and the United States—although "grievances" is hardly the word: intervention after the last war, open hostility to the Communist system, passivity in the face of the growing menace of Nazi Germany and Fascist Italy, Munich, a suspicion that a Russo-German war would not have brought us all to her side, that we helped her to help Britain and ourselves, and that she bled more and lost more than all the rest of us put together. Then there is the disturbing miracle of our war production, the atom bomb, the vitality of the competing capitalist system, British imperialism, and finally Britain and the United States joined by common language and traditions sitting on friendly territory, great resources and bases that encircle the globe from the eastern shores of the Atlantic to the western shores of the Pacific.

I think we had better face all these Russian concerns squarely and cease beating our breasts with self-righteous indignation.

Perhaps the Soviet rulers are insincere. It's hard to believe they are apprehensive any longer. Perhaps they *want* to rekindle the idea of two worlds—hostile and friendly; perhaps they *want* to cultivate the old suspicions of sinister capitalist encirclement. Certainly the new Five-Year Plans to rebuild and catch up will require iron discipline and public zeal for a long time. Perhaps they have internal problems—conflicts between collaborationists and expansionists, discontent among the returning soldiers who have had a glimpse of living standards further west.

I don't know whether the mistrust is sincere or for propaganda. But there it is. And this is the time to get everything they can—to establish "friendly" governments in their security zones, to expand their political and economic influence and improve their strategic position everywhere. Now, in the hour of confusion, fluidity and realignment which is the aftermath of global war. As the girl said, "A kiss on the wrist feels good, but a diamond bracelet lasts forever."

We must forsake any hope that the Soviet Union is going to lie still and lick her awful wounds. She's not. Peace treaties that reflect her legitimate demands, friendly governments on her frontiers and an effective United Nations Organization should be sufficient security. But evidently they are not and she intends to advance her aims, many of them objectives of the Czars, to the utmost.

What is our policy then? It was stated with unmistakable simplicity and clarity by the Secretary of State [Byrnes] on February 28:

We must get back to conditions of peace. We must liquidate the terrible legacy which war has left us. We must return our armies to their homelands. We must eliminate the breeding grounds of suspicion and fear.

Though the status quo is not sacred and unchangeable, we cannot overlook a unilateral gnawing away at the status quo. The Charter forbids aggression and we cannot allow aggression to be accomplished by coercion or pressure or subterfuge.

We must live by the Charter [and] the United States intends to defend the Charter.[58]

The world's hope is in the United Nations Charter. But the hope for the United Nations depends on the cooperation of the Big Three. And that means that they will act within the letter and the spirit of the Charter; that they will preserve the peace, not threaten it; that they will restrain aggression, not commit it; that they will abide by treaties, not break them; that they will adjust the status quo by negotiation, not intimidation.

Whether Russia will live up to her pledges under the Charter I don't know, but we will soon find out.

Some things are fairly clear. They have cooperated earnestly and energetically in building the United Nations. They like the United States, seem to trust us and want us to like and understand them. They are young, virile, and nationalistic. They want their share—and a share befitting their stature—in everything—and they mean to get it. They are realistic and respect power and prestige. They are victors and want spoils. And, *most of all*, they want a long period of recuperative peace.[59]

There is no one that can deal with them but us. We must be the peace-maker. It is a staggering responsibility, and it falls upon all of us. To succeed—to win their confidence, to justify the faith and hope of the rest of the world:

We must live by the Charter—it's the law.

We must be just and impartial—it will take more than words.

We must be strong—any decline in our power or prestige may be disastrous.

We must be independent—friendly with all and entangled with none.

We must be patient—making peace is harder than making war.[60]

Certainly this is no moment for maudlin optimism about UNO and the peace and progress of the world. Nor is it any moment for irritable pessimism.

After all, there was trouble aplenty after the last war. Civil war in Finland; German Free Corps fighting along the Baltic; Poles and Russians fighting; Lithuanians rowing with Poles; and Poles with Ruthenians and Czechs; Serbs and Croats squabbling; Croats and Italians; Albanians and Greeks; Greeks and Turks—the list seems endless. The Japs getting cocky. The Russians paralyzed by revolution and defeat. The French bled white. The Americans dropping out in impatient disgust, and the French and British endlessly quarreling. German putsches, Bolshevism in Hungary. The French occupying the Ruhr in defiance of Britain. And the Big Three of those days—the United States, France and Britain—were hardly models of collaboration!

Yet in spite of all discord and disunity of view, the world did settle down somewhat. We must give time—the healer—a little chance to do its work. We have another mighty healer now—the United Nations—and we can count on the organized opinion and support of most of the world.

But, in conclusion, let's not think for a moment that when this crisis is past and some political stability has been established that all will be sweetness and light.

On the contrary, there are unmistakable signs that hostilities have broken out again on the ideological front.

The war was just an interlude of mutual attraction for survival. We're back where we started, except that Britain is woefully wounded and the Soviet Union has emerged flushed with victory, a mighty power with a prestige and influence that Lenin only dreamed of, throughout a wretched world astir with new ideas. She's going to contest the leadership of Asia, a large part of Europe, perhaps the whole world.[61]

We are witnessing the twilight of the old imperialism and the dawn of a new imperialism of ideas and propaganda among the miserable masses of the world. Britain and the colonial powers will be the chief targets, but we will not escape.

But I see no reason to be alarmed. We too have emerged from this war with a majestic influence and opportunity. People believe in us and trust us. We have many, many friends in the many mansions of the world.

There have always been competing ideologies. There is room for their system and ours to exist side by side.

We have enough faith in our brand of democracy to risk it in fair contest for man's allegiance with theirs.

But it would be an unequal struggle if we, the United States, defaulted—if we didn't match their dynamism, if we didn't take the leadership that is ours, if we were not willing to pay the price in money, vision and conviction.

For to steal a phrase, the future belongs to him who rightly cares.[62]

[*A brief question-and-answer period followed, in which Stevenson answered one question about international loans being made through the international fund; one question about the role of the president of the Security Council postponing meetings on his own authority; and two questions relating to whether the United Nations members had made any amendments to change the Charter to a Constitution for World Government. His answer to the last questions was that no such efforts to amend the Charter had been offered.*]

Is This Peace or War?

JUNE 11, 1946

✡

This speech to the Chicago Bar Association given on June 11, 1946, was Stevenson's first postwar speech on a subject other than his "specialty: The United Nations." Drawing on his extensive travel in the Soviet Union in 1926, his efforts with the Soviet delegates to build the international organization, and his observations, he expressed his deep concern about the Russian intention to dominate the world economically, militarily, and ideologically, coupled with the American need to seek peaceful coexistence so that both could "avoid mutual suicide." This concern was repeated in his 1958 book Friends and Enemies, *when he asked, "Can we, will we, take the bold and costly measures to avert disaster in this contest?"[63]*

"IS THIS peace or war?"

Peace, some say. War, I say—and I hope this doesn't sound sensational. Because what I have to say is *not* sensational. It isn't even new. It's old stuff.

I submit that we are not at peace; that we are at war with—I'll give you one guess—and that we have been engaged in a global war of ideas with the Soviet Union for many years, except for a period of truce when we both fought Germany and happily—and only in the nick of time—eliminated that dangerous menace to both of us.

That threat was one of those world-dominion aberration intervals which seem periodically to enliven and stain the pages of history, but paradoxically sometimes leave the arts and sciences enriched, and even give men a moment of spiritual rebirth and insight

79

into the corrosive vanities of peaceful civilized life on this particular planet.

That the phenomenon could recur twice in twenty-five years in the same country is something I daresay history will note with interest, and perhaps with little credit to the intelligence of the rest of the nation-states—ours in particular—which did so little to prevent this historical error from happening again.

But to get back. With the Nazi-Fascist madness cured the hard way, the truce was over and the old conflict which began with the Third International was resumed with renewed energy and brighter prospects by the Russians,[64] while, of course, we relaxed and took a grand long terminal leave with the family before getting down to the serious business of earning a living, finding a house and getting a new car.

But we are always late starters. It's gallant, if a little expensive. And then we are always a little impatient with restless, aggressive peoples, and also a little incredulous. Sometimes if they tell us what they are up to—like Hitler did—we even refuse to believe them. We prefer good news and glad tidings, and didn't everyone say there was a bright, brave, new world of peace just beyond the horizon—just behind that shining new edifice—the United Nations?

Well, it's been almost a year now and some things, it seems to me, have begun to take form which we can't blink [at] any longer. It's all been said time and again. Russia believes in her system and we believe in ours. We both believe in peace and security. *We* believe that there is room for both philosophies to exist side by side in a peaceful world. But *Russia* believes that peace and security depend on general acceptance of *her* philosophy; that the way to avoid a conflict which would impede the development of a secure and prosperous Russia is to eliminate philosophical dissent over as large a portion of the globe as possible. It's a sound proposition. It is extending the doctrine of interdependence—the concept of One World—a step further, to One Communist World.

So they took steps to extend their influence and install like-minded governments up to the line of their armies from the Elbe River in Germany,[65] to Trieste on the Adriatic. The southern flank was unprotected. Hence the squeeze on Iran which was complicated by the intervention of the Security Council and which, incidentally, also demonstrated the difficulty of stopping political aggression by a great power in the present state of development of the world organization.

By one means or another Soviet power has been extended since the war began over at least 160 million more human beings. And the end is not yet. There is the Mongolian People's Republic; Northern Korea; Northern China is a battleground; Spain; Greece; claims in the Mediterranean; pressure on Turkey; flirtation with the Arab League; support for the French Communists; Germany is being partitioned; the hated Argentine government of Peron has resumed diplomatic relations; preparations are well advanced for a vigorous campaign among the exploited masses of South America, and, finally, championship of independent movements among dependent colonial peoples.

This is the battleground in the new thirty years' war of ideas. This is the outer zone. The middle zone, the contiguous area, is already well under control. It is well to remember that in Western and Central Europe is a large part of the world's technological and military elite; that in the strategic area of the Middle East are some of the world's most precious resources; that in Asia is a clear majority of the earth's inhabitants and, finally, that these areas and their peoples have all suffered cruelly from the war, are all more or less contiguous to Russian influence and a long way from ours.

At home in Russia, in the inner zone, Stalin has announced a new series of five-year plans to rebuild and develop the country; to establish staggering basic production figures, to raise the appallingly low standard of living. Propaganda and dark hints about the injustice of the Western democracies, about Britain and the U.S. ganging up, about dangers beyond the Iron Curtain and encirclement by a hostile capitalist world is a good antidote for letting down, for that tired, irritable feeling with which we in the West indulge ourselves. The same propaganda techniques preserve discipline and purity of thought at home and malign the motives of the "imperialistic" democracies abroad, without, of course, pointing out that the old imperialism is dead and that predatory capitalism is dying, or that Russia, with the weapons of propaganda and political penetration, is the new imperialist power in the world.

To summarize: the Soviets have capitalized by all the methods of force, coercion, persuasion and stubborn diplomatic negotiation, the confusion and fluidity of the war and postwar period, for all its worth. They have carried the ball into our territory. Almost overnight the power relationship has changed to our disadvantage. Russian control or influence has been extended over a vast area and a vast population. The whole world is conscious of the ferment. We in the United States least of all.

Their heroic war effort, their vigor, their sense of mission, the growth of Communist sentiment among hungry, miserable people amid the ruins of war, have given a few purposeful men in the Kremlin an influence and prestige throughout the world that has few historical counterparts.

And they mean to go right ahead extending their influence; stubbornly insisting on their terms (I wish I was more hopeful that the June 15 meeting of the Foreign Ministers in Paris was going to be more successful),[66] and vigorously selling Soviet thinking, if you please, whenever and wherever they can.

Let there be no mistake. This is a worthy antagonist. Change is the rule of life, and let no one think complacently that because our brand of representation, liberal democracy and individual freedom has been the people's choice for the last 150 years, that it is still in the ascendency.

We've locked horns at last with a mighty force in the everlasting contest for the allegiance of man everywhere. Moreover, if we get some comfort out of a secret conviction that communism (in whatever form it takes at any given place or time) can't stand the pace, that concentrated, ruthless power begets rebellion, that right and virtue always triumph, bear in mind that the Russians are thinking the same thing about us. What's more, they think our sins and extravagances and maudlin liberalism has about caught up with us; that Britain is a pushover, that the U.S. is a dying relic of eighteenth-century nonsense about economic and political freedom—to exploit and starve. Their assumption is that capitalism in America is sick unto death and won't survive another severe economic depression.

So I say again that the contest for man's allegiance between capitalism (or freedom or democracy or the dignity of the individual, or whatever overused words you want to use) and communism has been resumed throughout this shrunken globe. They've started fast with enhanced prestige and great momentum and we've started slowly. But the race is not always to the swift. What concerns me is not so much that we started slowly, as usual, but that a lot of us don't seem to know, or at least don't seem to care, that we are in a contest with a worthy, dynamic, powerful adversary—a missionary with a popular faith, an intolerant missionary who would like to convert the world and scotch all political heresy.

As someone said "with nearly a year of reconversion in back of us, we've done little to convince the hundreds of millions of shoeless spectators of the contest between ourselves and the Russians that ours is a better system. It's about time we started showing our real class."

You know what I mean. We are trying to build up a healthy international trade which is vital to our economy and all economies that believe in private commerce. But we are still debating the British loan.[67]

The Russians and most everyone else respect strength more than pious words. We are the most puissant state in the world. But we have vacillated for a year, while our military establishment melts away, trying to make up our mind whether to be strong or weak.

Food is a better weapon than cannon, or atomic bombs, right now. Have we starved, have we sacrificed really, that others might live and love the great white father of human freedom?

This is a time for greatness, for discipline self-imposed by free men, for vision, for example, for national purpose. Instead, we've given the world at least a good imitation of a free-for-all quarrel for selfish advantage.

Right and left we demand leadership, but it's peacetime now— politics as usual—and leadership is confounded in a babel of discordant voices.

You know what I mean. It hasn't been a good show.

But the news isn't all bad by any means. The audience likes us best of all. It is not just because of what we have, but because of what we are, that the organized public opinion of the world is on our side. In free elections the Communists seldom win. When I was in the Mediterranean theatre [of war] in 1943 and the European theatre in 1944, the commonplace assumption of many was that communism was in the ascendency and would sweep Europe. It hasn't, and the Soviets are not uniformly popular, even in their areas of control, by any means. We must not confuse fear with love.

Meanwhile, we are under close inspection and that there should be some misgivings about our leadership is not surprising. We can snap out of it. I think we are. I *know* we believe in our way of life devoutly. I think we realize it is challenged! I think the segments of the world that know something of the great liberal humane tradition have the same devout faith, and hope and pray that we will lead resolutely and wisely. But many of the world's inhabitants, let's not forget, know little or nothing of the blessings of freedom or the meaning of our brand of democracy.

War, shooting war, it seems to me, is not the danger. Russia knows quite well as we do that in the next war there will be no victor. But she must be convinced that the world can't be molded to her model and that we have not defaulted the race or the leadership which destiny has given us. Once she knows that we are strong and purposeful and healthy, things will change, the pendulum which has swung so far among the dislocations, fears, and sufferings of this elemental struggle will stabilize. Once she knows that the good will we enjoy is not going to be dissipated, power politics will subside and the Moscow line will be more conciliatory. Then we will settle down to contest the road to peace and security, to the best of all possible worlds. The new crusade is not something you can fight negatively, it is not something you "fight" at all. Ideas know no boundaries. It is something you compete with positively. An anti-Russian policy is not the answer. It's a prodemocratic policy, and nothing succeeds like success as the history of our institutions shows so well.

We will have to beware of the demagogues with all the answers; or reactionaries who think the nineteenth century is ahead of us; of false prophets of the status quo; of pre-atomic defeatists, be they editors or politicians, who damn everyone else indiscriminately; of defeatism about the United Nations which is a great leap forward toward international understanding.[68] We must beware of inconsistencies, of injustice to anyone, Russia particularly who has such good cause to suspect our motives and our sincerity. We'll have to face up to some awkward questions in the narrow waters and island bases of the world. We can't have our cake and eat it too. We can't mobilize world opinion behind inequity, behind a policy of heads I win, tails you lose.

We should reexamine our governmental equipment to initiate and execute foreign policy in competition with the parliamentary system in Britain and the authoritarian Soviet system where the executive doesn't have to cut and trim and time things for public and Congressional support. I've had a feeling for some time that I should reread Woodrow Wilson's *Congressional Government* written sixty years ago,[69] and which no one would dare write now if he was running for public office.

Peace cannot be preserved nor American objectives realized through better understanding of international problems by the American people *alone*. International events often move so rapidly that officials cannot wait for opinion to crystallize. Are we so organized and equipped as to operate with maximum effectiveness in dealing with our friends and rivals abroad? Is it true that "to divide power is to make it irresponsible"? What about the Senate's treaty marring power? How many government departments are involved in foreign affairs? How are they coordinated? Or rather, are they coordinated? Military policy has little meaning if divorced from objectives of foreign policy. Is there effective machinery for steady integration of foreign and military policy at the highest level? And so on.

As the English say, your public servants serve you right. In a free society, there is no substitute for a conscientious and responsible citizenry, which means competent public servants. The step the Senate took yesterday toward Congressional reorganization is good news.[70] But as an ex-public servant, you will permit me to raise a question as to whether in foreign policy our government structure isn't a luxury we can ill afford any longer.

I've talked too long. But I've been very continent. I haven't said one word about my specialty, the United Nations! And I hope you don't feel that I have been unfair to the Russians. I am not anti-Russian. Indeed, those who know me best have probably suspected a little too much of the contrary. What I have tried to say is that I think enduring peace rests as much with us as with the Russians; that we must let no one think that we are supine or apathetic. We dare not default. That is the road to war, because *we* know the American story is not ended. But we must make it convincing for the myriads of confused spectators. There is room for us all, but in the new era that dawned over Hiroshima we will have to wage peace with all the zeal and urgency of war—all of us.[71]

Well, I warned you that it would be all old stuff!

Wilson's Birthday–ABC Broadcast

DECEMBER 28, 1946

✡

*During the autumn of 1946, Stevenson's speeches focused upon the
United Nations. He inaugurated a series of lectures on the evolution, structure and operations of the U.N. at the Northwestern
University Law School. He also gave several speeches on the work
of the second session of the General Assembly, to which he was
again a delegate. Representing the United States position, he addressed a number of the Assembly's Committee II meetings on the
subject of economic relief and rehabilitation of refugees. Among
his nationwide radio speeches, his brief comments on the ABC
broadcast in honor of Wilson's Birthday, December 28, 1946, best
summarized his conception of the Assembly's accomplishments
during that session. Speaking from Chicago, he was joined through
the network by Raymond Swing, William Benton, Francis Sayre,
and William W. Waymack.[72] William E. Stevenson, Adlai's class-
mate at Princeton, and no relation, wrote of Wilson's possible
influence on Stevenson, "We shall never be sure how much . . .
the career and political philosophy of Woodrow Wilson may have
inspired him. . . . In his career, which developed in such a fasci-
nating way through his sixty-five years, he surely met the standard
for a university graduate which Wilson had defined many years
earlier, i.e. that he 'should be a man of his nation, as well as a man
of his time.' "[73]*

BORROWING much from the men and the memories of the
League of Nations, Woodrow Wilson's ill-fated dream of organized peace, borrowing much from the storehouse of his thinking and experience, our country took the lead again toward the

87

creation of this last, best hope for peace on earth—the United Nations. And this time, the best of teachers, time, had done its work and the people and the politicians eagerly followed the path Wilson had pointed out in vain a generation before.

Just a year ago I was in London. We had the Charter of San Francisco and we had a paper organization of the United Nations. Now, a year later, the first great General Assembly is over and we have conclusive proof that the United Nations works! I could say that in 1946 Wilson's vision was vindicated. But that would be melodramatic and premature, and I will only say that the United Nations not only works, but can even succeed.

And the test in New York was a severe one. The Assembly started in a mood of sober hope, followed by shock and pessimism when Mr. Molotov attacked the "atom" and "dollar" diplomacy of the United States.[74] It ended seven weary weeks later in a cordial atmosphere with a record of solid achievement.

If the delegates, a little incredulous and a little surprised, left for their homes all over the world in a state of temperate optimism it was no wonder.

Two significant things happened during those two months in New York which few would have predicted beforehand with any confidence. First, the General Assembly emerged as the organized conscience of the community of nations, an instrument of enormous power in the structure of the United Nations. And, second, those weeks were marked by improvement in cooperative spirit between Russia and the Western Powers.

Questions, scores of them, were debated with no holds barred, without fear or favor, debated in the open, in the presence of each other, in the presence of the press and radio. In the words of Dr. Spaak, the Foreign Minister of Belgium and the accomplished President of the General Assembly, "We dwelt under the sign of open diplomacy." And when the votes were counted, the Assembly, the organized public opinion of the world, had spoken and neither the Soviet Union nor the United States nor any other country rejected the verdict, however adverse.

We have the Soviet Union to thank for raising the question of disarmament and the resolution adopted is a historic first step on the long and tortuous road to reduction and regulation of armaments with adequate safeguards against the hazards of evasion. Had nothing but this one resolution been adopted, the meeting would have been worthwhile and established the resonance and authority of the Assembly in the world.

Although none of the great powers were prepared to modify the requirement of unanimity in the Security Council on which the very survival of the United Nations depends, the vigorous attack on the veto by some of the smaller powers served an educational purpose about the veto, and its use and abuse.

Again, the ventilation of conflicting views about Franco's Spain and his abhorrent Fascist regime served to clear the atmosphere and narrow the area of disagreement on this sad, perplexing problem.

Trusteeship agreements for eight dependent areas were approved and the Trusteeship Council, provided for in the Charter, was established.

A constitution for the International Refugee Organization was adopted at long last;[75] and, if the money is forthcoming, hundreds of thousands of wretched, homeless people can be cared for after UNRRA [the United Nations Relief and Rehabilitation Administration] ends and repatriated to their homelands or, if they do not wish to return, resettled elsewhere.

A plan was adopted for handling relief after the expiration of UNRRA next spring when starvation will again threaten some of the devastated areas. A budget of $27 million for the next year, the cost of a few minutes of total war, was adopted; economic commissions for Europe and Asia to help tie together the economy of interdependent areas were recommended. And many, many other significant measures were adopted attacking the sore spots in the world, and the political, economic and social obstacles to peace and prosperity.

Such was the record—33,000 pages, 5,000 documents, 20 million words—of two months of a town meeting of the world where the rich and the poor, the large and the small, the strong and the weak, sat down together around a table, each with one vote, and argued, conceded, and compromised in a common effort to save their people from a more awful recurrence of the fate which Wilson foretold a quarter century ago in these words: "I can predict with absolute certainty that within another generation there will be another world war if the nations of the world do not concert the method by which to prevent it."

As we look into 1947 there is no room for maudlin optimism. But we end a fateful year of 1946 in better heart than we entered it. Day by day, bit by bit, in the Council of Foreign Ministers, in the vast machinery of the United Nations, they are getting the habit of working together, getting to know each other better. As they do, suspicion and mistrust diminish, accord and accommodation become easier about the new problems and new frictions which growth and development of international living will surely bring.

Wilson said that permanent peace can grow in only one soil— the soil of actual good will and understanding. He was fond of a story about Charles Lamb who said he hated a certain man. Someone said, "Why, Charles, I didn't know you knew him." "Ah," he said, "I don't. I can't hate a man I know."

D.P.'s—The Saddest Chapter
in the Epilogue of the War

MARCH 12, 1947

☼

During 1947, Stevenson gave a number of speeches, some of which contained the same ideas he had expressed earlier about the United Nations and Soviet-American relations. An important example was his address to the Springfield, Illinois, Lincoln Library Forum on January 10, 1947, in which he traced American foreign policy since the atomic bombs fell on Hiroshima and Nagasaki eighteen months before. He also gave several speeches on the refugee problem and the work of the United Nations Relief and Refugee Administration. This speech, given to the Chicago Immigrants' Protective League on March 12, 1947, is illustrative of his concern for this problem.

OVER ten million people were herded into Germany and Austria during the war, most of them as slave laborers, some as prisoners of war, some as refugees from invading armies. Many died. When the Axis collapsed, a counterwave took place and the Allied armies, with the help of UNRRA, returned nearly 7 million to their homelands by rail, by truck, by foot, by air. It was the largest and quickest *Völkerwanderung* [mass migration] of all time.

But a million would not return. 850,000 of them, including a large portion of women and children, are living in camps in the American, British and French zones of Germany. I should have said "existing," for these displaced persons—D.P.'s they're called—are the saddest chapter in the epilogue of the war. And they have occasioned the bitterest and most prolonged controversy in the life of the United Nations. Driven into slavery by the Nazis, fleeing from persecution and invasion, these survivors who have suffered every abuse, every brutality and indignity, have still, after almost two years, had no chance to start again and rebuild their shattered lives.

The largest national group are Poles; many are Balts, from Latvia, Lithuania and Estonia which have been taken over by Russia. Some are Yugoslavs, and there are some other Eastern Europeans. For many reasons they do not want to return to their homelands. Some are anti-Communists who fear persecution at home; home to many is ashes and agony. Many are Catholics; about 20 per cent are Jews—the wretched remnant of Hitler's massacre.

They have been rounded up in camps and cared for by UNRRA and private relief agencies supplied by the armies. But UNRRA will expire in June, its mission completed, and this is not soldiers' work even if there were soldiers to do it. So what then? What to do about these unfortunates; how to support them, how to get them back to their own countries or how to get them re-settled elsewhere; how to enable them once more to become useful, productive human beings; how to weed out the Quislings and the traitors? This was the problem that confronted the First General Assembly of the United Nations in London a year ago last month.

After prolonged debate there; then at a special international conference last July; then in the Economic and Social Council; the General Assembly in New York in December of last year, after some six weeks of almost continuous debate, finally approved the Constitution of the International Refugee Organization. Seventy-nine amendments to the Constitution were proposed in the Assembly, mostly by the Soviet Union and the Eastern countries who sought relentlessly and tirelessly to compel the repatriation of political dissidents whom they seem to regard as war criminals or fascists. All these proposals were successfully resisted, largely under the leadership of the United States, represented by a great citizen and a great humanitarian—Mrs. Eleanor Roosevelt.

From the inception of the idea of an International Refugee Organization the United States, supported by Britain and France and [Nationalist] China, has insisted that no one should be forced to return home against his will. And that principle of political sanctuary, which brought so many of our ancestors to these shores, was overwhelmingly sustained by the United Nations.

Now a Preparatory Commission to organize the IRO is meeting in Geneva. Senator Vandenburg and Senator Connally introduced a resolution in the Senate authorizing American participation,[76] and yesterday it was unanimously approved by the Foreign Relations Committee. The President has asked Congress for $75 million for our share of the administrative and operational budget for the first year. The total budget is about $160 million to feed, clothe, shelter, repatriate and commence the work of finding new homes, for 1 million people. Lest America's share of 73 to 75 million appear very large it should be remembered that about two-thirds, 600,000, of these refugees in Germany, Austria and Italy, are the responsibility of the United States, and our contribution to the IRO will actually be substantially less than the Army's expenditures have been. General Hilldring has testified that it will cost the United States $130 million in the fiscal year ending June 30, compared to this contribution of $75 million to the IRO.[77]

All who know anything of this poignant problem fervently pray that the United States Congress will act promptly so that the organization will be prepared to take up its formidable burden the end of June. The other countries are waiting to see what we will do.

It is hoped that many of the Poles who are peasants and some of the Yugoslav peasants can be persuaded to go home. Of the remainder less than a third will be Jews. They will not return. There are too many mass graves in Eastern Europe. The Estonians, Latvians, and Lithuanians will not return to their Soviet-dominated homelands. 700,000 is a minimum hard core that will have to be resettled somewhere soon, before human deterioration sets in.

That will be the great task of the IRO. The sooner this humanitarian task is completed, the sooner this sad legacy of the war is liquidated, the better it will be for the refugees, and for the world. As the greatest, richest and one of the most sparsely settled countries in the world, we can easily find homes and useful occupation for many of them. More than half will be women and children. All are reminders that "the evil men do lives after them."[78]

Some Postwar Reflections

MAY 14, 1947

✡

Jacob Arvey, Chairman of the Cook County Democratic Central Committee in 1947, recalls that former Secretary of State James F. Byrnes suggested to him at a Washington luncheon that summer, "Mr. Arvey, you have a gold nugget in your own backyard. His name is Adlai Stevenson." Arvey writes,

This was the first time I ever heard the name of Adlai Stevenson in connection with politics. . . . Up to this time he meant to me only an upper-crust Chicago lawyer who had been connected with the founding meeting of the United Nations and previously had been assistant to the Secretary of the Navy, Frank Knox, another Chicagoan. . . . Just when I became aware of it I can't remember, but it gradually became evident that a Stevenson boomlet was in the making.[79]

A bit earlier, on May 14, 1947, Stevenson gave this well-received address to the Northwestern University Law School Alumni Association, of which he was a member. This version was the manuscript which he prepared for publication in the Illinois Law Review *of Northwestern University for the July–August issue. Although it is somewhat repetitive of earlier speeches, it is a polished effort in which the development of his ideas and of his style is seen at its best. The title is Stevenson's.*

DURING the past two years international organization has been rapidly extended into wider and wider areas—economic, social and political. The frustration of our hopes for prompt political settlements has obscured this remarkable development of the machinery of orderly international living and retarded its use.

But neither frustrations abroad nor preoccupations at home have retarded the growing curiosity about the new dimensions of our lives. The lively and sustained interest of the organized bar in the United Nations and its agencies is only one example of this anxious concern. And certainly lawyers, as the custodians of the legal tradition and as educated, privileged citizens whose influence is disproportionate to their numbers, have a responsibility to understand this process and these procedures whose success depends on a much broader popular base than governments.

If lawyers do not understand and cannot interpret the activities of a complex of deliberative bodies like the United Nations and its agencies, we cannot expect laymen to. If lawyers with an understanding of legislative and judicial procedures at the level of single states do not understand the difficulties of procedure and negotiation at the level of many states, we cannot expect laymen to. If lawyers are impatient and intolerant and ignorant about these first clumsy, faltering, awkward motions of complex, imperfect mechanisms, can we expect the rank and file to stand fast and keep faith?

But allegiance to the mechanisms of international cooperation cannot assure the happy issue of our times. Because they may add a little to our perspective, I want to suggest at random some considerations which lie in the background of this spectacular period.

Many people—many very wise people at home and abroad—were fearful that after the war the United States would soon revert to its traditional isolation. Many feared that we couldn't take it—that after a few frustrated efforts to mold the world based on our democratic system, the United States would angrily withdraw behind the door and pull down the shade. But we haven't. We did a ghastly dance keeping that peace indivisible, but apparently we've learned an enduring lesson. At least, we've kept at the business of global peace relentlessly for two grueling heart-breaking years, and I haven't seen a white feather.[80]

And during these past two years we have passed through successive waves of optimism and pessimism across the whole spectrum of emotion—from the happy illusion that the United Nations was somehow a substitute for power politics and a guarantee of automatic peace, to periods of black despair, talk of another war and visions of the ugly specter of two evil old worlds in hostile balance instead of one bright new world. But in spite of all the emotional gymnastics of the past two years, it would seem that the American people have matured very rapidly, that there is now a general awareness that making peace is harder than making war, and the obstacles and hazards infinitely more difficult to understand and to evaluate, that the hard realities of international life are no longer the monopoly of any region or group, that this is an era of world revolution and reorganization that has few historical counterparts, and that America is in the world to stay, not because it wants to be, but because it knows it can't keep out.

Another historic decision has been evolving for some time and culminated in the Greece and Turkey bill,[81] which I suppose it is fair to say passed the Congress not because they liked it but because they felt there was no safe alternative. From 1793 to 1917 American policy and legislation was based on three premises: (a) that wars were inevitable and a legal means of settling international disputes, (b) that since wars could be localized the United States should remain neutral, and (c) that international law protected neutral ships not carrying contraband and that, therefore, a policy of nonintervention and neutrality would not ruin our commerce. We sustained the doctrine of neutral rights with a fair degree of success for 100 years or more, although President Madison had to abandon neutrality and fight for our neutral rights in 1812, and of course the violation of our neutral rights by Germany was still President Wilson's ostensible reason for going to war more than 100 years later in 1917.

The Italian and Japanese wars of aggression put an unendurable strain on both the spirit and rationality of the neutrality and non-intervention policy. Under the Lend-Lease Act, which followed the principle of helping those who were helping to defend us, ended the fiction of neutrality. And now we have rejected all three of the basic premises on which our policy has rested since Washington's neutrality proclamation of 1793.[82] We no longer recognize war as a legal means of settling quarrels, we no longer believe that neutrality can be maintained even by abandoning neutral trading rights. Today we are on a new tack; we are attempting through the United Nations to settle international disputes at their inception; we propose through the "Truman Doctrine" to intervene, unilaterally if necessary, at the request of the aggrieved to support the principles of the Charter.

Now, assuming the conclusion that the United States is going to be a vigorous and permanent participant in world affairs is not premature, it is of historical importance for another and more obvious reason. Because we then see for the first time the world balanced between two non-European states, the highly developed United States with old ideas, and the underdeveloped Soviet Union with new ideas. Surrounding areas are attracted like satellites to these planets by dependence, by fear, by racial affinity. Large areas and populations are exposed to both magnetic fields. Russia has little and wants everything; the United States has everything and wants little. Both want peace and security—Russia to bind up her awful wounds and to develop her vastness and wealth; the United States to enjoy hers.

Must these two galaxies of power and influence some day collide? If we were ants we would probably have to answer in the affirmative. But we are not ants; we are rational human beings with at least the common spiritual heritage of the human race. The trouble is fear—fear of one another, fear of those ideas, old and new. Our old fear and mistrust of Bolshevism is aggravated by Russia's stubborn, acquisitive behavior. Russia's old fear of capitalist encirclement and counterrevolution is aggravated by a suspicion that we would have been glad to see Russia and Germany both bleed to death in the war. The Soviet press calls us fascist reactionaries and imperialists determined to dominate the world.

And so it goes—fear begets fear, epithet begets epithet. With each move the vicious circle tightens, the division between East and West sharpens—and the bystanders tremble. The arena is the United Nations, the Council of Foreign Ministers and many less publicized international meetings. The stakes are those great areas exposed to both gravitational pulls; largely Europe now, with first the Middle East and then Asia in the background. Meanwhile, Europe's economic recovery and integration proceeds with perilous and glacial slowness, perilous because without a healthy Europe there can be no peace.

How can we break this vicious circle of fear? How can we erase the tensions and get on with the business of redeeming this bloody century? With our technology and culture there's a golden age ahead. Can we get there—alive?

No one knows. But everyone knows that that's the most important job this country has ever faced. Because we want to live, and live in peace in a society that respects the sanctity of the human person.

What do the Soviets want? Just security, so that they, too, can live in peace? Or world communism? Who knows? And they won't oblige us with a bill of particulars. Perhaps they don't know themselves. But, after two years of painful, stubborn negotiation, one thing is clear; they are determined to get all they can while they can, whatever the ultimate objective—defensive or offensive.

So, confronted with uncertainty of Soviet ambitions, the expansion of Soviet power, and the encroachment of Soviet ideas, our policy for world order and security is unfolding: resistance and assistance. Resistance to further political expansion because we know all too well that appeasement doesn't work. If there are moderates in the Soviet hierarchy who are more concerned with security, recovery and development than expansion, appeasement won't help them: it will strengthen those who insist on further adventures. Just as it strengthened Hitler. But you can't resist with words and moral admonitions alone. The Soviet Union—any state for that matter, not excluding the United States—is more impressed with power than with words. It's apocryphal, but the remark attributed to Stalin illustrates what I mean: "The Pope—who is the Pope and how many divisions has he?" So to make resistance effective we must stay strong and never disarm unilaterally again, meanwhile doing our sincere best to further rational control and limitation of armaments through the United Nations.

But political resistance alone is not enough. Political resistance without economic assistance won't suffice, because we've learned another lesson. At least I hope we've learned that prosperity, like peace, is indivisible; that you can't have an island of prosperity in an ocean of want; that given a choice between life and liberty, people will choose life.

Order and security in the world will depend largely on those areas which have not made a choice between the old ideas and the new. Because ours is the only nation that has the *power* to *resist* and the *wealth* to *assist*, the burden falls squarely on us. It will be expensive and it may not succeed if it's too little and by default— and the cost of *not* resisting and assisting in the long run will make the cost of resisting and assisting now look like peanuts.

So I conclude, therefore, that the United States has made some historic decisions in these two years. Twenty-five years ago we would not even follow: today we are leading in the development of international concepts through the United Nations. We have given unmistakable evidence of permanent participation in world affairs. We are going to resist the spread of a new totalitarian threat to the peace. We are going to attack economic disintegration by collective action if possible, by individual action if necessary.

So the real question is no longer so much *what* the United States will do, but *how* we will do it. Will we use our economic abundance boldly and to the full to attack the breeding grounds of desperate political solutions? As the Chinese say, "You can't carve rotten wood and you can't paint on walls of sand." Until Europeans can eat regularly and live decently they are not going to think much about individual liberty.

Perhaps the greatest crisis in the world is the crisis of underproduction. Germany and Japan, the great producing centers, are crippled. In the economically advanced countries, devastated by the enemy and the liberator, production is still from 20 per cent to 50 per cent below the prewar level. The shortages are food to keep the people going, power—which means coal—on which the production depends, transportation to move commodities and goods, and dollars to buy food, industrial equipment and even coal.

The world is begging for our production while we talk of less work, more wages, higher prices and more profits. The higher prices go the less the precious foreign dollar buys and the more we will have to lend and give. Can a free economy arrest the creeping inflation and forestall disaster? Or are the Soviets right and is another depression in the United States inevitable? With it will the whole fragile house come tumbling down and result in (a) universal chaos, (b) the extinction of capitalism, (c) universal communism, or (d) war?

Are they also right who reason that Britain must collapse soon;

that, confronted with assumption of her additional burdens in Germany and elsewhere, the United States will wobble and begin to pull out of communism's path? Are they right who reason that with another severe economic depression in this country and the failure of democracy to solve its economic and social problems a man on horseback will ride in, millions will follow, just as they have elsewhere, and the United States will go fascist, with war as the inevitable result? Is it probable that the Russians are far more afraid of us than we are of them?

Let me remind you of some elementary things about the Russians. The factors of Communist ideology, ancient Russian habits of thought, and the internal conditions there, in combination, have produced a suspicion, fear, and evangelical zeal that underlie our difficulties with the Soviet Union. These difficulties cannot be resolved by angry name-calling and threats any more than you can break a colt by intimidation and roughness.

In the first place, Russia has never known peaceful, friendly neighbors. She has had to fight them all from the earliest times and the outside world has come to mean a hostile world. The external dangers of the past, real or fancied (and Germany and Japan were very real), and the traditional fear and suspicion of foreigners has fitted nicely into Soviet requirements of ruthless discipline and purity of thought.

In the second place, the dictatorship of the proletariat has functioned through decisions imposed from above, not from the proletariat. A minority of trusted party members controls the will of the majority. The result is that opposition has always existed, and the internal security of the regime has been the constant preoccupation of the Kremlin. But the Soviet government naturally could not admit the existence of opposition. So the internal danger is treated as reflection of the external. Hence the purge trials, the talk of wreckers and saboteurs, always as agents of foreign powers. The external enemy has been the convenient justification for the elaborate measures of protection against the internal one.

And bear in mind that the Soviets did not have to manufacture this fear psychosis. It was there, made to order, already. Czarist Russia was a police state.

Fear breeds abnormalities. A thread of persecution and appre-
hension runs through Russian literature. And there is a weird
ancient superstition that Mother Russia's, Holy Russia's destiny is
limitless. This messianic quality also fits nicely into the classical
Communist concept of world revolution.

But I won't enlarge. The point is that we are dealing not so
much with individuals, but on the one hand with deep-seated habits
of thought, conceptions and ways of looking at the world formed
over the space of centuries, and on the other with the magic of a
great idea.

Like all those who hold beliefs with deep-rooted, fanatic conviction the Soviets will seek to propagate theirs without dilution or
compromise. They are not hypocrites and the idea that we can
somehow buy them out is insulting. They are not frivolous and the
idea that we can somehow charm and talk them into acquiescence
is foolish.

But historically, Russian diplomacy has been very flexible. They
have always made sure they could retreat when they run into firm
and final resistance. We have seen that repeatedly. In a military
sense also their commitments never exceed their capacity. We must
not be rattled by the belligerent Soviet idiom—the discourtesy,
epithets, and abuse they pour on bourgeois governments and
peoples. Their potential power is enormous, but so is their present
weakness behind the rude, rough facade.

And history records the gradual cooling of the passions engen-
dered by all revolutionary movements. "The tendency," as E. H.
Carr says, "is for the revolutionary aspect to predominate in the
earlier stages, the positive aspect in the later. Primitive Christianity
was revolutionary until it had disrupted the old Roman civilization;
then it created a new and positive world order of its own, and
underwent a corresponding modification of its outlook. The Reformation began by being revolutionary and destructive, and
ended by becoming the basis of a new social order."

Competent observers suggest that the emotional power of Communist party doctrine in Russia is diminishing; that the urge for
better relations with the outside world—for freedom from fear—is
closer to the surface than we realize. The fact of a friendly

world—if it is a friendly world—will gradually penetrate, will gradually dissipate the hard shell of fear.

Gibbons pointed out that there is but a short step between enthusiasm and imposture. Our own conversion from isolationism proves that facts and reason and time can revise a nation's approach to world problems.

To summarize, we have made much progress in two years. The United Nations has been organized and many specialized agencies which are working across the whole front on the solution of political, economic and social problems face-to-face on an international basis. Peace treaties have been painfully worked out for all the satellite countries. Progress, more perhaps than we appreciate, has been made toward the German and Austrian treaties. But let's face it! The world is still very sick and very receptive to the new ideas moving from East to West, including the idea that the old Western democratic, political and economic institutions are no longer capable of solving the problems of mass civilization. We must face the fact that Asia is in revolt and struggling to rid herself of her European masters at the moment of Europe's greatest weakness. A billion people are demanding a share in the fruits of the twentieth century. We must face the fact that there are only about 600 million people in the world who share or know anything about the traditional democratic freedoms, as opposed to 1,600 million who do not. We must face the fact that Russia is contiguous to a large portion of these people and we are very remote. We must face the fact that at the present rate two-thirds of the population of Europe will be Slav in another generation.

And, complacent and remote, we dare not overlook that with two world wars, economic collapse and revolutions, the concepts of democracy and individual freedom which we have taken for granted for so long have lost some of their vitality and appeal, even in Western Europe where individualism was born. After the last war democratic institutions sprang up everywhere. But they didn't last long. When they failed to solve their problem (and we didn't help much) dictatorships took over. And after this war they didn't even spring up. The new political institutions in Europe more closely resemble collectivism than individualism.

It's worth inquiring whether the flow of men and ideas from

West to East which began in the Renaissance, the age of discovery and the Reformation, has been arrested; whether the tide has turned after 500 years and the flow is from East to West again; whether a new social order is in the making; whether it will be democratic or totalitarian, or a synthesis resembling current European socialism.

I think you will conclude that whether and how much of the democratic tradition survives depends less on ideological sympathies and more on the positive economic and social achievements of the democracies, and particularly in those great areas that are caught between the two magnetic fields, East and West. We cannot rest on our ancient laurels. We know that a full belly is a better defense against totalitarianism than an atomic bomb. We know that you can't stop ideas with soldiers; that in the long run there is only one defense against this creeping disease, and that's healthy flesh. To improve the well-being of the masses is today a mission commanding the same kind of moral fervor that once went into the task of winning their souls.

That an economic crisis is developing with appalling rapidity is all too apparent. With production crippled everywhere, the deficits of food, coal and goods have in effect been supplied from this hemisphere and largely this country. This year our export balance may exceed $8 billion, which of course is disastrous, for the only "favorable" balance this country can have for years to come will be what we used to call an "unfavorable" balance. The result is that the meager financial resources of Europe, even the gold reserves, are rapidly declining.

Confronted with that situation during the war, we passed the Lend-Lease Act. Now there is talk of peacetime lend-lease. The economic crisis of 1948 is clearly this country's major foreign-policy problem. But the time lags between policy formation by those who know the facts, public understanding and acceptance, and finally legislation and execution of the policy are sometimes very long and now the time may be very short.

Will we have the will and the wisdom to do the job? Is it too big for us? Obviously, even American resources are not inexhaustible. We will not be able to supply everything that is needed everywhere at once, if at all. But to talk of stopping communism without attacking its roots—hunger, want and insecurity—is illusory. Nor will the Western democratic tradition survive if we adopt policies of the nature we condemn in others.

The idea that individual will is the supreme arbiter of human destiny and the individual conscience the ultimate moral censor—and the idea that the state exists for the individual rather than the individual for the state—are the most precious things America has to defend. They *can't* be defended by words, by military power, by inaction. And they *won't* be defended by fascism in any indigenous disguise.

Our Foreign Policy Has Taken
a Seat at the Family Table

✿

After frequent luncheon meetings in late 1947 between Jacob Arvey and Stevenson in which the possibility of Stevenson as a senatorial candidate was discussed, Arvey decided that he wished Paul Douglas to run for Congress and Stevenson for Governor. When Stevenson was informed on December 26, 1947, that Arvey wanted him to run for Governor, he was highly negative—his experiences had led him to think of nothing else than the senatorial office. Because the Democratic State Committee was filling its 1948 slate for Illinois that week in Chicago, the hesitant candidate was given until noon on December 30 to decide whether he would run for Governor. Kenneth S. Davis writes that "At nine o'clock Dutch Smith [Stevenson's contact with Arvey and a lifelong friend] came to Stevenson's office. He found his friend 'in terrible shape,' as he later recalled. He argued, as Stevenson had argued with himself, that it was 'now or never' so far as a political career was concerned. 'They need you this year,' Smith said. 'If you say no when they need you, they won't take you when they don't need you.' "[83]

Stevenson later remembered, "I accepted. Why? I don't know exactly. . . . perhaps it was restlessness about settling down again after eight feverish years of war and peace. . . ."[84] When the decision was made to run, Stevenson began immediately to campaign. In January, 1948, at the Public Forum of the Chicago Athletic Club, he gave his first preserved speech in which he mentioned his announced candidacy. Typically, it dealt with for-

eign affairs and his concern for the deepening Soviet-American
ideological split at the recently concluded General Assembly of the
United Nations, which he had again attended as a delegate. He
made a strong plea for an American alternative to the Soviet threat
through the European Recovery Program, which was then being
debated in Congress.

SOME forty-odd years ago James Bryce's lectures at Yale University were published under the title "Hindrance to Good Citizenship."[85] He developed the familiar contrast between the requirements of democracy—in our sense of that word—and the actual behavior of citizens in a democracy.

He pointed out that no other form of government demands such intelligence, such civic virtue and such public spirit. Unhappily, he said, everywhere democracy had fallen short of expectations. And he enumerated three principal reasons why the practice of democracy had contradicted the basic assumption of classical democracy that the average man must be "an active, instructed and intelligent ruler of his country."

The first hindrance was the sin of indolence—the failure of citizens to inform themselves on public issues, their indifference to the privilege of voting, and the general unwillingness to serve in public office.

The second obstacle was private self-interest. He was referring to economic groups or lobbies which attempt to influence government for selfish reasons through bribery, political intimidation, etc.

The third hindrance to good citizenship was excessive partisanship—an allegiance to party, transcending loyalty to the nation. When party labels become a substitute for truth, democracy is mortally wounded.

What, with the passage of time, one might wish to add to or subtract from Bryce's list or quarrel with his emphasis on definitions here and there, but I think you will agree that what he said forty years ago is substantially true today.

And that, I take it, is why you hold these meetings: because you are aware of your responsibilities as citizens of a democracy; because you are not indolent and want to be informed; because you know that the public interest is greater than your self-interest; and, finally, because you know that blind intolerant partisanship is the political device of dictatorship and the deadly poison of democracy. I can illustrate the contrary state of mind by a story Carl Sandburg is fond of telling.[86]

Because I saw a lot of the war, of its waste, its horrible destruction and ghastly suffering; because I saw a lot of the peace-making, its difficulties and frustrations; because I've seen rather intimately the policies and methods of our Communist competitors unfold, I have developed a holy passion for our democratic system and the free way of life which, like many of us I am afraid, I had taken for granted. Hence, I've become more and more interested in these hindrances to good citizenship, these divergencies between the professions of democracy and its practice.

I even like to think that I was moved by some such noble motive when I agreed to run for Governor, and not just vanity!

But, Mr. Chairman, I promised you that I would not impose upon your good Republican membership and make a political speech. I won't, and as you suggested I'll take in a little more territory than Illinois and talk about foreign affairs.

I sometimes wonder, as the dramatic days of the revolutionary era in which we are destined to live march on, and the awful responsibility of the United States becomes more sharply apparent, if there is such a thing as "foreign affairs" for any American any longer.

A hundred years ago it took Queen Victoria's ambassador in Rome just as long to travel to London to report as it took a Roman general to travel from Britain to Rome to report to his emperor *eighteen hundred years ago*. Today it takes a few hours. The infant Republic of the United States was not consulted when the powers met at the Congress of Vienna to decide the future of Europe. A few weeks ago four powers were meeting in London and two of them could have decided the future of Europe, if only they could have agreed![87] The United States was one of these powers. Examples—economic, political and moral—could be multiplied to prove, as Secretary Marshall has said, that "our foreign policy has entered the American home and taken a seat at the family table." And I'll hazard a guess that foreign policy will continue to sit at the family table and to shoulder its way up and down every main street in America for a long, long time to come.

You can't turn out almost two-thirds of the entire world's production and not be concerned with customers. You can't be the richest man in town and not be concerned with insurance. And you can't be happy and free, surrounded by misery and slavery. It's not that way because we want it that way, but facts are stubborn and, to borrow a phrase from Dr. Aranha of Brazil, the President of this last General Assembly of the United Nations, "The people that disintegrated the atom now have the mission of integrating humanity."

So in my few minutes I want to comment on some aspects of the current scene which have a bearing on that rather extensive mission, and also a bearing on "Main Street" and on all the family firesides along "Main Street."

I spent three months of toil and turmoil in New York this fall and winter as a member of the American delegation to the 1947 General Assembly of the United Nations. Much as I should like to talk at length about that remarkable conference, let me just remind you that the United Nations is two years old. Its basic structure has been completed. It has faced the major international political problems, except the task of writing the peace treaties which is not within its province. It has furnished a parliament in which the bitterest political issues have been debated in unparalleled frankness. Through its Economic and Social Council and specialized agencies, it is already attempting to solve many of the world's economic and social problems. And the importance of its work in these fields must not be judged by some of the proposals that have been advanced, like a study of the effects of chewing cocoa leaves on certain Andean Indians! But its dramatic services to humanity through these agencies have been overshadowed by news of political tension.

It has approved liberal Trusteeship agreements in most of the mandated areas and a procedure by which nations report on economic, social and educational conditions in their colonies. Its Commission on Human Rights has produced a Declaration of Human Rights which if adopted will become part of international law.[88]

The United Nations has initiated processes of international community life which can assure political security, material prosperity, and the enjoyment of human rights—*if* the will of the nations will prompt them to use these processes, which brings me to some of the political developments of this Assembly which I want to mention.

The Assembly voted to establish a United Nations commission of inquiry on the Greek frontier to observe the guerrilla war and the participation, if any, of Greece's northern neighbors, Albania, Yugoslavia and Bulgaria, in a death struggle which has all but exhausted Greece. The Russians and their satellites violently opposed the creation of the commission and refused to serve on it after it was overwhelmingly approved.

The Assembly voted to establish a United Nations Commission to conduct elections and bring about at last the long-promised independence of Korea and the withdrawal of the Russian and American troops from our respective zones. Again the Soviet Union and its friends violently opposed and boycotted the Commission.

Likewise, they opposed and boycotted the interim committee to discuss and prepare questions for the next annual session of the Assembly, fearful that the constant focus of world opinion would bypass and undermine the authority of the Security Council where they have a vote [probably "veto"].

Although it was never contemplated that Greece and Korea— which are legacies of the war—would be responsibilities of the United Nations, which was created to keep the peace, not make it, these and many other actions by this Assembly may prove of positive constructive importance.

But of more immediate significance was the violent Soviet attack on the United States, launched, led and sustained by the brilliant and tireless Vishinsky throughout all those long weeks. Invective and noncooperation has been standing operating procedure for the Soviets from the time of the first controversies between the Mensheviks and the Bolsheviks. But this time it was worse than ever before.

Using bits and pieces of sensational, intemperate, hostile, even warlike talk gleaned from our free press, he charged us collectively and specifically with warmongering, imperialism, fascism, incitement to a new war, and a crazy plan to dominate the world. With a savagery and a vehemence that at first was stunning, he heaped on us all the abuse and epithets in the rich Soviet lexicon. "The speeches of Hitler seem by contrast the height of urbanity and elegance. The Russians and their camp followers succeeded in making the Assembly seem less like a body of grave and deliberate statesmen and more like a Saturday night in a mining town saloon."

In short, with the notable exception of Palestine, Soviet policy at this Assembly was purely negative. They stubbornly opposed in debate and by every parliamentary device almost every constructive proposal. They resisted every effort to get anything done of importance, unless it was something they wanted. They had almost nothing to offer but propaganda, threats and fear, fear, fear of an aggressive, selfish, profiteering, sinister United States that was determined to dominate the world politically and economically, sitting on its gold and atomic bombs, by precipitating a new war if necessary. Fear seemed to be the principal surplus commodity of the Soviet Union.

Now why was this and what did it reveal? Had the Russians come this year in an atmosphere of sweetness and light, they might have sharply divided opinion in this country at a time when unity and decision is vital. They might have confused and misled other smaller countries who are not anxious to take sides in this terrifying struggle. They might have made the United States look like the obstinate, uncompromising, irritable party instead of the Soviets. If that was their purpose they failed utterly by the tactic of unrestrained assault on the United States and its motives. They forced the other countries to take sides with the United States right down the line, and what commenced as a conflict between Russia and the United States ended as a conflict between Russia and the United Nations.

The Soviet performance in New York revealed, I think, how basically dissimilar our views are with respect to the evolution of the United Nations as a parliamentary body. On the one hand they object to the growth of power of the Assembly and will resist to the end any encroachment on the power of the Security Council which they have always conceived to be the heart and head of the organization, and where they can always protect their minority position by the veto. On the other hand, they are profoundly sensi-

tive to public opinion. "A government which muzzles every opposing voice at home and uses propaganda so extensively to sell
itself abroad must have an immense regard for public opinion. The
Assembly is the world's greatest sounding board, and the tendency
to give it the dominant position in the United Nations is a recognition that world sentiment is bigger than any of the big powers."

So, while they want to keep a firm hand on the organization
through the Security Council, use the organization where it serves
their ends and block it where it does not, they also want to exploit
the enormous resonance of the General Assembly, the town meeting of the world, for propaganda. But the two objectives are, of
course, incompatible. With the frustration of the Security Council
the power of the Assembly grows; with its use as the world forum
its power grows. As its power grows and the democratization of
the organization increases, the Soviet finds it harder to maintain
controls and at the same time more and more important to do so.
It's a dilemma for them and many prophesied that they would
withdraw and try to wreck the organization. But there was little
evidence of that intention at this session. My guess is that they
won't risk a break—at least not yet—because of the adverse effect
on world opinion and because it would tend to confirm the growing impression that the Soviet Union and its friends will cooperate
only when and where it is in their interest to do so; and also because they consider the Assembly too valuable for propaganda.

Why did they attack the United States with such unrestrained
violence? As I've said, they did not succeed in scaring the smaller
countries into a terrified neutrality. As I've said, they didn't succeed in dividing American opinion when they might have. On the
contrary, they hardened it, and it may have been a historic blunder. What then were they playing for?

The explanation seems to be that they concluded last summer
that the postwar economic collapse in the West which they have
confidently expected was not imminent after all, that the Marshall
Plan had a good chance of passage and that the battle for Europe
was entering a new phase which would prolong the final issue. In
these circumstances they decided to go on the defensive, to write
off American opinion, and to concentrate on forestalling discontent among their own people and among the satellite peoples, and

to inflame the Communist parties elsewhere to do as much damage as soon as possible.

Soviet dictators, like all dictators, want to keep their power and to increase it. To keep their own people in line, they must make it appear, therefore, that Soviet peace is constantly endangered. Many in Russia wonder why despotic power had not been relinquished in accordance with Communist doctrine. The answer has always been that they must keep dictatorial power because the Soviet Union is surrounded by enemies. Unless they can conjure up enemies, they cannot justify their power. That, for about thirty years, has been the constant theme of Soviet press and radio, and it requires constant replenishment.

In the next place, this propaganda attack on the United States was directed at the satellite countries—Poland, Czechoslovakia, Bulgaria, Rumania, Hungary, Albania and Yugoslavia. One must always remember that although their governments are friendly to Russia and under Russian influence, their people—the great mass of the people—include many who do not share this love of their great Slav neighbor. You can hardly imagine the historical antagonism of the Polish people suddenly converted into affection. Moreover, many people in these countries, including people in the government, don't enjoy the role of front-line soldiers in the Communist revolution; they are more interested in improving the lot of their people and want to participate with Western Europe in the Marshall Plan.

To combat disaffection and doubt, and maintain discipline in these countries, their Russian-influenced governments needed this deluge of propaganda about the imperialist, warlike designs of the United States. And of course the scrupulous fidelity of these areas behind the so-called Iron Curtain is essential to the existence of Soviet influence beyond the Curtain, first to Italy and France.

Also, the Communist parties in Italy, France and Western Europe need fuel to keep the fires of disorder and rebellion burning. In countries where people are far more intent on keeping alive, clothed and warm than they are on ideologies, the best way to counteract the effect of the prospect of an improvement in living conditions was to spread fear of the price an imperialist, heartless

United States would exact. And, of course, the strikes were timed to follow the propaganda preparation emanating from Flushing Meadows and Lake Success.

There is one other aspect of this propaganda drive that should not be overlooked. There is no more common technique than to distract attention by accusing others of doing and plotting what you are doing and plotting yourself. That was transparently the Russian theory of attack on our motives in Greece—that we, not they, were trying to gain control of that strategically located country. Repetition of falsehoods and half-truths more often and louder than others cause many to believe them and sufficiently confuses the issues to cause hesitation and doubt. I remind you that just before Hitler entered Prague he launched a violent attack on warmongers.

So it seems probable that the Soviet propaganda drive which characterized this session of the Assembly was directed largely at the people of the Soviet Union itself, at the satellite countries and to sharpen up the line for the Communist parties everywhere, and especially in the immediate battle areas of France and Italy. It's fair to say, in short, that Russia used the General Assembly principally as a base of attack on the Marshall Plan everywhere.

Which brings me to the Marshall Plan, and one of the great decisions in our history which will certainly have an important place in the future of individualism and human liberty on this earth. The question is simply, shall we pay the cost of establishing the conditions of free choice for the people of Western Europe? The condition of free choice is economic recovery from the war. We have already made a huge investment in recovery. Shall we press on, finish the job, or stop? This question is "our most intimate domestic concern."

When we speak of Western Europe in this connection, we are talking about sixteen countries and Western Germany. These sixteen countries contain the home of 275 million people—almost twice as many people as in the United States. They are industrious, largely industrialized, highly skilled people. Before the war they enjoyed the highest standard of living and the highest degree of literacy outside North America.

I wish to make but two points about the European Recovery Plan which will be the subject of public discussion for some time—and not too long I hope!

First, it is of prime importance to American security. It is essential to maintain the independence and restore the strength of the Western European nations and peoples. The loss of either gravely impairs our own safety and ends the hope of the United Nations. Second, the real issue in Congress is, not whether we shall have a European program, but whether it will be a recovery program or a relief program—whether it will cure the patient or merely prolong the illness, the cost and the danger.

In the world which confronts us in 1948, the European Recovery Program is the front line of American security. We have learned that vital as is the role of our military establishments, or of international military forces, our security and freedom depend in the first instance upon the actions of other nations and other peoples. These actions may gravely prejudice our security or greatly strengthen it. These actions are often forced by conditions largely or entirely beyond the control of the nations and people who take them—such as the ability to produce enough to live on. The course which the people of Western Europe take in the next four years is the most important decision affecting our national safety which is still open in the world today.

They and we want them independent of outside dictation and of inside dictatorship, self-supporting and healthy in their individual and national lives. Our own safety is immeasurably increased if this is so. It is immeasurably weakened if any of them are weakened and fall by internal action or external pressure, or both, into the closed, police, military and economic system which already stretches from the Elbe to the Pacific. It can happen. It has happened to others.

At the end of the war we thought that everyone believed that enduring peace and economic recovery from the war was best assured by political settlement and economic progress which were firmly founded on agreement between the great powers. The United Nations would, it was planned, go forward from this start on the basis of principle and organization which would bring to the settlement of international questions the conscience of mankind and the justice of laws and procedures which dealt equally with the strong and the weak.

It is now plain that the Soviet Union does not intend to join in the task of political settlement or economic recovery on any basis which the other powers, or any nation wishing to maintain its own integrity, can accept. On the contrary, the Soviet Union is doing its utmost to prevent recovery in Europe. The years of delay and obstruction have contributed to the exhaustion of resources and people and brought Western Europe to the crisis stage.

The European Recovery Program has replaced the long-sought great-power leadership as the last best hope for recovery abroad and American security at home. It calls for a joint European-American program to get the great workshop of Europe working and producing again. It is a workshop, just as the New England, Pittsburgh, Detroit, and Chicago areas are. It works the same way. The 275 million people who live there do not and cannot exist wholly on locally produced food and raw materials. Large amounts of both have to be brought from outside and paid for by sales of manufactured goods. Due to the war much of the producing plant has to be renovated and enlarged to produce enough to live on and sell. The job is to do this as fast as possible and to help the people who are doing it live and work in the meantime.

The program calls for a combined effort. The people and governments of Western Europe will renovate and expand the workshop, turn out more power, more goods. They will put their finances in order. They will work together to do this. From us they ask help in getting the additional food, fuel, raw materials, and machinery which will start and keep the wheels turning until the whole operation becomes self-supporting.

Relief is a wholly different operation. Relief does no more than keep people alive in an emergency. It does not bring self-support. It is costly because it is endless.

The real significance of the battle of the figures which is raging on the European Recovery Program is that it is a battle between a plan for recovery and a plan for relief. It is not simply a difference on the cost of recovery. Let me explain why this is so.

The Administration bill for European Recovery now before

Congress provides for help from the United States in the amount of $6.8 billion from April 1, 1948, to June 30, 1949—fifteen months in all. This money will go to provide goods to supplement other purchases which [the European nations] will make with funds advanced from the International Bank and private investment, and still other purchases which it is hoped will be financed by other countries in this hemisphere. The total import program is therefore much larger than $6.8 billion, and will amount to approximately $11 billion worth of goods, much of it financed by other sources.

All of these goods are for a productive program. Such a program requires different quantities and different goods from a relief program. Take food, for instance. People can exist on approximately 2,000 calories a day, but they cannot work on such a diet. Therefore a production program requires different foods and more foods than a relief program, and the whole production program will bog down if people do not have the necessary strength to work.

In the case of fuel, a similar situation exists. A production program requires that fuel be available so that factories, railways and mines can operate. A relief program would include fuel for heating, cooking and lighting. If the recovery fuel program is cut, production falters and may stop, since people have to be kept from freezing even though factories may not be able to run.

The same considerations affect the raw materials in a production recovery program. More cotton, for instance, has to be provided not only to clothe inhabitants of a particular country, but to permit the factories of that country to manufacture textiles which they can sell abroad in order to purchase more cotton and needed goods. Timber, in a production program, has to be provided for pitprops for mines, railway ties, packing cases for goods, as well as for shelter. If the quantity of timber is reduced, the production program suffers first.

Finally, in a production program equipment and machinery are essential. Without these items the production of more goods is impossible and self-support cannot be achieved.

In the light of these considerations you can see at once that if, as some have advocated, the amount of $6.8 is reduced to, say, $4 billion, the entire character of the program changes. It is not merely a reduced recovery program. It ceases to be a recovery program at all.

Also, a cut of $2 or $3 billion means a far larger cut because other sources of help will either be eliminated or reduced.

For instance, loans to the Western European countries by the International Bank can be made only if the chances of repayment are good so that American investors will buy the Bank's bonds. If items essential to bring recovery are omitted from the program, chances for repayment become poor, and the Bank cannot lend. Similarly, other countries in this hemisphere will be asked to make funds available with which European countries may purchase some of their needs. These other countries will regard quite differently a contribution to a recovery program, which will mean an end to assistance and a beginning of self-support, from contributions to a relief program, which might well be endless.

But the program would be reduced by even more than this if United States aid is seriously curtailed. As I have already pointed out, much of the imports will be paid for by the European countries themselves with the proceeds of their own exports. These exports depend upon continuing and expanding production. If the amount of foreign assistance is reduced, the amount of European exports is reduced, and again we descend into a vicious circle.

For this reason the battle behind the figures is the battle of recovery versus relief. This is a very different thing from saying that the amount asked of Congress is sacrosanct and that the Congress should vote the amount without careful consideration. Congress is entitled to and should investigate the figures with great care and either be convinced or, if it finds that there are any particular items or groups of items which can safely be eliminated, make that elimination.

But arbitrary cuts to achieve purposes not connected with the program will destroy the usefulness and prove in the end the most costly sort of economy. For a real recovery program requires the greatest expense in the first year in order to start production as soon and as vigorously as possible. The costs thereafter decline and shortly cease as self-support is attained. A relief program operates in exactly the opposite way. Costs increase as goods within the country become exhausted and as the productive power of the country slows down.

Very few of us can hope to have expert judgment on the exact figure of American aid which should be provided, but all of us know that what we are seeking is recovery, and we can and should insist if we are going into this great cooperative effort that we do it with funds sufficient to make recovery and success possible. Otherwise let's not do it at all, let's not risk aggravating our dangerous inflation, or let's do only an admittedly humanitarian relief job.

And now for the $64 question. If we conclude that it should be a genuine recovery program and not a misbranded relief program, and if we conclude that it can be done without injury to our economy and should be done in our self-interest, is there any guarantee that it will be successful? I think one must say with complete candor that there is no guarantee of success, and that even if it does succeed, even if Europe is sufficiently restored to make free choices, one cannot be sure that the choice will, or even can, be in our mold. Nor if it did succeed and Europe became self-supporting would it mean the end of communism's political power in the world, which now includes one-fifth of the inhabited earth with about 350 million inhabitants, with much larger potential populations and areas. But success may well mean whether that struggle goes on with or without Western Europe, the most highly industrialized area with the most literate and skilled population in the world outside this continent.

However, if success is uncertain, failure is *not*. If we do not make the effort, failure is *certain*. What then? Why should we worry?

The political institutions, the economic organization and the culture of Western Europe which so closely resemble ours cannot endure if the means of sustaining life, that kind of life, drastically shrinks. If the great inflow and outflow of goods from Western Europe on which it depends should dry up, a system will develop by which everyone is directed to believe, act and work in a certain way, not really as a result of choice, but because power will be seized as it always has been by a determined, militant minority after government and social organization have broken down.

Whether this authoritarian regime is initially Fascist or Communist will depend on local conditions, with odds on the Communists. Because if we fail or refuse to make possible the return of Western Europe to self-support by obtaining a chief part of the goods she needs through the cooperation of our system of production and trade, it must turn in major part to the East, even for survival with fewer numbers and a lower scale. Of course, Western Europe hopes and expects to continue and to expand its trade with Eastern Europe.

Trade has been increasing between Eastern and Western Europe. To date seventy-one bilateral trade agreements have been made. Since July, no less than six agreements have been concluded for the exchange of goods between the Western zone of Germany and various Eastern European countries. Poland is supplying coal westward as well as eastward. Sweden's trade agreement with the Soviet Union is being carried out, as is Finland's with Great Britain.

But the price of enforced dependence upon Eastern Europe would seem to mean for Western Europe, sooner or later, incorporation in the economic and political system of the Communists. It would mean a corresponding loss for the rest of the world.

It is hard for us, struggling with our day-to-day problems, to visualize the kind of world we will be facing if communism spreads to the English Channel. It is still harder to envisage the repercussions on our southern neighbors and the teeming millions of the Far East. Such a shift of power would be of incalculable importance to the security and well-being of the United States and the whole non-Communist world. It would be the major event of modern history.

And this is the year of decision—a year in which the Government is divided between a Democratic Administration and a Republican Congress and we are facing a Presidential election in which things are sometimes said and done which bear less resemblance to national interest than to personal or party interest.

It is a test, a severe one, and the results will measure us and our system for the myriads of people who are watching intently—some with malice, more with prayers.

Let me leave you with the words of a wise and devoted American, Henry L. Stimson:

It is the first condition of effective foreign policy that this nation put away forever any thought that America can again be an island to herself. No private program and no public policy, in any sector of our national life, can now escape from the compelling fact that if it is not framed with reference to the world, it is framed with perfect futility.

Our stake in the peace and freedom of the world is not a limited liability. Time after time in other years we have tried to solve our foreign problems with halfway measures, acting under the illusion that we could be partly in the world and partly irresponsible. Time after time our Presidents and Secretaries of State have been restrained, by their own fears or by public opinion, from effective action. It should by now be wholly clear that only failure, and its follower, war, can result from such efforts at a cheap solution.

The troubles of Europe and Asia are not "other peoples' troubles"; they are ours. The world is full of friends and enemies; it is full of warring ideas; but there are no mere "foreigners," no merely "foreign" ideologies, no merely "foreign" dangers, any more. Foreign affairs are now our most intimate domestic concern. All men, good or bad, are now our neighbors. All ideas dwell among us.[89]

Communism Is the Catfish
in the Western Herring Pond

OCTOBER 18, 1949

✡

In his campaign for Governor, traveling through the state and making six or more speeches daily, Stevenson concentrated on "intimate domestic issues" rather than foreign affairs. Jacob Arvey comments,

I shall always remember the first time I was exposed to his rare speaking ability. . . . he reminded me that he had never made a political speech before and asked whether our publicity director, James "Spike" Hennessy, who was with us, could "dash off" something for him. We suggested that he try it himself and then if necessary Spike would edit it. Editing was unnecessary because, when he came back ten or fifteen minutes later and read to us what he had scribbled on several telegraph blanks, we knew then that this was a new style in political speaking and it was bound to make an impression upon all those who heard him.[90]

The election victory, in which he received 527,067 votes, the largest number in Illinois history, suggests the possible influence of this style.[91] Although he gave few speeches on foreign affairs during the early part of his term of office, this brief one given to the Inland Daily Press Association Luncheon at Chicago on October 18, 1949, illustrates his constant concern for American alertness in the face of the Soviet threat.

NOW, I was asked to say a word about the foreign situation. It can be only a word; a relevant word, I hope. I said at the outset that if this proves, as I think it will, to be a very healthy era in

American life in which we demanded and got something cleaner and better in public management, we would have the Russians to thank for it. What I mean is this: The Soviet Union is not going to attack the Western world, nor are we going to attack them. But we are going to be incessantly engaged in an aggravating, exhausting cold war for longer than I like to contemplate. We have already been fighting this wretched war four years. Along with the troublesome irritations, the Red scares and the huge defense expenditures, it has produced some good. It has caused the world to reexamine colonial policies and aspirations for freedom. It has drawn the Western community closer together for common defense and social and economic survival. It has kept the United States an alert and positive participant. It has even brought the dream of peace by world government closer to realization. It has made the United Nations and the international forum more imperative than ever. And, finally, it has caused us in the midst of all the ferment of ideological conflict and realignment to look to our own housekeeping. While we have been loudly proclaiming the virtues of democracy and free enterprise, the Communists have been even more loudly calling attention to our real failures and hypocrisies and, of course, to a lot of false ones as well. While polishing up the facade of our splendid edifice for all the admiring and envious of the world to see, we've also been poking around among the long neglected fire hazards in our basement—and none too soon. And, of course, the Communists have been forcing us to spend money beyond our saddest dreams of precarious peace, with the result that the restive taxpayer is looking in the corners and under the rug for dirt and waste more diligently than he has for a long time—which is a very healthy thing.

All in all, this cold war and this relentless Communist pressure, which is the strongest competition our Western individualism has encountered since the Renaissance, has already and will continue to cause us to do all sorts of things and change all sorts of things, but in our own way, not their way. As Toynbee says, communism is the catfish in the Western herring pond. It may eat a few herring, but it prevents all the rest from getting soft and stale. And of course *if* we can only keep fresh and alert like the herring with the catfish; if we don't get rattled and develop and improve our way of life by this self-examination and rediscovery, as we put our house in better and better order, the less chance the Commies will have of imposing their way of life upon us. Indeed, our successes will be their downfall, because it will have the slow imperceptible effect on them they hope to have on us. They will be the converted, not we.

"The Nation Is Safe in His Hands"

OCTOBER 26, 1949

✡

When Stevenson introduced Pandit Jawaharlal Nehru to the Chicago Council on Foreign Relations on October 26, 1949, Nehru had been Prime Minister of India for two years. Twelve years later, on November 12, 1961, Stevenson, then beset by many problems at the United Nations, hosted the Prime Minister on his ABC biweekly program "Adlai Stevenson Reports" in New York. Nehru was asked, "You also made the statement, Mr. Nehru, on a previous occasion, that one must journey through life alone. To rely on others invites heartbreak. How heartbroken are you these days?" Nehru's response was "As one advances in experience and age, one gets a little tougher, used to all kinds of kicks of that type. In one's youth, the heart breaks easily, whether the political heart or any heart. Still one survives that. . . . Ultimately, . . . heartbreak is always greater in regard to matters affecting one intimately, I would say. I suffer more from something that happens in India which I think is wrong than even a major catastrophe outside."[92]

WE live in an age swept by tides of history so powerful they shatter human understanding. Only a tiny handful of men have influenced the implacable forces of our time. To this small company of the truly great, our guest on this memorable day in Chicago and Illinois belongs.

He does us honor to come here and we pay him our homage, not just because he is the Prime Minister of India, but because he is a great and a good man. Pandit Jawaharlal Nehru belongs to the even *smaller* company of historic figures who wore a halo in their own lifetimes.

"The nation is safe in his hands." Those were Mahatma Gandhi's concluding words when he publicly chose Pandit Nehru as his heir and successor—because of his bravery, his prudence and discipline, his vision and practicality, his humility and purity.

Three hundred and fifty million of his countrymen love him, follow him, bless him for his brilliant leadership in their struggle for independence, and some say, even more because of his character, spirit and sacrifice. Long ago he forsook ease and wealth and security, to risk life itself for his country.

A quarter of his life he has spent in prison for the same cause our own revolutionary ancestors pledged their lives, their fortunes and their sacred honor—freedom. Born to exalted station he knows the "art of being a king," yet he has a common touch that excites the devotion and understanding of all kinds and conditions of people, and he has a pen and tongue that stir the hearts of millions. In his address to Congress he said: "Even when preparing to resist aggression, the objective of peace and reconciliation must never be lost sight of, and heart and mind must be attuned to this supreme aim, and not swayed or clouded by hatred or fear." So spoke our own Abraham Lincoln. These are words we understand, Mr. Prime Minister, and we are grateful for the reminder.

My friends, I bid you mark well what he says to us, for he is the voice of India—the home of a sixth of the human race and the largest stable, solvent democracy in the East. India can be the anchor of freedom in all Asia, but around it swirl dangerous currents and in it live millions in incredible poverty. Bedeviled with the infinite problems of national infancy, of the partition with Pakistan, of welding innumerable classes and minorities into a single Eastern state based on the new liberal tradition of the West, his tasks beggar description.

Indeed I must acknowledge Your Excellency a personal debt. Whenever the problems of Illinois get too oppressive I think of India and you, sir, and immediately I feel much better! We welcome you to Illinois.

The Silence of Death
for the Voices of Freedom

✡

On March 9, 1950, Stevenson addressed the Masaryk Centennial Celebration at Cicero, Illinois, in memory of the birth of the founder of Czechoslovakia, Thomas Masaryk. In his speech, as in others during the 1950's, he offered an eloquent lament for the Soviet destruction of democratic institutions in Eastern Europe.

I AM honored to have a part in your program today. I sense in this meeting more than the routine recognition of the hundredth anniversary of the birth of a great statesman. To me it is an evidence that the ideal of political freedom of which Thomas Garrigue Masaryk was such a brilliant symbol has, in the minds and hearts of his American countrymen, been etched in even sharper outline by the events recently occurring in your unhappy homeland. I think it is a demonstration—inspiring and significant—that they are determined to do everything they can to bring back into the family of free nations the republic that Masaryk founded in 1918, only to be twice ruthlessly [devastated].

It was not my good fortune to know Thomas Masaryk personally. But I did know and greatly admired his son, Jan, whose death in a Prague courtyard was one of the most tragic events of the tragic postwar era. Jan Masaryk's death, by what means we cannot be certain, was a loss to the entire Western world and a blow to the cause of democratic government everywhere. Yet it served to bring out in crystal clarity the true import of the Communist coup of two years ago; it was dramatic testimony to the world that the new regime in Prague meant oblivion for the Czechoslovakia his father had wrought, and the silence of death for the voices of freedom. But his broken body on the stones of the courtyard broadcast the message that he tried to bring to his people in life—that the destiny of his homeland lay on the side of the democracies and that death was not too high a price to pay for freedom.

He was my friend of twenty years. He stayed in my house. I stayed in his. We collaborated in late years in the formation of the United Nations at San Francisco, London and New York. Jan Masaryk was a kind, wise, gay, earthy man. In those wild years of war and peace, of hope and despair, he was the most trusted Central European. No man saw better, perhaps none as well, the import of the developing conflict between East and West. With the great Beneš[93] he fought a long, resourceful, forthright battle to help his country steer a middle course—hoping, preaching, pleading that the Soviets and the democracies would learn to live with each other in peace, and that their beloved Czechoslovakia, the bridge between East and West, retain her freedom and sovereignty. When Masaryk's hopes faded and the Iron Curtain rolled ruthlessly down upon his people, he preferred death to servile silence. To me he will always be one of history's heroic figures—a martyr to the cause of Czech freedom for which his father also gave his genius, energy and life.

Thomas Masaryk's life, spanning the years from 1850 to 1937, embraced a period of manifold and dramatic changes in the destiny of Czechoslovakia. At sixty-five, after a full life of service to his nation and at a time when many retire weary and broken, Thomas Masaryk set out to do the greatest of all tasks he had undertaken. Risking his life and reputation, leaving the family he loved so well, he entered upon the great struggle from which emerged the Czechoslovakian republic. He was seventy then, yet full of vigor and purpose, he served his country for seventeen years more as President, an office in which he served longer even than Franklin Roosevelt! During his lifetime he became a legend to his people. There is no doubt that in the annals of history his will always stand out as one of the most purposeful, idealistic and fruitful lives fate ever granted to mortal man.

Thomas Masaryk was a humble man, as most great men are. "The lonely Slovak," who, as an Austrian writer described him in

1909, seemed to be "a mixture of Tolstoi and Walt Whitman," turned out to have some of the qualities of Abraham Lincoln as well. Indeed these great leaders had much in common. They placed above all else the interests of their country and the welfare of the people. Both had a consuming sense of social justice and a deep moral conscience. Both possessed the courage, the vision and the qualities of leadership that enabled them to bring their respective infant republics through periods of trial and stress. Both considered individual freedom to speak and worship and to determine one's own life the greatest goal toward which men could strive, the richest of human possessions.

I think it can be said that Masaryk was more than a great leader of his people. He was a rare combination of thinker and man of action—as a scholar unusually sensitive to some of the modern implications of social and economic change, and at the same time deeply aware of the ultimate dependence of all political and cultural achievement upon the strength of the ethical and moral foundations of public action. He was a perfect link between the Slav peoples and the English-speaking world, and his influence as a teacher reached deep into the Balkans among the Croats and the Serbs. He was a builder and the symbol of the cultural and intellectual bridge between Czechoslovakia and America.

But that bridge was broken by the shameful betrayal of Munich —the lowest point in the curve of democratic disintegration. And today even the ruins of the beautiful bridge are obliterated by the fundamental and irreconcilable differences on the nature of man and the meaning of history which divide us from the closed society of Russia.

Today we are told that there is no freedom as we understand it in Czechoslovakia. There is only the long night of repression, with no promise of dawn in the eastern sky. We are told that the concentration camp and the secret police haunt and silence those who would protest against the new regime. In recent weeks, the press reports, the regime is even busily attempting to wipe out the memory of Masaryk and Beneš from the minds of the Czech people. Postage stamps bearing the likeness of Masaryk have been invalidated. Pictures of Masaryk and Beneš have been banished from schools and other public buildings. Textbooks have been rewritten to picture Masaryk and Beneš as enemies of the Czech people.

Time and events will disclose whether this kind of repression can destroy the democratic traditions of your countrymen. In the light of history, which records the relentless and everlasting struggles of the Czech and Slovak peoples against oppression, it is hard to believe that the love of freedom ever can be stamped out by a policeman's boot or a censor's pen. History offers the more logical hope that in another time, under other circumstances, a new Masaryk will arise to lead your people to a happier destiny.

That is the hope which I know fills your hearts as you celebrate this anniversary, and the hearts of all Americans who know that we are all part of one another—politically, economically and morally. Americans cannot by nature be oblivious to human oppression, and they have learned by bitter experience that the rise of totalitarian power anywhere is a threat to freedom everywhere.

Czechoslovakia's plight has helped bring home to us the real issues in the cold war. It has helped arouse the free world to its new danger; it has clarified our concept of responsibility as a world power, and it has unified the democracies in the measures they are taking to check the spread of Soviet influence.

None can foretell when or how the freedom and independence of Czechoslovakia can be restored; but the spiritual kinship between our countries is close and will endure. It was from the example of this republic that Thomas Masaryk drew spiritual inspiration and constitutional guidance. It was in Independence Hall in Philadelphia that he proclaimed the establishment of the Czechoslovakian republic. Its constitution is patterned after our own. Its ambitions, its ideals, parallel ours. Its leaders, like Masaryk, father and son, and Beneš, have become an integral part of the tradition and the heritage of the democratic world.

A half century ago Thomas Masaryk asked his people the question: "When we recall our numerous struggles for existence in the past, such as our uprising at the White Mountain, which ended in defeat; our fall; our rebirth during the French Revolution and the enlightenment of the eighteenth century; the Revolution of 1848, the Polish rebellion, we, as thinking Czechs, are forced to decide: shall we choose violence or peace, the sword or the plow, blood or labor in the sweat of our brow, death or life?"

And his answer was: "Not violence but peace, not the sword but the plow, not blood but work, not death but life for the sake of life; this shall be the answer of the Czech spirit, this is the meaning of our history and the bequest of our great forebears."

That was the philosophy of Thomas Masaryk. Today, his abhorrence of war and his patient faith in ultimate justice are the most meaningful parts of the legacy of wisdom and truth we have from him. With this courage and honesty, and his firm faith, we must strive on resolutely to find peaceful means of solving the issues dividing the worlds in which we live.

So doing, we shall be true to the memory of Thomas Masaryk, who an English scholar said was the nearest historical example of Plato's ideal of the Philosopher-King. So doing, we shall be true to the great traditions of Western civilization he did so much to advance. To those traditions, let us fervently hope, his people can one day return.

Korea: An Incident in the Long Contest
for Mastery of the World

OCTOBER I, 1950

☼

Weaknesses inherent in the United Nations system of collective security were made highly apparent in the Security Council's actions in relation to the attack of North Korea against South Korea on June 25, 1949. The Council was able to apply the collective security provisions of the Charter and to initiate police action against the aggressors only because the Soviet delegation was then boycotting the Council meetings. With the Soviet return to the Council, the General Assembly was called upon to carry the burden of organizing the collective actions of the United Nations. Additionally, however, the Soviet delegation began to apply a consistent use of the veto on those matters involving Korea that were to be decided in the Council. About a month after Stevenson gave this speech to the United Nations Festival at the Chanute Air Force Base in Rantoul, Illinois, October 1, 1950, the General Assembly passed the "Uniting for Peace" Resolution, which attempted to establish the General Assembly as the principal agency for the organization of collective security.[94] Stevenson had long advocated strengthening the Assembly to make it more than a simple recommending body.

I AM greatly heartened by the fact that you people of Chanute Field have added to this honorable list—the United Nations!

That in this one corner of the great mid-continent area we are pulling the United Nations down out of the remoter reaches of the atmosphere and looking upon it like we do [at] our corn and grapes is a good thing. And I am glad that we are doing it gladly—in the same spirit of happy thankfulness with which we approach the eternal miracle of the harvest season.

You have, it seems to me, seized upon an appropriate point in time for this celebration. A short four months ago would have been too soon. I say this advisedly and in all candor, devoted as I personally have been to the cause of the United Nations Organization since its very inception. For there have been five long years during which the flame kindled so brightly at San Francisco at times burned perilously low. Disappointment has been piled on disappointment, frustration has followed frustration. A close and informed analysis of the record of the United Nations, its manifold special agencies and many missions, during the first years of its life discloses many major achievements, many dangerous fires quenched, which more than justify its existence even in the periods of apparent futility. But I cannot pretend that these accomplishments were sufficiently dramatic to satisfy the many who expected peace and security to rise full-grown from the ashes of the last war.

But Korea has changed all that. There is a new spirit abroad, a new feeling stirs the land about this greatest organized effort for peace. I sense it everywhere I go. Your festival is tangible and vivid evidence. We, as a people, almost for the first time have come to feel the great power that is latent in the United Nations, the kinship and common purpose of the free peoples around the globe—whatever their color, their religion, their social and political customs—who have joined hands in the common defense of their right to life and self-determination.

We in the United States have always gloried in our strength, our ability to take care of ourselves and to face our crises alone. But I do not, I believe, misread the feelings of most of us when I recall our unexpressed faintness of heart and loneliness of spirit those fateful hours in June when the first intimations filtered out from Washington that our government had, come what might, concluded to take its stand squarely on the Charter of the United Nations in a strange and bleak peninsula thousands of miles away. Our pride could not overcome the tell-tale misgiving that we were facing incalculable consequences in a vast and darkening world.

For once, I submit, the average citizen among us, in city and in village, in the factory and on the land, awaited the response of the other members of the United Nations with a suspense and prayerful anxiety which would have been unthinkable a few hours before. I need not remind you of what that response was, nor of how promptly it was given. Fifty-three nations all told instantly joined in the indictment of this ruthless, cynical breach of the peace. Aggression was identified in the most forthright terms; terms the timid would never have risked alone.

The United Nations embraced the fundamental task for which it was brought into being. This was no longer merely an interminable debate, or a mission to make educational studies in Africa, or a mission of economic experts to advance industrialization in Afghanistan. This was "it." And, as the man on the street could recognize the challenge, so could he measure the manner in which it was met. On that day the United Nations became a meaningful part of the life of the great mass of mankind. In the idiom of Americans, it took its place beside such institutions as the World Series, the Air Force, hot dogs, and fireworks on the Fourth of July. It became, if you please, something it might be a good idea to have a festival about!

The United States and the Republic of Korea have borne the brunt of the battle in Korea. But we have not been alone. Ground forces from other countries have joined in the painful ordeal. Foreign naval units have been at work in the waters around Korea and foreign aircraft have patrolled the skies. Medical and Red Cross teams from all over the world have supported the fighting men.

In scales of battle so delicately balanced, this help was not inconsiderable in and of itself. But its importance in nonmaterial terms was far greater. All of these military forces—our own, the Korean Republic's, and those of other countries—for the first time served under one flag. They were subject to one commander.

The flag and the voice of command were not those of any one nation, but of the United Nations. They bespoke not the interests or ambitions of any one country but the conscience of all the free peoples. They symbolized a dream come true—a dream of effective international cooperation to preserve peace by stopping aggression in its tracks, a dream from which there had earlier been the bitter awakenings of the brutal conquest of Ethiopia, the German reoccupation of the Rhineland, the rape of Austria. Hopes which were dashed at the Marco Polo Bridge in Manchuria,[95] dashed by the Pact of Munich and by Russian vetoes at Lake Success, have been rekindled at long last. As Secretary Acheson said a few days ago in his opening address to the current session of the General Assembly: "There is no longer any question: Will the United Nations survive? Will the United Nations suffer the fate of the League of Nations? This question has been answered. If by nothing else, it has been answered by United Nations action against aggression in Korea. Blood is thicker than ink."[96]

The United Nations has, thus, met and passed the supreme test which confronts any organization devised for collective security; when the chips were down, when words and pleas and protestations were no longer enough, it acted. The history of past civilizations shows us that the seeds of inevitable decline and fall are planted when the first major challenge is offered and is not squarely met and surmounted. The lesson of the past is plain. In our time the League of Nations was doomed from the day it first evaded the challenge of aggression. And so would have been the United Nations had it failed to meet the challenge in Korea.

This is, then, most certainly a time for thanksgiving, for rejoicing that the greatest postwar crisis is safely behind us. As we meet today, moreover, there is further cause for satisfaction in that the success of the first passage at arms by the United Nations seems assured after weeks of painful, bloody retreat and build-up.

We in the United States may properly take equal satisfaction from the course we have followed before Korea. There have been many times since the end of the war when our patience was sorely tried. The futilities of Security Council meetings with veto after veto, the disappointing communiqués issued by the successive meetings of the Council of Foreign Ministers, the stalemate of the Commission on the International Control of Atomic Energy—all combined to produce weariness and disappointment which could only result in disillusion and skepticism about the use and purpose of it all. There were bleak days when each of us must have asked himself whether the game was worth the candle, whether the patience, the effort, the money, the concessions to world harmony were not barren of any reward.

There were among us counsels of despair; there were those who urged the abandonment of international cooperation, the scrapping of the United Nations, or its reorganization as an alliance which would have obliterated its universality. Nor will those voices be stilled; they never are until time and events have silenced even the echo.

By our calm persistence in the face of provocation, by our long and honorable record of eager willingness to confer, to negotiate, to participate in and support common objectives, we have established the genuineness of our reliance upon peaceful procedures for all to see, to assay and approve. While we have identified in unmistakable outline the true source of the existing threat to peace, we have, at the same time, tendered both the pledge and the proof of our own good intentions.

Last June we reaped the harvest of our record. We were unembarrassed by any charge of having failed to exhaust the avenues of conciliation when the United Nations was called upon to approve our armed intervention in Korea. We could stand upon the record because the record was clear. Against the day when we may again be in a similar position, let us admit of no alternative which will obscure that record hereafter.

It is not, moreover, only in what others think of us that we find our power in these troubled times. Few of us are so corrupted by the layers of years that we do not recall from our school days Tennyson's line about Sir Galahad whose strength was as the strength of ten because his heart was pure.[97]

Korea, like the great issues that await us in the future, was a problem in morals. These problems are sometimes postponed but never really solved by mere weight of numbers of armed men or superiority in weapons. Involving, as they do, the elemental questions of human freedom and dignity and the destiny of man, they do not yield to force alone. To force must be added the purity of purpose we call justice—the clear conscience and the conviction that the peaceful alternative has been fully explored to no avail.

Our record of the last five years in this latter regard stood us in good stead in Korea. We had no stake there but a moral one and we came to the fray thrice-armed with good conscience and universal conviction that we had patiently struggled to prevent it. When there is talk of preventive wars, let us be alert to the price we would pay in these terms. Let us, none of us, fighting man or civilian, ever forget that force without justice is tyranny.

And, in conclusion, while we celebrate our blessings and our victory; while we marvel and glory in the might and majesty of our air force here at Chanute Field, let us also never forget that justice without force is impotent, futile and useless in the world we know. It was only a few years ago that people were clamoring to bring the boys home and liquidate the war and all its reminders quickly. It was only a few months ago that the press and the political platforms were ringing with demands for lower taxes and less defense spending. It was only a few weeks ago that the tune changed and they began hurling epithets about unpreparedness and demands for more spending.

We are, let's face it, a volatile people. Our consistency in the long run is the product of compensating peaks and valleys of inconsistency in the short run. And I bid you beware of the charlatans, the demagogues and the false prophets who have no convictions, no consistency, no vision, who drift with the erratic winds of opinion, clamoring today for this, tomorrow for that, with shameless, noisy self-confidence.

And, mark my words, they will be out in full force again now that the Korean crisis has subsided, preaching the soft doctrine of business as usual, politics as usual, eat your cake and have it too. We are suckers for good news; but we dare not be beguiled by a more conciliatory Soviet Union and by our strident, shallow voices who are its unwitting tools. Korea is only an incident in a long contest for mastery of the world. The millennium has not arrived; sweetness and light is still an illusion; objectives have not changed in Moscow, only tactics. The United Nations is the forum of international justice, but justice without force is still impotent. And the United States must be the big policeman of peace for a long time to come. So don't let down, don't relax; keep the boys flying!

Internationalism Is Now
a Life-and-Death Matter

FEBRUARY 26, 1951

☆

Profoundly disturbed that the Illinois legislature was considering a bill calling for the United States withdrawal from the United Nations, Stevenson gave the following speech at the Chicago American Association for the United Nations, where he had been invited to introduce Governor Youngdahl of Minnesota on February 26, 1951.

I READ this verse in a downstate paper the other day:

> The Dis United Nations is a disappointment rank.
> It's like a worthless rubber check that bounces from the bank.
> The Dis United Nations is a muddle and a miss.
> It was engineered at 'Frisco by a renegade named Hiss.
> The Dis United Nations should not have come to birth.
> The sooner it's disbanded, the better for our earth.

I get some comfort from the fact that it was written by a man in Wichita, Kansas, not Illinois.

But, there is pending in the Illinois legislature at Springfield a resolution calling on the United States to withdraw from the United Nations.

Now what accounts for this violent distaste for this best and only hope for collective security and peace in the world? What accounts for the unhappy fact that there are evidently thousands of adult, sober Americans whose disappointment with the Korean war and the continued tension in the world prompts them to cut off their nose to spite their face, to throw out the *baby* with the *bath*, to destroy the *good* because it is not *perfect?*

It was only a few years ago that people were clamoring to bring the boys home, liquidate the war and leave it all to the United Nations. It was only a year ago that the country was ringing with demands for lower taxes and less defense spending. It was only a few months ago that the time changed and they began hurling epithets about unpreparedness and demands for more defense spending. And now, after some reverses in Korea, there is clamor to junk the U.N. because there is no peace in the world.

We are a volatile people. Our consistency in the long run is the product of compensating peaks and valleys of inconsistency in the short run. Opinion tends to drift with the erratic winds of our fortunes. Today we clamor for this, tomorrow for that, with noisy self-confidence, but without consistency, conviction, vision—and most of all understanding.

But I did not come here to psychoanalyze my fellow Americans, nor have I any professional qualifications for such a diagnosis. Yet this sort of erratic impatience following on the very heels of last summer's applause and approval of the U.N. after the intervention in Korea reflects, at least to me, an alarming national instability that I can only charge to ignorance about our progress toward world order largely under American leadership.

Be that as it may, we quickly learned some years ago that the premise of the U.N., the common consent of the great powers to underwrite peace and security, was a false premise, and that Russia did not in fact consent. So for the past four or five years we have been connoting a system based on consent to a system based on force. And despite limited resources, public indifference, to put it mildly, and strong indigenous Communist influences in Europe we have made impressive progress in this conversion both in and out of the U.N. toward the organization and preservation of the free world. The stopgap Greek-Turkish aid program led directly to the Marshall Plan which all concede has reduced the Communist menace in Europe, raised the standard of living and reestablished confidence and hope. The Council of Europe, the Consultative Assembly, manifestations of political renaissance and unity in Europe have been fortified by the North Atlantic pact and the arms program.

But aggression came not in Europe but in Korea where we had

no like-minded allies. Yet fifty-three out of fifty-nine members of the U.N. promptly endorsed resistance and many have contributed military and material aid to this bloody battle for peace and security—the greatest experiment of its kind in history.

Now it seems to me that all these are no inconsiderable steps toward the goal of peace and security through the U.N., where possible, and outside the U.N. where necessary, by consent where possible, by force where necessary. These anxious years have demonstrated the U.N.'s virtues, flexibilities and also its deficiencies —deficiencies which were patent for all to see when the basic premise of sincere consent by the great powers was sabotaged by imperialist communism. And we should not forget that we helped to make the charter of the U.N. a limited instrument; that it has failed to do only what it was never given the power to do because the world was not ready to give it that power, including ourselves. But we do not say that the Constitution of the United States has failed because there is Jim Crow in the south, and gambling and lawlessness everywhere.

Is there an explanation of our failure of comprehension and our impatience in our long tradition of approaching international issues on idealistic and moralistic bases? Internationalism began here as a moral movement. Most of the public support for the U.N. has been of this character.

The idealist-moralistic approach to the U.N. has been useful in overcoming public inertia and in launching the organization, but it is now high time the public matured its thinking about the U.N. The lack of such maturity may account for much of the disillusionment today, and from time to time in the past, which has been expressed in despair and rejection of the U.N. because of its failure to relieve the growing world tension and because it has not by some miracle proved a full-blown, effective collective-security system able to maintain peace in a world divided by the ruthless ambitions of a strong and stealthy conspiracy. This frustration and disappointment has also been expressed at the other end of the spectrum by its most passionate friends in frustration and disappointment that so much international business is conducted outside the U.N. Again it is expressed in petulance about disagreements; the idea that the U.S. must always be right and that all states should look at issues from the same viewpoint that we Americans do and [should] always vote with us; in short, the concept of one world—in our own image and likeness.

But internationalism is now a life-and-death matter; not a matter of good will and idealism. We should look at the U.N., as we look at other political instruments, and see what it is *not*, disabuse ourselves of any illusions and recognize how useful it has been, is and can still be.

Of course, the U.N. is not a full-blown collective-security system and it is dangerous to think of it and operate within it as if it were. It's a council table, not a police force.

We all know that the disarmament provisions of the charter and the military contingents contemplated by Article 43 have never been implemented due to Russian intransigence. In short, the U.N. operates in a balance-of-power world, half of which is massively armed and the other half only beginning to arm. At best the organization now has only limited capabilities available from the free world. These must be developed and deployed and applied intelligently, flexibly, and not rigidly and dogmatically.

When one part of the world rejects the principles on which the U.N. is founded while retaining its membership, its role is inevitably modified. Increasingly it is becoming a political framework through which a broad coalition of the free world operates. A bridge to the Soviet Union is useful—indeed, when we cease to talk we will probably start to fight—but the U.N. cannot solve the Soviet problem. It is vital to our security to have this political framework as the maintenance and development of the coalition of the free world as our chief political task today. And if it did not exist it would have to be created even today.

I hope I've made it clear that the task of this organization, the American Association for the United Nations, is depressingly large: education and understanding of what's being done and why [, and] that with each change in the mind public opinion is not diverted. This is a conference on "Our responsibility for world leadership." But how can America lead if America doesn't understand?

Anything but Honest, Straightforward Talk
Borders on Treason

APRIL 22, 1952

✡

As the news media began to speculate in the spring of 1951 that Truman would not seek reelection as President, Stevenson was mentioned frequently as an important possibility. In January, 1952, Stevenson asked his friend Stephen A. Mitchell, who had played a major role in his initial election, to help him "establish a planning group to organize an independent campaign committee" for his renomination and reelection as Governor.[98] He also publicly filed his candidacy for renomination. However, on January 22, Truman announced to Stevenson in a secret meeting his intention not to run again for the Presidency and offered him his support for the nomination. Stevenson's refusal to run later prompted Truman to write, "I thought it strange at the time that he would reject a call to party leadership and service to the nation at so critical a moment in our history."[99]

Before his death Stevenson responded to a journalist's question about his refusal, "I declined for two reasons. One, I was already an avowed candidate for reelection as Governor of Illinois. . . . And, two, I didn't want to run for President. . . . Nobody can believe you when you say you're not a candidate. It's a curious thing. The more decisive you are in not seeking an exalted office, the more they say you're indecisive. My very decisiveness was attributed to what they called indecision."[100] Nevertheless, many rumors and articles began to appear which suggested that Stevenson was "the coy candidate." After Truman and Stevenson met again in March and Stevenson repeated his refusal to run, the Presi-

141

*dent's announcement at the national Jefferson-Jackson Day Dinner
on March 31 that he would not seek reelection caused the members
of the news media to stampede Stevenson for an answer.*

*Despite Stevenson's reiterations of his non-candidacy, Arthur
Krock wrote him shortly after, "Soon after the Illinois primary on
April 8, you will be an actively receptive candidate for the Democratic nomination for President. Want to bet?" Stevenson replied
on April 3, "Don't bet—with me or anybody else—a word to the
wise. A.E.S."[101] On April 16, he issued a formal statement, "I
have repeatedly said that I was a candidate for Governor of Illinois
and had no other ambition. To this I must now add that in view of
my prior commitment to run for Governor and my desire and the
desire of many who have given me their help and confidence in our
unfinished work in Illinois, I could not accept the nomination for
any other office this summer."[102] When he gave the speech below
to the Dallas Council on World Affairs on April 22, 1952, he was
very much in the front pages of the news. His views on foreign
policy, expressed as they were with freshness and their broad historical parallels of past turbulence and the nation's greatness, were
widely publicized. With new optimism, Stevenson devotees continued to create "Draft Stevenson" movements throughout the
country.[103]*

I SUPPOSE this will be known as one of those convulsive periods
in human history which witness the death of an old era and the
birth of a new. The process is painful and tumultuous, and accompanied by all manner of tension, disorder and torment. The teacher
in a grammar school asked the class: "What shape is the earth?"
and a small boy quickly answered: "My father says it's in the
worst shape it ever was." Perhaps it is. Bernard Shaw once remarked: "If the other planets are inhabited they must be using the
earth as their insane asylum."

But, of course, anxiety is nothing new. Long ago, Hezekiah,
King of Judah, facing a crisis in Judah's relations with Assyria,
said: "This is the day of trouble, and of rebuke, and of blasphemy."[104]

We commonly think of the nineteenth century as a calm and

hopeful age. Yet in 1806, William Pitt said: "There is scarcely anything around us but ruin and despair."[105] Even the fathers of our Constitution had their bad moments. In 1829, John Randolph of Virginia said: "The country is ruined past redemption."[106]

But all these dire forebodings came to nothing. A look at history from where we sit in the mid-twentieth century, confounded with difficulties and tormented with anxiety, should provide us a little perspective and much hope.

It seems as though the most creative and enterprising periods in human history have always been troubled and disorderly. The sixteenth century witnessed the flowering of the Renaissance, but a great contemporary, Erasmus, called that stirring era "the excrement of the ages."[107] So too the eighteenth century which we regard as one of the most creative, with the American and French Revolutions, was to Rousseau "this great rottenness in which we live."

I take some comfort from the contrast between the historical and contemporary view of violent and disturbed eras. But I take no satisfaction in the current habit of looking for scapegoats to blame for our difficulties—difficulties, anxieties and tensions which are the consequence of our present position of world leadership.

It is correct to say that this country never asked for or explicitly chose its present position. But we are not there because of some person's bad judgment or because of a historical accident. We made the choice unconsciously by making many decisions in our past that resulted in our present greatness. We expanded westward and settled a great continent bordering on two oceans. We developed our country industrially, largely on the basis of an expanding internal market. We developed a government on the principles of consent and accountability that gives us internal political strength. We fought in two wars, hoping to be free of great anxieties at their end, only to find that the power balance was changed by the outcome of the wars—England and France weakened, Germany and Japan eclipsed, the Soviet Union confronting us. We have great responsibilities, not because we wanted them, but because as a nation we made choices in our past that made them inevitable.

Jefferson foresaw this. Writing to John Adams in 1816 he foretold our position of influence and power: "We are destined," he said, "to be a barrier against the return of ignorance and barbarism." Of our continental strength he wrote: "What a stand will it secure as a ralliance for the reason and freedom of the globe!" He foresaw America assuming leadership: "Old Europe will have to lean on our shoulders . . . and to hobble along by our side. . . ." he said.

Now all this has come to pass (and probably come to stay) and it makes us miserable, so we exchange epithets and accusations and look for someone, preferably Democrats, to blame for it all. Instead of acting like Walt Whitman's "resolute breed of men" many of us react more like readers of the "whodunit" mystery thrillers. That mature people with any historical perspective should feel dismayed and betrayed if there is not perfect efficacy in foreign policy disturbs me. I recall a story told in Mexico. A man heavy in need and great in faith wrote a letter asking for 100 pesos. He addressed it to God and mailed it. The postmaster had no idea how to handle the letter. He opened it, seeking a clue. Touched by the man's story of need, he passed the hat among the postal employees. Thus 75 pesos were raised and placed in an envelope to await the return of the importuning man. A few days later he was back, inquiring for mail. He was given the envelope, opened it, counted the money and glowered. Then he went to the counter and painfully wrote out another letter. It read: "Dear God: I am still 25 pesos short. Please make up the difference. But don't send it through the local post office. I think it is full of thieves."

There can be no perfect efficacy in the conduct of foreign affairs and the "whodunit" approach to world problems will yield no solutions. Actually, the severity of the crisis in which we must, whether we like it or not, play a leading role, is due to a conjunction of separate crises no one of which would have been too formidable but all of which taken together put a fearful burden upon us. Of these separate crises, three, at least, are due to science:

1. A century of continuous social and economic revolution now reaching full speed largely because of the belief that modern techniques fully applied in peace could give a higher living standard to everyone, ergo, must.
2. Modern communications and transport that by transforming the entire planet into a single strategical area have made necessary think-

ing in terms of a world balance of power and increased the difficulty of localizing armed conflicts.

3. New weapons which, while no more lethal than the flu epidemic, are terrifying by the amount of killing and destruction they can accomplish at one clip—hence awakening greater fear of war.

4. Basic too, I think, is the decline in the belief in previous fixed values everywhere, thus making it more difficult to appeal to nations and groups to do what is necessary and to recognize dangers in time, while increasing their vulnerability to the new religion of communism.

5. The head start in territorial and arms expansion seized by the U.S.S.R. while our policy was to disarm unilaterally and try to tempt Stalin into cooperation rather than opposition; and—

6. The apparently uncompromisingly aggressive nature of Soviet communism.

Obviously, the first four of these would exist if there had never been a U.S.S.R. or if it underwent a drastic change tomorrow. And none of them are going to be spirited away by hysteria or political claptrap to catch unwary voters. I think we know that. McCarthyism and loose talk may take the headlines but they won't take the American people.

Foreign policy is now a life-and-death matter, and anything but honest, straightforward talk borders on treason. Most of us know that our difficulties and frustrations cannot be blamed on any single individual or group. Our troubles as well as our triumphs find their explanation in the full sweep of recent history for which we are all in part responsible. Our international position today is part and parcel of developments that result from actions of whole peoples and groups of peoples over a long period of time.

None of us can glibly toss off a share of responsibility for our present international position. And we won't find the architects of our woes hiding under the bed or sitting in public office.

Common sense tells us that the stuff of history is rich and complex and not within the sure control of any one nation. Our national power is enormous. But there is a lot of other power loose in the world—military power, historic traditions, ethnic loyalties, ideologies. Our position gives us a chance to influence and to beguile world history. But we cannot determine it. New faces in

Washington, whoever they are, cannot make everything come out just the way this nation wants it.

Of course, we are disappointed that prospects for tranquility are not brighter. But most of us know that life by its very nature is never free of trouble. Life is not so much getting one's way as working one's way. And I think most of us know that. Beneath the anxious, confused surface of our daily life something deep and sound has been happening. "Whodunit" is an irritable reaction from blithe optimism. Optimism is pleasant but it can never save the nation. It distorts facts, disguises issues, hides perils.

But it seems to me obvious that most Americans, irrespective of party, have a pretty sound outlook on the world and sense how dangerous an antagonist the Soviet Union really is. We were not the first to be attacked. But because of our power and our success this country is the Kremlin's chief concern. The United States is the one great obstacle to a world safe for communism. We are the symbol of hope to all men who aspire to be free and stand erect. Queen Juliana [of the Netherlands] said that what her children remember of New York is their last glimpse of the Statue of Liberty from the deck of the Queen Mary: "A hand sticking out of the fog, holding a torch." America is a torch in the fog, and the Soviet leaders would like to douse the torch.

My impression is that most of us are now also aware of the duplicity of Soviet strategy—the practice of "double diplomacy" —a set of slogans for home consumption, a set of slogans for foreign confusion; warfare against the Russian people, warfare against all foreigners; political and military warfare, simultaneous or interchangeable. Communism speaks with the voice of idealism but has the hand of the cynic. Perhaps its greatest influence springs from the fact that it has made the miserable of the world more conscious of their misery and lures them into dictatorship by the offer of "democracy," into tyranny by the promise of "justice," into servitude by the pledge of "freedom." Yet we know how it inflames the hearts and hopes of the ignorant and needy to whom elocution about democracy is meaningless.

I believe we have made up our minds about another matter. This nation has rejected isolation as the way to security in our shrunken world. Isolation was buried during World War II when we estab-

lished the United Nations. This was before the full peril of the
Soviet threat was clear, but that peril has only reinforced the national decision to go forward with allies. This country has emphatically and definitively concluded, I believe, that the time to stop
aggression is before it starts and that the way to do it is by organized action of the community of free peoples.

We have been engaged for some time in the formidable task of
building this community of free peoples—first through the United
Nations; then through the North Atlantic Treaty Organization to
strengthen the crucial Western European peninsula; simultaneously by developing the important Organization of American
States in our own hemisphere and by numerous other treaties,
agencies and policies.

We talk incessantly of our failures and Communist successes, but
it is well to remember that Communist encroachment was successfully opposed in Greece and Turkey, their blockade in Berlin was
met by ingenuity and countermeasures, and their aggression in
Korea was battled head-on. The prompt and firm response to the
North Korean aggression was part and parcel of a strategy of collective security which had been in the making for a long time and
which had been urged, welcomed, and agreed upon long since with
virtual unanimity by the American people.

Our immediate reaction through the United Nations to the
cynical North Korean attack was greeted at the time with the
applause of the entire country. The aggression has been stopped
and the aggressors driven back across the thirty-eighth parallel
from whence they came. Yet now, with the armistice negotiations
dragging out, possibly until after the elections, we hear ambitious
men in search of votes capitalize every discontent, every prejudice,
every credulity; we hear the repeated charge that the Korean war
is "Truman's war," that it is a "useless war," that "we stand exactly
where we stood three years ago." But what sort of logic is it to
argue that because the continuation of the war does not serve our
interests, it was futile from the start?

I do not know how soon we can expect an armistice in Korea, or
whether there will be an armistice at all. The decision rests with the
same Communist leaders who gave the signal for the attack on
South Korea. But perhaps never has a more important action re-

ceived less adequate explanation than the prompt intervention of the United States through the United Nations in Korea. The defense of South Korea was the first time in the world's history that military force was used by an international organization to turn back aggression. While Korea has not proved definitely that collective security will work, it has prevented the Soviet Union from proving that it won't work. And the Korean experience has hastened the development of the General Assembly of the United Nations as an agency for the enforcement of the United Nations' decisions against aggression, free from the Soviet veto.

Korea put the American rearmament effort into high gear. Now our increasing strength both inhibits and puts us in a better position to answer any new Communist aggression.

Also, the strong stand we took on Korea, together with a stepped-up rearmament program, has had an important effect on the morale of the peoples of Western Europe and encourages them to build up their own defenses. NATO would not have the strength it has today if we had not acted promptly and decisively to support the United Nations in Korea.

Our action in Korea also had valuable results throughout the Far East; it contributed greatly to the successful negotiation of a peace treaty with Japan, and to the conclusion of mutual security treaties with the Philippines, Australia and New Zealand, as well as Japan.

Finally, the Soviet Union now knows that the path of conquest is mortally dangerous. The Korean aggression very likely was planned as merely the first of a series of military actions—initially by satellites, finally to be undertaken by the Soviet Union itself. If so, the loss of Korea may be of historical importance.

Of course, speculation about possible adjustments in the thinking of the Kremlin must be cautious. Perhaps for the time the Soviet Union will now content itself with maneuvers in the cold war, like wooing Germany from the West; or perhaps Western strength of will is to be further tested by some other military challenge or even more sternly tested by a peace offensive calculated to retard the rearmament program. We dare not tie our policies to any one assumption regarding Soviet intentions. Whatever those intentions are, however, the Soviet miscalculation in Korea will make them harder of fulfillment, and to call a war launched by Moscow

"Truman's war" or a "useless war" is not only misleading but mischievous.

I believe our government has done well in diligently and painfully seeking to limit the war to Korea. We have been concerned not only to frustrate our immediate antagonists, but to use force to avoid a full-scale holocaust. For this reason, we have to be patient about the full settlement of the Korean problem. A satisfactory settlement—the unification of Korea as a free nation—is likely to take a long time and to wait upon settlements of other issues. And we may yet fail in our effort to keep the Korean fighting from spreading—the aggressor has a lot to say about that.

There is another matter on which I find wide agreement—the acceptance of the appalling cost of the rearmament and military-assistance program as a condition of security now, until, negotiating from strength, we can devise the means of coexistence on a tolerable basis with this inscrutable Russian power in the world.

In an earlier period of crisis, when Greece was challenged by Persia, Heraclitus said: "We have to defend our walls and our laws."[108] So do we and I suspect, thanks in large part to the impetus of Korea, that we are rapidly redressing the balance of power in the world. But certainly the Korean experience as a warning of the possibility of war any time and anywhere must remain in our calculations. The path of Soviet conquest must, until reason can prevail and disarmament safely commence, continue to be mortally dangerous as it was in Korea. Better to pay large insurance premiums than to rebuild the house after a terrible fire.

What is at stake between the free world and the Russians is primarily the decision as to who is going to decide the basis on which the social, economic and political problems of the world are going to be handled. The Soviet Union offers one method, we offer another. I am confident the American people intend to make sure that our democratic experiment will outlast the Soviet system on its merits, if we are fortunate enough to face chiefly that test. Marxist doctrine includes the expectation that the capitalist world will one day weaken and destroy itself, largely by its own inner contradictions. But in spite of our predilection for solving problems quickly and putting them behind us, I suspect we could do very well in a waiting contest. Americans are learning to live with some of their problems and we could become as effective in the cold war as we have always asked our military men to be in a hot war.

Each problem of our foreign policy must be tackled soberly, patiently, firmly, in the light of the total situation. We should refuse to be pushed into what looks like a brave policy before we are sure it is not a foolish one. That hard-headed activist, Winston Churchill, once wrote: "Those who are prone by temperament and character, to seek sharp and clear-cut solutions of difficult and obscure problems, who are ready to fight whenever some challenge comes from a foreign power, have not always been right. How many wars have been averted by patience and persisting good will."

No greater difficulty confronts us than the wise and thrifty allocation of our limited resources and capabilities in relation to all the demands upon us. We also have much to learn about how to talk and act with increasing relevance to the problems of the underdeveloped areas and the uncommitted peoples who stand so high on the Kremlin's list. There are ways to increase the brittleness of the Soviet and satellite system; we must find and exploit them.

Crucial to success is our ability to work with our allies. Let us not underestimate this undertaking. And likewise let us not underestimate the difficulty Stalin confronts with alliances maintained by ruthless central leadership. We, on the other hand, must rely on willing allies, drawn to us by a recognition of mutual interests and by confidence in our leadership. There still seem to be some Americans who think we can get along without allies. They admit that our interests and responsibilities are worldwide but they prefer to "go it alone," or assume we can pick up the necessary allies at the last moment. They seem to resent efforts to win allies in advance of trouble by mutual agreement to help each other, such as the Atlantic Pact. They somehow expect to have friends without being one. In some ways this brand of isolationism is more dangerous than the old-fashioned variety. America First argued we should leave the world alone, overlooking the fact that the world would not leave us alone. The ghost of America First asks us to assume world responsibilities but then advocates policies that would lose us our allies one by one.

Power attracts allies. But the whole tone and style in which we use our power is of primary importance. For power also repels. The nations we must count upon for help in a successful military defense and a promising political advance are weaker than we are. Some of these weaker nations, once alarmed at our isolation, are now worrying about how we will use our power. We should not be too surprised at this. A position of preponderant influence makes us the target of suspicion and criticism. We must admit there are some pretty headstrong people in our midst. Long ago, Ralph Waldo Emerson said: "Beware of the American peacock." Some of our allies are not completely convinced that along with our power and wealth we also know everything about leading a worldwide alliance. But we can show by what we do and say that we do not simply consult our own interests and views but give consideration to the concerns of our allies; that we in truth "have a decent respect for the opinions of mankind." I believe the eagle, and neither the ostrich nor the peacock, will continue to be the American emblem!

This is a dangerous time but it is also an exhilarating one! Indeed, we all must have moments when we feel it is a little too exhilarating! But we can still understand what that editor, about to be beheaded in the French Revolution, meant when he said: "It is too bad to take my head off. I wanted to see how all this is coming out."

Let's keep our heads. And it isn't always easy, particularly in an election year—and even if you are not running for office! We've come a long way from the myopic era that followed the First World War. The past is bright with promise for the future. And it is to the future we must look for more permanent and tolerable solutions than the present improvisations. As our muscles harden, will the Soviets sue for peace, permanent, secure peace? We can't assume that and there is little evidence for it. Is the hope then to devise means of coexistence with this ruthless and equal power in the world? How to coexist with evil without becoming evil? How long can we dissipate our national resources? How long can we endure such defense expenditures without fulfilling Marx's prophecy? Are the ultimate destinations, as Senator [James O'Brien] McMahon asked, military safety at the price of economic disaster,

Foreign Policy Is the Most Important
Consideration for the American People

JULY 30, 1952

✡

In his welcoming address to the Democratic National Convention in Chicago on July 21, 1952, Stevenson reminded the delegates:

For it is a very solemn hour indeed, freighted with the hopes and fears of millions of mankind who see in us, the Democratic Party, sober understanding of the breadth and depth of the revolutionary currents in the world. Here and abroad they see in us awareness that there is no turning back, that, as Justice Holmes said, "We must sail sometimes with the wind, sometimes against it, but we must sail and not drift or lie at anchor." They see in us, the Democratic Party that has steered this country through a storm of spears for twenty years, an under-standing of a world in the torment from an age that has died to an age struggling to be born. They see in us relentless determination to stand fast against the barbarian at the gate, to cultivate allies with a decent respect for the opinions of others, to patiently explore every misty path to peace and security which is the only certainty of lower taxes and a better life.[111]

Stuart Gerry Brown reflects on the significance of the address, "It would be hard to find a 'welcoming address' remotely like it in the annals of American party conventions. Stevenson had not only shocked, puzzled, annoyed, and aroused the convention to high enthusiasm almost simultaneously. He had also introduced himself unforgettably to his party and to the country. Henceforth no one who had heard him would fail to recognize his voice, or the quality of the man in the words he spoke. That he would be nominated was now certain."[112] After Stevenson's nomination, he offered his philosophy concerning domestic affairs, but especially concerning foreign policy in his often quoted Acceptance Speech on July 26:

And, my friends, more important than winning the election is governing the nation. That is the test of a political party—the acid, final test. When the tumult and the shouting die, when the bands are gone and the lights are dimmed, there is the stark reality of responsibility in an hour of history haunted with those gaunt, grim specters of strife, dissension and materialism at home, and ruthless, inscrutable and hostile power abroad.

The ordeal of the twentieth century—the bloodiest, most turbulent era of the Christian age—is far from over. Sacrifice, patience, understanding and implacable purpose may be our lot for years to come. Let's face it. Let's talk sense to the American people. Let's tell them the truth. . . .

Let's tell them that the victory to be won in the twentieth century, this portal to the Golden Age, mocks the pretensions of individual acumen and ingenuity.[113]

When Stevenson returned to Springfield on July 30, he held his first press conference:

REPORTER: What do you regard as the most outstanding issue of the campaign?

GOVERNOR: Foreign policy. It certainly is the most important consideration for the American people.

REPORTER: In the '44 campaign, President Roosevelt and Governor Dewey felt that it was essential during the campaigning to try to have some kind of bipartisan agreement to keep certain areas of foreign policy—for the country's security—out of the area of debate. Do you feel that at the present time there is any necessity for any agreement between the two parties and the two candidates?

GOVERNOR: I would regard that as worthy of serious consideration, but of course I think it is quite clear that General Eisenhower's views (and I am not presuming to say what the Republican platform means) as to Western Europe are clear; and that with respect to what menace we encounter, what goes on currently with respect to NATO, I don't know of anything which would make it necessary to reach such an agreement. I think we are in substantial agreement. I am not too clear about Germany or his views on it. I would hope that we would say nothing during the campaign which would be calculated in any way to diminish the allegiance of our allies and their dedication to our common cause. I will make no comment about the remark with respect to France, but I would feel, so far as I am concerned that it would be desirable if nothing of that kind were said in the future.[114]

REPORTER: Would you carry that forward into the present negotiations of the ratification of the German situation? Is it your view that that should go forward, or perhaps wait?

GOVERNOR: I would rather wait to speak on that. I would rather wait until later in the campaign and until I am a little clearer as to just what Germany is doing.[115]

If This Country Stands for Anything,
It Stands for Freedom

AUGUST 29, 1952

✡

Stevenson labeled his address to the Illinois State Fair's Governor's Day on August 14 the beginning of his campaign. In effect, it was his optimistic farewell address to the people of Illinois, even though his term as Governor was not to end until January. He made his first comments about the Republican criticism of Democratic foreign policy in this brief speech to the New York State Democratic Convention in New York City on August 29.

I AM disturbed by some of the Republican contributions to the foreign-policy debate. A Republican foreign-policy expert said the other day that the Democratic party was interested only in Europe and regarded all other nations only as "second-class expendables." This kind of statement is not simply absurd, it is also irresponsible and dangerous. And I hope that such excessive partisanship does not do irreparable damage to our country. Of course, we are interested in Europe. But if this country, and I mean Democrats and Republicans alike, stands for anything, it stands for freedom and against the expansion of Communist dominion everywhere in the world. Does Mr. Dulles think that President Truman by his prompt and courageous decision of June 27, 1950, treated Korea like "a second-class expendable"? If he does not think so, he would serve his party and his country and our friends in Asia better by more candor and less claptrap.

I hope that the Republican leaders will permit us to discuss our

157

somber foreign problems on the plane where they belong—not on the plane of demagoguery, but on the plane of serious, factual discussion, and in terms of alternatives that are real, rather than epithets that are false.

World Policy

SEPTEMBER 9, 1952

✡

During his campaign, by his own recollection, Stevenson gave 250 speeches which were preserved mostly by stenographic transcription and many other less important ones. Of the thirty-two major speeches that dealt with foreign affairs, he included sixteen in his book Major Campaign Speeches of Adlai E. Stevenson, *which he published after completing his term as Governor. This speech, given at San Francisco on September 9, 1952, is one of his major foreign-policy addresses during the campaign. It was published in his book as "World Policy" but with considerable differences between the published text and the unpublished speech that is printed here. The probability that the unpublished text was a pre-delivery copy is feasible. However, in other speeches during the campaign in which considerable variation between the texts occurs there are occasional indications in the unpublished versions that Stevenson was responding to an audience reaction or to an interference during the speech. For example, in his speech at Rome, New York, October 24, the text is interrupted by "(Train whistle and train movement)" and by Stevenson's response, "You know, that really isn't Republican sabotage, because all those guys are for us, that run those."*

WE who are free must have great strength in order that weakness will not tempt the ambitious.[116] We must have the strength to win if war should come. And the measure of the strength we must have is not what we would like to afford but what the adversary compels us to afford. With 85 per cent of our budget allocated to defense, it is the Soviet Union which now fixes the level of our defense expenditures and thus our tax rates. The only way to emancipate ourselves from this foreign control, and to substantially cut taxes, is first to develop our strength and then to find the means of ending the armaments race.[117]

No one can predict, and it would be foolish to try to predict, how and when the peaceful purpose of our power will succeed in creating a just and durable peace. But are our efforts conditional upon assurance of prompt success? To answer "yes" would be to accept the certainty of eventual defeat.

Coexistence is not a form of passive acquiescence in things as they are. It is waging the contest between freedom and tyranny by peaceful means. It will involve negotiation and adjustment—compromise but never appeasement—and I will never shrink from these if they advance the world toward secure peace. Though progress may be slow, it can be steady and sure. A wise man does not try to hurry history. Many wars have been avoided by patience and many have been precipitated by reckless haste.

In Europe, our efforts to build patiently for peace are meeting with success. The Marshall Plan has brought about a striking improvement in political and economic conditions. The North Atlantic Treaty Organization is building a strong system of defense. Europe is not yet wholly secure against subversion from within or attack from without, but this goal of security is in sight.

I wish I could say the same for Asia, but clearly I cannot, and there would be no greater disservice to the American people than to underestimate the gravity of the dangers that America faces in this area, perhaps for many years.

It is about America's relations with Asia that I want to talk with you tonight, soberly and realistically.

Across the continent of Asia more than a billion of the world's peoples are churning in one of history's greatest upheavals. All the struggles of man over the centuries—economic, political, spiritual—have come together in Asia and now seem to be reaching a climax. The causes behind that upheaval are many and varied. But there is nothing complicated about what the people want. They want a decent living—and they want freedom.

The word used most frequently by Asians to describe their aspirations is nationalism.

Nationalism to Asians means a chance to stand on their own feet, a chance to govern themselves, a chance to develop their resources for their own welfare, and a chance to prove that the color of their skins has nothing to do with their right to walk with self-respect among their fellowmen in the world. It means the end of a legalized inferiority. It means pride, spirit, faith.

This type of nationalism is not inconsistent with closer coopera-tion among nations nor with the need for an enforceable peace. The Asians actually regard freedom and national independence as the doorway to international order—just as we do.

The struggle in Asia and the hopes and longings of the Asian peoples have not gone unnoticed by Soviet Russia. Russia's interest in Asia is not new. The attempt to bring all of Asia under Russian dominion was clearly in evidence as long ago as 1897. The charge of aggressive imperialism was levelled against Russia no less than it was against the Western Powers.[118]

The expansionist aims of Russia did not change with the passing of the Czars. But today the Russian rulers have weapons far more powerful than those of their predecessors. The steel glove of a revolutionary ideology covers the heavy hand of imperialist ex-pansion.

The strategy of communism in Asia is to pose as the champion—the only champion—of the Asian peoples. Communism has not created the causes or the forces behind Asia's vast upheaval. It is attempting to give direction to those forces. It seeks to impose its own label on the multiple revolutions going on in Asia today by identifying itself with the deeply felt needs and hopes of the Asian peoples.

It constantly proclaims its sympathy for the goals of national liberation and independence. It promises human and social equality. It offers two bowls of rice a day where now there is one or none. It offers land to those who work the land.[119]

There is an important difference between communism as we view it and communism as some of the Asian peoples view it. When we think of communism we think of what we are going to lose. When many of the Asian peoples think of communism they think of what they are going to gain—especially if they believe they have nothing to lose.

something about India today rather than talking about China yesterday. Tearful and interminable post-mortems about China will save no souls for democracy in the rest of Asia, the Near East and Africa.

India is not caught up in civil strife. It can be helped in a way that is natural to us and best for it: help in the ways of peace and social progress. India has to grow more food. It has to restore its land. It needs new resources of power. In short, it needs a democratic helping hand in the development programs it has already charted.

The same is true in many other countries.

It is help of this kind that we can provide by sending agricultural experts, engineers, and other trained people to these countries, and through programs of assistance to economic development.

By working with each country to expand the production of goods which are needed by other countries in the region, a self-generating and self-financing cycle of trade and development can be initiated, which will reduce and can eventually eliminate the need for American aid. At the same time, we can enlarge our export markets and develop new sources of the products we need to import.

Land reform is, of course, fundamental to the problem of Asia. But in these ways and by this kind of friendly advice and counsel we can help to guide this economic development in ways which will give powerful support to democratic political institutions.

These programs are in accordance with our best traditions. And I want to assure our friends in Asia that America will never seek to dominate their political and economic development. We will not try to make their societies over in the image of our own. On the contrary, we respect the integrity of their institutions and the rich values of their cultures. We expect to learn as well as teach.

These programs are primarily concerned with the material needs and wants of individual men and women. Yet we do not make the mistake of believing that the answer to Communist materialism is a different brand of materialism. The answer to communism is, in the old-fashioned phrase, good works—good works inspired by love and dedicated to the whole man. The answer to the inhumanity of communism is humane respect for the individual. And the men and women of Asia desire not only to rise from wretchedness of the body but from abasement of the spirit.

In other words, we must strive for a harmony of means and ends in our relations with Asia—and indeed with the rest of the world. The means of our cooperation are primarily material. If we believe the Communist threat to Asia is dangerous to us, then it is in our own self-interest to help them defend and develop, adjusting our policies to the constantly changing circumstances in a world of accelerating change. But we must not, in our necessary concern for the urgent tasks of defense and development, permit the means to obscure the end. That end is the widening and deepening of freedom and of respect for the dignity of man.

Some will say to you that this is visionary stuff. To that I reply that history has shown again and again that the self-styled realists are the real visionaries—for their eyes are fixed on a past that cannot be recaptured. It was Woodrow Wilson, with his dream of the League of Nations, who was the truly practical man—not the Old Guard who fought him. And in the fateful summer of 1940 it took the vision of a Churchill to see beyond Dunkirk to victory.

I say that America has been called to greatness. The summons of the twentieth century is a summons to our vision, to our humanity, to our practicality. If these provide the common purpose of America and Asia, of our joint enterprise, of progress together, we need have no fear for the future. It will belong to free men.

First Fireside Speech

SEPTEMBER 29, 1952

✡

Adopting the style of Franklin D. Roosevelt, Stevenson planned a series of what he called "Fireside Chats" on radio and television to be paid for by the Volunteers for Stevenson. In this first Fireside Chat, from Chicago, he addressed the nation on WGN radio and NBC TV, September 29, 1952. By this time in the campaign, he felt it imperative to refute the charges that Truman's administration was culminating "twenty years of treason" and that somehow he himself was a traitor. Printed with the above title in Major Campaign Speeches, *the unpublished text leaves out the first six pages which are added in the book.*

FINALLY, now, peace and war. You know the kind of letters I receive; so many of you have written me about Korea and about your soldier sons. Every one of us knows in his heart why we have to stand up and to fight in Korea. We all know that when the Communists attacked across the thirty-eighth parallel that was the testing point for freedom throughout the world. The men in the Kremlin thought that they would be unopposed, and if they were, the whole question of the future could be settled in one blow. If they had been allowed to conquer free people in Korea, they could have picked away at the free world and engulfed more millions, piece by piece, one by one. Sooner or later we would have had to fight, and the later we made our stand, the bigger and the harder the war would have been. Stopping the enemy in Korea before Japan was threatened and before East Asia with all of its resources of manpower, rubber, tin, oil, etc., fell to the Communists was received with enthusiastic shouts of approval by the majority of the American people and even by the Republican leadership.

Now, however, they attempt to make you believe that it was almost an act of treason, but what do you think they would be saying now if we had not stopped the enemy in Korea, if Japan was threatened and if East Asia was falling bit by bit to the enemy? Would they not be saying now that Harry Truman and Joseph Stalin were boyhood friends in Outer Mongolia?

And another thing the Republican leadership is now telling us is that the danger to this nation is from within, not from without; the danger lies not with Moscow but in Washington; your enemy is not Joseph Stalin but Harry Truman—or even possibly Adlai Stevenson.

A campaign addressed not to men's minds and to their best instincts, but to their passions, emotions and prejudices, is unworthy at best. Now, with the fate of the nation at stake, it is unbearable; with the darkest evil, the mightiest force ever gathered on earth arrayed against us and our friends, this is no time for such talk. It is not for me to stand in judgment upon the men who pilfer the truth and say such things, but for your sake and for mine—for the sake of my sons and your children, and the future of millions of our friends overseas, and the future of our nation and for those who languish imprisoned behind the Iron Curtain, we must know the truth and come to grips with the facts of life, look them in the face and stare them down, and in so doing, triumph over them.

We are not, I take it, a race of whimpering adolescents who can't face the truth, but a race of men and women, proud, courageous and unafraid. I shall state the facts as they appear to me from some years of experience, not only in domestic affairs but in foreign affairs. The Republican leadership blows thin drafts of crafty words down your neck, but it fails to tell you the following things. Eighty-five per cent of the federal budget goes for past wars and for preserving our present and our future liberty. The world has been at war almost continuously now for forty years. The intervals between the wars grow shorter; the wars increase in dimension and in destructiveness. The last war was man's first true world war. The revolutions of our times are man's first revolutions; their flames burn from one end of the globe to the other. The intercontinental airplane makes counties of continents; it makes lakes of oceans. In the words of the song, "There is no hiding place down there."

Much of mankind is changing its entire outlook upon the world; whatever was is cast out; whatever is, is questioned. Mankind and its hundreds of millions is on the march toward what good and with what destruction on the way no man can foretell. Whole nations have sunk out of sight behind iron curtains; whole peoples have disappeared from view. Today there is less communication between the great, great groups of men than there was in the roadless world of a thousand years ago. So, we can no more communicate with half of mankind than we can raise the dead. While the anti-Christ stalks around, organized communism seeks even to dethrone God from his central place in this universe. It attempts to uproot everywhere it goes the gentle and restraining influences of the religion of love and peace. One by one the lamps of civilization go out and nameless horrors are perpetrated in darkness.

All this is done by an enemy of a kind that we have never faced before. He is primitive but he is also advanced. He goes with a piece of black bread in his hand but in his mind he carries the awful knowledge of atomic energy. He is careful, cool, calculating, and he counts time not impatiently like we do, not by the clock, but by decades, in terms of centuries. Much of what he is trying to do today his ancestors were attempting to do 400 years ago. The problems of a tortured, convulsive humanity stagger the nation. Unprecedented times demand of us unprecedented behavior. The task that confronts us will try our souls. It will exact a high price in discipline of mind and in austerity of spirit. It will determine whether we are worthy of our high place in the world, whether we are worthy of our forefathers who converted a wilderness into a country, fair and free, and left to us all the riches, material and spiritual, that they wrought in pain.

Long ago we asserted a great principle on this continent: that men are, and of right ought to be, free. Now we are called upon to defend that right against the mightiest forces of evil ever assembled under the sun.

This is a time to think, a time to feel, a time to pray. We shall need all of the resources of the stubborn mind, the stout heart, the soul refreshed, in the task that confronts us.

It is the most awesome task that any people has ever faced. For we are become the leader and mainstay of one great wing of humanity in conflict with another wing of humanity. As such, we must play the principal part in saving ourselves, our friends, and our civilization.[120]

The Destiny of Asia May Rest
in the Hands of Japan

MARCH 12, 1953

✡

Toward the end of the campaign, Stevenson demonstrated his discouragement about the low level of discussions on foreign policy. Speaking at the Rensselaer Polytechnic Institute at Troy, New York, on October 24, 1952, he remarked, "And there isn't any clear, decisive statement at all of the Republican foreign policy. Why? Because oil and water don't mix, and neither do isolationists and internationalists, and they are all in the front ranks of this queer crusade." In his final foreign-policy campaign address at the Brooklyn Academy of Music, October 31, 1952, he said, "I thought for a time that the issues of foreign policy and of our future could be freely and honestly debated between us on a level worthy of the American people. But the Republicans have concentrated not on discussing, but on systematically disparaging the policies which, with all their defects, have brought the United States to a peak of world prestige and power and responsibility never before dreamed of."[121] In his Introduction to Major Campaign Speeches *he wrote: "As the battle of words progressed, I felt more and more that people cared little about the issues and party records, or about precise definition of positions. They were weary of conflict, impatient and eager for repose."[122]*

After the election, he decided to make a "self-educating" trip as a private citizen through the world with emphasis on Asia. One of his traveling companions, Barry Bingham, later editor and publisher of the Louisville Courier-Journal *and the* Louisville Times, *and during the 1956 campaign the national chairman of Volunteers for Stevenson-Kefauver, writes that Stevenson had no idea how much ardent interest his presence would stir among the Asians: "The surprise began the moment we touched down in Tokyo. Almost unmanageable crowds thronged the airfield." Bingham comments that the English-language Tokyo* Evening News *printed Stevenson's acceptance speech to the Democratic Convention with the statement that it "demanded rereading because it contained one of the most cogent interpretations of the spirit of democracy—humility coupled with a recognition of the obligation to serve the general welfare."[123] Although this speech to the Japan-America Society in Tokyo delivered at the beginning of the Asian phase of his tour, March 12, 1953, was partially a recap of his San Francisco Fireside Speech in September, 1952, his audience was highly pleased by his belief that Japan's actions had deep influence on the survival of a free Asia. Ernie Hill of the Chicago* Daily News *cabled from Tokyo: "Stevenson has evidently made a firm resolve that he will not be the new American pop-off. People are amazed at his firmness in this determination. For that and other reasons, he made a tremendous hit in Japan and Korea. He is regarded here as a statesman with intellect and wit."[124]*

IT GOES without saying, of course, that I am traveling as a private citizen with no official or, indeed, semi-official mission to accomplish. But perhaps all the more on that account the reasons that impelled me to come straight to Asia rather than Europe and to plan my journey with most of the emphasis on the Orient might be of interest because they are reasons which, I think, are those the great majority of my fellow countrymen would share. It goes without saying also that I have long wanted to see Japan with my own eyes. I heard tales of it from my infancy from my father who came and stayed here before the turn of the century. I am distressed that our visit is so short, but perhaps it's better on the whole because your hospitality and courtesy has been so gracious that perhaps if my visit were to be longer I should never go home at all.

To speak these days of the increased importance of the Orient to the United States, is, of course, to deal in a cliché of the most resounding sort. In fact, to use another ponderous bromide, we are living in the age of communication and all parts of the world are increasingly important to all other parts. However, there is, I think, a special significance for all of us and one felt especially keenly by all of you here today, in the increased importance of the relations between our two countries in particular. Though we celebrate its centenary this year, it's only a moment in historical time since the day the Black Ships of Admiral Perry sailed into Yedo Bay. That moment marked the final meeting of Eastern and Western civilizations in their courses around the globe. It was a moment that could not, indeed cannot, for in a sense we are still living in it, ever come again. It was and is a unique moment in world history and one that brackets Japan and America together indelibly in a relationship that no other two nations in the world can ever hope to share.[125]

We think sometimes of the migration of the center of gravity in historical times. The center of gravity in world affairs from the Tigris and the Euphrates Basin to the Egypt of the Pharaohs; to the great Attic civilization of Greece, thence to Rome; and moving ever westward to the France of Charlemagne; to London and then, only in our time, that great leap across the Atlantic to the United States of America. Moving ever westward . . . the rim of the Pacific . . . the other rim of the Pacific . . . Japan . . . once [far, now] closer and closer toward the center of gravity in world affairs. It's obvious to anyone I suppose that Asia [is] in what might be called this era of decision, this area of decision as well, in our modern world. Evidences of that, some tragic as in Red China or in war-wrecked Korea, some heartening, as in the Philippines, India, Pakistan, confront us on all sides.

But what seems to me to be more pertinent at the moment, here in Tokyo for the first time, is that we in the United States and Japan are also, in this centennial year of Japan's reemergence into the community of nations, at a crucial time of decision. And that, in a very real sense, this nation is the one in whose hands the destiny of Asia and thus of the world may rest. Whether it is to be a free or a slave world is, of course, the decision that we all face in the era of decision. But the point I should like to make is that Americans, all of them, not just sight-seeing travelers such as myself and my associates are aware of Japan's critical importance in the way that the decision will finally be made.

What we Americans foresee is of course not only a free world but especially a community of Pacific nations to balance the great free community of European nations to both of which, and to one no more than the other, the countries of the Western Hemisphere belong. Well, that sums up, if I may say so, as best I can on short notice and in short order the basic reasons that set us forth on this trip in a westerly direction. We have a billion neighbors in the world. It was to see some of our billion neighbors of the free world that I thought it a suitable time to travel a bit. And yet, as I take it for granted that my basic conceptions about Asia in general, and Japan in particular, are shared by most Americans, I presume that it is my job on this trip less to tell Asians about Americans than to find out something about Asians to tell Americans when I get back. To say that we have a basic awareness of Asia's importance is not, I regret to admit, to say that we have any considerable part of the knowledge we must develop as to how we can best build our Pacific community and make it live up to its undreamed-of potentialities.

I felt at the outset, as we used to say, "this trip was necessary," if only, as I say, to diminish my own ignorance. If I can bring information that will do the same for any of my fellow countrymen, I shall feel that it has all been well worthwhile.

The questions that history asks and which Japan as well as America must answer is whether this idea, this ancient idea of individualism—the idea of personal freedom for you and for me—is equal to the idea of collectivism—the idea of personal subordination to the state; whether the idea of maximum personal liberty is equal to the idea of maximum personal discipline.

This old contest between freedom and despotism, which is renewed in every generation, is acute within ours, and likewise the conflict between national independence and national subordination.

I don't think that war is an inevitable part of this gigantic contest. Even the most ambitious and ruthless men don't deliberately invite destruction on the basis of their power. They can throw, to be sure, the iron dice, but they cannot foretell the fortunes of war. . . .

(. . . recap of San Francisco address, September 9, 1952).[126]

. . . This lovely land and this government and these friendly people, whose destiny, whose hopes are linked inextricably with our own, to them I am profoundly grateful for their welcome here in Tokyo. We in our country ask of no nation anything for ourselves, we ask nothing that we could not ask for humanity itself. We know how sorely tried this great country is, how appalling are the economic obstacles it faces, but we know and Japan knows that security and peace in this tormented world is not a gift but a prize. In the struggle for that prize I pray that Americans and Japanese will rub shoulders for generations to come. And in conclusion, may I add but another word and that is that before I set off on this long journey I lunched with the President of the United States. He asked me particularly to bring his good wishes, his respect and his friendship to our friends throughout the world. I know of no better place than this meeting of the Japanese and Americans here in Tokyo to bring you the greetings of the President of the United States. Thank you.

A Truce in Korea Is the Best News
in the World

JUNE 9, 1953

✿

On June 9, 1953, Stevenson issued this brief statement at the American Embassy in Tel Aviv as he ended the Asian phase of his world tour.

I AM concluding here in Israel a journey of more than three months through East Asia, South Asia and the Middle East. From here we go on to Cyprus, Turkey, Greece and Western Europe.

My journey in Asia has left few countries unvisited. It has been a vastly fruitful experience and it ends here in the Holy Land as a truce is imminent in Korea. This is the best news in the world for years. And we should not overlook the sudden Soviet decision to end eight years of interzone traffic control in Austria. But a truce is not peace and I venture to say that we should temper our joy by asking ourselves what Communist intentions are in Malaya and Indo-China where there is no truce. While we hope and pray that a new day is dawning on this tormented world we should not, I think, relax our exertions or our vigilance. Strength, resistance and assistance, have borne fruit again as they did in Greece and Turkey, in the Berlin blockade and in Western Europe. The end of our difficulties, I suspect, is not yet.

In Asia, mostly new countries only recently independent, I found a great emerging expectation of a better way of life for those myriad peoples who freely compare totalitarian and free institutions as the ways and means of realizing their rising expectations. Happily the leaders of all these countries are faithful to the voluntary, free democratic philosophy of government and that

175

solution of their exacting economic, political and social problems.

Can they do it? I have no ready answer, but great hopes that they can and that the policy of the U.S. will take a total view of the wide world; while raising relentlessly *our* defenses and their defense that it [U.S. policy] will never forget that it is safer and easier to prevent fires than to quench them; that bullets don't stop ideas and that our friendly efforts should be directed to economic improvement and the positive encouragement of free institutions as well as mere military defense.

Traveler's Report

SEPTEMBER 15, 1953

⬡

Barry Bingham describes Stevenson's effectiveness as a traveler: "People listened to Adlai in Asia because he listened to them. He told them his ideas with clear conviction, but he did not shout to them."[127] *When 250 reporters and photographers greeted Stevenson and his companions as he returned to the United States on August 20, 1953, Stevenson thanked them "for your presence here this morning" and gave as his reason for such an extensive trip: "I wanted to see and hear for myself. And what I have seen and heard is both encouraging and sobering." He warned the reporters: "While there is much misunderstanding in America, there is as much or more misunderstanding of America." Still, he indicated his own feeling of responsibility as a traveling citizen: "While abroad, I have never criticized the Administration's handling of our foreign affairs; rather I have sought to explain American attitudes and positions when I had to and as best I could." On September 14, speaking to 1500 Chicago Democrats at a $100-a-plate dinner, he expressed his surprise that the Republicans had failed to take credit for frightening the recently deceased Stalin to death and lashed out at their apparent attitude toward the Communists: "One false move by you guys and we'll cut the national defense budget by another billion dollars."*

On September 15, under nonpartisan auspices at the Chicago Civic Opera House, Stevenson gave his "Traveler's Report," which he later considered among his five most important speeches between the 1952 election and the beginning of his 1956 campaign.[128] *Assessing this address, Alden Whitman suggests:*

Two of the threads that Stevenson the internationalist wove through his speech that night in Chicago were to appear and reappear throughout his public career: the first, the need to seek accommodation between the Western and Communist world; the second, the need to narrow the gap between the affluent and the impoverished nations. Certainly by making these questions subject to public debate Stevenson helped show the way toward a more enlightened, a less bellicose foreign policy other men could follow.[129]

Although it was printed in Stevenson's What I Think, *the text which he prepared for publication varies considerably from this version in his unpublished files. The title is Stevenson's.*

ALMOST thirty years ago an inquisitive young man traveled across Europe, up the Black Sea and across Western Russia. When he got home, bursting with his trials and adventures, something had gone wrong—there was no band, no welcoming committee to meet him at the station in Bloomington, Illinois. In sad fact, there was no one at all, except the old baggage man, and his greeting was, "Hi, Adlai; you been away?"

I've been traveling again and I must say that this welcome compares quite favorably with that! I am touched and deeply grateful. You do me a great honor. But the trip itself was a reward, and I wish everyone concerned with his country's place in the world could have the opportunity I've had to hear and see—especially anyone who doesn't know how lucky he is to be an American![130]

For six months I have traveled across this vast and troubled world, for tens of thousands of miles—which were just as exhausting as the campaign, but I didn't encounter as much opposition! My mind is filled with recollections of people I talked with from Syngman Rhee and the Emperor of Japan, to Pope Pius and Queen Elizabeth; of the sights I've seen, roving and beautiful, sordid and sickening; of that rugged front in ravaged Korea where, pray God, the strife has stopped for keeps; of the ugly war in the wet, green rice paddies of Indo-China where communism, masquerading as nationalism, imperils the whole of Southeast Asia; and of millions of refugees huddled in squalid camps and hovels stretching from Korea across Asia to Western Europe—remnants of many more

victims of the wars, revolutions, intolerance, and savagery that
have cursed our time on earth.

A trip like mine is a sobering experience. It is more than a privilege; it is a responsibility to be an American in this world. It isn't
one world; it's more like three worlds—the allied world, the Communist world, and the uncommitted world. Almost a billion people
live along the route I took. Most of them live in Asia and most of
the so-called uncommitted peoples live in Asia. They don't belong
to the white minority of the human race, and tragically many of
them are poor, undernourished and illiterate.

Asia is in revolution. Civilizations are very old, but political independence is very young. In the new states the economies are
shaky, public administration is weak; they are hungry and poor,
sensitive and proud. Nationalism is rampant. And the West, identified with the hated colonialism, is suspect. Utterly preoccupied
with their own overwhelming problems, they see little of the
world conflict and don't appreciate America's global responsibilities. They know from experience a lot about feudalism, landlords,
money lenders, and oppressors, and the theories of Karl Marx
sound pretty good to many of them, who know surprisingly little
about the ugly realities of communism in practice. Nor is there the
perception one would expect of international communism as a new
imperialism.

There is little tradition of democracy in these new states, but
independence, won at long last, is a passion, which partly accounts
in some quarters for their opaque view of Communist China where
to many Asians it appears that the foreigners have been thrown out
and the ignominy of centuries [is] erased by Asians. There is
reverent admiration for the ideas of the American Revolution, the
Bill of Rights, and the great utterances of human freedom. But
they think they see contradictions in the current wave of conformity and fear at home, and hypocrisy in our alliances with the
colonial powers and professed devotion to freedom and self-determination.

The ideological conflict in the world doesn't mean much to the
masses. Anti-Communist preaching wins few hearts. They want to
know what we are for, not just what we are against. And in nations
like India, Indonesia and Burma they don't accept the thesis that

everyone has to choose sides, that they have to be for us or against us. Nor do I believe that we should press alliances on unwilling allies. After all, we had a long record of neutrality and noninvolvement ourselves, and the important thing is that such nations keep their independence and don't join the hostile coalition.

But in spite of all their doubts and difficulties, I was impressed by the devotion of the leaders of Asia to the democratic idea of government rather than force, and by the decisive manner in which so many of the new countries of Asia have dealt with violent Communist insurrections and conspiracies. Their revolutions have not produced Utopia and they are struggling with infinite difficulties to raise living standards and satisfy the rising tide of expectations. They want rice and respect, and they want to believe in wondrous America that sends friendly, earnest people to help them and who believe in them, and the aspirations of all God's children for peace, dignity, and freedom.

We are on the eve of great decisions in Asia. Korea is the first step. Will Red China yield at the conference table what it fought to prevent on the battlefield? It would seem to me unlikely if we adopt arbitrary positions in advance and have no room for maneuver and negotiation. I hope our leaders will not be prisoners of domestic political propaganda or hobbled by inflexibility.[131]

Personally I am skeptical of Red China's intentions, but when we search for settlements we have to *search*, and when we negotiate we have to have something to negotiate *with* as well as *for*. Many of our friends think China wants peace and trade above all, as they themselves do. With so much at stake in Asia—the unification of Korea, Formosa, peace and security in Indo-China—it would seem to me that we owe it to ourselves as well as to our friends at least to find out, if we can, what Communist China's ultimate intentions are.

Let me add here that I emphatically approve what our government is doing to leave no doubt about our concern for the security and independence of Indo-China, which is the gate to all Southeast Asia.

I wish I had an hour for Asia,[132] for if I may risk a prophecy the hostile world is going to pay more and more attention to Asia, especially huge, uncommitted India. And I suspect that as Europe's Eastern empires shrink, there will be left to us more of the burden of defense and of helping to guide the great forces which great changes have unleashed in Asia.

The Middle East is largely a power-and-defense vacuum, except for doughty little Israel and tough, strong Turkey. Peace is imperative in the Middle East—peace between Egypt and Britain, and between the Arab states and Israel, which is engaged in a historic effort to provide refuge and new hope to oppressed people.[133]

In Europe, the recovery since the war is spectacular. In Western Germany, which doesn't have to support an army, navy and air force, it looks ironically as though the vanquished were better off than the victors. In France, the progress has not kept pace; there is grave social unrest and political frustration which can be remedied and will be, pray heaven, by heroic measures. Among Frenchmen the conviction is growing that France can no longer maintain the defense effort in Europe, fight communism in Indo-China with weapons and at home with larger social and economic expenditures, all at the same time. We should bear in mind that many Frenchmen vote Communist not from conviction, but in protest. Hence the increasing clamor to get out of Indo-China altogether and spend more on housing, industrial development, and social betterment at home.

The most urgent problem in Europe today is, of course, Germany: how to channel its developing strength and resources into paths that will benefit both Europe and the world, how to resolve the age-old rivalries of France and Germany, and how to satisfy the intense German desire for reunification, whetted by the gallant workers' revolt in the Soviet Zone which exhilarated the whole free world.

In short, the difficulties are many and the hazards great everywhere. But things are better. There is hope in the air, born of America's postwar policy of assistance and resistance, of growing strength and self-confidence, and of Stalin's death followed by shifting winds from Moscow, truce in Korea, rebellion in Eastern Europe, troubles behind the Iron Curtain.

But the world is weary; there is universal anxiety and impatience to ease the tensions, to explore every possibility of settlements by conference and negotiation. The Soviet will exploit discord in our ranks at every opportunity in order to divide and enfeeble the grand alliance of the free. There is uncertainty abroad about America and our objectives; is our objective to discover through negotiation ways to relax tensions, or is it intensification of the cold war; is it coexistence or extermination of Communist power?

Some of the misunderstandings may seem incredible to us, but it is well to try to see ourselves as others see us. Many think we are intemperate, inflexible, and frightened. And people who have lived in insecurity for centuries don't understand how there can be insecurity in America, which has never been bombed or lived in thralldom. Also, like ourselves, proud nations resent any real or suspected interference in their domestic affairs. Nor can they reconcile our exhortations about the peril of the deep costs in our defense budget. And everywhere people think they recognize the dominant mood [of] America in what is called "McCarthyism," now a worldwide word. Inquisitions, purges, book-burning, repression, and fear have obscured the bright vision of the land of the free and the home of the brave.

Most of our friends want and need trade, not aid. There is an uneasy feeling that the U.S. is showing signs of economic nationalism, of a drift toward no trade and no aid. But our friends must trade to live, and not many are going to go hungry, I suspect, to prove to us just how anti-Communist they are.

Just as there are many misconceptions about us, we have many illusions about others, and one of them is that irritations, doubts and disagreements are symbols of ingratitude or anti-Americanism. Some hostile feeling is inevitable, particularly in occupied areas, but I found surprisingly little. Misgivings about our wisdom, unity and clear purpose, yes, but also widespread admiration and gratitude for our faith and fortitude, and prayerful hopes for the sobriety, good judgment and moral vitality of American leadership. At my journey's end Winston Churchill said to me with emotion: "America has saved the world."

Our foreign assistance programs have succeeded, especially in Europe. They have cost us dearly, but I bless the day when Presi-

dent Truman went to the aid of Greece and Turkey and commenced the Marshall Plan. Stronger, more self-reliant, our friends
are feeling more independent of Washington, and are talking back
to us now, which seems to me a healthy sign.

I think we are winning the cold war step-by-step. The spread of
communism has been arrested. And while Moscow has military
potency, the Communist idea has little appeal any longer, at least in
Europe.

But though the imminent danger has receded, this is no time to
wobble or lower our guards, not with the hydrogen bomb and no
certain evidence that the seductive music from Moscow reflects
any basic change in the Soviet design of world domination. And it
is no time for arrogance, petulance or inflexibility either.

If I am not mistaken, holding our allies together is going to be an
ever harder job, which will tax mightily our patience, resolve and
statesmanship. For we can't "go it alone." Unilateralism is but the
new face of isolationism and it spells disaster.

Looking to the future, it seemed to me clearer than ever that the
economic, military, and political integration of Europe is the best
hope for balancing Soviet power and for enabling the states of
Europe to exercise a powerful, positive and peaceful influence in
the modern world. We have already invested years of effort and
encouragement and billions of dollars toward this bold and imaginative end.

Europe has already made important progress toward unification
on the economic front. On the political front, a draft constitution
for a federated Europe is already under consideration.

For years we have been encouraging military integration and a
contribution from Germany for the defense of the free world. Dr.
Adenauer is a vigorous advocate, and with his victory last week,
about all that lies in the path of the European army plan is France's
natural fear of a bigger, stronger and rearmed Germany.

I think our government should now bend every effort to encourage and hasten federation. Yet threats of insensitivity to many
difficulties and basic fears will only impede progress. One is the
natural French fear of a federal institution which may be dominated by the Germans. Another is that Russia will prevent the

reunification of Germany if Germany joins the West because of the Soviet fear, alleged at least, that a United Europe and a European army is an aggressive bloc aimed at Russia.[134]

So we must surmount a thicket of difficulty; we must bring the discussion back to the level where once again it challenges the imagination and the hopes of all Europe. We must think afresh, in terms of a European system of durable assurances of nonaggression —for Russia, as well as for France, Germany and the rest of us.

If the Soviet Union rejects assurances of nonaggression, if the Red Army will not withdraw behind its borders, if an Austrian peace treaty and German unification are impossible except on the Soviet's terms, then we will at least have cleared the air. We will have resolved the uncertainties of many about Soviet sincerity and intentions.[135]

But whatever commitments we make to our European allies to buttress such assurances of nonaggression we must be prepared to make on a long-term basis. For there is anxiety lest the shaping of our policy may be slipping from the respected hands of President Eisenhower into the hands of men less concerned with strengthening our alliances abroad than with appeasing our isolationists at home.

And at this moment a new fact confers a grim and pressing urgency on the international situation—the hydrogen bomb. For some years efforts toward the limitation and control of armaments have been stalemated. Once more, I think we should fix our sights high, as we did in 1947, and resume the initiative in reexploring the possibility of disarmament. The alternative to safety through an effective plan for arms limitation is safety through more massive military spending and more frightening weapons development.

As it is, we seem now to be taking the initiative in unilateral disarmament. We've tried that before, and I am as opposed to unilateralism in our disarmament policy as I am in our foreign policy.

In the past, new initiatives have had little impact on the Kremlin. I do not know that they would have any more today. But conditions have changed. The Soviet threat has aroused the massed military power of the free peoples. Russia learned in Korea that the West has the will to meet force with force. The death of Stalin and revolt in the satellites has altered the situation inside the Soviet Union.

In these circumstances we should press forward—not under any foolish illusion that one grand conference would yield security, but rather with realistic recognition that the foundations of stability must be laid, stone by stone, with patient persistence. We owe it to ourselves and our anxious, weary friends to expose Communist intentions if we can; to confer when we can; to reduce tensions and restore hope where we can. The door to the conference room is the door to peace. Let it never be said that America was reluctant to enter.

Under our Constitution, foreign policy is the responsibility of the executive. The Democrats in Congress have shown that they are eager to help the President carry out an effective foreign policy, restore the leadership of America and give fresh inspiration and confidence to the great alliance which is indispensable to our security. If it brings the President great personal success we will all rejoice, because the nation and the free world will be the beneficiaries.

And, finally, we must bear in mind, that the world's troubles do not all spring from aggressive communism. Many of them would be here anyway, and always will be. The quest for peace and tranquillity isn't a day's work; it is everlasting. We will have to learn to think of the responsibility of leadership not as a passing annoyance but as a status in an interdependent world that we as Americans, Democrats and Republicans alike, must live in, must trade in, work in, and pray for in the accents of mercy [and] justice in a power greater than ours or any man's.

We may be approaching the end of the first phase of this era—stopping the spread and influence of communism. Will strength and perseverance prevail in the second phase and the great threat wither? We haven't the resources to remedy all the ills of man. And we can't remake the world in our image and likeness. But we have erected here in the United States man's happiest home. Respect for our own principles and the courage to live by them, at home and abroad, will be a potent force in the world, and, in the long run, our greatest contribution to a world in which peace is a prayer.

The Future Will Belong to Free Men

OCTOBER 16, 1954

✡

In March of 1954, Stevenson served as the lecturer for the Godkin Lectures at Harvard University, a series created to explore annually "The Essentials of Free Government and the Duties of the Citizen." He jested that when he accepted the invitation after his 1952 defeat, "with gracious and intoxicating applause ringing in my ears from many centers of learning," the idea of his lecturing at Harvard seemed less absurd than during the actual presentation of his lectures. He emphasized that he focused on world affairs in these lectures, later published as Call to Greatness, *because "it seems to me that the historic drama of the twentieth century in which we are inextricably involved dwarfs in immensity all our other concerns and places in new perspective the essentials of free government and the duties of the citizen."[136]*

Although the Godkin Lectures remained bipartisan in their scope, shortly before, on March 7, Stevenson rebuked the Republicans, following Senator McCarthy's attacks on the Democratic Administrations as "Twenty Years of Treason," and Secretary of State John Foster Dulles's statement of the Republican policy of "massive retaliation." Appearing in What I Think *as "Crusades, Communism, and Corruption," the speech given to the Democratic National Committee Southern Conference and Dinner in Miami Beach, reminded his partisan audience, "When demagoguery and deceit become a national political movement, we Americans are in trouble; not just Democrats, but all of us." Stuart Gerry Brown writes, "Few addresses in American history have been so effective in their immediate consequences. Stevenson had intended to put the*

186

matter so strongly that the Administration could not ignore what he said nor delay any longer the sort of vigorous action which would bring an end to McCarthyism. He succeeded."[137] *Shortly after, Vice President Nixon answered Stevenson's speech and firmly repudiated McCarthy for his "reckless talk and questionable method." McCarthy's disgrace soon followed, with a motion in the Senate for censure proposed that spring and passed overwhelmingly after the autumn Congressional elections.*

The issue of massive retaliation and Republican irresponsibility remained a critical issue to Stevenson. During the autumn elections, he gave several addresses criticizing this negative approah to foreign policy. In the campaign speech printed below, given October 16, 1954, at San Francisco, Stevenson attacked strongly this concept and urged that the Republicans repudiate it. Ending on a hopeful note, he recalled his 1952 campaign plea that he had made in San Francisco: "America has been called to greatness. The summons of the twentieth century is a summons to our vision, to our humanity, to our practicality. If these provide the common purpose of America and Asia (and I might have added, of the free world) . . . we need have no fear for the future. Because it will belong to free men."

MR. NIXON expresses his views on foreign policy and everything else, freely and frequently, and changes them in the same manner. Senator Knowland tells off President Eisenhower and denounces Secretary Dulles also freely and frequently and loudly, which is the more remarkable considering that he is the President's leader in the Senate.

While the President talks about peaceful coexistence with the Communists, Senator Knowland talks of war with Red China. When he publicly demands that we sever diplomatic relations with Russia the President has to issue a quick and angry "No."

In March Mr. Nixon, the Administration's chief spokesman those days, took to the television to tell us that massive atomic retaliation is the key to peace and we want no more small wars, no more Koreas; we are not going to be "nibbled to death."[138] Yet the following month he was in favor of sending American forces to fight in Indo-China. Then after the Communist triumph, he told political meetings that the Truman Administration was to blame for the French disaster in Indo-China. (I think that kind of political trip must be an ill-will tour.) But meanwhile the President was talking amiably about bipartisanship. This, I understand, is known as the smile and smear technique of campaigning: The President smiles while the Vice-President smears. Finally, to complete this story, now that the fighting is over and the free world has lost half of Viet-Nam to the Communists, our agile Vice President points to peace in the world as an achievement of the Eisenhower Administration.

Of course, there are many explanations for the catastrophic loss of our moral and political prestige in the non-Communist world during recent months, losses which we and our world can ill afford at a time when the first objective of Soviet policy is to drive a wedge between us and our friends and enfeeble our grand alliance. The reasons for our sudden decline in world esteem stem mostly, it seems to me, from the unhappy divisions that have all but paralyzed the Republican party's initiative and effectiveness as an instrument of government. I warned you about the Old Guard, about the men who have had to be dragged, screaming and kicking, into the twentieth century. Just two years ago yesterday I said here in San Francisco (and I'm not embarrassed about repeating what I said during that campaign for you see I wasn't a very promising candidate):

These men opposed our policy of strength at home. They opposed labor's right to organize and bargain collectively. They opposed effective supports for farm income. They opposed the whole conception of security in economic life. They wanted labor to be weak, the farmers to be weak, government to be weak—and only themselves to be strong. They never understood the central truth—that the strength of the nation resides in the strength of the whole, and not in the strength of one of its parts.

That was two years ago and meanwhile in the giveaway of our natural resources, in the economic retreat, in tax legislation for the benefit of corporations and the well-to-do, we have seen emerge the traditional Republican platform of government of the many, by the few and for the few.

But two years ago here in San Francisco I also said that the Old Guard would not support even the foreign policy of their own Republican candidate. As an illustration I specifically mentioned foreign trade on which our allies, like Britain, Japan and Germany, are wholly dependent and on which we are becoming more dependent as our productive capacity exceeds our needs, especially in agriculture. And what happened was even worse than I foresaw. In the last session of Congress even President Eisenhower's modest proposals received not a single Republican vote and the best he could get was a one-year extension of the old Democratic Reciprocal Trade Law.

Our foreign affairs take, in effect, two-thirds of our federal taxes, and the question of war or peace in the hydrogen age is the question of survival or extinction. So foreign affairs are our most important affairs, and, as in 1952, I want to talk soberly about foreign policy tonight—here on the rim of the Pacific where the destiny of the world for long years to come may well be decided.

What I want to say, briefly, is that in spite of all the domestic reasons for electing a Democratic Congress this fall there are even better and more insistent reasons in the foreign field where our loss of prestige and confidence and the spread of anti-Americanism is alarming.

Why is this? Why has the impression got around that we are heedless of the risks of war in the atomic age? Why are our friends fearful that a distant United States—that has never been occupied or bombed—may drag them into another war? How has the Administration continued to increase worldwide fears of America's belligerence while steadily reducing America's effective strength?

There are many contributing reasons for our present plight. Among them the Republicans have to bear the responsibility for nourishing our thinking since the war for myths—the myth, for example, that Truman and Acheson and a few sinister men in the State Department caused the Chinese Revolution; the myth that Roosevelt gave Eastern Europe to the Communists at Yalta and Teheran; the myth that other peoples have to be for us or they are against us, and so on.

The Republicans created and cultivated those myths to discredit the Democrats. Now the Republicans are in power and the victims of their own mythology. With unsolved problems on all sides, they still mumble the old myths and waste our national reputation trying to give meaning to empty words, and to prove that the Truman foreign policy which saved Europe, forged the grand alliance and held the walls of the free world for years, was made in Moscow.

Also, the violence which has lately marked our domestic politics is not unrelated to the alarming deterioration of our world position. The Republicans have painted a picture of bitterly divided America for all the world to see. The image is not one to evoke confidence in our leadership but one of an uncertain and unreliable ally, powerful beyond compare and all the more disturbing for that reason.

While the rest of the free world drew courage and inspiration from our defense of freedom in Korea, Governor Dewey of New York, twice his party's candidate for the office of President, told the American people that the word Democrat was synonymous with murder and treachery; the Republican National Committee celebrated Lincoln's birthday last winter with a series of speeches by Senator McCarthy entitled "Twenty Years of Treason"; and the Attorney General of the United States [Herbert Brownell] impugned the very loyalty of a former President—a man who has done more to fight communism than all the Republican politicians put together—and I mean Harry S. Truman.

With mounting wonder and disbelief the world has seen and heard many other strange sights and sounds. McCarthyism, fear and mistrust have tarnished the bright vision of strong, confident, free America. Books were banned, respected people slandered, and frightening, arrogant slogans followed one another—into oblivion: "Let Asians fight Asians," "liberation" of the satellites (which sounded like war in Europe), "unleashing Chiang Kai-shek" (which sounded like war in Asia), the "new look" in defense, "massive retaliation" (which sounded like total atomic war everywhere), "agonizing reappraisal," etc. At first our friends trembled lest the government of the United States meant what it said, but then they gradually learned that the Administration did not mean what it said—a lesson, by the way, which the American people have had to learn about farm policy, public power, labor relations, balancing the budget, etc.

Is it any wonder that the leaders of other nations and their peoples have begun to doubt whether they can have confidence in America and the continuity of our policy? What's wrong? Why is this?

Basically, it is because the Administration is trapped in a dilemma of its own making—it is trying to conduct a responsible foreign policy and appease the extremist wing of the Republican party at the same time. It is trying to reconcile the irreconcilable. And it acts as though it was more important to unite the Republican party than to unite our country and the free world. They talk tough to satisfy the extremists and reduce the Army and the Air Force to satisfy the budget cutters. Driven by the extremists, they announce goals exceeding their willingness or ability to act. Secretary Dulles demands united action on Indo-China and settles for united inaction, with nothing to show for our part in the Geneva Conference[139] but the preposterous boast that we had refused to speak to our adversaries, because the right-wing Republicans have successfully identified negotiation with appeasement. The President announces firm support of a liberal trade policy and not only accepts defeat without a struggle, but actually raises various tariffs.

Over and over we are wobbly when we should be firm and rigid when we need flexibility. We shake our fist and then our finger. Repeatedly we have bluffed friends and foe alike. Repeatedly Secretary Dulles has waved the diplomatic big stick and threatened our allies.

The Administration acts as if bluff and bluster were the essence of statesmanship. Its public utterances are designed more often to impress not our friends abroad, nor even our adversaries, but the right wing of the Republican party at home—the gentlemen who aid and abet the Communist policy of breaking up our alliances by abusing our allies. In order to achieve good relations with these gentlemen the Administration has impaired our relations with Britain, France, India. For harmony in the Republican party it has paid the price of harmony in the free world.

Some of you may wonder why the issue of foreign policy arises in a political campaign. Let me make it absolutely clear that it is in this campaign through no desire of the Democrats. The leaders of my party have expressed again and again their hope that the kind of bipartisanship in foreign policy which existed in the days of Truman and Roosevelt would be brought back to Washington.

Why is there no bipartisanship in the formulation of our foreign policy these days? Why are there no Democrats in high positions in President Eisenhower's Administration when there were so many Republicans in President Truman's Administration? Is it because the Republicans are imprisoned by their own irresponsible slander? Only this week the Administration is playing its cynical numbers game again about the subversives and security risks they have fired, but I haven't heard of a single Communist or traitor that they have exposed. Or has bipartisanship in the State Department been subordinated by job hunger and the Republican spoils system?

Why have they sharply cut our Air Force and Army while warning us about growing enemy strength—cuts, by the way, which account for most of the budget reduction to which they point with such pride? Has tax reduction, for the few, taken priority over national defense? Why have they cut economic and technical assistance programs, just as the Soviets venture into that field?

Why have they failed to keep their foreign-trade promises just as the Moscow-Peiping axis dangles seductive trade proposals before our hard-pressed friends?

Why have the State Department and Foreign Service been terrorized by a protégé of Senators Knowland, Bridges and McCarthy?

Why, indeed, are all the tools of our foreign policy in disarray? Why is our economic assistance program today a tool of little or no value? Why is our Point IV program limping aimlessly? Why is our foreign information program disorganized and voiceless? Why, indeed, do we even have to talk about the foreign policy and performance of this great nation in a Congressional political campaign when the goals, the objectives and ambitions of all of us, Democrats and Republicans alike, are identical?

The answer to all these questions is the same: political expediency, appeasement of the Republican extremists, party unity at the price of national unity and international influence.

After all these months of babble and bewilderment is it any wonder that we have become unpredictable to our friends and predictable to our enemies? In Europe and Japan they fear we may heedlessly involve them in unnecessary war. Our enemies look at cutbacks in our defense expenditures, withdrawal of troops from the Pacific, the bluff that failed in Indo-China, delays in our continental defense program, tensions in our relations with our allies, our withering programs for building economic strength and unity, our reliance on military strategy and neglect of the underlying political and social problems. Our enemies look at these hard facts rather than Mr. Dulles's hot words—and believe they have little to fear.

Yet the President said the other night in Los Angeles: "Over the world we have brought strength where there was weakness. We have brought realism where there was wishful thinking. We have brought frankness, candor and force to foreign policy."[140]

Well, if he really believed that, it would be positively dangerous, because the success of our foreign policy far transcends in importance the political success of his party or mine. And until our leaders distinguish words from reality and foolish elocution from effective action, we will be in trouble, and our alliances, our security, in jeopardy.

I could add, too, that we will be in trouble as long as the Administration tries to placate the implacable, and yields to that little band of right-wing Republicans. At the risk of mixing my metaphors, perhaps here in San Francisco I could remind our leaders of an old Chinese proverb: "He who rides a tiger may not dismount."

But with the great losses of the past months there have been some gains too. I would even add that while Republicans, like Mr. Nixon, still blame the Democrats for the Communist conquest in China, I don't blame the Republicans for the Communist conquest in Indo-China. I don't even think there are many traitors among the responsible Republicans in Washington. In fact, I think they are just as patriotic and just as loyal, if not quite as wise and intelligent, as we Democrats.

But I must add about Indo-China that I hope I never again see the United States in such nervous disorder and confusion. Unable to fight, unable to negotiate, we ended up unable even to speak coherently, while the Communists drove a wedge into Southeast Asia and the free world suffered its greatest disaster since the fall of China.

But, as I say, there have been gains. In Iran the long negotiations have come to a happy end, and our government is, I believe, entitled to a large share of the credit.[141]

In the Middle East the British and the Egyptians have settled the menacing dispute over Suez.[142] But after seven years there is no peace between the Arabs and Israel whose fears are now aggravated by our government's plan to arm her Arab neighbors. Yet we can hope that the important and conciliatory proposals Israel has lately made may point the way at least toward direct negotiation with the Arabs.

At long last a settlement has been reached between Yugoslavia and Italy over Trieste which is solid progress.[143]

In Guatemala a Communist cell in the New World has been exposed and eliminated.[144]

While we lost the European Defense Community on which we banked too heavily and [that we] threatened too much, the position and participation in European defense of Germany has been worked out through NATO. And if Mr. Dulles played a passive, secondary role I don't criticize, I applaud him. The time has come for us to calm down a bit, step aside and let our allies take some initiative—those allies, by the way, like Britain and France whom the Republican extremists constantly vilify.

And in the East the debacle of Indo-China ought to make it clear that military power in Asia is nationalism and the greatest problems are political and social. But the Southeast Asian Defensive Alliance Secretary Dulles has negotiated has definite military value,[145] and it could and will, we hope, become far more than what the Asians call the "White Man's Protective Association."

So, I repeat, there have been some gains in the past two years and certainly our government and Secretary Dulles are entitled to credit and gratitude for their contribution. But I pray let us understand the full significance of our situation and let us state our successes with modest realism and not boastful reassurance. For we confront a trembling alliance in Europe, less than confidence in

Asia, growing attraction of monstrous China, Russia's military and economic might, a restless Africa, and a South America we have too long taken for granted.

We exclude as solutions either world destruction or world tyranny; we exclude, in short, preventive war or surrender as offering any possible solutions of the predicament of Western civilization. The only course remaining is coexistence, and I confess I get a little impatient with the semantic debate for and against coexistence, for it is either co-existence or no-existence—until the evil of the dread design of imperialist communism is clear for all to see.

But coexistence with our obnoxious, aggressive and perfidious neighbors can never be peaceful. Workable coexistence can only be based on a balance of effective strength, military, economic and moral, with evil neighbors who will relentlessly and tirelessly expand whenever they scent weakness or vulnerability. So military power is essential.

But imperialist communism is not just an armed threat and an underground conspiracy. It is also a special movement which grows and prospers, especially in the great underdeveloped areas of discontent, while we concentrate on combatting the conspiracy. Having checked their military efforts we would be foolish to let them win easy victories in the social and economic battle. So we must push steadily forward in developing the economic and moral strength of the non-Communist world.

Can the U.S. meet this vast challenge? I doubt it so long as the Administration in Washington places the welfare of the Right Wing of the Republican party above the welfare of the country. The "agonizing reappraisal" and the "liberation" which Secretary Dulles has talked about must begin at home and now, before we lose any more precious, hard-won ground. And the way to liberate our government from its present thralldom is to elect a Democratic Congress in November.

By electing a Democratic Congress, we can turn the Republican Old Guard out of control of the committees of Congress. We can demonstrate that this small group has no mandate from the American people. We can even encourage the Secretary of State to be himself and to sponsor a foreign policy which will represent the country as a whole and not just a reactionary minority; a policy which is not a hydra-headed compromise that frightens everyone, and pleases no one, and demeans our country.

But a Republican victory in November would confirm the Administration in its futility and error. It would encourage the spirit of "go it alone" in the world and "go it alone" in the nation. It would postpone indefinitely the restoration of genuine bipartisanship and mutual confidence in foreign affairs.

Only a Democratic Congress can free foreign and defense affairs from those suffocating influences which the Administration seems to regard with such fear and trembling.

With a Democratic Congress perhaps we can all join to rebuild our unity, our strength, the tools of our policy, respect for our word in the world, the faith and constancy of our allies, the confidence of mankind everywhere in the essential honor, decency and good will of America. Then we would merit the respect, and even the just fear, of those who choose to be our enemies.

A Democratic victory in November can lay the basis for national unity. For we Democrats do not believe that to be a Republican is to be a traitor, to be corrupt, or even always to be confused. We have, in fact, prided ourselves on the cooperation and service of able Republicans in matters affecting the welfare of our country, particularly in the great areas of foreign affairs and national security.

With a Democratic Congress we can review the problems of our defense budget, the level to which our economy can be expanded, and the nature of an equitable tax structure to give us financial stability while meeting our proper defense and foreign policy outlays.

With a Democratic Congress perhaps the President and Mr. Dulles will no longer feel compelled to tolerate insubordinate agents of right-wing Republican senators. The morale and efficiency of the State Department could be rebuilt; new and talented men could be trained for its work; honest reporting and careful analysis could once again become subject to reward, not reproach.

With a Democratic Congress we could address ourselves once more to the interrupted task of building that better-functioning world economy so necessary not only to give others economic hope, but indispensable to our own continued growth and prosperity.

With a Democratic Congress we could address ourselves once more to the interrupted task of assisting the underdeveloped areas of the world in making the transition to the opportunities of the world of the future.

We could then speak to our allies again in accents which they can understand and believe. We could strengthen our alliances and contribute leadership commensurate with our other contributions. We could move from disunity, mutual recrimination and antagonism to that mutual respect and well-wishing which are the preconditions of political maturity and responsibility.

We could stand prepared to meet whatever thrusts our enemies might plot against us with unity at home, with growing military and economic strength, with efficient organs of government, with our allies' understanding of our purposes and of the limits of those purposes.

And, finally, remembering that strength is not an end in itself but a means to an end, we could explore with greater confidence the possibilities of negotiation with our friends, yes, and with our enemies—negotiations, for settlements here and there and for safe and sound disarmament, thus inching our way along the weary path to peace.

Negotiation without strength, which some of our European friends seem to want, is madness. Strength without negotiation is futility. Negotiation on the basis of strength and solidarity is the only policy which can hold out hope to patient and suffering mankind.

The world at the moment is in a long and dark valley. Science offers us mass suicide. But it also offers the world a greater abundance than we have ever known. Our generation will have to make a fateful choice.

Just two years ago, here in San Francisco, I said that: "America has been called to greatness. The summons of the twentieth century is a summons to our vision, to our humanity, to our practicality. If these provide the common purpose of America and Asia (and I might have added, of the free world) . . . we need have no fear for the future. Because it will belong to free men."

I am still content to leave it there, adding only that the Democratic party is faithful to this vision and ready to work with all like-minded men and women in answering this summons.

The Formosa Crisis: A Peaceful Solution

APRIL 11, 1955

✡

In early 1955, a year of impending crisis in foreign affairs, the news was dominated by the fear of a possible attack by Communist China against the Republic of China, consisting of Formosa and a number of smaller islands. While Congress was debating a mutual defense treaty with Formosa, mainland forces began a series of small daily attacks against the islands. After Yikiang Island was occupied in January, the Tachen Islands were evacuated as unnecessary to the defense of Formosa. Before his trip to Formosa to sign the treaty, during his visit there, and after his return to the United States, Secretary of State Dulles made a number of oblique remarks about American determination to defend Quemoy and Matsu, small Formosan-held islands off the coast of mainland China. By late March and early April, national opinion focused around whether Communist China would attack these islands, thus precipitating an American attack on Communist China. Stevenson considered it his duty to offer a major address to help ease the tension and to offer reasonable alternatives. Addressing the nation by radio from Chicago on April 11, 1955, he gave what he later considered one of the most important speeches in his career. The following day, Secretary Dulles announced that Stevenson's alternatives for a peaceful solution concerning Formosa had copied those of the Administration and had "in fact endorsed the Administration's program in relation to Formosa."[146] No further discussion of the importance of defending Quemoy and Matsu was offered. This speech, printed also in What I Think, *was given its title by Stevenson.*

MY fellow countrymen—

I have not spoken to you for more than four months. And I do
so tonight only because I have been deeply disturbed by the recent
course of events in the Far East and because many of you have
asked me for my views. I have waited until the first excitement
about the islands, Quemoy and Matsu, has subsided and we can
more calmly examine our situation in the Straits of Formosa and in
Asia. In matters of national security emotion is no substitute for
intelligence, nor rigidity for prudence. To act coolly, intelligently
and prudently in perilous circumstances is the test of a man—and
also a nation.

Our common determination, Republicans and Democrats alike,
is to avoid atomic war and achieve a just and lasting peace. We all
agree on that, I think, but not on the ways and means to that end.
And that's what I want to talk about—war, and ways and means to
a peaceful solution in the present crisis in the Straits of Formosa.

On this April evening, I remember vividly that it was in April
just ten years ago that the largest conference in all diplomatic
history met at San Francisco to write the Charter of the United
Nations—a charter of liberation for the peoples of the earth from
the scourge of war and want.

The spirit of San Francisco was one of optimism and boundless
hope. The long night was lifting; Hitler's armies were on the eve of
collapse; the warlords of Japan were tottering. Our hearts were
high in that bright blue dawn of a new day—just ten years ago.

But tonight, despite the uneasy truces in Korea and Indo-China,
our country once again confronts the iron face of war—war that
may be unlike anything that man has seen since the creation of the
world, for the weapons man has created can destroy not only his
present but his future as well. With the invention of the hydrogen
bomb and all the frightful spawn of fission and fusion, the human
race has crossed one of the great watersheds of history, and mankind stands in new territory, in unchartered lands.

The tragedy is that the possibility of war just now seems to
hinge upon Quemoy and Matsu, small islands that lie almost as
close to the coast of China as Staten Island does to New York—
islands which, presumably, have been fortified by the Chinese
Nationalists with our approval and assistance.

Having loudly hinted at American intervention in Indo-China just a year ago, and then backed away, having forced General Chiang Kai-shek to evacuate the Tachen islands when the Communists made menacing gestures just a couple of months ago, we now face the bitter consequences of our government's Far Eastern policy again: either another damaging and humiliating retreat, or else the hazard of war, modern war, unleashed not by necessity, not by strategic judgment, not by the honor of allies or for the defense of frontiers, but by a policy based more on political difficulties here at home than the realities of our situation in Asia.

Given these unhappy choices it appears that President Eisenhower will decide what to do if and when the attack comes, depending on whether in his judgment it is just an attack on these islands or a prelude to an assault on Formosa. While our President has great military experience, perhaps it is not improper to ask whether any man can read the mind of an enemy within a few hours of such an attack and determine whether, at some later date, the enemy plans to go further and invade Formosa. Is it wise to allow the dread question of modern war to hinge upon such a guess?

Many of the President's most influential associates—including the Republican leader in the Senate [William Knowland] and the Chairman of the Republican Policy Committee [Styles Bridges]—have been insisting that he pledge us to the defense of these islands. They say that another bluff and backdown, another retreat in Asia, would add substance to what the Chinese Communists say about the U.S. being a "paper tiger."

Those who demand a pledge to go to war also say that having gone this far with Chiang Kai-shek to let him down now, when he is reinforcing these islands and preparing an all-out stand, would deal a heavy blow to the morale of his forces and endanger the defenses of Formosa itself.

Now there is undeniable merit to these and other arguments, but I must say in all candor that they seem to me overborne by the counterarguments, and I have the greatest misgivings about risking a third world war in defense of these little islands in which we would have neither the same legal justification nor the same support as in the defense of Formosa. They are different from Formosa. They have always belonged to China. But Formosa belonged to Japan and was ceded by the Japanese Peace Treaty.[147] We have as much right to be there as anybody, except perhaps the real Formosans.

But, of course the President's judgment must be final. He asked for and got from Congress the sole responsibility for making this decision. His word is our law, and, as Senator Lyndon Johnson, the majority leader, has said: "we are not going to take the responsibility out of the hands of the constitutional leader and try to arrogate it to ourselves." So the ultimate decision must rest with the constitutional leader, the President, and he will have my prayers for his wisdom and fortitude in making this critical decision, if he must and when he must. I only hope that the inflammatory voices in his party and his Administration do not unbalance his consideration of these critical questions:

Are the off-shore islands essential to the security of the U.S.?

Are they, indeed, even essential to the defense of Formosa—which all Americans have agreed upon since President Truman sent the Seventh Fleet there five years ago?

Or is it, as the Secretary of Defense [Charles E. Wilson] says, that the loss of Quemoy and Matsu would make no significant military difference?

Can they be defended without resort to nuclear weapons?

If not, while I know we now have the means to incinerate, to burn up, much of living China, and quickly, are we prepared to use such weapons to defend islands so tenuously related to American security?

Finally, are we prepared to shock and alienate not alone our traditional allies but most of the major non-Communist powers of Asia by going to war over islands to which the United States has no color of claim and which are of questionable value to the defense of Formosa?

Are we, in short, prepared to face the prospect of war in the morass of China, possibly global war, standing almost alone in a sullen or hostile world?

These are questions that must be answered, this time I hope with more concern for realities in Asia and for unity with our allies, than for fantasies in Formosa and for placating implacable extremists in America.

At this late date there may be no wholly satisfactory way of resolving the dilemma. But if we learn something from this experience, then perhaps we can turn our present difficulties to good account and devise an approach more in keeping with the realities of Asia and of the hydrogen age.

And that causes me to say that the division of our coalition over these offshore islands, the weakening of the Grand Alliance of free nations pledged to stand together to defend themselves, is in my judgment a greater peril to enduring peace than the islands themselves.

I know some politicians tell us that we don't need allies. Life would certainly be much simpler if that were so, for our friends can be highly irritating. But it is not so. We need allies because we have only 6 per cent of the world's population. We need them because the overseas air bases essential to our own security are on their territory. We need allies because they are the source of indispensable strategic materials. We need, above all, the moral strength that the solidarity of the world community alone can bring to our cause. Let us never underestimate the weight of moral opinion. It can be more penetrating than bullets, more durable than steel. It was a great general, Napoleon, who wrote that: "In war, moral considerations are three-quarters of the battle."[148]

Should we be plunged into another great war, the maintenance of our alliances and the respect and good will of the uncommitted nations of Asia will be far more important to us than the possession of these offshore islands by General Chiang Kai-shek ever could be. Moreover, the maintenance of a united front is of vital importance to the defense of Formosa itself, since, in addition to the material and military support our friends might contribute, their moral support and the knowledge by the Communist leaders that they would be facing a united free world, would be a much more effective deterrent to an assault on Formosa than is our present lonely and irresolute position.

How shall we mend the walls of our coalition? How shall we frustrate the supreme aim of the Moscow-Peiping axis—to drive a wedge between America and her allies? And is there any hope of a peaceful solution of the offshore-island question?

I think so. Senator [Walter F.] George, the Chairman of the Foreign Relations Committee, has recently pointed the way: "We nations of the free world," he said, "must understand each other and reach a measure of unity before any hopeful approach can be made to a reexamination of our Far Eastern problems."[149]

And Governor Harriman of New York, long familiar with the problems of maintaining a coalition, warned us the other day that in Asia: "The whole world is a party at interest, and that it has been not only illogical but deadly dangerous," he said, "to arrogate to ourselves the sole responsibility for decisions which involve the future of many peoples."[150]

So I would urge our government to promptly consult our friends, yes, and the uncommitted states too, and ask them all to join us in an open declaration condemning the use of force in the Formosa Strait, and agreeing to stand with us in the defense of Formosa against any aggression, pending some final settlement of its status—by independence, neutralization, trusteeship, plebiscite, or whatever is wisest.

Nor do I see any reason why we should not invite Soviet Russia, which is united by treaty with Red China, to declare its position, to indicate whether it prefers the possibility of ultimate settlement by agreement to an unpredictable, perhaps limitless conflict, started by an arrogant, foolhardy Communist China, either by miscalculation or by design.

Fortified by such an international declaration denouncing the use of force; with the assurance of such collective support for the defense of Formosa; and with the addition, thereby, of moral solidarity to military strength, I should think Quemoy and Matsu would have little further importance to the Nationalists, let alone to us—and that they could then be relinquished, before we stumble any further down the dismal road to war that nobody wants.

Diplomacy prescribes no rigid formula for accomplishing our objectives, and another major avenue in the quest for a peaceful solution in the Far East remains unexplored: the United Nations. I should think that the United States, together with friends and allies in Europe and Asia, could submit a resolution to the United Nations General Assembly, calling upon the Assembly likewise to condemn any effort to alter the present status of Formosa by force, and I think we could afford to go further and call upon the United Nations Assembly to seek a formula for the permanent future of Formosa, consistent with the wishes of its people, with international law, and with world security.

One of the weaknesses of our position is that we have been making Formosa policy as we thought best regardless of others. We have not made it clear that we are helping to hold Formosa not as an offensive but as a purely defensive measure. We have not made it clear because the Administration has not been clear itself. But we can't expect other nations to support policies they disagree with, let alone ambiguous and dangerous policies.

Joint action along the lines I've indicated would put Formosa policy on a much broader and more comprehensible basis. In the eyes of the Asian nations we would thereby achieve a consistent and morally unquestionable position in providing for the protection of the Formosans according to the principles and ideals of international law. In the eyes of our European friends we would once more have asserted our full belief in the value, indeed in the indispensability, of maintaining the alliance of the free world against the slave world. And in the eyes of our Nationalist friends on Formosa, surely the understanding and support of the bulk of the non-Communist world is a much stronger defense of Formosa than these islands can possibly be.

But, if the Chinese Communists refuse; if they insist on force and reject any peaceful solution, then at least it would be clear to everyone who the aggressors were. And, clearly, if the Chinese are so bent on violence, so intoxicated by their success, so indifferent to the grisly realities of modern war, then we have no alternative but to meet force with force. But let us at least meet it with our allies beside us and the blame placed squarely where it belongs— not on America's fantasies and inflexibility, but on the unteachable and unquenchable ambition and the indifference to human life of China's Communist regime.

To profit from this unhappy experience we might ask ourselves how we ever got into this position, how the prestige and honor of the great United States, not to mention the peace of the world, could be staked on some little islands within the very shadow of the China coast in which we have no claim or interest?

The answer, of course, lies partly in the fact that domestic political considerations have influenced our Formosa policy lately. Domestic politics should not enter our foreign affairs, least of all factional conflict between the two wings of the President's party, but they have, and too often our hot and cold, vacillating behavior has reflected efforts to please both of the views that divide our government and the Republican party, especially on Far Eastern policy.

And, while I do not belittle some recent achievements in the foreign field, for the same reasons too much of our foreign policy of late has disclosed a yawning gap between what we say and what we do—between our words and deeds.

For example, you recall that just a year ago as the Communist pressure rose in Indo-China, so did our warlike, menacing words. The Vice-President of the United States even talked of sending American soldiers to fight on the mainland of Asia. But what happened? Nothing.

Likewise all the bold, brave talk about "liberation" that raised such vain hopes among the peoples behind the Iron Curtain has long since evaporated, with the loss of half of Viet-Nam and of much of our prestige and influence.

So also we hear no more of last year's dire threats of instantaneous and massive atomic retaliation. Instead, the President has spoken lately of pinpoint retaliation with tactical weapons. I fear, however, that the psychological effect of the use of atomic weapons, large or small, will be most unfortunate.

Now let me be clear. I am not criticizing the Administration for abandoning these extravagant positions; I am criticizing it for taking such positions, for making threats which it is not prepared to back up, and thereby undermining faith in the United States. Theodore Roosevelt said: "Never draw unless you intend to shoot," and I fear this wordy warfare has made more friends in Asia for China than for us.

Another example of these winged words, as we have seen, was President Eisenhower's dramatic announcement two years ago that he was unleashing Chiang Kai-shek, taking the wraps off him, presumably for an attack on the mainland to reconquer China.

However, it was apparent to everyone else, if not to us, that such an invasion across 100 miles of water by a small, over-age, under-equipped army against perhaps the largest army and the largest nation on earth could not possibly succeed without all-out support from the United States.

Since it seemed incredible to sober, thoughtful people that the government of the United States could be bluffing on such a matter, the President's "unleashing" policy has caused widespread anxiety that we planned to support a major war with China which might involve the Soviet Union. Hence we find ourselves where we are today—on Quemoy and Matsu—alone.

What, then, are the lessons to be drawn from the past two years?

In the first place, I think we should abandon, once and for all, the policy of wishful thinking and wishful talking, the policy of big words and little deeds.

We must renounce go-it-aloneism.

We shall have to face the fact that General Chiang's army cannot invade the mainland unless we are prepared to accept enormous burdens and risks—alone.

The world will respect us for recognizing mistakes and correcting them. But if our present posture in the offshore islands, for example, is a wrong one, who will respect us for stubbornly persisting in it? If we cease to deceive ourselves over the hard realities of power in the Formosa situation, we shall have taken the first step toward our first essential—the restoration of unity of purpose and action between ourselves and our allies in the free world. But our friends have made it clear that so long as fantasy, rigidity and domestic politics seem to stand in the way of peaceful Formosa settlement, they will not support us if, in spite of our endeavors, a conflict should break out.

So, finally, let us face the fact that keeping friends these days calls for more statesmanship than challenging enemies, and the cause of world peace transcends any domestic political considerations.

But preoccupied as we all are these days with the immediate problem of these islands, we must try to keep things in perspective somehow, and not lose sight our main objectives. For beyond Quemoy and Matsu, and even Formosa, lie the urgent and larger problems of Asia—the growing attraction of enormous, reawakened China, the struggle of the underdeveloped countries to improve their condition and keep their independence, and the grave misgivings about America.

It is not only over the offshore-islands crisis that we need a new sense of direction and to mend our fences. Too often of late we have turned to the world a face of stern military power. Too often the sound they hear from Washington is the call to arms, the rattling of the saber. Too often our constructive, helpful economic programs have been obscured, our good done by stealth. Thus have we Americans, the most peaceful and generous people on earth, been made to appear hard, belligerent and careless of those very qualities of humanity which, in fact, we value most. The picture of America—the kindly, generous, deeply pacific people who really are America—has been clouded in the world, to the comfort of the aggressors and the dismay of our friends.

As best we can, let us correct this distorted impression, for [we] will win no hearts and minds in the new Asia by uttering louder threats and brandishing bigger swords. The fact is that we have not created excess military strength. The fact is that compared to freedom's enemies we have created if anything too little; the trouble is that we have tried to cover our deficiencies with bold words and have thus obscured our peaceful purposes and our ultimate reliance on quiet firmness, rather than bluster and vacillation, on wisdom rather than warnings, on forbearance rather than dictation.

We will be welcome to the sensitive people of Asia, more as engineers and doctors and agricultural experts, coming to build, to help, to heal than as soldiers. Point Four was an idea far more stirring, far more powerful, than all the empty slogans about "liberation" and "retaliation" and "unleashing" rolled together. So I say, let us present once more the true face of America—warm and modest and friendly, dedicated to the welfare of all mankind, and demanding nothing except a chance for all to live and let live, to grow and govern as they wish, free from interference, free from intimidation, free from fear.

Let this be the American mission in the hydrogen age. Let us stop slandering ourselves and appear before the world once again—as we really are—as friends, not as masters; as apostles of principle, not of power; in humility, not arrogance; as champions of peace, not as harbingers of war. For our strength lies, not alone in our proving grounds and our stockpiles, but in our ideals, our goals, and their universal appeal to all men who are struggling to breathe free.

Reduce the Volume of Loose Words
and Catchy Slogans!

OCTOBER 29, 1955

✡

Throughout the spring and fall of 1955, Stevenson continued to challenge the Republicans for their "tough talk and timid action, bluff and backdown, and blowing hot and cold." Although the Geneva Summit Conference seemed likely to relax the cold-war relations, Stevenson believed the "Geneva Spirit" was shattered in September of 1955 when the Middle East crisis was initiated by the large arms deal between the Egyptians and Soviet bloc countries. Despite the Eisenhower policy of giving military assistance to countries or regions for the common purpose of opposing communism, he refused to sell $50 million worth of arms to the Israelis which they had requested for their defense. Eisenhower's pronouncements seemed as questionable to Stevenson as this statement the President made later in the fall: "While we continue willing to consider requests for arms needed for legitimate self-defense, we do not intend to contribute to an arms competition in the Near East." Stevenson's speech at Duluth, Minnesota, to the Democratic Rally, October 29, printed below, was a sharp attack on such policies by the Republican Administration.

NOWHERE is it so important that we stop the politics of misleading talk as in the field of our foreign relations.

We do not belittle the "Geneva spirit." We thank God that no guns are firing today. We are grateful for even an uneasy peace and we are grateful to the Republican Administration for the constructive steps it has taken. We are proud, too, of the Democratic record for bipartisanship in foreign policy—and especially proud that we have resisted even the provocation of those Republicans who have smeared that record with the charge of treason, and every lesser epithet as well.

But we insist on putting a stop to the loose talk and erratic behavior that has marked the conduct of our foreign affairs these past three years and that has confused our purposes and frightened our friends if not our enemies.

I mean the contemptuous talk about containing the spread of communism as a "negative, futile and immoral policy"; I mean the loose talk of rolling back Communist power, while at the same time cutting down our military establishment, balancing the budget and reducing taxes.

I mean the threats of massive atomic retaliation as a national defense policy.

I mean the boast of "unleashing" Chiang Kai-shek for an attack on the China mainland.

I mean the talk of intervention in Indo-China.

I mean tough talk and timid action; I mean bluff and backdown; I mean blowing alternately hot and cold, and confounding everyone in the process, themselves included.

And I mean creating or encouraging the illusion that all is well, or at least better, that miracles happened at Geneva last summer, that peace and security are around the corner, like some other Republican blessings I can think of.

Well, the fact is that our foreign affairs are not prospering any more than agriculture is prospering. The fact is that we should pray the more fervently for the success of the Foreign Ministers' Conference in Geneva because our world situation has sadly deteriorated.

You have but to look at the violence in North Africa, at France's difficulties, at growing misgivings about Germany's future direction, at the smoldering Middle East, at Greece and Turkey quarreling, at Japan's economic dilemma, at the unsettled Formosa Strait —and I could name half a dozen other unhealthy spots, every one of which our adversaries will exploit.

My purpose is not to be alarming. My purpose is to be realistic, and not to be misled by the new Soviet charm policy or the

Republican peace chorus. Moscow has discovered that war and the constant threat of war is a political and economic dead end. Has Washington discovered that a rigid military diplomacy is too? All our bases, arms and alliances are no better and stronger than the good will and political strength of the nations involved.

One of our greatest tasks in the years ahead will be to reduce the volume of loose words and catchy slogans, both hot and cold, and increase the volume of sobriety, realism and flexibility in our foreign affairs.

The Road Away from Revolution

NOVEMBER 11, 1955

✪

*Pressure on Stevenson to announce his candidacy for the 1956
Presidential nomination increased during the summer and autumn
of 1955. President Truman indicated that he would lend his support if Stevenson declared himself a candidate before Labor Day.
His decision was made more difficult partly because Eisenhower
was recuperating from his heart attack and also because, as James
Reston wrote of him in* The New York Times: *"He is going to run
all right, but he is having his troubles. He has no staff to speak of.
He has no funds. He has no political organization, and he is almost
entirely out of touch with the political leaders of the Democratic
Party on Capitol Hill."*[151] *Additionally, by October, Truman was
actively supporting Governor Averell Harriman, and it seemed
likely that Senator Estes Kefauver of Tennessee would also enter
the race for the nomination. Stevenson announced his candidacy
on November 15 and offered three main reasons for his decision:
"In the first place, I believe it important for the Democratic Party
to resume the executive direction of our national affairs. Second, I
am assured that my candidacy would be welcomed by representative people in and out of my party throughout the country. Third,
I believe any citizen should make whatever contribution he can to
search for a safer, saner world."*[152]

*Shortly before, on November 11, Stevenson was the principal
speaker for the opening of the Woodrow Wilson Centennial at the
University of Virginia in Charlottesville. While he continued to
attack recent American mistakes in connection with the Middle
East and other crises, this nationally acclaimed speech, printed
below and also in* What I Think, *focused on his more characteristi-*

cally optimistic approach to foreign affairs. It is suggestive of the considerable influence Wilson's ideas on foreign policy contributed to Stevenson's broad international understanding. The title is Stevenson's.

WE have come tonight to celebrate the hundredth birthday of another Virginian, a "brave ancestor," who profoundly impressed Americans with the "measures to secure their freedom." While the centennial year of Woodrow Wilson will not begin officially until December 28, it is wholly fitting that the Woodrow Wilson Foundation should have chosen November 11 as the date on which to open the year of commemoration. There could hardly be a moment more appropriate for a national rededication to Woodrow Wilson than this day when we pause in memory of those who died in the first global war for democracy and freedom.[153]

We can see now a painful but just irony in the designation "Armistice Day." For November 11, 1918, brought only an armistice; it did not bring peace. The years since 1918 have been a parody of peace, a series of intervals between wars; and war itself has grown more ghastly and more appalling. The crisis in human history which Wilson perceived with such clarity thirty-five years ago is now upon us with redoubled urgency. In an age when total war threatens not just a setback to civilization, but its total destruction, it will profit us to revisit Wilson and reconsider his contributions to the struggle for peace.[154]

The Wilsonian reforms thus helped produce the vast material abundance we have today. But, more important still, they contributed to a renewal of the American moral purpose. They gave meaning in a world of affairs to the fact that we are, in the words of [St.] Paul, members, one of another; they reminded us that the vital community depends on integrity, upon generosity and decency in human relationships, and on equality in human opportunities.

What Wilson saw in the nation he came to see even more urgently in the world. In the international anarchy of his day—an anarchy which plunged Europe into war within eighteen months of his election—he saw, all over again, the strife, the bitterness, the disaster which must follow if uncontrolled forces are allowed to struggle with each other with no restraints imposed by the community as a whole. As the flames enveloped Europe, President Wilson had the vision to see that unrestrained national interests, like unbalanced economic forces at home, do not invariably work toward the general good. The philosophy behind the League of Nations, indeed, was Wilson's guiding idea of the common good as applied to international society.

As we all know, he failed to convey this vision to his people, or at least to a sufficient number of their leaders. Our nation took no part in the world's first experiment in international order. But, looking back today with the hindsight of over thirty years, we also know that his vision of a community of nations under law was—and is—the only road to lasting peace. The dream of 1919 has become the reality of the United Nations. And so, once again, if we look for monuments to the work of Wilson, we can find them with us, built into the foundations of our postwar world.

This does not mean that, for Wilson, the League then—or the United Nations today—would constitute the whole of a strategy of peace. The grounds of the universal unrest and perturbation lie deeper; they lie, Wilson himself suggested, "at the sources of the spiritual life of our times."[155] Underneath the recriminations of diplomats and the conflicts of nation-states, there boiled up then—as there boil up today—the hopes, resentments and aspirations not just of leaders, but of great masses of people, seeking for themselves and their children the rights and privileges which, Wilson said, "all normal men desire and must have if they are to be contented and within reach of happiness."[156]

This, it seems to me, is the heart of the matter—and the heart not only of democracy and of freedom but of peace itself. Violence is, after all, the confession that mutual relations of respect and good will have broken down and the web of common life has been torn apart. The most urgent task before any society, domestic or worldwide, is to check grievances, clashes, blind opposition of interest, long before they reach the flashpoint of war.

These subterranean pressures rising round the world—of dire need, of hunger and disease, of awakened hope, of nationalism, of envy, of impatience to make up for lost centuries—these are the explosive stuff of international life. And this Woodrow Wilson knew, just as he knew that poverty and underprivilege and the

gulfs between rich and poor, were fire hazards in America's basement. In one of his last public utterances, he discussed the phenomenon which so threatens and alarms us today—the rise of
communism. He was one of the first Americans to call attention to
the danger of communism; and thirty years later we still spend
more time calling each other's attention to the danger than to its
causes.

"The sum of the whole matter is this," Wilson said: "That our
civilization cannot survive materially unless it is redeemed spiri-
tually." What we require, he said, must include "sympathy and
helpfulness and a willingness to forego self-interest in order to
promote the welfare, happiness, and contentment of others and of
the community as a whole." This, he said, thinking of the terror of
the Communist alternative—this "was the road away from revolution."[157]

I would suggest that Wilson still has much to say to us today.
And what he has to say is that we must wage more fiercely than
ever the same twofold struggle of a generation ago: the war against
want and oppression, and the war against war itself.

We have made a start in the war against poverty and oppression.
But our world is not moving by the action of some inscrutable
"hidden hand" toward spreading prosperity, rising standards and
the extension of freedom. On the contrary, the drift is the other
way, to population outstripping resources in backward lands, to
wealth accumulating in the already wealthy West, and to the
Communists' propaganda and infiltration. If they succeed in cap-
turing the revolution of the underdeveloped areas—the uncommitted third of the world—as they have already captured the
revolutions of Russia and China, the circle of freedom on earth will
dangerously shrink.

Yet anticommunism and self-interest should not be our only
motive in offering a helping hand to people struggling for dignity
and independence. Unselfishness and magnanimity are also part of
the American record. And there is much we can do to help reverse
the fatality in less fortunate lands whereby poverty breeds ever
more poverty and hatred breeds ever more hatred. We can set our
overwhelming resources of wealth and skill to work to improve the
productivity and standards of life. We can furnish more of our
brain power for activity abroad and widen the opportunities for

giving education and training to our foreign friends here in the United States. And we can convince the peoples of the world that we do this not just to check communism or to impose Americanism or to perpetuate colonialism, but because we believe that the dream of a fearless, free and equal society, first cherished within these shores, is more potent than ever and can be spread around the world.

But perhaps the most urgent struggle of all is the war against war itself. Our past failures to control war caused great wreckage in the world and took many lives, but they did not destroy the world itself. Total war in the nuclear epoch will not let civilization off so lightly.

What humanity now demands is a great leap ahead in our thinking and in our action. We talk of "limiting" war. But that is not enough. War in the hydrogen age resists limitation: one cannot keep a chain reaction on a leash. So the ultimate goal is not limitation, it is not an uneasy balance of weapons, or of terror, but the abolition of war by the abolition of the means of war.

The difficulties in the way of achieving an enforceable system of disarmament are immense. Maybe the problem is insoluble now as it has been in the past. But it seems to me that the urgency is such that we can settle for nothing less than a sustained and dogged search for effective disarmament with the best brains we can muster, and that we have no greater foreign-policy objective.

That we must move ahead creatively and decisively along all the world's fronts in the struggle for the common good of freedom daily becomes more imperative. Each day's news is another plea for sober realism. For now that the rosy mists around last summer's meeting at the Summit are rising we see all around us signs of the disintegration of our whole security system. The fabric is unraveling. Most recently Arab-Israel hostility has risen to a new pitch of intensity along the Egyptian frontier, just as the Soviet design to split the Arab world from the West becomes more apparent.

It is interesting and relevant to recall that Wilson believed in encouraging Jewish settlement in Palestine and took an active part in making the Balfour Declaration a vital part of the Palestine mandate under the League of Nations. Since then the state of Israel has become a fact, and, unhappily, so also has the bitter hostility of its Arab neighbors. For five years violence along the armistice lines has been mounting. Unless these clashes cease there is danger of all-out war developing while we debate which side was the aggressor.

A major effort of statesmanship is required if we are to avert a political disaster in this troubled area. We have shown little initiative within or outside the United Nations in devising measures to prevent these border incidents. After years of experience it would seem evident that the only way to avoid bloodshed and violence along the border is to keep the troops of these antagonists apart. And I wonder if United Nations guards could not undertake patrol duties in the areas of tension and collision. Certainly both sides would respect United Nations patrols where they do not trust each other.

In this country we have lately been dismayed by the arms deal between Egypt and Russia. Of course, there should be an equitable balance of armed strength so that neither side feels that it lives by the grace of its none too kindly neighbor. We must help, if need be, to counteract any Soviet attempt to upset such a balance, and we must make it emphatically clear that the status quo shall not be changed by force. But we do not want to see an arms race in this area where the principles of Woodrow Wilson's Fourteen Points once shone like a lighthouse after centuries of dark oppression.[158]

The Middle East has long been an area of Russian ambition. And we trust our friends there have neither overlooked the fate of nations which have listened to the siren songs of Moscow, nor forgotten that the Soviet Foreign Minister [Viacheslav Molotov] told the Nazi Foreign Minister [Joachim von Ribbentrop] in 1940 that one of the conditions of a Nazi-Soviet agreement was that the Persian Gulf was to be a sphere of Soviet influence.

The contagious flames of undeclared war between Israel and her neighbors have smoldered too long. We applaud the peaceful efforts of the Secretary-General of the United Nations [Dag Hammarskjold] and we must bestir ourselves to help create conditions which will work toward peace, not conflict, in this troubled area. The United States does not choose sides when it chooses peace.

Let us, I say, not deceive ourselves. The Soviets have recognized the limits of force and threat and intimidation in the face of growing Western strength. Since the death of Stalin they have sharply altered their tactics and stepped boldly forth from the shadows of conspiracy and secrecy. To our dismay they are competing openly and directly with the West. We must take care lest the illusions of their charm policy further weaken our defenses, moral and physical. And we must take care, too, lest rigid military-security diplomacy hobble our foreign policy. We cannot meet each new problem in the war against war and the war against want just in terms of air bases, military alliances and nuclear stockpiles. If we do, our influence will steadily ebb away in those crucial areas of the world where progress and peace are the major concerns.

So, let us keep our powder dry, our minds supple, our hearts warm and our spirits high as the great contest of our times moves forward into a new, even more perilous phase.

As Woodrow Wilson devised new methods to promote the common good among men and peace among nations, so must we devise new methods to meet the challenges of our times. Surely this is what the spirit of Wilson has to say to us today. And it commits us to the institutions for world understanding and for peace, which Wilson tried so nobly to establish.

It commits us to labor relentlessly against the causes of war and against the means of war—a labor which must go on and on until men everywhere can live in the sunlight without oppression and fear.

This image from the greatness of America's bright past commits us most of all to enliven the new international spirit without which Wilson knew that neither institutions nor material programs could succeed. It is the spirit that recognizes that justice transcends victory, that "humanity is above all nations," that "every man beareth the stamp of the human condition," that in the words of our Illinois poet [Carl Sandburg]:

There is only one man in the world and his name is All Men.
There is only one woman in the world and her name is All Women.
There is only one child in the world and the child's name is
All Children.[159]

Let us take this occasion to consecrate ourselves to these purposes, until at last Wilson's words will no longer mock us—until at last the world will be truly safe for democracy.

H-Bomb, Defense and Foreign Policy*

APRIL 21, 1956

✡

One of Stevenson's most potent speeches during his campaign for the Presidency in 1956 was his address to the American Society of Newspaper Editors in Washington, on April 21, 1956, printed below in the text from The New America. *Seymour E. Harris and Arthur Schlesinger, Jr., editors of his 1956 collection of campaign speeches, write in their introduction:*

Discussions with atomic scientists the winter before had convinced him both that the radiation problem was assuming dangerous proportions and that a cessation of H-bomb testing would leave the United States in a favorable position relative to the Soviet Union. . . . Moreover, it seemed to him essential that the United States take some initiative to break the disarmament deadlock and restore our moral leadership, especially in Asia where we dropped the atom bomb. Finally, it seemed to him imperative that the hydrogen bomb problem be brought under control before a Nasser or Peron got his hand on a bomb—a condition which the administration's disarmament expert, Harold Stassen, had declared to be imminent. . . . The President's charge that Stevenson's proposal was "a theatrical gesture," the refusal of the Republican campaigners to debate or even discuss the issue on the merits, and the constant charge that Stevenson was proposing to give away our bombs were effective. On the whole, the proposal undoubtedly lost Stevenson more votes than it gained him . . . [and] gave a distorted impression of Stevenson's position on foreign policy.[160]

After passing through the difficult and tiring primary battles successfully in the spring with major emphasis on domestic policies,

* "H-Bomb, Defense and Foreign Policy"—April 21, 1956 from The New America by Adlai E. Stevenson. Copyright © 1957 by Adlai Ewing Stevenson. Reprinted by permission of Harper & Row, Publishers.

Stevenson wanted to utilize his expertise on foreign affairs for the campaign against Eisenhower. However, as Herbert J. Muller writes: "By Stevenson's standards, the platform was least satisfactory in its declarations on foreign policy, his principal concern. Among other things, it not only pledged 'determined opposition to the admission of Red China to the United Nations' but attacked the Republicans for 'fraternizing with Communists,' thus adopting the tactics of Richard Nixon."[161] Even though Stevenson believed his concept of "the New America" should be focal to his campaign, as Schlesinger and Harris comment, "he acquiesced reluctantly in the decision to minimize foreign affairs. He believed (as, indeed, did most of his advisers) that foreign policy confronted the electorate with the most important decisions it had to make in 1956; and he believed in addition (as did few of his advisers) that, if the people heard more about the alarming situation, they would listen and respond."[162]

Eisenhower declared on a nationwide broadcast on October 12: "I've got the best announcement that I think I can possibly make to America tonight. The progress made in the settlement of the Suez dispute this afternoon at the United Nations is most gratifying. . . . It looks like there's a very great problem behind us." Angered by the statement and by his own comparative silence, Stevenson denounced what he called the "most serious failure of the Republican administration. I mean its failures in conducting our foreign policy. . . . He [Eisenhower] announced that he had 'good news' about Suez. But there is no 'good news' about Suez. Why didn't the President tell us the truth? Why hasn't he told us frankly that what has happened in these past few months is that the Communist rulers of Soviet Russia have accomplished a Russian ambition that the czars could never accomplish?"[163] Mary McGrory called this address "the most impassioned speech of the campaign—an eloquent denunciation of Eisenhower's foreign policy as 'timid, naive, sterile' at the height of the Suez crisis."[164]

Later, on November 1, Stevenson gave a major address on the Middle East in which he said:

*The condition which confronts us is stark and simple—our Middle
Eastern policy is at an absolute dead end. . . .*

*The first Communist victory is the establishment in the Middle East
of Russian influence.*

*The second Communist victory is the breakdown of the Western
alliance. This has been a supreme objective of Soviet policy since the
end of the Second World War. . . .*

*A foreign policy which has brought about these results—which has
benefited Communism and has cut our own country off from our
democratic friends—is a foreign policy which has failed. . . .*

*We have lost at every point in the game. I doubt if ever before in
our diplomatic history has any policy been such an abysmal, such a
complete and such a catastrophic failure.*[165]

*Despite the seriousness of the Middle East and Hungarian crises,
Stevenson's outspoken criticism of Republican failures in foreign
policy was overshadowed by "the uproar over two issues only:
Reconsidering the draft (and possible replacement with a professional army), and suspending hydrogen bomb tests. The result, as is not uncommon in heated political campaigns, was a
noisy argument over two points, not a sober discussion of the
whole range of foreign policy."*[166] *Even with his late efforts
to concentrate on foreign policy, his defeat was more overwhelming than before. Stevenson himself believed that these
foreign crises had increased Eisenhower's plurality to 456 electoral
votes versus his 74 and Eisenhower's 35,581,003 popular votes
versus his 26,031,322.*

I HAVE often confessed that I am a frustrated newspaperman. So
you will understand the personal feelings that crowd in upon me as
a renegade journalist turned politician rises to address this austere
society.

Yet I have never thought that my transformation from newspaperman to politician involved very radical changes. After all,
newspapermen—and especially editors—have much in common
with politicians, though you may not perhaps be as ready to

acknowledge this resemblance as we are. We all have messages to put over. We all deal in words. At our worst we all falter in the face of temptation to dissemble and deceive. At our best we all like to think that we elevate the national discourse and clarify the issues of our age.

But if we are going to rise to this high responsibility, we must have the information on which sound judgment is based. I know that you gentlemen are much concerned about improving the quantity and quality of the information the nation gets about the great issues of our time. I know something about the good work of your Freedom of Information Committee, and I was pleased to hear its praise from Congressman Moss for helping strengthen the awareness in federal agencies of the "public's right to know." The American people are in your debt for these efforts.

But the very need for a Freedom of Information Committee points to a danger. Government secrecy, as your president, Mr. Kenneth Macdonald, has said, has become "entrenched behind a host of statutes and regulations." Indeed, one of the most serious criticisms I would make of this Administration is that it has had so little respect for the public's right to know. We have to rethink the whole question of governmental secrecy, for without facts democracy dies at the roots. And we have not only been denied facts we ought to have, we have all too often been deliberately, intentionally misinformed. We have been sold rather than told. That is a long and dangerous step toward being told what we are permitted to think.

Peace and security are the nation's most important business. Yet nowhere has our government told us less and kidded us more. It has used foreign policy for political purposes at home. Unwilling to admit its failures, it has been unwilling to take us into its confidence. Reverses have been painted as victories. And if the Administration has not succeeded in misleading the enemy, it has succeeded wonderfully well in misleading us.

When the Eisenhower Administration first came to power, there was considerable talk about "operation candor"—they were going to tell us the facts of international life and national defense. But since then "operation candor" has been replaced by "operation bromide"—by vague and comforting assurances to allay anxiety and persuade us that we were comfortably ahead in the armaments race and had the love and esteem of our fellowmen.

Was Secretary Dulles informing us or misleading us when he told a House committee on June 10, 1955, that the Soviet Union was "on the point of collapsing"? Was he giving us the facts when he said last November 29 that "we have the initiative, very distinctly" in the Middle East and in South Asia?[167] Was he serious when he told the Senate Foreign Relations Committee as recently as February 24 that the free world is in a stronger position than it was a year ago and that the new Soviet economic and political challenge was a confession of failure?[168] Was he the responsible Secretary of State of the greatest power in the world when he recently boasted that he and the President had conducted the nation three times to the brink of war and then averted catastrophe by his own peerless statesmanship?

We must do better than this. Underlying every other freedom, especially freedom of the press, is the freedom to know, to know the facts, especially the facts about our own prospects for life or for death.

Given the facts, Americans will not retreat in confusion or dissolve in terror, but will respond with determination to do whatever is necessary to assure the nation's safety.

And it is about some of the things which I think we must do and not do to ensure the nation's safety that I want to talk with you today.

Let me commence with a speech President Eisenhower made to this society here in Washington on "The Chance for Peace" exactly three years ago.[169] It endorsed the principles which had guided American policy since 1945 under President Truman; it placed the blame for the fears that gripped the world squarely on the Soviet government, and Stalin, who had died a few weeks earlier; and it held out to the new Soviet rulers a chance to work with us in building a hopeful future for mankind. You hailed it in your papers as the authentic voice of leadership in the new Administration. Your reporters described the response as one of "universal acclaim."

What has happened? What has gone wrong since that speech?

But, first, let us try to recall hurriedly the context of that speech—what our position was three years ago when it was delivered.

You will recall how, in one act of constructive statesmanship after another, President Truman's Administration met the postwar challenges and crises.

The United Nations and a new international order came into existence with tireless American encouragement.

Western Germany was forged into a strong nation, with a democratic constitution and a self-supporting economy.

Japan was reestablished with a humanitarian constitution dedicated to the arts of peace.

In 1947, when Russian power threatened the Eastern Mediterranean, the Truman Doctrine was proclaimed and Greece and Turkey were saved.

Berlin was saved by decisive action to break the blockade.

Then there followed in dramatic succession the Marshall Plan—a bold act of statesmanship that revived the economy, the self-esteem and defenses of Western Europe, to their benefit and ours; President Truman's Point Four Program, which gave new hope to the underdeveloped nations and underprivileged peoples of the world; the North Atlantic Treaty Alliance, which confronted Russia in the West not only with economic strength but the military potential of the great coalition.

Those were great, creative years in American foreign policy. Years of achievement. Years of success.

Then, 1950, war came to Korea. A psychopathic Stalin challenged world democracy and the United Nations. Under the decisive leadership of President Truman, that threat was stopped in its tracks. The United Nations was saved and a third world war was prevented.

This is a record in foreign affairs that we, as Americans, can all be proud of, regardless of party. In those years we confidently, courageously took the political and the moral leadership of the free peoples of the world. Compare that extraordinary outburst of creativity with the sterility of the past three years—a sterility which even the exuberance of Mr. Dulles's slogans cannot disguise.

We desperately need today a rebirth of ideas in the conduct of our foreign affairs. I would urge you, three years after that speech by the President, to think a little about America's position in the world today.

Is the United States more secure or less than it was three years ago?

Are our relations with our allies stronger or weaker? Is the mounting criticism of the United States, from Britain and France and Iceland and Turkey, in the West, to Japan and Formosa and Pakistan and Ceylon, in the East, really without foundation and justification?

Does our Secretary of State enjoy the trust, the respect and the confidence of the peoples and governments of the free world?

Is the moral position of the United States clear and unambiguous and worthy of us and our real aims? Is the image of the United States one that inspires confidence, respect and cooperation?

Do you think we are winning or losing ground in the competition with the Communist world?

I very much hope that the President will address himself to these vital questions when he speaks to you tonight.[170] For these are the vital questions of our day. And the fact that such questions must be asked three years after his speech of 1953 shows, I fear, what all the world has discovered—that our admirable sentiments mean little when unsupported by positive and sustained action. Virtuous words are easy, but they are no substitute for policy.

The fact is that that speech never really served as a guide to policy. The tone it set found few echoes in what the President or the Vice-President or the Secretary of State and the Secretary of Defense did in the months that followed.

This is too bad. Our position in the world, I believe, would have been vastly different had we followed the guidelines laid down here before this society three years ago. Now, where are we today—at this period of an extraordinary age which has witnessed the coincidence of three revolutions:

1. The technological revolution that has split the atom, devastated distance and made us all next-door neighbors.
2. The political revolutions that have liberated and subjugated more peoples more rapidly than ever before in history.

3. The ideological revolution, communism, that has endangered the supremacy of Western ideas for the first time since Islam retreated from Europe.

It is against this background of violent, sudden change in all directions that the drama—or melodrama—of foreign policy must be played. This is a time of change in world affairs. The peoples sense it, even if the statesmen don't, for the peoples are, in a deep sense, forcing change. No one knows just where these changes will lead.

The Administration has been slow to respond to this new mood. The Russians, on the other hand, have exploited it adroitly. Their objectives, we are told almost every day, have not changed. Of course they haven't. No one said they had. The Soviet rulers frankly state that their goal is a Communist world. But they have changed their approach; and we have not changed ours.

I seem to recall a slogan from 1952—something about "It's time for a change." It is indeed time for a change—in a number of ways—especially in foreign policy. Our old policies are no longer adequate in the new situation. At least they are not if reports from all around the world are to be believed, and I think they are. From every corner of the globe your reporters are saying what has been apparent for a long time—that U.S. policy is rigid, unimaginative and fails to take advantage of new opportunities. And the realities of our situation bear little resemblance to the press releases.

I do not propose to chronicle here the whole long list of tension points in the world today. We know their names: Israel, Algeria, Formosa, Indochina, and Indonesia, Kashmir, Cyprus, and now the whole NATO area.

What is more basic and ominous and infinitely harder for us to accept is that in these last three years the United States has come dangerously close to losing, if indeed it has not lost, its leadership in the world—economically, militarily, and worst of all, morally. On all three of these fronts we have manifestly lost the initiative—and that is the prelude to the loss of leadership itself.

It is tragic irony that the people of America, who believe more firmly and fervently in peace and human freedom than anyone else, are not recognized as their sympathetic friend by the millions of mankind who are struggling out of the poverty and squalor and colonial bondage of ages. Instead it is Communist imperialism, which has enslaved scores of millions in a decade, that is usurping the role.

And only a few years back we seemed to those people the hope of the earth. America had gained freedom itself through revolution against European colonialism. Our great documents, from the Declaration of Independence to the Atlantic Charter, had spoken the aspirations of independence and growth. Our own colonial policies had been generous and forbearing. Our great leaders had affirmed the ideals of freedom with an eloquence that had won the allegiance of men and women everywhere. It was to us that new nations instinctively looked for sympathy, for support and for guidance.

Yet today, in the great arc from North Africa through Southeast Asia, the Russian challenge is developing rapidly and with great flexibility and force. Everywhere people seeking a shortcut to raise their own standards of life are told that the Soviet Union alone has mastered the secret of converting a peasant economy into a modern industrial state in a single generation.

In the meantime, we, whose position is fundamentally decent and honorable and generous, have so mismanaged ourselves of late that we must now try to prove that we love peace as much as the Russians, and are as concerned with the problems of economic development and national independence as they are. It is fantastic but true.

Today the peoples of the proud, poor, new nations can find little in official United States policy which seems addressed to them and their problems, little which holds out promise of contributing to their social and national self-fulfillment.

Why is this?

It is compounded of many factors. One is the price we have been paying ever since the bomb was dropped on Hiroshima. The world is on edge and wants to blame somebody for not being able to sleep at night. And since America dropped the first bomb on Asians, and then the Japanese fishermen were burned, America has been unfairly suspected of caring precious little about Asians and peace.

False and unfair as this is, we contribute to it in many ways.

On the one hand, we exhort the world about the virtues of the United States. On the other hand, most of our official dealings seem to be in terms of military threats, military alliances and military values. During the 1952 campaign, General Eisenhower and Mr. Dulles talked loosely about the liberation of the satellite countries. Since then the Administration has noisily "unleashed" Chiang Kai-shek, huffed and puffed about Indochina, threatened massive atomic retaliation, and scolded, boasted and bluffed—while at the same time presiding over the reduction of our armed·strength. And all this has been more visible outside the United States than inside.

At a time when the new leadership in Russia has been very successfully playing on the universal desire of people everywhere for an end of the cold-war tensions, the Administration has clung stubbornly to its military emphasis on pacts, foreign aid, trade and international exchanges of all kinds. Much of the world has come to think of us as militarist, and even a menace to peace. In a survey last year in Calcutta people thought the United States more likely to start a war than Russia in the ratio 19 to 1.

Also, on the question of colonialism the Administration has done nothing to evolve a reasoned and sound American position, linked to our own traditions as well as to respect for our friends and a due concern for world stability. In the absence of a rational attitude, we have floundered, trying to be all things to all people and thereby antagonizing everyone.

We have persisted in construing the Communist threat to the underdeveloped world as essentially military. For people hungering after economic growth, we offer SEATO and place a defense effort ahead of the struggle against poverty. For people hungering after national independence, we offer little more than a policy of insensitive arrogance—witness the official derision of the Bandung Conference,[171] and the clumsy reference to Goa.

We had earlier this month, at Mr. Dulles's press conference on April 3, a pitiful summation of all this—and a revealing commentary on the cause of so much of it. Asked to comment on the present state of the reputation of the United States in the world, Secretary Dulles answered, and I quote from the *New York Times* report, that he "agreed that the United States was being criticized all over the world, but concluded that this was a fine 'tribute' to the United States because it proved nobody was afraid to criticize us."[172]

This, of course, is dangerous nonsense. For what this criticism reflects is the infinitely sterner, more ominous fact that we have lost the moral initiative—and the rest of the world knows it.

Equally sobering is the realization that we are also losing the military advantage. Three years ago the United States had a clear margin of military superiority in the field of air-atomic power—in the production of the new weapons and in our capacity to deliver them. Today we have lost that margin of superiority.

It was, of course, inevitable that when the Soviet Union built its stockpiles to a certain level the fact that we retained a lead in the number of weapons would lose significance, and that an atomic stalemate might require us to develop more conventional forces. But it was not inevitable that we should fall behind in air strength and in weapon development.

I trust I've made it clear that armed might should not stand as the symbol of our foreign policy. But military power is diplomacy's indispensable partner during this period when the ramparts of peace are still to be built and genuine arms control is still in the future.

To summarize: Three years ago this nation was looked to by all the free world as equipped by faith, history, accomplishment and authority to lead the peoples of the world to the promised land of security and peace. That is no longer the case. And we must squarely face the fact that there is no time to lose in reexamining and in redefining our policy to meet the challenge of today.

I know well the willfulness of the forces which affect the conduct of a nation's foreign policy. I make no pretense that there are one or two or three sure steps which would solve our problems. Wars may be won by secret weapons, but there are no secret weapons which will guarantee peace.

But I recognize the obligation to measure criticism by affirmative suggestion. So let me make some suggestions which are inherent, I think, in what I have said.

First of all, a decent respect for the opinions of others is still a basic requirement of a good foreign policy. Foreign policy is not only what we do, it is how we do it. The wisest policy will be poisonously self-defeating if mishandled. Smugness, arrogance, talking big are poison. Impulsive, abrupt actions create the impression that we are impulsive and abrupt. The restoration of composure, confidence and an impression of knowing-what-we-are-about is thus of first importance.

We want to be recognized not as bold, but as prudent, and that rules out boasting about brinks and the like. We want to be recognized as sensitive to the implications of modern warfare, and that rules out talk of massive retaliation. We want to be recognized as responsible, and that rules out trying to reconcile the irreconcilable wings of the Republican party. We want to be regarded as reasonable, and that rules out nonsense about the imminent collapse of the Soviet system. And we must reveal that craving for peace which is the true heart of America.

Second, I believe we should give prompt and earnest consideration to stopping further tests of the hydrogen bomb, as Commissioner Murray of the Atomic Energy Commission recently proposed.[173] As a layman I hope I can question the sense in multiplying and enlarging weapons of a destructive power already almost incomprehensible. I would call upon other nations, the Soviet Union, to follow our lead, and if they don't and persist in further tests we will know about it and we can reconsider our policy.

I deeply believe that if we are to make progress toward the effective reduction and control of armaments, it will probably come a step at a time. And this is a step which, it seems to me, we might now take, a step which would reflect our determination never to plunge the world into nuclear holocaust, a step which would reaffirm our purpose to act with humility and a decent concern for world opinion.

(After writing this last week down south, I read last night in Philadelphia that the Soviet Union has protested a scheduled H-bomb test. After some reflection I concluded that I would not be intimidated by the Communists and would not alter what I had written. For this suggestion is right or wrong and should be so considered regardless of the Soviets.)

Third, we should seriously consider basic revision of our method of giving aid; specifically, we should, I think, make greater use of the United Nations as the economic aid agency. We should try to remove economic development from the arena of the cold war. We believe, to be sure, that anything which strengthens economic growth, national independence, human welfare and democratic processes will improve a nation's resistance to the virus of communism. But our first purpose is human betterment, and anything else is a by-product.

Also, if we propose to make economic aid most effective, we will have to stop demanding that recipient nations pass loyalty tests, and stop using our money to bribe feeble governments to set up rubber-check military pacts which will bounce as soon as we try to cash them. Rather we must convince the peoples of the underdeveloped world that we want no dominion over them in any form, and that we look forward to the end of colonialism in the world.

I don't believe we have explored all possible uses of our agricultural surpluses as raw materials of diplomacy. Surely there are ways of using our abundance, not as an embarrassment but creatively as part of a comprehensive plan of foreign assistance.

There is, too, the vast potential in peaceful use of atomic energy. It will be our ultimate ironical failure if the Soviet Union rather than the United States should provide the underdeveloped needful nations with atomic power. Our mastery of the atom, our willingness to make it mankind's public utility, should be one of our greatest contributions to human betterment.

I emphasize again, however, that all the bushels of wheat and the nuclear reactors and dollars in creation will do us little good if they seem only to be the bait with which a rich but uncertain nation seeks to buy protection for itself. If our attitude is wrong, no amount of money can do the job; and if our attitude is right, less money will go further.

These poor nations have discovered that poverty, oppression and disease are not the immutable destiny of man. They mean to improve their lot and quickly—by the methods of consent, our Western way, if possible. But if they can't, they will turn away from us—to forced labor and forced savings, the totalitarian way —because they mean to industrialize one way or another.

If the United Nations administered economic development funds supplied by its members, it would strengthen international cooperation and the United Nations. It would remove economic development from the arena of the cold war. It would permit objective priorities on the needs of various backward sections of the world. It would stop competitive bidding. And if contributions were apportioned according to the existing formula, for each dollar contributed by the United States two dollars would be contributed by other U.N. members.

And, finally, it would involve the Soviet Union in responsible international cooperation all over the world. As it is now, there is nothing to prevent Russian penetration anywhere on a unilateral basis to serve its separate ends.

The Soviets refused to participate in a similar arrangement when we proposed the Marshall aid program in 1948. But that was Joseph Stalin—of now dishonored memory. And if his heirs should similarly reject multilateral economic assistance, the implications would be clear to all the world.

In this connection, a first step in this direction might well be taken in the Middle East, it seems to me. We all welcome the good news that a partial cease-fire agreement has been arranged.

But there are many tasks ahead, of course, before any genuine peace in that area can even be foreseen. Without reciting them here, let me just suggest that a coordinated attack on poverty in the Middle East might well be a profitable field for a United Nations economic program such as I have suggested.

Finally, it seems to me that any aid program we devise will be effective only as it expresses a healthy relationship between free and self-respecting peoples. We must show that we care about others in the world, not as bodies we would hurl into the military breach, but as men and women and children who we hope will live lives of dignity and fulfillment.

So long as we overmilitarize our international thought and statement, so long as we picture the differences between Russia and the West as part of a great military contest, hot or cold—for so long will our efforts prove futile and our motives suspect. For there is little about that struggle which penetrates the minds and hearts of the people of Asia or Africa.

Let us, rather, rally the nations for a worldwide war against want. And let us then—for men do not live by bread alone—

identify what we do in the world with the one export which we can offer as no one else can. I mean liberty, human freedom, independence, the American idea—call it what you please—which is more precious and more potent than guns or butter.

For from the word "go"—which is to say, from our very first national statement in 1776—America spoke for freedom in terms so inspiring, so sublime and so inexorably appealing to men's consciences that the Old World was shaken to its foundations. Tyrannies dissolved; hope sprang up like a fresh breeze; movements of liberation mushroomed. This was the greatest foreign-aid program in history and no one has ever improved on it or ever will.

We have drifted and stumbled long enough. It is time to restore the true image of America, once so well-known and well-loved, which gave birth to the Declaration of Independence and the Four Freedoms—a nation marked, not by smugness, but by generosity; not by meanness, but by magnanimity; not by stale conservatism and a weary reliance on dollars and arms, but by broad vision and moral and social passion.

It is time to regain the initiative; to release the warm, creative energies of this mighty land; it is time to resume the onward progress of mankind in pursuit of peace and freedom.

The Political Relevance of Moral Principle

JANUARY 18, 1959

✡

Barbara Ward, a long-time friend of Stevenson, accompanied him on a part of his travels through Africa during the spring of 1957 and was with him when the honorary Doctor of Laws degree was conferred upon him at Oxford University on May 24, 1957. In presenting his citation, Oxford's Public Orator called him: "Adlai Stevenson, amid the strains and stresses of national and international politics, the champion of humanism in word and deed, and himself the source." Reflecting on this event, Barbara Ward writes: "He won all hearts at the beginning by referring to the saying that Oxford is reputed the home of Lost Causes. Whom, then, could they more fitly distinguish than the man who was probably the world's greatest living exponent of the Lost Cause."[174]

In November of 1957, Stevenson accepted the Administration's invitation to help provide ideas for the forthcoming NATO meeting in Paris; he felt the gravity of the world situation impelled him to work with the Republicans, "regardless of partisanship or personal convenience." After three and a half weeks Stevenson ended his assignment declaring that he sensed no urgency but only an overemphasis on the military and an underemphasis on the economic-social-political war around the world. Not until 1960, when Under-Secretary of State Douglas Dillon signed the articles establishing the Organization for Economic Co-operation and Development, did the Republican Administration adopt Stevenson's proposals. John B. Oakes, writing in The New York Times, *commented: "Stevenson's influence abroad is probably greater now than it is at home. . . . It is quite possible, now that he has returned to public*

*life, that he will be heard more frequently than in the recent past
on various aspects of his favorite subject, foreign affairs."*[175]

*During the summer of 1958, Stevenson, two of his sons, and
friends, traveled through Russia and the Soviet Union. In his Introduction to* Friends and Enemies, *his collection of brief reports
about this visit, he wrote:*

*Like all Americans I am curious about Russia, which has contradicted
our ideas, organized a vast empire, raised our taxes, and challenged the
United States to political, economic and military competition everywhere—all in forty years. That is why I went back—to see the Russia of
today and its leaders for myself. . . .*

*The journey confirmed my impression that no relaxation in the
Communist offensive is imminent and that there are no visible signs of
internal weakness or upheaval in the Soviet Union. . . . Nor could I
detect that our negative policy toward the Soviet Union was likely to
induce the Soviet collapse which has been periodically foretold from
official Washington in recent years, or even contain the expansion of
Soviet influence. . . .*

*But I came away from this vibrant country with a much clearer
feeling for the people's hunger for peace and dread of another
war. . . . Assuming we do not invite Soviet military adventure by
our weakness, I do not fear a third world war.*[176]

*On January 18, 1959, Stevenson gave the first annual lecture at
Constitution Hall in Washington, D.C., printed below, in memory
of A. Powell Davies, a Unitarian minister who for many years had
"argued for deciding political questions in fundamentally moral
terms." Devoting the key chapter in his* Conscience in Politics *to
this speech of Stevenson's, Stuart Gerry Brown comments:*

*The occasion permitted him a better opportunity than he had yet had
to speak from his heart on the subject which meant most to him and
which had led him into politics. . . . This address, more than any
other of his many speeches and writings, explains why Adlai Stevenson could not have been elected to the Presidency of the United States
in the "Age of Eisenhower." But it explains, too, why he had established for himself a high place in the history of his time and his country,*

and why, on transcendent issues, he could and did articulate the will and the vision of America as no other of his contemporaries could do.[177]

Stevenson also included this lecture in his collection of speeches given in 1959, Putting First Things First: A Democratic View. *He entitled it in that volume "Our Broken Mainspring" and abbreviacted it somewhat from what appears below with his original title, "The Political Relevance of Moral Principle." In 1962, the speech was also printed, with its original title, in E. J. Wrage and B. Baskerville's* Contemporary Forum.

I AM profoundly flattered by your invitation to inaugurate these annual lectures in memory of Dr. A. Powell Davies. It is an honor to be asked to help in any way in the commemoration of a man so eminently worthy of being remembered.[178] But it is hard indeed to pay adequate homage in words to a man whose own were so fresh, so apt and so fitting to the important issues of the day.

But I am encouraged by one fact. Dr. Davies did not feel that his office as a minister of religion debarred him from comment upon contemporary problems. On the contrary, he saw that he could make his message relevant to his people only by showing it at work in the concrete issues of their daily lives.

I think of a story my grandfather Stevenson, a devout Scotch-Presbyterian of Southern descent, told about the preacher who was driving along a back road when he espied a parishioner wearily clearing up a poor, stony field. "That's a fine job you and the Lord have done cleaning up that rocky field," he shouted. "Thank you, parson," the man replied. "I wish you could have seen it when the Lord had it all to himself."

Dr. Davies believed that God is dependent on man, as man is on God. He believed that the clergy above all were responsible for making a reality of the bond between God and man and he was fearless in letting his congregation and the world know the truth as he saw it and a sensitive awareness of peril to the individual in our day of bigness, of statism and conformity. Therefore he was impelled to fight for the oppressed and the persecuted; to fight for equal justice for all and the rights inherent in our citizenship. Ardently he defended freedom of the mind, free speech, the right of the dissenter to speak and the duty of the conformist to listen. And his compassion was boundless.

It was the tardiness of the American social conscience in understanding the severity of its ordeal with authoritarianism that made Dr. Davies impatient, that made him work so hard to awaken us to the perils. He literally wore himself out trying to mobilize public opinion and induce every American to hold himself personally responsible for the preservation of freedom.

From the mountain of vision, Dr. Davies constantly proclaimed the political relevance of moral principle and of religion as a "judgment of righteousness." From the dusty plains of politics I would like in my turn to reaffirm this relevance. I like to believe that there may be some value in echoing testimony from a layman who has spent his middle life in the press and confusion of great events in government service, in diplomacy and in politics.

All politics is made up of many things—economic pressures, personal ambitions, the desire to exercise power, the overriding issues of national need and aspiration. But if it is nothing more, it is without roots. It is built on shifting, changing sands of emotion and interest. When challenged, it can give no account of itself. When threatened, it is in danger of collapse.

Today, when the threat and challenge to free society seems more total and powerful than ever before, it is not a political luxury or fruitless pedantry to reexamine our fundamental principles. I think it more likely to be the condition of survival.[179]

There is a phrase of Dr. Davies's that stays in my mind. I do not know when I have heard a more terse and pregnant summing-up of our predicament. "The world," he said, "is now too dangerous for anything but the truth, too small for anything but brotherhood."[180] This I believe to be in broad measure a correct estimate of the condition of human society, which is now capable, with a few hydrogen bombs, of extinguishing itself. Today we can all be killed by the same bombs or atomic fallout. In that sense we have a desperate physical solidarity. But moral and social solidarity in the family of man is still to be found.

Not so long ago I visited Dr. Albert Schweitzer in his primitive jungle hospital in French Equatorial Africa, and he told me he considered this the most dangerous period in history, not just modern history, but all human history. Why? Because, he said, heretofore nature has controlled man, but now man has learned to control elemental forces—before he has learned to control himself.[181]

Many of us seem to rely on some mythical God-given superiority of the white Western world to save us. And my concern is that there is more evidence that the Communists accept the reality of the human condition than we do.

It is impossible to spend weeks traveling around the Soviet Union as I did this summer without taking away an overwhelming impression of thrust and purpose in most aspects of Soviet life. The revolutionary ardor has cooled with time but even the very pragmatic political leaders seem to believe profoundly in the truth of their way of life, and they are quietly confident that it will sweep the world in time. I think they sincerely believe that their methods, their aspirations, their dreams, make up the final truth about the nature of man and society; that collective man in the collective state is the ultimate unfolding of human destiny, the end of history, the "far off divine event" for which mankind has been in long travail, the vision of "all things made new" that has haunted men's minds ever since Christianity thrust into human thought the intoxicating ideal of a perfected humanity.

From this conviction, if I have not overstated it, flow two consequences. The first is that no effort, no dedication, no sacrifice is too great that may help to realize the Communist party's goals in Soviet society. The second is that no corner of humanity can be a matter of indifference to the Communists, because the whole human race is destined to become one in Communist brotherhood.

These are not abstract generalities. Russia is a vast powerhouse of energy all harnessed to the communal task of building the Soviet dream. The thrust of economic growth which adds a 9 or 10 per cent increase each year to industrial expansion is one aspect of this energy. The vast sums available for science and research are another. The self-discipline and long hours put in by school children to train themselves as the scientists, technicians, administrators and linguists of the new world order are perhaps the most significant measure of the resources of energy, work and skill upon which Soviet leaders hope to draw. And if these people are in deadly earnest, what about the 600 million Chinese whose dream is even newer and who have so much further to go? In Moscow, Serge Obraztsov, the brilliant director of the famous puppet theatre, said: "I visited China five years ago. It was the most extraordinary experience of my life. People in China have had nothing—nothing! Now several hundred million people are dreaming of tomorrow; I cannot describe to you the feeling of excitement there—much, much more even than here in the Soviet Union."

The energy, the drive, the dedication in the U.S.S.R. spill over into international affairs. In part, of course, this is the restless concern which all imperialist powers must exercise, especially when the peoples they control are as restive and unreliable as the captive peoples in Russia's European empire. But Communist activity, planning and efforts in trade and aid are not confined to areas of Communist control. They are worldwide, and there is no corner of the earth's surface which they think too insignificant for their attention. While trade missions are busy in Latin America trading Soviet machinery and oil for coffee and wool, academic representatives are touring West Africa, Arab and Asian students are being trained in Moscow, technical advisers dispatched to India and Burma and Indonesia, and the glossy flood of propaganda depicting the Soviet millennium of bumper harvests and happy workers is pumped out all round the world.[182]

All this we know—or begin to know. But I wonder how often we try to grasp the scale of dedication that lies behind it. Why should they be so busy? Why so much work and thought? Why such diversion of resources? Why such patience through every setback, such forward thrusts through every point of Western weakness? Heaven knows, we only want to stay home. Why don't they? Why do we never meet an isolationist Communist? These are the questions that haunted me while I confronted at firsthand this iron, forceful and formidable way of life.

And I don't think there is any doubt about the answer. Part of it is simply needed foreign trade. Part is fear, the search for security through friends. And part is the historical centrifugal forces in Russia that have been pressing outward for a hundred years—to the Pacific, the Balkans and the Middle East. But the important thing is that the Soviet Russians believe in their truth, as the men of the Western world once believed in theirs. They, not we, are firing the shots that are heard round the world—and also the satellites that orbit above it. The fact that their faith is in many ways an evil perversion of the great propositions that once made the blood course in our Western veins does not alter the fact that their tempo is dynamic and ours sluggish—even, I think, to ourselves.

The reason cannot be that we Americans have lost our vision of truth and brotherhood. No country on earth owes the sense of community more explicitly to the fact that it is united not by race or nationality but by fidelity to an idea. We were born "dedicated to a proposition" and our greatest leaders—the Jeffersons, the Lincolns, the Woodrow Wilsons—were not great because they achieved purely American purposes, but because they were able to speak for humanity at large and extend their vision to the whole family of man.

Nor, I believe, can we find fault with the American dream. Its truths are still "self-evident." The possession of liberty and the pursuit of happiness—rightly understood—have not been overthrown as the highest goods of human society. Indeed, the ferment of our freedom works inexorably and dangerously in the Communist world. No one can have visited Poland without seeing how little the Polish people accept their servitude and how they look beyond their neighbors to the free world as the reservoir of power and hope.

But, alas, on the basis of the record, one would hardly suspect that the Western world possessed so powerful a weapon. All our talk—in diplomacy, in strategy, in aid and trade, in all the intricacies of our worldwide relations—has been to a depressing degree purely defensive. We have offered aid not to help others but to shield ourselves. We have reacted to countless Soviet initiatives; acted on our own initiative barely at all. We watch the skies for other people's sputniks and listen to the telegraph wires for other people's moves. Yet we are the free men of this universe, the children of liberty, the beneficiaries of unequaled abundance, and heirs of the highest, proudest political tradition ever known to man!

Why this lack of initiative? Why this paralysis of will? What have we done to our truth and our brotherhood—the supreme truth of freedom, the Christian truth of brotherly love? Have they failed? Or have we?

There is no more urgent duty than to discover why we have failed and to get back into the arena, aspiring, striving, fighting once more for what we believe. An examination of what you might call our collective conscience is to my mind far more important than particular projects or progress. You can have a perfect assembly of pieces for your watch but they are worthless if the mainspring is broken. I am not basically worried about our various pieces—our technology, our science, our machines, our resources. But I am concerned, desperately concerned, about our mainspring. That it has run down, we know. But is it broken beyond repair? In the last analysis, no question is worth more consideration in America today.

And I would like to suggest some of the ways in which it seems to me we have enfeebled the great central pulse of freedom, the great truth of liberty, which, more than any other nation, we first set working in the modern world.

The great German poet, Goethe, who also lived through a crisis of freedom, said to his generation: "What you have inherited from your fathers, earn over again for yourselves or it will not be yours."[183] We inherited freedom. We seem unaware that it has to be remade and re-earned in each generation of man. One reason for this failure is, I believe, passing at last. In recent years we were stifled with complacent self-confidence. We believed ourselves dominant in every field. We talked of "the American Century." We forgot the ardors and efforts that had given us a measure of preeminence. Complacency made us impervious to ideas, even the obvious idea that we are in danger. So we assumed that all we needed was to sit still and enjoy the "peace and prosperity" that was our right.

I believe that phase is passing. Our foolish languor has been shaken, if not shattered. We are more ready to examine ourselves and our record. And it is a privilege of our society that every citizen should make his own inquiry. If I stress one other aspect of our problem, this is simply my angle of vision. You have yours. The urgent thing is to feel the need for rethinking and to set to work the ultimate energies of free society—which cannot be done by the fiat of government but only by the troubled conscience of responsible men and women.

It is simply as a citizen as concerned as you are that I want to suggest what seem to me to be the obstacles to a full understanding of our great mission in this time of testing.[184]

I believe—as I have said before—that we have confused the free with the free and easy. If freedom had been the happy, simple, relaxed state of ordinary humanity, man would have everywhere been free—whereas through most of time and space he has been in chains. Do not let us make any mistake about this. The natural government of man is servitude. Tyranny is the normal pattern of government. It is only by intense thought, by great effort, by burning idealism and unlimited sacrifice that freedom has prevailed as a system of government. And the efforts which were first necessary to create it are fully as necessary to sustain it in our own day.

He who offers this thing we call freedom as the soft option is a deceiver or himself deceived. He who sells it cheap or offers it as the by-product of this or that economic system is knave or fool. For freedom demands infinitely more care and devotion than any other political system. It puts consent and personal initiative in the place of command and obedience. By relying upon the devotion and initiative of ordinary citizens, it gives up the harsh but effective disciplines that underpin all the tyrannies which over the millennia have stunted the full stature of men.

But of what use is escape from external restraint if given the opportunity men simply stunt themselves? If freedom means ease alone, if it means shirking the hard disciplines of learning, if it means evading the rigors and rewards of creative activity, if it means more expenditure on advertising than education, if it means "bachelor cooking" and "life adjustment" courses in the schools, and the steady cult of the trivial and the mediocre, if it means— worst of all—indifference or even contempt for all but athletic excellence, we may keep for a time the forms of free society, but its spirit will be dead.

I believe we have had enough of adjustment, conformity, easy options as the least common denominator in our system. We need instead to see the "pursuit of happiness" in terms which are historically proven and psychologically correct. The dreary failure in history of all classes committed to pleasure and profit alone, the vacuity and misery accompanying the sole pursuit of ease—the collapse of the French aristocracy, the corruption of imperial Rome, the decline and fall of the resplendent Manchus[185]—all these facts of history do not lose their point because the pleasures of today are mass pleasures and no longer the enjoyment of an elite. If we become a nation of Bourbons, numbers won't save us. We shall go their way. Vacuity and indifference are not redeemed by the fact that everyone can share in them. They merely restrict the circle from which regeneration can come.

I say this in no Puritan or pleasure-hating spirit. On the contrary, there is no boredom or misery to equal the pursuit of distraction alone. We do not slip into happiness. It is strenuously sought and earned. A nation glued to the television screen is not simply at a loss before the iron pioneers of the new collective society. It isn't even having a good time. No society has ever spent as much as we do on drink and tranquilizers. Can one argue that this is evidence of universal fun? I ran across a quotation of [Jean de] La Bruyère on the court of Louis XIV that struck me as relevant. "Les joies sont visibles, mais fausses, et les chagrins, cachés, mais réels"—its joys are visible, but artificial, and its sorrows hidden, but real.

But perhaps this misunderstanding of the true nature of happiness and of the conditions of its pursuit is simply an aspect of something else—our misunderstanding of the real nature of freedom. I recall the words of the wise Judge Learned Hand, who warned us that freedom would not survive in our Constitution if it had already died in the hearts of the people. We shall not have a free society unless we have free men.

And how often do we reflect upon what this inner freedom entails? "Give me the man," cries Hamlet, "who is not passion's slave."[186] But this is what we are in danger of becoming, slaves to a tyranny more intimate and inescapable than any Stalin or Mao Tse-tung could impose. We can be made slaves simply by the clutter and complexity of modern living—which notoriously leaves no time for serious thought and offers every means of distraction so that we can avoid such thought. Between aircraft that take us everywhere more rapidly, newspapers that grow in weight and coverage, news that flashes round the globe, ceaseless and competitive entertainment, fashions—God help us!—that change from sack to trapeze and back again, we can fill up every "unforgiving minute" with enough trash and preoccupation to still forever the deeper voices of the soul. Like Matthew Arnold, we can

> . . . see all sights from pole to pole,
> And glance and nod and bustle by,
> And never once possess our soul
> Before we die.[187]

How are we to defend freedom if, for the tyranny of external control we substitute the clattering, cluttering tyranny of internal aimlessness and fuss? This freedom for our souls, freedom at the profoundest level of our being, is not a gift to us by our contemporary way of life. On the contrary, much of this life is a direct conspiracy against it. And if we cannot—by a certain discipline, by readiness for reflection and quiet, by determination to do the difficult and aim at a lasting good—rediscover the real purpose and direction of our existence, we shall not be free. Our society will not be free. And between a chaotic, selfish, indifferent, commercial society and the iron discipline of the Communist world, I would not like to predict the outcome. Outer tyranny with purpose may well triumph over the inner, purposeless tyranny of a confused and aimless way of life.

I doubt if any society in history has faced so great a moral challenge as ours, or needed more desperately to draw on the deepest sources of courage and responsibility. Ours is the first human community in which resources are so abundant that almost no policies lie beyond our capacity for purely physical reasons. What we decide to do, we can do. The inhibitions of poverty—lack of resources, lack of capital, lack of power—do not hold us back. We can accomplish what we aim at. Thus, perhaps for the first time in the world, choice, not means, ends, not instruments, are decisive.

Then again we have proved—drably and dangerously—over the last decade that defensiveness is not a sufficient reason for action. All the policies we have pursued in self-defense have left us still on the defensive. But if we do not act from fear, we must find some other motivation. In free society there is no other alternative but to tap the vigor, faith and imagination of the people themselves. We must find out once more who we are, as the psychologists say. And I would earnestly appeal especially to the women of America to organize an "Operation Wisdom" and to lead the way to a new self-examination and self-discipline.[188]

But perhaps the most urgent reason why the quality of our moral response has become the decisive issue in politics is quite simply that most of the major problems of our day present themselves in moral terms, and are probably insoluble without some stirring of generosity, some measure of vision. Let me give you three instances. In the wealthiest nation in the world, at least 5 million families still live in squalid but remediable poverty. They are a minority. They don't have the votes to force the issue of their misfortune into the front rank of public issues. They depend, for remedies, upon the alert conscience of the majority. But how do we keep the conscience sensitive and alert? By concentrating on our own concerns and adding the dishwasher to the television and to the air conditioner? By griping over taxes and attacking that great bogey we call "the welfare state"? By closing our minds every time our shiny car takes us through a slum? No—we shall have the dedication and drive to wipe poverty out of this rich land only if the well-to-do majority of today do not repeat the selfish indifference which, in many communities, has been the epitaph of yesterday's wealthy elite.

Or take the issue of the rights and status of our colored citizens. This is our small share of a worldwide problem. The 400 years' dominance of men of white skin is ending. The vast colored majority of mankind are seeking the opportunity and the respect which white people have been lucky enough to enjoy for so long— sometimes at the colored people's expense. But, within this world-wide crisis, we in America, with our colored minority, have a major role to play—for good or evil. "The unfinished work" which Lincoln left us, of creating a society in which all men can hold up their heads as equals and self-respecting citizens, can never be accomplished unless there are enough white men and women who resist in the core of their being the moral evil of treating any of God's children as essentially inferior.

Nor is this simply a question of our own national community. I come back to the painful fact that the Communists show a world-wide concern which is largely lacking among the men of the West. The whole human race is their horizon. Their "brotherhood" is materialist, collectivist, atheist, and we dislike it, but it embraces everybody, and it is the framework of policies which take the missionaries of their new order to the ends of the earth. I say with all the emphasis I can command that we have no corresponding commitment to our fellow men. For hundreds of years, we have preached the Christian principles of brotherhood, but today, when vanishing space and scientific revolution have turned our planet into a single neighborhood, the ideal means little in terms of concern or conviction, in terms of policy or action.

Here we are in the Atlantic world, 16 per cent of the world's peoples consuming 70 per cent of the world's wealth. We cannot be indifferent to the moral implications of this gap. I do not know how we can gain a new perspective about the narrow world of plenty and poverty in which we live unless moral insights of justice and compassion stir us to understand the privileged position in which we live.

We are not going to be stirred to action by our own needs. We are the cushioned, protected, fortunate minority. It is not the measure of our morals or the lesson of our history to be spurred on only by fear of Russian encroachments. What we have done has largely had this motivation, and it has left us on the defensive. Our hope is to accept the implications of our own faith, make concrete the image of brotherhood which we profess, and set to work to express our dedication in whatever effort or sacrifice the world's needs may dictate. And, if we must always think in terms of contest with the Soviets, the ability to create the good life for the greatest number will be decisive.

This age has been defined in many ways—as a time of conflict in ideology, as a time of ferment in technology, as a period of revolution in science, as an era when at last the means lie at hand to free mankind from the ancient shackles of pain and hunger. It is all these things—but I believe the true crisis of our times lies at a deeper level. We have indeed conquered means and resources unknown to earlier ages. We have had thrown open to us frontiers of choice which would leave earlier ages stupefied by their scale and scope.

But all this freedom and elbowroom only thrusts onto us with more force the fundamental issue of the faith that is in us. We can use our wealth and capacity for some vision of truth, some ideal of brotherhood, or we can imprison ourselves within the selfishness of our own concerns and the limitation of a narrow nationhood. This is the dimension of our crisis.

You may argue that these qualities—of dedication and selflessness—are pretty remote from the realities of politics. They are all very well for private life, but what part can they play in the rough-and-tumble of partisanship, of primaries, conventions and election campaigns? Ambition, drive, material interests, political skills, the art of maneuver—all these, you say, have their part, but do not let us pretend that the democratic process is primarily a school of virtue or an arena of moral combat.

And yet, I wonder. It has been the view of great philosophers and great statesmen that our system of free government depends in the first instance upon the virtue of its citizens. Montesquieu made virtue the condition of republican government; Washington declared that it could not survive without it. We have had 175 years of it since their time and no one can deny that the system has survived a remarkable amount of skulduggery. In fact, it is probably a tougher system than its founders imagined. Yet I believe they are right. For no democratic system can survive without at least a large and active leaven of citizens in whom dedication and selflessness are not confined to private life but are the fundamental principles of their activity in the public sphere.

Naked interest and naked ambition will carry a lot of people naturally and inevitably into politics. We do not need societies for the promotion of lobbies. Interests, good and bad, will promote themselves. Nor, in any generation, do we lack politicians whose only principle of action is the advancement of their own career—the starry-eyed opportunists and all the other eager men in a hurry to the top. But into what state must politics degenerate if that is all we find active in the political arena? That and sectional interests played upon by personal ambitions? There have been such periods— the roaring nineties, the time from Harding to the Wall Street crash—but our democratic system survived because such epochs were followed and cleansed by periods of disinterested reform.

But there has never been any disinterested reform without dis- interested reformers. And here we come to the essential contribu- tion made by dedication and selflessness to the public good. No one ever did any good in politics without readiness for endless hard work—for the grinding, boring, tedious work, as well as the glamorous, high-sounding, headline-hitting work. The painstaking hours collecting the facts, the hours in committees and confer- ences, the hours in persuasion and argument, the hours of defeat and disappointment, the hours of disgust and revulsion at the darker sides of human behavior—these cannot be supported with- out energy and devotion. No reforms come easy; even the most obvious will have its entrenched enemies. Each one is carried to us on the bent and weary backs of patient, dedicated men and women.

They are not only dedicated in their readiness to give energy and hard work to the cause; they must also have sufficiently clear sight and open minds and hearts to see the need for reform in the first place. But clear sight and an open heart for others' needs is again something that hardly "comes naturally." We have so many needs of our own—our families, our jobs, our homes and fortunes, our prospects. We are hemmed in with needs and interests, weighty, urgent, honorable, human needs and interests, even if they are exclusively our own. It takes an extra dimension of vision to see beyond our inner circle of interest. Most people, most of the time, do not possess it—which is one reason why self-regarding interests make up so much of the stuff of politics. And this, I suppose, is why the men and women of genuine, imperturbable public spirit seem so few and far between.

I sometimes think there is a danger of this element of vision vanishing almost wholly from our political life. In the main we are so comfortable; so many evils of the past have shrunk in size and almost out of sight. At the same time, people marry much younger, have larger families and are profoundly involved in earning a living, making careers and safeguarding the future of their children. It is more difficult, they say, to give time to public affairs when private life is so urgent and absorbing.

Yet is it, I wonder, more urgent and absorbing than a hundred years ago when young men not only married young, had large families and built up careers, but also opened up the new frontiers, created new cities from the wilderness and gave to new states and communities the framework of active political life?

If one reads the life of young Abe Lincoln, it is hard to believe that his struggles as a young lawyer and his difficulties as a young parent were less than those of young men today. Yet there was no time when the deepest issues of the day did not occupy his mind or the call of statecraft make itself heard above the claims and clamor of everyday life. Nor was he alone or exceptional. Stephen A. Douglas's life was no different. The prairie towns were filled with earnest, active citizens deeply, profoundly concerned with the great issues of a nation "half slave, half free." When the multitudes gathered, a hundred years ago, to listen in rapt attention for hours to the Lincoln-Douglas debates, had they fewer responsibilities and duties than the citizens of today to many of whom the great issues of politics seem to be most usefully conveyed in fifteen-second television flashes of subliminal advertising?

Is it not possible that the pressures of personal responsibilities are not greater but that the dedication and selflessness needed to discern and influence public issues have shrunk? In a century in which so many of the mentors of the public mind—from the psychiatrists to the ad-men—speak to us in terms of "what we owe to ourselves," may there not indeed have been a slackening of devotion compared with those days, not so long distant, when what man owes to God and his neighbor was a common theme of public discourse?

If so, this is a dangerous hour for our politics and for government by consent of the governed. For at no time have so many of the great issues of the day demanded clear, real moral vision to bring them into focus—the vision of A. Powell Davies, who loved the truth and believed in man's capacity and right to govern himself.

"The Earth Belongs Always
to the Living Generation"

APRIL 12, 1960

✡

Among Stevenson's significant speeches on foreign affairs in the spring of 1960 were his Founder's Day Address at the University of Virginia, April 12, which is printed below; his speech to the Conference on World Tensions at the University of Chicago, May 12, later printed as "Full Promise of a Distracted World" in The Promise of World Tensions; *and his address to the Eleventh Biennial Convention of the Textile Workers Union of America in Chicago, June 1. In these speeches and in his address at the Cook County Democratic Dinner, May 19, in which he charged that while Khrushchev had wrecked the Paris Summit Conference, "Eisenhower had handed him the crowbar and the sledgehammer to wreck it," his topic was consistently the Summit Conference. In his May 12 speech, Stevenson said: "I hope and pray that the prospect for a test-ban agreement at the Summit has not been harmed by this confusing announcement [Eisenhower's statement of May 7 that the United States would resume underground nuclear test explosions] just when everything looked as if there was for the first time a real chance—perhaps a last chance—to bring the development of nuclear weapons under reasonable control before they spread further through the world and before they become still more lethal and versatile." Later, speaking to the Textile Workers, he urged these "priorities for peace":*

1. Build up a "deterrent power and a limited war capability that does not depend on the 'budget bureaucrats.'"

2. *Strengthen the political and economic unity of the Western Alliance by setting up an Atlantic Council.*

3. *Join with our allies in a long-range aid program to poor nations.*

4. *Make it plain that "general and complete disarmament under international control is an imperative for all of us."*

5. *"Put first things first here at home" to show the world that freedom works in meeting basic needs for schooling, research, health, housing, urban renewal, and in guaranteeing civil rights for all Americans.*

Stevenson's Founder's, or Jefferson, Day Address combines his attacks against the Republicans with his broad philosophical approach to foreign affairs that was later characteristic of his speeches in the United Nations. It demonstrates also the likelihood that Jefferson's ideas, like Wilson's, played a significant role in the development of his own concept of an enlightened foreign policy.

THIS is the fifteenth anniversary of the death of Franklin D. Roosevelt at Warm Springs, Georgia. It was at Warm Springs, after he had been crippled by paralysis, that he said, "We will build a cottage here and begin a new life."[189]

To build a cottage and begin a new life seems to me a peculiarly Jeffersonian idea, for that is what he helped to do in this country, and that is what he wanted for the world. I was reminded of this in South America, from whence I have just returned. When Jefferson was Ambassador to France in 1787, he met a young Brazilian patriot who was seeking aid for their struggle for independence. Jefferson explained to Senhor da Maia that he had no authority to discuss such a delicate subject, but that while the very young government of the United States could not get involved, the American people could and should be concerned with Brazil's freedom. He made a distinction between the acts of governments and the acts of citizens, who played such a significant part in the independence struggle in Latin America.[190]

I like to think about that talk long ago in a little French provincial inn and of what Jefferson may have said to the eager young Brazilian. Historians have long since released Jefferson from the narrow partisan and states' rights prisons that could never confine his universal dimensions. And he must have revealed that his great hope, as expressed in some magnificent letters, was not to extend our national power but to spread the dominion of our national ideals: "May it be to the world what I believe it will be (to some parts sooner, to others later, but finally to all) the signal of arousing men . . . to assume the blessings and security of self government."

South America must have been much in his mind when he wrote that. And I wonder if he didn't warn his young friend about the evils of the European social order as well as the colonial system of that time; how, as he put it, "they have divided their nations into two classes, wolves and sheep." While he loved Europe, he was horrified by a system in which, in words he quoted from Voltaire, every man was either the hammer or the anvil.[191]

"Cherish therefore," Jefferson wrote, "the spirit of our people, and keep alive their attention. Do not be too severe upon their errors, but reclaim them by enlightening them. Once they become inattentive to public affairs, you and I, and Congress and . . . judges and governors shall all become wolves."[192]

Jefferson today would, I suspect, scent some wolves and prescribe a large dose of enlightenment to keep alive "the people's attention." To be sure, the agrarian society that delighted Jefferson is a lost world, and he would have been dismayed by the urban, industrialized, automated society in which we live today. But he would have understood that, as the population swelled from 5 million to 180 million, it brought profound changes; that with the machine age would come tremendous pressures toward impersonalized conformity. For Jefferson knew full well that the world does not stand still. "The earth," he said, "belongs always to the living generation," and, "Nothing is unchangeable but the inherent and inalienable rights of man."[193]

So Jefferson today would be plunged into a battle that was familiar to him, even though the terrain is different. The challenge of free men to stay free in a swiftly-changing world would absorb all his energies. As he fought for the Bill of Rights in his own lifetime, so would he be fighting today for their application to all Americans. What mattered to him, as to all liberals, was the extension of freedom and the rights of the individual. And he would be shocked to hear his name invoked in defense of doctrines no longer designed to extend civil rights, but to curtail them.

He would, I think, be quick to remind the Americans of today that they cannot take their freedom and security for granted, that they can no longer indulge in the comfortable illusion as one historian put it, that "history does not happen to us." For we are no longer far removed from the tidal waves of history, and the Western world is no longer the center of gravity on our planet. And our common culture and convictions are challenged as they have not been since Islam's challenge to Christianity hundreds of years ago.

I also believe that Jefferson would be deeply disturbed by the slowness with which this reality is sinking in. Not only has our society become infinitely more complex, but life itself has become infinitely more perilous. Not long ago, I visited Dr. Albert Schweitzer in his jungle hospital in equatorial Africa. He told me he thought this the most dangerous period in all human history. Why? Because, he said, man is no longer controlled by nature. He has learned to control the elemental forces of nature—before he has learned to control himself.

To one who spent a dauntless, restless lifetime in the services of his fellowmen, some other symptoms of our times would also be profoundly disturbing. Jefferson thought of democracy as a moral principle. What of our public morals today? He knew how hard it was to win and preserve freedom. But the freedom many people want today is freedom from responsibility. Jefferson toiled night and day to serve his country. But in our time, millions of Americans are seemingly so indifferent to public affairs that they do not even feel an obligation to vote.

We can hear his pleading again: "Cherish the spirit of our people, and keep alive their attention . . . by enlightening them." Would he not say to us—man your defenses, and reaffirm your faith in salvation by works? Would he not say—strengthen the morals and might of your society to meet and master the new challenge of tyranny? Would he not say—rise up to the altitude of man's peril to prevent forever the thermonuclear tragedy?

What would he say about leadership? Jefferson's whole philosophy was based on belief in the ability and decency of the average man. But would he not caution us to beware of easy options and of men on horseback? Would he not remind us again that any dominant group, however ostensibly enlightened, would, if given a chance, exploit the people? (The way beekeepers do to bees, was the way he put it.) Would he not decry our anti-intellectualism and the cult of the lowest common denominator at a time when terrible and dangerous decisions have to be made?

There is no doubt in my mind where Jefferson would stand. He was—to use a contemporary term—an egghead, and proud of it. "Of all the charges brought against me by my political adversaries," he said on leaving the Presidency, "that of possessing some science has probably done them the least credit. Our countrymen are too enlightened themselves that ignorance is the best qualification for their service." He would see that our national leadership has not prepared us for the tasks of this searching century; that it has not summoned us to our duty; that it has not, in his words, "kept alive our attention." Too often—and I wish I could call Jefferson as a witness—our leadership has been hesitant and half-hearted, and has concealed from us the nature and dimensions of the crisis.

Such failure of leadership and communication touches the roots of the idea of democratic society. Our system of government was founded, as Jefferson declared, "not in the fears and follies of man, but on his reason, on his sense of right, on the predominance of the social over his dissocial passions." For the people can neither grant nor withhold consent on rational or just grounds unless they are informed—enlightened, to use Jefferson's word. Government by concealment, by soothing assurances rather than candid communication, cannot be long tolerated if our system is to endure.

Concealment of the true nature of the crisis—even assurances from a Secretary of State, as late as 1956, that communism is "a gigantic failure"—has been accompanied by an attitude on the part of our leaders that seems almost to equate discussion with disunity and criticism with disloyalty. When some of our most distinguished citizens and generals express concern about the obvious fact that our defenses are not as strong as they were, the President

becomes angry, Mr. Nixon considers that it undermines our security, and the Republican national chairman [Thruston Morton]
contributes a sarcastic remark about their "paper hats and wooden
swords."

And this recent history of truth-trifling and misrepresentation
goes way back to the talk about "liberating" Eastern Europe, "unleashing" Chiang Kai-shek, "Communists in government," and a
long procession of impostures born of political expediency and
cynical salesmanship.

But these impostures also derive from misunderstanding or dis-
respect for our system—from a vague feeling that the best kind of
government is one in which the people turn their hopes and fears
over to a kind of caretaker for the national welfare and conscience,
to a benign chief magistrate who countenances little criticism and
comforts the people with good news or none. This concept of
leadership is in sharp contrast to Jefferson's conviction that the
people must be kept attentive by enlightening them, and that
democracy needs the fertilization of dissent if it is not to wither
like a plant without water.

But if what I have been saying seems too contemporary for a
memorial lecture, my excuse is that these attitudes about leadership
are not new. Thomas Jefferson knew them well. Indeed, they
represent one of the two enduring polarities of thought around
which our political life has centered. What distinguished the Fed-
eralists, the Whigs and in our day the Republicans from the party
that Jefferson founded is that their leaders never really trusted
what he called "the good sense of the people." Instead, they felt
that the business of government should be left in the hands of those
who believed they knew best.

This distinction was perceived by Tocqueville more than a
hundred years ago. He called it a division "between two opinions
which are as old as the world . . . the one tending to limit, the
other to extend indefinitely the power of the people." This is a
moral issue that has always kindled strong feelings, and he concluded that whenever America lost this distinction dividing two
parties, "her morality . . . suffered by their extinction."[194]

Jefferson, too, discerned a natural division of men into opposing
parties in every free and deliberative society—with each taking his

side according to his fear of or confidence in the good sense of the people. And although historical parallels are never exact, we can see similarities between the central issue of today—the right of the people to know—and the one that the nation faced in what Jefferson called "the momentous crisis" of 1800.

Then, too, the nation had recently experienced an effort to suspend political debate, a drift away from government through discussion and toward a curbing of criticism. Even Washington, a military and world hero, cautioned in his Farewell Address against those self-created societies that had fomented so much political dissent. He spoke warmly of respect for law and order, little upon the subject of liberties and not at all upon the right to criticize. And at the close of the 1790's, this tendency reached its most extreme form in legislation which sought, in the name of national security, to apply a checkrein to criticism of public officials.

To Jefferson, this tendency to stifle debate struck at the very heart of our idea of government by consent, the moral foundation on which government rested. That is why I think he would be dismayed at today's public-relations techniques which are designed to smother political debate with images, slogans and catchwords. In 1952, you remember, it was "Communism and Corruption" and "I shall go to Korea." In 1956, it was "I like Ike" and "Peace, Progress and Prosperity." And in 1960 it will probably be something about "seven wonderful years"(—or more accurately "seven comfortable years"!).

But whatever the slogans that are being tooled for us this year, we who trust in the good sense of the people must report the facts and raise the questions the people must answer. In Jefferson's phrase, we must "cherish the spirit of our people," even though we will no doubt be accused of "gloom and doom," extravagance, hysteria, socialism and, if Mr. Nixon again lets himself go, of something just short of treason. For, as Jefferson once said, "No experiment can be more interesting than that which we are now trying, and which we trust will end in establishing the fact that man may be governed by reason and truth. Our first object should therefore be to leave open all the avenues to truth."[195]

In the months ahead, I hope his party, the Democratic party, will open up the avenues to many truths, avenues that have been ob-

scured too long. The people have a right to know why we have
lost our once unquestioned military superiority; why we have
repeatedly allowed the Soviets to seize the diplomatic initiative; why
we have faltered in the fight for disarmament; why we are not
providing our children with education to which they are entitled;
why—nearly a century after the Fourteenth and Fifteenth Amendments—all of our citizens have still not been guaranteed the right to
vote; why we spend billions of dollars storing surplus food when
one-third of humanity goes to bed hungry; why we have not
formulated an economic development program geared to the
worldwide passion for economic growth; why we have failed to
win the confidence and respect of the billions of impatient people
in Asia, Africa and Latin America; why millions of Americans lead
blighted lives in our spreading urban slums; why we have fewer
doctors per capita than we did fifty years ago and pay more for
our medical care than ever before; why we spent more money last
year on tranquilizers than on space exploration, and more on leisure
than on learning; why the richest nation in the history of the world
cannot support the public services and facilities we must have not
only for world power but for national growth and opportunity.

The people have a right to know—and their leaders have a duty
to tell them—the truth about the nature of our crisis and the
dimensions of the problems that will have to be faced by the next
Administration. We are entering a decade of great decisions affecting our nation, our civilization and our very survival as human
beings—a decade as fateful for the Republic as the one that began
with Jefferson in 1800, and the one that began with Lincoln just a
hundred years ago, in 1860. And one of the first of these decisions
will be to select new leadership—leadership that will treat Americans as grown-up people, that will help us understand our choices
and our dangers, and how to cope with them. The next President's
task is heavier than any autocrat's because in the decade of the
1960's democracy and the slow progress of persuasion must match
the efficiency of central planning and the swiftness and certainty of
dictatorial decision. Our chief executive will have to be a man who
agrees with Franklin Roosevelt's definition of the Presidency as
"preeminently a position of moral leadership," and who deeply

believes, as Jefferson did, that "the spirit of liberty, when conducted by public virtue, is invincible."

Jefferson was this kind of President. In 1800, we as a nation were a defenseless confederation standing at the mercy of two great world powers. Yet this was the nation that Jefferson proclaimed to be the strongest on earth, not because of its military might or its productive capacity—for it had little of either—but because its people believed profoundly in a moral purpose from which they could not be swayed, even when men in office sought to curb their energies and suppress their criticisms.

Jefferson believed that the American revolution belonged to all mankind. "The inquiry which has been excited by our revolution and its consequences," he said, "will ameliorate the condition of men over a great portion of the globe." There was no lethargy in 1800, no confusion about our values or objectives. Excitement was in the air, for we stood as a nation at the head of a crusade for freedom that was just beginning to unshackle humanity from the servitude of centuries.

Today we are no longer poor and defenseless. We are by far the richest nation on earth and, until recently, the most impregnable. Yet, ironically, our actions have been timid and irresolute. Our leaders talk of freedom—and embrace dictators. We do not act as frightened as we did during the shameful McCarthy era. But to millions of people just emerging from feudalism or colonialism we still look like a nation that has forgotten its revolutionary heritage and moral purpose, and that prefers its political status quo, business profits, and personal comforts to the traditions on which our republic was founded.

Rich and endowed as we are, the dominant concerns of our leadership have been almost wholly defensive. Our foreign policy has been dominated by sterile anticommunism and stupid wishful thinking, our domestic policy by fear of inflation and mistrust of government. We offer aid less to help others than to shield ourselves. We have been reassured on the one hand that America has never been stronger or more prosperous or more respected in the world. And on the other hand we have been warned that in spite of a gross national product of $500 billion, bankruptcy stares us in the face if we divert any more of our wealth from private self-indulgence to the urgent task of meeting the challenge of a totalitarian society, already growing faster than ours, whose leaders are determined to remake the whole world in their own image.

And our leaders tell us in effect that if we can just balance the budget and produce more consumer goods, the Soviet challenge will somehow disappear.

This is dangerous deception. It is impossible to spend years traveling around the world, as I have, without a disquieting awareness of the thrust and purpose of Soviet society. The leaders believe in their revolution as the leaders of the American Revolution believed in theirs. They are quietly confident that it will sweep the world, that collective man in a collective state is the ultimate unfolding of human destiny. Their agents are everywhere. No effort is too great that may help to realize their goals; and no corner of humanity is too insignificant to those who believe the whole human race is destined to become one in Communist brotherhood.

And beyond Russia, in a nation that our leaders pretend does not exist, there is an even greater thrust of power and purpose by 650 million Chinese under a system even more disciplined and under leaders even more dedicated to the triumph of their fanatical dream.

Our own leaders have deceived us by underrating the magnitude of the crisis. But haven't we, as a people, also deceived ourselves? The harsh verdict of history will be that our nation was quiescent and complacent, content with illusions; that we failed to insist, through our press and other agencies of opinion, that all the avenues to truth be kept open.

Our strength does not lie in the iron discipline of the state. Nor does it lie in the balance of a budget. It does not even lie in the productive capacity of our farms and factories. These are instruments of power, and we must wield them to accelerate our growth. In the final analysis, as Jefferson said, our national strength lies "in the spirit and manners of the people."[196] And late in life, Jefferson reflected upon the good fortune that "the full experiment of a government democratical, but representative, was reserved for us." But knowing that we would never be a perfected society and should never think of ourselves as one, he added, "and is *still* reserved for us."

The experiment, he knew, could never be concluded. Political action alternates endlessly between the great poles of attitude that determine policy. Periods of high purpose and endeavor yield to periods of complacency and relaxation, eras of energy and innovation are supplanted by eras of static timidity, stages of high public virtue are succeeded by stages of moral confusion, long years of struggle over mountainous terrain are followed by years of slumber in green valleys.

We are emerging—we must emerge—from one of these valleys today—with leaders who will have the courage to tell us the truth, the heart to inspire us and the energy and wisdom to show us the way. We do not have such leadership now. Early this year Richard Nixon admitted that a crisis provokes demands that the President "lead the people up to the mountain top." And he added that this was the easy way, but not often the wise way.

Mr. Nixon is wrong. It is the wise way. But it is not the easy way.

And today, Jefferson would not understand why anything should stop us from showing this restless, inquisitive world—only now beginning to sense its common humanity—that our civilization is just as vigorous as the Soviet civilization, and that we Americans are just as capable of great deeds as we were when our frontier was not the wilderness of space but the wilderness of our own continent.

"We are never permitted to despair of the commonwealth," said Jefferson. To do so would be the ultimate treason, the last refuge of the faithless citizen. But hope, in the face of universal and revolutionary change, cannot be sustained by platitudes and pieties. Publicity photographs are no substitute for making decisions; [nor are] personal appearances in foreign capitals, for the hard work of imaginative diplomacy. Nor can we longer let our fears and mistaken priorities deter federal action where federal action is needed on defense, on education, on civil rights, on housing and slums, on industrial strife, on the cost of medical care—on all the problems that affect the strength and well-being of the whole nation.

These have been tranquil, comfortable years, but the great decisions have been postponed. This is why the year 1960, like the [year] 1860 and the year 1800, is one in which the issues transcend all the usual political passions of a quadrennial election. This year we will be making a choice between two approaches. We shall have to decide whether to go on putting private consumption first or shift the first priority to our public needs. Not long ago, the Chairman of the President's Council of Economic Advisers [Raymond J. Saulnier] said, "As I understand our economy, its ultimate purpose is to produce more consumer goods. This is the objective of everything we are working at: to produce things for consumers."

This preference for private indulgence to public need is a far cry from the ideals expressed by Thomas Jefferson. So long as this kind of thinking prevails in our leadership, America will continue to entice talented young people into entertainment rather than teaching; into high-priced psychiatry rather than low-cost public health. And America, as a nation, will be the weaker for it.

We can no longer pretend that the challenge of the twentieth century can be met with better detergents and more toothpaste, with private opulence and public squalor. It can only be met with better education and more attention to our public needs.

But to achieve a greater tempo in the development of national power, our President has told us that we will have to "take our country and make it an armed camp and regiment it . . . and get people steamed up like you did in wars."

Is the President saying that we cannot meet the Communist challenge without changing our system and giving up our freedoms? Is he saying that our system of liberty is so fragile that it cannot keep up the pace in this great contest of national power? Is he saying that with a $500 billion economy the nation will be imperiled if it devotes a somewhat larger share of its resources to public purposes?

This is the language of those who fought Jefferson in 1800. It is the language of those who fought Roosevelt's great initiative, the New Deal, at another time of decision nearly thirty years ago. It is the language of those who have no confidence in the good sense of the people.

But our national character has not deteriorated beyond repair in this period of leaderless lassitude. Whatever their condition, Jefferson believed in the capacity of the people to rise to greatness once they know, once they are told, once they are summoned. In 1800 he brought a drifting nation back to a sense of its proper mission, not for the sake of any narrow, selfish nationalism but for those maxims of a free society that Lincoln reaffirmed in 1860.

So now he would call upon this still young, still vigorous nation to rouse itself and resume the everlasting work of preserving "the blessings and security" of self-government.

His power—his leadership—did not come just from the fact that he was a philosopher-statesman, a teacher, and that, in Henry Adams's phrase, he dared to legislate for all humanity. Rather his power lay in his unshaken confidence based not on fatuous illusions but on a clear, hard-headed realization that only on such a foundation could "the last best hope of earth" endure.

Jefferson's use of the power of the Presidency communicated a respect for the intelligence as well as the virtue of the people. As the avenues to truth are opened up, he would expect the people to understand the gravity of the issues and the decisions that lie before them. This is the Jeffersonian mission—the sacred obligation that confronts all Americans who honor his name today—the overwhelming challenge, the exciting opportunity to show the world that the American Revolution still belongs to all mankind.

The Principles That Guide Us

FEBRUARY 1, 1961

☆

Amid considerable speculation during the spring of 1960 that Stevenson would be a candidate for the Presidency again, James Doyle officially announced the formation of a "Draft Stevenson" movement, which spread to forty-two states. Mrs. Eleanor Roosevelt's statement that he would be a candidate embarrassed Stevenson and forced him to deny his candidacy. His failure to endorse one of the declared candidates seemed to his partisans a clear indication that he would serve if summoned. In July, he indicated that it was "possible but not probable" that he would be nominated and that he would do "his utmost to win" if nominated. Senator Eugene McCarthy's eloquent nomination speech for him is reminiscent of Stevenson's own oratory and search for an ethic.

Do not reject this man. He has fought gallantly. He has fought courageously. He has fought honorably. In 1952 in the great battle. In 1956 he fought bravely. And between those years and since, he has stood off the guerrilla attacks of his enemies and the sniping attacks of those who should have been his friends. Do not reject this man who made us all proud to be called Democrats. Do not reject this man who, his enemies said, spoke above the heads of the people, but they said it only because they didn't want the people to listen. He spoke to the people. He moved their minds and stirred their hearts, and this was what was objected to. Do not leave this prophet without honor in his own party. Do not reject this man.[197]

After the convention's tumultuous reception for Stevenson, it proceeded quickly to nominate Kennedy on the first ballot with 806 votes to Johnson's 409 votes, Symington's 86 votes, and Stev-

enson's 79½ votes. James Reston wrote in the New York Times: *"Adlai Stevenson is free at last of the long anguish of Presidential politics, but he is still not entirely at peace. . . . Nevertheless, he still has an extremely important role to play. . . . He carries more weight in both the Allied and the Communist worlds than Kennedy, Nixon or Lodge. He is more experienced and more articulate in this field than either candidate, which is why Kennedy said during the primary campaign that he 'assumed' any Democratic President would nominate Stevenson as Secretary of State."*[198]

Stevenson's nomination for Secretary of State was not forthcoming. On December 8, with Stevenson at his side, Kennedy told the press of his decision to appoint him as the Ambassador to the United Nations. Stevenson said to the newsmen: "The United Nations is the very center of our foreign policy and its effectiveness is indispensable to the peace and the security of the world." Still, he deferred acceptance of the position until he knew who would be Secretary of State and was assured that he himself, with Cabinet rank, would "play a key role in the formulation of foreign policy."

On January 18, 1961, Stevenson spoke to Congress after the confirmation of his appointment:

. . . the assignment which President-elect Kennedy has given me, with—I hope—your advice and consent, represents something of a homecoming for me.

I welcome this opportunity to serve the United States in the United Nations. I do not minimize its difficulties, but I also regard it as a great opportunity. . . .

The identity of the United Nations with our deepest convictions about the nature and destiny of man is a central fact we need to keep in mind as we move through a period of relentless turmoil and travail. . . .

We should use it not as a device in this cold war, not just in defensive reaction to Soviet initiatives, but affirmatively to advance its great purposes—to liberate men from the scourges of war, poverty, disease, ignorance, and oppression.[199]

On January 21, he was sworn in as Ambassador Extraordinary and Plenipotentiary, Permanent Representative of the United States to the United Nations, and a member of the Kennedy Cabinet. He presented his credentials to Secretary-General Dag Hammarskjold on January 23, 1961, and assumed his duties. On February 1, 1961, in his first speech in the Security Council, printed in Looking Outward *and below, he outlined several key objectives of the Kennedy Administration.*

MR. PRESIDENT [Sir Patrick Dean of Great Britain],

First, let me say that I am very happy to come to this table for the first time in many years under your chairmanship. Under the rules I understand that I must succeed you as President the first of next month and I wish I did not suspect that you would relinquish that honor with the same enthusiasm that Mr. [Omar] Loutfi [Ambassador of the United Arab Republic] has relinquished it today.

Listening to such kindness and flattery as I have heard here today, I have begun to wonder if you have confused me with Thomas Jefferson whom Ambassador Helena Z. Benitez of the Philippines was good enough to mention and whose name is always agreeable to a Democrat!

I deeply appreciate, Mr. President, the kind words and good wishes of you and my colleagues. I must apologize for my voice. I wish I could say that it was a casualty of the battle for peace instead of New York weather.[200] I have sometimes said that flattery is all right, Mr. President, if you don't inhale. Well, you have made it very hard for me not to inhale thanks to the charity and the kindness which has touched me so deeply. In the days—and perhaps nights—ahead of us, I shall always remember with gratitude this hour. And may all of our wishes be as good for all of the peoples of the world as your kind words have been good for me today.

As some of you know, I had a part in the birth of the United Nations in San Francisco in 1945, and in its early walks as an infant in London and then in New York in 1946 and 1947. And now it is fifteen years old and I am pleased to be sharing in the problems of its adolescence. The problems of adolescence are largely those of young love. I believe this is true in all countries. Would that all of our problems in this Council were as amiable.

Although some of our problems may not be amiable, I hope that we may deal with even the thorniest of them in an atmosphere of tolerance and of good will. We are, to use the French phrase, the Nations United. Let us *be* united, united in a patient and persevering attempt to find the things we can agree upon and to build upon them a structure of understanding and of cooperation against which whatever storms may be ahead shall beat in vain.

To one who has been long absent from these Councils, it is striking and heartening that the United Nations has not only survived the turmoil and the conflict of these fifteen years but has grown to nearly twice its original membership and has become an ever more potent factor in the shaping of world events.

We of the United States wish the United Nations to be still more potent—for the grave dangers of this nuclear age demand much more unity among the nations. The common yearning of all men expressed in the Charter is to achieve freedom from war, poverty, disease, ignorance and oppression. That is what binds us all together. Our security and our salvation is the ability of the nations and the governments to see through the clouds of conflict and discern the truth about our common interests—and then, boldly and in concert, to act. Only the actions of states, both large and small, can impart vigor to this organization and can redeem the pledges of the Charter. And we in the United States believe that the times are too dangerous for anything except the truth.

The United Nations is a sensitive measure of the tremors which shake the community of nations—tremors which have built up to dangerous levels. But we are not helpless spectators. The tremors are man-made and man can still them. To help the organization to meet that task, we of the United States will be guided by certain principles, and I hope you will indulge me for a moment while I mention some of them.

First, we know the great importance which the newer and less developed nations attach to the United Nations. In their search for peace, for mutual tolerance, for economic development, for dignity and self-respect, our interest is theirs. We don't seek military allies among them, nor do we wish to impose our system or our philosophy upon them—indeed, we cannot; freedom cannot be imposed on anyone.

Our concern for these nations is that they should be truly independent members of the peaceful community of nations.

As the oldest anticolonial power, the United States is in favor of freedom and of self-determination for all peoples. We rejoice in the rapid and peaceful revolution which has brought into being and into our midst at the United Nations so many new sovereignties. Our great desire is that this transition should proceed peacefully and in good order, with the least possible suffering, bitterness and new conflicts. We applaud what has been done to bring about this orderly transaction both by the emerging nations and by their former rulers. And we applaud the efforts of this Council to assist the orderly transition in the Congo through the Secretary-General.

Equally important, if not more so, is the work which this organization can do to further economic development, without which political independence cannot be sustained. The United States attaches the highest importance to improving the conditions of life of the peoples in the newly developing countries. In that work the United Nations has already proved its effectiveness as a source of technical assistance, of expert knowledge on potential capital investment, and of administrative personnel to help those who are determined to help themselves, and without any political condition or any ulterior motive. So we shall support the work of the United Nations in the whole field of economic betterment.

We shall also, Mr. President, do all in our power to use the United Nations as "a center for harmonizing the actions of nations."[201] We believe the United Nations is an opportunity for preventive diplomacy which can identify and solve potential disputes before they reach the acute stage sometimes induced by the glare of publicity.

The United States Government is giving its most earnest attention to the impasse over disarmament. We know, as President Kennedy said the other day, that "the instruments of war have far outpaced the instruments of peace." We know that progress toward disarmament becomes daily more imperative and we are ceaselessly aware of the vital interest in this problem which is felt by all of the members of the United Nations.

May I also say that if the United Nations is to continue to function, two things are also essential. It must be properly financed and the integrity of the office of the Secretary-General and of the Secretariat must be preserved. We hope all members from every region will join in fulfilling these indispensable minimum conditions.

And finally, with such a fateful agenda, Mr. President, it is more than ever important that, in these councils, we avoid useless recrimination. Free debate is an essential part of the United Nations process. But let us not demean free debate, as you have so eloquently said, Mr. President.

In his address to Congress the other day, the new President of the United States said that he regards the United Nations "as an instrument to end the cold war instead of an arena in which to fight it."[202] We devoutly hope that all of the governments here represented will share his view and that our deliberations in this Council may be uniformly directed toward the calm and constructive solution of the problems that confront us. May peace among the nations begin with peace among the members of the Council.

We are the Security Council, my colleagues, and it should be to us that the people of the world look for the security they so desperately long for. They are looking to us, I believe, for leadership, for strong, sober, constructive leadership. If they don't look to this body with confidence, it is our fault. So I wholeheartedly pledge myself to the high and the challenging task of cooperating with you in our common endeavor to provide the leadership that the world is asking of us. I devoutly hope and pray that we may fulfill this solemn obligation.

A Time for Action: The Developing Crisis
in the Congo

FEBRUARY 15, 1961

✡

In his May, 1960, article for Harper's Magazine, *"The New Africa," Stevenson compared his two visits to the Belgian Congo, one in 1955, when*

the country was full of the hustle and preparations for a visit from the beloved young King Baudouin, and his triumphal progress across the vast colony was attended by a frenzied noisy welcome. . . . [and the second in 1957, when] something was different. People were uneasy. There was a minor race riot in Leopoldville over "nothing"—a referee's decision in a soccer match. . . . And when King Baudouin returned after the bloody riots in 1959, prosperity still reigned in Africa's richest land, but the King's path was lined with armed soldiers and the people were shouting not "Vive le Roi!" but "Independence!"—as they are all over Africa, whether ready for self-government or not.[203]

When the Congo received its independence in the summer of 1960, its lack of readiness for self-government was immediately apparent. Ambassadors Lodge and Wadsworth, Stevenson's predecessors, initially were involved with the Congo problem and Stevenson inherited it at a most critical point in its history. Later, reflecting on its significance, he said:

Joining the Cuban crisis as a predominant factor in any appraisal of this session of the General Assembly—although, again, you will not find it on the agenda as such—is the Congo. Here, once more, the United Nations looms large in the picture with 18,000 troops from 34 nations participating from time to time in the U.N. effort to maintain law and order.

Nonetheless, time is running out, and the unification of the Congo cannot be put off much longer.[204]

Between December 1960, and February 1961, the situation had worsened steadily. On November 27, Patrice Lumumba, the Prime Minister of the Congo, and two associates had been arrested and transferred to Thysville. When United Nations troops there reported a mutiny by the Congolese army on January 13, 1961, rumors spread that mutinous soldiers had killed or freed Lumumba. Moise Tshombe, leader of Katanga, confirmed the report that Lumumba had been transferred secretly to Elisabethville. On February 10, Mr. Munongo, Minister of the Interior for Katanga, announced that Lumumba and his comrades had overpowered their guards and escaped. Three days later, he declared that Lumumba had been apprehended and killed, and praised the villagers for their action: ". . . We cannot honestly blame [them] for having rid Katanga, the Congo, Africa and the world of a problem . . . which threatened to be a source of trouble to mankind. . . . I should be lying if I said that Lumumba's death grieves me. You know how I feel about him: he is an ordinary criminal. . . ."[205] *When the Security Council met that day to consider Lumumba's assassination, Ambassador Zorin of the Soviet Union blamed Belgium and its allies and the Secretary-General with his United Nations command in the Congo: "After all that has happened in the Congo and Katanga, one can no longer have any confidence in the Secretary-General or his staff." The next day, he circulated a statement and a resolution condemning the colonialists and "the shameful role that is being played in Congolese affairs by the Secretary-General."*[206]

In preparing his maiden speech on a matter of substance in the Security Council for February 15, Stevenson wished to minimize the Soviet-American differences if possible. Still, he strongly planned to reaffirm American support for the United Nations Congo operation and the Secretary-General. After the speech, Zorin caustically labeled it as "non-constructive, evasive, and distorted." Members of the Western and neutral nations joined in defending

the integrity of the Secretary-General and stated their opposition
to the introduction of such a new unilateral influence in the Congo
as the Soviet Union, which Zorin's statement had seemed to an-
nounce. On February 20, after the reported death of six additional
Congolese leaders, the Council passed a resolution offered by the
representatives of Ceylon, Liberia, and the United Arab Republic
condemning the arrests and executions and calling for an impartial
international investigation. It rejected the radical Soviet resolution.

Stevenson's speech to the Council on February 15, printed
below, appears also with the above title in his book Looking Outward *without mention, however, of the disturbing situation that*
evolved during the middle of his speech.

MR. PRESIDENT,

A few days ago a new Administration took office in the United
States. This is the first occasion for the United States, under the
leadership of President Kennedy, to speak formally in the Security
Council on a question of substance.

But first let me thank you again, all of you both here and abroad,
who have welcomed my arrival at this table so graciously and so
hopefully. While I cannot fulfill your expectations of miracles to
come, I can commit my country, my colleagues and myself, to a
tireless effort to make the United Nations successful—to make this
great experiment in international collaboration fulfill the dreams of
its founders—that one day reason would rule and mankind would
be liberated from the everlasting scourge of war.

It seems to be my lot, Mr. President, to address you and my
colleagues for the first time,[207] in a moment of grave crisis in the
brief and tragic history of the Congo, and in a moment of equally
grave crisis for the United Nations itself. I had hoped it would be
otherwise.

Within recent days we have seen successively the withdrawal of
two national units of the United Nations Forces, the violent death
of former Prime Minister Patrice Lumumba, the reported recognition of the Gizenga regime in Stanleyville by the United Arab
Republic and a threat by the U.S.S.R. to provide unilateral assistance outside the United Nations. What we decide here in the next

few days may, we believe, determine whether the United Nations will be able in the future to carry on its essential task of preserving the peace and protecting small nations.

This is a time for urgent and constructive action. In the midst of passions it is a time when the Security Council must be calm. In the midst of efforts to destroy the United Nations action in the Congo it is a time when we must persevere in the interests not only of the Congo but of all of us, large and small. The choice, as always, is a choice of us the members of the United Nations. Either we will follow a path toward a constructive and workable solution or we will follow a path of negative recrimination and self-interest.

As a new arrival listening and talking to delegates, I have wondered sometimes in the past ten days if everyone is actually thinking about the Congo—a new Republic struggling to be born—or if the Congo has been obscured by passions and prejudices about the doctors—Kasavubu, Lumumba, Gizenga, Tshombe, and so forth.

Opinion seems to be polarizing about them, not about the patient. So it is more important than ever to rally strong support to the United Nations in order to save the patient.

For the past fortnight, my country has been consulting on a United Nations program to save the patient, both here and abroad —a program on which there might be agreement by a large majority of United Nations members. That effort in which so many of us have taken part, must not be abandoned. Indeed, its urgency is only accentuated by the impact of subsequent events.[208]

As I said, Mr. President, I had hoped that my first formal remarks to the Security Council on the vexed problems of the Congo could be directed solely to constructive suggestions which would be helpful to the Congolese people in working out their own independence, free of outside interference.

Instead, I find myself compelled to comment not on constructive suggestions but on a statement and a proposed resolution by the Soviet Union published in this morning's newspapers which is virtually a declaration of war on the United Nations and on the principle of international action on behalf of peace.

Permit me to analyze what, stripped of intemperate rhetoric, this statement and this resolution propose. They propose the abandonment of the United Nations' effort for peace in the Congo and a surrender of the United Nations to chaos and to civil war.

But the statement and the resolution say many things which we are glad to see, things which support positions that my country has always maintained. As to colonialism, my country fought colonialism in 1776 (when, if I may say so, the ancestors of the authors of this statement in the newspapers and this resolution had scarcely stirred beneath their bondage). And we have fought it ever since. My countrymen died to end colonialism in the Philippines, and my countrymen have assisted the Philippine people to attain their present high destiny of complete independence. And my countrymen have died to end colonialism in Cuba, though some Cubans seem to have forgotten it.

We rejoice, too, to hear the Soviets denounce political assassinations with such vehemence. In this country it has always been condemned by whomever committed, whether by Congolese, by colonialists or by Communists. We condemn any violation of human rights, any death without due process of law, whether of African politician, Hungarian patriot, or Tibetan nationalist. The United States stands squarely for the rights of man, individual man, man himself, as against any tyranny, whether it be the tyranny of colonialism or the tyranny of dictatorship or the tyranny of the majority.

We note that the Soviets demand that Belgian foreign military and paramilitary aid be withdrawn. We, the United States, insist that all foreign military aid from whatever source and to whatever end be removed from the Congo and that no such aid be permitted to interfere with the free and independent working out by the Congolese people themselves of their own political destiny. We mean this and we intend to keep on meaning it. And we mean it with particular reference to the threat—which we hope we misinterpret—by the Soviet Government that—and I quote, "It is ready to render all possible assistance and support" to a so-called Congolese government in Stanleyville which has no legal status.

The United States intends to use its utmost influence and, within the framework of the United Nations, to see to it that there is no outside interference, from whatever source, with the Congolese people's working out of their independence.[209]

So, Mr. President, we rejoice that the Soviet Union shares the distaste of the United States for colonialism and joins with us in condemning political assassination and in condemning foreign interference in the Congo.

I pass lightly over the Soviet Government's petulant attack on the Secretary-General and that great office. He needs no defense from me nor does the institution. His record is an open book, a book which all peace-loving peoples recognize as the record of a dedicated international civil servant whose only loyalty is to international justice and international peace. Let the Soviet government, if it wishes, pretend that he does not exist; it will find that he is far from a disembodied ghost and it will find that peace-loving states will continue to support his patient search for the right road to security and peace in the Congo and for all peoples. The United Nations may have made mistakes in the Congo, as who has not, but nothing justifies an intemperate and unjustifiable attack on the integrity of the office itself.

We know that the United Nations has been denounced with equal vehemence by Kasavubu, by Gizenga, by Tshombe, while they also attack each other with equal vehemence. But could there be better testimony of impartiality? And I recall that Christian scripture says: "Woe unto him when all men speak well of him." Neither the United Nations nor the Secretary-General seem likely to suffer from the affliction of universal approval.

We regret, Mr. President, that the Soviet Government does not as yet seem to have seen fit to cooperate with states who truly seek peace in attempting to work out constructive steps for the co-operative solution of the agonizing problems that the Congolese people are now facing.

Instead the Soviet Government proposes the complete abandonment of the United Nations operation in the Congo in one month. What does this mean? It means, my colleagues, not only the abandonment of the Congo to chaos and to civil war, to, if you please, the cold war, but it means abandonment of the principle of the United Nations itself.

Does anyone doubt that the removal of the United Nations Forces would mean chaos? Does this Council, the *Security* Council, favor abandoning security for insecurity and anarchy?

Do we want to withdraw the only elements that stand four-square against civil and tribal war? Does the Soviet Government really want Africans to kill Africans? The United States does not, and it devoutly hopes that the Soviet Government does not too, and that it will join the United States and other peace-loving states in supporting and strengthening the only force that can prevent Congolese civil war—the United Nations.

And now the cold war. Does the Soviet Government really want to chill what should be warm and temperate in Africa with the icy blasts of power politics? The United States does not. Its only interest in the Congo is to support the Congolese people in their struggle for real independence, free from any foreign domination from *any* source.

The United States deplores any war, cold or otherwise. Its only desire is to live in peace and freedom and to let all other peoples live in peace and freedom. It will resist with all of its power all assaults on its own peace and freedom, and it proposes to join with all other peace-loving peoples in resisting, in the cooperative framework of the United Nations, all assaults on the peace and freedom of other peoples.

In that spirit we declare that so far as we are concerned, Africa shall never be the scene of any war, cold or hot. But we also declare that Africa for the Africans *means* Africa for the Africans, and not Africa as a hunting ground for alien ambitions. And we pledge our full and unstinted support against any attempt by anyone to interfere with the full and free development by Africans of their own independent African future.

We believe that the only way to keep the cold war *out* of the Congo is to keep the United Nations *in* the Congo, and we call on the Soviet Union to join us in thus ensuring the free and untrammeled exercise by the Congolese people of their right to independence and to democracy.

But, Mr. President, the position apparently taken by the Soviet Government involves more than the unhappy and despicable fate of three Congolese politicians. It involves the future of the 14 million Congolese people. They are the ones with whom we are concerned. We deplore the past and we condemn those responsible for it, no matter who they may be. But we submit that it is the future that is all-important now, and that the best efforts of this Council should be concentrated on the future security of the Congo and, indeed, on the future security of all peoples.

For, Mr. President, it is the security of all peoples which is threatened by the statement and by the proposals of the Soviet Government. Let me make my meaning abundantly and completely clear, if I can. The United States Government believes and profoundly believes that the single best and only hope of the peoples of the world for peace and security lies in the United Nations. It lies in international cooperation, in the integrity of an international body rising above international rivalries into the clearer air of international morality and international justice.

The United Nations has not achieved perfection, nor has the United States, and they probably never will. The United States, like the United Nations, is composed of humans, it has made mistakes, it probably always will make mistakes; it has never pleased all people, it cannot please all people; in its desire and wholehearted determination to do justice it may offend one group of states in 1952, another in 1956, and perhaps still another in 1961. But always the United States has tried, and we believe it will always try, to apply even-handedly the rules of justice and equity that should govern us all.

Are we callously to cast aside the one and only instrument that men have developed to safeguard their peace and security? Are we to abandon the jungles of the Congo to the jungles of internecine warfare and internal rivalry?

The issue, Mr. President, even transcends the fate of the suffering 14 million Congolese people. It involves the fate of all of us, of all mankind.

The issue, then, is simply this: shall the United Nations survive? Shall the attempt to bring about peace by the concerted power of international understanding be discarded?

> *At this time, an obviously organized group of American Negroes or Africans began a disturbance in the visitors' gallery. More than 100 began to shout and chant: "Viva Lumumba," "Down with the United Nations," "Drive the U.N. out of the Congo," "Out with Dag Hammarskjold," "Save the*

Congo," "Freedom or death," and "Africa for the Africans."
This last remark probably was directed to Stevenson's state-
ment shortly before: " . . . but we also declare that 'Africa
for the Africans' means 'Africa for the Africans' and not as a
hunting ground for alien ambitions." During the disturbance,
Stevenson sat calmly while the Council President, Sir Patrick
Dean, ordered the gallery cleared. Because the microphones
remained on, one diplomat was heard muttering: "What are
those SOB's trying to do?" As the crowd was being ejected
bodily, it added such phrases to its chant as, "Go to Hell, you
SOB's," "You're pinching me," "You white bastards," "Segre-
gation in the U.N.," and "Someone should throw a goddamn
bomb into this shitty place and send the whole goddamn U.N.
SOB's to Hell." Some few began to sing, "We shall over-
come." It was twenty minutes before order could be restored
so that Stevenson could resume his speech.[210]

Mr. President, may I say that I deeply deplore this outrageous and
obviously organized demonstration. To the extent that Americans
may have been involved, I apologize on behalf of my Government
to the members of the Security Council.

To continue, shall any pretense of an international order, of
international law, be swept aside? Shall conflicts of naked power,
awful in their potential, be permitted to rage in Africa or elsewhere, unchecked by international cooperation or authority?

These are questions, Mr. President and my colleagues, which call
for an answer, not so much by the great powers as by the smaller
ones, and the newer ones. My own country, as it happens, is in the
fortunate position of being able to look out for itself and for its
interests, and look out it will. But it is for the vast majority of
states that the United Nations has vital meaning and is of vital
necessity. I call on those states to rise in defense of the integrity of
the institution which is for them the only assurance of their freedom and their liberty, and the only assurance for all of us of peace
in the years to come.

And I also call upon the Soviet Union to reconsider its position. My Government is earnestly determined to cooperate with all

governments in an attempt to improve international relationships and to further friendships among peoples, and it has welcomed evidences of cooperation toward that end by the Soviet Government. Let those evidences be buttressed by concrete steps by the Soviet Government looking toward constructive solution of the difficult problems that confront us all. Let us join in condemning the past but let us join in facing the future with calm determination to support steadfastly and strengthen sturdily the United Nations, the United Nations which is the last best hope of us all.

Now let me turn to the Congo and to what can be done to arrest the sad deterioration in that divided country. There are certain fundamental principles concerning the Congo which have had and will continue to have the full support of the American people and of the United States Government. It is on the basis of these principles that we have undertaken consultations this past fortnight. We believe that they are shared by others and we are willing to work with any and all who show a willingness to find a solution. The essential principles of such a solution are, we believe, apparent to all.

In the first place, that the unity, the territorial integrity, the political independence of the Congo must be preserved. I am sure Sir Patrick will not object if I repeat that the United States was one of the first anticolonialists and that during the 186 years since we have stood steadfastly for the right of peoples to determine their own destiny. The United States desires nothing for the Congo but its complete freedom from outside domination and nothing for its people but the same independent freedom which we wanted for ourselves so long ago and have resolutely defended ever since.

Much as the United States was once beset by internal dissensions, so the Congo since its independence has been beset by secessionist movements—previously in the Katanga and now in Orientale Province too. The United States supports the continued territorial integrity of the Congo. So far as we are concerned, its borders are identical with its borders on July 1, 1960. The United States is ready to join with other states which support its independence and integrity to maintain this principle within the framework of the United Nations.

Second, the Congo must not become a battleground, as I have

said, either for a cold or a hot war among the big powers. When the United States was first requested to provide troops for the Congo, we told the Congolese government to appeal to the United Nations. We then supported the United Nations military assistance to the Congo. In contrast to others, the United States has never at any time provided a single tank, a single gun, a single soldier, a single piece of equipment, that could be used for military purposes to anyone in the Congo.

We have, on the other hand, responded to every request made to us by the United Nations promptly and vigorously so that the entire control over our assistance passed from our hands to those of the United Nations. We remain firmly determined, as I have said, to do everything in our power to keep the cold war out of Africa.

Third, we support the United Nations action in the Congo to the fullest measure of our power. The best way to keep the cold war and the hot war out of the Congo, as I have said, is to keep the United Nations in. To those members who are still contemplating withdrawal, I suggest a long, hard, careful look at what might happen in the Congo if the United Nations Force collapses or if the United Nations mission fails because of lack of support from its members.

Finally, we believe that the Congolese people must be allowed to develop their own political settlement by peaceful means, free from violence and external interference. The Congo's political problems must in the last analysis be worked out by the Congolese themselves. The United Nations can assist in this effort—by helping create peace and stability and through extending its good offices as it has done in the Conciliation Commission. But only a settlement demanding the support of the Congolese people will long endure.

On these principles, the maintenance of territorial integrity and political independence, the isolation of the Congolese from big power and small power interference, continued vigorous United Nations assistance and the settlement of internal political controversies by peaceful means—on these principles rest, in our opinion, the only possibility for a solution.[211]

We are faced now with the necessity for urgent and effective steps to bring these principles closer to reality. The threat of civil war, of increased unilateral intervention in the Congo on all sides is increasingly grave. If the United Nations does not take effective action immediately, not only may conflict break forth in full fury in the Congo but the hopes of African unity may be destroyed for many years to come by the divisions which will be produced among African nations. What then, in these circumstances, needs to be done?

First, all foreign intervention outside the framework of the United Nations should cease immediately and any foreign military or paramilitary personnel in the Congo should be withdrawn. The injunction of the General Assembly resolution adopted with the support of all members of the United Nations, except the Soviet bloc, against any unilateral military aid whatever, whether direct or indirect, should be adhered to fully by all United Nations members. This applies to those Belgians who are providing military advice and assistance to the Congo. It applies equally against military assistance to the forces in Orientale [Province].

The United States, for its part, does not intend to sit by if others consciously and deliberately seek to exacerbate the present situation. We are prepared to use all of our influence, if other members of the United Nations do likewise, to prevent such assistance from coming to the Congo, no matter from what quarter it comes.

Equally urgent and immediate steps are needed to avert the extension of civil war in the Congo and to protect the lives of innocent civilians and refugees should the present passions result in widespread outbreaks of violence. United Nations political and military authorities on that ground should consult immediately with the chief of state and with other civilian and military leaders if necessary to agree on measures which would best maintain peace and stability and protect the lives of citizens.

Such measures must be accompanied also by immediate steps to assure long-range stability and progress. The Secretary-General proposed to us less than two weeks ago that measures should be taken to unify, reorganize, retrain the Congolese army and other armed forces in the Congo with a view to eliminating force as a political element in that afflicted country. The United States supports this proposal. We believe that negotiations to bring this about should be undertaken with the same urgency as the measures I have just mentioned.

On Monday here in the Security Council I deplored the reported death of Mr. Lumumba and his colleagues and supported the Secretary-General's request that a preliminary investigation be included on the agenda. On every occasion when the arrest of Mr. Lumumba has been discussed in the United Nations, the United States has taken the position that he must be treated humanely and with all protection of law and order. We have similarly expressed ourselves through diplomatic channels to the appropriate authorities in the Congo. I believe it has been long known that in our consultations during the past week we had advocated the release of all political prisoners and their participation in the political process once law and order had been restored to the Congo and the possibility of civil war averted. We continue to believe that this must be done for those political prisoners, such as Minister Sangolo, about whom the world press has been less aware. In the case of Mr. Lumumba we support the Secretary-General's investigation and we believe that it should be continued vigorously until the true facts are known. I earnestly hope that the Katanga forces will cooperate so that the full facts may be brought to light.

The ultimate objective of such steps should be to promote the reconciliation of the political elements in the Congo and a full return to constitutional processes in a form to be designated by the people themselves. The Government recently appointed by the chief of state is a step in the right direction; indeed any step in the direction of moderation and breadth of base is a step in the right direction. The provision of unfilled cabinet places for other elements is encouraging. Determined future efforts must be made to broaden the base of the Congolese Government, and parliament should be convened as soon as conditions of security, law and order permit. Encouragement by the United Nations of such steps is of fundamental importance we believe.

The measures which I have outlined can only be carried out with dispatch and with effectiveness through the Secretary-General and the United Nations mission in the Congo. To attempt to discredit and dismiss the Secretary-General at this critical moment would not only wreck the United Nations mission in the Congo, it would dangerously weaken the United Nations itself.

This is the measure of the gravity of our crisis, and we call upon all members around this table to face soberly and solemnly these realities. We are eager to continue consultations with other nations at this table with a view to producing a draft resolution to carry out measures such as these. We are prepared to meet in the Council by night and by day until we can reach consensus and agreement. The occasion for, the time for effective action in the Congo is now. We must seize it and we must seize it quickly.

Angola Is Entitled to All of the Rights
Guaranteed by the Charter

MARCH 15, 1961

✶

The first important self-determination issue to concern Stevenson at the United Nations was the Angola question. The impact of this speech given in the Security Council on March 15, 1961, and printed below, stems from its apparent shift in American foreign policy toward issues like colonialism and self-determination. Before the Kennedy Administration, the United States delegation usually voted with the American allies on resolutions concerning Angola or colonialism. Rather than cast negative votes on these issues, the delegation normally had abstained, which seemed a negative approach to the sensitive Afro-Asians. ·

Since its admittance to the United Nations in 1955, Portugal had consistently denied the Assembly and Security Council any competence to discuss or recommend action regarding its "overseas territories." In February, 1961, nationalists in Angola began military action against the existing government. A full-scale guerrilla rebellion erupted against the Portuguese government in Angola on March 15. The Council met that day under Stevenson's presidency to consider inscribing the "Angolan situation" on its agenda. While the Western delegations spoke against the inscription because "there is [not] in fact, in Angola, a situation likely to endanger the maintenance of international peace and security,"[212] Stevenson, although expressing American friendship for Portugal, urged the Portuguese representative, Dr. Vasco Viera Garin, to accept the proposed Afro-Asian resolution as "an effort toward genuine cooperation in the achievement of goals which are shared by all of us

and which are recognized in the Charter of the Organization."
This speech, though mild and conciliatory, nonetheless evoked
Zorin's condemnation for failing to condemn Portuguese actions in
Angola and for failing to admit that the United States and other
NATO countries supplied the weapons to Portugal so that the
natives could be suppressed. Other reactions were immediate. It
caused consternation from the Western delegates, anger from the
Portuguese with threats of a reevaluation of Portuguese-American
relations, and suspicion from the Afro-Asian delegates.[213]

WHEN he first raised the question of Angola in the Security
Council, the distinguished representative of Liberia, Ambassador
[George A.] Padmore, recognized that the recent disturbance in
Angola was not of itself an immediate threat to the maintenance of
international peace and security. At that time he said, "I believe
that there is still time for us to help build in Angola a future of
which neither the Portuguese nor the Africans need be afraid. But
we no longer have centuries or even decades in which to accomplish what should be a simple and humanitarian task."

He emphasized several problems with which the United Nations
must concern itself: the urgency in this era of rapid communication of acting with dispatch, the recognition of Angola's problem
being a part of the larger African scene, and the desirability of
Portugal availing itself of United Nations cooperation and help in
the development of its territories in Africa.

It was clear from his remarks that Ambassador Padmore was
anticipating conditions which, if unchanged, might endanger the
peace and security of Africa, if not of the world.

It is in a spirit of seeking a constructive elimination of not just
the symptoms but the sources of friction that the United States
approaches this problem. I regret to find myself in disagreement
with the distinguished representative of China and other members
of this Council who present their position with such logic and
force. We recognize full well that while Angola and the conditions
therein do not today endanger international peace and security, we
believe they may, if not alleviated, lead to more disorders with
many unfortunate and dangerous consequences.

We in the United States deplore the violence which occurred in Luanda and the tragic loss of life involving all elements of the community. Nothing we can do here will restore these people to life, but perhaps we can discourage further violence which can only make constructive efforts toward the solution of basic problems more difficult.

It is only prudent to view the disorder in Luanda in the context of dramatic changes which have taken place in so much of Africa in the past few years. Angola is but a part of the overall picture of evolution on the African continent.

The views of the United States have not changed since Jefferson wrote, "We hold these truths to be self-evident, that all men are created equal, that they are endowed by their Creator with certain inalienable rights, that among these are life, liberty and the pursuit of happiness. That to secure these rights, Governments are instituted among men, deriving their just powers from the consent of the governed. . . ." These words reflect, we believe, the basic principles which all governments would do well to observe and to implement with all of the energy at their command.

It is no secret that the General Assembly has been interested for years in conditions within Portugal's African territories. There can be no doubt that the people of Angola are entitled to all of the rights guaranteed them by the Charter, the right of unfettered opportunity to develop their full economic, political and cultural potentialities. I am sure that Portugal recognizes that it has a solemn obligation to undertake a systematic and rapid improvement of the conditions of the peoples of its territories, an evolution which is contemplated by the Charter.

The United States would be remiss in its duties as a friend of Portugal if it failed to express honestly its conviction that step-by-step planning within Portuguese territories and its acceleration is now imperative for the successful political and economic and social advancement of all inhabitants under Portuguese administration—advancement, in brief, toward full self-determination.

The practical difficulties facing Portugal in the immediate future are formidable. If the people of Angola are not given reason to believe that they too may hope to participate in determining their own future, the tension which exists today will grow and may well result in disorders which will indeed pose a threat to international peace and security.

On the other hand, we all know and know all too well the tragic events which have occurred in the Congo, that huge unhappy state which lies just to the north of Angola. I do not think I would be straining the truth to conclude that much of the Congo's problems result from the fact that the pressure of nationalism rapidly overtook the preparation of the necessary foundation essential to the peaceful and effective exercise of sovereign self-government. The important thing for us then is to ensure that similar conditions do not exist for the Angola of tomorrow. We believe that a beginning should be made promptly within that territory to foster that educational, social and economic development of which political development is an integral part, and to ensure the rapid attainment of political maturity within this area. As we know, political maturity is the crying need everywhere.

Last fall by Resolution 1542 the General Assembly considered that a number of Portuguese territories were non-self-governing within the meaning of Chapter XI of the Charter. The assembly spoke of an obligation which exists on the part of Portugal to transmit information under Chapter II of the Charter concerning these territories. The Assembly further invited the Government of Portugal to participate in the work of the Committee on Information from Non-self-governing Territories.[214]

I mention this because, in the view of my Government, the best course of action for Portugal and the best course of action to promote the interests of the people of Portuguese territories seems to be through cooperation with the United Nations. In our view the resolution to which I have just referred was an invitation to Portugal to work with members of this organization to ensure the more rapid progress of the peoples in Portuguese territories. I stress, gentlemen, the words "work with." The United States does not read any dark dangers into this resolution. This is a gesture of concern, a gesture of good will, and beyond that, an effort toward genuine cooperation in achievement of goals which are shared by all of us and which are recognized in the Charter of this organization.

Hence we hope that Portugal will proceed in accordance with

the resolution now before the Council. In doing so, it would, in the words of the Charter, work "to develop self-government, to take due account of the political aspirations of the peoples, and to assist them in the progressive development of their free political institutions, according to the particular circumstances of each territory and its peoples and their varying stages of advancement."

I hope that what I have said will be taken in the spirit in which it is intended—to encourage the peaceful evolution of a society in Angola in which men of all races can live together in harmony, with mutual respect for the different cultures and ways of life which now exist there.

The Cuban Complaint

APRIL 17, 1961

✡

*On October 18, 1960, the Cuban government had requested that
its complaint of United States aggression against Cuba be placed on
the General Assembly agenda. Assigned to the First Committee for
discussion, this complaint was not added to the agenda until April
17, 1961. Dr. Roa, Cuba's Minister of Foreign Affairs, opened the
debate by charging that on that very day Cuba had been invaded
by forces from Guatemala and Florida that were financed by the
United States.[215] Stevenson's forty-minute address to the First
Committee, printed below, was a categorical denial of any material
American support to an invasion. He said, however, that the
American people gave their complete moral support to Cuban patriots seeking to recover their betrayed homeland. Zorin sharply
chided Stevenson for his "clumsy attempt to distract Committee
members from the American interference in the affairs of Cuba."
Later that evening, Roa announced that an air attack was in
progress, which, he said, proved that the "mercenary invasion,
instigated, organized, provisioned, armed and financed by the Government of the United States is now progressively becoming a
direct military invasion."[216]*

*On April 18, Zorin presented Khrushchev's letter to Kennedy
and the official Soviet statement condemning the United States for
aiding the invaders and urging it to halt the aggression. Stevenson
spoke to the Committee, reading Kennedy's reply to Khrushchev,
and again argued that Castro had betrayed his own revolution.
Ahmed Shukairy, Minister of State for United Nations Affairs of
Saudi Arabia, stressed that if the Cuban charges were true, the
implied threats in the statements by Kennedy and Khrushchev*

might lead to a world conflagration. Seven Latin-American delega-
tions presented a draft resolution, which was passed on April 21,
urging the Organization of American States to assist in achieving a
solution to the crisis and requesting all members of the world
organization to refrain from any action that might further aggra-
vate existing tensions. On the evening of April 20, Stevenson gave
his third major address on the Cuban complaint. Although he re-
peated the denial of American aggression, he failed to answer the
pointed questions offered him by the representatives of the neutral
countries. When the Minister of Saudi Arabia pondered the seri-
ousness of the situation and quipped: "I doubt if the invaders have
come from the moon, but if not from the sky, nor Guatemala, nor
the shores of Florida, where indeed did they come from?" Steven-
son was silent.[217]

Later, when President Kennedy accepted full responsibility for
what came to be known as the "Bay of Pigs Fiasco," Stevenson's
further usefulness in the United Nations seemed, to some close
observers of the diplomatic scene, utterly destroyed. It was ap-
parent that Stevenson's image of the United States as a peace-
loving state and his high ethical values were tested severely during
this crisis. Herbert J. Muller writes:

. . . shortly after this speech on April 20 friends found Stevenson in a
shocked daze: he had at last been told the truth, learned that unwittingly
he had told the U.N. a clumsy lie. Feeling that he could never hand in
his resignation at so critical a moment as this, he felt worse when gossip
had it that Kennedy had referred to him as "my official liar." At the
U.N. he was pained most of all by the conclusion a foreign delegate
expressed to Norman Thomas: "What American can we ever be-
lieve?"[218]

Kenneth Davis writes: "His credibility was destroyed, his effec-
tiveness destroyed. He would have to resign. . . . And yet he
couldn't do that either! His resignation now would be a betrayal of
the President and the country at a moment of gravest peril, adding
to the already terribly high price of folly. What then could he do?
Nothing it seemed. He could only suffer helplessly in a trap whose

iron jaws mangled his spirit."[219] *Muller reflects: "Stevenson's book* Looking Outward *makes no mention, however, of another affair that engrossed him in the early months of his ambassadorship, the Bay of Pigs invasion. A disaster too complete and indefensible perhaps to deserve the name 'crisis,' this gave Stevenson the most humiliating experience of his whole public career.*"[220]

Fortunately, following the debate and the passage of the moderate Latin-American resolution, the General Assembly adjourned until autumn. Kennedy's remark to Ted Sorensen, "How could I have been so stupid?" showed that the President blamed himself as bitterly as ever Stevenson could blame him. Davis writes:

Stevenson also learned from Schlesinger, from [Harlan] Cleveland, from the President himself, that the White House had had no intention of deliberately deceiving its UN representative in order that he might function unwittingly (hence more convincingly) as part of the cover. . . . On the day before sending Schlesinger to New York to give Stevenson the first briefing on the forthcoming operation [his trip to Latin America that summer], Kennedy said: "The integrity and credibility of Adlai Stevenson constitute one of our great national assets. I don't want anything to be done which might jeopardize that."[221]

MR. CHAIRMAN, members of the committee,

Dr. Roa, speaking for Cuba, has just charged the United States with aggression against Cuba and invasion coming from Florida. These charges are totally false and I deny them categorically. The United States has committed no aggression against Cuba and no offensive has been launched from Florida or from any other part of the United States.

We sympathize with the desire of the people of Cuba—including those in exile who do not stop being Cubans merely because they could no longer stand to live in today's Cuba—we sympathize with their desire to seek Cuban independence and freedom. We hope that the Cuban people will succeed in doing what Castro's revolution never really tried to do: that is, to bring democratic processes to Cuba.

But as President Kennedy has already said, "There will not, under any conditions, be an intervention in Cuba by United States armed forces. This Government will do everything it possibly can, and I think it can meet its responsibilities, to make sure that there are no Americans involved in any actions inside Cuba." I wish to make clear also, that we would be opposed to the use of our territory for mounting an offensive against any foreign government.[222]

Dr. Roa has also charged my country—which fought for Cuban independence—with literally everything else, including releasing hounds against children and keeping slavery alive, and crucifying the mandates of man and God.

I must say if such lurid oratory is a fair example of Dr. Roa's literature, that I shall read more for entertainment if not for enlightenment.

We have heard Dr. Roa's colorful challenges and his denunciation of the United States paper on Cuba as the most low and astigmatic literature he has ever seen. Well, when it comes to astigmatism, I would remind Dr. Roa what the gospel says in the Book of Matthew, "And why behold thou the mote that is in thy brother's eye but consider not the beam that is in thine own eye."[223]

It is my privilege now to discuss some of the beams in Cuba's eyes about the United States.

But first let me say that on Saturday Dr. Roa paid me the compliment of saying that he was familiar with my books and writings and was therefore surprised by my attitude about events in Cuba. He said there must be two Stevensons.

Well, I confess that I am flattered that Dr. Roa has read some of my writings, but I am not sure that I equally appreciate his suggestion that I am so versatile that there are two of me.

Dr. Roa will find that on the subject of tyranny—be it of the Right or the Left—be it of the minority or the majority—be it over the mind, or spirit, or body of man—that I have only one view—unalterable opposition. That he evidently has not read what I think on that subject very carefully does not surprise me.

But if there are not two Stevensons, I suggest that on the subject of uprisings and communism Dr. Roa seems to have two views. Perhaps there are two Roas. In his book entitled *En Pie*, published in 1959, Dr. Roa included an essay on the Hungarian Revolution and its suppression by the Soviet Army. I should like to quote, if I could, certain brief portions of Dr. Roa's essay, in an English translation which although it may not do justice to the eloquence of the original language, nevertheless indicates Dr. Roa's views at that time: At that time he wrote:

The brutal methods employed by the Soviet army to suppress the patriotic uprising of the Hungarian people have given rise to the strongest feelings of repulsion on the part of the free world, and the repercussions of these feelings in the intellectual areas subject to the Kremlin are breaking up the dogmatic unity of the communist movement on the cultural level. The crimes, excesses and outrages perpetrated by the invaders have evoked strong censure and numerous desertions among the trained seals and charlatan lackeys of Moscow. The implacable brainwashing and systematic hardening of the sensibilities to which the heralds and palfreys of Marxist dichotomist doctrine are subject seems to have failed in this case.

Dr. Roa then cited what he called "representative opinions, judgments and pronouncements" of intellectuals in many countries of many political creeds, including the Communist, in condemnation of "Soviet infamies and depredations in Hungary," to use his own words. His essay concluded with this summation:

In Belgium, Holland, Norway, Sweden, England, Denmark and the United States of America, the most elevated men of science and the most eminent writers have closed ranks with the Hungarian patriots. The free voice of our America has already let itself be heard in a ringing document which I had the honor of signing. And also that of the Asiatic and African peoples who are fighting for the advent of a world wherein will reign justice, equality and respect for human rights.

If valor is not always accompanied by good fortune, nevertheless, the battles fought on behalf of liberty and culture against despotism and barbarism are never lost. The case of Hungary once more corroborates the patent validity of this statement.

Now, though it may seem paradoxical, Mr. Chairman and gentlemen, I must tell you that I am in entire agreement with the judgments in Dr. Roa's essay of 1959.

But in October, 1960, the Cuban Foreign Ministry under Dr.

Roa's direction gave an orientation lecture to its employees in which the Hungarian Revolution was characterized as follows:

The Hungarian counterrevolution of 1956 was directed by North American imperialism to divert world attention from the Suez aggression: participating in the counterrevolution were fascist elements of the former Nagy Government of Hungary, war criminals from West Germany and other foreign countries, leaders of the Roman Catholic church who had lost lands and political power, and members of the Hungarian Labor party, intellectuals and students who desired the restoration of capitalism; Soviet troops entered Hungary at the request of the legitimate government, and the U.S.S.R. also gave economic aid.

Well, gentlemen, for flexibility and agility, I am afraid I would have to concede that even two Stevensons are no match for one Roa.

In reading these conflicting characterizations of the Hungary Revolution, one by Dr. Roa and the other by his Ministry of Foreign Affairs, I was reminded of certain other parallels between Hungary and Cuba. The Castro regime and its foreign collaborators are using the same methods now to suppress the patriotic uprising of the Cuban people as were used in 1956 to suppress the Hungarian people. Cuban patriots are now called traitors, mercenaries, criminals and tools of imperialism, in the same way as the patriotic Hungarian workers of 1956 were then and are still being slandered by such false allegations.

Patriots become traitors and mercenaries evidently very quickly in the idiom of Dr. Roa. My recollection is that Batista said the same things using the same identical words to describe Dr. Castro, Dr. Roa and their countless associates who have fled from the tyranny in Cuba.[224]

No, Dr. Roa, our great champions of human freedom, Jefferson and Lincoln, will not have to be reburied because of our sympathy for today's freedom fighters, wherever they are.

Dr. Roa's description of the detailed reports in the United States papers and magazines about the activities of the Cuban refugees illustrates something that I hope no member here will overlook. It illustrates how free the press is in this country. We don't have to wonder what would happen if a newspaper in Havana exercised the same freedom. We don't have to wonder because it has already happened; the free press of Cuba has long since been crushed.

I want to remind the Committee that there was great sympathy in the United States for the proclaimed goals of the Cuban Revolution when it took place. As soon as the Castro regime came to power the United States accorded it prompt recognition; that in the spring of 1959 the United States stood ready to supply the Castro Government with economic assistance; that the hope of my fellow citizens has always been that Dr. Castro would live up to the pledges of freedom and democracy that he uttered from Sierra Maestra to the Cuban people.[225]

Instead, Dr. Castro chose to embark on a systematic betrayal of these pledges. He has presided over a methodical and shameless corruption of his own revolution. To conceal his program of betrayal, he has followed the classical course of all tyrants: he has raised the specter of a foreign enemy whose alleged malevolence can serve as an excuse for tightening the screws of tyranny at home. And so in the course of 1959 he began the anti-United States campaign that in recent months has risen to so strident a crescendo. He closed his door to the American Ambassador in Havana. He conjured up the ghost of a Yanqui imperialism. By demanding that the American Embassy in Havana be reduced to a handful of persons, he eventually forced our Government to break diplomatic and consular relations with his regime.

What is even more important, Dr. Castro has accompanied his attack on my country by an ever-widening assault on the entire hemisphere. We must not forget that Dr. Roa has described President Frondizi of Argentina in terms so revolting that I will not repeat them.[226] The official Cuban radio has poured shrill invective on the governments and on the leaders throughout the hemisphere—and the more democratic and progressive the government, the more the Castro regime recognizes it as a mortal enemy, and the more savage becomes its abuse.

In time his assault has expanded to include the whole conception of the inter-American system and the Organization of American States. Dr. Castro has repeatedly proclaimed his purpose, to quote his own words, "to convert the Cordillera of the Andes into the

Sierra Maestra of the hemisphere." He has avowed his ambition to overthrow the free governments of the Americas and to replace them by regimes modeled in his own tyrannical image. If Dr. Castro stands today an outlaw in the hemisphere, it is through his own desire, his own determination, his own decision to establish a new tyranny in Cuba. If the Castro regime is perishing it is from self-inflicted wounds.

What Dr. Roa seeks from us today is the protection of the Castro regime from the natural wrath of the Cuban people. We have all read the recent newspaper stories about these activities which he has described with such lurid oratory—of men who hope to return to Cuba for the purpose of establishing a free government in their homeland. At least some members of such groups have been captured or imprisoned or executed by Cuban firing squads. We have given asylum to tens of thousands of Cuban citizens who have been forced to flee from their homeland to these shores. These exiles nurse a natural burning desire to bring freedom to Cuba, and toward that end they work with the dedicated concentration which José Marti and other Cuban exiles in the United States have shown in the tradition which is now nearly one hundred years old.[227]

But what does the present Cuban regime have to fear from these groups? What accounts for Dr. Roa's agitation? Is Dr. Roa demanding that the Cuban exiles through the Americas be suppressed and controlled in the same ruthless manner as the people within Cuba today?

It cannot be that he fears the armed might of small armed bands of resistance fighters. His Prime Minister has often boasted of the armed strength of Cuba. Cuba has by far the largest ground forces of any country in Latin America, possessed, by Dr. Castro's own admission, with ample supplies of automatic rifles, machine guns, artillery, grenades, tanks and other modern armament obtained from his new friends. Well over 30,000 tons of Soviet equipment has arrived in the last few months. This includes at least 15 Soviet 50-ton tanks, 19 Soviet assault guns, 15 Soviet 35-ton tanks, 78 Soviet 76-mm field guns, 4 Soviet 122-mm field guns, and over 100 Soviet heavy machine guns. Over 200 Soviet and Czechoslovak military advisers are in Cuba, and over 150 Cuban military personnel have been sent to the bloc for training.

In view of all of this, we must look for the answer to Castro's fears somewhere else: in the internal situation in Cuba and in Prime Minister Castro's own experience with the difficulties which small dissident groups can cause for a dictator who has betrayed his own revolution, as in the case of Batista.

If the Cuban Government is so deeply concerned about a few isolated groups, it must be because Dr. Castro has lost confidence in his own people. He evidently really believes that small armed groups are likely to find support enough to become dangerous. If this is the case, it seems a remarkable confession of doubt as to whether his own people approve his regime and its practices and Dr. Castro is surely right to be afraid. Even with full government control of the press, the radio, television, all forms of communication, every evidence, including the daily defections of his close associates and supporters, suggests that the people of Cuba are rejecting this regime.

Let me make it clear that we do not regard the Cuban problem as a problem between Cuba and the United States. The challenge is not to the United States but to the hemisphere and its duly constituted body, the Organization of American States. The Castro regime has betrayed the Cuban revolution. It is now collaborating in organized attempts by means of propaganda, agitation and subversion to bring about the overthrow of existing governments by force and replace them with regimes subservient to an extra-continental power. These events help to explain why the Cuban Government continues to bypass the Organization of American States, even if they do not explain why Cuba, which is thus in open violation of its obligations under inter-American treaties and agreements, continues to charge the United States with violations of these same obligations.

Soon after the Castro government assumed power, it launched a program looking to the export of its system to other countries of the hemisphere, particularly in the Caribbean area. The intervention of Cuban diplomatic personnel in the internal affairs of other nations of the hemisphere has become flagrant. Cuban diplomatic

mercenaries. He is familiar with their contribution to the Revolution. The reasons for their defection are no mystery to him. Many
of them are his friends and associates of long standing both in
government service and at the University of Havana. Mr. Zorin,
on the other hand, might be excused perhaps for not being familiar
with the revolutionary background of some of these Cuban patriots. I think it might be instructive for him and for the members
of the Committee to know who some of these people are. They
make an impressive list: the first provisional President of the
Revolutionary Government, Dr. Manuel Urrutia, who had asserted in defiance of Batista and in defense of Castro the right of
Cubans to resort to arms to overthrow an unconstitutional government; the First Prime Minister, Dr. José Miro Cardona, who is
Chairman of the Revolutionary Council which seeks the rescue of
the betrayed revolution; and the first President of the Supreme
Court, Dr. Emilio Menendez.[231]

It also includes nearly two-thirds of Castro's first Cabinet, such
as Minister of Foreign Affairs Roberto Agramonte, Minister of
Treasury Rufo Lopez Fresquet, Minister of Labor Manuel Fer-
nandez, Minister of Agriculture Humberto Sori Marin, and Minister of Public Works Manuel Ray. In other fields a similar compila-
tion can be made: companions-in-arms of Fidel Castro such as
Sierra Maestra commanders Hubert Matos, Mino Diaz and Jorge
Sotus and rebel air force leaders such as Pedro Diaz Lanz and the
Verdaguer brothers; labor leaders such as David Salvador and
Amaury Fraginals; editors and commentators such as Bohemia
Director Miguel Angel Quevedo, Luis Conte Aguero, and the
notoriously anti-American José Pardo Llada; and even such confi-
dants as Juan Orta, the head of the Prime Minister's own offices.

The roster of disillusioned, persecuted, imprisoned, exiled, and
executed men and women who originally supported Dr. Castro—
and who are now labelled as "traitors and mercenaries" by Dr. Roa
because they tried to make the Castro regime live up to its own
promises—is long and getting longer. These are the men who are
now leading the struggle to restore the Cuban Revolution to its
original premises.

In his letter of February 23, circulated in Document A/4701,
Dr. Roa claims that it is the policy of the United States "to punish

the Cuban people on account of their legitimate aspirations for the political freedom, economic development and social advancement of the underdeveloped or dependent peoples of Latin America, Africa, Asia and Oceania." Such a ludicrous charge deserves no serious reply. But I should remind Dr. Castro that he had many friends in the United States at the time he took power in Cuba. The ideals which he then expressed of establishing honest and efficient government, perfecting democratic processes, and creating higher standards of living, full employment and land reform were welcomed warmly both in the United States and in other parts of the Western Hemisphere. I sincerely wish that was still the case.

The problem created in the Western Hemisphere by the Cuban revolution is not one of revolution. As President Kennedy said on March 13:

. . . political freedom must be accompanied by social change. For unless necessary social reforms, including land and tax reform, are freely made—unless we broaden the opportunity of all of our people—unless the great mass of Americans share in increasing prosperity—then our alliance, our revolution, and our dream and our freedom will fail. But we call for social change by free men—change in the spirit of Washington and Jefferson, of Bolivar and San Martin and Marti—not change which seeks to impose on men tyrannies which we cast out a century and a half ago. Our motto is what it has always been—progress yes, tyranny no.[232]

No, the problem is not social change—which is both inevitable and just. The problem is that every effort is being made to use Cuba as a base to force totalitarian ideology into other parts of the Americas.

The Cuban Government has disparaged the plans of the American states to pool their resources to accelerate social and economic development in the Americas. At the Bogota meeting of the Committee of Twenty-One in September, 1960, the Cuban Delegation missed few opportunities to insult the representatives of other American States and to play an obstructionist role. They refused to sign the Act of Bogota and thereby to take part in the hemisphere-wide cooperative effort of social reform to accompany programs of economic development. The Cuban official reaction to President Kennedy's "Alliance for Progress" program for the Americas was in a similar vein.[233] In a speech on March 12, 1961, Dr. Castro denounced the program, portraying it as a program of "alms" using "usurious dollars" to buy the economic independence and national dignity of the countries which participate in the program. This is insulting to the countries which participate in the program. But equally important, he chose to ignore the underlying premise of the program: a vast cooperative effort to satisfy the basic needs of the American peoples and thereby to demonstrate to the entire world that man's unsatisfied aspiration for economic progress and social justice can best be achieved by free men working within a framework of democratic institutions. The hostility of the Castro regime to these constructive efforts for social and economic progress in the Americas—and even the language—recalls the similar hostility of the U.S.S.R. to the Marshall Plan in Europe.

Dr. Castro has carefully and purposefully destroyed the great hope the hemisphere invested in him when he came to power two years ago. No one in his senses could have expected to embark on such a course as this with impunity. No sane man would suppose that he could speak Dr. Castro's words, proclaim his aggressive intentions, carry out his policies of intervention and subversion—and at the same time retain the friendship, the respect and the confidence of Cuba's sister republics in the Americas. He sowed the wind and reaps the whirlwind.

It is not the United States which is the cause of Dr. Castro's trouble: it is Dr. Castro himself. It is not Washington which has turned so many thousands of his fellow countrymen against his regime—men who fought beside him in the Cuban hills, men who risked their lives for him in the underground movements in Cuban cities, men who lined Cuban streets to hail him as the liberator from tyranny, men who occupied the most prominent places in the first Government of the Cuban Revolution. It is these men who constitute the threat—if threat there is—to Dr. Castro's hope of consolidating his power and intensifying his tyranny.

It is Dr. Castro's own policy which has deprived these men of the hope of influencing his regime by democratic methods of free elections and representative government. It is Dr. Castro who, by denying Cuban citizens constitutional recourse, has driven them toward the desperate alternative of resistance—just as Batista once did.

Let us be absolutely clear in our minds who these men are. They are not supporters of Batista; they fought as passionately and bravely against Batista as Dr. Castro himself.

They are not champions of the old order in Cuba: they labored day and night as long as they could to realize the promises of the Cuban Revolution.

They will not turn the clock back, either to the tyranny of Batista or to the tyranny of Castro: they stand for a new and brighter Cuba which will genuinely realize the pledge which Dr. Castro has so fanatically betrayed—the pledge of bread with freedom.

The problem which the United States confronts today is our attitude toward such men as these. Three years ago many American citizens looked with sympathy on the cause espoused by Castro and offered hospitality to his followers in their battle against the tyranny of Batista. We cannot expect Americans today to look with less sympathy on those Cubans who, out of love for their country and for liberty, now struggle against the tyranny of Castro.

If the Castro regime has hostility to fear, it is the hostility of Cubans, not of Americans. If today Castro's militia are hunting down guerrillas in the hills where Castro himself once fought, they are hunting down Cubans, not Americans. If the Castro regime is overthrown, it will be overthrown by Cubans, not by Americans.

I do not see that it is the obligation of the United States to protect Dr. Castro from the consequences of his treason to the promises of the Cuban Revolution, to the hopes of the Cuban people, and to the democratic aspirations of the Western Hemisphere.

It is because Dr. Castro has turned his back on the inter-American system that this debate marks so tragic a moment for all citizens of the Western Hemisphere. It is tragic to watch the historic aspirations of the Cuban people once again thwarted by tyranny. It is tragic to see bitterness rise within a family of nations united by so many bonds of common memory and common hope.

It is tragic to watch a despotic regime drive its own people toward violence and bloodshed. The United States looks with distress and anxiety on such melancholy events.

Our only hope is that the Cuban tragedy may awaken the people and governments of the Americas to a profound resolve—a resolve to concert every resource and energy to advance the cause of economic growth and social progress throughout the hemisphere, but to do so under conditions of human freedom and political democracy. This cause represents the real revolution of the Americas. To this struggle to expand freedom and abundance and education and culture for all the citizens of the New World the free states of the hemisphere summon all the peoples in nations where freedom and independence are in temporary eclipse. We confidently expect that Cuba will be restored to the American community and will take a leading role to win social reform and economic opportunity, human dignity and democratic government, not just for the people of Cuba, but for all the people of the hemisphere.

[*In a further intervention Ambassador Stevenson said:*]

I will detain you only a moment because I agree with Mr. Zorin's suggestion that we adjourn until this afternoon.

But I must intervene long enough to say that, while I was not here at the United Nations at that time, I recall no such complaints of aggression against a small country from Mr. Zorin when Castro's followers were organizing their revolt against Batista on the shores of the United States. Why is it that the distinguished Representative of the Soviet Union is so concerned about a revolt against Dr. Castro? Cuba is no smaller today than it was then, and far more defensible—thanks to the U.S.S.R.

An Ethic for Survival

MAY 23, 1961

✡

On May 23, 1961, Ambassador Stevenson was honored by the creation of a Foundation in his name at the Jewish Theological Seminary in New York City. In the speech, printed below, he pondered: "Strangely enough, in 1961, millions of persons the world over appear to be groping for new ethical guidelines as if they had never before been traced, or as if the old ones were no longer relevant. This seems to me curious, and I wonder if we can trace this uneasiness and search for a new ethic to the nuclear power balance between East and West. . . . It is no wonder that this is the anxious age and that we want an ethic—an ethic for survival." In this speech, he took pains to sketch the components of such an ethic, as it seems to me that he did throughout his public life, and as the title of this collection suggests.

On June 7, the Herbert H. Lehman Institute, of which the Stevenson Foundation was a part, took a full-page ad to solicit contributions to the Foundation. Stevenson called the Foundation in the ad: "an eloquent call for 'an ethic for survival' creating a $1,500,000 fund for the immediate establishment of the AES Foundation [which] will undertake a searching study of ethical traditions and will seek to discover how these concepts can help us cope with the urgent problems of our day."[234]

I CANNOT pretend to be an expert in a subject so vast and complex as ethics. But as an ex-politician I can assure you that it is very flattering to be asked to discuss it.

Dr. [Louis] Finkelstein and his associates at the Jewish Theological Seminary have devoted lives to study and reflection on this subject, and in their presence I feel most humble about expressing any views of my own.

But I *can* express my gratitude to all of you whose contributions have created a foundation in my name for the study of ethics in international relations. In my years in public life I have enjoyed many honors and I have been richly rewarded with the loyalty and confidence of many friends. But nothing has moved or pleased me more. I am grateful that you should consider my name to be a fitting symbol for such a noble undertaking. I hope your generosity has not exceeded your judgment!

But I am sure that the Stevenson Foundation, under the wise and understanding guidance of Dr. Finkelstein and this famous center of theology and thought, will make valuable contributions to the search for those enduring values which transcend the day-to-day frictions which beset the world.

Over the centuries scores of great men have laid down a mosaic of ethical concepts treating with almost every aspect of human life. Yet, strangely enough, in 1961 millions of persons the world over appear to be groping for new ethical guidelines as if they had never before been traced, or as if the old ones were no longer relevant. This seems to me curious, and I wonder if we can trace this uneasiness and search for a new ethic to the nuclear power balance between East and West. Certainly men everywhere are now living under a new shadow of fear as the horrendous and universal implications of nuclear holocaust become more apparent.

We are, it seems, inextricably caught up by a devouring Frankenstein of our own creation—so complex and so volatile that even those directing it appear unable to control it. I suppose that many of us even long for the good old days of limited war with conventional weapons. But with such mistrust in the world, while we dread to go forward we seem to be unable to go back or even to stop this death march.

As the apprehensions caused by this Damoclean power struggle have mounted in the breasts of men everywhere, they have responded with ineffective, piecemeal protests. War is no longer rational, we say, yet the response to our mistrust of one another is more lethal weapons. And then to loudly proclaim that we never plan to use them.

It is no wonder that this is the anxious age and that we want an ethic—an ethic for survival.

Yet the very fact that man is acutely aware that he can no longer resolve his differences by force may well prove to be the key to his salvation. But practical steps are needed—and quickly.

Mere awareness of peril has never been known to eliminate it. The world is still very much a pressure cooker, and new ways must be found to release its tensions through nondestructive channels.

I think a relevant precept to remember in our quest for a world ethic was first stated by Plato when he said: "The creation of a world of civilized order is the victory of persuasion over force." Implicit in Plato's practical thinking is the axiom that men will always be at odds over one thing or another. If such is the case, and so far there is little reason to doubt it, then we must devise means of equal durability for settling our contentions in a nonviolent manner.

It is for the realization of this end that the United Nations was founded. And for an organization so young and still so vulnerable, it has, in good measure, been successful. Its attempts to establish some international ethical standards, of international conduct and human rights, has made it a symbol of hope for millions of people all over the world.

A second and equally important precept is that men have as many similarities as they have differences and, as Prime Minister Nehru said: "We must learn to stress these similarities in order to create a harmonious atmosphere in which we can quietly and amicably work out our disagreements."[235]

These are grand precepts of incontestable validity, but what is to be done about implementing them, and who will do the job? It seems to me that most of the institutions and people needed to further better understanding among men or to arbitrate their differences already exist.

Most countries in the world have religions, laws, educated leaders, scholars, and great institutions of learning. Almost every country has access to the United Nations.

Buttressing all this are millions of other human beings who would like nothing better than to live in peace and friendship with their neighbors, be they down the block or on the other side of the world.

But, whether we care to admit it or not, diplomacy until very recently has been rooted in the Machiavellian principle that: "Where the safety or interests of the homeland are at stake there should be no question of reflecting whether a thing is just or unjust, humane or cruel, praiseworthy or shameful . . . one must take only that course of action which will secure the country's life and liberty."[236]

I suspect that many statesmen still hold to this basic tenet and certainly the Communists acknowledge no greater interest than their own.

But today's statesmen must seek to improve the state of the world as well as the state of the nation. If it was once true that decisions were based solely on the interests of the state, it is now equally true that power politics and war are anachronistic. Today the ideals of individual dignity and liberty, and a human community transcending national boundaries, are the growing notions and the unfolding hope of world community and peace.

In relations among men, it is not enough to help those who are at a disadvantage, but it is necessary also to save, and if possible to increase their self-respect. Perhaps the most significant contribution of the New Deal to our life was not the fact that it brought security and help to many who lacked both before, but that it gave it to them as a right, as citizens of our country, and not as charity, for which one expected gratitude and which was to be accepted with appropriate humility.

The problem of our time hinges to some extent on whether this principle can be applied also among nations. We in America are certainly expending more on the help of less advantageously placed peoples than has ever been expended by any other people. Yet something more is needed—a contribution to the sense of self-respect, of dignity of these ancient societies and civilizations, which are now emerging into effective influence on the world.

How to develop this self-respect among peoples who have never known it as individuals, and having dimly felt it as tribes and nations are losing it in confrontation with the powerful of the earth, is a challenge to our ingenuity, and our wisdom.

Much has already been achieved through the establishment of the United Nations. Once more, we have created an institution, in which the weakest of peoples has a voice, and a vote, which in difficult moments is sought by the powerful.

Yet there remains one aspect of the self-respect of peoples. Like the individuals composing them, so nations and states are more than bodies. They also are minds, and their minds require a sense of dignity, no less than their bodies.

When this sense of dignity is denied them, it is frequently replaced with belligerent and even chauvinistic, unrealistic and unthinking nationalism, which astounds the older and more highly developed peoples. We see this so often among the new countries. But the ferocity and narrowness which are born out of self-depreciation, cannot be exorcised except by appreciation. And this appreciation should itself be offered not as charity, but as a human right. That the small states exercise such decisive influence in the United Nations, for example, is a major contribution to this appreciation, this right, and we can hope that the consciousness of their power in this new forum can and will help to develop self-appreciation, self-confidence and dignity among the new states.

If there were no reason to respect ancient, and what are often called primitive societies and cultures, we could not by sheer will develop that feeling toward them. But fortunately for mankind, there is, in every culture and every society, much that everyone can respect, and from which everyone can learn. There is no group of people so mean and so humble that they have only to be our pupils, and cannot in any respect offer us instruction. That in fact is one of the distinctive qualities of *Homo sapiens*. Wherever he has organized himself as a society (and he has done so wherever he exists), he has created a tradition, a system of sanctions and habits which we might properly call "law," a language, a collective, as well as an individual, conscience.

In each of these traditions, systems of sanctions, and dialects of morals, there is a residue of what might be called wisdom. Much of what is done in the name of this wisdom may seem to us of another world, utter folly, just as no doubt much of what we do must seem bizarre to peoples of other backgrounds.

Certainly, we of the West can scarcely boast of the manner in which we have twice in our time fumbled our way into the most ferocious of all wars, and seem to be preparing for a third even more destructive. No folly perpetrated in any simple and primitive culture can approach the collective folly, as exhibited in the tragedy of the two world wars of the first half of this century, and the menace of a possible third one in the second half.

Yet despite these follies, and those attendant on them, like the worldwide rise in the rate of crime, especially among the youth, Western civilization certainly contains, as no one will deny, much that is wise, and which other peoples could ponder to their benefit. May this not be likewise true of the primitive races? And may it not be that one of the gravest failures of Western thought has been its underestimate of this residue of wisdom in other societies than its own?

Perhaps none of us has ever thought of the Tibetan people, who in our time have been exposed to so much suffering, as one by whom we could be instructed. Their manners and ways certainly seemed strange to most people. What was one to think of a people which considered it wrong to destroy even the most pestiferous insect? And yet is there not something for us to learn from this astonishing respect for life, where it is impossible for a cultured person to kill a fly, as it might be for a similarly situated person among us to walk naked through the streets?

Is it possible that one of the world's urgent needs in our time is really a collective Socrates, who was in his time called by the Oracle of Delphi, the wisest of men, solely, he maintains, because he alone knew his shortcomings and tried so hard to learn from all men.

What a remarkable pedagogue he was, who was able to give his young disciples instruction, while at the same time increasing their self-confidence in their own ability to think. And what a glorious place in the annals of history awaits that group of people, and that institution, which seeks above all to make sure that those whom it encounters, realize that they have much to teach.

So I therefore applaud the efforts being made by your Seminary under the guidance and leadership of Dr. Finkelstein to create just such a forum and institution. What has been achieved by your Institute for Religious and Social Studies and by the Conference on Science, Philosophy and Religion, which it sponsors, by the Herbert H. Lehman Institute on Ethics, by your radio and television programs in this area is already impressive. It is perhaps significant that while it cannot be said that the publications of the Conference on Science, Philosophy and Religion are popular reading in this country, I am told some of them have gone through eight editions in Japan.

It is not an accident that an institution, which stands at the apex of your own Jewish tradition, should be so concerned with the problem of mutual respect of men. All great religions and philosophies share the doctrine that men must learn to love and respect one another, and that they have to discover in each other that which demands respect and love. But in your instance, history fortifies this tradition, in a special way. You know as scripture puts it "the spirit of the stranger," for during centuries you have suffered indignity and persecution, probably unparalleled both in extent and continuity in the history of any other people.

And surprisingly in our own civilized century and our highly civilized Western world, your brethren underwent greater torment and suffering than any recorded in your own long history. Yet throughout this period of suffering and indignity, your ancestors knew how to preserve their soul and mind: seeing in their tradition something worth not only dying for but for which they were willing to court contumely and disdain. They had a purpose to fulfill in the human drama, and the cost to themselves as individuals or as a group mattered little, if at all. Not all peoples have such a built-in machinery for the preservation of their own sense of dignity; but intuitively, you, scholars and laymen alike, recognize its importance.

From this, I take it springs the desire manifested by so many of you here tonight to continue and to expand this aspect of the labors of the great institution in whose name you are gathered here.

Your desire to expand and perpetuate the aspect of your work dealing with ethics and human relations, your aspiration to hold conferences under the aegis of your institute for religious and social studies in other parts of the world, and your ultimate goal of a world academy, which will devote itself solely to the extraction of the wisdom implicit in various intellectual and cultural traditions, seems to me not only praiseworthy, but to hold forth a promise of great good to mankind.

So it is important for religions to explore those common human values which give people everywhere a sense of belonging to a common world community. For if the growing self-consciousness of national cultures increases, the creedal differences in religious systems may be exploited to accentuate tension in the world society.

We would then have, as we have had in the past, the anomaly of universalist religions undermining world brotherhood.

So I see a great opportunity here to further the search for those enduring values which transcend the divisive frictions between nations. While each country supports its national interest through an ethical rationalization, human progress can only be achieved if a way is found to identify the ethical ideas which are the basis for long-range goals helpful to all men.

I am proud and grateful to be identified with such healing scholarship. And I would be even more honored and grateful if the foundation just established in my name held an occasional seminar for statesmen. If they could be induced to divorce themselves for even a few days from the griminess of daily politics and plunge into this new Walden Pond, they will, I feel, be much better leaders the rest of the year.

The First Business of This Dangerous World:
Disarmament
NOVEMBER 15, 1961

✡

The problem of disarmament, which Stevenson called the General Assembly's most pressing single issue, was the first order of business in 1945. Speaking during the sixteenth session, he recalled that the American delegation in 1945 had offered to destroy its atomic weapons and to prohibit the future manufacture of such weapons.[237] On August 30, 1961, the Soviet Union announced its intention to resume its atmospheric tests of nuclear and thermonuclear bombs. Stevenson denounced the breaking of the moratorium in a brief but sharply-worded press release. Still, negotiations between the Soviet Foreign Minister and the American Secretary of State continued. On September 20, Zorin and Stevenson submitted a Joint Statement of Agreed Principles for Disarmament Negotiations. In an address to the General Assembly on September 25, entitled "Let Us Call a Truce to Terror," President Kennedy urged the adoption of such a disarmament treaty. In October, eighty-seven national delegations approved a resolution appealing to the Soviet Union to refrain from exploding its pre-announced fifty-megaton bomb. On October 30, when Zorin stated that a bomb even larger than fifty megatons had been set off, Stevenson stated tersely:

By this arrogant act, the Soviets have added injury to insult.
They broke the moratorium on nuclear weapons testing.
They have raised atmospheric pollution to new heights.
They have started a new race for more deadly weapons.
They have contemptuously spurned the appeal of the

United Nations and of all peace-loving peoples.
They have advanced no justification for exploding this
monstrous and unnecessary weapon.
They have been wholly unmoved by the dangers of radio-
active fallout.
The United States Delegation deeply deplores this great
leap forward—by the Soviet Union—in the direction of
disaster.[238]

He further called the explosion "a violence unheard-of in human
history" and "the greatest and most lethal explosion in human
history."

Zorin began the debate on the "Question of Disarmament" in the
First Committee on November 15 by offering a noble theme: "The
essence of disarmament is simple; to prevent the use of the horrible
weapons for the destruction of human beings; such weapons them-
selves must be destroyed."[239] *While he praised the joint statement*
of the Soviet and American delegations on agreed joint principles,
he argued that the aggressive policies of the United States and its
insistence on a system of controls seriously complicated the
problem.

In his fifty-seven-minute reply, Stevenson agreed that the issue
was the most important discussion of the entire United Nations
history and for the survival of mankind. He painted a grim word-
picture of the alternative to a "warless world" when

great areas and great places have been turned into radioactive waste-
land—when millions upon millions of people are already dead while
debris from those great mushroom clouds drifts ghoulishly over the
living; when great parts of our institutions, ideologies, faiths and be-
liefs—even our art and literature—lie smashed in the smoke and rubble
of material destruction.

In his reply, immediately after Stevenson's speech, Zorin chided
him for "upbraiding" the Soviet Union, saying:

Excuse me, Mr. Representative of the United States, you came out
against our position not from the point of view of the general demand
of mankind, but from the point of view of your own military

interests. . . . There is not a shred of humanism, not an iota of human-
itarian consideration that you need now; what you need, what you
preserve, is the military interest of the United States. There is your
humanism; there is your morality, Mr. Representative of the United
States. Therefore, it is not suitable for you to preach to us.[240]

Stevenson's rebuttal was immediate and stinging: "I must say that I
have underrated Mr. Zorin's capacity for talking. I have him to
thank, however, for one of the crudest lessons in hypocrisy that I
have ever listened to. . . . Let us cut out this rhetoric and get
down to the business of our meeting here. You voted for a mora-
torium and then you broke it. When we vote, we mean it."[241]

The speech printed below is also published in a much abbrevi-
ated form and with the same title in Looking Outward.

THE earlier portions of the remarks by the distinguished Representative of the Soviet Union were devoted to a repetition of the
Soviet version of the problem of Berlin and of Germany. While
this is quite irrelevant, I must remind the committee for the record
that it is clear that the Berlin problem is a problem created by the
Soviet Union for its own purposes. It is the Soviet Union which is
trying to breach the agreements on Berlin. It is the Soviet Union
which has illegally erected a wall which divides that city. It is the
Soviet Union which is seeking to perpetuate the division of
Germany.

Regarding the Soviet desire to liquidate what they call the
vestiges of the war, I would remind the committee that the Soviet
Union regards as vestiges of the war only what is not to its liking,
that is, the Western presence in Berlin, the freedom of movement
within that city, and the hope for the reunification of Germany. It
evidently does not regard as a vestige of the war such things as the
division of Germany and of Berlin.

It calls this a situation brought about by life itself. But this problem of Germany is not before us today and I have no intention of
pressing this matter further, but rather propose to turn my attention to the item on our agenda which is disarmament.

If I understood Mr. Zorin, he said that the American plan was
ambiguous about the production, for example, of arms and fission-

able materials. I would invite his attention to Paragraph C of Stage Three which reads as follows: "The manufacture of armaments would be prohibited except for those of agreed types and quantities to be used by the United Nations peace force and those required to maintain internal order. All other armaments would be destroyed or converted to peaceful purposes." But such misstatements will be dealt with when the details of disarmament are discussed.

I agree with Mr. Zorin that this subject of disarmament is the most important question before this committee and, indeed, before this General Assembly. I only wish that his misleading and frequently abusive speech had produced something new and some encouragement for real disarmament. I earnestly hope that on examination the draft resolution which he has presented to me just now will give us some greater hope than the speech portends.[242]

War is one of our oldest institutions. It is deeply imbedded in the traditions, the folkways, the literature, even the values of most all countries. It has engaged talented men and produced national heroes. At the same time, civilized men and women for centuries past have abhorred the immorality of organized killing of men by men.

Yet let us confess at once, to our common shame, that this deep sense of revulsion has not averted wars, nor shortened one by a day.

While I do not say that all wars have been started for unworthy purposes, let us also confess—morality to the side—that most all past wars have served to promote what was conceived to be the national or princely or religious interests of those who fought them—or at least those who won them. For in past wars, there have been winners as well as losers—the victors and the vanquished —the decorated and the dead. In the end, valuable real estate and other riches have changed hands. Thrones have been won—regimes transferred—rule extended—religions and ideologies imposed—empires gained and lost—aggressions halted or advanced. Thus, wars in the past have sometimes been a means of settling international disputes, of changing political control, of inducing social transformation, and even of stimulating science and technology.

And I suppose that on moral grounds it is only a difference of degree whether millions are killed or only thousands—whether the victims include children in the debris of a big city building or only young men lying on a battlefield in the countryside. Nor has war been a very efficient way of settling disputes. Yesterday's enemies are today's friends. First, the victor pays for destruction of his enemy, then for reconstruction of his friend.

But war in the future would differ fundamentally from war in the past—not in degree but in kind. It is this which seems so difficult to grasp. Thermonuclear war can not serve anyone's national interest—no matter how moral or immoral that interest may be—no matter how just or unjust—no matter how noble or ignoble—regardless of the nation's ideology, faith or social system.

It is no satisfaction to suggest that the issue of morality in war thus has become academic. Yet this is the fact and perhaps it will serve to clarify the dialogue of war and peace. For we can now free our collective conscience of nice ethical distinctions, and face the stark, amoral fact that war has ceased to be practical—that no nation can contemplate resort to modern war except in defense against intolerable exaction or aggression. Therefore we must abolish war to save our collective skins. For as long as this nuclear death dance continues, millions—tens of millions—perhaps hundreds of millions are living on borrowed time.

I suggested a moment ago that war is such an ancient institution —so deeply entrenched in tradition—that it requires a strenuous intellectual effort to imagine a world free from war. So it does, and I shall have more to say about this later.

But I submit that the alternative effort is to imagine a world at the end of another war—when great areas and great places have been turned into radioactive wasteland—when millions upon millions of people are already dead while debris from those great mushroom clouds drifts ghoulishly over the living; when great parts of our institutions, ideologies, faiths and beliefs—even our art and literature—lie smashed in the smoke and rubble of material destruction.

I submit that however difficult the vision of a world *without war* may be, it is not only a happier but an easier vision to imagine than one of a world *after war*. In any event, we must choose between them.

It is against this bleak reality that we meet once again, Mr. Chairman, to take up the subject of disarmament.

The story of man's efforts to do away with armaments is a long and sorry one.

At various times this or that measure of disarmament has seemed within our grasp.[243] My own country has a proud record in this respect. We supported the two Hague Conferences.[244] We took the lead in naval disarmament after World War I. We did our utmost to make the comprehensive Disarmament Conference of 1932 a success.[245] And after World War II we stripped our armed forces to the bone, in the hope and belief that we had made some progress toward a peaceful world.

Disarmament was one of the first orders of business for the United Nations. Fifteen years ago, at the first meeting of this Assembly, the United States Delegation, of which I was a member, made a proposal as revolutionary as the scientific discovery which prompted it.

At that time we proposed to destroy the few atomic weapons which the United States alone possessed—to outlaw forever the manufacture of such weapons—to place the development of atomic energy in all its forms under the full control of the United Nations and to turn over to this organization all facilities and all information bearing on atomic science and technology; all this to prevent an atomic arms race.

The world does not need to be reminded here of the tragic consequences of the rejection of that initiative of a decade and a half ago. Since then there has been a long series of commissions, committees, subcommittees and conferences, inside the United Nations and out, which have tried to deal with the question of general disarmament and first steps toward it.

After the Soviet Delegation walked out of the Ten-Power General Disarmament talks in June 1960,[246] our main hopes were focused on the Three-Power negotiations at Geneva for a treaty to ban the testing of atomic weapons.

After two and a half years of patient negotiations—in the course of which significant progress was made—the United States and Britain tabled a comprehensive treaty which they had every reason to believe would meet the remaining points of difference with the Soviet Union. The United States and Britain were prepared to sign a comprehensive treaty at once—and still are.

Then on the last day of last August came the shocking news that the Soviet Union would break the moratorium which it had advocated and vowed never to break. The United States and Britain immediately offered to agree with the Soviet Union to ban at once all tests in the atmosphere without inspection—to spare mankind the hazards of radioactive fallout. We regret that, like the Baruch proposals,[247] this offer was also rejected by the Soviet Union.

Since that time the Soviet Union has carried on a series of nuclear weapons tests with unprecedented pollution of the atmosphere. It was climaxed by the explosion of history's most appalling weapon, a super-bomb of more than 50 megatons, or more than 50 million tons of TNT. This weapon's destructive power exceeds any known military requirements. So its principal purpose is to serve the political strategy of terror.

This action was taken in disregard of pleas from governments and peoples all over the non-Communist world—and, finally, in defiance of an unprecedented resolution of the United Nations General Assembly supported by eighty-seven nations.

To all our pleas the Soviet Union, for months past, has invariably replied that it will agree to a ban on nuclear tests only as part of an agreement for general and complete disarmament. By insisting on this link between an issue which we had nearly resolved and the difficult issue of disarmament, the Soviet Union has tightened the knot and made it harder than ever to untie. Only last Thursday the General Assembly rejected the idea of delaying a test-ban treaty by calling once again, by a vote of 71 to 11, for the urgent resumption of negotiations to outlaw nuclear tests.

So let me point out at once to the distinguished Representative of the Soviet Union that it is his country alone which insists on making a genuine and effective test ban dependent on the achievement of general disarmament. And because it does so insist, the Soviet Union, as we now move into the debate on general and complete disarmament, becomes *doubly* answerable to world opinion. The world will look to them in this debate to answer not one but two burning questions: do you or don't you want disarmament? and—once again—do you or don't you want an end to nuclear weapons, in fact or just in rhetoric?

And yet there is this much connection between the two subjects: the advance in weapons technology as a result of tests must ultimately increase our common peril. It is a measure of the tragic failure of all our efforts to reach disarmament agreements. And it is a compelling challenge to my government to try again—to make a fresh start—to insist with the utmost urgency that the weapons which have made war an obsolete institution be laid aside quickly before others are forced in self-defense to carry this insensate race yet another stage toward ultimate folly.

No doubt there are those who will ask how we can dare realistically to speak of disarmaments today—when the winds of conflict blow all about us. There are those who will ask whether this is mere wishful thinking—whether this is more than escapism.

To that we would reply: escapism, no—escape, yes. For man *must* escape—not in wishful dreams, but in hard reality. We *must* escape from this spiral of fear from the outmoded illusion that lasting security for peoples can be found by balancing out the wildly destructive power in the hands of their governments.

As President Kennedy said to the General Assembly on September 25:

Today, every inhabitant of this planet must contemplate the day when it no longer may be habitable. Every man, woman and child lives under a nuclear sword of Damocles, hanging by the slenderest of threads, capable of being cut at any moment by accident, miscalculation, or madness. The weapons of war must be abolished before they abolish us.

President Kennedy informed the General Assembly then that the United States has prepared a new set of proposals for general and complete disarmament. These proposals were circulated subsequently to all members.

He also outlined my Government's conception of what is needed to create a world without war. It is a view which embraces first steps, subsequent steps, and the ultimate goal at the end of the road. And it goes far beyond the technical steps in arms reduction. It requires the reservation of outer space for peaceful uses. It includes international programs for economic and social progress. And it insists especially upon the essential need to build up the machinery of peace while we tear down the machinery of war—that these must go hand-in-hand—that these, indeed, must be but two parts of a single program.

For in a world without arms, military power would be taken out of the hands of nations; but other forms of power would remain—and mostly in the hands of the same states which are the most powerful military states today.

Conflicting ideologies would still be with us.

Political struggles would still take place.

Social systems would still be subject to disruptive pressures from within and without.

Economic strength would still be a factor in—and an instrument of—national foreign policies.

And the world would still be the scene of peaceful transformation—for it cannot and should not remain static.

Let us be clear about all this:

Disarmament alone will not purify the human race of the last vestiges of greed, ambition and brutality—of false pride and the love of power. Nor will it cleanse every last national leader of the least impulse to international lawlessness. No sane and honest man can pretend to foresee such a paradise on earth—even an earth without arms. But it would be a safer earth where the contest and conflict could be waged in peace.

Clearly, then, disarmament will not usher in utopia. But it will prevent the wanton wastage of life and the wholesale destruction of material resources. And it will free the energies of man to engage in beneficent pursuits. How much could be done to improve the conditions of man—his education, his health, his nutrition and his housing—if even a small portion of the funds and the ingenuity of man now devoted to improving the art of killing were transferred to improving the art of living!

Who would keep the peace in a disarmed world? How would our disputes get settled when arms have been taken away?

If we can answer these questions we are much nearer to a solution of the problem of disarmament. For these questions open up the unexplored ground between first steps toward disarmament and the vision at the end of the road. And the vision of a world free from war will remain a utopian illusion until means for keeping the peace lend it reality.

It, therefore, seems clear to me that the only way to general and complete disarmament lies along two parallel paths which must be traveled together. One leads to the absence of arms; the other to the presence of adequate machinery for keeping the peace. As we destroy an obsolete institution for the settlement of disputes we must create new institutions for the settlement of disputes—and simultaneously.

Let me repeat for emphasis. We do not hold the vision of a world without conflict. We do hold the vision of a world without war—and this inevitably requires an alternative system for coping with conflict. We cannot have one without the other. But if we travel the two roads together—if we build as we destroy—we can solve the technical problems of dismantling the vast apparatus of war.

Let me come now to the United States proposals for dismantling the towering and costly machinery of war.

To begin with, the United States emphatically embraces the commitment to general and complete disarmament. We proclaim the goal—without reservation—and in the shortest possible span of time. And we take this terminology to mean exactly what it says— the general and complete disarmament of all national forces capable of international aggression, and the safe disposal of all their arms.

It is interesting to note that the Conference of Non-aligned Nations which met in Belgrade in September of this year demonstrates how widely shared our goal is. I quote their words:

"The participants in the Conference consider that disarmament is an imperative need and the most urgent task of mankind. A radical solution of this problem, which has become an urgent necessity in the present state of armaments, in the unanimous view of participating countries, can be achieved only by means of a general, complete and strictly and internationally controlled disarmament."[248]

Mr. Chairman, the United States proposal is, indeed, a "radical" one.

It calls for large reductions of armaments even in the first stages—both conventional and nuclear armaments.

It calls for an end to production of fissionable materials for weapons purposes—and the transfer of such materials from existing stocks for non-weapons use.

The program calls for a stop in the further development of independent national nuclear capabilities.

It calls for the destruction or conversion to peaceful uses of strategic nuclear weapons delivery vehicles.

It calls for an end to the production of such delivery vehicles.

It calls for the abolition of chemical, biological and radioactive weapons.

In short, the United States program calls for the total elimination of national capacity to make international war. And, to ensure that all these steps are actually carried out by each side, every step of the way, the plan calls for the creation of an International Disarmament Organization within the framework of the United Nations.

If the United States program is comprehensive, it also is flexible. It does not pretend to be the final word—nor would we wish it to be. We expect it to be examined exhaustively—to be altered and to be improved. It certainly is not perfect, but it can stand up to close scrutiny—for it has been prepared at great pains and in good faith. It is presented in dead earnest—and in the conviction that propaganda on the subject of disarmament is a cynical and cruel mockery of man's deepest hope.

At one point and one point alone the United States is, and will remain, inflexible—this is on the familiar question of verification—on the indispensable need for the world to know that disarmament agreements are, in fact, being carried out. Because of the confusion that persists on this point, I must dwell upon it for a moment.

First of all, verification must be understood not as a technical point but as a fundamental principle—as the essential condition for any significant progress in disarmament—as its *sine qua non*. To pretend that there is enough confidence between the major armed powers to accept disarmament without verification is to deny the existence of the arms race itself. For the arms race is nothing if not living proof of the absence of mutual trust, and confidence has been rudely shaken by recent events.

I will say quite bluntly that mistrust exists on our side—and how could it be otherwise? The hostility of Soviet leaders toward my country, its institutions and its way of life is proclaimed, documented and demonstrated in a thousand ways. Yet we earnestly seek agreement with them—through diplomatic methods—and through agreements recorded in words and deeds. So we may be excused, it seems to me, if we are wary of agreements deeply involving our national security with a nation whose recent leader wrote this: "Good words are a mask for the concealment of bad deeds. Sincere diplomacy is no more possible than dry water or iron wood."[249]

These are the words of the late Marshal Stalin. I am aware that his former absolute authority has been subject to a certain reevaluation recently. But the present Premier of the Soviet Union, who served Stalin so loyally, still proclaims his indebtedness to Lenin. And after the Treaty of Brest-Litovsk[250] Lenin said this: "We must demobilize the army as quickly as possible, because it is a sick organ; meanwhile we will assist the Finnish Revolution. Yes, of course we are violating the Treaty; we have violated it thirty or forty times."

More recently we have seen wholesale violation of agreements pledging self-determination to the peoples of Eastern Europe—not to mention so contemporary an event as the erection of a wall through the middle of a city in violation of a postwar agreement.

Mr. Chairman, I do not mention these matters to belabor the dead, nor to rub salt in wounds both old and fresh, nor to becloud the disarmament problem with irrelevant questions. They are not irrelevant—because there can be no disarmament without agreement—and because clear warnings and harsh experience have taught us to insist upon independent and international verification of agreements with the Soviet Union.

Our deepest hope—our most fervent prayer—is for proof that this acquired lack of trust will no longer be justified. Meanwhile, we do not ask that those who are suspicious of us take us at our word. We offer to them the same guarantees that we have the right and duty to demand of them. We offer to submit to verification procedures under international control at each step of disarmament.

Let me assure you, Mr. Chairman [Mario Amadeo of Argentina], that the United States has no interest in controls for the sake of controls. We do not wish to buy control or to trade something for it. We have no stake in playing the host to teams of foreign inspectors within our borders. But there is no other way to dispel mistrust—to exorcise suspicion—to begin to build the mutual confidence upon which peaceful cooperation ultimately depends.

So we accept the need for adequate verification procedures. We recognize the right of others to assure themselves that we in fact do what we say we shall do with respect to disarmament.

But in the meantime we must find a basis for workable agreement.

Last spring, as delegates here will recall, this committee agreed to postpone further discussion of disarmament so that the United States and the Soviet Union could "exchange views on questions relating to disarmament and to the resumption of negotiations in an appropriate forum whose composition was to be agreed upon."

Beginning on June 19 and ending on September 19, meeting in Moscow, Washington, and New York, representatives of the Soviet Union and the United States discussed these two questions. The results of these talks were reported to the General Assembly by the United States and the Soviet Union in a Joint Statement of Agreed Principles, which is before this committee, Document A/4879.

This report shows that, although our conversations did not bring complete success, neither did they bring complete failure.

We were unable to agree on a forum for negotiations. But we did agree on a set of principles to guide negotiations on disarmament.

The U.S. Government welcomed this limited agreement with some hope—especially since the Soviet and American delegates agreed quite explicitly to the implementation of all disarmament measures from beginning to end, under international control. This looked like a very bright spot on a dark horizon—perhaps a real breakthrough toward a world without arms.

But, Mr. Chairman, our hopes have been restrained by the Soviet refusal to follow through on this aspect of the agreed principles. In his address to the Plenary Meeting of the General Assembly on September 26, Mr. Gromyko made the following statement:

After all, no one knows right now what armaments and armed forces the states possess. This is quite normal. For perfectly obvious reasons states do not reveal that kind of information and the same situation will endure after the implementation of disarmament measures provided for in this or that state, pending the completion of general and complete disarmament.[251]

What can this possibly mean? The meaning is that to our Soviet colleagues, inspection should apply to the destruction of armaments—but not to existing armaments or the production of new ones.

Apparently we are being asked to establish an elaborate international inspection force simply to witness the destruction of certain quantities and categories of arms with no knowledge of what remains—to watch while one weapon is junked without seeing whether two others are in production to take its place—perhaps in reality to certify the disposal of inventories of obsolete equipment. I am reminded of the story of the little boy who was showing off his conjuring tricks and said to his parents: "I am going to do some magic for you, but you have to promise not to look."

The Soviet position thus seems to be the same as it was when the Representative of the Soviet Union, Mr. Zorin, addressed a letter to the U.S. Disarmament Representative, Mr. McCloy, on September 20, at the conclusion of the bilateral Soviet-American disarmament negotiations. Mr. McCloy had noted that the Soviet Union had refused to accept, in the statement of Agreed Principles, a clause reading "such verification should ensure that not only agreed limitations or reductions take place, but also that retained armed forces and arms do not exceed agreed levels at any stage."

Now, Mr. President, this sentence seemed to us to represent a *sine qua non* for any effective verification and control. But in his reply Mr. Zorin insisted that such control—that is, control over the armed forces and armaments retained by states at any given stage of disarmament—would turn into what he called an international system of recognized espionage.

If it is the position of the Soviet Union that verification of agreed levels of armaments retained by states under a disarmament plan is espionage, then clearly there can be no general and complete disarmament agreement, for armaments destroyed are of less concern to us than armaments retained. It is the latter and not [the] former which states attacked in war would have to fear. No matter how many weapons were destroyed it would be the weapons which were left that would be utilized in a military operation. This is a stumbling block which could be crucial. Unless we can get a clear and satisfactory agreement on this particular point, it is difficult to envisage very substantial progress in disarmament negotiations.

For under the Soviet concept of disarmament inspection, the arms race could continue and the arsenals of war could be larger and deadlier at the end of the first stage of "disarmament" than at the beginning. In short, we would disarm in public and be perfectly free to rearm in secret.

Mr. Chairman, this interpretation turns common sense on its head and makes mockery of logic. This turns reason into gibberish, meaning into nonsense, words into water.

The purpose of disarmament is to abolish war precisely by abolishing the means of making war—which is to say the armaments and armed forces with which wars are fought. If disarmament does not mean the reduction of the actual levels of armament it has no meaning at all.

I can only hope that Soviet delegates will not persist in their attitude. If I have misunderstood the position, I shall be happy to be informed, and we can go forward. For on their face, the principles agreed between the United States and the U.S.S.R. do provide sound and workable guidelines for serious disarmament negotiations—and I prefer to think that they represent an important step in the right direction.

This brings us to the question of the proper forum. During our exchanges with the Soviet Union on this point, we of the United States tried to reach agreement on a formula which could then be recommended to the other states concerned. Our position on the exact representation was and still is flexible. These proposals can be found in Document A/4880. In fact, we suggested four possible alternative solutions, but to no avail. The Soviet Union continued to insist on a formula which we felt was restrictive and based on artificial and arbitrary criteria.

Quite frankly, we have grown a little weary of the repeated Soviet demands for changes in the negotiating forum on disarmament. The history of the disarmament talks is full of them. The Ten-Nation Committee was established at Soviet insistence. This was because they seemed to set great store by what they called "parity" in numbers of delegations between their side and the West—even though on the Western side there are several major powers, and on their side there has been only one. Then when the Soviets found that the negotiations in the Ten-Nation Committee were not to their liking, they abruptly broke off the talks and demanded an entirely new forum.

Now the latest Soviet proposal for altering the forum into three "groups" is all too reminiscent of the Soviet view, which is quite extraneous to disarmament and quite unacceptable to many other nations—the view that the world can be neatly divided into three so-called blocs.

The United States recognizes that all nations have a vital stake in the cause of peace and disarmament. On that basis we supported in past years the expansion of the United Nations Disarmament Commission to include all members of the United Nations.

We recognize, in fact, that the world outside the old Ten-Nation Committee is much larger and more populous than the countries represented in that Committee. Therefore, if we do expand its membership we would be inclined to include additional members to ensure the representation and the advice of the world at large. This is the sense of our proposal to add ten members to the Ten-Nation Committee which was carrying on disarmament negotiations in 1960, on the basis of equitable geographic distribution.

We hope the Soviet Union is ready to discuss with us the composition of the negotiating forum. I am sure most of the members of the Committee would welcome an agreement on this point which would enable us to get started on the substantive negotiations which have been interrupted ever since the U.S.S.R. decided it did not like the Ten-Nation Forum it had demanded. The world wants disarmament and so do we, and not everlasting negotiations about the number of negotiators.

While we consider the first moves toward disarmament, we can begin right away to strengthen our machinery for keeping the peace. We can do this without hampering our efforts to reach agreement on disarmament. Every step to improve the machinery of peace will make it easier to take the next step in destroying the machinery of war.[252]

We need not even be at a loss as to where to begin or how to proceed. The experience of the United Nations itself gives us a starting point and a guideline. In its earliest years the United Nations had successful experience with mediation and conciliation. It defended collective security and the independence of small nations against their assailants in Korea. Then, at a time of urgent need in the Middle East, the United Nations acquired an effective power to police the lines of an armistice agreement. At another time of great need in the Congo—it added an effective power to use force, if necessary, to restore order and to prevent a civil war. Out of such emergencies, the United Nations is becoming a stronger instrument for keeping the peace.

It will have to be much stronger still. Our task, now, is to strengthen, refine and develop more fully the peace-keeping structure of the United Nations.

We can begin by drawing lessons from the United Nations' most recent experience in the Congo. From this operation it is not difficult to see that effectiveness in such peace-making missions depends in large measure on four things: first, the ready availability and mobility of national units; second, their discipline and training and capacity to work with contingents of other nationalities; third, the length of their commitment; and, fourth, a clear chain of command flowing from United Nations Headquarters.

When the United Nations is so often pitted in a race against time, we risk a dangerous vacuum during the interval while military forces are being assembled. And we further risk a dangerous erosion in the political and moral authority of the United Nations if troops trained for national forces are thrust without special training into situations unique to the purposes and methods of the United Nations—or, if such troops are either kept on the job without rotation, are precipitately withdrawn when no replacements are at hand, or are insufficiently supported for lack of adequate financial resources.

We are all deeply in the debt of those officers and men who have served and are serving the cause of peace under the United Nations flag. We must proceed without delay to strengthen the context in which they act in this pioneering work of the United Nations as the guardian of peace.

The United States has suggested that all nations indicate the kind and quality of military units they might be prepared to send for service with the United Nations. My own country has provided very important logistic support for both UNEF in the Middle East,[253] and the United Nations Forces in the Congo. We now suggest that member countries make available to the United Nations an inventory of the forces, equipment and logistic support which they would be prepared to put at the disposal of the United Nations for peace-preserving functions.

But to commit such facilities on paper is not enough. The functions of a United Nations Force are likely to be different from those of national forces. The United States believes that national units should be specially trained for the special character of United Nations operations. Recent United Nations experience should be studied, so manuals can be prepared to assist the United Nations in officer training and to help member countries in training noncommissioned personnel.

Such steps would strengthen the United Nations capacity to serve as an international police force. But a stronger and better organized police force would be needed only when threats to peace have reached dangerous proportions. The police force, therefore, must be supplemented with improved machinery for settling disputes before they reach an explosive stage. Our task, here again, is to build on the existing resources of the United Nations, including the International Court of Justice, and to avail ourselves more fully of the potentials for action within these existing resources.

The Secretary General may wish to present to the United Nations members his own ideas for the expansion and improvement of

United Nations machinery for observation, fact-finding, conciliation, mediation and adjudication. He undoubtedly will wish to make use of senior members of his staff in his conciliation activities. The political organs themselves may wish on occasion to avail themselves of the services of rapporteurs.[254]

Moves such as these—and I hope other members will have other suggestions—would permit us to get on with the job of creating the kind of peace-keeping machinery that will be essential for dealing with conflicts in a world free from war. And we·can start them at once—even without waiting for agreement on disarmament.

Every such move will help to reduce danger, help to lower distrust, help to blunt fear. The way to start is to start; and a good place to start is ready [at] hand. I refer to the proposed treaty whose objective it is to outlaw further testing of atomic devices in space, in the atmosphere, on the ground, or under the ground or the water, which is still tabled at Geneva. We are flexible about first steps; we are adamant only on the point that we begin at once—immediately—to disarm.

Mr. Chairman: We can begin at once to disarm. To start now in no sense limits or postpones the goal of general and complete disarmament; indeed, this is the way to reach it faster. For some steps can be taken sooner than others—without disadvantage to any nation or groups of nations.

Let no one doubt our seriousness. Six weeks ago the President of our nation presented in person to this session of the General Assembly the boldest and most comprehensive plan for disarmament that my nation has ever offered to the world. Since then he has signed into a law an Act creating a new Arms Control and Disarmament Agency, directly under his authority and containing an array of expert talent whose counterpart I would be very happy to see in a similar agency in the Soviet Union.

Mr. Chairman, as I said earlier, it is extremely difficult for the mind to grasp a clear vision of a world without arms, for it is a condition totally foreign to the human experience. But as I also said earlier, it is even more difficult to envision a world turned to a radioactive wasteland—which may well be the alternative. Difficult as it is, then, we must grasp the easier and happier vision.

And I do think we can see—however dimly—the general out-
lines of such a world. A world disarmed would not be utopia—but
one suddenly blessed by freedom from war. It would not usher in
world government—but the world community would have the
capacity to keep the peace. It would not end national sovereignty
—but the sovereign right to commit national suicide would be
yielded up forever.

A disarmed world would still be a world of great diversity—in
which no one nation could seriously pretend to have the wit and
wisdom to manage mankind.

It would be a world in which ideas—for the first time—could
compete on their own merits without the possibility of their impo-
sition by force of arms.

It would be a world in which men could turn their talents to an
agenda of progress and justice for all mankind in the second half of
the twentieth century.

In short, it would not be a perfect world—but a world both
safer and more exhilarating for us all to live in.

There is nothing inherently impossible in creating the conditions
for a world without war. Our basic problems are not technical,
mechanistic, or administrative. The basic question is whether every
nation will agree to abandon the means to coerce others by force.

If they will not, the arms race will go on. For those who love
freedom and have the power to defend it will not be coerced. And
uncertain as it is, free people prefer to live on borrowed time than
to yield to terror.

Conceivably the world could survive on this perpetual brink of
universal disaster. Conceivably fortune would spare us from the
fatal act of a lunatic—and miscalculation of an uninformed leader
—the false step of a nervous young sentry.

But on behalf of my Government and my people I propose that
this assembly set the world on the road toward freedom from war.

And I propose that this committee take the first steps by approv-
ing a negotiating forum, endorsing the statement of agreed principles already worked out by the United States and the Soviet
Union, and recommending that the new forum get on at once with
the first business of this dangerous world—general and complete
disarmament.

I ask Mr. Zorin whether his country cannot so conduct negotiations now, that we and our respective allies may be able to turn to the rest of the members here, and to the hundreds of millions for whom they speak, and say: "We have not failed you."

The Failure of the Security Council
Is a Failure of the United Nations

DECEMBER 18, 1961

✿

The Goa question, one of the most short-lived but explosive issues
presented in the Security Council, prompted Stevenson to offer a
potent and damning accusation against the Indian government for
its invasion of Goa. Between December 8 and 19, 1961, the presi-
dent of the Council received communications both from Portugal
and from India relating to the deteriorating situation in Goa,
Damao, and Diu, Portuguese territories on the Indian frontier. On
December 18, Ambassador Vasco Vierira Garin of Portugal
charged that India had launched a full-scale attack against these
territories. The Council discussed the issue in two meetings that
day. Garin concluded his speech: "The conscience of mankind is
shocked. World public opinion has expressed itself in no unmistak-
able terms expecting that the Security Council will immediately
denounce and rectify this new lawless action of the Indian Govern-
ment."[255] Ambassador C. S. Jha of India called the Portuguese
presence on Indian territory an "echo of the past. . . . the point
of view of a colonial Power of 400 years ago."[256] Stevenson's
speech caused one United Nations news correspondent to com-
ment, it was "so pessimistic . . . that most of the gloomy com-
ments . . . were provoked by this speech in which you compared
the fate of the United Nations with the League of Nations."[257]
Jha criticized Stevenson's speech, saying: "Does not that statement
show some kind of disregard, some kind of indifference, towards
the motivations, the feelings of people, the great movement of our

times, the yearning for freedom—the passionate yearning for freedom?"[258]

When the Council reconvened that evening, the Western representatives again joined Stevenson's denunciation against the Indian use of force. Jha denied that an invasion had occurred: "We have gone into Goa to assist the freedom movement of Goa, to help the resistance movement of Goa. . . . The patriots have risen, and if they were not able to do more previously it was because they were ruthlessly suppressed. We have gone there for that purpose; they are our people. They must come back to the motherland."[259] *Stevenson's resolution, cosponsored by four delegations, urged the Indians to cease hostilities and withdraw their troops and asked that both governments work toward a peaceful settlement of the issue. Three Afro-Asian delegations sponsored a separate resolution charging Portugal as the aggressor and appealing to the Portuguese for cooperation with India in liquidating their colonial empire. When Ambassador Barnes requested that the vote be delayed until morning so that he could telephone his government in Liberia for instructions, Stevenson protested: "This is an urgent and pressing matter. This is war. People are being killed."*

Both resolutions were defeated. Speaking briefly after the vote was taken, Stevenson again urged India to abandon its use of force. When asked in his December 21 press conference why he had not taken the issue to the General Assembly under the Uniting for Peace Resolution, he replied that by the morning of December 19, the Goan defenses had surrendered and the cease-fire was no longer an issue.[260] *He might have added that the action of the Afro-Asian delegations in the Council made it patently clear that no support would be forthcoming from the neutral nations in the General Assembly.*

Although the crisis lasted but one day and is not listed among his "crises" in Looking Outward, *both addresses showed his courage to speak for the rights of the Goans despite his overwhelming loss of Afro-Asian support. His broad philosophizing about the fate of the United Nations, as seen in the two brief speeches printed below, serve as his stark reminders of the responsibility of the United Nations and its frailty in working for peaceful settlements.*

I SHOULD like to express the views of the United States at this fateful hour in the life of the United Nations. I will not detain you long but long enough, I hope, to make clear our anxiety for the future of this organization as a result of this incident.

When acts of violence take place between nations in this dangerous world, no matter where they occur or for what cause, there is reason for alarm. The news from Goa tells of such acts of violence. It is alarming news and, in our judgment, the Security Council has an urgent duty to act in the interests of international peace and security.

We know as the world knows, and as has been said countless times in the General Assembly and the Security Council, that the winds of change are blowing all over the world. But the winds of change are man-made and man can and must control them. They must not be allowed to become the bugles of war.

Our Charter begins with the determination "to save succeeding generations from the scourge of war" and pledges its members to "practice tolerance and live together with one another as good neighbors."

In that connection it deserves to be said that all of us at the United Nations owe much to India. The largest contingent in the United Nations effort to establish peace in the Congo are the troops of India. India has also contributed of its resources in the Middle East. Few nations have done more to uphold the principles of this organization or to support its peace-making efforts all over the world and none have espoused nonviolence more vehemently and invoked the peaceful symbolism of Gandhi more frequently. That nation is led by a man whom I regard as a friend, who has been a lifelong disciple of one of the world's great saints of peace, whom many have looked up to as an apostle of nonviolence and who only this year addressed this Assembly with a moving appeal for a United Nations Year of International Cooperation.

These facts make the step which has been taken today all the harder to understand and to condone. The fact is, and the Indian Government has announced it, that Indian armed forces early this morning, on December 18, marched into the Portuguese territories of Goa, Damao and Diu. Damao and Diu have been occupied and there is fighting at this moment within the territory of Goa.

Here we are, Mr. President, confronted with the shocking news of this armed attack and that the Indian Minister of Defense, so well-known in these halls for his advice on matters of peace and his tireless enjoinders to everyone else to seek the way of compromise, was on the borders of Goa inspecting his troops at the zero hour of invasion.

Let us be perfectly clear what is at stake here, gentlemen. It is the question of the use of armed force by one state against another and against its will, an act clearly forbidden by the Charter. We have opposed such action in the past by our closest friends as well as by others. We opposed it in Korea in 1950, in Suez and in Hungary in 1956, in the Congo in 1960, and we do so again in Goa in 1961.

The facts in this case are unfortunately all too clear. These territories have been under Portuguese dominion for over four centuries. They have been invaded by Indian armed forces. The Government of India regards these territories as having the same status as the territories of Britain and France on the subcontinent from which those countries have voluntarily withdrawn. The Government of India has insisted that Portugal likewise withdraw. Portugal has refused, maintaining that it has a legal and moral right to these territories.

Mr. President, we have repeatedly urged both of the parties to this dispute to seek by peaceful processes the resolution of a problem which has its roots in the colonial past.

I do not at this time propose to concern myself with the merits of this dispute. We are not meeting here today to decide the merits of this case. We are meeting to decide what attitude should be taken in this body when one of the members of these United Nations casts aside the principles of the Charter and seeks to resolve a dispute by force.

But, Mr. President, what is at stake today is not colonialism. It is a bold violation of one of the most basic principles of the United Nations Charter, stated in these words from Article 2 of paragraph 4: "All members shall refrain in their international relations from the threat or use of force against the territorial integrity of political independence of any State, or in any other manner inconsistent with the purposes of the United Nations."

We realize fully the depths of the differences between India and Portugal concerning the future of Goa. We realize that India maintains that Goa by rights should belong to India. Doubtless India would hold, therefore, that its action today is aimed at a just end. But if our Charter means anything, it means that states are obligated to renounce the use of force, are obligated to seek a solution of their differences by peaceful means, are obligated to utilize the procedures of the United Nations when other peaceful means have failed. Prime Minister Nehru himself has often said that no right end can be served by a wrong means. The Indian tradition of nonviolence has inspired the whole world, but this act of force with which we are confronted today mocks the faith of India's frequent declarations of exalted principle. It is a lamentable departure not only from the Charter but from India's own professions of faith.

What is the world to do if every state whose territorial claims are unsatisfied should resort with impunity to the rule of armed might to get its way? The Indian sub-continent is not the only place in the world where such disputes exist.

The fabric of peace is fragile, and our peace-making machinery has today suffered another blow. If it is to survive, if the United Nations is not to die as ignoble a death as the League of Nations, we cannot condone the use of force on this instance and thus pave the way for forceful solutions of other disputes which exist in Latin America, Africa, Asia, and Europe. In a world as interdependent as ours, the possible results of such a trend are too grievous to contemplate.

This action is all the more painful to my country because we have in recent weeks made repeated appeals to the Government of India to refrain from the use of force. This has included not only a series of diplomatic approaches in Washington and in New Delhi but also a personal message from President Kennedy to Prime Minister Nehru on December 13 indicating our earnest hope that India would not resort to force to solve the Goa problem.

As a culmination of these efforts, the United States Government last Saturday made an appeal to Prime Minister Nehru both through the United States Ambassador in New Delhi and through the Indian Ambassador in Washington to suspend preparations for the use of force in connection with a direct offer of United States help in seeking a peaceful solution to the problem. This resort to armed action is a blow to international institutions such as our United Nations [and] the International Court of Justice, which are available to assist in the adjustment of disputes.

This is our principal concern. This body cannot apply a double standard with regard to the principle of resort to force. We appeal to India to recognize that its own national interests, as well as those of the entire world community, depend on the restoration of confidence in the processes of law and conciliation in international affairs. Indeed, Mr. President, this tragic episode reveals clearly—if nothing else—the need for urgent review of peaceful settlement procedures to deal with the problems of peaceful change. The United States will have more to say about this at an appropriate occasion.

The Council has an urgent duty, in our judgment, to bring this dispute back from the battlefield, so fraught with danger for the world, to the negotiating table. We earnestly urge the Government of India to withdraw its armed forces from the territories which they have invaded. We earnestly appeal for a cease-fire. And we earnestly urge the Governments of India and of Portugal to enter into negotiations to achieve a solution. We must ask for an immediate cease-fire, in our judgment; we must insist on withdrawal of the invading forces; and we must insist that the two parties negotiate on the basis of the principles of the Charter.

The law of the Charter forbids the use of force in such matters. There is not one law for one part of the world and another law for the rest of the world. There is one law for the whole world, and it is, in our judgment, the duty of this Council to uphold it.

DECEMBER 18, 1961

Stevenson's Second Statement

✡

MR. PRESIDENT,

I am the only delegate, I think, at this table who was present at the birth of this organization. Tonight we are witnessing the first act in a drama which could end with its death. The League of Nations died, I remind you, when its members no longer resisted the use of aggressive force. So it is, sir, with a most heavy heart that I must add a word of epilogue to this fateful discussion, by far the most important in which I have participated since this organization was founded sixteen years ago. The failure of the Security Council to call for a cease-fire tonight in these simple circumstances is a failure of the United Nations. The veto of the Soviet Union is consistent with its long role of obstruction. But I find the attitude of some other members of the Council profoundly disturbing and ominous because we have witnessed tonight an effort to rewrite the Charter, to sanction the use of force in international relations when it suits one's own purposes. This approach can only lead to chaos and to the disintegration of the United Nations.

The United States appeals again to the Government of India to abandon its use of force, to withdraw its forces. We appeal to both parties again to negotiate their differences. This is the course prescribed by the Charter. It is the course of wisdom. The inability of the Council to act because of a Soviet veto does not alter this fact. We will consult overnight with other members of the Council about further steps which the United Nations might take and we reserve the right to seek a further meeting at any time.

A Premeditated Attempt:
The Dread Realities
and the Building of the Sites

OCTOBER 25, 1962

☆

The Soviet and Cuban representatives renewed their verbal attacks on the United States for its "aggression against Cuba" during the General Debate at the opening of the seventeenth session of the General Assembly on September 21, 1962. Stevenson exercised his right of reply by saying:

Now in direct answer, let me say to the representatives of the Soviet Union and of Cuba, that we are not taking and will not take offensive action in this hemisphere, neither will we permit aggression in this hemisphere. . . . While we will not commit aggression, we will take whatever steps are necessary to prevent the Government of Cuba from seeking to subvert any part of this hemisphere. . . . The threat to peace in Cuba comes not from the United States but from the Soviet Union. . . . If the Soviet Union genuinely desires to keep the peace in the Caribbean, let it stop this warlike posturing, this stuffing of Cuba with rockets, military aircraft, advanced electronic equipment and other armament all out of proportion to any legitimate needs.[261]

On October 8, after President Dorticos of Cuba addressed the Assembly, Stevenson charged that he had "seen fit to use this rostrum to attack my country with unparalleled calumnies, slanders and misrepresentations." He gave his reply outside the Assembly because he did "not want to descend even by reply to the levels of the chief of state we have just heard on this ceremonial occasion." Stevenson stated: "Let no one mistake the impact of this

341

Soviet intervention in Cuba on the hope we all share for world peace. If the Soviet Union persists in the course it has chosen, if it continues to try to prevent the peaceful social revolution of the Americas, it will increasingly excite the deep indignation of the people of my country and the other American states. . . . A consequence of this gratuitous Soviet initiative is to postpone even further the hope for world stabilization. I cannot state this point with sufficient gravity."[262]

On October 22, Stevenson requested an urgent meeting of the Security Council to deal "with the dangerous threat to the peace and security of the world caused by the secret establishment in Cuba by the Union of Soviet Socialist Republics of launching bases and the installation of long-range ballistic missiles capable of carrying thermonuclear warheads to most of North and South America." He also introduced a draft resolution asking the Security Council to: 1. Call for the immediate dismantling and withdrawal from Cuba of all missiles and other offensive weapons; 2. Authorize and request Acting Secretary-General U Thant to despatch to Cuba a United Nations observer corps to assure and report on compliance with the resolution; 3. Call for termination of the American quarantine directed against military shipments upon the United Nations certification of Soviet compliance with Part One of the resolution; and 4. Urgently recommend that the United States and Soviet Union confer on measures to remove the existing threat to the security of the Western Hemisphere and the peace of the world.[263]

Stevenson's speech on October 23 in the Security Council, one of his major addresses in the United Nations, described the nature of the secret Soviet build-up of missiles in Cuba. The speech consisted of a minutely detailed expansion of President Kennedy's statement the evening before which announced:

Within the past week, unmistakable evidence has established the fact that a series of offensive missile sites is [are] now in preparation on that imprisoned island. The purpose of these bases can be none other than to provide a nuclear strike capability against the Western Hemisphere. . . .

The characteristics of these new missile sites indicate two distinct types of installations. Several of them include medium range ballistic missiles, capable of carrying a nuclear warhead for a distance of more than 1,000 nautical miles.

Additional sites not yet completed appear to be designed for intermediate range ballistic missiles—capable of traveling more than twice as far—and thus capable of striking most of the major cities in the Western Hemisphere. . . .[264]

Stevenson urged Cuba that if it wished to renounce communism and establish normal relations with its hemispheric neighbors, "the way is clear, and the choice is Cuba's." Robert and Selma Schiffer, editors of Looking Outward, write that it "was a speech that none who heard it will forget."[265] After the Security Council adjourned that evening, Stevenson announced to the press that the Soviet Union did not deny that Soviet MRBM and IRBM sites and missiles had been installed secretly in Cuba and that it was now apparent that President Dorticos was admitting their existence when he told the Assembly on October 8: "we have sufficient means with which to defend ourselves; we have indeed our inevitable weapons, the weapons which we would have preferred not to acquire and which we do not wish to employ."[266]

According to Robert and Selma Schiffer, "Perhaps the single most dramatic moment of any UN meeting occurred in the Security Council on October 25, 1962. For two days the world had stood at the abyss. . . . In the hushed Security Council chamber the discussion of the United States complaint ended abruptly after a memorable exchange between Governor Stevenson and Ambassador Zorin."[267] After President Kennedy and Chairman Khrushchev reached agreement on the removal of the missiles, delicate and prolonged negotiations replaced the dramatic exchanges in the Council and Zorin was recalled to Moscow not long after. The two statements that Stevenson gave to the Council on October 25 are printed below as a single unit and also in Looking Outward *under*

the titles, "A Premeditated Attempt: The Dread Realities" and "A
Premeditated Attempt: The Building of the Sites."

TODAY we must address our attention to the realities of the situation posed by the build-up of nuclear striking power in Cuba.

In this connection, I want to say at the outset that the course adopted by the Soviet Union yesterday to avoid direct confrontations in the zone of quarantine is welcome to my Government. We also welcome the assurance by Chairman Khrushchev in his letter to Earl Russell that the Soviet Union will "take no reckless decisions" with regard to this crisis.[268] And we welcome most of all the report that Mr. Khrushchev has agreed to the proposals advanced by the Secretary-General. Perhaps that report will be confirmed here today.

My Government is most anxious to effect a peaceful resolution of this affair. We continue to hope that the Soviet Union will work with us to diminish not only the new danger which has suddenly shadowed the peace but all of the conflicts that divide the world.

I shall not detain you with any detailed discussion of the Soviet and the Cuban responses to our complaint. The speeches of the Communist delegates were entirely predictable. I shall make brief comment on some points suggested by these speeches and some other points which may have arisen in the minds of members of the United Nations.

Both Chairman Khrushchev in his letter to Earl Russell and Ambassador Zorin in his remarks to this Council argued that this threat to the peace had been caused not by the Soviet Union and Cuba but by the United States.

We are here today and have been this week for one single reason—because the Soviet Union secretly introduced this menacing offensive military build-up into the island of Cuba while assuring the world that nothing was further from their thoughts.

The argument, in its essence, of the Soviet Union is that it was not the Soviet Union which created this threat to peace by secretly installing these weapons in Cuba but that it was the United States which created this crisis by discovering and reporting these installations.

This is the first time, I confess, that I have ever heard it said that the crime is not the burglary but the discovery of the burglar—and that the threat is not the clandestine missiles in Cuba, but their discovery and the limited measures to quarantine further infection.

The peril arises not because the nations of the Western Hemisphere have joined together to take necessary action in their self-defense but because the Soviet Union has extended its nuclear threat into the Western Hemisphere.

I noted that there [are] still at least some delegates in the Council, possibly, I suspect, very few, who say that they do not know whether the Soviet Union has, in fact, built in Cuba installations capable of firing nuclear missiles over ranges from 1,000–2,000 miles.

As I say, Chairman Khrushchev did not deny these facts in his letter to Earl Russell, nor did Ambassador Zorin on Tuesday evening. And if further doubt remains on this score, we shall gladly exhibit photographic evidence to the doubtful.

One other point I would like to make is to invite attention to the casual remark of the Soviet Representative claiming that we have thirty-five bases in foreign countries. The facts are that there are missiles comparable to these being placed in Cuba with the forces of only three of our allies. They were only established there by a decision of the heads-of-government meeting in December, 1957, which was compelled to authorize such arrangements by virtue of a prior Soviet decision to introduce its own missiles capable of destroying the countries of Western Europe.

In the next place, there are some troublesome questions in the minds of members that are entitled to serious answers. There are those who say that conceding the fact that the Soviet Union has installed these offensive missiles in Cuba, conceding the fact that this constitutes a grave threat to the peace of the world, why was it necessary for the nations of the Western Hemisphere to act with such speed? Why could not the quarantine against the shipment of offensive weapons have been delayed until the Security Council and the General Assembly had a full opportunity to consider the situation and make recommendations?

Let me remind the members that the United States was not looking for some pretext to raise the issue of the transformation of Cuba into a military base. On the contrary, the United States made no objection whatever to the shipment of defensive arms by the Soviet Union to Cuba, even though such shipments offended the traditions of this hemisphere.

Even after the first hard intelligence reached Washington concerning the change in the character of Soviet military assistance to Cuba, the President of the United States responded by directing an intensification of surveillance. And only after the facts and the magnitude of the build-up had been established beyond all doubt did we begin to take this limited action of barring only these nuclear weapons equipment and aircraft.

To understand the reasons for this prompt action, it is necessary to understand the nature and the purpose of this operation. It has been marked, above all, by two characteristics—speed and stealth. As the photographic evidence makes clear, the installation of these missiles—the erection of these missile sites—has taken place with extraordinary speed. One entire complex was put up in twenty-four hours. This speed not only demonstrates the methodical organization and careful planning involved. But it also demonstrates a premeditated attempt to confront this hemisphere with a *fait accompli*. By quickly completing the whole process of nuclearization of Cuba, the Soviet Union would be in a position to demand that the status quo be maintained and left undisturbed.

If we were to have delayed our counteraction, the nuclearization of Cuba would have been quickly completed. This is not a risk which this hemisphere is prepared to take.

When we first detected the secret offensive installations, could we reasonably be expected to have notified the Soviet Union in advance, through the process of calling the Security Council, that we had discovered its perfidy, and then to have done nothing but wait while we debated and then have waited further while the Soviet representative in the Security Council vetoed a resolution, as he has already announced that he will do? In different circumstances, we would have. But today we are dealing with dread realities and not with wishes.

One of the sites, as I have said, was constructed in 24 hours. One of these missiles can be armed with its nuclear warhead in the middle of the night, pointed at New York, and landed above this room five minutes after it was fired. No debate in this room could affect in the slightest the urgency of these terrible facts or the immediacy of the threat to the peace.

There was only one way to deal with that urgency and with that immediacy, and that was to act, and to act at once—but with the utmost restraint consistent with the urgency of the threat to the peace.

And we came to the Security Council, I remind you, immediately and concurrently with the Organization of American States. We did not even wait for the OAS to meet and to act. We came here at the same time. We immediately put into process the political machinery that, we pray, will achieve a solution of this grave crisis. And we did not act until the American republics had acted to make the quarantine effective.

We did not shirk our duties to ourselves, to the hemisphere, to the United Nations, or to the world. We are now in the Security Council on the initiative of the United States precisely because, having taken the hemispheric action which has been taken, we wish political machinery—the machinery of the United Nations—to take over, to reduce these tensions, and to interpose itself to eliminate this aggressive threat to the peace and to assure the removal from this hemisphere of offensive nuclear weapons and the corresponding lifting of the quarantine.

There are those who say that the quarantine is an inappropriate and extreme remedy—that the punishment does not fit the crime. But I ask those who take this position to put themselves in the position of the Organization of American States to consider what you would have done in the face of the nuclearization of Cuba. Were we to do nothing until the knife was sharpened? Were we to stand idly by until it was at our throats? What were the alternatives available?

On the one hand, the Organization of American States might have sponsored an invasion, or destroyed the bases by an air strike, or imposed a total blockade on all imports to Cuba, including medicine and food. On the other hand, the OAS and the United States might have done nothing. Such a course would have confirmed the greatest threat to the peace of the Americas known to history and would have encouraged the Soviet Union in similar adventures in other parts of the world. And it would have discredited our will, our determination, to live in freedom and to reduce—not increase [—] the perils of this nuclear age.

The course we have chosen seems to me perfectly graduated to meet the character of the threat. To have done less would have been to fail in our obligation to peace.

To those who say that a limited quarantine was too much in spite of the provocation and the danger, let me tell you a story— attributed like so many of our American stories to Abraham Lincoln—about the passer-by out in my part of the country who was charged by a farmer's ferocious boar. He picked up a pitch- fork and met the boar head on. It died and the irate farmer de- nounced him and asked him why he didn't use the blunt end of the pitchfork. And the man replied, "Why didn't the boar attack me with his blunt end?"

Some here have attempted to question the legal basis of the de- fensive measures taken by the American republics to protect the Western Hemisphere against Soviet long-range nuclear missiles.

I would gladly expand on our position on this but in view of the proposal now before us presented last night by the Secretary-Gen- eral, perhaps that is a matter and a discussion in view of its com- plexity and length which could be more fruitfully delayed to a later time.

Finally, let me say that no twisting of logic, no distortion of words can disguise the plain, the obvious, the compelling common- sense conclusion that the installation of nuclear weapons by stealth, weapons of mass destruction in Cuba poses a dangerous threat to the peace, a threat which contravenes Article 2 paragraph 4, and a threat which the American republics are entitled to meet, as they have done, with appropriate regional defensive measures.

Nothing has been said by the representatives of the Communist states here which alters the basic situation. There is one fundamen- tal question to which I solicit your attention. The question is this: What action serves to strengthen the world's hope of peace?

Can anyone claim that the introduction of long-range nuclear missiles into Cuba strengthens the peace?

Can anyone claim that the speed and stealth of this operation strengthens the peace?

Can anyone suppose that this whole undertaking is anything more than an audacious effort to increase the nuclear striking powers of the Soviet Union against the United States and thereby magnify its frequently reiterated threats against Berlin? When we are about to debate how to stop the dissemination of nuclear weapons does their introduction in a new hemisphere by an outside state advance sanity and peace?

Does anyone suppose that, if this Soviet adventure should go unchecked, the Soviet Union would refrain from similar adventures in other parts of the world?

The one action in the last few days which has strengthened the peace is the determination to stop this further spread of weapons in this hemisphere.

In view of the situation that now confronts us and the proposals made here yesterday by the Acting Secretary-General, I am not going to further extend my remarks this afternoon. I wish only to conclude by reading to the members of the Council a letter from the President of the United States which was delivered to the Acting Secretary-General just a few minutes ago in reply to his appeal of last night. He said to Mr. U Thant:

I deeply appreciate the spirit which prompted your message of yesterday.

As we made clear in the Security Council, the existing threat was created by the secret introduction of offensive weapons into Cuba, and the answer lies in the removal of such weapons.

In your message and your statement to the Security Council last night, you have made certain suggestions and have invited preliminary talks to determine whether satisfactory arrangements can be assured.

Ambassador Stevenson is ready to discuss these arrangements with you promptly.

I can assure you of our desire to reach a satisfactory and peaceful solution of this matter. [269]

I have nothing further to say at this time, Mr. President.

OCTOBER 25, 1962
Stevenson's Second Statement

✡

I want to say to you, Mr. Zorin that I do not have your talent for obfuscation, for distortion, for confusing language and for double talk. And I must confess to you that I am glad that I do not!

But if I understood what you said, you said that my position had changed, that today I was defensive because we did not have the evidence to prove our assertions that your Government had installed long-range missiles in Cuba.

Well, let me say something to you, Mr. Ambassador—we do have the evidence. We have it and it is clear and it is incontrovertible. And let me say something else—those weapons must be taken out of Cuba.

Next, let me say to you that if I understood you, with a trespass on credibility that excels your best, you said that our position had changed since I spoke here the other day because of the pressures of world opinion and the majority of the United Nations. Well, let me say to you, sir, you are wrong again. We have had no pressure from anyone whatsoever. We came in here today to indicate our willingness to discuss Mr. U Thant's proposals, and that is the only change that has taken place.

But let me also say to you, sir, that there has been a change. You—the Soviet Union has sent these weapons to Cuba. You—the Soviet Union has upset the balance of power in the world. You— the Soviet Union has created this new danger—not the United States.

And you ask with a fine show of indignation why the President did not tell Mr. Gromyko on last Thursday about our evidence, at the very time that Mr. Gromyko was blandly denying to the President that the U.S.S.R. was placing such weapons on sites in the New World.

Well, I will tell you why—because we were assembling the evidence, and perhaps it would be instructive to the world to see how a Soviet official, how far he would go in perfidy. Perhaps we wanted to know if this country faced another example of nuclear deceit like that one a year ago when in stealth the Soviet Union broke the nuclear test moratorium.

And while we are asking questions, let me ask you why your Government, your Foreign Minister deliberately, cynically deceived us about the nuclear build-up in Cuba?

And, finally, the other day, Mr. Zorin, I remind you that you did not deny the existence of these weapons. Instead, we heard that they had suddenly become defensive weapons. But today, again if I heard you correctly, you now say they do not exist, or that we haven't proved they exist, with another fine flood of rhetorical scorn.

All right, sir, let me ask you one simple question: Do you, Ambassador Zorin, deny that the U.S.S.R. has placed and is placing medium- and intermediate-range missiles and sites in Cuba? Yes or no—don't wait for the translation—yes or no.

[*The Soviet representative refused to answer, saying he was not in an American courtroom.*]

You can answer yes or no. You have denied they exist. I want to know if I understood you correctly.

I am prepared to wait for my answer until hell freezes over, if that's your decision. And I am also prepared to present the evidence in this room.

[*The President, Ambassador Zorin, called on the representative of Chile to speak, but Ambassador Stevenson continued as follows:*]

I have not finished my statement. I asked you a question. I have had no reply to the question, and I will now proceed, if I may, to finish my statement.

I doubt if anyone in this room, except possibly the representative of the Soviet Union, has any doubt about the facts. But in view of his statements and the statements of the Soviet Government up until last Thrusday, when Mr. Gromyko denied the existence or any intention of installing such weapons in Cuba, I am going to make a portion of the evidence available right now. If you will indulge me for a moment, we will set up an easel here in the back of the room where I hope it will be visible to everyone. [*Enlarged aerial photographs were then placed on display.*]

The first of these exhibits shows an area north of the village of Candelaria, near San Cristobal, southwest of Havana. A map, together with a small photograph, shows precisely where the area is in Cuba.

The first photograph shows the area in late August, 1962; it was then, if you can see from where you are sitting, only a peaceful countryside.

The second photograph shows the same area one day last week.

A few tents and vehicles had come into the area, new spur roads had appeared, and the main road had been improved.

The third photograph, taken only twenty-four hours later, shows facilities for a medium-range missile battalion installed. There are tents for four or five hundred men. At the end of the new spur road there are seven 1,000-mile missile trailers. There are four launcher-erector mechanisms for placing these missiles in erect firing position. This missile is a mobile weapon, which can be moved rapidly from one place to another. It is identical with the 1,000-mile missiles which have been displayed in Moscow parades.

All of this, I remind you, took place in twenty-four hours.

The second exhibit, which you can all examine at your leisure, shows three successive photographic enlargements of another missile base of the same type in the area of San Cristobal. These enlarged photographs clearly show six of these missiles on trailers and three erectors.

And that is only one example of the first type of ballistic missile installation in Cuba.

A second type of installation is designed for a missile of intermediate range—a range of about 2,200 miles. Each site of this type has four launching pads.

The exhibit on this type of missile shows a launching area being constructed near Guanajay, southwest of the city of Havana. As in the first exhibit, a map and small photograph show this area as it appeared in late August, 1962, when no military activities were apparent.

A second large photograph shows the same area about six weeks later. Here you will see a very heavy construction effort to push the launching area to rapid completion. The pictures show two large concrete bunkers or control centers in process of construction, one between each pair of launching pads. They show heavy concrete retaining walls being erected to shelter vehicles and equipment from rocket blast-off. They show cable cars leading from the launch pads to the bunkers. They show large reinforced concrete buildings under construction. A building with a heavy arch may well be intended as the storage area for the nuclear warheads. The installation is not yet complete and no warheads are yet visible.

The next photograph shows a closer view of the same intermediate-range launch site. You can clearly see one of the pairs of large concrete launch pads with a concrete building from which launching operations for three pads are controlled. Other details are visible, such as fuel tanks.

And that is only one example, one illustration of the work being furnished in Cuba on intermediate-range missile bases.

Now, in addition to missiles, the Soviet Union is installing other offensive weapons in Cuba. The next photograph is of an airfield at San Julian in western Cuba. On this field you will see twenty-two crates designed to transport the fuselages of Soviet Ilyushin-28 bombers. Four of the aircraft are uncrated and one is partially assembled. These bombers, sometimes known as Beagles, have an operating radius of about 750 miles and are capable of carrying nuclear weapons. At the same field you can see one of the surface-to-air antiaircraft guided-missile bases, with six missiles per base, which now ring the entire coastline of Cuba.

Another set of two photographs cover still another area of deployment of medium-range missiles in Cuba. These photographs are on a larger scale than the others and reveal many details of an improved field-type launch site. One photograph provides an overall view of most of the site; you can see clearly three of the four launching pads. The second photograph displays details of two of these pads. Even an eye untrained in photographic interpretation can clearly see the buildings in which the missiles are checked out and maintained ready to fire—a missile trailer—trucks to move missiles out to the launching pad—erectors to raise the missiles to launching position—tank trucks to provide fuel—vans from which the missile firing is controlled—in short, all of the requirements to maintain, load and fire these terrible weapons.

These weapons, gentlemen—these launching pads—these planes —of which we have illustrated only a fragment—are a part of a much larger weapons complex, what is called a weapons system.

To support this build-up, to operate these advanced weapons systems, the Soviet Union has sent a large number of military personnel to Cuba—a force now amounting to several thousand men.

These photographs, as I say, are available to members for detailed examination in the Trusteeship Council Room following this meeting. There I will have one of my aides who will gladly explain them to you in such detail as you may require.

I have nothing further to say at this time.

[*After another statement by the Soviet representative, in which he questioned the authenticity of the photographs, Ambassador Stevenson replied as follows:*]

Mr. President and gentlemen, I won't detain you but one minute.

I have not had a direct answer to my question. The Representative of the Soviet Union says that the official answer of the U.S.S.R. was the *Tass* statement that they don't need to locate missiles in Cuba. Well, I agree—they don't need to. But the question is not do they need missiles in Cuba; the question is have they missiles in Cuba—and that question remains unanswered. I knew it would be.

As to the authenticity of the photographs which Mr. Zorin has spoken about with such scorn, I wonder if the Soviet Union would ask its Cuban colleague to permit a U.N. team to go to these sites. If so, I can assure you that we can direct them to the proper places very quickly.

And now I hope that we can get down to business, that we can stop this sparring. We know the facts and so do you, sir, and we are ready to talk about them. Our job here is not to score debating points. Our job, Mr. Zorin, is to save the peace. And if you are ready to try, we are.

The Human Race *Is* a Family

MAY 9, 1963

☿

A subject that Ambassador Stevenson continued to develop during the spring of 1963 was patriotism. In his address as recipient of the Tenth Annual Patriotism Award of Notre Dame University's Senior Class on February 18, 1963, he said: "It is not easy to be a patriot these days—not because it is difficult to love one's country. The difficulty lies not with the love, but with loving one's country in the right way."[270] Considering one's patriotism in regard to the human race, he was fond of quoting Carl Sandburg's lines from "Time Sweep" that read: "There is only one man in the world and his name is all Men. / There is only one woman in the world and her name is all Women. / There is only one child in the world and the child's name is all Children." In his address at the Annual Scholarship Dinner, printed below, which he gave at De Paul University on May 8, 1963, he developed the theme: "The human race is a family. Men are brothers. All wars are civil wars. All killing is fratricidal—as the poet Owen put it, 'I am the enemy you killed, my friend.' "[271]

COMING back to Chicago and visiting with old friends is the best kind of therapy for a transplanted Chicagoan—even if I *must* sing for my supper.

I am happy to be home again; and to have a place on this program, thanks to Father O'Malley and my old friend and colleague, Donald Walsh, because what brings us together is important to De Paul University and De Paul is important to higher education, and education is all-important to our Republic.

Now, as I understand our respective roles, I am to contribute a speech to De Paul, and you are to contribute something more tangible. This is a nice division of labor; much like the relation of Big Ben to the Leaning Tower of Pisa. That is to say, I've got the time if you've got the inclination. And it appears obvious that all of you incline very much toward the De Paul Scholarship Fund.

Since 1875, De Paul University has helped to enlighten the young people of this city and region on an ever wider scale. And now De Paul has students from thirteen states and thirty foreign lands.

So I would like—in this vigorous and growing Catholic university—to take my theme from a great Catholic leader who, in recent years, has shown the world what vigor, what energy a profoundly paternal love can bring to the great concerns of humanity. I refer, of course, to Pope John XXIII. It is clear that for him the human race is not a cold abstraction, but a single precious family whose life, interest, responsibilities and well-being are a constant and loving preoccupation. Innumerable messages, two great encyclicals, and—now most recently—his moving Easter broadcast all underline the same theme.

The human race *is* a family. Men *are* brothers. All wars are civil wars. All killing is fratricidal—as the poet Owen put it, "I am the enemy you killed, my friend." Peace is, moreover, the one condition of survival in the atomic age. So our human family must be organized for peace, and this entails the building, at world level, of the civil authority, the peace-keeping functions, the effective social institutions, the solidarity of economic and social burden [of] sharing without which human communities cease to be peaceful, civilized societies and become, as St. Augustine reminds us, not "human kingdoms," but "robber bands."[272]

The great "robber band" of our present divided world—this is the core of the Pope's preoccupation. How can it be transformed into a society of civilized men? How can the nations advance beyond their blind self-concerns—which destroy them as egoism destroys a man? How can they ensure that moral commitment and concern flow across the world's frontiers and the nightmare ends in which vile words or lethal missiles seem to exhaust the dialogue of humanity?

The Pope, we may notice, is not content to leave the problem at a high order of abstraction. In "Mater et Magistra," he specifically underlined the duty of the rich nations to conduct their economic policies in such a way that the development of poorer communities is fostered.[273] In "Pacem in Terris," he recommends a world authority as the crown of the subsidiary authority of states and communities, and specifically commends the United Nations Organization in these words:

It is our earnest wish that the United Nations—in its structure and in its means—may become ever more equal to the magnitude and nobility of its tasks and that the day may come when every human being will find therein an effective safeguard for the rights which are inalienably his as a human being.[274]

Notice well the Pope's emphasis. He accepts the fact that in a world made one by science and threatened by universal destruction, some personal rights—above all the right to life and security —can no longer be safeguarded by the individual national government. Just as the tribe has proved over millennia too small an area of authority to meet the needs and promote the energies of man, so today our separate parochial nation-states have moved toward the same condition. World society has to achieve the minimum institutions of order—police, law courts, means of equalizing the economic burden, an organization to oversee these activities—and as the Pope looks around the world today, he sees only one embryo of such an order, the United Nations system.

Though it still exercises minimal authority, it does represent the will of governments to recognize more than national interests; it has policing functions, an international court, functional agencies in fields such as health, education and labor. Day by day it attempts to conciliate, mediate, discuss, compromise, or, if need be, simply delay the conflicts which play, like earthquake tremors, across the frail political crust of our great society.

Indeed, if I were not here I would be engaging in such an activity between Haiti and the Dominican Republic this minute.[275]

Now—with this theme of the Pope as my point of departure— let me explore a remarkable paradox. The Pope is pontiff and leader of the world's most ancient Christian faith—a faith which is felt, by its very venerability, to be custodian of ancient tradition and to stress in its teaching man's instinct to conserve as well as to innovate. We should thus expect a conservative stamp to his thinking. Yet here he is proclaiming in the name of tradition itself the need for the boldest innovation in the ordering of our international relations.

Yet, at the same time, here in America—still a new country, and formed moreover in a mood of radical and even utopian vision— here in America, self-styled patriots denounce all aspects of international action as betrayal, urge the removal of the United Nations from American soil, bombard senators and excite credulous people about plots to police America with African troops and hand it over to the U.N., censor books for mentioning UNESCO, and brood over heaven knows what dark connections between internationalism and communism.

I know this fringe is thin. But it is the foam on the crust of a larger wave of opinion, which still construes patriotism as the narrowest, most exclusive nationalism, and seeks to limit its human commitment to the shores of the United States. This I believe to be not only a danger to the world, but a betrayal of America's profoundest vision.

For, never forget, America began in a unique way and the Founding Fathers precisely did *not* see the new state in terms of narrow bonds of tribe or land. There was a universality in our country's soul from the birthday of our Republic that sets us apart from more traditional communities—formed by pre-existing civilizations, or by conquest, or by tribal links.

None of these routes was followed by America. Our people have come from every "tribal" group, they have largely had to create their own civilization as they went along to absorb a continent. They have never been conquered or had any sort of synthesis imposed upon them. Their community had, in fact, a unique beginning—it was from the moment of its birth a land "dedicated to a proposition"—that men are born equal, that government is a government of laws, not men, and exists to serve them, that "life, liberty and the pursuit of happiness" are man's inalienable right.

America is much more than a geographical fact. It is a political and moral fact—the first community in which men set out in principle to institutionalize freedom, responsible government, and human equality. And we love it for this; it must give our patriotism a universal aspect. In founding the Republic, our fathers spoke for man himself. Can we speak for less in preserving it?

We cannot afford to lose this vision of freedom at any level. The child affronted in its racial dignity in the American South, the child starving in the Congo in an abundant world—they belong with us to the family of man, and our concern must be stretched to include them both.

The spiritual health of our community depends upon this wider commitment. If the effort to realize our citizens' birthright of freedom and equality in a world of freedom and equality is not constantly renewed, on what can we fall back? As a going concern, we can no doubt survive many shocks and shames. It was Adam Smith who remarked that "there is a great deal of ruin in every state." But can we survive, as a great, dynamic, confident and growing community, if the essentially liberal thrust of our origins is forgotten, if we equate liberty with passive noninterference, if we exclude large minorities from our standards of equality, if income becomes a substitute for idealism, consumption for dedication, privilege for neighborly good will—above all, if we lose our vision of humanity in the narrow pursuit of narrow national self-interest?

Well, you may say, "Why be so concerned; after all, one of the most forceful elements of our free society is precisely our discontent with our own shortcomings." You may say "Governor Stevenson, you have said that 'self-criticism is our secret weapon' yourself." You may say, "Because we are free, because we are not the victims of censorship and manipulated news, because no dictatorial government imposes on us its version of the truth, we are at liberty to speak up against our shortcomings." You may say, "We don't confuse silence with success: we know that 'between the idea and the reality falls the shadow,' and we are determined to chase away that shadow in the uncompromising light of truth."

But are we? All too often, voices are raised, again in the name of some superpatriotism, to still all criticism and to denounce honest divergences as the next thing to treason. The intolerant spirit which equates responsible criticism with "selling the country short" or "being soft on communism" or "undermining the American way of life" or "handing over America to the foreigners" is still abroad in the land of the free and the home of the brave.

You will meet it—no doubt you have met it already—and I can give you no comfort in suggesting that there is an easy way out and around this type of criticism. Our position today *is* equivocal. We *are* in one sense a very conservative people—for no nation in history has had so much to conserve. Suggestions that everything is not perfect and that things must be changed do arouse the suspicion that something *I* cherish and *I* value may be modified. Even Aristotle complained that "everyone thinks chiefly of his own, hardly ever of the public interest." And our instinct is to preserve what we have, and then to give the instinct a colored wrapping of patriotism.

This is in part what the great Dr. Johnson meant when he said: "Patriotism is the last refuge of scoundrels." To defend every abuse, every self-interest, every encrusted position of privilege in the name of love of country—when in fact it is only love of the *status quo*—that, indeed, is the lie in the soul to which any conservative society is prone.

If the world's first experiment in the open society uses patriotism as a cloak for inaction or reaction, then it will cease to be open and then, as a social organism, it will lose its fundamental reason for existence.

Do not, therefore, regard the critics as questionable patriots. What were Washington and Jefferson and Adams but profound critics of the colonial *status quo?* Our society can stand a large dose of constructive criticism just because it is so solid and has so much to conserve. It is only if keen and lively minds constantly compare the ideal and the reality and see the shadow—the shadow of self-righteousness, the shadows of slums and poverty, the shadow of delinquent children, the shadow of suburban sprawls, the shadow of racial discrimination, the shadow of worldwide misery, the shadow of national self-assertion, the shadow of war—it is only then that the shadows can be dispelled and the unique brightness of our national experiment and our international commitment can be seen and loved.

The patriots are those who love America enough to wish to see her as a model for mankind. They love her, of course, as she is, but they want the beloved to be more lovable. This is not treachery. This, as every parent, every teacher, every friend must know, is the truest and noblest affection.

Since our patriotism and our love for country are profoundly and totally rooted in our sense of the rights and dignities of man—for our own people, for our neighbors, for all the world—it is precisely in America that the fervor to create a more just and more coherent international order should be at its most enlightened and sustained.

And so in a sense it has been, for it was a great President, Woodrow Wilson, who conceived the first sketch of a functioning world community, and another great President, Franklin Roosevelt, who launched the labors which set up the constitution of our present United Nations. Moreover, at an international level—below the level of universality, but beyond our own frontiers—we Americans have since the war made new and notable experiments in effective action with other governments—to safeguard legitimate interests and to forward legitimate hopes.

Take our reaction to the problems of Communist pressure—not the imaginary plots of the hysterical—but the solid fact of Communist power backed by Soviet weapons. We know that we face in Communist hostility and expansionism a formidable force, whether Mr. Khrushchev and Mr. Mao Tse-tung pull together or apart. Their disagreement so far only turns on the point whether capitalism should be peacefully or violently buried. They are both for the funeral! So long as this fundamental objective remains, we must regard the Communist bloc as a whole with extreme wariness.

Even if the Communists are divided and confused everywhere, even if they have scored of late none of the victories in Africa, East Asia and the Middle East our doomsayers predicted, still the Communist bloc is aggressive and powerful and determined to grow more so.

So we have sensibly concluded in the NATO Alliance that our separate sovereignties and nationalisms must be transcended in a common, overwhelming union of deterrent strength. Together our weight keeps the balance of power firmly down on our side, and it removes from each state the temptation of playing off one against another and weakening the overall power in order to strengthen its own. Thus, creatively, we transcend our narrow nationalism.

Or take our economic interdependence. The Atlantic world has taken 70 per cent of world trade and absorbed 70 percent of its own investments for the last seventy years. We are an interwoven international economy. Bank rates in Britain affect investments in New York. Restrictions here affect carpet makers in Belgium. Restrictions there affect poultry producers in Arkansas. We can only avoid the failure of our interwar mismanagement of this community if we pursue joint policies: expansion of demand, currency stability, overseas investment, more commerce with the developing nations, reserves for world trade. Without joint policies here, we could easily slip back to the debacle of the period between the great civil wars of Europe of 1914 and 1939.

In this context, separate, divisive nationalism is not patriotism. It cannot be patriotism to enlarge a country's illusory sense of potency and influence and reduce its security and economic viability. True patriotism demands that in some essential categories, purely national solutions be left behind in the interest of the nation itself. It is this effort to transcend narrow nationalism that marked the supremely successful Marshall Plan. It marks the great enterprise of European unification—after so many tribal wars. It could mark the building of an Atlantic partnership as a secure nucleus of world order. The fact that there are discordant voices in Europe must not deter us. We can reexamine the terms of our alliance, but surely the world is not yet so safe that anyone can afford to break it up.

But these partial achievements of supranational cooperation and order do not exhaust our responsibilities, I cite them to show the fatuity of "going it alone." I do not pretend that they amount to the vision of a world in which all men can live in peace. We come back here to the urgent exhortations of Pope John. However dark the prospects, however intractable the opposition, however devious and mendacious the diplomacy of our opponents, we ourselves have to carry so clear and intense a picture of our common humanity that we see the brother beneath the enemy and snatch at every opportunity to break through to his reason and conscience, and, indeed, enlighten self-interest.

We have constantly to rebegin—or carry on—the work of building the institutions and practices of a nonviolent world. It may be here a matter of mutual inspection, there of blocking the spread of nuclear weapons, or an elusive agreement on the peaceful uses of outer space, or joint research for human health, or to extend the boundaries of human knowledge; above all, the continuing, frustrating, yet essential work of disarmament. We must neglect none of the openings, keeping clearly in mind, beyond the setbacks and disappointments, our *own* vision of a peaceful future for man.

And here again we encounter ambiguity, even among ourselves. There are misguided patriots who feel we pay too much attention both to problems of world order—which is, heaven help us, the problem of peace itself—and to the opinions and reactions of other nations. Well, let me remind you that "a decent respect for the opinions of mankind" was the first order of business when the Republic was created. The Declaration of Independence was written, not to proclaim our separation, but to explain it and win other nations to our cause. The Founding Fathers did not think it was "soft" or "un-American" to respect the opinions of others. And I want to put it to you that today for a man to love his country truly, he must also know how to love mankind, and this love must be the sustaining force in the search for world order. The two appalling wars of this century, culminating in the atom bomb, have taught all men the impossibility of war. Horace may have said: "It is sweet and fitting to die for one's country." But to be snuffed out in the one brief blast of an atomic explosion bears no relation to the courage and clarity of the old limited ideal.

Nor is this a simple shrinking from annihilation. It is something much deeper—a growing sense of our solidarity as a human species on a planet made one and vulnerable by our science and technology. That cry of John Donne, "Send not to ask for whom the bell tolls,"[276] echoes round the world, reaching, I believe, deeper and deeper levels of consciousness.

For, on this shrunken globe, men can no longer live as strangers. Men can war against each other as hostile neighbors, as we are determined not to do; or they can coexist in frigid isolation, as we are doing. But our prayer is that men everywhere will learn, finally, to live as brothers, to respect each other's differences, to heal each other's wounds, to promote each other's progress, and to benefit from each other's knowledge. If the evangelical virtue of charity can be translated into political terms, aren't these our goals?

Aristotle said that the end of politics must be the good of man. Man's greatest good and greatest present need is, then, to establish world peace. Without it, the democratic enterprise—one might even say the human enterprise—will be utterly, fatally doomed. I need not belabor that point. It is clear to all of us that war under modern conditions is bereft of even that dubious logic it may have had in the past. With the development of modern technology, the "victory" in war has become a mockery. What victory—victory for what or for whom?

Perhaps younger people are especially sensitive to this growing conviction that nowadays all wars are civil wars and all killing is fratricide. The movement takes many forms—multilateral diplomacy through the United Nations, the search for world peace through world law, the universal desire for nuclear disarmament, the sense of sacrifice and service of the Peace Corps, the growing revulsion against Jim Crowism, the belief that dignity rests in man as such, as all must be treated as ends, not means.

But whatever its form, I believe that, far from being in any sense an enemy to patriotism, it is a new expression of the *pietas* and respect for life from which all true love springs. We can truly begin to perceive the meaning of our great propositions—of liberty and equality—if we see them as part of the patrimony of all men. We shall not love our corner of the planet less for loving the planet too, and resisting with all our skill and passion the dangers that would reduce it to smoldering ashes.

I would like to end as I began. You are members of a great Catholic university, and to you I would like to repeat my belief that no leader today so radiates a sense of paternal regard for all God's children as Pope John XXIII. Again and again he returns to this concept of "the human family"—"the sons of God," "the brotherhood of all mankind." Whether he is inviting all men of good will to pray for spiritual unity, or pleading with all wealthy nations to acknowledge their obligations to the less fortunate, or proposing proper organs of world government, one feels that before his eyes the vast restless species of mankind appears indeed as a true family—troublesome, no doubt, confused, bewildered, easily misled, easily cast down, but one which must be loved and sustained, and treasured as parents love their family and patriots their land. He adds, in short, the extra dimension of a universal patriotism and makes the brotherhood of man not a cliché, but a living, burning truth.

I can, therefore, wish no more for your profound dedication as Americans than that you will add to it a new devotion to the worldwide brotherhood of which you are a part and that, together with your love of America, there will grow a wider love which seeks to transform our earthly city, with all its races and peoples, all its creeds and aspirations, into Saint Augustine's "Heavenly City where truth reigns, love is the law, and whose extent is eternity."

The Most Important Single Step in the Field
of Arms Control and Disarmament

OCTOBER 15, 1963

✡

When the Test-Ban Treaty was signed in Moscow during July, 1963, Stevenson felt justified that his long efforts to bring about such an agreement had reached a measure of success. Addressing the Security Council on July 26, he reminded his colleagues that he had first proposed a nuclear test-ban treaty during the Presidential campaign of 1956. He cautioned them: "Bear in mind, gentlemen, that it is not a reduction of arms, that it does not even halt the growth of weapons, but it is the first big step forward that we have been able to take in this vital field. . . . It is hoped that even more important than this test-ban agreement is the new direction in which it points toward a progressive relaxation of tension and danger in all directions."[277] On October 15, 1963, Stevenson gave this speech, printed below, to Committee One and called the treaty an event by which "we have moved a little closer to a world ruled by reason [rather] than by force."

FOR the last nine years we have gathered here to discuss the urgent problem of nuclear weapons testing, without results as Sudan has pointed out. But this time a significant step has been taken since our Committee last met: a partial test ban is a reality and more than 100 countries have committed themselves to it. Like everyone else I can't refrain from saying something about this treaty which was officially registered this morning with the Secretary General by the Representatives of the United Kingdom, the United States and the U.S.S.R. This treaty is the final chapter of a long story and represents the most important single step which has been taken in the field of arms control and disarmament. Reason has triumphed. The treaty is a clear demonstration of the fact that when the nuclear powers have a *common* interest and *act* upon it, we can make progress in improving man's environment. In the future, the air we breathe will be *cleaner*, our children will have a better chance of growing up to contribute to the well-being of mankind rather than to its destruction.

The achievement of agreement is a matter of great personal gratification because, as some of you may know, I have believed a test-ban agreement possible and advocated it for many years.

We take heart from the test-ban treaty, and also from the fact that the direct communications link we have sought is now in operation between Washington and Moscow. With the test-ban treaty we have moved a little closer to a world ruled by reason rather than by force. We are that much closer to an agreement on a comprehensive test-ban treaty. It should also improve the prospects of achieving agreement on other measures which might in turn lead to general and complete disarmament.

The overwhelming vote of the Senate of the United States in favor of the test ban is a reflection of the strong support the treaty has in the United States. We have been pleased, too, at the favorable response the treaty, the essentials of which we put forward at Geneva and in this Committee over a year ago, has received elsewhere in the world. We echo the earnest hope so often expressed that it will receive universal acceptance in order to ensure that all nuclear weapons tests in the atmosphere, in outer space, and underwater are ended *everywhere*.

Throughout the world it is recognized that the treaty is useful in helping to (1) halt the nuclear arms race, (2) discourage the search for ever larger, more destructive weapons, (3) make more difficult the development of nuclear weapons in any country which has not begun to test, (4) end the danger of radioactive fallout, and (5) facilitate agreement on other measures.

In considering benefits of the partial test ban, it is also important to note what the treaty will *not* do. The fact that we have a test-ban treaty must not lull us into believing that the task we have set for ourselves has more than just begun. As the President of the

United States has said of the treaty, it is a milestone but not the millennium. The treaty does not stop underground testing nor does it put an end to all weapons development. It does not reduce the nuclear arsenals of states. It does not eliminate the threat of war. These are serious problems and we must continue to work toward the solution of them.

We share emphatically the view expressed by the distinguished Delegate of India—that we must continue to seek urgently an agreement on an adequately verified comprehensive test-ban treaty ending all nuclear weapons tests. While we recognize the difficulties in this task, we are nevertheless convinced that such an agreement can be reached.

The General Assembly of the United Nations and the participants in the Geneva Conference of the Eighteen-Nation Committee on disarmament were influential in helping the U.S., the U.K. and the U.S.S.R. to reach agreement on a partial test ban. We feel that the efforts of the General Assembly and of the Eighteen-Nation Committee have been useful in stimulating negotiations and furthering progress toward a comprehensive test ban with adequate verification. The efforts of the eight nonaligned participants have reenforced our conviction in the usefulness of the Geneva Conference.

The United States also believes that a ban on underground testing is an important next step forward in stopping the nuclear arms race.

The United States, however, remains steadfastly opposed to a voluntary unverified moratorium on underground testing. We know that a moratorium on testing does not facilitate agreement—but will only engender suspicion and increase tension.

The scientific facts point to the amount and type of verification necessary to reach agreement. The United States has already spent over $150 million on trying to improve our knowledge of the detection and identification of nuclear events so that we would not need to ask for any more verification than that which is required by the scientific facts. The core of our effort to improve our knowledge of seismology and nuclear test detection is what we call "Project Vela." This effort and this project continue to receive our urgent attention. The memorandum tabled by the United Kingdom and the United States at Geneva on 1 April, 1963, sets forth in general terms the type of agreement which could be achieved in short order. We ask only for as much verification as is necessary to give adequate assurance of compliance with the provisions of a comprehensive treaty and, in the case of underground tests, adequate assurance requires on-site inspection in order to make it possible to dispel questions of doubt as to the nature of certain seismic events.

In the past, the Soviet Union has complained that on-site inspections might be used for purposes of espionage. We have done all we could to offer safeguards against such abuse of inspections. For example, the area to be inspected in any on-site inspection would be limited; a sensitive installation, consisting of buildings or similar facilities, could be excluded from inspection; all the safeguards considered necessary to assure the security of military and other sensitive defense installations, provided that inspection teams could still arrive promptly, could be taken; the receiving state could use its own aircraft, its own pilots, and could choose its own flight routes, its personnel could accompany the teams which would include members of an international staff.

The United Kingdom and the United States in their memorandum have indicated what elements we regard as necessary for effective verification of a test-ban treaty. It would be helpful to the negotiations if the Soviet Union similarly were to indicate for us the necessary elements of a properly safeguarded agreement in accordance with the present state of the science of nuclear test detection and identification.

As recognized in the test-ban treaty, the goal remains the ending of all nuclear weapon tests and the achievement of general and complete disarmament. When the participants in the Eighteen-Nation Disarmament Conference return to Geneva, efforts should be renewed to reach agreement on an adequately safeguarded comprehensive test-ban treaty.

From the time the Baruch Plan was first presented to the United Nations on 14 June, 1946, to the present, the United States has sought to place the atom under control so that it will be developed for the good of mankind rather than for mankind's destruction. In this country we feel that we must continue our efforts to control the power and the danger of the atom so that hope, not despair, may reign, so that confidence replaces fear, and so that safe and sound competition becomes the way of international life.

The Government of Peiping Is Not Peace-Loving

OCTOBER 16, 1963

✡

During each session of the General Assembly at which Stevenson was the American representative, the issue was raised whether the Communist Chinese government should replace the Nationalist Chinese government in the United Nations. Norman A. Graebner, writing of Secretary of State Dean Acheson's policy toward the problem of recognition for the Chinese Communists in 1949, says:

What pleased the British was the apparent American decision to recognize the new Chinese government and thus extricate the United States from its involvement in that nation's internal affairs. The Secretary had declared in September, 1949: "We maintain diplomatic relations with other countries primarily because we are all on the same planet and must do business with each other. We do not establish an Embassy in a foreign country to show approval of its Government." British officials assumed that the United States would follow their lead and shortly recognize Peiping.[278]

Graebner reflects that the efforts to push the Nationalist Chinese position by leaders such as William Knowland and Herbert Hoover, attacks on the patriotism of Acheson and other members of the State Department by Senators Jenner and McCarthy, and Acheson's " 'continued insistence that the problem of Asia stemmed, not from American foreign policy, but from vast revolutionary changes blanketing the Orient' kept him in the direct line of fire. . . . To men who believed China more essential to American security than England, and Chiang's cooperation more important than that of Clement Attlee or Winston Churchill, the Europe-first orientation of Acheson's policies appeared weak and un-Ameri-

can."[279] *In December, 1950, a Republican caucus in the House of Representatives adopted a resolution declaring that Acheson had "lost the confidence of the Congress and the American people." No single member of Congress defended his integrity or the soundness of his policy toward the two Chinas.*

Hans J. Morgenthau believes that Secretary of State Dulles was determined not to allow the same lack of domestic confidence to cripple his handling of foreign affairs and therefore Dulles permitted himself to be intimidated on the China policy by right-wing Republicans like Jenner and McCarthy. Morgenthau comments:

Public opinion with regard to Communist China [during the Eisenhower Administration] was dominated by two strong contradictory desires: to make good somehow the defeat which the United States had suffered through the defection of China to the Communist camp and to do so without getting involved in a major war on the continent of Asia. The opposition [Jenner and McCarthy] . . . promised the overthrow of the Communist regime of China and the restoration of Chiang Kai-shek's rule through aerial bombardment and a naval blockade, using Formosa as a springboard.[280]

During the 1950's, Stevenson again and again argued against such a negative policy toward the Chinas and indicated in his earlier speeches that the American government must eventually come to terms with the Communist Chinese. Stevenson's treatment of the question in the United Nations seems at variance with his private attitudes toward it. Kenneth Davis writes:

In the most widely reported of his speeches on Kennedy's behalf during the 1960 campaign, Stevenson had called for a reexamination of our China policy with a view to admitting (and thus committing) Communist China to the United Nations. It was his opinion that some kind of two-China UN representation—one delegation from Taiwan, another from Peking—could and should be worked out, and that the U.S. ought at the same time to establish direct diplomatic relations with the Red Chinese. . . . Domestic political opposition to doing the right and reasonable thing remained strong (Eisenhower, for instance, had warned the President-elect that any "threat" of Red Chinese admittance would bring him into open opposition) and Kennedy was determined to postpone facing it at least for a year. The postponement became annual. Stevenson was thus condemned to lead the battle against Communist China's membership every year that he was UN Ambassador, an exercise that disgusted him and did nothing to discourage Mao's abhorrent tyranny (indeed it helped persuade the Chinese that the tyranny was necessitated by capitalist hostility) while doing a good deal to encourage Mao's mad-dog rage against nearly all the world beyond China's borders.[281]

Still, Stevenson's own ethic compelled him to support the government's policy "this side short of madness or treason." This speech, printed below, was given to the Plenary Session of the General Assembly on October 16, 1963.

NOTHING has happened in the world in the past year to justify the General Assembly seriously re-debating the item which we now have before us; indeed quite the opposite is the case. For many years this issue has been dealt with in decisive fashion by the United Nations; in 1961 proposals to seat the Communist Chinese and expel the Representatives of the Republic of China were defeated by a vote of 36 to 48; last year they were defeated by 42 to 56. In 1961 also the Assembly decided by a vote of 61 to 34 that any proposals to change the representation of China would come under the provisions of Article 18 (3) of the Charter and this requires a two-thirds vote. Since then the leaders of Communist China have further demonstrated both in word and deed that they do not accept the most basic principles of the Charter. The Albanian proposal is consequently totally inappropriate and should be decisively rejected.

Given the behavior of the Communist Chinese in the past year, it is even more unfortunate that the constructive mood of this Eighteenth Session of the General Assembly, a mood in which all, or almost all, of us have taken such satisfaction, should be interrupted in the strident and discordant rhetoric of the cold war. As President Kennedy said in his address at the outset of this session, the whole world is now looking to the United Nations to see if the current "pause in the cold war" can be stretched into a period of cooperation during which both sides can gain "new confidence and experience in concrete collaboration for peace."[282] The Albanian proposal to expel one of our founding members and to replace its representatives with those of the world's most warlike regimes is in essence a proposal to install the chilliest advocate of both cold and hot wars in our halls.

Two years ago on the eve of our debate on this subject Communist China had subjected Tibet to its domination. Last year it was engaged in aggressive warfare against India, and by its own admission was using its influence during the crisis over Soviet missiles in Cuba to try to prevent the solution which the rest of the world welcomed. And now this year we find Communist China not only embroiled in both old and new disputes, on all of its peripheries, but also being the unique and aggressive advocate, alone in the councils of the world, of the inevitability and desirability of war as a means of solving international disputes.

Mr. President, in the past two years nineteen plenary meetings have been devoted to substantive debate on the representation of China. Nearly all members have expressed their views. In both 1961 and 1962, proposals to expel the representatives of the Government of the Republic of China and to admit Chinese Communist representatives were decisively rejected, not by "less and less support," as claimed by the Representative of Albania [Budo Halim] in his statement of September 27, but by a "no" vote of 48 in 1961 and by an absolute majority of 56 in 1962. One of the preceding speakers, furthermore, has based his case in part on the erroneous assumption that a majority of member states recognize Communist China. The fact is, of course, that an absolute majority of member states— namely 59—recognize the Government of the Republic of China.

The Albanian request that this Assembly reverse itself, that we throw out a loyal Charter member and make room here for representatives of a regime which is not a "peace-loving" state will not bear scrutiny.

In contrast to the Albanian Delegate's protestations about the "peace-loving" nature of the Peiping leaders and their dedication to "peaceful coexistence," the Chinese Communists have demonstrated repeatedly that they will not meet the qualifications of Article 4 of the Charter. The Government in Peiping is not peace-loving; it does not concur in the obligations which the Charter imposes; and it is clearly neither able nor willing to carry them out.

A recent example is Communist China's reaction to one of the most significant international developments since our last debate on Chinese representation. I refer of course to the Test-Ban Treaty, the first successful step in seventeen years of effort to limit the nuclear arms race. What has the Chinese Communist regime said about this agreement? Unlike the virtually unanimous majority of United Nations member states represented here, which have adhered to the Treaty, the Peiping regime rejected it out of hand as a "fraud," a "trap," a "deceit." "It is rotten to the core" is their specific reaction to this first momentous step on the path to peace and security by arms control.[283]

The Chinese Communists' rejection of the Test-Ban Treaty, while disappointing, cannot be said to come as a surprise in view of their known attitude toward other efforts to diminish international tension and the danger of war.

Their objection to the strenuous efforts of the United Nations to bring about disarmament has also been repeated within the last sixty days. "Universal and complete disarmament can be realized only after imperialism, capitalism, and all systems of exploitation have been eliminated," they say. "To make propaganda about the possibility of realizing 'a world without weapons, without armed forces, and without wars' through universal and complete disarmament while imperialism still exists is to deceive the people of the world and is detrimental to the struggle for world peace."

Just ponder this for a moment. As we know, "imperialism" has long been a Communist synonym for the democracies of the West. Peiping is saying that only when these free, peaceful, economic and political systems have been eliminated, can we talk of general disarmament. In other words they are opposed to the work of the Eighteen-Member Committee in Geneva; they are opposed to actions such as the resolution we have just adopted in Committee One forbidding the placing of weapons of mass destruction in orbit; and they are prepared to talk about disarmament only when those who don't accept their ideology have been erased.

Such an attitude hardly is a recommendation for admission to the

United Nations. But it is also hardly new. Long ago Mao Tse-tung expressed the iron maxim of Chinese communism in the words: "All political power grows out of the barrel of a gun."[284] Only recently he was confirmed by one of his spokesmen as having said in 1957: "If the worst came to the worst and half of mankind died, the other half would remain while imperialism would be razed to the ground and the whole world would become Socialist (i.e. Communist)."[285] We must conclude that they accept nuclear war, because the death of half of the human race would improve the prospects for Chinese communism in the remaining half of the world.

In spite of all this evidence of the dangerous mood of Communist China, there may be delegations here who are still essentially unmoved. People who see Communist China's attitude as only one more aspect of the "cold war"; who regard this as a remote dispute—even if important—between big powers but with little real relevance and importance to them; who may even secretly take some comfort in the attitude of Communist China on the assumption that it to some degree assists them in the struggle against colonialism.

To those who are so inclined I urge that the real objective and aims of the Chinese Communists be studied more carefully. For their true objective is not the objective of African or Asian democratic nationalism; their true objective is to use this nationalism as a way station to world domination.

The efforts of peoples still under colonial rule to achieve freedom are to be supported, but the Communist party in those countries is enjoined to work "independently among the masses" and to "guide the revolution onto the road of socialism" by which, of course, they mean communism. And lest there be any misunderstanding of what this means to the social fabric and leadership of those states, the leaders of Communist China add that "all forms of struggle, including armed struggle" are to be mastered and that "the transition from capitalism to socialism (that is, communism) in any country can only be brought about through the proletarian revolution and the dictatorship of the proletariat in that country." These words speak *for* themselves and they should speak *to* all of us.

No, Mr. President, while the Communist Chinese continue by

word and deed to reject the obligations of the United Nations
Charter—while they treat the organization with contempt and
arrogance—they block their own admission to it. They—who have
been branded as an "aggressor" by the United Nations—charge
that the "United Nations flag has been imprinted with the igno-
minious hallmark of aggression against Korea." And they persist in
asserting the right to use force if necessary to eliminate the Government of the Republic of China and take the island of Taiwan.

The Chinese Communists, according to Albania, consider "the
liberation of Taiwan and the other Chinese islands . . . a legitimate right of this People's Republic of China . . . ," an objective
made more specific in a report of a political work conference of the
Chinese Communist People's Liberation Army issued on March 6,
1963, which says: "We will speed the revolutionary and moderniz-
ing buildup of our army . . . to liberate Taiwan . . ."[286] For
many years the United States has sought without success to persuade the Chinese Communists to abandon the use of force as a
method of pursuing their policies in the straits. It is no wonder, in
the light of such an attitude, that we participate in a mutual assistance treaty with the Republic of China.

The standards of this Organization were established after serious
deliberation. Every member that has joined this Organization is
pledged to accept those standards. The Chinese Communists cannot amend or contradict them in the way they do and still expect
the members of the Organization to consider them seriously committed to obey them and undertake the responsibilities and obligations of membership.

The recurrent theme of "universality" running through the
arguments of those in favor of the admission of Red China surely
cannot be considered in isolation from such facts. We agree that
universality represents a goal toward which the United Nations
must strive. But the people of China are already properly and legiti-
mately represented in the United Nations by the Government of
the Republic of China. The United Nations must not weaken its
dedication to the principles on which it was founded and which
have been spelled out in its Charter. It is these principles that
should be universal. If we were to admit those who deny their
validity, we would be creating an illusion of universality, which in

time would probably turn out to be no more than a universal delusion.

Nor are the "realists," who maintain that the composition of the United Nations should simply reflect the world as it is, realistic if they disregard these principles of international conduct. The argument that it is "unrealistic" to exclude the representatives of a regime that for fourteen years has controlled hundreds of millions of people on the mainland of China brushes aside realities that have a direct bearing upon the issue before us. These realities include the unrepresentative and aggressive nature of the Chinese Communist regime; the fact that China is already represented in the United Nations by a Government which is both able and willing to carry out its obligations under the Charter; the fact that the Charter of the United Nations sets forth explicitly the requirements for membership; and finally the monstrous reality of the Albanian proposal to expel a member that has always supported the Charter in order to make room for a regime whose creed and actions are diametrically opposed to the letter and spirit of the Charter.

This argument of "realism" also overlooks still another reality, namely that what keeps the people of Mainland China from participating in the work of this organization is an unscrupulous regime that has interposed itself between the people of China and the rest of the world. The people of the United States have always been close friends of the people of China, and we are much concerned with their well-being and that they take their proper place in the modern world. But we believe we could do the Chinese people no greater disservice than to give them the impression that we are siding with their oppressors.

It has also been suggested that the Chinese Communists can best be "tamed" by admitting them into the United Nations. Although I still feel, as I said in 1961, that "this is a most tempting thought which all of us would like to share," unfortunately the weight of the evidence points the other way. In their bilateral relations they have been aggressive, expansionist and unfriendly to their neighbors. On the rare occasion when Chinese Communists have spoken in international meetings they have fostered disharmony and conflict. Even in the recently completed Centenary Congress of the International Red Cross the Chinese Communist delegate, Peng Yen, refused to support a resolution which "welcomed the efforts being made by the Governments to dispel the menace of armed conflict by the reduction of armaments, the banning of nuclear tests and weapons and the resort to peaceful methods of negotiation."

We have another concrete illustration of Chinese Communist behavior after they were brought into the international conference arrangement on Laos. Whenever the ICC has taken action to forestall the possibility of a resumption of full-scale hostilities on Laos, it has been subjected to attack by the Chinese Communists. Despite their protestations of peaceful intent the Chinese Communists have refused to cooperate and have, through their proxies in North Viet-Nam, sought to defeat the purpose of the international agreement to which they have become a signatory, thereby keeping this unhappy neighbor country in a constant state of turmoil.

Nor need we look beyond the speech of the Foreign Minister of Albania, the spokesman of Communist China in this Assembly. His two speeches to this Assembly have constituted a brutal reversion to the most extreme demagoguery of the cold war and have given the Assembly a vivid example of what would happen in our incessant struggle for mutual understanding and accommodation in the halls of the United Nations if Communist China should become a member.

In conclusion, Mr. President, the fact of the matter is that the General Assembly has ruled and ruled again on this matter.

In 1961 the General Assembly after a long, full and a fair debate decided that it was not prepared to throw out one loyal member of this Organization and to replace it by a regime which defies the Charter and the Organization itself, and which has the temerity to demand a license to permit armed aggression as the price of its admission to an organization dedicated to peace. That decision was reaffirmed with even greater conviction in 1962. Nothing has happened in the interim to cause us to reconsider that carefully considered decision. On the contrary, everything that has happened confirms the wisdom of that decision. The evidence mounts from month to month that Communist China does not believe in world peace and collective security nor the Charter of this organization.

The United Nations: Hope for the Future

OCTOBER 24, 1963

✡

On October 24, 1963, Stevenson addressed approximately 1,750 persons at a United Nations Day Rally in Dallas, just a month before President Kennedy's assassination there. Part of the speech's impact lies in Stevenson's statement that the deepening rift between Communist China and the Soviet Union demonstrated that "the cold war will never be the same again. We are moving into a new era." Equally important were his attacks against "the logic of these superpatriots who decry the United Nations; who talk of peace but who object to every attempt at negotiation and conciliation and offer no alternative save weapons that will destroy friend and foe alike."

During the speech, which received two standing ovations, Stevenson was spat upon and heckled by members of his audience, who told newsmen that they were members of the John Birch Society, the Young Americans for Freedom, and still others who were Cubans in Alpha 66, a counterrevolutionary group. When Frank McGehee, an organizer of the ultraconservative National Indignation Convention, heckled Stevenson and asked him how he could believe in the worth of the United Nations, the Ambassador received extensive applause with his reply: "For my part, I believe in the forgiveness of sin and the redemption of ignorance." Following the speech, approximately 100 hecklers jostled Stevenson as he left the auditorium and Mrs. Cora Fredrickson of Dallas struck him with a sign reading "Adlai, Who Elected You?" When he asked her what was wrong, she replied: "If you don't know what's wrong, I don't know why. Everybody else does." After his return to Wash-

ington, he unsuccessfully urged President Kennedy to cancel his planned trip to Dallas because of the right-wing hostility against American involvement in the United Nations which he had found there, and to prevent possible violence against the Presidential party.

The title of the address is Stevenson's.

AS I speak to you today, on this, the eighteenth anniversary of the United Nations Charter, it is cheering to note that all the predictions of an early demise for the U.N. have so far failed to come true. For this millions of us—all of us—have reason to be thankful. Still, there are some who continue to criticize.

Constructive criticism is justified, for we have not yet developed a perfect instrument for peace with justice. But as William Penn said: "They have a right to censure that have a heart to help."[287] The critics I refer to have no heart to help. Worse, perhaps, they fear to hope. And if anything, this eighteenth anniversary of the United Nations is an occasion that offers hope.

I don't mean to imply that we are suddenly threatened in the United Nations—and the world—with harmony or that the light of sweet reason is about to shine forth everlastingly. I would say such prospects are remote. But I would say, too, that more and more nations are less and less flouting the general consensus of what most nations and men believe to be the law of the Charter.

Nonetheless, if we are to believe our ears on some occasions— when the small vocal opposition to the U.N. is at its shrillest—we might think some threat to our independence accompanies our participation in this worldwide alliance of sovereign nations pledged to preserve the peace. I understand that some of these fearful groups are trying to establish a U.S. Day in competition with U.N. Day. This is the first time I have heard that the United States and the United Nations are rivals!

At the House of Burgesses in Williamsburg, Virginia, a quaintly costumed guide shows visitors a draft prepared there in 1775 for the new nation's Constitutional Convention. She tells visitors proudly that the draft was incorporated into the United States

Constitution, and that its principles, in turn, were incorporated into the United Nations Charter. How can we fear our own invention, born in the original colonies, nurtured in our city of brotherly love, and adopted by the world at our Golden Gate? We would hold our principles less dear, if we wanted to keep them exclusively for ourselves.

In celebrating the ratification of the Charter of the United Nations, we are paying homage to this universal adoption of the fundamental principles of the United States. Moreover, the truth is that our membership in the United Nations is overwhelmingly in the national interest—if peace in the world is in our national interest, and I know of no higher national interest of the United States than peace and security.

It becomes increasingly difficult, therefore, to understand the logic of those superpatriots who decry the United Nations; who talk of peace but who object to our only institution for peaceful settlement; who decry every attempt at negotiation and conciliation and offer no alternative save weapons that will destroy friend and foe alike.

Well, we can't afford to prove them wrong. When I consider the possibility my mind goes back to an old Gaelic toast:

> Here's to us
> And those like us
> Of which there are few
> And they are all dead.

Or when I consider some of the suicidal fallacies that have been advanced over the years in the name of patriotism, I think about the man who rushed in to see Oscar Hammerstein, the producer, and wanted $50,000 for the greatest act on earth. "What do you do?" asked Mr. Hammerstein. "I stand on stage and blow my brains out," was the answer. "Marvelous," said Mr. Hammerstein. "But what do you do for an encore?"

In a nuclear production, my friends, there won't be any encores. Those of us who hold public office and are involved in life and death responsibilities cannot afford either reckless language or deeds. We have the sobering job of trying to make appraisals which will lead to intelligent, effective policy. And it is in this sensitive area of appraisal that we differ so much with the proponents of the illusion of so-called instant victory.

I stress this today because victory will not be won in an instant—only mutual annihilation can be attained that fast in our age. And we must not only possess the common sense to recognize this fact—we must also have the courage, the persistence, and the patience to forge ahead even if the progress is slow and frustrative and the goal is far away.

But if we do, perhaps we shall in our time disprove Plato's dire prediction that "Only the dead have seen the last of war."

And this is no mere shrinking from annihilation. It springs from something much deeper—a growing sense of our solidarity as a human species. For that cry of John Donne, "Send not to ask for whom the bell tolls," echoes round the world today, reaching, I believe, deeper and deeper levels of consciousness.

In the eighteen years since the United Nations became a viable, vibrant organization, that sense of solidarity has grown, it seems to me, as never before in the history of man. But what responsibilities to assign to an eighteen-year-old stripling!

As Mr. Dooley said, however, speaking of the youngest man ever to be President, Theodore Roosevelt, "A man is old enough to vote when he can vote, he's old enough to work when he can work. And he's old enough to be President when he becomes President. If he ain't, it will age him."[288]

The United Nations *has* aged quickly, in part because the youngest nations in it are maturing quickly. Peoples long divided by race and political subjugations, with all the lingering resentments that flow from that condition, now meet in a community of equals, and they are learning respect for law and order and parliamentary procedure. For they are citizens of our planet and, with few exceptions, they belong to no bloc. Certainly there is no such thing as an Afro-Asian bloc—save on colonial issues—and the sense of community, of interdependence, of common peril and hope they feel, weighs heavily on the scales of peace in this dangerous world. Meantime, the older nations are also learning—

even as the newer ones—that the most rewarding task of civilized man today is that of reconciling different points of view. And perhaps that is the most valuable lesson of all.

Reasonable men, of course, will question whether we are learning fast enough, whether the pace being set by the U.N. is too slow. But the great challenge of our time—the challenge the United Nations *is* meeting day in and out—is in striking the proper balance in promoting changes for the better in the condition of mankind. This is the purpose and the meaning of the whole system of world order we have been trying to construct for the past eighteen years.

And in these eighteen years the United Nations has been tougher and more resilient than faint hearts predicted and cynical hearts hoped. It has survived all manner of assaults and misfortunes—like the Korean war, 101 Soviet vetoes, the three-headed monster theory of executive management called the "Troika," Dag Hammarskjold's sudden death, imminent bankruptcy and the gloomy prediction of the Cassandras in our midst who began prophesying its doom even before the ink was dry on the Charter.

Meanwhile, it has performed some prodigious feats of peace-keeping and nation-building—in Iran, Palestine, Kashmir, Tunisia, Suez, the Congo, West New Guinea, Yemen, Malaysia.

The United Nations' record in the peace-keeping field speaks for itself: A phenomenon all the more remarkable because it still has no armed forces of its own or available at its call. Its accomplishments have been made possible only by reason of the willingness of its members—many from the smaller, newly independent countries—to contribute the forces needed. And if we were to analyze how the United Nations has done its job in each instance, we would discover some little known and less understood facts.

First of all, when one mentions peace-keeping, one thinks immediately of the major confrontations that were averted: Cuba, the Congo, the Middle East, to name only a few. Those of you who are familiar with the history of the First World War know just how senseless and needless that conflict was, beginning as it did with a small incident in the Balkans. We now realize how it could probably have been averted had there been an institution like the

United Nations where steam could have been let off, national face saved, mediation instituted, and so on. One remarkable factor is the flexibility the United Nations has developed in dealing differently with different kinds of crises. In some cases it has used troops; in others it has used surveying and observing teams; in others it has turned to mediators; in still others to fact-finders. But regardless of the method, the pervading principle is that the United Nations seeks no victories for itself, only a victory for the rule of law.

And what does all this cost the American taxpayer? Without going into any involved accounting, in the eighteen years that the United States has been a member of the United Nations it has cost us slightly over $100 million a year, or one-fourth the cost of the aircraft carrier Enterprise. Or to be even more Scotch about it, the cost of the entire operation has been approximately 75 cents a year per man, woman and child. Compare that with our $50 billion a year defense budget, and one sees how much cheaper it is to prepare for peace than to prepare for war.

The range and variety of the United Nations' work is, of course, a reflection of the real world of the second half of the twentieth century—a world of multiple revolutions, of vast ferment, of pervasive change, of political turmoil. It is a reflection of the fact that with the discovery of the secret of the atom, the whole purpose of the armed struggle is becoming meaningless, and the conventional wisdom about national security, which has instructed the leaders of all states in all times past, has suddenly become obsolete.

Within the very recent past, too, scientific discoveries have so extended the average span of life that the population expansion threatens to cancel out our best efforts to improve living standards.

Within the very recent past nearly half a hundred new nations have gained independence—and with it the risks and perils of self-government.

Within the very recent past we have become grimly aware of the intolerable contradiction of want in the midst of plenty—of surplus food in the midst of hunger—of burgeoning knowledge in the midst of ignorance. And we have become aware, too, only very recently, of the complex ways in which our nations are interdependent. Science, transport, communications, economics, and politics have become international concerns and have made the world one.

For many, our age is one of contradiction, paradox and crisis, and there are good reasons for all the ferment and turbulence of our times, for all the complexity and danger of our affairs, and therefore, for all the variety and scope of the work and labors of this parliament of man.

Reflecting the realities of this world as it does, the U.N. for the most part is a symbol of the aspirations of 111 nations working, talking together, arguing, agreeing and disagreeing together in the search for peace, for decency, for human dignity. The agenda at the General Assembly which is now in session in New York numbers nearly 100 items, ranging from atomic energy to Zanzibar. Take 100 items, multiply by 111 nations and you wind up with a figure of 12,000 decisions to be made, 12,000 decisions each affecting the future of the world!

Now I would not wish to give the impression that the United States will be in accord with each one of these decisions—or that it has been in accord with all past decisions. It will not and it has not. And there will be many more to come. After all we can seldom agree among ourselves in Congress! The United Nations is not a wing of the State Department and we can't control everything it does. I doubt if we would want to even if we could. But I am saying that, overall, we have every reason to think that our views will continue to be the majority view as they have in the past on issues of substance.

Just the other day, as one example, the Assembly voted again not to admit Communist China on its terms, and the vote for our position was even larger than last year's. I do not cite this instance because I take any particular pleasure in barring any country from membership. The United Nations, after all, is for all the people in the world. But the admission of the Communist Chinese and the expulsion of the Republic of China, a founding member, would, in my view, have installed in the United Nations the world's most warlike regime—a regime not representative of the people—and would have given at least implicit approval of war as an instrument of national policy.

We have reason to be pleased, too, with the action taken by the

United Nations on extending the United Nations operation in the Congo for the first six months of 1964. The formula that was adopted reduces the United States' share of the financing by about 10 per cent below what we paid in past years, and distributes the burden more widely.

The peace-keeping operation in the Congo has, of course, been one of the U.N.'s greatest undertakings. Unfortunately, it has also been one of its most costly. Actually there would have been no such financial peril for the Organization had all the members paid their fair share of the costs. Some, I am glad to report, are now meeting their peace-keeping obligations. The Congo has taught us all the lesson that if the Organization is to meet its full potential as peace-keeper, the financial responsibility of the membership is essential. It has also revealed the difficulty of launching and sustaining peace-keeping operations which some countries feel are against their national interests.

The Congo, though, was just one step, albeit a big one, in the rapid progress of decolonialization. The remnants of colonialism will continue as one of the most perplexing and emotional issues before the United Nations. While the pace of national freedom for the former colonies has been swifter than anyone foresaw when the Charter was drafted, it does not satisfy people who are not yet free.

The emphatic and indignant position of the African nations with regard to the repugnant policy of apartheid in South Africa is, however, not without growing realization of the difficulties of the racial situation there. And their insistence on self-determination for the African population of the Portuguese Territories has also been confined within temperate limits. One can even hope that the talks now taking place between the Portuguese Foreign Minister and the African representatives in New York may be the first step toward a peaceful solution of that stubborn situation.

There are other serious problems confronting the United Nations. For one, there is the disturbing situation in Yemen where progress toward disengagement and peaceful settlement has been slow. And now we have Indonesia's threatening gestures toward the newly formed Federation of Malaysia and the conflict between Algeria and Morocco. And I haven't begun to exhaust the list of reasons why there is never a dull day in the United Nations—or night—for that matter.

I haven't mentioned disarmament or all the other items before the General Assembly. Some we may solve this year; those we don't will be back on the agenda next year—part of the continuing, never-ending search for peace. In this search, it is not enough for nations merely to look at each other. They must look in the same direction. So the big question we face today, of course, is whether the Communist bloc will ever look in the same direction as we do. The answer may be a long time coming. But the recently concluded nuclear test-ban treaty, now signed by more than 100 countries, is the most important single step taken since the war in the field of arms control and disarmament. Perhaps even more important than the treaty, which the Russians emphatically rejected when I proposed it in the General Assembly just a year ago—is the clear demonstration that when the nuclear powers have a common interest and act upon it—when they look in the same direction— they can make progress.

As for the test-ban treaty, in the future the air we breathe will be cleaner and our children will have a better chance of growing up to contribute to the well-being of mankind rather than to its destruction. And, being human, I must add that it was a great personal satisfaction and gratification to me because, as some of you may recall, I urged such a treaty during the Presidential campaign in 1956—and probably lost a few million votes in the process. Now, seven years later, the overwhelming approval of the Senate is a reflection of the strong support the treaty has in the United States—and with it we have moved a little closer to safety and sanity in the world.

The unanimous resolution of the General Assembly proposed by the United States and the Soviet Union, not to orbit or station weapons of mass destruction in outer space, is another hopeful sign. It adds to our hope for further progress in disarmament rather than the resumption of cold-war rhetoric that has been the chief ingredient of all the meetings in Geneva up to now. Much remains to be done in these talks; the surface has just been scratched and now it is time for second steps. If Premier Khrushchev is as interested as we are in peace and disarmament, and I think he is, then we share a great common cause, and progress should be possible.

It in no way detracts from the significance of recent agreements, however, to remember that the basic conflicts and differences in ideologies still remain.

The Foreign Minister of Pakistan put it well some days ago in the General Assembly: "The world," he said, "is asking itself the question: Will the test-ban treaty be a turning point in history? We cannot see past the veil which obscures the future. Dangerous questions are still outstanding. There has been no change as yet in the position of the East and the West on Viet-Nam, Laos, Germany, Berlin and Cuba—even though their frozen positions have somewhat melted."[289] This list, I could add, is far from complete.

In tempering our optimism, too, we must bear in mind that differences between the East and the West are not the only ones that threaten the world. I have mentioned the last stubborn racial and colonial problem in Africa. We cannot ignore the growing pressure of the Chinese Communists, and what some darkly hint is the attempt to divide the world between the whites and the non-whites. And in Latin America in recent weeks we have witnessed some serious blows to democratic government; while in Asia—in Laos and Viet-Nam, to mention only the obvious—the long struggle for peace and progress still goes on.

Our imagination, our courage, our will, therefore, face remorseless tests everywhere we look. How we meet them may determine the future course of world history. There is, for example, much dissatisfaction about our foreign-aid programs. But we must not lose sight of the fact that, in the long run, equal chance and equal dignity for the emerging masses—the guiding philosophy of our aid program—may have more to do with peace and security in the future than the outcome of the ideological conflict between East and West that has held our attention for so long.

I was reminded of this recently when reading about the death of Edith Piaf, and how she always helped lesser known artists. When you reach the top yourself, she said, "You have to send the elevator back down so that others can also get to the top."

As I have said so many times, for so many years, we dare not neglect any opening that will help us advance our belief in a peaceful and equal future for all men. To seize every opportunity to break through to the reason and conscience of others is, indeed, nothing less—or more—than enlightened self-interest.

Understanding, therefore, that very real dangers and conflicts still grip our world today, the fact remains that the United Nations observes its eighteenth anniversary in a moment of relative calm. And it is in this calm that we must see and put into perspective the gigantic tasks that are still before us.

In our own land, for one, we cannot rest until the last vestiges of indignity or discrimination are abolished forever—until every man in America can look his neighbor in the face and see a friend—not a color. For the very essence of freedom, after all, is nothing less than dignity.

I recently told a committee of the United Nations, during a debate on racial discrimination, that we in this country are now living through our third revolution in the name of freedom.[290]

It has been essentially peaceful; and nearly all Americans, Negro as well as white, are determined to keep it that way. But today, even as in our first revolution in 1776, we are in anguish and our anguish is evident to all. We make no effort to hide or disguise it, which is more than many can say. And the fact is that what troubles we have today are the result of progress made yesterday. We are moving through a period of social change in the direction of equal rights for all in the last corner of our land. That much still remains to be done is self-evident. But our greatness as a nation demands that the shadow be dispelled and our international commitment to freedom and justice for all be redeemed.

And if some among you question why I refer to a national dilemma when speaking about the United Nations, it is because as one who loves America, I wish to see her as a model for all mankind. For it is in America, I believe, that the fervor and will to create a more just and more coherent international order should and can be at its most enlightened and sustained.

And the attainment of equality for all in America will give the twin causes of freedom and human rights a great impetus throughout the globe. For the rights of man—the quality of life on earth in our time—is, after all, the key to peace.

It has been precisely that quality of life on earth with which the United Nations has been concerned since 1946. Looking back, most of us remember with what hopes and dreams the United Nations was launched. For many Americans, the adoption of the Charter was a kind of expiation of our earlier rejection of the League of Nations, and those who believed this noble experiment might have worked if the United States had participated in it pinned extravagant expectations on this new experiment.

There was desperation in our hope then, considering the alternative—a chaotic world, war and total destruction. And there was still the question—could the nations of the world unite to keep the peace? Many orators answered with an emphatic *yes;* but few could forget that the previous answer had been *no!*

Today our hope is based on eighteen years of experience, of building the United Nations into a going concern. It has survived repeated threats to its existence and its effectiveness. It helped create a climate that has contributed some progress in disarmament, detente and hope for the future. And in urging the great powers to take the next step, it is helping us decide today whether the family of man shall live as in the past—in anarchy and violence—or build a new, decent world community with freedom as its political habit and peace as its goal. Has mankind ever made a more fateful decision?

We have been victims of the past. We don't intend to be victims of the future. For we Americans are deeply committed to living in a free and peaceful world. In this convulsive atomic age the only way to live is to live in peace. And because the Charter of the United Nations is both the vision of this new world and the road map, we are resolved by necessity and desire to make the United Nations system work.

As I look back on these eighteen years—and I was one of the jubilant midwives present at the birth—this anniversary, therefore, seems to me to be the brightest one of all. At first, as I said, we had only hopes. Now our hopes are firmer and more confident. True, when we look back it is to eighteen years of tumult and danger.

But we are confident now that we are building an effective organization which can deal with crises—because it has done so again and again. And each success, each humble effort at pacification accomplished at any level, brings peace that much closer.

The journey of a thousand leagues, we say, begins with a single step. So we must never neglect any work of peace that is within our reach, however small. We have constantly to carry on, or rebegin, the work of building the institutions and practices of a nonviolent world, keeping always in mind, beyond the setbacks and disappointments, that a free people should ever be seeking their greatest adventure in the works of peace—that even in the midst of conflict they must never surrender the creative and compassionate attitudes proper to a peaceful community.

Let me emphasize again, no one claims that we have developed a perfect instrument in the United Nations. Certainly it is no magic lamp. It is not the whole answer to lasting peace. It never was from the day the world divided after the war. And it is not a world government. But world society has to achieve the minimum institutions of order, and the only embryo of such an order is the United Nations system which represents the will of most governments to recognize more than national interests.

Above all perhaps, the consensus of the members represents a moral force that cannot be lightly ignored, one that day-by-day attempts to conciliate, mediate, discuss, compromise or, if need be, simply [to] delay the conflicts which play, like earthquake tremors, across the frail political crust of our society.

I have ranged widely in these remarks, but such is the complexity of a world in which one thing always leads to another; and the business before the General Assembly this autumn ranges more widely still.

Our task is to build the Organization to help us master our physical environment, foster peaceful change, and promote human rights.

Our task is to use the Organization—its facilities, its resources, its talents, its procedures—to work at the problems that lie right before us, plain to view.

Vast opportunities may have been opened up by modern science, by the fluid state of international relations just now, and by the rising impatience everywhere about the achievement of full personal freedom and equality.

History and our own peoples enjoin us to probe every opening —to explore every international device—to take every step that reflects our common interest in progress and in peace.

Our efforts will be erratic, and the world will remain a dangerous place to live. But we have our wits and our resources; we have the United Nations in which to pool them for peace-keeping and nation-building; we have the beginnings of a habit of cooperation on a good many kinds of problems.

And we have a simple conviction: that it is not beyond man's capacity to act human!

On this United Nations Day, therefore, let us renew our hope that, finally, men will learn to live as brothers, to respect each other's differences, heal each other's wounds, promote each other's progress, and benefit from each other's knowledge.

Human Rights Still Remain the Great
Unfinished Business of All Men

DECEMBER 9, 1963

✡

While the United States and much of the world was still in a state of shock over the assassination of President Kennedy, and was attempting to determine the resolve of President Johnson, Stevenson addressed the Plenary Session of the General Assembly in its commemoration of the fifteenth anniversary of the Universal Declaration of Human Rights on December 9, 1963. As he suggested, rather than quote from his own statements on human rights, as a demonstration of the continuity of the American dedication to the pursuit of universal human rights, he chose to quote from John F. Kennedy, Lyndon B. Johnson, and Eleanor Roosevelt.

AS a common standard of achievement for all, the Declaration was a milestone in history. It was a great stride along the road to justice and peace. For the first time an international forum accepted the proposition that the precondition to peace was human rights—the rights of man that tyranny, bigotry, and oppression had too long denied him.

We meet here today to commemorate this act. In the words of an immortal champion of those rights, it is altogether fitting and proper that we should do this.

For the United States, in particular, this ceremony has added significance. In conjunction with marking the fifteenth anniversary of the Declaration of Human Rights, we celebrate this week, too, the 172nd anniversary of our own Bill of Rights. It is a matter of pride for us that the two have so much in common—that from our distant past we can take increased hope for the world's future, a future in which dignity and equality shall be the inalienable right of all men everywhere.

As a bridge to the future there is profound significance in the anniversary of the Universal Declaration of Human Rights which we celebrate today. Let me emphasize, however, unless we cross that bridge, unless we use it as an instrument to right the wrongs that still oppress so much of the human family, the Declaration will sometime wither on the shelves with all the other pious affirmations of good intentions.

Today, gratified though we may be that the Declaration has gathered reverence for fifteen years, human rights still remain the great unfinished business of *all* men.

So this is not an occasion for lighthearted celebration. It is a moment for sober reflection. The war it declared is not yet won. Only when *every* man in every land can truly say he has attained *every* right that is his due, only then will we have the right to truly celebrate. And perhaps none of us will be here for that celebration.

In marking this anniversary today I would like to call your attention to some words recently spoken by the new President of the United States, Lyndon Johnson.

"Justice," he said, "is not a partial thing which can be measured in terms of percentages. Any degree of injustice is complete injustice. And until we achieve complete justice we can regard progress only as a series of steps toward the goal. Each step should hearten us; but should not lull us into self-satisfaction that the job has been done."[291]

And so it is that the Universal Declaration of Human Rights must not be regarded as an end. Noble it is, but it is only one step toward the establishment of a universal standard of justice, a precondition of the enduring world peace we seek.

It should hearten us, yes, "but should not lull us into self-satisfaction that the job has been done."

President Kennedy, in the last address he was to make at this rostrum, told us truthfully, bluntly, what that job was, and he was equally candid, whether referring to the United States or to others. And if I may digress for a moment, I would suggest that all world leaders who come to this rostrum discuss with equal candor the stubborn ills that plague their own societies.

Would that we did not have such ills in America! But until they are cured—and they will be and soon—I can assure you that we will never be secret or furtive about them; we shall continue to battle them and discuss them openly where all may see and hear. For this, too, is a human right—the right of men to know what is being done to combat the evils among us.

". . . man does not live by bread alone," President Kennedy said,

and members of this organization are committed by the charter to promote and respect human rights. Those rights are not respected when a Buddhist priest is driven from his pagoda, when a synagogue is shut down, when a Protestant church cannot open a mission, when a cardinal is forced into hiding, or when a crowded church service is bombed. The United States of America is opposed to discrimination and persecution on grounds of race and religion anywhere in the world, including our own nation. . . .

We are opposed to *apartheid* and all forms of human oppression. We do not advocate the rights of black Africans in order to drive out white Africans. Our concern is the right of all men to equal protection under the law—and since human rights are indivisible, this body cannot stand aside when those rights are abused and neglected by any member state.

New efforts are needed if this Assembly's Declaration of Human Rights, now fifteen years old, is to have full meaning. And new means should be found for promoting the free expression and trade of ideas— through travel and communication and through increased exchanges of people and books and broadcasts. For as the world renounces the competition of weapons, competition in ideas must flourish—and that competition must be as full and as fair as possible.

I have taken the liberty of quoting extensively not what I have said but what two Presidents of this country have said, because it could have been said anywhere in the world by leaders concerned with prejudice, oppression, social irresponsibility, discrimination, and man's inhumanity to man. To press forward the frontiers of the human intellect and spirit is the task of all leaders everywhere.

And the United Nations by this historic declaration has charted the way to lift from the conscience and the shoulders of man the ancient burden of inequality.

It is for us to follow the chart, to get on with the great unfinished business of human rights which are at the core, the very heart, of our effort to bring about a peaceful change in the affairs of the human family.

The history of tyranny and injustice is much older than the history of freedom and justice. Yet now we know full well that no society, national or international, can prosper or long endure if it does not grant the people full human, political, and economic rights.

When the battle for the rights of man will be won is not predictable, but this must not lessen our determination that, in the end, it will be won and that it will be won peacefully.

Eleanor Roosevelt, the beloved First Lady of our era, who gave so much of her great heart and tireless energy to the Declaration, once asked: "Where, after all, do universal rights begin?" And she answered: "In small places close to home, so close and so small that they cannot be seen on any map of the world . . . they are the world of the individual person. . . ."

Let us, each of us, go forth from here to places close to home, and there let each of us strive to finish the work that we, in this Assembly, have solemnly proclaimed "the highest aspiration of the common people."

The People of the Republic of Vietnam
Are the Victims of Armed Aggression

MAY 21, 1964

✡

Reflecting on the American entrance into the Vietnamese conflict, Herbert J. Muller writes:

"No doubt," concluded Arthur Schlesinger in his book on Kennedy, "he realized that Vietnam was his great failure in foreign policy, and that he had never really given it his full attention." If the public record gives some reason to doubt that he realized this, unquestionably he failed to give Vietnam sufficient attention. . . . it became ever plainer to all but American policy-makers that most of the South Vietnamese had little heart for this war of liberation. . . . Washington's attention became so absorbed by Vietnam that all the rest of the world was neglected, and we overlooked the disagreeable truth that most of the world disapproved of the war we were fighting. . . . He had some good reasons for nevertheless deciding to defend South Vietnam—reasons that would induce Stevenson to support our basic policy there until the end of his life. . . .[292]

In the spring of 1964, the discussions in the United Nations focused on border incidents between Cambodia and Vietnam. Stevenson defended the American policy of military support in South Vietnam, not yet enlarged as it was to become, in several speeches in the Security Council.

These border incidents gained their importance as symptoms of the worsening military and political situation in Southeast Asia. In his first speech on the issue which he gave to the Council on May 21, printed below, Stevenson stressed that the United States had no national military objectives there but to serve the South Viet-

*namese government upon its own request in the search for peace.
"There is," Stevenson urged, "a very simple, safe way to bring
about the end of United States military aid to the Republic of Viet-
Nam. Let all foreign troops withdraw. . . . When their neighbors
decide to leave them alone—as they must—there will be no fighting in Southeast Asia and no need for American advisers to leave
their homes to help these people resist aggression."*

THE facts about the incidents at issue are relatively simple and
clear.

The Government of the Republic of Viet-Nam already has
confirmed that, in the heat of battle, forces of the Republic of Viet-
Nam did, in fact, mistakenly cross an ill-marked frontier between
their country and Cambodia in pursuit of armed terrorists on May
7 and May 8, and on earlier occasions. That has been repeated and
acknowledged here again today by the representative of Viet-
Nam.

The Government of Viet-Nam has expressed its regrets that
these incidents occurred with some tragic consequences. It has
endeavored to initiate lateral discussions with the Cambodian
Government to remove the causes of these incidents.

But these incidents can only be assessed intelligently in the light
of the surrounding facts: namely, the armed conspiracy which
seeks to destroy not only the Government of Viet-Nam but the
very society of Viet-Nam itself.

Mr. President, it is the people of the Republic of Viet-Nam who
are the major victims of armed aggression. It is they who are fighting for their independence against violence directed from outside
their borders. It is they who suffer day and night from the terror
of the so-called Viet Cong. The prime targets of the Viet Cong for
kidnaping, for torture, and for murder have been local officials,
schoolteachers, medical workers, priests, agricultural specialists,
and any others whose position, profession, or other talents qualified
them for service to the people of Viet-Nam—plus, of course, the
relatives and children of citizens loyal to their Government.

The chosen military objectives of the Viet Cong—for gunfire or
arson or pillage—have been hospitals, schoolhouses, agricultural

stations, and various improvement projects by which the Government of Viet-Nam for many years has been raising the living standards of the people. The Government and people of Viet-Nam have been struggling for survival, struggling for years for survival in a war which has been as wicked, as wanton, and as dirty as any waged against an innocent and peaceful people in the whole cruel history of warfare. So there is something ironic in the fact that the victims of this incessant terror are the accused before this Council and are defending themselves in daylight while terrorists perform their dark and dirty work by night throughout their land.

Mr. President, I cannot ignore the fact that at the meeting of this Council two days ago, Ambassador [N.T.] Fedorenko, the distinguished representative of the Soviet Union, digressed at great length from the subject before the Council to accuse the United States Government of organizing direct military action against the people of the Indochinese peninsula.

For years—too many years—we have heard these bold and unsupported accusations. I had hoped that these fairy tales would be heard no more. But since the subject has been broached in so fanciful a way, let me set him straight on my Government's policy with respect to Southeast Asia.

First, the United States has no, repeat *no,* national military objective anywhere in Southeast Asia. United States policy for Southeast Asia is very simple. It is the restoration of peace so that the peoples of that area can go about their own independent business in whatever associations they may freely choose for themselves without interference from the outside.

I trust my words have been clear enough on this point.

Second, the United States Government is currently involved in the affairs of the Republic of Viet-Nam for one reason and one reason only: because the Republic of Viet-Nam requested the help of the United States and of other governments to defend itself against armed attack fomented, equipped and directed from the outside.

This is not the first time that the United States Government has come to the aid of peoples prepared to fight for their freedom and independence against armed aggression sponsored from outside their borders. Nor will it be the last time unless the lesson is learned once and for all by *all* aggressors that armed aggression does not pay—that it no longer works—that it will not be tolerated.

The record of the past two decades makes it clear that a nation with the will for self-preservation can outlast and defeat overt or clandestine aggression—even when that internal aggression is heavily supported from the outside, and even after significant early successes by the aggressors. I would remind the members that in 1947, after the aggressors had gained control of most of the country, many people felt that the cause of the Government of Greece was hopelessly lost. But as long as the people of Greece were prepared to fight for the life of their own country, the United States was not prepared to stand by while Greece was overrun.

This principle does not change with the geographical setting. Aggression is aggression; organized violence is organized violence. Only the scale and the scenery change; the point is the same in Viet-Nam today as it was in Greece in 1947 and in Korea in 1950. The Indochinese Communist party, the parent of the present Communist party in North Viet-Nam, made it abundantly clear as early as 1951 that the aim of the Vietnamese Communist leadership is to take control of all of Indochina. This goal has not changed—it is still clearly the objective of the Vietnamese Communist leadership in Hanoi.

Hanoi seeks to accomplish this purpose in South Viet-Nam through subversive guerrilla warfare directed, controlled, and supplied by North Viet-Nam. The Communist leadership in Hanoi has sought to pretend that the insurgency in South Viet-Nam is a civil war, but Hanoi's hand shows very clearly. Public statements by the Communist party in North Viet-Nam and its leaders have repeatedly demonstrated Hanoi's direction of the struggle in South Viet-Nam. For example, Le Duan, First Secretary of the Party, stated on September 5, 1960, "At present our Party is facing [a] momentous task: . . . to strive to complete . . . revolution throughout the country. . . ." He also said this: "The North is the common revolutionary base of the whole country." Three months after the Communist Party Congress in Hanoi in September 1960, the so-called National Front for the Liberation of South Viet-Nam was set up pursuant to plans outlined publicly at that Congress.

The International Control Commission in Viet-Nam, established by the Geneva accords of 1954,[293] stated in a special report which it issued in June, 1962,[294] that there is sufficient evidence to show that North Viet-Nam has violated various articles of the Geneva accords by its introduction of armed personnel, arms, munitions, and other supplies from North Viet-Nam into South Viet-Nam with the object of supporting, organizing, and carrying out hostile activities against the Government and armed forces of South Viet-Nam.

Infiltration of military personnel and supplies from North Viet-Nam to South Viet-Nam has been carried out steadily over the past several years. The total number of military cadres sent into South Viet-Nam via infiltration routes runs into the thousands. Such infiltration is well documented on the basis of numerous defectors and prisoners taken by the armed forces of South Viet-Nam.

Introduction of Communist weapons into South Viet-Nam has also grown steadily. An increasing amount of weapons and ammunition captured from the Viet Cong has been proven to be of Chinese Communist manufacture or origin. For example, in December, 1963, a large cache of Viet Cong equipment captured in one of the Mekong Delta provinces in South Viet-Nam included recoilless rifles, rocket launchers, carbines, and ammunition of Chinese Communist manufacture.

The United States cannot stand by while Southeast Asia is overrun by armed aggressors. As long as the peoples of that area are determined to preserve their own independence and ask for our help in preserving it, we will extend it. This, of course, is the meaning of President Johnson's request a few days ago for additional funds for more economic as well as military assistance for Viet-Nam.

And if anyone has the illusion that my Government will abandon the people of Viet-Nam—or that we shall weary of the burden of support that we are rendering these people—it can only be due to ignorance of the strength and the conviction of the American people.

We all know that Southeast Asia has been the victim of almost incessant violence for more than a decade and a half. Yet despite this fact, it has been suggested that we should give up helping the people of Viet-Nam to defend themselves and seek only a political solution. But a political solution is just what we have already had, and it is in defense—in support—of that political solution that Viet-Nam is fighting today. The United States has never been against political solutions. Indeed, we have faithfully supported the political solutions that were agreed upon at Geneva in 1954 and again in 1962.[295] The threat to peace in the area stems from the fact that others have not done likewise.

The Geneva accords of 1954 and 1962 were—quite precisely— political agreements to stop the fighting, to restore the peace, to secure the independence of Viet-Nam and Laos and Cambodia, to guarantee the integrity of their frontiers, and to permit these much-abused peoples to go about their own business in their own ways. The United States, though not a signatory to the 1954 accords, has sought to honor these agreements in the hope that they would permit those people to live in peace and independence from outside interference from any quarter and for all time.

To this day there is only one major trouble with the political agreements reached at Geneva with respect to Viet-Nam, Cambodia, and Laos in 1954 and again with respect to Laos in 1962. It is this: The ink was hardly dry on the Geneva accords in 1954 before North Viet-Nam began to violate them systematically with comradely assistance from the regime in Peiping. Nearly a million people living in North Viet-Nam in 1954 exercised the right given to them under the Geneva agreement to move south to the Republic of Viet-Nam. Even while this was going on, units of the Viet Minh were hiding their arms and settling down within the frontiers of the Republic to form the nucleus of today's so-called Viet Cong[296]—to await the signal from outside their borders to rise and strike. In the meantime they have been trained and supplied in considerable measure from North Viet-Nam—in violation of the Geneva agreement, the political settlement. They have been reinforced by guerrilla forces moved into the Republic of Viet-Nam through Laos—in violation of the Geneva agreement, the political settlement.

This is the reason—and the only reason—why there is fighting in Viet-Nam today. There is fighting in Viet-Nam today only because the political settlement for Viet-Nam reached at Geneva in

1954 has been deliberately and flagrantly and systematically violated.

As I say, Mr. President, this is the reason why my Government —and to a lesser extent other governments—have come to the aid of the Government of the Republic of Viet-Nam as it fights for its life against armed aggression directed from outside its frontiers in contemptuous violation of binding agreements. If the Government of the Republic of Viet-Nam is fighting today, it is fighting to defend the Geneva agreement which has proven undefendable by any other means. If arms are being used in Viet-Nam today, it is only because a political solution has been violated cynically for years.

The same disregard for the political settlement reached at Geneva has been demonstrated—by the same parties—in Laos.[297] Violation has been followed by a period of quiet—and then another violation. Limited aggression has been followed by a period of calm—and then another limited aggression. Throughout the period since July, 1962, when the Laotian settlement was conceded, the Prime Minister of Laos, Prince Souvanna Phouma, has with great patience and fortitude sought to maintain the neutrality and independence of his country. He has made every effort to bring about Pathet Lao cooperation in the Government of National Union.

Now, in the past few days, we have seen a massive, deliberate, armed attack against the forces of the coalition government of Prime Minister Souvanna Phouma. The attack was mounted by a member of that coalition government, with the military assistance of one of the signatories of the Geneva accords. These violations are obviously aimed at increasing the amount of Lao territory under Communist control.

The military offensive of recent days must be seen as an outright attempt to destroy by violence what the whole structure of the Geneva accords was intended to preserve. Hanoi has persistently refused to withdraw the Vietnamese Communist forces from Laos despite repeated demands by the Lao Prime Minister. Hanoi has also consistently continued the use of Laos as a corridor for infiltration of men and supplies from North Viet-Nam into South Viet-Nam.

It is quite clear that the Communists regard the Geneva accords of 1962 as an instrument which in no way restrains the Communists from pursuing their objective of taking over Laos as well as South Viet-Nam.

The recent attempt to overthrow the constitutional government headed by Prime Minister Souvanna Phouma was in large part attributable to the failure of the machinery set up with the Geneva accords to function in response to requests by the Government of Laos. This machinery has been persistently sabotaged by the Communist member of the International Control Commission, who has succeeded by misuse of the so-called veto power in paralyzing the machinery designed to protect the peace in that area and thereby undermining support of the Souvanna Government. Today, however, that government which was created under the Geneva Agreements remains in full exercise of its authority as the legitimate government of a neutral Laos.

The other Geneva signatories must live up to their solemn commitments and support Prime Minister Souvanna Phouma in his efforts to preserve the independence and neutrality which the world thought had been won at Geneva. These solemn obligations must not be betrayed.

Mr. President, my Government takes a very grave view of these events. Those who are responsible have set foot upon an exceedingly dangerous path.

As we look at world affairs in recent years, we have reason to hope that this lesson has at last been learned by all but those fanatics who cling to the doctrine that they can further their ambitions by armed force.

Chairman Khrushchev said it well and clearly in his New Year's Day message to other heads of government around the world. In that letter he asked for "recognition of the fact that territories of states must not, even temporarily, be the target of any kind of invasion, attack, military occupation or other coercive measures, directly or indirectly undertaken by other states for any political, economic, strategic, boundary, or other considerations, whatso-ever."[298]

There is not a member of this Council or a member of this organization which does not share a common interest in a final and total renunciation—except in self-defense—of the use of force as a means of pursuing national aims. The doctrine of militant violence has been rendered null and void by the technology of modern weapons and the vulnerability of a world in which the peace can-not be ruptured anywhere without endangering the peace every-where.

Finally, Mr. President, with respect to Southeast Asia in general, let me say this. There is a very easy way to restore order in South-east Asia. There is a very simple, safe way to bring about the end of United States military aid to the Republic of Viet-Nam.

Let all foreign troops withdraw from Laos. Let all states in that area make and abide by the simple decision to leave their neighbors alone. Stop the secret subversion of other people's independence. Stop the clandestine and illegal transit of national frontiers. Stop the export of revolution and the doctrine of violence. Stop the violations of the political agreements reached at Geneva for the future of Southeast Asia.

The people of Laos want to be left alone.

The people of Viet-Nam want to be left alone.

The people of Cambodia want to be left alone.

When their neighbors decide to leave them alone—as they must—there will be no fighting in Southeast Asia and no need for American advisers to leave their homes to help these people resist aggression. Any time that decision can be put in enforceable terms, my Government will be only too happy to put down the burden that we have been sharing with those determined to preserve their independence. Until such assurances are forthcoming, we shall stand for the independence of free peoples in Southeast Asia as we have elsewhere.

Now, Mr. President, if we can return to the more limited issue before this Council today: the security of the frontier between Cambodia and the Republic of Viet-Nam. My Government is in complete sympathy with the concern of the Government of Cambodia for the sanctity of its borders and the security of its people. Indeed, we have been guided for nearly a decade, in this respect, by the words of the final declaration of the Geneva conference of July 21, 1954:

In their relations with Cambodia, Laos and Viet-Nam, each member of the Geneva Conference undertakes to respect the sovereignty, the independence, the unity and the territorial integrity of the above-mentioned states, and to refrain from any interference in their internal affairs.[299]

With respect to the allegations now made against my country, I shall do no more than reiterate what Ambassador [Charles W.] Yost, the United States delegate, said to this Council on Tuesday morning:[300] The United States has expressed regret officially for the tragic results of the border incidents in which an American adviser was present; our careful investigations so far have failed to produce evidence that any Americans were present in the inadvertent crossing of the Cambodian frontier on May 7 and May 8; and there is, of course, no question whatever of either aggression or aggressive intent against Cambodia on the part of my country.

Let me emphasize, Mr. President, that my Government has the greatest regard for Cambodia and its people and its Chief of State, Prince Sihanouk, whom I have the privilege of knowing. We believe he has done a great deal for his people and for the independence of his country. We have demonstrated our regard for his effort on behalf of his people in very practical ways over the past decade. We have no doubt that he wants to assure conditions in which his people can live in peace and security. My Government associates itself explicitly with this aim. If the people of Cambodia wish to live in peace and security and independence—and free from external alignment if they so choose—then we want for them precisely what they want for themselves. We have no quarrel whatsoever with the desire of Cambodia to go its own way.

The difficulty, Mr. President, has been that Cambodia has not been in a position to carry out, with its own unaided strength, its own desire to live in peace and tranquillity. Others in the area have not been prepared to leave the people of Cambodia free to pursue their own ends independently and peacefully. The recent difficulties along the frontier which we have been discussing here in the Council are only superficially and accidentally related to the Republic of Viet-Nam. They are deeply and directly related to the fact that the leaders and armed forces of North Viet-Nam, supported by Communist China, have abused the right of Cambodia to live in peace by using Cambodian territory as a passageway, a source of supply, and a sanctuary from counterattack by the forces of South Viet-Nam, which is trying to maintain its right to live in peace and go its own way, too. Obviously Cambodia cannot be secure, her territorial integrity cannot be assured, her independence cannot be certain, as long as outsiders direct massive violence within the frontiers of her neighboring states. This is the real reason for troubles on the Cambodian border; this is the real reason we are here today.

Now it is suggested that the way to restore security on the Cambodian-Vietnamese border is to reconvene the Geneva conference which ten years ago reached the solemn agreement which I just read to you.

Mr. President, we can surely do better than that. There is no need for another such conference. A Geneva conference on Cambodia could not be expected to produce an agreement any more effective than the agreements we already have. This Council is seized with a specific issue. The Cambodians have brought a specific complaint to this table. Let us deal with it. There is no need to look elsewhere.

We can make, here and now, a constructive decision to help meet the problem that has been laid before us by the Government of Cambodia—to help keep order on her frontier with Viet-Nam and thus to help eliminate at least one of the sources of tension and violence which afflict the area as a whole.

Let me say, Mr. President, that my Government endorses the statement made by the distinguished representative of Cambodia [Voeunsai Sonn] to the Council on Tuesday when he pointed out that states which are not members of the United Nations are not thereby relieved of responsibility for conducting their affairs in line with the principles of the charter of this organization. We could not agree more fully. Yet the regimes of Peiping and Hanoi,

which are not members of this organization, are employing or supporting the use of force against their neighbors. This is why the
borders of Cambodia have seen violence. And this is why we are
here today. And that is why the United Nations has a duty to do
what it can do to maintain order along the frontier between Cambodia and Viet-Nam—to help uphold the principles of the charter
in Southeast Asia.

As for the exact action which this Council might take, Mr. President, my Government is prepared to consider several possibilities.
We are prepared to discuss any practical and constructive steps to
meet the problem before us.

One cannot blame the Vietnamese for concluding that the International Control Commission cannot do an effective job of maintaining frontier security. The "troika" principle of the International Control Commission, which is to say the requirement under
Article 42 of the Geneva Agreement on Viet-Nam that decisions
dealing with questions concerning violations which might lead to
resumption of hostilities can be taken only by unanimous agreement, has contributed to the frustration of the ICC.

The fact that the situation in South Viet-Nam has reached the
crisis stage is itself dramatic testimony of the frustration to which
the International Control Commission has been reduced. With the
exception of the special report on June 2, 1962, to which I referred, condemning Communist violations of the Geneva accords,
the Commission has taken no action with respect to the Communist
campaign of aggression and guerrilla warfare against South Viet-
Nam.

The representative of Cambodia has suggested that a commission
of inquiry investigate whether the Viet Cong has used Cambodian
territory. We have no fundamental objection to a committee of
inquiry. But we do not believe it addresses itself to the basic problem that exists along the Viet-Nam–Cambodia border. More is
needed in order to assure that problems do not continue to arise.

Several practical steps for restoring stability to the frontier have
been suggested, and I shall make brief and preliminary general remarks about them. I should like to reiterate what Ambassador Yost
said, that we have never rejected any proposal for inspection of
Cambodian territory.

One suggestion is that the Council request the two parties directly concerned to establish a substantial military force on a bilateral basis to observe and patrol the frontier and to report to the Secretary-General.

Another suggestion is that such a bilateral force be augmented by the addition of United Nations observers and possibly be placed under United Nations command to provide an impartial third-party element representing the world community. We also could see much merit in this idea.

A third suggestion is to make it an all-United Nations force. This might also be effective. It would involve somewhat larger U.N. expenditures than the other alternatives. But if this method should prove desirable to the members of the Council, the United States will be prepared to contribute.

We would suggest, Mr. President, that whether one of these or some other practical solution is agreed, it would be useful to ask the Secretary-General of the United Nations to offer assistance to Cambodia and the Republic of Viet-Nam in clearly marking the frontiers between the two countries. One of the difficulties is that there are places where one does not know whether he stands on one side of the frontier or the other. Certainly it would help reduce the possibility of further incidents if this uncertainty were to be removed.

In conclusion, Mr. President, let me repeat that I am prepared to discuss the policy and the performance of my Government throughout Southeast Asia. But the issue before us is the security of the Cambodia–Viet-Nam border. I have expressed my Government's views on that subject. I hope other members of the Council also will express their views on that subject and that the Council, which is the primary world agency for peace and security, can quickly take effective steps to remedy a situation which could threaten peace and security.

"We Still Seek No Wider War"

AUGUST 5, 1964

☼

Alden Whitman writes that "escalation in South Vietnam and the Marine Corps landing in the Dominican Republic raised new problems, or rather new versions of the ones that had plagued him [Stevenson] during the Kennedy years. These were a lack of involvement in the making of the Dominican and Vietnamese policy (at times he felt he was being simply ignored). . . . For many of Stevenson's warmest supporters, including artists, writers and scientists, his public pronouncements were, quite simply, not to be believed."[301] In the same vein, Herbert Muller, commenting that "this may truly be called 'Johnson's war,'" speculates:

Stevenson was again unhappy over the war. He was deeply worried by the policy of escalation, knowing the pressures the President was always under to carry it further, even to an all-out war that might bring in China. . . . In any case we were endangering our improved relations with the Soviet, forcing it to join China in condemning our aggression on a Communist country. . . . Meanwhile Johnson was ignoring the United Nations, where Stevenson was kept aware that world opinion was against us. . . . Apparently he was most shaken by an affair that did not come to light until after his death—the failure of U Thant's efforts to arrange the negotiations he always preferred to military action.[302]

Whitman states that in June, 1965, as the Vietnam build-up continued, a group calling itself Artists and Writers Dissent, sent Stevenson a declaration that the Administration policies in Vietnam and the Dominican Republic had "clearly violated the United Nations Charter, international law and those fundamental prin-

410

ciples of human decency which alone can prevent a terrifying, world-wide escalation of suffering and death." They urged him to resign as the American ambassador to the United Nations and to become again "the spokesman for that which is humane in the traditions and in the people of America." Whitman comments that although the declaration "shook Stevenson," a "spokesman for Stevenson said that he would look on any resignation [in protest] as a betrayal and that he was concentrating his efforts rather on 'getting the United Nations back on its feet!' "[303]

In the speech printed below, given to the Security Council on August 5, he charged that North Vietnamese torpedo boats had attacked American ships in international waters. Later called the "Gulf of Tonkin" incident, which provided the base for wide escalation of the war by the United States, the event caused the Czech and Soviet delegates to charge that the United States had violated its own standards of international law by its retaliatory bombing of North Vietnamese torpedo boat bases. Soviet Ambassador Platon Morozov insisted that the American right of self-defense was separate and different from any "right to reprisal," which he argued was "categorically denied by contemporary international law." Both the Communist delegates in the Council charged that the United States was guilty of aggression and criminally irresponsible, and should be condemned. French Ambassador Roger Seydoux argued that the increasing tension proved that the United States must return to "strict and scrupulous respect" for the 1954 Geneva accords. In reply, Stevenson said: "You will find us ready to cooperate 100 per cent. Let North Viet-Nam leave its neighbors alone, let it comply scrupulously with the accords of 1954, and the U.S., as well as South Viet-Nam, will have no cause for military defensive measures."

I HAVE asked for this urgent meeting to bring to the attention of the Security Council acts of deliberate aggression by the Hanoi Regime against naval units of the United States.

Naval vessels of my Government, on routine operations in international waters in the Gulf of Tonkin, have been subjected to deliberate and repeated armed attacks. We therefore have found it necessary to take defensive measures.

The major facts about these incidents were announced last night by the President of the United States and communicated to other governments at the same time I was instructed to request this meeting. I shall recount these facts for you, Mr. President, in chronological order so that all the members may have all the information available to my Government.

At 8:08 A.M. Greenwich Meridian Time, August 2, 1964, the United States Destroyer *Maddox* was on routine patrol in international waters in the Gulf of Tonkin, proceeding in a southeasterly direction away from the coast about 30 miles at sea from the mainland of North Viet-Nam.

The *Maddox* was approached by three high-speed North Vietnamese torpedo boats in attack formation. When it was evident that these torpedo boats intended to take offensive action, the *Maddox*, in accordance with naval practice, fired three warning shots across the bows of the approaching vessels. At approximately the same time, the Aircraft Carrier *Ticonderoga*, which was also in international waters and had been alerted to the impending attack, sent out four aircraft to provide cover for the *Maddox*, the pilots being under orders not to fire unless they or the *Maddox* was fired upon first.

Two of the attacking craft fired torpedoes which the *Maddox* evaded by changing course. All three attacking vessels directed machine-gun fire at the *Maddox*. One of the attacking vessels approached for close attack and was struck by fire from the *Maddox*. After the attack was broken off the *Maddox* continued on a southerly course in international waters.

Now, Mr. President, clearly this was a deliberate armed attack against a naval unit of the United States Government on patrol in the high seas—almost 30 miles off the mainland.

Nevertheless, my Government did its utmost to minimize the explosive potential of this flagrant attack in the hopes that this might be an isolated or uncalculated action. There was local defensive fire. The United States was not drawn into hasty response.

On August 3, the United States took steps to convey to the

Hanoi regime a note calling attention to this aggression stating that United States ships would continue to operate freely on the high seas in accordance with the rights guaranteed by international law, and warning the authorities in Hanoi of the "grave consequences which would inevitably result from any further provoked offensive military action against United States forces." This notification was in accordance with the provisions of the Geneva accords.

Our hopes that this was an isolated incident did not last long. At 2:35 P.M. Greenwich Meridian time, August 4, when it was nighttime in the Gulf of Tonkin, the destroyers *Maddox* and *C. Turner Joy* were again subjected to an armed attack by an undetermined number of motor torpedo boats of the North Vietnamese navy. This time the American vessels were 65 miles from shore, twice as far out on the high seas as on the occasion of the previous attack. This time numerous torpedoes were fired. The attack lasted for over two hours.

There no longer could be any shadow of doubt that this was a planned deliberate military aggression against vessels lawfully present in international waters. One could only conclude that this was the work of authorities dedicated to the use of force to achieve their objectives regardless of the consequences.

My Government therefore determined to take positive but limited and relevant measures to secure its naval units against further aggression. Last night aerial strikes were thus carried out against North Vietnamese torpedo boats and their support facilities. This action was limited in scale—its only targets being the weapons and facilities against which we had been forced to defend ourselves. Our fervent hope is that the point has now been made that acts of armed aggression are not to be tolerated in the Gulf of Tonkin any more than they are to be tolerated anywhere else.

I want to emphasize that the action we have taken is a limited and measured response fitted precisely to the attack that produced it, and that the deployments of additional U.S. forces to Southeast Asia are designed solely to deter further aggression. This is a single action designed to make unmistakably clear that the United States cannot be diverted by military attack from its obligations to help its friends establish and protect their independence. Our naval units are continuing their routine, patrolling on the high seas with orders to protect themselves with all appropriate means against any further aggression. As President Johnson said last night, "We still seek no wider war."

Mr. President, let me repeat that the United States vessels were in international waters when they were attacked.

Let me repeat that freedom of the seas is guaranteed under long-accepted international law applying to all nations alike.

Let me repeat that these vessels took no belligerent actions of any kind until they were subject to armed attack.

And let me say once more that the action they took in self-defense is the right of all nations and is fully within the provisions of the Charter of the United Nations.

The acts of aggression by the North Vietnamese in the Gulf of Tonkin make no sense whatsoever standing alone. They defy rational explanation except as part of a larger pattern with a larger purpose. As isolated events, the kidnaping of village officials in the Republic of South Viet-Nam makes no sense either. Neither does the burning of a schoolhouse—or the sabotage of an irrigation project—or the murder of a medical worker—or the random bomb thrown into a crowd of innocent people sitting in a café.

All these wanton acts of violence and destruction fit into the larger pattern of what has been going on in Southeast Asia for the past decade and a half. So does the arming of terrorist gangs in South Viet-Nam by the regimes in Hanoi and Peking. So does the infiltration of armed personnel to make war against the legitimate government of that nation. So does the fighting in Laos—and all the acts of subversion—and all the propaganda—and the sabotage of the international machinery established to keep the peace by the Geneva Agreements—and the deliberate, systematic, and flagrant violations of those agreements by two regimes which signed them and which by all tenets of decency, law, and civilized practice are bound by their provisions.

The attempt to sink United States destroyers in international waters is much more spectacular than the attempt to murder the mayor of a village in his bed at night. But they are both part of the pattern, and the pattern is designed to subjugate the people of Southeast Asia to an empire ruled by means of force of arms, of rule by terror, of expansion by violence.

Mr. President, it is only in this larger view that we can discuss intelligently the matter that we have brought to this Council.

In his statement last night, President Johnson concluded by emphasizing that the mission of the United States is peace. Under the explicit instructions of President Johnson, I want to repeat that assurance in the Security Council this afternoon: Our mission is peace.

We hoped that the peace settlement in 1954 would lead to peace in Viet-Nam. We hoped that that settlement, and the supplementary Geneva Accords of 1962, would lead to peace in Laos. Communist governments have tried aggression before, and have failed. Each time the lesson has had to be learned anew.

We are dealing here with a regime that has not yet learned the lesson that aggression does not pay, cannot be sustained, and will always be thrown back by people who believe, as we do, that people want freedom and independence, not subjection and the role of satellite in a modern empire.

In Southeast Asia, we want nothing more, and nothing less, than the assured and guaranteed independence of the peoples of the area. We are in Southeast Asia to help our friends preserve their own opportunity to be free of imported terror, alien assassination, managed by the North Viet-Nam Communists based in Hanoi and backed by the Chinese Communists from Peking.

Two months ago, when we were discussing in this Council the problems created on the Cambodia–South Viet-Nam frontier by the Communist Viet Cong, I defined our peace aims in Southeast Asia. I repeat them today:

There is a very easy way to restore order in Southeast Asia. There is a very simple, safe way to bring about the end of the United States military aid to the Republic of Viet-Nam.

Let all foreign troops withdraw from Laos. Let all states in that area make and abide by the simple decision to leave their neighbors alone. Stop the secret subversion of other people's independence. Stop the clandestine and illegal transit of national frontiers. Stop the export of revolution and the doctrine of violence. Stop the violations of the political agreements reached at Geneva for the future of Southeast Asia.

The people of Laos want to be left alone.

The people of Viet-Nam want to be left alone.

The people of Cambodia want to be left alone.

When their neighbors decide to leave them alone—as they must—there will be no fighting in Southeast Asia and no need for American advisers to leave their homes to help these peoples resist aggression. Any time that decision can be put in enforceable terms, my Government will be only too happy to put down the burden that we have been sharing with those determined to preserve their independence.

Until such assurances are forthcoming, we shall stand for the independence of free peoples in Southeast Asia as we have elsewhere.

That is what I said to this Council in May. That is what I repeat to this Council in August.

When the political settlements freely negotiated at the conference tables in Geneva are enforced, the independence of Southeast Asia will be guaranteed. When the peace agreements reached long ago are made effective, peace will return to Southeast Asia and military power can be withdrawn.

The United States Reviews the
U.N. Constitutional Crisis

JANUARY 26, 1965

☼

In his biography of Stevenson, Stuart Gerry Brown writes:

If there was any important failure in Stevenson's five-year record as American Representative at the United Nations, it was in his persistent but unrewarding effort during the General Assembly of 1965 to persuade the Soviet Union, France, Belgium, and some other nations, to pay, at least in part, their financial dues to the UN. . . . It was American policy to hold to this provision [Article 19 of the Charter, which states that a member nation two years in arrears with its financial payments to the United Nations would automatically lose its vote in the General Assembly] on the ground that if it were not enforced the UN executive effort, at least, would be frustrated.[304]

Since the Assembly could not function without the Soviet Union, a variety of attempts at compromise were made with the decision that no vote on a substantive issue would be taken during that session in the General Assembly. This speech was presented in the Plenary Session of the Assembly on January 26, 1965. As did so many of his earlier speeches, it reflects his broad philosophical approach to the usefulness of the United Nations and the dangers besetting it.

MR. PRESIDENT [Alex Quaison-Sackey of Ghana]:
  This is my first opportunity to express publicly, on behalf of the delegation of the United States, our congratulations to you on your election as President of this Assembly, and our admiration—I

shall now add—for the manner in which you have conducted that office in most difficult circumstances.

I have asked to speak at this late date so that I can share with all delegations, in a spirit of openness, with candor and with simplicity my Government's views on the state of affairs at this United Nations as our annual general debate comes to its conclusion. Certain things which I shall say here today have to do with law, with procedures, with technical and administrative matters. So I want to emphasize in advance that these are but manifestations of much deeper concerns about peace and world order, about the welfare of human society and the prospects of our peoples for rewarding lives.

There can be little doubt that we have reached one of those watersheds in human affairs. It is not the first, of course, and surely not the last. But this is clearly a critical point in the long, wearisome, erratic, quarrelsome but relentless journey toward that lighter and brighter community which is the central thread of the human story.

Twenty years ago we took a giant stride on that historic journey. We negotiated and signed and ratified the Charter of the United Nations. The first purpose of the United Nations was to create a new system of world order. Those who drafted the Charter were acutely conscious of earlier efforts to find collective security against war and were determined to do better this time.

I speak to you as one who participated in the formulation of the Charter of this organization, both in the Preparatory Commission in London and in the Charter Conference in San Francisco, under circumstances so eloquently recalled by Dr. Lleras Camargo in his memorable address in this hall last evening.[305] I too recall vividly the fears and hopes of those days as the World War ended in the twilight of an old era and the fresh dawn of a new one—fears and hopes which brought us together determined to ensure that such a world catastrophe would never again occur. At those Conferences we labored long and diligently; we tried to take into account the interests of all states; we attempted to subordinate narrow national interests to the broad common good.

This time we would create something better than static conference machinery, something solid enough to withstand the winds of controversy blowing outside and inside its halls. This time we would create workable machinery for keeping the peace and for settling disputes by nonviolent means, and we would endow it with a capacity to act. This time we would create working organizations to stimulate economic growth and social welfare and human rights —and put resources back of them. And this time we would create a constitutional framework flexible enough to adapt to an inevitably changing environment and to allow for vigorous growth through invention, experiment and improvisation within that framework.

Twenty years ago nobody could see, of course, what the post-war years would bring. But there was a widespread feeling, in those bright, cool days on the rim of the Pacific, that the United Nations was our last chance for a peaceful and secure system of world order, that we could not afford another failure. For the character of war had evolved from a clash of armies for strategic ground to the possibility of the destruction of populations and the indiscriminate destruction of wealth and culture; the weapons of war had evolved from field artillery to block-busting bombs, and then to a single warhead that could wipe out a city; and recourse to war had evolved from what was cruel to what could be suicidal insanity.

Twenty years ago there was a widespread feeling, too, that it already was late in the day to begin loosening the strait jackets of unbridled sovereignty and unyielding secrecy, to begin systematically to build the institutions of a peaceful, prosperous international community in the vulnerable, fragile, interdependent neighborhood of our planet. For science and technology were making the nations interdependent willy-nilly and interconnected whether they liked it or not. Science and technology were making international cooperation and organization a modern imperative, in spite of ideology and politics, and were paving the way for a practical assault on world poverty, if the world was up to the challenge.

It may well be that twenty years ago people expected too much too soon from this organization. In the workaday world we quickly discover that social and scientific and institutional inventions—even important and dramatic ones—do not swing wide the doors to Utopia, but only add new tools to work with in the solution of man's problems and the abatement of man's ills. In the workaday world we also discover, over and over again, that man himself is a stubborn animal, and in no way more stubborn than in his reluctance to abandon the iron luggage of the past that encumbers his journey toward human community. In the workaday world we discover, too, that to be effective an international organization must be relevant to contemporary world realities, and that there may be conflicting views as to just what those realities are.

So we have learned how real are the limitations upon a single enterprise so bold and so comprehensive in its goals as the United Nations. We have learned how heavy are the chains of inherited tradition that inhibit man's journey towards wider community. We have learned that the United Nations will be no less—and can be no better—than its membership makes it in the context of its times.

And yet, we have seen that the Charter of this organization has made it possible to maintain a hopeful rate of dynamic growth; to adapt to changing realities in world affairs; to begin to create workable international peace-keeping machinery; to begin to grapple with the complex problems of disarmament; to stimulate effective international cooperation; and so to move, however erratically, down the road toward that international community which is both the goal of the Charter and the lesson of history. I am proud to say that not only has the United States given of its heart and mind to this endeavor, but that over the years we have contributed more than $2 billion to the support of the United Nations and its activities.

The progress which this institution has fostered has been accomplished despite the unprecedented character of the organization, despite the intractable nature of many of the problems with which we have dealt, despite the so-called cold war which intruded too often in our deliberations, and despite a series of debilitating external and internal crises, from which the organization has, in fact, emerged each time more mature and better able to face the next one.

In the short space of two decades, the United Nations has responded time after time to breaches of the peace and to threats to the peace. A dozen times, it has repaired or helped repair the rent

fabric of peace. And who can say that this has not made the difference between a living earth and an uninhabitable wasteland on this
planet?

During that time, the United Nations has sponsored or endorsed
all the efforts to halt the armaments race and to press on toward
general and complete disarmament in a peaceful world. Its efforts
were not fruitless. Agreement was reached on a direct communications link between Washington and Moscow—a step lessening the
risk of war through accident or miscalculation. A treaty was
signed—long urged by the General Assembly—banning nuclear
weapons tests in the atmosphere, outer space and under water. The
two states presently capable of stationing nuclear weapons in outer
space expressed in the United Nations their intent to refrain from
doing so, and we adopted a resolution here calling on all other
states to do likewise. In short, the efforts of the last twenty years
have at last begun to arrest the vicious spiral of uncontrolled
nuclear armament.

In the short span of twenty years, the United Nations also has
created a versatile range of international agencies which are surveying resources, distributing food, improving agriculture, purifying water, caring for children, controlling disease, training technicians—researching, planning, programming, investing, teaching,
administering thousands of projects in hundreds of places, so that,
to quote the Charter, "we the peoples of the United Nations" may
enjoy "social progress and better standards of life in larger freedom." These activities are now being financed at the impressive
level of some $350 million a year.

In its brief life the United Nations also has taken major strides
toward creating an open community of science—for the peaceful
use of atomic energy, for the application of technology to industry
and agriculture and transport and communications and health, for
a worldwide weather reporting sytem, for shared research in many
fields, and for cooperative regulation of the growing list of tasks—
like frequency allocation and aerial navigation—which cannot even
be discussed except on the assumption of international cooperation
and organization.

We have proved in practice that these things can be done within the Charter of the United Nations whenever enough of the members want them done and are willing to provide the means to get them done.

In the process we have left well behind us the outdated question of whether there should be a community of international institutions to serve our common interests. The question now is how extensive and effective these organizations should become—how versatile, how dynamic, how efficient—and on what assumptions about the sharing of support and responsibility.

And yet, in spite of this history, we have reached a fork in the road ahead of this organization—and thus in our search for world order and our journey toward a wider community.

Is this to over-draw the picture—to over-dramatize the situation in which we find ourselves? Not, I think, if we recollect the historic character of warfare.

I assume that we are all convinced that the revolutionary advance in destructive capability—and the danger that little wars anywhere can lead to bigger wars everywhere—has made war an obsolete means for the settlement of disputes among nations. Yet World War II, I remind you, occurred after it already was clear to intelligent men that war had become an irrational instrument of national policy—that another way must be found to settle international accounts and to effect needed change.

The reason is not hard to find: the level of destruction does not obliterate the inherently double character of warfare. In our minds we tend to associate war—and correctly so—with the ancient lust for conquest and dominion; we tend—rightly—to identify war as the instrument of conquerors and tyrants.

Yet in every war there is a defender who, however reluctantly, takes up arms in self-defense and calls upon others for aid. And this is the other face of war: war has been the instrument by which lawlessness and rebellion have been suppressed, by which nations have preserved their independence, by which freedom has been defended. War is an instrument of aggression—and also the means by which the aggressors have been turned back and the would-be masters have been struck down.

As long ago as 490 B.C., Miltiades and his heroic spearmen saved Greek civilization on the Plain of Marathon. Nearly 2,500 years later, the gallant flyers of the Royal Air Force fought in the skies over Britain until the invading air armadas were turned back, while the indomitable legions of the Soviet Army fought on and on at Stalingrad until at last they broke the back of the Nazi threat to the Russian homeland.

All through the years we have been taught again and again that most men value some things more than life itself. And no one has reminded us more eloquently and resolutely that it is better to die on your feet than to live on your knees than the noble spirit that left us the other day in London—Sir Winston Churchill.

As long as there are patriots, aggression will be met with resistance—whatever the cost. And the cost rises ever higher with the revolution in weaponry. At Marathon 200 Athenians lost their lives. At Stalingrad 300,000 invaders lost their lives.

There, precisely, is the difficulty we are in. Now, in our day, the end result of aggression and defense is Armageddon—for man has stolen the Promethean fire. Yet resistance to aggression is no less inevitable in the second half of the twentieth century than it was 2,500 years ago.

The powers of the atom unleashed by science are too startling, too intoxicating, and at the same time too useful as human tools for any of us to wish to abandon the astonishing new technology. But, if we will not abandon it, we must master it. Unless the United Nations or some other organization develops reliable machinery for dealing with conflicts and violence by peaceful mean, Armageddon will continue to haunt the human race; for the nations will—as they must—rely on national armaments until they can confidently rely on international institutions to keep the peace.

This, it seems to me, makes the present juncture in our affairs historic and critical. This, it seems to me, is why the Assembly should be able to perform its proper functions in the event of an emergency, and why this issue before us must be resolved.

What then is the issue before us? It is, in essence, whether or not we intend to preserve the effective capacity of this organization to keep the peace. It is whether to continue the difficult but practical and hopeful process of realizing in action the potential of the Charter for growth through collective responsibility, or to turn toward a weaker concept and a different system.

This choice has not burst upon us without warning. Some three and a half years ago, the last Secretary-General, Dag Hammarskjold, in what turned out to be his last report to the General Assembly, foreshadowed this choice quite clearly.

There were, he said:

. . . different concepts of the United Nations, the character of the Organization, its authority and its structure.

On the one side, it has in various ways become clear that certain members conceive of the Organization as a static conference machinery for resolving conflicts of interests and ideologies with a view to peaceful coexistence, within the Charter, to be served by a Secretariat which is to be regarded not as fully internationalized but as representing within its ranks those very interests and ideologies.

Other members have made it clear that they conceive of the Organization primarily as a dynamic instrument of Governments through which they, jointly and for the same purpose, should seek such reconciliation but through which they should also try to develop forms of executive action, undertaken on behalf of all members, and aiming at forestalling conflicts and resolving them, once they have arisen, by appropriate diplomatic or political means, in a spirit of objectivity and in implementation of the principles and purposes of the Charter."[306]

If that language of Mr. Hammarskjold's seems mild and diplomatic, the warning was nevertheless clear. If it was relevant then it is no less relevant now. If we needed an Organization with capacity for executive action then, how much more do we need it now.

There have been many challenges to the United Nations' ability to act, from the abuse of the right of the veto to the effort to impose a troika to replace the Secretary-General. Now we are faced with a challenge to the Assembly's right even to engage in peace-keeping functions or to determine how they are to be financed and to adopt assessments to support them.

The decision to invest this assembly with the power over the United Nations' finances, its power of assessment, was made in 1945 when the Charter was adopted.[307] Ever since then, an overwhelming proportion of the Members have been paying their assessments on the assumption and understanding that this was, in fact, the law—and that the law would be applied impartially to one and all.

Almost from the outset these assessments have included peace-keeping activities. Starting in 1947, the United Nations Truce Supervisory Organization in the Middle East, the United Nations military observer in Kashmir, the United Nations observation mission in Lebanon and other similar missions, were financed by mandatory assessments under Article 17. For ten years no member of the United Nations thought to refuse—as some are now doing—to pay these assessments, or to condemn them as illegal—as they now do.

With the assessments for the United Nations Emergency Force in the Middle East and the Congo, operation[s] were passed year after year by large majorities in this Assembly; the members clearly understood them also as mandatory obligations.

This was the understanding of states when they made voluntary contributions above and beyond their regular scale of assessments to reduce the burden on members less able to pay.

This was the understanding on which the members approved the United Nations bond issue, and it was the understanding on which the Secretary-General sold—and over sixty Member states bought—some $170 million of these bonds.

As the Secretary-General so aptly put it last Monday, the question is whether the United Nations will, in the days ahead, be in a position "to keep faith with those who have kept faith with it."[308]

When the argument was pressed, in spite of the United Nations' unfailing practice, that peace-keeping assessments were not mandatory because peace-keeping costs could not be expenses of the Organization within the meaning of Article 17, that question was taken to the International Court of Justice for an opinion. We all know that the Court confirmed the principle which the Assembly had always followed: Peace-keeping costs when assessed by the Assembly—and specifically those for the Congo and the United Nations Emergency Force—are expenses of the Organization within the meaning of Article 17. We also know that the General Assembly by resolution at the last session accepted that opinion by an overwhelming vote—thus confirming that the law was also the policy of this Assembly as well.

The Assembly's most important prerogative may well be its power of assessment. It is the heart of collective financial responsibility and as the Secretary-General also said last week:

policy of improvisation, of *ad hoc* solutions, of reliance on the generosity of a few rather than the collective responsibility of all . . . cannot much longer endure if the United Nations itself is to endure as a dynamic and effective instrument of international action.[309]

It is your power of assessment which is being challenged. It is the power of each member of this Assembly—and particularly those smaller nations whose primary reliance for peace and security and welfare must be the United Nations. And—make no mistake about it—it is your power to keep or to abandon.

We can live with certain dilemmas and paradoxes; we can paper over certain ambiguities and anomalies; we can ignore certain contradictions of policy and principle in the interests of pursuing the common interest of majorities in this Assembly. And we can, of course, change our procedures and devise new procedures, within the framework of the basic law, for handling our affairs in the future. Or we can indeed change the law. But we cannot have a double standard for applying the present law under which we have been operating in good faith for the past two decades.

We cannot have two rules for paying assessments for the expenses of the Organization: one rule for most of the members and another rule for a few. If this Assembly should ignore the Charter with respect to some of its members, it will be in no position to enforce the Charter impartially as to others, with all the consequences which will follow with respect to the mandatory or voluntary character of assessments.

This is not to say that the procedures under which the Assembly exercises its authority should not conform to changed conditions and to political realities. Indeed, it is all-important that they do.

That is why my Government has suggested that a special finance committee, perhaps with a membership similar to the Committee of Twenty-One, be established by the Assembly to recommend to the General Assembly in the future the ways and means under which it should finance any major peace-keeping operations—and that this committee should consider a number of alternative and flexible financing schemes whenever it is called upon for such recommendations.

We are not dogmatic about this proposal and we are prepared to examine patiently variations and alternatives with other members— we have been for months and months. Certainly it should not be beyond the ingenuity of such a committee, on a case-by-case basis, to devise ways of assuring financing arrangements for the future which are generally acceptable, particularly to the permanent members of the Security Council.

But in favoring procedural changes we do not challenge the basic law of the Charter: we seek improved working procedures. We do not seek to undo the past—but to smooth the future.

We support the primacy of the Security Council in the maintenance of peace and security and would support an increase in its role; but we seek to maintain the residual right of this Assembly to deal with such questions in the event the Security Council fails to do so.

We support the right, under the Charter, of this Assembly to assess the membership for the expenses of this Organization, so long as it enforces this power equitably and impartially; we will also support steps to assure that the views of all are taken fully into account.

We believe, as I have said, that the Assembly should continue, within the scope of its powers, to be able to deal, free of a veto, with problems of peace and security should the need arise. We are prepared to seek ways of accommodating the principle of sovereign equality and the fact of an unequal distribution of responsibility.

The question here is whether the United Nations will demonstrate again, as it has in the past, a capacity for flexibility and adaptation, which has permitted it to grow and to prosper in the past, and whether we continue to adhere to the prevailing principle of collective financial responsibility for world peace.

It will, of course, be up to the Member Governments to decide whether this Organization is going to continue to work under the Charter as it has been accepted by most of us, interpreted by the Court, and endorsed by this Assembly.

My Government is quite clear about its own choice, lest that be a secret to any of you. We want to continue to do our full share in designing and supporting—morally, politically and materially—any sound expansion of the peace-keeping machinery of this Organization. We feel that there are possibilities for a more diversified family of weapons of peace in the United Nations arsenal—from conciliation procedures, to small teams available for investigation of complaints and for border inspection, to logistical plans for peace-keeping missions.

My Government also intends to continue the search for meaningful and verifiable steps to limit and, hopefully—hopefully, I repeat—to halt the arms race. For a peaceful world delivered of the burden of armament, we will pursue with the urgency it merits the objective of stopping the spread of lethal weapons and of halting the multiplication of nuclear arms. This most urgent objective is in the common interest of all mankind. For if we fail to achieve it soon, all the progress attained thus far would be brought to naught and the goal of general and complete disarmament would become more distant than ever.

My Government is prepared to support a further enlargement of the capacity of the international agencies to wage the war against poverty. We would, for example, like to see the combined Special Fund and Technical Assistance Program raise its budgetary goal well beyond the present $150 million once the two programs have been merged satisfactorily. We would like to see a further expansion of capital for the International Development Association. We would like to see a further expansion in the use of food for development. We would like to see some major experiments in bringing to focus the whole family of United Nations agencies.

We would like to see, among other things, the Center for Industrial Development intensify its work and become an effective laboratory for spreading the technology of the industrial revolution to the far corners of the planet. We feel that there are good opportunities for building up the institutions and programs dealing with the transfer and adaption of science and technology, and for developing the wise use of the world's most precious resources.

And, too, we wish to see the final chapter written in the drama of decolonization, and written peacefully. We, too, wish to explore the desirability of creating some new United Nations machinery in that most neglected area of the Charter called human rights. We, too, want to press on in such fields as weather forecasting, nuclear energy, resources conservation, and the conversion of sea water.

My Government is as anxious as any delegation represented in this Assembly to get on with these priority tasks, to press ahead toward the peaceful solution of disputes, toward cooperative development, toward building the law and institutions of a world community in which man can someday turn his full talents to the quality of society and the dignity of the individual.

This is what we have believed in and worked for at the United Nations for two decades now. This is what most of the members have believed in and worked for as long as they have been members.

What, then, is the alternative? What if the Assembly should falter in the exercise of its own authority? What if the Assembly should repudiate its own history, reject the opinion of the International Court, reverse its own decision with respect to that opinion, and shut its eyes to the plain meaning of the Charter, and thereby the treaty which gives it being?

I have no prophetic vision to bring to the answer to this question —for this would be a step in the dark, down an unfamiliar path. I can only say with certainty that the United Nations would be a different institution than most of the Members joined and a lesser institution than it would otherwise be.

I do not have to draw a picture of the uncertainties, the delays, the frustrations and no doubt the failures that would ensue were Members able to decide with impunity which activities they, unilaterally, considered to be legal or illegal and which, unilaterally, they chose to support or not to support from year to year. And so our world would become not a safer but a more dangerous place for us all, and the hopes for a strengthened and expanded and more useful United Nations would have been dimmed.

I must say in all earnestness that my delegation would be dismayed if at this stage in history the members of this Assembly should elect to diminish the authority of this Organization and thereby subtract from the prospects for world order and world peace. If the General Assembly should now detour on the long journey toward an enforceable world order, I fear we will set back the growth of collective responsibility for the maintenance of peace.

Wise men drew a lesson from World War I and established the League of Nations. President Woodrow Wilson took the lead in that great experiment, and my countrymen, in hindsight, deeply regret that the United States did not take up its share of the burden in that historic enterprise. But the lesson of World War II was not wasted on this country as our active leadership in establishing the United Nations and its Charter attests.

Who can say whether we shall have another chance to draw a lesson from another global conflict and start again? But this we know full well: We, the human race, are fellow travelers on a tiny spaceship spinning through infinite space. We can wreck our ship. We can blow the human experiment into nothingness. And by every analogy of practical life, a quarrelsome ship's company and many hands on the steering gear is a good recipe for disaster.

In such a world there can be only one overriding aim—the creation of a decent human order on which we can build a reasonable peace—not simply the precarious peace of balances and alliances, not simply the horrifying peace of mutual terror, but the peace that springs from agreed forms of authority, from accepted systems of justice and arbitration, from an impartial police force.

That is why our commitment to an effective, working, tenacious United Nations is so deep, and why, in the most literal sense, the United Nations carries with it so much of the hope and future of mankind.

This is our position not because we, among the Members, are uniquely dependent upon the United Nations for the security and safety of our citizens.

This is our position not because we, among the Members, especially look to the United Nations for guidance and help for our economic development.

This is our position not because we found it advantageous to our narrow national interests to treat assessments as mandatory; we found it a price worth paying in recognition that others also shared the principle that all Members bear some measure of responsibility for maintaining the peace.

This is our position, rather, because we believe that in the nuclear age the only true national security for all Members lies in a reliable and workable system of dealing with international disputes by nonviolent means—because we believe that we shall continue to face crises and problems which, by definition, can only be dealt with internationally—because we believe that workable, effective international institutions are a plain necessity of our day and age—because we believe that in every secure community shared privileges demand shared responsibility—and because we believe it unwise and unsafe and unnecessary to take a side road at this stage of the journey on which we set out together two decades ago.

Beneath all the complexities of the issue that now threatens the future capacity of this organization, there are some very simple, very basic, very plain points to remember.

My nation, most nations represented here, have paid their assessments and have kept their accounts in good standing.

My Government, most Governments represented here, have accepted the principle of collective financial responsibility and have striven to uphold the prerogatives of this Assembly.

My Government, most of the Governments represented here, want to resolve this crisis without violence to the Charter and to get on with our international business.

That is why we have all stood available to discuss this issue at all times.

What we have sought is not defeat for any Member of this Organization. What we have sought is the success of the United Nations as a living, growing, effective international organization.

But the Assembly is now nearing a fork of the road, and I have attempted to put the issue frankly because the Assembly may soon again have to decide which branch of the road it will take.

And the very least that we can do is to be absolutely clear just what we are doing when we exercise that option.

Finally, I, for one, cannot escape the deep sense that the peoples of the world are looking over our shoulder—waiting to see whether we can overcome our present problem and take up with fresh vigor and with renewed resolution the great unfinished business of peace—which President Johnson has called "the assignment of the century."

The United States Has No Intention to
Dictate the Political Future
of the Dominican Republic

MAY 3, 1965

✡

*Kenneth Davis writes that in early May of 1965 Stevenson and
other officials met with President Johnson to consider the crisis in
the Dominican Republic, where civil war threatened to endanger
the lives of American citizens. Johnson read to the group a statement that he would shortly make public announcing that a small
detachment of marines would be sent in to rescue imperiled foreigners. Davis comments:*

*Stevenson . . . was disturbed by a sentence in the President's state-
ment to the effect that the U.S. stood ever ready to help the Dominican
Republic to preserve its freedom. He asked what that meant. Was this
to be a strictly limited rescue operation or was it to be a full-scale
armed intervention in Dominican Republic affairs? By his own later
account, he received no direct answer to his direct question, and no
support from others in the room, who seemed intimidated by Johnson.
But the President himself finally said to Stevenson, "I think you're
right," and drew a line through the questionable sentence. But a few
days later, Stevenson watched and listened with dismay as the President
of the United States, on TV, announced that we were intervening,
and massively (we sent in no fewer than 20,000 marines) to put down
a Communist-led rebellion and prevent the Dominican Republic from
becoming "another Cuba." He did not believe at the time, he never did
believe, that this action was justified. Indeed, two months later, in a
private, presumably off-the-record talk with correspondent David*

Schoenbrun in Paris, he termed it "a massive blunder." But he never-theless had to defend the action in a public speech at the U.N.[310]

Stevenson gave this speech in the Security Council on May 3, 1965. It was the first of many that he was to give in the Council on the Dominican Republic question that spring before his death.

MR. PRESIDENT, we have heard from the distinguished representative of the Soviet Union about the Congo, about Viet-Nam, about Panama, about Cuba. We have even heard some comments about Alabama and about American business. After the recent experience that we have had in the bodies of the United Nations with Soviet polemics reminiscent of the days of Stalin and Vishinsky, I must say that I am not surprised that the Soviet Union has again used a United Nations body, this time the Security Council, to digress into a whole catalogue of complaints about United States resistance to Communist expansion or assistance to those resisting aggression.

I used to marvel at the audacity of the Soviet Union in pointing an accusing finger at others—the Soviet Union which signed a pact with Hitler, which forcibly added 264,000 square miles and over 24 million people to its own territory and population in the aftermath of World War II, which subjugated all of Eastern Europe, crushed the uprisings in East Germany and Hungary, and which has persistently sought to enlarge its domination elsewhere beyond its borders.

When one hears, as we did this morning, the Soviet Union, which has politically enslaved more people than any nation in this century, attack the good faith, the sincerity and honesty of the Government of the United Kingdom, which has politically liberated more people than any nation in this century, one gets the measure of the Soviet's cynical disdain for fact or fairness in the pursuit of its goals.

Whenever there are difficulties in the Western Hemisphere in which the United States is in any way involved, we know from experience that the Soviet Union will issue a loud and self-righteous blast accusing the United States of aggression or intervention—or both. Of course, it did not do so when it itself installed long-range nuclear missiles in Cuba. Nor does it hesitate to denounce the United States while itself aiding and abetting the Castro regime to foment the forceful overthrow of established governments through the Caribbean area. But whenever any defensive action against subversion or disorder is taken, it is the first to cry "aggression."

Of course, the Soviet Government knows perfectly well that the Western Hemisphere has an active and effective regional organization, the OAS, to which the Republics of the Western Hemisphere are deeply attached, and which they prefer to be the vehicle for resolving the problems of this hemisphere. The Soviet Government also knows that the OAS has for several days been dealing with the situation in the Dominican Republic and has made substantial progress.

But since the Soviet Union cannot use the OAS Council for its customary attacks, it always hastens to bring such matters to the United Nations Security Council, where it can. Most of the members of the United Nations are quite familiar with these tactics and the traditional charges they always involve. You will remember similar charges last year, that the United States was committing aggression against Panama. I believe it is now apparent to all that Panama continues to enjoy its full sovereignty and independence. The same will be true of the Dominican Republic—if the agents of the Cuban dictator do not succeed in first exploiting and then taking over a democratic revolution as they did in Cuba, and as they have tried and are trying to do in Venezuela and in other countries of the region. That this is the objective in the Dominican Republic is apparent from the very eagerness of the Soviet Union and of Cuba to exploit the present ambiguous situation in the Security Council before the full facts about this desperate strike for a Communist take-over in the Dominican Republic become more obvious.

I do not propose here to review in great detail the history of the Dominican Republic over the past five years or to speculate at any length on the origins or the political motivations of the mixed forces which have led to a state of anarchy in that unfortunate country. However, I do believe it relevant to our discussions to recall that the people of the Dominican Republic have suffered from constant turmoil and political conflict following in the wake of the long tyrannical reign of the former dictator, Trujillo.

It is also relevant to recall that the final overthrow of that regime was brought about, in part, by the action of the Organization of American States in adopting diplomatic sanctions against the Trujillo dictatorship. At that time, and in the period both preceding and following the election of Juan Bosch as President of the Dominican Republic, the Government of the United States supported every effort of the Dominican people to establish a representative democracy.

After the last remnants of the Trujillo regime had departed and the Council of State was established, my Government in conjunction with the OAS, assisted in the preparation of an electoral code, made available information and procedures on the mechanics of elections and finally, again in conjunction with the OAS, observed the actual elections, the first free elections held in the Dominican Republic in over thirty years. Both prior to and following this election my Government has pursued extensive efforts to build a stable and free society capable of economic, social and political development. Let there be no doubt in anybody's mind of our devotion to the cause of representative government.

The members of this Council know well the instability which often follows the end of authoritarian regimes and the difficulties of a people unfamiliar with the practices of democracy in establishing effective government. The Soviet Union itself has had some experience with the difficulties of transferring power without public participation and approval.

About a week ago the instability which has plagued the Dominican Republic since the fall of Trujillo erupted and the officials who had governed there for a year and a half were violently forced out; rival groups strove to capture power; fighting broke out between and among them; and the Dominican Republic was left without effective government for some days.

As the situation deteriorated, certain of the contending forces indiscriminately distributed weapons to civilians; armed bands began to roam the streets of Santo Domingo—looting, burning, and sniping—law and order completely broke down.

The Embassies of Mexico, Guatemala, Peru, Ecuador and the

United States were violated and the Embassy of El Salvador burned.

The great majority of those who joined in this insurgent cause in the Dominican Republic are not Communists. In particular, my Government has never believed that the "PRD"—the Dominican Republican party led by President Bosch—is an extremist party. United States cooperation with President Bosch and his Government during his tenure following the ouster of Trujillo speaks for itself.

But while the "PRD" planned and during its first hours led the revolutionary movement against the Government of Reid Cabral, a small group of well-known Communists, consistent with their usual tactics, quickly attempted to seize control of the revolution and of the armed bands in the street.

Quite clearly this group was acting in conformity with directives issued by a Communist conference that met in Havana in late 1964 and printed in *Pravda* last January 18. These called for assistance and continuing campaigns in support of the so-called freedom fighters to be organized "on a permanent basis so that this work will not dwindle to sporadic manifestations or disunited statements."

"Active aid," it went on to say, "should be given to those who are subject at present to cruel repression—for instance, the freedom fighters in Venezuela, Colombia, Guatemala, Honduras, Paraguay and Haiti."

This deliberate effort of Havana and Moscow to promote subversion and overthrow governments in flagrant violation of all norms of international conduct is responsible for much of the unrest in the Caribbean area.

In the face of uncontrollable violence, the Government which had replaced the Reid Cabral Government also quickly crumbled in a few days. Many of its leaders, and also others from the initial leadership of the revolt against the Reid Cabral Government, also sought asylum.

In the absence of any governmental authority Dominican law enforcement and military officials informed our Embassy that the situation was completely out of control, that the police and the

Government could no longer give any guarantee concerning the safety of Americans or of any foreign nationals and that only an immediate landing of American forces could safeguard and protect the lives of thousands of Americans and thousands of other citizens of some thirty other countries.

At that moment, the United States Embassy was under fire; the death toll in the city, according to estimates of the Red Cross, had reached 400; hospitals were unable to care for the wounded; medical supplies were running out; the power supply was broken; and a food shortage threatened.

Faced with this emergency, the threat to the lives of its citizens, and a request for assistance from those Dominican authorities still struggling to maintain order, the United States on April 28 dispatched the first of the security forces we have sent to the island. Since their arrival, nearly 3,000 foreign nationals from 30 countries have been evacuated without loss, although a number of United States military personnel have been killed and wounded.

We have made a full report to the Organization of American States; we have successfully evacuated some 2,000 Americans and about 1,000 persons of other nationality; we have established the secure zone of refuge called for by the OAS; we have supported the dispatch by the OAS of a committee which is at present in Santo Domingo; we have proposed that other American states make military forces available to assist in carrying out the mission of the committee—and OAS is considering such a resolution today.

To refresh your recollection of last week's events, let me remind the Council of the sequence.

On Tuesday, April 27, this situation was considered by the Peace Committee of the OAS. On Wednesday, April 28, also, the OAS was formally notified by the Ambassador of the Dominican Republic about the situation in this country, and my Government called for an urgent meeting of the Council of the Organization of American States to consider ways to bring an end to the bloodshed by a cease-fire and to restore order so that the people of the Dominican Republic could settle their own political affairs without further recourse to arms.

At the same time my Government notified the President of the

Security Council of the action it had taken to evacuate its citizens and other foreign nationals and to set in motion the machinery of the Organization of American States.

The Council of the OAS met on Thursday, April 29, and as a first step—called for an immediate cease-fire on all sides, and addressed an appeal to the Papal Nuncio in Santo Domingo requesting him to use his good offices to help effect a cease-fire and a return to peace.

The Council continued in session and in the early hours of April 30, took a second action urgently calling upon all parties to "pursue immediately all possible means by which a cease-fire may be established and all hostilities and military operations suspended in order to prevent any further tragic loss of life." This same resolution made "an urgent appeal to the same authorities, political groupings and forces on all sides to permit the immediate establishment of an international neutral zone of refuge encompassing the geographic area of the City of Santo Domingo immediately surrounding the embassies of foreign governments, the inviolability of which will be respected by all opposing forces within which nations of all countries will be given safe haven."

At the same time, on the initiative of the Delegate of Venezuela, an urgent meeting of the Foreign Ministers of the Organization of American States was called for May 1 to consider what further measures should be taken to restore peace to the Dominican Republic.

The Security Council was immediately informed by the OAS of all these actions in accordance with Article 54 of the Charter. In accordance with the OAS Resolution of April 30, U.S. Forces in the Dominican Republic have now established a zone of safety. Three thousand persons, as I have said, have now been evacuated— not only United States citizens, but nationals of 30 countries, including 14 countries of this hemisphere. More than 5,000 persons, 1,500 of whom are American. The others, of other foreign nationality, are still awaiting evacuation.

These evacuations continue, and efforts are being made to secure the safety of some 5,000 people awaiting evacuation, including more than 1,000 American citizens and 500 citizens of other countries who remain in peril throughout the Dominican Republic.

In addition, my Government has distributed more than 6,000 tons of food and medical supplies, to all elements in Santo Domingo, to relieve the suffering of the population.

The Council of the OAS, on the afternoon of April 30, dispatched the Secretary-General of the Organization, Dr. José Mora, to the Dominican Republic. He departed on Saturday and is now working with the Papal Nuncio and others to restore order.

On Saturday the OAS again convened at a meeting of consultation of ministers of foreign affairs. This time it despatched a five-member committee composed of Argentina, Brazil, Colombia, Guatemala, and Panama "to go immediately to the city of Santo Domingo, to do everything possible to obtain reestablishment of peace and normal conditons." The committee was directed to give priority to two tasks: In the first place, to offer its good offices "to the Dominican armed groups and political groups and to the diplomatic representatives, for the purpose of obtaining: A cease-fire, the orderly evacuation of the persons who have taken asylum in the embassies and of all foreign citizens who desire to leave the Dominican Republic." Second, "to carry out an investigation of all of the aspects of the situation existing in the Dominican Republic that has led to the convocation of this meeting." This Committee is now actively at work in the Dominican Republic.

Members are no doubt aware that as a result of these repeated appeals a cease-fire was first agreed to—on the initiative of the Papal Nuncio—late in the afternoon of April 30 by the military leaders and by some of the leaders of the opposition forces, and on May 1 also by Colonel Camana. Although the leaders of the opposition forces declare that they no longer control many elements who are still shooting in Santo Domingo, this agreement began to take effect among organized forces Saturday and Sunday, and the situation in the city was much improved by Sunday afternoon.

However, lawlessness and disorder have by no means been eliminated. It has become clear that Communist leaders, many trained in Cuba, have taken increasing control of what was initially a democratic movement, just as they once did in Cuba, and many of the original leaders of the rebellion, the followers of President Bosch, have taken refuge in foreign embassies. The American nations will not permit the establishment of another Communist government in the Western Hemisphere. This was the unanimous view of all the American nations when in January, 1962, they declared, and I quote, "The principles of Communism are incompatible with the principles of the inter-American system."

This is and this will be the common action and the common purpose of the democratic forces of the hemisphere, as President Johnson has said. For the danger is also a common danger and the principles are common principles. So we have acted to summon the resources of this entire hemisphere to this task.

At the same time, we have increased our own forces in the light of the urgency of the situation.

The OAS Committee now in the Dominican Republic has called for the urgent shipment of more food and medical supplies to be made available to Dr. Mora, Secretary-General of the Organization, and the OAS adopted a resolution to that effect this morning. The United States will respond promptly.

The OAS has before it today a resolution which would "request governments of the American States that are capable of doing so to make available to the OAS contingents of their military, naval or air forces—to assist in carrying out the mission of the committee." The same resolution also would provide for the meeting of consultation "to continue in session in order to—take the necessary steps to facilitate the prompt restoration of constitutional government in the Dominican Republic and the withdrawal of foreign forces."

In this connection, I want to reaffirm the statement made by Ambassador Bunker, representing the United States, in the OAS meeting on Saturday: "My Government regrets that there was no inter-American force available to respond to the request of the authorities and the needs of the people of the Dominican Republic, and for the protection of the lives and the safety of other nationals. And my Government would welcome the constitution of such a force, as soon as possible."

Mr. President, the efforts of the OAS to deal with this tragic crisis in the Dominican Republic have been carefully considered, prudent and reasonable. Heroic efforts to end the bloodshed by cease-fire have been made by the Papal Nuncio. The Secretary-General of the OAS, Dr. Mora, is on the island contributing his prestige and abilities to this effort. The Inter-American Committee is also in Santo Domingo and functioning actively.

The Soviet effort—in the face of these energetic and productive steps—to exploit the anarchy in the Dominican Republic for its own ends is regrettable, if familiar.

But, my delegation welcomes the discussion in the Security Council of the situation in the Dominican Republic. Members of the Council are well aware, however, that Article 33 of our Charter states that efforts should be made to find solutions to disputes "first of all" by peaceful means, including "resort to regional agencies or arrangements."

This, of course, does not derogate from the authority of this Council. It merely prescribes the procedures and priorities envisaged by the authors of the Charters of the United Nations and the OAS for dealing with disputes of a local nature, procedures and priorities that have been followed consistently in analogous situations in the past.

In light of all the action by the OAS, it would be prudent, constructive, and in keeping with the precedents established by this Council to permit the regional organization to continue to deal with this regional problem. The United Nations Charter in Article 52 specifically recognizes the authority of regional organizations in dealing with regional problems. The Council recognizes the desirability of encouraging regional efforts, and I may add, the confidence of this Council in the abilities of regional organizations to deal with their own problems has been justified by the historical record.

In closing, Mr. President, I wish to make two things clear.

First, the United States Government has no intention of seeking to dictate the political future of the Dominican Republic. We believe that the Dominican people under the established principle of self-determination should elect their own government through free elections. It is not our intention to impose a military junta or any other government. Our interest lies in the reestablishment of constitutional government and to that end to assist in maintaining the stability essential to the expression of the free choice of the Dominican people. This intent is in full accord with the basic demo-

What We Require Above All
Is a Truce to Terror

JUNE 26, 1965

✡

On June 25 and 26, 1965, President Johnson and Ambassador Stevenson attended the twentieth anniversary commemorative meeting of the founding of the United Nations at San Francisco. In April, Stevenson had prepared a draft for Johnson's speech which would carefully refrain from attacking Communist China and would urge a workable solution to the unpaid-dues issue in the General Assembly. Whitman writes: "At the San Francisco gathering Stevenson, according to Donald Grant of the St. Louis Post Dispatch, *was 'a sobered man, his face twisted with inner pain.' He knew then, Grant wrote, that Johnson 'had rejected his suggestions.' "[312] Kenneth Davis comments: "James Reston's column in* The New York Times *predicted with remarkable accuracy the proposals Johnson would make in San Francisco, whereupon Johnson (presumably for this reason) refused to make them. He ordered the speech rewritten in Washington and gave orders that the final draft be shown to no one, including (he made a point of it) Adlai Stevenson. And Stevenson was told this by a Presidential assistant when he called the White House to ask that the final draft of the speech be read to him."[313]*

Several authors note Stevenson's decision to resign. William Benton, who had been with him earlier on the day he died, July 14, 1965, recalls: "He promised to spend the next weekend playing tennis with me at my home at Southport, Connecticut. We were to talk about his future after his anticipated resignation as U.S. Ambassador to the United Nations at the end of 1965."[314] Before his death, Stevenson asked Eric Sevareid of CBS: "How can I

444

honorably and decently leave this United Nations job? What I would really like is just to sit in the shade with a glass of wine in my hands and watch the dancers."[315] *Irving Howe, in his criticism of Stevenson for not resigning, excluded him from the true liberal tradition and argued that the best excuse for Stevenson remaining in his post was that he had nowhere to turn, "no arena of liberal criticism in which he could speak," and since our political life provided no such support, he was doomed to failure because he "tried to act by civilized standards within the present society."*[316]

In his speech at the United Nations' anniversary meeting in San Francisco, on June 26, printed below, and in his last public address at the United Nations Economic and Social Council meeting in Geneva on July 9, he demonstrated his concern for the creation of peace through the reduction of terror and for the building of reasonable social and economic alternatives to provide a peaceful coexistence. These last statements characterize him, much as Barbara Ward described him: "even when policies and interests diverged violently, [he was] a symbol of America's readiness to live within the limits of civilized and responsible power."[317] *His last public discussion of the grave troubles affecting the world, tempered by his optimistic hope of finding their solutions, was recorded in London, on July 14, the day he died. Britain's BBC TV program "Panorama" broadcast the discussion a few days after his death. Hearing of his death as he was preparing to host a luncheon for visiting Japanese Cabinet members, President Johnson said: "We realize that America has lost its foremost advocate and its most eloquent spirit and one of its finest voices for peace in the world. The world of freedom has lost, I think, perhaps its most dedicated champion."*[318]

Stevenson's search for an ethic—an ethic for survival—had ended.

THIS is the end of a commemorative occasion. Some of us here today who were midwives at the birth of the United Nations can never forget those days here in San Francisco in the twilight of the war, when an old world was dying and a new world was coming to birth.

We shared an audacious dream—and launched a brave enterprise.

It seemed so easy then—when all was hope and expectation. I remember my own sense of pride, of history, of exultation—and the special responsibility that fell upon the host country to that historic conference.

Inescapably I remember, too, both the triumphs and the failures. For over these churning, fearful, and expectant years, we have been up and we have been down.

But up or down, my Government and my people have never lost faith in the United Nations.

The hope, the expectation, was mirrored by the vote—89 to 2—by which the United States Senate approved the ratification of the Charter of the United Nations in 1945—a few weeks after the Charter was signed here in San Francisco in this very hall.

And our Congress only this week—in a rare mood of unanimity —reaffirmed that support and dedicated this country, once again, to the principles of this Organization.

This Concurrent Resolution referred specifically to this twentieth anniversary event, to International Cooperation Year, to the "important and, at times, crucial role" which the United Nations has played in defense of the peace—and to its other "valuable service" to human rights and the fight against hunger, poverty, disease and ignorance.

The Resolution then stated:

Now therefore, be it
Resolved . . .
That it is the sense of the Congress that the United States of America rededicates itself to the principles of the United Nations and to the furtherance of international cooperation within the framework of law and order . . .

Thus in this week of memory and anticipation did the representatives of our democratic diversity declare again our unity and our commitment in matters that touch the peace of the world.

We welcome the counsel of all our brethren, large and small, on this long, rough voyage to world community.

We make no claim to omniscience or omnipotence; we, too, believe that to the humble many things are revealed that are obscure to the mighty.

Out of twenty years of humbling experience, we all know that we need the United Nations more today than we needed it twenty years ago—that we shall need it more twenty years from now than we do today—that the United Nations is a simple necessity of our times.

We know that the issue therefore is not one of survival but of how rapidly or how slowly, how surely or how hesitantly, how skillfully or how clumsily, we shall get on with the work we took up here so short a time ago.

And the record of the United Nations is full of evidence of skillful action by men and women of many nations.

There is time, even in a short address, to salute the Secretary-General and the international civil servants of the U.N. family of agencies who pioneer day in and day out in our emerging world community.

We have time to extend our congratulations to those delegates from the younger nations who have joined our ranks since the Charter first was signed—who have added diversity to our company—who have given us all an intimate sense of wider community —who have contributed their minds and talents, their vision and wisdom to the conduct of our affairs.

We have time, too, to pay our respects to those hundreds of men of the United Nations who have given their lives in the cause of peace—to those tens of thousands from fifty-four countries who have helped the United Nations keep the peace—and to those other thousands of Blue Berets who at this moment stand guard for peace in Gaza, Cyprus, and Kashmir, even as we meet here, peacefully, in San Francisco.

We have time here to offer thanks to those unsung heroes of the United Nations who are responsible for curing 37 million children of the yaws, and 11 million more of trachoma, and another million of leprosy—and to those who have protected 162 million people against tuberculosis, and lowered the incidence of malaria by over 100 million people a year—and to those nameless men and women of the United Nations who have helped find new homes and new lives for more than a million refugees.

These are a few—and only a few—of the things that we the people of the United Nations have done together in the time-speck of two tearing decades.

In the bright glow of 1945 too many looked to the United Nations for the full and final answer to world peace. And in retrospect that day may seem to have opened with the hint of a false dawn.

Certainly we have learned the hard way how elusive is peace—how durable is man's destructive drive—how various are the forms of his aggressions.

We have learned, too, how distant is the dream of those better standards of life in larger freedom—how qualified our capacity to practice tolerance—how conditional our claims to the dignity and worth of the human person—how reserved our respect for the obligations of law.

Our world is still as brave, though not so new, as it seemed in this place two decades past. But the world's leaders, and their peoples, are deeply troubled—and with cause:

There is war in Viet-Nam—and in other places, too.

There has been revolution and bloody violence in the Dominican Republic—and in other places, too.

There are still border troubles in Kashmir, communal bitterness in Cyprus, violence in the Congo.

There is shattering ideological conflict; there is subversion and aggression—overt and clandestine; there is tension and mistrust and fear.

The nuclear threat is spreading and the means of self-destruction are still uncontrolled.

Meanwhile the economic gap between the developed and developing nations grows wider. Human rights and political rights and self-determination are cynically denied. Hunger, disease and ignorance still afflict the majority of God's children.

I agree with Ambassador Bindzi of the Cameroon that these are symptoms of an unstable, dangerous world—too dangerous and too unstable, for the General Assembly to remain in its present deadlock.

We all know that the deadlock must be broken before we sit down again in the General Assembly nine weeks hence.

If there be disputes which keep us apart—there is much, much more to be done which draws us together.

Change, guaranteed by the inventions of science and the innovations of technology, accelerates, threatens and promises.

Already science has destroyed any rational excuse for war between states.

Already science induces statesmen to reach for national prestige not in the conquest of someone's territory, but in the conquest of everyone's environment.

Already science and technology are integrating our world into an open workshop where each new invention defines a new task, and reveals a shared interest, and invites yet another common venture.

In our sprawling workshop of the world community, nations are joined in cooperative endeavor: improving soils—purifying water—harnessing rivers—eradicating disease—feeding children—diffusing knowledge—spreading technology—surveying resources—lending capital—probing the seas—forecasting the weather—setting standards—developing law—and working away at a near infinitude of down-to-earth tasks—tasks for which science has given us the knowledge, and technology has given us the tools, and common sense has given us the wit to perceive that common interest impels us to common enterprise.

Common enterprise is the pulse of world community—the heartbeat of a working peace—the way to the great society.

Yet we are all impatient. We are all concerned that the scope of our work is still too narrow—that the pace of our work is still too slow—that our best efforts to date risk being overwhelmed by the enormity of the tasks and challenges that press upon us from all sides.

We need time to perfect our peace-keeping machinery to the

point where no nation need use its own armed forces save in the service of the international community.

We need time to adjust to the thundering impact of science and technology upon human society and human tradition.

We need time to get on with international cooperation toward disarmament, toward a decent world diet, toward peaceful exploration of outer space, toward international development.

And we the members of the United Nations need time at home to struggle with all those great domestic tasks of welfare and justice and human rights which cry out for the priority attention of all national leaders, regardless of the size or the wealth of or the social system of any particular country.

Is there no way to quicken the pulsebeat of our common enterprise? Is there no shortcut to a better world society? Is there no way to make time our ally—and use it better to serve us all?

Of course there is. For the enemy is not change but violence. To induce needed change without needless murder what we require above all is a truce to terror. We need a moratorium—a breathing spell free from acts of international violence.

We need—all of us—a respite from the malignant claims which violence levies upon our energy and our attention and our resources.

There is not a single dispute in this world—however sharply the issues may be drawn—which would not look different two decades from now, after time and change have done their erosive work on the sharpest corners of conflict.

If we could somehow bring about a Truce to Terror we would soon discover that world order will come not through the purity of the human heart nor the purge of the human soul, but will be wrought from a thousand common ventures that are at once possible and imperative.

Mr. President, on behalf of myself, on behalf of my Government, on behalf of the vast bulk of my countrymen, let me say this:

We believe in the United Nations; we support the United Nations; and we shall work in the future—as we have worked in the past—to add strength, and influence, and permanence to all that the Organization stands for in this, our tempestuous, tormented, talented world of diversity in which all men are brothers and all brothers are somehow, wondrously, different—save in their need for peace.

For all our desperate dangers, I do not believe, in the words of Winston Churchill, "that God has despaired of His children."

For man in his civil society has learned how to live under the law with the institutions of justice, and with a controlled strength that can protect rich and poor alike. This has been done, I say, within domestic society. And in this century, for the first time in human history, we are attempting similar safeguards, a similar framework of justice, a similar sense of law and impartial protection in the whole wide society of man.

This is the profound, the fundamental, the audacious meaning of the United Nations. It is our shield against international folly in an age of ultimate weapons. Either we shall make it grow and flourish, arbitrator of our disputes, mediator of our conflicts, impartial protector against arbitrary violence, or I do not know what power or institution can enable us to save ourselves.

We have the United Nations. We have set it bravely up. And we will carry it bravely forward.

Appendix A: The United Nations Memorial Ceremony for Ambassador Stevenson

JULY 19, 1965

✡

On July 19, 1965, a memorial ceremony was held for Ambassador Stevenson in the General Assembly. The speeches included below are those of U Thant, Secretary-General; Carlos Sosa Rodriguez, President of the General Assembly; Archibald MacLeish, American poet and playwright and Stevenson's close friend; and Secretary of State Dean Rusk. The texts are those found in the Department of State Bulletin, *August 9, 1965.*

Secretary-General U Thant

When I first was told last Wednesday, a little before 1:00 P.M., that Ambassador Stevenson had died in London, I could not believe my ears. I had seen him only recently, in Geneva, less than a week before, and he was so alive and looked so well. When the news was confirmed, it took me some time to accept the fact that Adlai Stevenson had really passed away.

My first thought was to send a message of condolences to President Johnson. In my message I referred to the respect, admiration and affection of all of his colleagues at the United Nations, which Ambassador Stevenson had earned over the last four and a half years by reason of his extraordinary human qualities.

The same afternoon I referred, in a public statement, to my sense of grief and shock because, suddenly and without warning, death had struck and we had lost a good friend and a highly esteemed colleague. As I stated in that tribute, in his years at the United Nations Ambassador Stevenson has demonstrated with rare distinction how it was possible to combine the highest form of patriotism with loyalty to the idea of international peace and cooperation.

When on December 8, 1960, it was announced that Mr. Stevenson was to be Permanent Representative of the United States of America to the United Nations, it seemed to everybody to be such a natural and right appointment. He was, in truth, one of the founding fathers of the United Nations, having been present at the signing of the Charter in San Francisco in June, 1945, and also having been closely associated with the negotiations leading up to that historic event.

Thereafter, he was the head of the United States delegation to the Preparatory Commission and Executive Committee of the United Nations in London, and I believe his offices were located in Grosvenor Square, close to the very spot where he collapsed last Wednesday.

Subsequently, of course, he had entered domestic politics and his direct association with the United Nations was only intermittent. But I have no doubt in my own mind that his presence at the birth of the United Nations was an important factor in the evolution of his own political thinking and in his own dedication to the noble principles and purposes of the Charter.

I remember how many tributes were paid to him when he took over his duties at the United Nations. There were so many encomiums, both within and outside these walls, that they could have turned the head of a lesser man. Not so with Ambassador Stevenson. On one occasion he observed: "Flattery is like smoking—it is not dangerous so long as you do not inhale."

During the four and a half years that he served at the United Nations, he stood as the embodiment of dedication to the principles of the United Nations. His many speeches, which expressed so well his whole mental and intellectual approach, in the championship of fundamental rights, in defense of the dignity and worth of the human person, in support of the equal rights of nations large and small, were cheered and applauded by all sides of the house. He not only spoke with a rare gift of phrase but with such an obvious sincerity that his words carried conviction.

My first contact with Ambassador Stevenson came about in

1952, when I was one of the members of the Burmese delegation to the seventh General Assembly. This was at the time when he was the Democratic candidate for the Presidential election. His speeches were naturally fully reported in the newspapers, and I followed his campaign closely. His speeches were not only master-pieces of oratory; they were also the incisive reflections of a great man and of a great mind, in line with the best traditions of American liberal thought.

There were some during his lifetime, of course, who rated him as too liberal and too far ahead of the times. Others sought to dis-count his effectiveness on the score that he was too much the idealist and therefore not practical enough. This does him injustice.

The line of distinction between idealism and vision is obscure at best. Vision, certainly, is an essential attribute of statesmanship, and he was a fine statesman. In any case, what a dismal world it would be, and how unpromising its future, without spiritual lift given to mankind by the idealists who, in the courage of their conviction, chart the course and mark the goals of man's progress!

At that time I did not have any personal acquaintance with Mr. Stevenson. For me the chance came a year later when he visited Burma in 1953. On that occasion I had the opportunity to talk to him and to discuss with him many issues of current interest. Again I was greatly impressed, not only by the depth of his intellect but equally by his breadth of vision.

From the time that Mr. Stevenson became the Permanent Repre-sentative of his country at the United Nations and while I was still the Permanent Representative of Burma, we developed very close ties of friendship. These ties became even closer toward the end of the year when I assumed my present responsibilities and continued to be so during the last three and a half years. I found it easy to discuss with him any current issue of importance with complete freedom and in full frankness and friendliness.

No one can serve his country in the United Nations for long without having his moments of frustration. Ambassador Stevenson had his share of such moments, and on such occasions he confided to me his innermost thoughts and I was struck by his completely human approach to our common problems. He seemed not only to think about them but also to feel about them as a human being. In all such discussions I was repeatedly impressed by his dedication to the basic concepts of peace, justice, and freedom.

So many tributes have been paid to Mr. Stevenson since his sudden and tragic passing away. So many of his friends and admirers have eulogized his fine intellect, his modesty, and humility. Many have praised his felicitous style and his ready wit. Tributes have been paid to his great learning, which he carried so lightly because he was truly an educated man, a cultured man, a civilized man.

Speaking in San Francisco on June 26, 1965, on the twentieth anniversary of the United Nations, Ambassador Stevenson said:

Some of us here today who were midwives at the birth of the United Nations can never forget those days here in San Francisco in the twilight of the war, when an old world was dying and a new world was coming to birth.

We shared an audacious dream—and launched a brave enterprise.

It seemed so easy then—when all was hope and expectation. I remember my own sense of pride, of history, of exultation. . . .

He went on to reflect:

In the bright glow of 1945 too many looked to the United Nations for the full and final answer to world peace. And in retrospect that day may seem to have opened with the hint of a false dawn.

Certainly we have learned the hard way how elusive is peace, how durable is man's destructive drive. . . .

We have learned, too, how distant is the dream of those better standards of life in larger freedom, how qualified our capacity to practice tolerance, how conditional our claims to the dignity and worth of the human person, how reserved our respect for the obligations of law.

He then proceeded to restate, on behalf of himself, his Government, and the vast bulk of his countrymen, his faith in the United Nations in the following words:

We believe in the United Nations; we support the United Nations; and we shall work in the future, as we have worked in the past, to add strength and influence and permanence to all that the organization stands for in this, our tempestuous, tormented, talented world of diversity in which all men are brothers and all brothers are somehow, wondrously, different—save in their need for peace.

And he concluded by saying:

We have the United Nations. We have set it bravely up. And we will carry it bravely forward.

Unfortunately Adlai Stevenson is no longer with us to keep step with us in the march forward to the goals he had stated so well.

On this occasion, when we are paying homage to the memory of one who has left us so large a legacy, it is fitting, I believe, to give some thought to the momentous questions of war and peace which were so close to his heart.

In my view, many governments, while unwilling to wage war and at the same time unable to make peace, seem to have resigned themselves to the prospect of an interminable cold war. While admittedly the cold war cannot bring down the physical holocaust on our heads, it has nevertheless already inflicted on us a tremendous moral and psychological injury which is intangible but equally destructive. The long, uneasy cold war has destroyed and mutilated not our bodies but our minds. Its weapons are the myths and the legends of propaganda.

It has often been said that in war the first casualty is truth. The cold war is also capable of inflicting the same casualty. The weapons designed and utilized to crush and mutilate the human mind are as potent as any of the weapons designed for physical destruction. The weapons of the cold war contaminate our moral fiber, warp our thinking processes, and afflict us with pathological obsessions. These are the invisible but, nevertheless, the most devastating effects of the cold war on humanity. I believe Adlai Stevenson, in his innermost thoughts, realized these truths.

There is no doubt that Adlai Stevenson has earned a place in history—not only a place in the history of his own country but a place in the history of this world organization. He brought to international diplomacy, in his dignity, his gentility, and his style, a special dimension. Even more, he has earned the admiration and affection of millions of people to whom he was but a name and a legend.

This was so, I think, because so often his voice rang true as the voice of the people, his eloquence expressed the hopes and aspirations of the common man the world over. He was, in our times, in a quite unique way the people's friend. Equally, he has earned a permanent place in the hearts of all those who knew him, and today I mourn his passing not just as a great historical figure, a famous man, but as a true and trusted friend. As the poet says: "Friendship is a nobler thing; Of friendship it is good to sing."

Mr. Sosa Rodriguez

Mr. Secretary-General, Mr. Secretary of State, fellow delegates, ladies and gentlemen:

It is sometimes difficult to put into words the true magnitude of a feeling, the sorrow that takes hold of the spirit in the face of the irreparable, the sadness that invades the soul in the face of hard reality. And yet, we must find words to reflect the pain that grips us at the loss of a friend who knew how to win our hearts, of a colleague who knew how to conquer our admiration, for such was for us Adlai Stevenson, the Governor, as we, his friends, used affectionately to call him.

The impact of the unexpected news, while I was on holiday in Madrid, was a hard blow for me: "Adlai Stevenson died suddenly in London." Only three weeks earlier we had been together in San Francisco at the commemoration of the twentieth anniversary of the United Nations, and he appeared so jovial, as ever so full of life.

Why is it that it is the good men, the men necessary to mankind, that we lose so suddenly? We must bow, however, before the inscrutable dictates of Providence and resign ourselves to the will of God. Yet the vacuum left by the death of a friend we cannot but feel profoundly. We, his colleagues in the United Nations, have lost a dear and admired friend. But America has lost one of its most enlightened sons and the United Nations one of its most faithful champions.

In this time of mourning, in which, gathered here in the General Assembly, witness to so many of his brilliant interventions, we pay tribute to his memory, it seems to us that we still hear the echo of his eloquent and tempered words, the expression of a noble spirit and a high culture placed at the service of his country but placed also at the service of the ideals of peace and justice advocated in the United Nations Charter.

Of the many qualities that adorned the shining personality of Adlai Stevenson, perhaps the most outstanding were his moderation and his profound human feeling. Perhaps this is the reason why he never inspired hatred but only affection, and always respect. Adlai Stevenson, like all public men, has been known to have devoted admirers and formidable adversaries, but he has never been known to have enemies. And it is because the goodness and sincerity that flowed from his personality could not allow for feelings of enmity to be forged against him.

In his distinguished public life, and especially in the United Nations where we better knew him, Stevenson always highlighted the great sense of equanimity and his constant preoccupation with the search for truth and justice. Perhaps these qualities, combined with so vast a culture which perforce opened for him horizons of doubt, at times deprived him of the necessary impetus for political triumph but gave him instead the universal and broad understanding of the problems of our time and an acute and penetrating vision of the future, clouded neither by prejudice nor by preconceived notions.

Adlai Stevenson was a great patriot. He placed at the service of his country, unstintingly and unsparingly, the full fountain of his extraordinary intelligence, of his profound culture, and of his personal charm. And while in the service of his country he was struck down by death.

Adlai Stevenson lived and died for his country. Perhaps better than any other public figure, Adlai Stevenson gave the world an image of a modern and liberal North America, conscious of the outstanding role it is called upon to play in history and conscious of the enormous responsibility derived for her from her great military and economic power. It would be difficult to classify Adlai Stevenson, from the political standpoint, as a man of the right or a man of the left. Stevenson was a liberal in the true sense of the word. He was a man free of extremism, ever respectful of the opinions and viewpoints of others, but always convinced of the force of reason, not of the reason of force. His liberal spirit was reflected in all his acts as a public figure and especially in his performance as a diplomat.

For him, negotiation and conciliation were the methods *par excellence* for the attainment of his aspirations, and he never lacked moderation, patience, and understanding in the fulfillment of the delicate functions entrusted to him. As an orator he was brilliant, eloquent, witty. When it was necessary to enter into polemics he could be sharp and even ironical but at all times courteous and considerate. Socially, he was a man of the world, of great personal charm, with the simplicity and the natural manner of great men.

Adlai Stevenson leaves of his passage through life a profound imprint. He leaves in his country that owes him so much a profound mark. He leaves a mark in the United Nations, which he so vigorously defended. He leaves a mark in the world, which he understood so well. He leaves his imprint in the hearts of his friends, who will never forget him. The death of Adlai Stevenson opens a great vacuum in the intellectual world, in the world of letters, in the world of politics, in the world of diplomacy. It leaves a vacuum in his country, and it leaves a vacuum in the world.

His understanding of the true causes of present-day problems, his great concern with social affairs, his untiring defense of peace and concord among nations, his knowledge of man and his staunch defense of the ideals in which he believed—all of this manifested in his public acts, in his words, his writing, and his actions—had made of him the prototype of the intellectual who uses his culture for the benefit of mankind.

Stevenson was not happy with the egotistical pleasure of having a vast culture for himself. His constant preoccupation with the well-being of the less favored in the world and with the true grandeur of his country made him at all times place that culture at the service of others. That is why he will always be remembered with admiration and respect, both by his partisans and his adversaries.

The death of Adlai Stevenson will be felt most especially in the United Nations, where we had become used to having him as head of his country's delegation. There were those who agreed with the views he upheld and those who did not, but no one can deny that Stevenson, because of his great love for peace, his profound human feeling, and his faith in negotiation, was at all times a guarantee in the most difficult situations. It will not be easy to fill the void that he leaves with his death.

To the great American people, to President Johnson, to Mr. Stevenson's family, I convey my words of condolence. May the good and generous man, the true and sincere statesman, the refined diplomat, the perfect gentleman, who was Adlai Stevenson rest in peace.

May these words of mine be accepted as the modest tribute of a sincere friend to the great man whose memory will continue to guide future generations in the search for peace and justice in our world.

Mr. MacLeish

I am deeply conscious of the privilege of speaking of Adlai Stevenson in this company and in this place, this room which has heard his remembered voice so often.

I am conscious too of the responsibility and burdened by it, for it is here, and perhaps only here, that something might be said of him which would touch, or almost touch, the indefinable, rare thing he was. When Adlai Stevenson spoke at the memorial service for Eleanor Roosevelt, who had come home, he said, to the rose garden at Hyde Park for the last time, he told her friends that it was not her life they had lost—she had lived that out to the full: It was the thing she was—"and who can name it?"

Who can name what he was? Not I certainly. But if there is a room anywhere in which it can be spoken of, it is this one. Not because—not only because—the United Nations was, for so many years, the center of his life and of his concern, but for a different reason: because the organization itself, the nature of the organization, creates a perspective in which a life like Adlai Stevenson's might perhaps be seen—in which it might assume the nobility, the significance, which are its inward form.

In the ordinary context, the context to which our age is increasingly accustomed, a life like his becomes a puzzle, a contradiction which even those who love him—and this room is full of those who love him—cannot readily resolve. Our generation—and not in the United States alone—not only in the United States—is obsessed by a view of human life which leaves no room for any human greatness or magnificence but one. Power fascinates us, and the exercise of power, and we judge our public figures by the power they dispose of, by the offices they hold which give them access to the thrust of power.

Adlai Stevenson cannot be measured by these measures, cannot be known or recognized by them, or even named. He had no taste for power, no desire for it. The unforgettable speech in which he accepted the inevitability of his nomination for the Presidency was a portrait of himself as ill-advised politically as it was personally honorable. And the two disastrous and superb campaigns which he conducted were proof that his reluctance at the start was not the reluctance of political calculation but of passionate belief.

When he said, years afterward, that he would like to be remembered for those unsuccessful ventures, for those two defeats, he meant that there are some things in the life of a democracy more important than to come to power—more important, ultimately, than the possession of the power.

And yet, as the last few days have demonstrated, it is in terms of power or of the failure to come to power, that his life is still most commonly conceived. In the shock and sorrow of his sudden death, the minds of those who wrote and spoke of him went back again and again, over and over, with admiration and regret and more sometimes than admiration or regret, to what were called the contradictions and the paradoxes of his history. He was, we were reminded, a great political figure who had never held a great political office; a master of the art of government who had governed only in his own State; a public man unsuccessful somehow in public life—too fine for it perhaps; a Hamlet who thought too long too deeply, who doubted too scrupulously, who could never permit himself to be as sure as an American politician in the fifties was supposed to be sure, that that voice beneath the battlements urging to violence and revenge was the king his father's voice.

Well, it was true in part of course—true that he thought long and deeply—true that he had the courage of his doubts—true, too, that he was skeptical of hatred and its prophets in a day when the great majority of his fellow citizens were listening to those prophets and believing them. But the conclusions most often drawn from these observations are not true. Hamlet dies to those heartbreaking words in which the pity overwhelms the grief: "Good-night, sweet prince." In Adlai Stevenson's death there is no room for pity. Those of us who mourn him and will always mourn him think of him not as a man defeated in his purpose but as a man victorious in it; not as a man whose life was a contradiction and a paradox, but as a man whose life had a particular singleness, an unusual wholeness, its own law.

And it is here in this room, I think, that that wholeness best appears. For the United Nations, though it knows and suffers from our contemporary trust in power, is dedicated to another end: the subordination of power to the hope for peace—which is to say the hope for humanity. Those qualities in Adlai Stevenson which seemed, in other surroundings, to be traits of character, attributes of personality—his warmth, his charm, his considerateness, his intelligence, his humor, his devotion, his incisiveness, his eloquence—were fused here, in their employment in the noblest of all causes, to compose a complete man, a man so balanced, so harmonious as a human being, that his greatness passed almost unnoticed while he lived.

His effectiveness here, his services to this organization and to the country to which his life was given, others have spoken of and will speak. They were great services, greatly rendered. But the most important thing about them, or so it seems to me, was their humanity. It is not, in the long history of civilization, the accomplishment which counts but the manner of the accomplishment. Works of will are notoriously short-lived, and even works of intellect can fail when the intelligence is cynical or dry. It is only when the end is reached through the human heart as well as through the human mind that the accomplishment is certain to endure. And it is for that reason that Adlai Stevenson seems certain of remembrance.

His great achievement was not political triumph or, indeed, triumph of any kind. His great achievement was the enrichment of his time by the nature of his relationships with his time. If his intelligence was remarkable, it was remarkable, even more than for its clarity, by its modesty, its humor, its total lack of vanity or arrogance. If he was one of the great articulators of his time, one of the few, true voices, it was because the words he spoke were the words of his own thought, of his deepest and most personal conviction. It was himself he gave in word and thought and action, not to his friends alone but to his country, to his world. And the gift had consequences. It changed the tone and temper of political life in the United States for a generation. It humanized the quality of international exchanges throughout a great part of the world. It enlightened a dark time.

Which means, I suppose, that Adlai Stevenson's great achievement was himself. What we have lost, as he said of his friend Mrs. Roosevelt, is not his life. He lived that, if not to the full, at least more fully than almost any other man. What we have lost is himself. And who can name the warmth and richness of it?

Secretary Rusk

Colleagues and friends: His family and his fellow countrymen are grateful that so many from so many lands are gathered in this great hall to pay respect to Adlai Stevenson. Today he returns to the soil which gave him birth, as we gather here at the United Nations which had become the very fiber of his life.

We have been deeply moved by what has been said here today and by the messages which have come from all over the earth. For these are messages which leap over the frontiers of nation, cultural tradition, or ideology, messages which brush aside the passing differences of present controversy and recall that Adlai Stevenson's hopes, dedication, and passionate concern encompassed all mankind.

You and we who have worked alongside him day by day have lost a talented colleague in our most stimulating profession—a profession corporately bound together in the unrelenting search for peace. And what an inspiring colleague he was!

His restless conviction that things were never good enough sustained his zest and joy in public service. But his exultation in a further step toward peace was short-lived, for there was always the unfinished business still to be done—the *next* step which consumed his energy and imagination.

Adlai Stevenson deeply respected the colleagues with whom he labored in this United Nations and treasured the friendships nourished in this place. It is true that he had the capacity for forceful advocacy—when advocacy was needed. But he also had the perception to see that all issues worthy of debate are complex and are seen differently—and honestly—from other points of view. Thus, if his talents blazed bright from the public platform, his skills were no less luminous in the professional arts of quiet diplomacy. For he had the wisdom to seek always to see problems as they are seen by others, even though he might himself not be able to share their view.

He had the discrimination to separate the important from the unimportant. And he had the endless patience—and the tolerance and restraining moderation—to sustain him through the sometimes exhausting work of mediation and accommodation.

He knew, as do all who are schooled in the great traditions of diplomacy, that it is never too early to anticipate difficulty in order to prevent it and never too late to lay the hand of reason upon a crisis in order to solve it.

His colleagues were never bored; perhaps it was with Adlai Stevenson in mind that one editor defined a liberal as "independent and surprising." In private this public man was a warm and entertaining friend, perceptive of the ironies of politics and statecraft, given to illuminating shafts of sardonic wit, obviously worried about the behavior of nations but deeply confident about the nature of man. Because he believed so thoroughly in what he was doing and enjoyed so immensely the doing of it, he poured out his energies to the full—and to the very end.

In these past few days it has been said, over and over again, that Adlai Stevenson was a universal man. And so he was. But not merely because he was informed, well traveled, urbane, sophisticated, eloquent, and gifted. He was all of these; but his universality did not rest upon his being a prince among plain men, but rather upon his being a plain man even among princes. His was the simplicity of fundamental human values—what is common in the midst of diversity—what is permanent in the midst of change: the love of peace, the instinct of tolerance, the feeling of compassion, the devotion to human rights, the urge to act for human welfare.

This philosophy which animated Adlai Stevenson lay deep in him—permanent and indestructible. Perhaps this is what attracted him so powerfully, almost irresistibly, to the United Nations and its noble tasks. For he was committed to the principles of the charter before it was written. The preamble and the first two articles of the charter put into words what had already guided his life. And so it seems most natural that he should have spent so much of his energies in the cause of the United Nations.

He began in 1945 as an assistant to the Secretary of State and adviser to the United States delegation at the charter conference in San Francisco. He was the chief of our delegation at the Preparatory Commission in London, then a delegate to the first and second sessions of the General Assembly. It was altogether fitting that his life work was crowned in these halls and that his last mission was to the United Nations Economic and Social Council.

The words of the charter—and his own ringing phrases which will live in literature—were more than symbols to him. They were calls to action. He used language as few man have—but used it to summon himself and others to work.

The work to which he summoned our reason and our feelings remains still to be done. The charter he kept on his desk contains only 5 pages of philosophy, followed by 50 pages of procedures.

He knew that the philosophy could lift men's vision and sustain their energies. But he also sensed that its meaning was contained not in eloquent words but in agreed procedures, in workable machinery, in arrangements that enabled the nations to work together on particular tasks—while continuing to argue about why they are working together and why they sometimes disagree.

He had early learned the dictum of Justice Oliver Wendell Holmes that general propositions do not decide concrete cases, and he worked hard and long to build that executive machinery for peace which is the real alternative to the system of war by which men and nations have always lived—by which they no longer dare to live.

And so we pay tribute to a working colleague—to a professional diplomat, to a practitioner, a craftsman, an indefatigable worker for peaceful change. And in honoring him we are affirming our determination that the peace of the world will be secured.

You and I, who worked with him, will remember Adlai Stevenson not only as an inspired voice of the conscience of man; we shall remember him and miss him and honor him, as well, as a valued professional colleague—as a brilliant public servant in the broadest and noblest sense of that term.

There is no institution which deserves such talents more than the United Nations; it calls out for the best that can be produced by the societies of man. Three Presidents of the United States sent Adlai Stevenson to the United Nations. They sent you our best.

Now that he is gone I think of the line from *Pilgrim's Progress:* "So he passed over, and all the trumpets sounded for him on the other side." Yet something of him remains with us in this great Assembly Hall.

Appendix B: "A Privilege Abused:
100 Soviet Vetoes"

JUNE 22, 1962

✿

Ambassador Stevenson's address in the Security Council, June 22, 1962, in which he condemned the Soviet misuse of the veto, is historically important and deserves a place among the speeches included in this volume. However, it is printed here, in the appendix, to provide an opportunity to consider it in relation to the problems he faced in delivering it. Since I was present in the Council for the address, I heard the extensive interruptions by Soviet Representative Platon Morozov and saw Stevenson's extensive writing before the speech and during the interruptions. I asked his Protocol Officer, Miss Rosemary E. Spencer, to photocopy the draft of the speech from which he spoke so that I would have his changes, deletions, and additions in his own handwriting. Although she was unable to do this, she allowed me to copy his exact changes from the original draft, which totaled fifty-eight penned comments in a speech intended to be about ten minutes long.

Stevenson, his political advisers, the Soviet and International bureaus (and later the Southeast Asian and Asian bureaus) of the State Department had considered the feasibility and complications involved in delivering a major address against the Soviet misuse of the veto whenever the Soviet delegation would cast its one-hundredth veto in the Security Council. Although the United States had not yet utilized the veto, its possible use in the future barred outright condemnation. Additionally, such an address could further provoke the cold-war politics between the Communist and Western nations. In the spring of 1962, it became evident that this

469

veto would most likely be cast during the heated and sensitive debate on the Kashmir question, the unsettled border dispute between India and Pakistan, which had been discussed in the Council intermittently since 1948. State Department officials urged Stevenson to use extreme caution to avoid offending either of the disputant nations, since Krishna Menon, then Indian Defense Minister, who had flown in to argue his country's position, believed that even the American suggestion to discuss the issue in the Council was an "unfriendly act toward his Government."

Because Menon, Stevenson, and Morozov were expected to give major addresses on June 22, accredited members of the press and guests of the various missions filled the galleries to capacity. As was expected, Morozov vetoed the resolution on the Kashmir question presented by the Irish delegation. Stevenson requested permission to speak first following the vote. During the speech, Morozov interrupted him on three occasions and delivered four additional statements, consuming more time than Stevenson's whole speech; the President, Armand Bérard of France, spoke eight times in an effort to clear up the points of order that Morozov raised; and Alex Quaison-Sackey of Ghana spoke once. What was expected to be a potent but brief speech ended as an hour-long spectacle with considerable attempts on Morozov's part to minimize its effectiveness.

Printed below, the text is a combination of the Security Council verbatim text, including the interruptions, and the copy of Stevenson's original draft from which he spoke. His additions to the original draft are indicated by italics, his deletions by parentheses. My comments are set in brackets. Where Stevenson has italicized a word, it is shown by small capitals. The speech was also printed in Looking Outward *but without the changes or interruptions indicated below. The title is that found in* Looking Outward.

MR. STEVENSON:
(Mr. President:

This is an historic day for the Security Council. It should not pass without notice. A permanent member has just cast its 100th veto.) *I hope the members of the Security Council will not object and will indulge me while I make a few remarks on this historic day in the Security Council. It is a day that should not pass without notice. A permanent member of the Security Council has just cast its 100th veto.*

(Insert A—see attached)

From the beginning of the United Nations, one of its special characteristics has been the voting procedure in the Security Council.

We all recall the serious deliberations which took place at San Francisco concerning the NATURE (,) and the import for the FUTURE (,) of the veto right for the permanent members of the Security Council.

The veto was given to the permanent members primarily because it would be *their* military and economic power which would have to be used to sustain and enforce Security Council decisions directly affecting vital world interests.

Representatives of small and middle-sized states emphasized their anxiety that the veto might be used to hamstring the Security Council. In order to meet such fears (,) the four sponsoring members of the conference set forth their conception at that time of the unanimity rule, with which the delegation of France also associated itself.

The big powers, including the (USSR) *Soviet Union*, specifically stated "It is not to be assumed . . . that the permanent members, any more than the nonpermanent members, would use their veto WILLFULLY to obstruct the operation of the Council."

That was the way we started, Mr. President, at San Francisco seventeen years ago, this very week, I believe. (w) What happened since? Before the first year was out the Soviet Union had cast nine vetoes. The Soviet member of the Council has today cast its 100TH veto. For fifteen years the U.S.S.R. on occasion after occasion has sought to obstruct the operations of the Council, sometimes where Soviet plans and prestige were directly and clearly involved (,) and at other times when (Soviet interests were not directly involved, save that) the continuation of friction might contribute to Soviet objectives.

The Soviet Union has used the veto lavishly to prevent states from assuming their rightful place in the United Nations. In fact, fifty-one of these vetoes were cast on applications for membership in the United Nations. Ireland, a member of this Council, was denied membership for nine years. So were Jordan and Portugal. Austria, Finland and Italy were kept out for eight years. Ceylon was kept out for SEVEN years. (and) Nepal *for* SIX *years*. Mauritania was vetoed in 1960, and Kuwait in 1961. Korea (and Viet-Nam are) *is* still not a member. The veto has been used to tie the admission of clearly qualified states for which there was widespread support (,) to the admission of states and regimes about whose qualifications for membership there were grave doubts. This despite the fact that the tying of the admission of one applicant to that of another has been specifically held by the International Court of Justice to be contrary to the Charter.

The Soviet Delegate used the veto THIRTEEN times to assist Soviet bloc activities against the territorial integrity and the political independence of other states. When the Soviet subverted Czechoslovakia in 1948, the Soviet Delegate vetoed Security Council moves to investigate the case. When Communist-supported guerrillas tried to overturn the independence of Greece in 1946 and 1947, the Soviet again vetoed a Security Council (investigation) *resolution*. And when Thailand asked the Security Council to act against attempted infiltration from Indochina in 1954, the Soviet again vetoed . . .

THE PRESIDENT [Ambassador Armand Bérard of France—interpretation from French]: I call on the representative of the Soviet Union on a point of order.

MR. MOROZOV, Union of Soviet Socialist Republics [interpretation from Russian]: We are obviously hearing a very interesting lecture, no doubt; it is a survey of all the occasions when the veto was used, the veto of the Soviet Union. I would be quite ready to listen to this lecture and to this summing-up if it were on the agenda. But the item on the agenda is not entitled "Summary of the utilization of the veto by the Soviet Union in the Security Council since the inception of the United Nations." When this item is included in the agenda then I myself and the other members of the Council will be more than happy to hear what the members of the Council, and especially the representative of the United States, have to say on this subject. But for the moment, since we are not considering such an item but another item entitled "The India-Pakistan question," which is well-known all over the world as "The India-Pakistan question," it might be a good thing if the President, in full implementation of the powers vested in him by the provisional rules of procedure of the Security Council, were to indicate to the representative of the United States exactly what subject we are discussing in the Council. If, after the vote that was cast on the draft resolution that was inspired by the United States—but which was not defended by it—the representative of the United States has nothing to say, although he supported it by his vote, then perhaps the representative of the United States would be good enough to postpone this most popular and interesting lecture to some future date. In the meantime, in view of the stage at which we have now arrived, I think it would be quite in order to hear explanations of the vote. That is why I am raising this point of order and requesting you, Mr. President, if you will be objective in the application of the rules of procedure, to call the representative of the United States to order. As far as the delegation of the Soviet Union is concerned, we shall make use of our right to explain our vote on that resolution when the right time to do so has arrived. I therefore beg you, Mr. President, to be good enough to settle the point of order that I have just raised.

THE PRESIDENT [interpretation from French]: The representative of the Soviet Union has just referred to my powers as President of the Council, but I cannot entirely agree with him. The powers of the President flow from the provisional rules of procedure and from the practice in the Security Council. Referring to my own experience in the Council, I note that it has been the practice of this body to allow its members to express their opinions or their feelings after a vote has been taken. The vote that was taken this afternoon has, no doubt, an exceptional degree of importance, and this being the case I would point out to the representative of the Soviet Union that I do not believe I have the power to call the representative of the United States to order. I can, however, appeal to all members of the Council to be good enough to limit their statements as much as possible and to be as brief as they can while, at the same time, remaining within the scope of the item which is before us. If the representative of the Soviet Union asks for the floor in due course, I shall certainly not fail to call upon him.

MR. STEVENSON: *When interrupted, I was reciting the instances in which Soviet bloc activities of the veto have been used some thirteen times to assist Soviet bloc activities against the territorial integrity and political independence of other states.*

After realizing its mistake in boycotting the Council during the North Korean aggression against the Republic of Korea in 1950, *I remind the members of the Council that* the (USSR) *Soviet Union* returned to the Council in August and immediately began to veto Security Council decisions designed to uphold the independence of that country. Fortunately for the Korean people and for this organization, that effort failed because we were able to proceed through the General Assembly. Similarly, in 1956, the United Nations was forced to move in the General Assembly to condemn Soviet intervention in Hungary after the Soviet Union (had) supported its aggression against the Hungarian people by invocation of the veto.

And most recently in 1960 the Soviet vetoed a resolution on the Congo sponsored by Ceylon and Tunisia because the resolution was designed in part to resist Soviet efforts to intervene in the Congo despite the fact that the United Nations peace-keeping operation was already in action; again an emergency session of the General Assembly was required before the United Nations could do what was necessary.

There are still more areas in which the veto has been used to obstruct the operation of the Council.

The veto has been frequently used to prevent the United Nations from investigating . . .

MR. MOROZOV [in English]: Point of order.

MR. STEVENSON: *The gentleman, I am sure, will have an opportunity to speak after I have concluded what I have to say, which I submit, Mr. President, is entirely consistent with the rules and entirely proper for me to speak.*

MR. MOROZOV [in English]: I ask for the floor on a point of order.

THE PRESIDENT [interpretation from French]: I call upon the representative of the Soviet Union on a point of order.

MR. MOROZOV [interpretation from Russian]: I expected, Mr. President, that the representative of the United States would adhere not to the first part of your ruling in which you gave approval to his having said certain things which had absolutely no bearing upon the subject under discussion but to the second part of your appeal which had compelled me temporarily to be silent in order to see what would happen to your ruling. In the second part of your appeal there was a recommendation or an enjoinder to all members of the Council, and therefore to the representative of the United States, to keep to the subject under discussion and not to endeavor here to engage in cold war maneuvers in their worst manifestation, such as fortunately we have not heard in the precincts of this Organization for a long time.

In making this statement I request that your ruling be put to the vote so that we may see which members of the Council will support in a positive manner what a member of the Council who happens to be the representative of the United States permits himself to do after a vote. He has made statements dealing not with his motives in voting but with all sorts of political implications which, if the representative of the United States wanted to put them on the agenda of the Security Council as an individual subject, we could deal with and give him a hearing. This we cannot do at the present time and accordingly once again Mr. President, I would request that you call the representative of the United States to order and ask him to deal merely, if he wishes, with the Soviet Union vote on the subject which is—or was—under discussion here. Even then we should be making a serious compromise, as a gesture of conciliation, because after all that has been said here on the substance of the matter to discuss the reasons for my vote in explanation of his own is something no one has any right to do. After all, the discussion has come to an end and some kind of order must be followed. If, Mr. President, you do not come to this legitimate and logical conclusion upon which I insist, on the basis of the provisions of the Charter, on the basis of the practice and the rules of procedure of the Council, I ask that your ruling be put to the vote, because I shall of course vote against it. Others may vote for it or they may abstain or they may do whatever they wish. Then, of course, if a decision is taken on this procedural matter which is contrary to the one upon which I insist with full justification on the basis of the Charter and rules of procedure, it will become apparent that the right of veto in the Security Council is not such a bad thing but is rather a wise thing which compels even some great Powers to remain within the limits which are proper and which obliges them to keep their feet off the table whenever they put them on the table in proper American fashion. That is the question I raise now.

THE PRESIDENT [interpretation from French]: The representative of the Soviet Union has challenged the interpretation of the custom of the Council, as I saw it. My ruling has been challenged and, hence, in accordance with Rule 30, we have to submit this to the vote.

Therefore, I request those members of the Council who disagree with my interpretation of the Council's usage to be good enough to signify by raising their hands.

We have already announced the voting, and at this point I should not call on the representative of Ghana. However, I understand that it is on a point of order.

MR. QUAISON-SACKEY of Ghana: I raised my hand before you spoke, actually I was going to say that I did not know exactly what you were going to say in response to the request made by the representative of the Soviet Union. But according to Rule 30, it is only when you make a ruling that there can be a challenge to that kind of ruling; and in that case, this is put to the vote. However, in so far as my delegation can make out, you never made a ruling; you merely appealed to the members of the Council to restrict themselves to the points under discussion. Therefore, my delegation finds itself in a quandary as to what action you would require us to take in response to the request of the Soviet Union. I would again repeat that you have not made a ruling; you have only made an appeal; and I think the matter should rest with the appeal, and not with the ruling, unless of course, you are going to make a ruling. In that case, my delegation would have to consider its position again.

MR. PRESIDENT [interpretation from French]: I think the situation is perfectly clear. Earlier when I spoke, I was giving my interpretation of the custom of the Council; and the first word spoken by the representative of the Soviet Union was one of challenge, and therefore, he challenged my interpretation.

Rule 30 is crystal-clear on this point. Accordingly, I must submit to the vote the challenge that was made to my ruling or to my interpretation; and according to Rule 30, the ruling shall stand unless overruled. That being the case, I request those members of the Council agreeing with the challenge of the representative of the Soviet Union to be good enough to raise their hands.

MR. MOROZOV [interpretation from Russian]: I would like to speak on the order in which you put the matters to the vote. Therefore, this is a point of order, although you have already started the procedure of the vote.

The point is: in Rule 30, the following is stated:

"If a representative raises a point of order, the President shall immediately state his ruling. If it is challenged, the President shall submit his ruling"—his ruling, stressed—"to the Security Council for immediate decision"—in the Russian there is a semicolon there —"and it shall stand unless overruled."

Accordingly, the subject of the vote in this case may be but a single matter: who among the members of the Council will support your ruling?

I am not going to argue about the ruling as to substance. You have formulated it, and I wish to remain strictly within the framework of procedure and not [to] exacerbate unnecessarily the already exacerbated situation, although it is not the fault of my delegation.

Inasmuch as your ruling is subject to the vote, would you be good enough, please, to so put it to the vote?

If your ruling receives seven votes in its favor, it means that the decision will have been confirmed by the requisite number of votes of Members of the Council for your ruling to be in force. If, on the other hand, it is not confirmed, then your ruling will have been overruled, with all the consequences stemming therefrom. Then, apparently, some other decision will have to be taken. I am not· quite sure what will happen later; but in any event, I cannot agree, since we are now speaking on the question that you raised, that your ruling be put to the vote in a form not in accordance with Rule 30 of the rules of procedure.

I would request you, Mr. President, to show the same generosity to the Soviet delegation as has been shown in the previous meetings of the Security Council. I would request that you put your ruling to the vote in positive form, as called for in Rule 30 of the rules of procedure. If you come to some other conclusion, naturally there would be no reason for a vote, anyway, because there would not be any posing of the question for the vote other than I have done. At least, I have the right to do that, and you certainly cannot deprive me of that particular right.

If the Council, by a majority of votes, deems that waging of the cold war is the most appropriate activity for the Security Council, then, of course, we will reply, upon the conscience of those who have voted for that decision. I will have no recourse but to resort to my right and explain my own vote on this matter—if you really wish to have the matter clarified, a situation which is constantly being beclouded by certain delegations.

I think my request is a clear one. I wish to have the question put to the vote in the form in which I have requested.

THE PRESIDENT [interpretation from French]: The representative of the Soviet Union may rest assured that I shall deal with this matter in a manner which will be most favorable to his delegation.

I know of only one precedent which will permit me to settle this difference that has arisen between the representative of the Soviet Union and myself and, on the basis of that precedent, I shall follow the interpretation made by the delegation of the Soviet Union, which was also that of the delegation of France.

At the 330th Meeting of the Security Council on July 7, 1948, when the Palestine question was being discussed, the President, having proposed to put his ruling to the vote, the representative of the Soviet Union was opposed to that proposal and said:

[in English]: "It seems to me that the correct way to proceed would be exactly the reverse. We should vote on the question: Who is against the President's ruling? The results of the vote would decide that question. If I am not mistaken, this would be more consistent with the rules of procedure." From *Security Council Official Records, Third Year, 330th Meeting*, page 8.

[continued in French]: The record goes on to say:

[continued in English]: "Then the ruling of the President was put to the vote in the form suggested by the representative of the U.S.S.R. and upheld."

[continued in French]: I do not think that I can do better than to abide by that precedent and follow the custom of the Soviet delegation.

Mr. Morozov [interpretation from Russian]: Mr. President, you are wrong if you think you made a discovery when you quoted this record. A question such as this occurred in the Security Council on many occasions and indeed such a statement as you quoted was made here. But in respect of the interpretation of the procedure given then, I can say that on many occasions it was the ruling of the President that was put to the vote. Perhaps, on the particular occasion, when the question was not as complex as the ruling which you made today, the interpretation suggested then could have been right, and the Soviet representative was right in giving this interpretation then. [Extensive laughter from gallery audience.]

The audience may find it hilarious, but I feel that while he was right then, I can prove that I am right today. The point is that your ruling, Mr. President, consists of two parts. The first part indicates your opinion that nothing in the statement of the United States representative today contains anything that is outside the item of the agenda under discussion. The second part of your ruling, as can be seen clearly from the verbatim records or the sound recordings of today's meeting, consists of the fact that you made an appeal to the members of the Security Council—and since the representative of the United States is a member of the Council, this appeal was made to him too—to adhere closer to the subject.

Now I would vote for the second part of your ruling, but I am not ready to vote for your opinion that what has been said by the representative of the United States—and this is exactly what we challenge—is part of the item under discussion. Therefore, you must put the first part separately to the vote. The second part is not being challenged by us and is thus a different matter. Now the first part which you have to put to a vote must receive seven votes in favor for it to remain in force.

I would also like to indicate, Mr. President, that since you found the records for 1948 so quickly, I consider this an indication of very good stage direction. It would not be so easy to find records for 1948 unless you knew in advance what was coming. In conclusion, I would like to say that it is almost seven o'clock now and we should find out who in the Security Council is ready to support the first part of your ruling. As to the second part, as I have indicated on many occasions, we have not challenged it.

THE PRESIDENT [interpretation from French]: I agree with the representative of the Soviet Union that we should put an end to this sterile discussion that has lasted too long already. But since he tells me that as President I have discretionary powers, I can therefore put to the vote his challenge to my ruling. I have this formal right, according to him, and I may do this if I please. However, in order to meet his wishes I must once again state my interpretation, namely, that there is nothing in the rules of procedure regarding this question of speakers who take the floor after a vote. There is nothing in the practice of the Council either that obliges me or makes it my duty to prevent speakers from speaking on any subject after the vote, if they wish to speak after the vote.

This is my interpretation and this is what I shall put to the vote which will be held valid unless it is overruled. This is in accordance with Rule 30 of the rules of procedure and I shall now put this to the vote.

MR. MOROZOV [interpretation from Russian]: Mr. President, it is obviously time to put an end to this question. I am rather satisfied that apart from yourself, no one in the Security Council has supported the position of the United States. I think we should put a full stop here. I am therefore withdrawing my challenge for reasons which are all too clear. I will, on the other hand, use my right to explain my vote and use the other rights in respect of your actions as President.

THE PRESIDENT [interpretation from French]: I thank the representative of the Soviet Union and I call on the representative of the United States again. In view of the lateness of the hour, may I appeal to him to be as brief as possible and to keep as close as possible to the subject at hand.

MR. STEVENSON [penned in on original draft of speech]: (I haven't much more to say Mr. Pres, but before I proceed I must say I wasn't aware that my shoes were on the table, if I undr the delg of the USSR correctly. I suspect he has [the preceding four words stricken out] could he have confused me with someone else—who has still other uses for a shoe on a table. Now when I was interrupted for the 2nd time—) *I haven't more to say, Mr. President, but before I proceed I must say that I was not aware, if I understood the representative of the Soviet Union correctly, that my shoe was on the table.* [Laughter.] *I wonder if he could have had me confused with someone else* [Khrushchev] *who still has other uses for shoes and tables.* [Laughter.]

When I was interrupted for the second time, Mr. President, I was saying that the veto has been frequently used to prevent the United Nations from investigating charges brought to the Council by the Soviet Union *itself.* On at least four occasions, with the use of six vetoes, the Soviet Union refused, after using the Security Council (as a propaganda sounding board for) *to air* its charges , to let its own assertions be examined. I invite your attention to 1950 when the Soviet Union charged the United States Air Force with the bombing of Communist-held areas of China (,). (the) *The* Soviet *Union* vetoed a commission of investigation. In 1952, the Sovict representative climaxed one of the most shameless (despicable lies) *falsehoods* in history—the long crescendo of accusations that the United States and the United Nations troops were employing germ warfare in Korea—by bringing the issue before the Security Council and then promptly vetoing a proposal for an impartial examination.

In 1958, when the Soviet Union purported to be concerned about United States flights over the Arctic Circle, the United States proposed an Arctic Inspection Zone. That too, was vetoed. In 1960, when Soviet fighter planes destroyed a United States RB–47 airplane over international waters, the (USSR) *Soviet Union* vetoed two separate proposals for investigations, one of them asking only that the International Red Cross be permitted to assist any surviving (crew) member of the plane.

In each of these cases the Security Council tried to exercise its proper peace-keeping function through systematic investigations. In each case, after having brought the charge, the Soviets vetoed the attempt at a remedy.

One of the most disturbing facts also revealed in the history of 100 vetoes is the consistent effort to prevent the Security Council from developing processes of peaceful settlement. Not only do many of the vetoes I have referred to fall into this category (,) but most of the remaining ones were also cast AGAINST efforts to promote peaceful settlements: (—twice now in Kashmir) four times with respect to Spain in 1946; once again (on) a resolution on troop withdrawals from Syria and Lebanon in 1946, not because the resolution was wrong but because it was not extreme enough; twice in connection with problems arising at the time of Indonesian independence; once against the Security Council recommendations for a solution of the Berlin blockade in 1948; (once on Goa) [contained in original draft, then stricken out by Stevenson, then added again] *once on Goa;* twice to prevent extension of United Nations peace-keeping functions in 1958; and five times since 1960 in the Security Council's consideration of the Congo. The U.S.S.R. also vetoed four resolutions in the field of disarmament.

(Today we see the pattern again—a Soviet veto of a moderate and reasonable peace-keeping proposal backed by seven members of this Council and objected to only by the Soviet Union and Romania. And again the Council is prevented from exercising its role of keeper and promoter of peace.) [The preceding was penned in the original draft by Stevenson, and then stricken.]

Distortion of the veto power has been a fact of life in (the Security) *this* Council. It is a fact that has led to the Unifying for Peace procedure, adding to the United Nations peace-keeping machinery a flexible means whereby United Nations members *can* assure that the United Nations' primary function of preserving the peace will be carried out.

The veto does exist, within its proper context, as a recognition of political reality, but it is a privilege to be USED (,) not ABUSED, and abused it has been, for the Soviet Union HAS willfully obstructed the operation of this Council. It has violated that part of the Four Power Declaration at San Francisco—(a declaration which must be read as a whole—) in which the powers agreed not to use their veto willfully to obstruct the operation of (the) *this* Council. (I am confident no historian of tomorrow will have to mark some cenotaph of the Security Council with the graven words "Soviet Veto.")

Now, so much for yesterday and for today. (what) *What* of the future? The Council is a vital and purposeful (organ) *organization of the United Nations* (which) in spite of the veto (,). (it) It provides vital and purposeful direction and leadership. And (,) in areas of its work where the veto does not apply, we believe the Council might well widen its activities and increasingly provide that direction and that leadership *to our affairs*. [New paragraph began here on original draft.] As for the veto itself, we hope that long before the Soviet Union approaches its 200th veto, it will realize that its own interests lie (,) not in national obstruction(ism) but in international cooperation, not in willful vetoes for narrow ends but in willing ASSENTS for the broad and common good for which the (United Nations) U.N. stands.

Thank you, and my apologies—and I assure you I have had my shoes on all afternoon. [Applause from gallery audience.]

Appendix C: Chronological List of Stevenson's Addresses and Statements on International Affairs, 1936–1965

✡

This list is compiled from Stevenson's unpublished volumes of speeches on "Foreign Affairs," including his speeches from 1936 to 1958; from a group of unpublished speeches during 1959 and 1960 called "Doc's Stock"; from his various published books of speeches; and from the press releases issued by the United States Mission from 1961 to 1965 cited as US/UN. Some of the speeches, especially earlier ones, are no longer extant unless they are now preserved among Stevenson's papers at Princeton University. These are listed below as lost since they are not included in Stevenson's unpublished volumes except by name and identification. This collection is presently closed to the public. The list includes all of Stevenson's speeches on international affairs that have come to my attention.

1936

1. Address to the Junior Association of Commerce, Chicago, May 18 (copy lost).
2. Campaign address for F. D. Roosevelt on the reciprocal trade agreements. Carleton College, Northfield, Minnesota, October 23 (last third extant). Included in this volume as "The Reciprocal Trade Agreement."

1937

3. Address to the Advertising Men's Post, American Legion, Chicago, January 4 (copy lost).
4. Address to the Oak Park Lions Club and Young Men's Club, Oak Park, Illinois, December 9 (copy lost).

5. Text in long-hand on the present state of foreign affairs, unidentified as to occasion of original usage (copy lost).

1938

6. Text for illustrated talk, an "inventory in the most general terms of the present state of foreign affairs," Wayfarer's Club, February 15 (copy lost).

7. A fuller, typed text on the general state of American foreign policy, Oak Park American Legion, April 11 (copy lost).

1940

8. Address to a Zionist mass meeting, Chicago, January 31. Included in this volume as "I Am a Zionist!"

9. Suggested Plank on Foreign Affairs, Democratic National Convention, July 14. Included in this volume as "No American Wants War!"

10. Address on the threat of Hitler, League of Women Voters, Chicago, October 4. Included in this volume as "Aid to Britain Will Keep America Out of War."

11. Address on same subject as above, William Allen White Committee, Chicago, December 16.

1945

12. Address on the founding of the United Nations, Chicago Bar Association, June 28. Included in this volume as "The United Nations: Collaboration Based on National Self-Interest."

13. Radio newsreel on a brief description of the United Nations Preparatory Committee meetings, London, November (?) (copy lost).

14. NBC broadcast on "The United States is not seeking to influence the location of the United Nations," with Philip Noel Baker and Wellington Koo, London, November 4 (copy lost).

15. Address to the American Chamber of Commerce, Savoy Hotel, London, November 12 (copy lost).

16. Address on American efforts to establish the United Nations, British-American Forces Dining Club, London, November 13 (last third of speech extant).

17. NBC University of the Air program on "The United Nations: A Forecast," with Philip Noel Baker, Wellington Koo, and a fourth unidentified participant, London, November 24 (copy lost).

18. ABC broadcast on the United Nations, December 23 (only copy, in French, which was lost).

1946

19. Radio recording on the choice of the General Assembly for locating the United Nations in the United States, London, February 15.

20. Address to the Commercial Club, on "Building the UNO: Political Situation," Chicago, March 9 (copy lost).

21. Address to the Council on Foreign Relations, entitled "UNO Gets Under Way," with a question-and-answer period, Chicago, March 22. Address included in this volume with the same title.

22. Address to the Chicago Bar Association, on the global war of ideas with the Soviet Union, Chicago, June 11. Included in this volume as "Is This Peace or War?"

23. Address to the Democratic County Committee of Illinois, on Democratic contributions to foreign policy in the past fifteen years and their responsibility for the future, Springfield, Illinois, October 4.

24. Address to the Northwestern University Law School, on the evolution, structure and operations of the United Nations, Chicago, October 15.

25. ABC broadcast on the beginnings of the General Assembly of the United Nations to which Stevenson was a delegate, New York City, October 19.

26. CBS broadcast entitled "America's Program for Peace Through the United Nations," from the General Assembly, New York City, October 26.

27. Statement in the General Assembly Committee II, entitled "World Shortage of Cereals," New York City, November 13 (copy lost).

28. Statement in the General Assembly Committee II on the development of the United Nations Relief and Rehabilitation Administration (UNRRA), New York City, November 14.

29. Town Hall of the Air, on the subject "Should the Veto Be Abolished in the UN?" Stevenson was asked to comment on "The UN Cannot Function Effectively If the Veto Is Abolished," November 14 (copy lost).

30. Walgreen Foundation Lecture, entitled "Civil-Military Relations in the United Nations," University of Chicago, Chicago, November 21.

31. Remarks in the General Assembly Committee II on economic reconstruction of devastated areas and on a proposed Economic Commission for Europe, New York City, November 25 (copy lost).

32. Remarks in the General Assembly Committee II on the relief program and criticism of the La Guardia proposal on relief, New York City, December 6 (copy lost).

33. Remarks in the General Assembly Committee II on the formation of a committee to review imports and exports and the foreign

exchange deficits of claimant countries, New York City, December 9 (copy lost).

34. Remarks in the General Assembly Plenary Session on the report of Committee II concerning relief needs after the termination of UNRRA with special comments on the basic elements of peace, New York City, December 11 (copy lost).

35. ABC broadcast in honor of Woodrow Wilson's Birthday, with Stevenson speaking from Chicago, other participants Raymond Swing, William Benton, Francis Sayre, and William W. Waymack, December 28. Included in this volume as "Wilson's Birthday—ABC Broadcast."

1947

36. Address on United States relations with Russia, Winnetka, Illinois, early January (copy lost).

37. Lincoln Library Forum Address, on the directions of American foreign policy in the eighteen months since Hiroshima, Springfield, Illinois, January 10.

38. Address to the Commonwealth Club, on Stevenson's personal experiences in Italy in 1944, relevant to the United Nations, the demands on American and especially conservative leadership, the thirty years' war with Russia, and the image of America, Chicago, January 22 (handwritten copy lost, but Stevenson's address on behalf of the Jewish Welfare Fund Campaign contains some of the same material).

39. Introduction of Mrs. Eleanor Roosevelt to the Chicago Council on Foreign Relations, Chicago, March 3.

40. Lincoln Birthday Banquet Address to the Peoria County Bar Association, Peoria, Illinois, specific date not known (perhaps a final draft reworked for subsequent use and virtually the same coverage as the Jewish Welfare Fund Campaign Address).

41. Address on the possible establishment of an International Refugee Organization in which the United States would play a substantial role, Immigrants' Protective League, Chicago, March 12. Included in this volume as "D.P.'s—The Saddest Chapter in the Epilogue of the War."

42. Address on behalf of the Jewish Welfare Fund Campaign, in which he talked about the major national American objective—peace on an enduring and equitable basis, Congress Hotel, Chicago, March 17.

43. Address to the Italian-American Meeting, on his experiences in wartime Italy, Chicago, April 25.

44. Address at the Jefferson Day Dinner, Pontiac, Illinois, May 13 (copy lost).

45. Address to the Northwestern University Law School Alumni Association, entitled "Some Postwar Reflections," Chicago, May 14; later printed in the *Illinois Law Review of Northwestern University*, July–August, 1947. Included in this volume with the same title.

46. Address to the Board of Governors' Meeting of the Investment Bankers Association, French Lick, Indiana, May 20 (copy lost).

47. Julius Rosenthal Foundation Lecture, on development of international law, particularly under the United Nations; the Marshall Plan; American principles of economic aid; and basic American objectives in dealing with Russia and United States foreign policy, Northwestern University Law School, Chicago, June 27 (apparently developed from the May 14 Address but with a number of additional points; copy is lost).

48. Address to the South Shore Kiwanis Club, on displaced persons, Woodlawn, Chicago, July 23 (apparently only notes and no written text; copy lost).

49. Statement in the General Assembly Committee I, on admission of new member nations, Eire, Portugal, Transjordan, Italy, and Finland; extensive comments on the situation in the Eastern Europe satellite countries Rumania and Bulgaria; position on Gromyko threat of veto, New York City, November 10 (copy lost).

50. Introduction of Secretary of State George C. Marshall, who was about to attend the Council of Foreign Ministers meeting in London, Palmer House, Chicago, November 18.

51. Bloomington Forum on the 1947 United Nations General Assembly; American-Soviet relations; and the Marshall Plan, Bloomington, Illinois, December 15 (copy lost).

1948

52. Address, unidentified forum, Geneva, Illinois, January (?) (substantially same as Chicago Athletic Club Forum; copy lost).

53. Public Forum of Chicago Athletic Club, outlining his philosophy regarding American involvement in foreign affairs and especially future U.S. relations with the Soviet Union, Chicago, January (?). Included in this volume as "Our Foreign Policy Has Taken a Seat at the Family Table."

54. Address to the Lions and Rotary clubs, on peace as a major goal of the American foreign policy and American military establish-

ment and of the United Nations through collective security, Quincy, Illinois, February 17.

1949

55. Address to the Inland Daily Press Association Luncheon, on the cold war and how Soviet pressures have strengthened and affected the concept of Western individualism, Chicago, October 18. Included in this volume as "Communism Is the Catfish in the Western Herring Pond."

56. Introduction of Prime Minister Nehru of India to the Chicago Council on Foreign Relations, Chicago, October 26. Included in this volume as "The Nation Is Safe in His Hands."

1950

57. Address to the Masaryk Centennial Celebration, on Masaryk's efforts to establish a free Czechoslovakian state and its present subjection to Communist rule, Cicero, Illinois, March 9. Included in this volume as "The Silence of Death for the Voices of Freedom."

58. Address to the First International Trade Fair Luncheon, on the growth of international trade, Chicago, August 7.

59. Introduction of Trygve Lie, Secretary-General of the United Nations, Chicago, September 8.

60. Address at the United Nations Festival, on the progress of the United Nations in entering the Korean conflict, Chanute Air Force Field, Rantoul, Illinois, October 1. Included in this volume as "Korea: An Incident in the Long Contest for Mastery of the World."

61. Brief statement on Presentation of the United Nations Flag by Navy Mothers, Executive Mansion, Springfield, Illinois, October 17.

1951

62. Introduction of Governor Youngdahl of Minnesota to the American Association for the United Nations. In this address Stevenson commented on the bill pending in the Illinois Legislature calling for United States withdrawal from the United Nations, Chicago, February 26. Included in this volume as "Internationalism Is Now a Life-and-Death Matter."

63. Address to the Chicago World Trade Conference, on American trade and aid, Chicago, February 27.

64. Address to the Crusade for Freedom Luncheon, on Radio Free Europe and the establishment of a Radio Free Asia, Peoria, Illinois, September 19.

1952

65. Address to the Chicago Teachers' Union on the progress made by the United States in foreign policy since World War II, Chicago, March 22.

66. Address to the Council on World Affairs in which Stevenson reviewed key American involvement in foreign affairs from the founding of the Republic until the present, Dallas, April 22. Included in this volume as "Anything but Honest, Straightforward Talk Borders on Treason."

67. Address to the Norwegian National League, on Norwegian Independence Day and its parallel to American independence, Chicago, May 17.

68. Address to the Lithuanian Chamber of Commerce of Illinois, on the subjugation of Lithuanian freedom, Chicago, May 18.

69. Address at the Hamden-Sydney College Commencement on the concept of the 1950's being a period of international transition, Hamden-Sydney, Virginia, June 9.

70. Address at the African Methodist Episcopal Church, on universal civil rights, Sparta, Illinois, July 9.

71. Press Conference, Springfield, Illinois, July 30. Included in this volume as "Foreign Policy Is the Most Important Consideration for the American People."

72. Statement to the New York State Democratic Convention, New York City, August 29. Included in this volume as "If This Country Stands for Anything, It Stands for Freedom."

73. Armed Services overseas broadcast, August 31. Published as "War and Peace" in *Major Campaign Speeches*.

74. Labor Day Rally, Grand Rapids, Michigan, September 1. Published as "Bipartisan Foreign Policy" in *Major Campaign Speeches*, and as "World Policy" in *Stevenson Speeches*.

75. Labor Day Rally, Hamtramck, Michigan, September 1. Published as "Is It Liberation?" in *Major Campaign Speeches*, and as "World Policy" in *Stevenson Speeches*.

76. Address, Cheyenne, Wyoming, September 6. Published as "The New West" in *Major Campaign Speeches*.

77. Address, San Francisco, September 9. Included as "World Policy" in *Major Campaign Speeches*, in *Stevenson Speeches*, and in this volume.

78. Address, Albuquerque, New Mexico, September 12. Published as "The Threat of Communism" in *Major Campaign Speeches*, and as "On Communism" in *Stevenson Speeches*.

79. Address, Bushnell Memorial Auditorium, Hartford, Connecticut, September 18. Published as "The Atomic Future" in *Major Campaign Speeches* and *Stevenson Speeches* (but not included among Stevenson's own unpublished "Foreign Affairs" volumes).

80. Address, Memorial Auditorium, Louisville, Kentucky, September 27. Published as "Korea" in *Major Campaign Speeches* and *Stevenson Speeches*.

81. First Fireside Chat, in which he answered the charges of corruption and softness on Communism, WGN Radio and NBC TV, Chicago, September 29. Included as "First Fireside Speech" in this volume and in a considerably extended form in *Major Campaign Speeches*.

82. Address on the charges of his softness on Communism, Detroit, Michigan, October 7. Published as "Safeguards Against Communism" in *Major Campaign Speeches*.

83. Address at the University of Wisconsin, Madison, October 8. Published as "The Area of Freedom" in *Major Campaign Speeches* (but not included in his own unpublished volumes).

84. Address on American foreign policy in Europe, Milwaukee, October 8.

85. Address on the question of peace and the continuance of the present foreign policy and collective security, Oklahoma City, Oklahoma, October 10.

86. Address to the Democratic Rally, New Orleans, October 11. Published as "Tidelands Oil–Foreign Trade" in *Major Campaign Speeches*.

87. Second Fireside Chat, in which he discussed the Korean conflict, Los Angeles, October 16. Published as "Second Fireside Speech" in *Major Campaign Speeches*.

88. Address at Oklahoma City, Oklahoma, October 16 (this is a recap of another speech; copy lost).

89. Address on the isolationism of the Republican party, San Diego, October 17.

90. Address, Alamo Plaza, San Antonio, October 18. Published as "The Idea of Human Freedom" in *Major Campaign Speeches*.

91. Statement in honor of United Nations Week, October 19.

92. Address on American trade and aid, Houston, October 19.

93. Women's Broadcast Number 2, in which he discussed Korea, Springfield, Illinois, October 20.

94. Third Fireside Chat, in which he discussed world peace, Chicago, October 21.

95. Address to the *New York Herald Tribune* Forum, New York City, October 21. Published as "Leadership for Peace" in *Major Campaign Speeches* (but not included in his unpublished volume).

96. Address on the United Nations, Rochester, New York, October 24.

97. Address on his experiences in Italy during the war, Rome, New York, October 24.

98. Address on Republican cricitism of the United Nations, Rensselaer Polytechnic Institute, Troy, New York, October 24.

99. United Nations Day broadcast, Springfield, Illinois, October 24. Published as "The United Nations: Our Hope and Our Commitment" in *Major Campaign Speeches*.

100. Address to the Volunteers for Stevenson on fuller application by Americans of the Judaeo-Christian ethic to neighboring nations, Boston, October 26. Published as "On Religion and Politics" in *Major Campaign Speeches*.

101. Address, Providence, Rhode Island, October 27 (recap of an earlier speech; copy lost).

102. Address, New Haven, Connecticut, October 27 (recap of an earlier speech; copy lost).

103. Address on the need for continued American efforts to fight the spread of Communism, Kline Auditorium, Bridgeport, Connecticut, October 27.

104. Address, Pittsburgh, October 30 (recap of an earlier speech; copy lost).

105. Address, York, Pennsylvania, October 30 (recap of an earlier speech; copy lost).

106. Address, Academy of Music, Brooklyn, October 31. Published as "The Fundamental Issues" in *Major Campaign Speeches*.

1953

107. Address to the Japan-America Society, Tokyo, Japan, March 12. Included in this volume as "The Destiny of Asia May Rest in the Hands of Japan."

108. Statement as Stevenson was completing the Asian phase of his tour, American Embassy, Tel Aviv, Israel, June 9. Included in this volume as "A Truce in Korea Is the Best News in the World."

109. Statement to assembled newsmen at his return to the United States, New York City, August 20.

110. Traveler's Report, Civic Opera House, Chicago, September 15. Included in this volume and published in *What I Think* with the title "Traveler's Report."

111. Address at the Woodrow Wilson Foundation in honor of former Secretary of State Dean Acheson, New York City, October 1.

112. Welcome at dinner honoring King Paul and Queen Frederica of Greece, Conrad Hilton Hotel, Chicago, November 7.

113. Statement at reception honoring King Paul and Queen Frederica of Greece, Opera House, Chicago, November 8.

114. Statement on American sacrifices in Korea, Association of American Law Schools, Chicago, December 28. Published as "The Reputation of the Government" in *What I Think*.

1954

115. Statement on the proposed Bricker Amendment, Chicago, January 28.

116. Introduction of Celal Beyar, President of Turkey, Chicago Council on Foreign Relations, Chicago, February 5.

117. Address to the Southern Conference of Democrats, in which he denounced McCarthyism and Secretary of State Dulles's "Massive Retaliation," Miami Beach, Florida, March 7. Published in *What I Think* as "Crusades, Communism and Corruption."

118. First Godkin Lecture, Harvard University, Cambridge, Massachusetts, March 17. Published as "Ordeal of the Mid-Century" in *Call to Greatness*.

119. Second Godkin Lecture, Harvard University, Cambridge, March 18. Published as "Perpetual Peril" in *Call to Greatness*.

120. Third Godkin Lecture, Harvard University, Cambridge, March 19. Published as "America's Burden" in *Call to Greatness* (but entitled "Cautionary Comments" in his unpublished volumes).

121. Statement on Republican Administration announcement that it would "unleash Chiang Kai-Shek," Charlotte, North Carolina, April 2.

122. Statement at the National Hillbilly Music Day, Meridian, Mississippi, May 26 (copy lost).

123. Statement on the collapse of American foreign policy toward Asia, Anchorage, Alaska, July 25.

124. Address, Omaha, Nebraska, August 7 (recap of an earlier speech; copy lost).

125. TV spot to campaign for the election of a Democratic Congress, August 19 (copy lost).

126. Statement on deteriorating American foreign policy, *Christian Science Monitor*, August 19.

127. Statement on deteriorating American foreign policy, August 25 (copy lost).

128. Address, Hollywood Bowl, Los Angeles, October 9. Published as "A Truth Beyond Politics" in *What I Think*.

129. Address in which he denounced the Administration policy of "instant and massive retaliation," San Francisco, October 16. Included in this volume as "The Future Will Belong to Free Men."

130. Address on the attempts of Republican extremists to destroy bipartisan foreign policy, Rochester, New York, October 26.

131. Address at Public School 197, on the dilemma of the divided Republican party concerning foreign policy, Brooklyn, October 27.

132. Address to the American Committee for the Weizmann Institute of Science, New York City, December 2. Published as "Israel and the Arabs: Ancient Glory and New Opportunity" in *What I Think*.

133. Address at the Democratic National Committee Conference and Dinner, New Orleans, December 4. Published as "The Challenge to Political Maturity" in *What I Think*.

134. Address, Democratic Dinner, Harrisburg, Pennsylvania, December 8 (recap of earlier speech, perhaps one in New Orleans; copy lost).

1955

135. Statement on deteriorating foreign policy in relation to Asia, *Look* Magazine, January 11.

136. Statements, January 21 (copies lost).

137. Radio speech to the nation, Chicago, April 11. Included in this volume and in *What I Think* as "The Formosa Crisis: A Peaceful Solution."

138. Address at the American Jewish Tercentenary, on the responsibilities of freedom, New York City, June 1.

139. Address at the Jamaica Tercentenary Industrial Exhibition, Kingston, Jamaica, September 15.

140. "Great Issues" Lecture, University of Texas, Austin, September 28. Published as "America, The Economic Colossus" in *What I Think*.

141. Address on Canadian-American relations, Queen's University, Kingston, Ontario, October 15. Published as "Partnership and Independence" in *What I Think*.

142. Address at the United Nations Award Luncheon, Congress Hotel, Chicago, October 24.

143. Address on the misleading Republican talk on foreign policy, Democratic Rally, Duluth, Minnesota, October 29. Included in this volume as "Reduce the Volume of Loose Words and Catchy Slogans!"

144. Address at the Woodrow Wilson Centennial, University of Virginia, Charlottesville, November 11. Included in this volume and in *What I Think* as "The Road Away from Revolution."

145. Address, Democratic National Committee Dinner, Chicago, November 19. Published as "On Giving Government Back to the People" in *What I Think*.

146. Address to the AFL–CIO Unity Convention on Labor's responsibility in promoting reasonable foreign policy, December 8.

1956

147. "Face the Nation," CBS Radio and TV, Chicago, January 8.

148. Statement, *Life* Magazine, on Secretary of State Dulles's boast of "brinkmanship," January 14.

149. Statement on the Republican cut in military spending and "brinkmanship," Minnesota, January 17.

150. Statement on the Republican Administration's policy of "atomic intimidation," Tucson, Arizona, January 23.

151. Statement requesting the Secretary of State to cooperate in American foreign policy, Phoenix, January 24.

152. Statement about the Declaration of Washington, San Mateo, California, February 2.

153. Address to the Democratic Council State Convention on "brinkmanship," Fresno, California, February 4.

154. Address, Seattle, Washington, February 14 (copy lost).

155. Address, stressing foreign affairs as America's most important affairs and denouncing Republican blunders, University of Minnesota, Minneapolis, March 2.

156. Press Conference, Atlanta, Georgia, April 3. *

157. Address, Veterans Businessmen's Club, Daytona Beach, April 11.

158. Address, Banquet, San Carlo Hotel, Pensacola, Florida, April 14.

159. Address to the American Society of Newspaper Editors, Washington, D.C., April 21. Included in this volume and published in *The New America* as "H-Bomb, Defense and Foreign Policy."

160. Address on Latin America, Miami, April 26 (recap of earlier speech).

* Files of the actual unpublished speeches from this date through 1958 are not in my possession, which accounts for the lack of description in many cases.

161. California whistle-stops and speeches on the Middle East, May.
162. Addresses on Israel's attack against Egypt, Fairfax and Beverly, California, May 5.
163. Address, University of Oregon, Eugene, May 15.
164. Kefauver-Stevenson TV discussion on deteriorating American foreign policy, May 21.
165. Florida election eve broadcast, May 28.
166. Town Hall luncheon address, Los Angeles, May 31. Published as "Liberalism" in *The New America*.
167. Address at the Democratic Picnic, Bloomington, Illinois, July 4.
168. Address on Labor Day, opening the 1956 campaign with references to the deteriorating situation around the world, Pontiac, Michigan, September 3.
169. Address to the Polish War Veterans Meeting, Detroit, September 3.
170. Address to the American Legion Convention, Los Angeles, September 5.
171. Address for the Israel Bond Drive, New York City, September 11.
172. Statement, Washington, D.C., September 17.
173. Address, Miami, September 25.
174. Address, Minneapolis, September 29. Published, with deletions, as "The Draft and Defense" in *The New America* (but not listed among his unpublished volumes).
175. Address, Fairleigh Dickinson University, Teaneck, New Jersey, October 2. Published as "Peace" in *The New America* (but not listed among his unpublished volumes).
176. Statement, Pulaski Day, October 11.
177. Telecast, Chicago, October 15. Published as "Testing Bombs" in *The New America* (but not listed among his unpublished volumes).
178. Address, Youngstown, Ohio, October 18. Published as "An Armed Service of Professionals" in *The New America*.
179. Address, Louisville, Kentucky, October 19. Published, with deletions, as "The War Party?" in *The New America* (but not listed among his unpublished volumes).
180. Address, Cincinnati, Ohio, October 19. Published as "Foreign Policy" in *The New America*.
181. Statement, Chicago, October 22.
182. Address, Madison Square Garden, New York City, October 23.
183. Address to the Liberal Party Women's Campaign Committee,

New York City, October 24 (recap of a campaign speech on the Middle East).

184. Address, Los Angeles, October 27. Published as "Leadership" in *The New America* (but not listed among his unpublished volumes).

185. Program Paper on the H-Bomb, issued from Washington, D.C., October 29. Published in *The New America*.

186. Address, Boston, October 29 (recap of an earlier campaign speech).

187. Address, Reyburn Plaza, Philadelphia, October 30.

188. Telegram to President Eisenhower on war in the Middle East, October 30.

189. Address, Pittsburgh, October 31.

190. Address to the Garment Workers, New York City, October 31.

191. Address, Union Square, New York City, October 31 (recap of an earlier speech).

192. Address, Buffalo, November 1. Published as "Middle East" in *The New America*.

193. Address, Detroit, November 2.

194. Address, Cleveland, November 2.

195. Address, Chicago Stadium, Chicago, November 3.

196. Telegram to President Eisenhower, November 4.

197. Telecast from Boston, November 5. Published as "The Fateful Decision" in *The New America* (but not listed among his unpublished volumes).

198. Address, Minneapolis, early November.

199. Program Paper on Foreign Aid, prepared late in the campaign but not released. Published in *The New America*.

1957

200. Press Conference, January 3.

201. Address to the Democratic National Conference, San Francisco, February 16.

202. "Meet the Press," NBC Radio and TV, May 5.

203. Address, accepting Honorary Degree, Oxford University, Oxford, England, May 24.

204. Address to the English-Speaking Union Dinner, London, May 27.

205. Address, Accra, Ghana, June 4.

206. Statement, Jan Smuts Airport, Johannesburg, South Africa, June 5.

207. Press Conference, Jan Smuts Airport, Johannesburg, South Africa, June 12.

208. Statement, Bonn, Germany, July 20.

209. Press Conference, New York City, August 6.
210. Statement, Paris, France, September 1.
211. "Face the Nation," CBS Radio and TV, Chicago, September 8.
212. Address to the Institute of International Education, Chicago, September 29.
213. CARE Press Conference, October 7.
214. Statement, October 7.
215. Statement, Libertyville, Illinois, November 7.
216. Address given over WIBH–TV entitled "Search for Truth in Foreign Affairs," November 10.
217. Statement, New York City, November 12.
218. Address to the New York County Laywers' Association, 44th Annual Bar Dinner, New York City, December 9.
219. Address for the Bill of Rights Day, Sherman Hotel, Chicago, December 16.

1958
220. Address at the Roosevelt Day Dinner to the Americans for Democratic Action, New York City, January 31.
221. Address at the Harry S Truman Dinner, Washington, D.C., February 22 (apparently recap of an earlier speech).
222. Address at the Conference on Foreign Aspects of U.S. National Security, Washington, D.C., February 25.
223. "Radio Beat—Russia and the West: An 'Opposition' View," CBS Radio, New York City, March 12.
224. Address to the National Conference of Organizations on International Trade Policy, Washington, D.C., March 27.
225. "Look Here," NBC–TV, March 30.
226. Statement on arriving in Leningrad, Russia, July 12.
227. Statement on Russian trip, August 7.
228. Statement, Moscow, August 8.
229. Statement, December 3.

1959
230. "The Political Relevance of Moral Principle," A. Powell Davies Memorial Lecture, Constitution Hall, Washington, D.C., January 18. Published as "Our Broken Mainspring" in *Putting First Things First;* included in this volume and also in *Contemporary Forum* with the original title.
231. "Today's Most Fateful Fact," Address at McGill University on receiving the Doctor of Letters, *honoris causa*, Montreal, May 29. Published in *Putting First Things First*.

1960

232. Founder's Day Address, University of Virginia, April 12. Included in this volume as "The Earth Belongs Always to the
Living Generation."

233. Address to the Conference on World Tensions, University of
Chicago, Chicago, May 12. Published as "Full Promise of a Distracted World" in *The Promise of World Tensions*.

234. Address to the Eleventh Biennial Convention of the Textile
Workers Union of America, Chicago, June 1.

235. Campaign Address for John F. Kennedy, University of California,
Berkeley, September 28.

236. Campaign Address for John F. Kennedy, University of Wisconsin, Madison, October 10.

237. Address to the Commonwealth Club, San Francisco, November 4.

238. Address to the Primrose Club Dinner on goals of the Kennedy
Administration, Toronto, December 3.

1961

239. Statement before the Senate Committee on Foreign Relations after
approval as Ambassador to the United Nations, Washington,
D.C., January 18.

240. Transcript of remarks at a press conference held at United Nations Headquarters, January 27 (US/UN press release 3642).

241. Statement in the Security Council (*hereafter referred to as S. C.*)
on assuming his seat as representative of the United States,
February 1 (US/UN 3643). Included in this volume and in
Looking Outward as "The Principles That Guide Us."

242. Statement in the S. C. on the death of Lumumba, February 13
(US/UN 3645).

243. Remarks at a luncheon of the United Nations Correspondents
Association, at the United Nations, February 14 (US/UN 3646).

244. Statement in S. C. on the Congo, February 15 (US/UN 3647).
Included in this volume and in *Looking Outward* as "A Time for
Action: The Developing Crisis in the Congo."

245. Statement in S. C. on the Congo, February 17 (US/UN 3648).

246. Statement in S. C. on the Congo, February 17 (US/UN 3649).

247. Statement in S. C. on the Congo, February 20 (US/UN 3651).

248. Statement in S. C. on the Congo, February 20 (US/UN 3653).

249. Statement in S. C. on the Congo, February 21 (US/UN 3655).

250. Statement in S. C. on the Congo, February 21 (US/UN 3656).

251. Statement to the press on the Congo, February 24 (US/UN 3658).

252. Address at a luncheon given by Robert F. Wagner, Mayor of New York City, Waldorf-Astoria Hotel, New York City, March 2 (US/UN 3661). Published as "Let Us Leave Rivalries Behind" in *Looking Outward*.

253. Remarks on a nationwide closed-circuit television program organized by the American Association for the United Nations, New York City, March 2.

254. Statement to the press on the agenda, March 7 (US/UN 3663).

255. Statement in S. C. on assuming the position of President for the month of March, March 10 (US/UN 3664).

256. Statement in S. C. on Angola, March 15 (US/UN 3668). Included in this volume as "Angola Is Entitled to All of the Rights Guaranteed by the Charter."

257. Statement in the Plenary Session of the General Assembly (*hereafter referred to as G. A.*) on the Congo, March 21 (US/UN 3670).

258. Statement in the First Committee (*hereafter referred to as Com. I*) on the agenda, March 21 (US/UN 3671).

259. Statement in Com. I on Africa, March 23 (US/UN 3674).

260. Statement in Com. I in reply to the Representative of Nigeria on the African Item, March 23 (US/UN 3675).

261. Statement and press conference on the United States proposal in G. A. on a development program for Africa, March 28 (US/UN 3677).

262. Statement in Com. I on Disarmament, March 30 (US/UN 3682).

263. Statement in Com. I on Korea, April 10 (US/UN 3685).

264. Statement in Com. I on Korea, April 11 (US/UN 3688).

265. Statement to the press on manned Soviet orbit, April 12 (US/UN 3689).

266. Statement in Com. I on Korea, April 12 (US/UN 3690).

267. Statement in G. A. on the Congo, April 14 (US/UN 3695).

268. Statement in Com. I on the Cuban Complaint, April 15 (US/UN 3696).

269. Statement in Com. I on the Cuban Complaint, April 15 (US/UN 3697).

270. Statement in Com. I on the Cuban Complaint, April 17 (US/UN 3699) and included in this volume as "The Cuban Complaint."

271. Statement in Com. I on the Cuban Complaint, April 18 (US/UN 3701).

272. Statement in Com. I on the Cuban Complaint, April 18 (US/UN 3704).

273. Statement in Com. I on the Cuban Complaint, April 20 (US/UN 3706).
274. Statement in G. A. on the deferral to the 16th General Assembly of the African, Korean, and Outer Space Items, April 21 (US/UN 3710).
275. Introductory remarks at a dinner honoring Prime Minister Caramanlis of Greece, Commodore Hotel, New York City, April 21 (US/UN 3711).
276. Statement in G. A. on the report of the Credentials Committee, April 22 (US/UN 3712).
277. Note to correspondents on the Peace Corps and similar U.N. volunteer agencies, April 25 (US/UN 3714).
278. Address at the annual dinner of the Conference Group of United States National Organizations of the United Nations, Carnegie Endowment Building, New York City, May 2 (US/UN 3717).
279. Address at a dinner celebrating the ground-breaking ceremonies for the new building program of the Albert Einstein College of Medicine of Yeshiva University, Waldorf-Astoria Hotel, May 7 (US/UN 3720).
280. Address at the annual banquet of the Princeton Club of Washington, Washington, D.C., May 17 (US/UN 3724).
281. Address at a dinner held by the Jewish Theological Seminary at the Jewish Museum, celebrating the creation of the Stevenson Foundation in the Herbert Lehman Institute of Ethics, New York, May 23 (US/UN 3725). The title of this address—"An Ethic for Survival"—is also the title of this volume.
282. Remarks at Memorial Services at President Franklin D. Roosevelt's Grave, Hyde Park, New York, May 30 (US/UN 3737).
283. College Commencement Address (read by the College President because Stevenson was heading a special mission to Latin America), Amherst College, Amherst, Massachusetts, June 11.
284. Remarks to the National Press Club on his mission to Latin America, Washington, D.C., June 26 (US/UN 3739).
285. Statement at the thirty-second session of the Economic and Social Council, Geneva, July 10 (US/UN 3744). Published as "A Better Life" in *Looking Outward*.
286. Excerpts from an address at a meeting of the Italian Society for International Organization, Rome, July 26 (US/UN 3750). Published as "A Lost Sense of Mastery" in *Looking Outward*.
287. Remarks before the International Astronomical Union, Berkeley,

California, August 15 (US/UN 3757). Published as "A Parable for Statesmen" in *Looking Outward*.

288. Statement at the Special Session of the General Assembly on the Bizerte Question, August 22 (US/UN 3758).

289. Statement at the Special Session on the Bizerte Question, August 24 (US/UN 3760).

290. Statement at the Special Session on the Credentials Committee Report, August 25 (US/UN 3761).

291. Statement to the press on the Collet Incident, August 29 (US/UN 3762).

292. Statement to the press on the Soviet announcement of resumption of nuclear testing, August 31 (US/UN 3764).

293. Informal remarks at the annual reception of the American Association for the United Nations, Waldorf-Astoria Hotel, September 17 (US/UN 3768).

294. Statement to the press on the death of Secretary-General Dag Hammarskjold, September 18 (US/UN 3770).

295. Statement in G. A. on the death of Hammarskjold, September 20 (US/UN 3771). Published as "He Belongs to All Mankind" in *Looking Outward*.

296. Statement in the General Committee on the inscription of the item entitled "The urgent need for a treaty to ban nuclear weapons tests under effective international control," September 21 (US/UN 3772).

297. Statement in the General Committee on the Cuban item, September 21 (US/UN 3774).

298. Statement in the General Committee on the Hungarian item, September 21 (US/UN 3775).

299. Statement in S. C. on membership applications, September 26 (US/UN 3779).

300. Statement in S. C. on membership applications, September 26 (US/UN 3780).

301. Statement in S. C. on the membership application of Sierra Leone, September 26 (US/UN 3781).

302. Statement to the press on the hate letter sent to the African delegations, September 28 (US/UN 3782).

303. Remarks on Secretary-General Hammarskjold at the Prime Minister's dinner, Stockholm, September 29. Published as "Uppsala Was the World Today" in *Looking Outward*.

304. Transcript of the ABC Radio and TV program "Adlai Stevenson Reports" (all of the programs were conversations between Steven-

son and Arnold Michaelis, often with a prominent guest), with Dean Rusk as his guest, October 1.

305. Statement to the press on the Soviet troika proposal, October 2 (US/UN 3783).

306. Remarks at a convocation at Brandeis University, Waltham, Massachusetts, October 8 (US/UN 3787).

307. United Nations Day Message, recorded for broadcast by CBS on October 22, made on October 9 (US/UN 3788).

308. Statement in G. A. in reply to the statement of the Cuban Representative, October 10 (US/UN 3792).

309. Statement to the press on the United States abstention in the vote censuring the speech of the Foreign Minister of the Republic of South Africa, October 11 (US/UN 3794).

310. Transcript of "Adlai Stevenson Reports," with Ambassaador Wechuku of Nigeria as his guest, October 15.

311. Address at the Inter-American Press Association luncheon, Waldorf-Astoria Hotel, October 16 (US/UN 3796).

312. Statement to the press on the independence of Western Samoa, October 18 (US/UN 3803).

313. Statement in the Political Committee on nuclear testing, October 19. Published as "Nuclear Death Dance: The Need for a Test Ban Treaty" in *Looking Outward.*

314. Statement to the press on the award of the Nobel Peace Prize to the late Dag Hammarskjold, October 23 (US/UN 3809).

315. United Nations Day Address to the San Francisco Chapter of the American Association for the United Nations, Masonic Auditorium, San Francisco, October 24 (US/UN 3810). Published as "Let None Mock Its Weakness" in *Looking Outward.*

316. Transcript of "Adlai Stevenson Reports," with U Thant, Representative of Burma, as his guest, October 29.

317. Statement to the press on the Soviet explosion of a fifty-megaton bomb, October 30 (US/UN 3816).

318. Statement in Com. I on nuclear testing, October 30 (US/UN 3818).

319. Statement in Com. I in reply to Soviet statement on nuclear testing, October 30 (US/UN 3819).

320. Statement to the press calling for immediate settlement of filling the office of Secretary-General, November 1 (US/UN 3820).

321. Statement in G. A. on the election of U Thant as Acting Secretary-General, November 3 (US/UN 3826).

322. Transcript of "Adlai Stevenson Reports," with Jawaharlal Nehru, Prime Minister of India, as his guest, November 12.

323. Statement in S. C. on the Congo, November 13 (US/UN 3835).

324. Statement in Com. I on disarmament, November 15 (US/UN 3837). Included in this volume and published in *Looking Outward* as "The First Business of This Dangerous World: Disarmament."

325. Statement in Com. I in reply to the statement of the Soviet Representative concerning disarmament, November 15 (US/UN 3838).

326. Address at the dedication ceremonies of the Fordham University Law School Building, Lincoln Square, New York City, November 17 (US/UN 3843).

327. Statement in S. C. on the Congo, November 21 (US/UN 3848).

328. Statement in S. C. on the Congo, November 21 (US/UN 3849).

329. Statement in S. C. on the Congo, November 21 (US/UN 3850).

330. Statement in S. C. on the Cuban complaint, November 22 (US/UN 3854).

331. Statement in S. C. on the Congo, November 24 (US/UN 3858).

332. Transcript of "Adlai Stevenson Reports," with Edward R. Murrow, Director of the United States Information Agency, as his guest, November 26.

333. Text of a letter dated November 25, addressed to the President of the G. A., transmitting the comments of the United States on the Soviet memorandum regarding colonialism, November 28 (US/UN 3862).

334. Statement in S. C. on the Cuban complaint, November 28 (US/UN 3863).

335. Remarks on accepting the American Jewish Congress Award to the United States Mission, November 29.

336. Remarks on receiving the first annual "World Humanitarian Award," sponsored by MEDICO, at a dinner at the Astor Hotel, New York City, November 29 (US/UN 3865).

337. Statement in G. A. on the representation of China in the United Nations, December 1 (US/UN 3872). Published as "An Invitation to Aggression" in *Looking Outward*.

338. Statement in Com. I on international cooperation in the peaceful uses of outer space, December 4 (US/UN 3875). Published as "To Narrow the Gap" in *Looking Outward*.

339. Note to correspondents denying that he wished to be a candidate for the United States Senate, December 5.

340. Transcript of "Adlai Stevenson Reports," with Dr. Mario Adadeo, Representative of Argentina as his guest, December 10.

341. Statement in Com. I on disarmament, December 13 (US/UN 3888.)
342. Statement in S. C. on Tanganyika's membership application, December 14 (US/UN 3889).
343. Statement in G. A. on the Chinese representation question, December 14 (US/UN 3891).
344. Statement in G. A. on the priority of the resolutions on Chinese representation, December 15 (US/UN 3894).
345. Statement in S. C. on the Goa situation, December 18 (US/UN 3897). Included in this volume with the next statement below as a single unit entitled "The Failure of the Security Council Is a Failure of the United Nations."
346. Statement in S. C. on the Goa situation, December 18 (US/UN 3898).
347. Statement in S. C. on the Goa situation, December 18 (US/UN 3900).
348. Statement in G. A. on the Hungarian item, December 21 (US/UN 3904).
349. Press Conference, held at United Nations Headquarters, December 21 (US/UN 3906).
350. Transcript of "Adlai Stevenson Reports," December 24.

1962

351. Remarks on the Armstrong Circle Theatre telecast on CBS, January 3 (US/UN 3908). Published as "By Consent of the Governed" in *Looking Outward*.
352. Draft of suggested acceptance speech for the America's Democratic Legacy Award by the Anti-Defamation League of B'nai B'rith, January 14.
353. Address before the Anti-Defamation League on the reception of the America's Democratic Legacy Award, Plaza Hotel, New York City, January 14 (US/UN 3910).
354. Transcript of "Adlai Stevenson Reports," special topic, "The Congo," January 21.
355. Address at the 61st Annual Meeting of the Bloomington Association of Commerce, Bloomington, Illinois, January 23 (US/UN 3912).
356. Statement in G. A. on Angola, January 25 (US/UN 3914).
357. Address to the Association of the Bar of the City of New York, New York City, January 29 (US/UN 3915).
358. Statement in S. C. on the Congo, January 30 (US/UN 3916).
359. Statement in G. S. on Angola, January 30 (US/UN 3917).

360. Statement in S. C. on the Kashmir question, February 1 (US/UN 3919).

361. Address at the Roosevelt Day Dinner of the Americans for Democratic Action, February 1.

362. Transcript of "Adlai Stevenson Reports," with Philip M. Klutznick, United States Ambassador to the Economic and Social Council, as his guest, February 4.

363. Statement in Com. I on the Cuban Complaint, February 5 (US/UN 3921).

364. Statement to the Foreign Relations Committee of the United States Senate in support of S.2768, a bill to promote the foreign policy of the United States by authorizing the purchase of United Nations Bonds, February 7 (US/UN 3924).

365. Transcript of "Adlai Stevenson Reports," with Jonathan B. Bingham, United States Representative to the Trusteeship Council, as his guest, February 18.

366. Address at the Women's National Press Club, Washington, D.C., February 22 (US/UN 3930).

367. Transcript of "Adlai Stevenson Reports," with Mrs. Agda Rossel, Representative of Sweden, and Paul Hoffman, Managing Director of the United Nations Special Fund, as his guests, March 4.

368. Letter to U Thant concerning United States objects launched into sustained orbit or beyond, March 5 (US/UN 3933).

369. Address at Colgate University, Hamilton, New York, March 6 (US/UN 3934).

370. Address at North Carolina State College, Raleigh, North Carolina, March 7 (US/UN 3935).

371. Address at the 12th Annual Conference of National Organizations, American Association for the United Nations, Statler Hilton Hotel, Washington, D.C., March 13 (US/UN 3937). Published as "Glenn's Law: Or National Vigor" in *Looking Outward*.

372. Note to correspondents on the purchase of U.N. bonds by the Federal Republic of Germany, March 15 (US/UN 3939).

373. Statement in S. C. on the Cuban Complaint, March 15 (US/UN 3940).

374. Statement in S. C. on the Cuban Complaint, March 16 (US/UN 3941).

375. Transcript of "Adlai Stevenson Reports," with Francis Plimpton, United States Deputy Ambassador to the United Nations, and

Dr. Franz Matsch, Representative of Austria, as his guests, March 18.

376. Statement in S. C. on the Cuban Complaint, March 23 (US/UN 3948).

377. Statement in S. C. on the Lake Tiberias incident, March 28 (US/UN 3955).

378. Transcript of "Adlai Stevenson Reports," with Hubert H. Humphrey, United States Senator from Minnesota, as his guest, April 1.

379. Text of letter to U Thant concerning the registration data about objects launched into sustained orbit or beyond by the United States, April 3 (US/UN 3962).

380. Address at an African Seminar at Lake Forest College, Lake Forest, Illinois, April 13 (US/UN 3976). Published as "The Upheaval of a Continent" in *Looking Outward*.

381. Transcript of "Adlai Stevenson Reports," with Mrs. Marietta Tree, United States Representative to the United Nations Commission on Human Rights, and Mrs. Gladys Tillett, United States Representative to the United Nations Commission on the Status of Women, as his guests, April 15.

382. Address at the Annual Membership Meeting Luncheon of the United States Committee for the United Nations, United Nations, April 17 (US/UN 3978).

383. Statement to the press on the United States resumption of nuclear testing, April 25 (US/UN 3980).

384. Transcript of "Adlai Stevenson Reports," with William C. Foster, Director of the United States Arms Control and Disarmament Agency, as his guest, April 29.

385. Transcript of "Adlai Stevenson Reports," with Barbara Ward (Lady Jackson) as his guest, May 13.

386. Transcript of "Adlai Stevenson Reports," with no guest, May 27.

387. Excerpts from an address at the United Nations Correspondents Association Luncheon in his honor, May 29 (US/UN 3997).

388. Transcript of the question-and-answer part of the United Nations Correspondents Association Luncheon, May 29 (US/UN 3998).

389. Commencement Address, Boston University, Boston, June 3. Published as "The Road to an Open World: Our International Aim" in *Looking Outward*.

390. Address to the Fortieth Reunion of the Class of 1922 at Princeton University, Princeton, New Jersey, June 8 (US/UN 4003).

391. Commencement Address at Tufts University, Medford, Massachusetts, June 8 (US/UN 4004). Published as "Dreams Come True: Goals for Americans" in *Looking Outward*.

392. Statement in G. A. on Southern Rhodesia, June 12 (US/UN 4007).

393. Address at the Seattle "Century 21" Exhibition, Seattle, June 15 (US/UN 4009).

394. Statement in S. C. on Kashmir, June 15 (US/UN 4010).

395. Statement in S. C. on Kashmir, June 22 (US/UN 4015). Included in this volume and published in *Looking Outward* as "A Privilege Abused: 100 Soviet Vetoes." (See Appendix B.)

396. Statement on the United Nations Loan Bill, to the Committee on Foreign Affairs of the House of Representatives, Washington, D.C., June 27 (US/UN 4016).

397. Statement in G. A. on the adjournment of the 16th General Assembly, June 28 (US/UN 4020).

398. Statement at the 34th session of the Economic and Social Council, Geneva, July 9 (US/UN 4022).

399. Remarks to a group of visiting French leaders, members of the French Association for the Atlantic Community, who were visiting the United States Mission, August 29 (US/UN 4031).

400. Statement in S. C. on the membership application of Jamaica and Trinidad and Tobago, September 12 (US/UN 4037).

401. Statement on the passage of the U.N. Bond Bill by the House of Representatives, September 14 (US/UN 4039).

402. Transcript of "Adlai Stevenson Reports," with Secretary of State Dean Rusk as his guest, September 16.

403. Statement concerning the proclamation presented to U Thant by Mayor Wagner, September 18 (US/UN 4041).

404. Statement in G. A. on the convening of the seventeenth session of the General Assembly, September 20 (US/UN 4043).

405. Statement in G. A. in reply to the Soviet Representative, September 21 (US/UN 4045).

406. Address at the Emancipation Proclamation Ceremonies, Lincoln Memorial, Washington, D.C., September 22 (US/UN 4044). Published as "A Call to a New Battle" in *Looking Outward*.

407. Address, "A Lincoln Portrait," Lincoln Center, New York City, September 25.

408. Statement at the signing of the International Coffee Agreement, September 28 (US/UN 4049).

409. Transcript of "Adlai Stevenson Reports," with Lord Home, Secretary of State for Foreign Affairs of the United Kingdom, as his guest, September 30.

410. Statement in S. C. on the membership application of Algeria, October 4 (US/UN 4052).

411. Point of order after address by President Dorticos of Cuba, October 8 (US/UN 4055).

412. Statement in reply to President Dorticos, October 8 (US/UN 4056).

413. Statement in G. A. on admission of Algeria, October 8 (US/UN 4057).

414. Statement in Com. I on the Nuclear Test item, October 10 (US/UN 4060).

415. Transcript of "Adlai Stevenson Reports," with Ahmed Ben Bella, Prime Minister of Algeria, as his guest, October 14.

416. Text of a United Nations Week address, recorded for distribution through the United States Committee for the United Nations to radio stations throughout the United States for broadcast during United Nations Week, October 15 (US/UN 4064).

417. Statement in S. C. on the membership application of Uganda, October 15 (US/UN 4065).

418. Statement in G. A. on the Chinese representation question, October 22 (US/UN 4068).

419. Letter and resolution delivered to the President of the S. C. on Cuba, October 22 (US/UN 4069).

420. Statement in S. C. on Cuba, October 23 (US/UN 4070). Published as "A Threat to the World" in *Looking Outward.*

421. Statement to the press on Cuba after S. C. adjourned, October 23 (US/UN 4071).

422. Statement in S. C. on Cuba, October 25 (US/UN 4073). Published as "A Premeditated Attempt: The Dread Realities" in *Looking Outward;* included in this volume, together with the next statement below, with the title "A Premeditated Attempt: The Dread Realities and the Building of the Sites."

423. Statement in S. C. on Cuba, October 25 (US/UN 4074). Published as "A Premeditated Attempt: The Building of the Sites" in *Looking Outward.*

424. Text of letter to U Thant, transmitting the text of the White House statement on Ballistic Missile Build-up in Cuba, October 26 (US/UN 4077).

425. Statement on presentation of United States Bond Purchasing Check to U Thant, November 2 (US/UN 4081).

426. Statement in G. A. in tribute to Mrs. Eleanor Roosevelt, November 9 (US/UN 4088). Published as "She Would Rather Light Candles" in *Looking Outward*.

427. Transcript of "Adlai Stevenson Reports," with Arthur H. Dean, the United States Representative to the Eighteen-Nation Disarmament Conference, as his guest, November 11.

428. Text of letter to Senator Barry Goldwater, November 13 (US/UN 4092).

429. Text of eulogy at Memorial Service for Mrs. Eleanor Roosevelt, Cathedral of St. John the Divine, New York City, November 17 (US/UN 4096). Published as "Her Journeys Are Over" in *Looking Outward*.

430. Transcript of "Adlai Stevenson Reports," with B. N. Chakravarty, Representative of India, as his guest, November 25.

431. Statement in G. A. on the election of U Thant as Secretary-General, November 30 (US/UN 4109). Published as "One Can Not Ask More of Any Man" in *Looking Outward*.

432. Letter by Stevenson and Zorin to the Secretary-General with documents relating to an American-Soviet agreement reached on cooperation in the peaceful uses of outer space, December 5 (US/UN 4114).

433. Statement in Com. I on the international cooperation in the peaceful uses of outer space, December 5 (US/UN 4115).

434. Address at the First International Awards Dinner of the Joseph P. Kennedy, Jr., Foundation, Washington, D. C., December 6.

435. Statement on the occasion of the fourteenth anniversary of the adoption of the Universal Declaration of Human Rights, December 8 (US/UN 4117).

436. Transcript of "Adlai Stevenson Reports," with Senators Gordon L. Allott and Albert Gore, as his guests, December 9.

437. Address to the Nigerian American Chamber of Commerce, New York City, December 12.

438. Remarks at Dinner in Honor of U Thant, New York City, December 13.

439. Statement at United Nations Headquarters on the adjournment of the seventeenth session of the General Assembly, December 21 (US/UN 4137).

440. Transcript of "Adlai Stevenson Reports," with no guest, December 23.

441. Statement on the death of Warren P. Austin, former United States Representative to the United Nations, December 26 (US/UN 4139).

1963

442. Transcript of "Adlai Stevenson Reports," with Paul G. Hoffman, Managing Director of the United Nations Special Fund, as his guest, January 6.

443. Note to correspondents on the announcement of the termination of the Katanga secession, January 15 (US/UN 4141).

444. Statement on the death of Hugh Gaitskell, January 18 (US/UN 4142).

445. Transcript of "Adlai Stevenson Reports," with Dr. Ralph J. Bunche, United Nations Under-Secretary for Special Political Affairs, as his guest, January 20.

446. Address at the Tenth Anniversary Convocation, Center for the Study of Democratic Institutions, Fund for the Republic, Americana Hotel, New York City, January 22 (US/UN 4145). Published as "The Essence of Democracy" in *Looking Outward*.

447. Transcript of "Adlai Stevenson Reports," with Dr. Isidor I. Rabi, United States Representative to the United Nations Scientific Advisory Committee, as his guest, February 3.

448. Transcript of "Adlai Stevenson Reports," with Senator William Fulbright as his guest, February 17.

449. Address in acceptance of the Tenth Annual Patriotism Award of the Senior Class of the University of Notre Dame at the University's Washington's Birthday Exercises, South Bend, Indiana, February 18 (US/UN 4149). Published as "The Principles of Patriotism" in *Looking Outward*.

450. Address on the Fortieth Anniversary Kick-Off Luncheon of the Chicago Council on Foreign Relations, Chicago, February 19 (US/UN 4151).

451. Transcript of "Adlai Stevenson Reports," with Harlan Cleveland, Assistant Secretary of State for International Organization Affairs, as his guest, March 3.

452. Statement before the Senate Subcommittee on International Organization Affairs of the Committee on Foreign Relations, Washington, D.C., March 13 (US/UN 4159). Published as "What's In It For Us?" in *Looking Outward*.

453. Transcript of "Adlai Stevenson Reports," with George W. Ball, Under-Secretary of State, as his guest, March 17.

454. Transcript of "Adlai Stevenson Reports," with Thomas K. Finletter, United States Representative to NATO, March 31.

455. Address to the Organization of American States on Pan-American Day, Pan-American Union, Washington, D.C., April 15 (US/UN 4179). Published as "Two Views of History" in *Looking Outward*.

456. Statement in S. C. on the requests by Gabon and Congo (Brazzaville) to participate in the discussion of the Senegalese complaint, April 18 (US/UN 4181).

457. Statement at a luncheon held by the United Nations Correspondents Association, April 22 (US/UN 4182).

458. Text of question-and-answer portion at United Nations Correspondents Association luncheon, April 22 (US/UN 4183).

459. Statement in S. C. on the Senegalese Complaint, April 24 (US/UN 4187).

460. Statement in S. C. on the membership application of Kuwait, May 7 (US/UN 4201).

461. Address at the closing luncheon of the American Red Cross Annual Convention, Bellevue Stratford Hotel, Philadelphia, May 8 (US/UN 4200).

462. Address at the Annual Scholarship Dinner, De Paul University, Chicago, May 9 (US/UN 4203). Included in this volume as "The Human Race *Is* a Family."

463. Remarks at a luncheon meeting upon receiving an award from the United States Committee for the United Nations and the American Association for the United Nations, "For his dedication to public education," United Nations, May 13 (US/UN 4205).

464. Statement in G. A. on the admission of Kuwait, May 14 (US/UN 4206).

465. Address in acceptance of the American Liberties Medallion, at the Fifty-Sixth Annual Meeting of the American Jewish Committee, Hotel Commodore, New York City, May 18 (US/UN 4209).

466. Transcript of "Adlai Stevenson Reports," with Sir Muhammed Zafrulla Khan, President of the United Nations General Assembly, as his guest, May 26.

467. Text of a letter, entitled, "Dangerous United States Activities in Outer Space," to U Thant on a Soviet statement, June 6 (US/UN 4219).

468. Address at the dedication of the Memphis Metropolitan Airport, Memphis, June 7 (US/UN 4220).

469. Statement in S. C. on the question of Yemen, June 11 (US/UN 4222).
470. Commencement Address at Radcliffe College, Cambridge, Massachusetts, June 12 (US/UN 4221).
471. Statement in Com. V on U.N. Financing of Peace-keeping Operations, June 21 (US/UN 4224).
472. Message to His Holiness Paul VI on his election, June 21 (US/UN 4225).
473. Text of question-and-answer portion of press conference, June 25.
474. Statement as Chairman of the Eleanor Roosevelt Memorial Foundation at a press conference, New York City, June 25.
475. Statement at the 36th session of the Economic and Social Council, Geneva, July 10 (US/UN 4227).
476. Statement in S. C. on the Portuguese territories, July 26 (US/UN 4230).
477. Statement in S. C. on the signing of the Test-Ban Treaty, July 26 (US/UN 4231).
478. Statement in S. C. in explanation of the United States vote on the Portuguese territories resolution, July 31 (US/UN 4232).
479. Statement in S. C. on the South African question, August 2 (US/UN 4233).
480. Statement in S. C. on the Israeli-Syrian question, August 28 (US/UN 4237).
481. Text of remarks on presenting a check for $500,000 to the Under-Secretary of the United Nations Department of Economic and Social Affairs, as the United States contribution to the 1963 program of the United Nations High Commissioner for Refugees, September 11 (US/UN 4244).
482. Statement in S. C. on Southern Rhodesia, September 11 (US/UN 4245).
483. Note to correspondents in response to Mr. Gromyko's speech, September 19 (US/UN 4246).
484. Address at the Consecration Ceremony, Church Center for the United Nations, September 22 (US/UN 4247).
485. Note to correspondents on the ratifying of the Nuclear Test-Ban Treaty by the Senate, September 24.
486. Note to correspondents on a speech by the Foreign Minister of Albania in the General Assembly, September 27 (US/UN 4248).
487. Statement in Com. III on the Draft Declaration on the Elimination of All Forms of Racial Discrimination, October 1 (US/UN 4249).

488. Statement in G. A. in reply to the statement of the Cuban Representative, October 7 (US/UN 4253).

489. Address at the Annual Banquet of Planned Parenthood–World Population, The Plaza Hotel, New York City, October 15 (US/UN 4262).

490. Statement in Com. I on Nuclear Weapons Testing, October 15 (US/UN 4264, Rev. 1). Included in this volume as "The Most Important Single Step in the Field of Arms Control and Disarmament."

491. Statement in Com. I on general and complete disarmament, October 16 (US/UN 4248).

492. Statement in G. A. on Chinese Representation, October 16 (US/UN 4267). Included in this volume as "The Government of Peiping Is Not Peace-loving."

493. Statement in G. A. on the Draft Resolution on Orbiting of Weapons of Mass Destruction in Outer Space, October 17 (US/UN 4268).

494. Text of a United Nations Day message recorded for use during intermission of the Special Concert of the New York Philharmonic, dedicated to United Nations Week, and broadcast over Station WOR, October 18 (US/UN 4270).

495. Remarks at the "International Tribute to Eleanor Roosevelt," presented by the Eleanor Roosevelt Memorial Foundation, Lincoln Center, October 21 (US/UN 4271).

496. Statement as Chairman of the Eleanor Roosevelt Memorial Foundation, delivered at a press conference, at the United States Mission, October 23 (US/UN 4273).

497. Address at a luncheon sponsored by the Los Angeles World Affairs Council, the Los Angeles Bar Association and the Southern California Council of the American Association for the United Nations, Los Angeles, October 23 (US/UN 4275).

498. United Nations Day Address, Memorial Theatre, Dallas, October 24 (US/UN 4276). Included in this volume as "The United Nations: Hope for the Future."

499. Statement in G. A. on the Agreement between the Republic of Indonesia and the Kingdom of the Netherlands concerning West New Guinea (West Irian) and the Report of the Secretary-General, November 6 (US/UN 4288).

500. Statement in G. A. on the Report of Committee V concerning administrative and budgetary questions, November 6 (US/UN 4289).

501. Address at the Memorial Services for Mrs. Eleanor Roosevelt, Hyde Park, New York, November 7 (US/UN 4292).

502. Statement in Com. I on the Latin-American Nuclear Free Zone, November 13 (US/UN 4299).

503. Statement in Com. I in reply to the Soviet Representative on the Federal Republic of Germany, November 13 (US/UN 4300).

504. Address at a testimonial dinner honoring William J. Pachler, President of the Utility Workers Union of America, AFL–CIO, for the benefit of the AFL–CIO Committee for the United Nations, New York Hilton Hotel, New York City, November 18 (US/UN 4308).

505. Statement in G. A. on the Declaration on the Elimination of All Forms of Racial Discrimination, November 20 (US/UN 4312).

506. Statement on the death of President Kennedy, November 22 (US/UN 4317).

507. Statement in G. A. on the death of President Kennedy, at the United Nations Memorial Service, November 26 (US/UN 4318).

508. Statement in S. C. on Apartheid in South Africa, December 4 (US/UN 4328).

509. Statement on the death of Herbert H. Lehman, December 5 (US/UN 4331).

510. Statement in Com. I with texts of resolutions (adopted December 13), December 2.

511. Statement in G. A., special Plenary Session, on the fifteenth anniversary of the Universal Declaration of Human Rights, December 9 (US/UN 4335). Included in this volume as "Human Rights Still Remain the Great Unfinished Business of All Men."

512. Note to correspondents on the House Appropriations Committee cut of funds for American voluntary contributions to international agencies, December 15 (US/UN 4344).

513. Statement in S. C. on the admission of Kenya and Zanzibar, December 16 (US/UN 4345).

514. Statement in G. A. on the admission of Kenya and Zanzibar, December 16 (US/UN 4346).

515. Toasts at luncheon for President Johnson, December 17 (US/UN 4347).

516. Statement at the close of the eighteenth General Assembly, December 17 (US/UN 4348).

517. Statement on the adjournment of the General Assembly at a press conference at United Nations Headquarters, December 18 (US/UN 4349).

1964
518. Statement in S. C. on the Panamanian Complaint, January 10 (US/UN 4353).
519. Address at a New England regional conference sponsored by Brown University and the Plans for Progress Advisory Council of the President's Committee on Equal Employment Opportunity, Brown University, Providence, Rhode Island, January 28 US/UN 4358).
520. Text of letter to Carlos Alfred Bernardes, President of the Security Council, informing the Council of the Cuban Fishing Boat Incident, February 7 (US/UN 4360).
521. Statement in S. C. on Kashmir, February 14 (US/UN 4362).
522. Statement to the Press that the United States is not seeking to isolate Archbishop Makarios, February 17 (US/UN 4363).
523. Statement in S. C. on the Cyprus question, February 19 (US/UN 4364).
524. Statement to the press on the Cyprus question, March 4 (US/UN 4367).
525. Dag Hammarskjold Memorial Lecture, Princeton University, March 23 (US/UN 4374).
526. Address at Charter Day Convocation, University of California, Berkeley, April 2 (US/UN 4377).
527. "The Anatomy of World Leadership," Address to the Commonwealth Club, San Francisco, April 3.
528. Statement on the death of General Douglas MacArthur, April 5 (US/UN 4375).
529. Statement in S. C. on the Yemen situation, April 6 (US/UN 4379).
530. Address at the Eleanor Roosevelt Memorial Foundation Luncheon in honor of Mrs. Lyndon B. Johnson, New York Hilton, New York City, April 9 (US/UN 4380).
531. Statement in S. C. in explanation of the vote on the Yemen resolution, April 9 (US/UN 4381).
532. Address at the Preview of the State of Illinois' "Land of Lincoln" Pavilion, New York World's Fair, Flushing Meadows, New York, April 20 (US/UN 4385).
533. Address at Convocation and Dinner of the New School for Social Research, Park Lane Hotel, New York City, April 28 (US/UN 4387).
534. Address at Honors Day Convocation, University of Illinois, Urbana, May 1 (US/UN 4388).

535. Statement in S. C. on the Cambodian Complaint, May 21 (US/UN 4395).
536. Statement in S. C. on the Cambodian Complaint, May 21 (press release 249). Included in this volume as "The People of the Republic of Vietnam Are the Victims of Armed Aggression."
537. Statement in S. C. on the Cambodian Complaint, May 26 (US/UN 4398).
538. Statement in S. C. on the Cambodian Complaint, May 26 (US/UN 4399).
539. Statement on the death of Prime Minister Nehru, May 27 (US/UN 4400).
540. Remarks at the 1964 Selznick Golden Laurel Trophy Awards Ceremony held at the United States Mission, May 27 (US/UN 4403).
541. Address at the 20th Anniversary Dinner of the Citizens' Committee for Children of New York, Waldorf-Astoria Hotel, June 1 (US/UN 4406).
542. "Strengthening the Machinery for Peace," Address to the Women's National Democratic Club, Washington, D.C., June 2 (press release 264).
543. Statement in S. C. on the Cambodian Complaint with text of resolution adopted that day, June 4 (US/UN 4408).
544. Statement in S. C. on the question of race conflict in South Africa, June 16 (US/UN 4415 and 4415 Corr. 1).
545. Statement in S. C. on the question of race conflict in South Africa, June 18 (US/UN 4416).
546. Statement on the passage by the United States Senate of the Civil Rights Bill, June 19 (US/UN 4418).
547. Statement in S. C. on the attacks by the Hanoi Regime on United States Naval vessels, August 5 (US/UN 4424). Included in this volume as "We Still Seek No Wider War."
548. Statement in S. C. on a point of order regarding the United States request for a Security Council meeting, August 5 (US/UN 4425).
549. Statement in S. C. on the appearance of North and South Vietnamese representatives before the Council, August 5 (US/UN 4426).
550. Statement in S. C. on the situation created by attacks by the Hanoi Regime on United States Naval vessels, August 7 (US/UN 4428).

551. Statement in reply to the Representative of Czechoslovakia, August 7 (US/UN 4429).

552. Statement in S. C. on Cyprus, August 9 (US/UN 4430).

553. Statement in S. C. on Cyprus, August 9 (US/UN 4431 and 4431 Corr. 1) .

554. Address to the American Bar Association, Waldorf-Astoria Hotel, August 13 (US/UN 4434).

555. Text of letter to Acting President of the Security Council on the United Nations Mission Report concerning Cambodia and Vietnam, September 9.

556. Statement in S. C. on the Malaysian Complaint, September 10 (US/UN 4436).

557. Statement in S. C. on the Greek-Turkish Complaint, September 11 (US/UN 4437).

558. Statement in S. C. on the Malaysian Complaint, September 17 (US/UN 4439).

559. Statement in S. C. on the Greek-Turkish Complaint, September 17 (US/UN 4440).

560. Excerpts from an address at the World Affairs Council Luncheon, Philadelphia, September 24 (US/UN 4441).

561. Excerpts from an address at the Centennial Banquet of the St. Louis Bar Association, St. Louis, October 6 (US/UN 4445).

562. Letter of transmittal of memorandum on the United Nations Financial Crisis, October 8.

563. Address at an Anniversary Banquet at Cornell University, Ithaca, New York, October 9 (US/UN 4446).

564. Remarks at a stamp preview ceremony honoring the Agreement on Cessation of Nuclear Testing held at United Nations Headquarters, October 21 (US/UN 4453).

565. United Nations Day Address, War Memorial Auditorium, Nashville, October 22 (US/UN 4454).

566. Address to the American Jewish Congress, Waldorf-Astoria Hotel, October 25 (US/UN 4456).

567. Address at the World Affairs Council Luncheon, Los Angeles, October 30 (US/UN 4460).

568. Text of letter to Chief Adebo on question of United Nations Financing, November 9 (US/UN 4465).

569. "The Promise of Science and Technology," Address to the Xerox Corporation Symposium, Rochester, New York, November 12 (US/UN 4466).

570. Text of letter to President of Security Council on United States cooperation with Belgium in rescue of hostages from the Congo, November (Security Council document S/6065).
571. Text of letter to President of Security Council on withdrawal of Congo rescue mission, December 1 (Security Council document S/6075).
572. Statement on the "no-voting agreement in the General Assembly," December 1 (US/UN 4472).
573. Statement in G. A. on the admission of new members, December 2 (US/UN 4473).
574. Statement in S. C. on the Israeli-Syrian Complaint, December 3 (US/UN 4474).
575. Statement to the press on Foreign Minister Gromyko's address to the General Assembly, December 7 (US/UN 4475).
576. Statement in S. C. on the Congo Complaints, December 9 (US/UN 4476).
577. Statement in S. C. on the Congo Complaints, December 9 (US/UN 4477).
578. Statement in G. A. in reply to the statement of the Cuban Representative, December 11 (US/UN 4478).
579. Statement in S. C. on the Congo question, December 14 (US/UN 4479).
580. Statement in S. C. on the Congo question, December 24 (US/UN 4486).
581. Statement to the press in explanation of the United States vote on the Ivory Coast-Moroccan resolution on the Congo question, December 30 (US/UN 4487).

1965

582. Statement on the death of Sir Winston Churchill, January 24 (US/UN 4491).
583. Statement in G. A. during the General Debate on the United Nations Constitutional Crisis, January 26 (US/UN 4492). Included in this volume as "The United States Reviews the U.N. Constitutional Crisis."
584. Statement in G. A. on the death of Prime Minister Ali Mansur of Iran, January 26 (US/UN 4493).
585. Address at the Memorial Service for Sir Winston Churchill, National Cathedral, Washington, D.C., January 28 (US/UN 4495).
586. Statement to the press on the recess of the General Assembly, February 1 (US/UN 4496).

587. Statement at the special meeting of the United Nations Children's Fund Executive Board in memory of Maurice Pate, February 2 (US/UN 4497).

588. Text of letter to President of the Security Council concerning retaliatory attacks against North Vietnam by the United States and South Vietnamese Forces, February 7.

589. Statement on closed-circuit television to the New York Police Academy, February 8 (US/UN 4498).

590. Statement in G. A. on the "no vote agreement," February 18 (US/UN 4503).

591. Statement to the press on the "no vote agreement," February 18 (US/UN 4504).

592. Statement in G. A. in reply to the Soviet statement, February 18 (US/UN 4505).

593. Address to the University of the West Indies, Kingston, Jamaica, February 20 (US/UN 4506).

594. Text of letter to President of the Security Council, transmitting United States report on Vietnam, February 27 (US/UN 4508).

595. Note to correspondents pledging American funds to the United Nations Development Program for 1965, and text of letter to Secretary-General, March 2 (US/UN 4509 and 4510).

596. Address to the Overseas Writers Association, Willard Hotel, Washington, D.C., March 11 (US/UN 4512).

597. Address in acceptance of the John Dewey Award, at the Spring Luncheon Conference of the United Federation of Teachers, New York Hilton Hotel, March 13 (US/UN 4513).

598. Statement in S. C. on Cyprus, March 19 (US/UN 4515).

599. Statement to the press on disarmament, March 31 (US/UN 4517).

600. Text of letter to the President of the Security Council denouncing circulation of the Soviet Note on American use of gas in Vietnam, April 2 (US/UN 4519).

601. Address at the Dedication of the Prudential Center, Boston, April 20 (US/UN 4527).

602. Address at a joint session of the Massachusetts State Legislature, Boston, April 20 (US/UN 4528).

603. Address at the Annual Dinner of the Bureau of Advertising of the American Newspaper Publishers Association, Waldorf-Astoria Hotel, April 22 (US/UN 4530).

604. Statement to the United Nations Disarmament Commission, April 26 (US/UN 4532).

605. Note to correspondents on the death of Edward R. Murrow, April 27 (US/UN 4533).

606. Text of letter to President of the Security Council concerning the threat in the Dominican Republic, April 29 (US/UN 4536).

607. Statement in S. C. on the Dominican Republic question, May 3 (US/UN 4538). Included in this volume as "The United States Has No Intention To Dictate the Political Future of the Dominican Republic."

608. Statement in S. C. on the Dominican Republic question, May 3 (US/UN 4539).

609. Statement in reply to the statement of the Soviet Representative on the Dominican Republic question, May 3 (US/UN 4540).

610. Statement in S. C. on the Dominican Republic question, May 4 (US/UN 4541).

611. Statement in S. C. on the Dominican Republic question, May 4 (US/UN 4542).

612. Statement in S. C. on the Dominican Republic question, May 5 (US/UN 4543).

613. Statement in S. C. on the Dominican Republic question, May 5 (US/UN 4544).

614. Statement in S. C. on the question of Southern Rhodesia, May 5 (US/UN 4545).

615. Statement in S. C. on the Dominican Republic question, May 6 (US/UN 4547).

616. Statement in S. C. on the Dominican Republic question, May 7 (US/UN 4549).

617. Statement in S. C. on the Dominican Republic question, May 11 (US/UN 4550).

618. Statement in S. C. on the Dominican Republic question, May 13 (US/UN 4551).

619. Statement in S. C. on the Dominican Republic question, May 14 (US/UN 4552).

620. Statement in S. C. on the Senegalese Complaint, May 19 (US/UN 4554).

621. Statement in S. C. on the Dominican Republic question, May 19 (US/UN 4556).

622. Statement in S. C. on the Dominican Republic question, May 20 (US/UN 4557).

623. Statement in S. C. on the Dominican Republic question, May 21 (US/UN 4558).

624. Statement in S. C. on the Dominican Republic question, May 22 (US/UN 4560).

625. Statement in S. C. in explanation of the United States vote on the Uruguayan resolution of the Dominican Republic question, May 22 (US/UN 4561).

626. Statement in S. C. on the Dominican Republic question, May 22 (US/UN 4562).

627. Statement in S. C. on the Dominican Republic question, May 22 (US/UN 4564).

628. Text of letter to Ambassador Paul Tremlay, Chairman of the Committee for the International Cooperation Year, May 24 (US/UN 4563).

629. Statement in S. C. on the Dominican Republic question, May 24 (US/UN 4566).

630. Address at a convocation of the University of Toronto, Toronto, May 28 (US/UN 4567).

631. Address at the 67th Annual Meeting of the Arkansas Bar Association, Arlington Hotel, Hot Spring National Park, Arkansas, June 4 (US/UN 4575).

632. Statement in S. C. on the Dominican Republic question, June 9 (US/UN 4580).

633. Remarks at the opening of the Handicrafts and Handlooms Center of India, New York City, June 9 (US/UN 4581).

634. Address at Williams College, Williamstown, Massachusetts, June 13 (US/UN 4585).

635. Address at the Annual Commencement Meeting of the Harvard Alumni Association, Cambridge, Massachusetts, June 17 (US/UN 4588).

636. Statement in S. C. on the Dominican Republic question, June 18 (US/UN 4594).

637. Statement in S. C. on the Dominican Republic question, June 18 (US/UN 4595).

638. Address at a dinner celebrating the dedication of the Equitable Building, Palmer House, Chicago, June 23 (US/UN 4596).

639. Text of a letter to the Secretary-General pledging United States funds for the United Nations program to train South Africans, June 25 (US/UN 4598).

640. Address at the Commemorative Meeting on the Twentieth Anniversary of the Signing of the United Nations Charter, June 26 (US/UN 4597). Included in this volume as "What We Require Above All Is a Truce to Terror."

641. "Strengthening the International Development Institution," Statement to the 39th session of the Economic and Social Council, Geneva, July 9.
642. Panorama Program on BBC Television, London, recorded on July 14.

Footnotes to Introduction

[1] Ernest G. Bormann, "Ghostwriting and the Rhetorical Critic," *Quarterly Journal of Speech*, XLVI (October, 1960), p. 284.

[2] Debs Myers and Ralph Martin, "A Brief Biography of Adlai Stevenson," *Speeches of Adlai Stevenson*, Foreword by John Steinbeck (New York, 1952), p. 10.

[3] Hermon Dunlap Smith, "Politics and R + R," *As We Knew Adlai: The Stevenson Story by Twenty-two Friends*, Ed. and Preface by Edward P. Doyle, Foreword by Adlai E. Stevenson III (New York, 1966), p. 30. See also Jacob Arvey's comments on Stevenson's request to have "something dashed off for him" in "A Gold Nugget in Your Backyard," *Ibid.*, p. 54.

[4] John Steinbeck, Foreword, *Speeches of Adlai Stevenson*, pp. 6–7.

[5] George Ball, "With AES in War and Politics," *As We Knew Adlai*, p. 147.

[6] "Stevenson's Ghost Writers: Big Names Lend Hand—New Dealers Chip In Too—But Adlai Distills His Own Quips," *U.S. News and World Report* (September 25, 1952), pp. 57–59. See also Raymond Yeager, "A Rhetorical Analysis of the 1952 Presidential Campaign Speeches of Adlai E. Stevenson," Unpublished Ph.D. dissertation, Ohio State University (1956), p. 196.

[7] Stephen A. Mitchell, "Adlai's Amateurs," *As We Knew Adlai*, p. 81.

[8] George Ball, pp. 149–150.

[9] William Attwood, "Pencils, Pads and Chronic Stamina," *As We Knew Adlai*, pp. 154–155.

[10] *Ibid.*, pp. 156–157.

[11] Russel Rayl Windes, Jr., "The Speech-Making of Adlai E. Stevenson in the 1956 Campaign" (unpublished Ph.D. dissertation, Northwestern University, 1959), pp. 42–43.

[12] Arthur Schlesinger, Jr., and Seymour Harris, Introduction, Adlai E. Stevenson, *The New America*, Edited by Arthur Schlesinger, Jr., Seymour Harris, and John Bartlow Martin (New York, 1957), p. xxi.

[13] Russel Rayl Windes, Jr. "Adlai E. Stevenson's Speech Staff in the 1956 Campaign," *Quarterly Journal of Speech*, XLVI (February, 1960), p. 35. See Schlesinger and Harris, pp. xx–xxi for a full list of those who assisted Stevenson's hard-core research team and for those who assisted him editorially in connection with his speeches, see p. xxii. Russel Windes argues that the hard-core writers included: Wirtz, Schlesinger, Martin, Robert Tufts, and William Lee Miller. The last two were included by Schlesinger and Harris as important, but not as members of the hard core. See Windes, p. 35.

[14] *Ibid.*, pp. 36–37.

[15] *Ibid.*, p. 43.

[16] Mary McGrory, "The Perfectionist and the Press," *As We Knew Adlai*, p. 176.

[17] William Benton, "Ambassador of Good Will in Latin America," *As We Knew Adlai*, p. 202.

[18] William Attwood, p. 161.

[19] *Ibid.*, p. 165.

[20] "The United States Mission to the United Nations," Unpublished, mimeographed, and released by the United States Mission (December, 1961), p. 1.

[21] Miss Elinor Green, the former Public Affairs Officer at the Mission, and my host there during the summer of 1962, in a conversation with me at the Mission, June 19, 1962.

[22] Wallace Irwin, former Director of Public Services at the Mission, taped interview with me at the Mission, June 26, 1962.

[23] Adlai E. Stevenson, *Looking Outward: Years of Crisis at the United Nations* (New York, 1963), p. xvii.

[24] Francis T. P. Plimpton, "They Sent You Our Best," *As We Knew Adlai*, p. 260.

[25] Green, interview, June 1962.

[26] Irwin, interview.

[27] Michael Moynahan, taped interview with me at the Department of State, Washington, D.C., July 26, 1962.

[28] Irwin, interview.

[29] Dean Rusk and Adlai E. Stevenson, "Adlai Stevenson Reports," ABC Radio and TV transcript (October 1, 1961). It may be here that Stevenson coined the term "corridor diplomacy" which he used repeatedly since.

[30] But see Michael H. Prosser, "Adlai E. Stevenson's United Nations Audience," *Central States Speech Journal*, XVI (November, 1965), pp. 262-271.

[31] Sydney D. Bailey, *The General Assembly of the United Nations: A Study of Procedures and Practice* (New York, 1960), p. 111.

[32] Stevenson, as quoted by Alden Whitman, *Portrait: Adlai E. Stevenson: Politician, Diplomat, Friend* (New York, 1965), p. 214.

[33] Robert T. Oliver, "The Rhetoric of Power in Diplomatic Conferences," *Quarterly Journal of Speech*, XL (October, 1954), p. 292.

[34] ————, *Culture and Communication: The Problem of Penetrating National Boundaries* (Springfield, Illinois, 1962), p. 12.

[35] Moynahan, interview.

[36] Irwin indicated to me that a speech such as this one was long in preparation and would be sent back and forth between the State Department and the Mission by regular mail or telegram. In a crisis period, speech drafts and revisions were transmitted by telephone, often in code.

[37] Moynahan, interview.

[38] Ernest G. Bormann, "Ethics of Ghostwritten Speeches," *Quarterly Journal of Speech*, XLVII (October, 1961), p. 267.

39 Plimpton, p. 261.
40 Adlai E. Stevenson, Statement in Security Council (February 15, 1961), S/P34, pp. 5–6.
41 Stevenson, Statement in Committee I (November 15, 1961), US/UN3837, p. 5.
42 Irwin, interview.
43 Moynahan, interview.
44 Stevenson, *Looking Outward*, pp. xvi–xvii.

Footnotes to Stevenson's Addresses

[1] Alfred Mossman Landon was elected Republican Governor of Kansas in 1932 despite a bitter intraparty struggle and was reelected in 1934, the only Republican incumbent to win that year. This led to the "Landon boom" and his candidacy against Roosevelt in 1936. *Encyclopaedia Britannica* XIII (1966), 653–654.

[2] Roosevelt's Reciprocal Trade Agreement went into effect January 1, 1936. It contained lower-tariff duties on goods exchanged with Brazil and Canada and, in return for halting French double taxation of American businesses in France, gave French imported goods reduced tariffs. *New York Times* (January 1, 1936), p. 30.

[3] President Hoover signed the Smoot-Hawley Tariff Bill in the hope that it would aid the hard-pressed staple farmers. Raising duties higher than ever before in American history, by 1932 it caused twenty-five countries to enact retaliatory tariffs. *Oxford Companion to American History* (1966), p. 366.

[4] Alexander F. Kerensky, the Prime Minister of Russia from July to November, 1917, was overthrown by the Bolshevik Revolution. Still, he believed it "an epic sweep toward the eternal and universal ideal of human liberty." *Encyclopaedia Britannica*, XIII (1966), 313.

[5] As quoted by Russel Windes, Jr., and James A. Robinson, "Public Address in the Career of Adlai E. Stevenson," *Quarterly Journal of Speech*, XLII (October, 1956), 277.

[6] Judge Harry Fisher, Circuit Court Judge in Cook County, Illinois, brought Stevenson together with Colonel Jacob M. Arvey, the Democratic power in Illinois, which began Stevenson's path to the governorship. *Martindale-Hubbell Law Directory I* (New York, 1950), 376.

[7] The White Paper on Palestine was issued by the British government in May of 1939, offering three objectives: 1. the establishment of an independent Palestine, a state both for Arabs and Jews, 2. retention of mandatory British power during the transitional period, and 3. the limitation of 75,000 Jewish immigrants to Britain over the next five years. *New York Times* (May 18, 1939), p. 4.

[8] Stuart Gerry Brown, *Adlai E. Stevenson: A Short Biography* (Woodbury, New York, 1965), p. 35.

[9] This paragraph was added by Stevenson in handwriting at the last moment.

[10] Clay Judson of the *Chicago Tribune* and spokesman of the America First Committee, was apparently the first speaker to whom Stevenson made allusions during the speech. Shortly after the speech, Judson stated: "The

United States can by itself keep out of war . . . there is nothing which could happen in South America, Europe or Asia which would make war obligatory." *New York Times* (October 30, 1940), p. 22.

[11] Stevenson penciled in "omit" for this paragraph, suggesting that when the speech was given it was left out.

[12] White, as chairman of the national committee, supported Wendell Willkie for President, while Stevenson as the Chicago chairman supported Roosevelt. *New York Times* (October 30, 1940), p. 22.

[13] When the peace treaty was signed on June 28, 1919, between the Allied and Associated Powers and Germany at Versailles, the delay in signing other peace treaties with Austria, Hungary, Bulgaria, and Turkey made this treaty seem first in importance, thus giving unexpected weight to Germany as a vanquished nation. *Encyclopaedia Britannica*, XXIII (1966), 93.

[14] Professor Adolf Lasson, a German Hegelian philosopher, wrote *The War* in 1868.

[15] Otto von Bismarck, the Prussian Premier from 1862 to 1871 and German Chancellor from 1871 to 1890, united the German empire and wielded it into one of the great powers of that period. Hans J. Morgenthau, *Politics Among Nations: The Struggle for Power and Peace*, 3rd ed. (New York, 1961), p. 613.

[16] The Center party, an offshoot of the Catholic Center party founded in Germany in 1848, held the majority in the legislature from 1895 to 1906 and was the chief support of the Imperial government as a war party. Koppel Pinson, *Modern Germany: Its History and Civilization* (New York, 1966), p. 185.

[17] Count Alfred von Schlieffen developed the Schlieffen Plan in 1911 for a war on two fronts based on a right-wing attack to annihilate France and on a move into Russia before it had time to mobilize. Helmuth von Moltke modified the plan in 1914 and it had lasting strategy effects in both World Wars. *New Century Cyclopedia of Names* (1954), III, 3517.

[18] Ludwig von Edelsheim assisted the Grand Duke in his plans to attack Prussia in 1866 and had formulated plans for attack on the then weakened United States. *Grand Larousse Encyclopedia* (1964), VIII, 362.

[19] Written to Lodge from Oyster Bay, New York, March 27, 1901. *The Letters of Theodore Roosevelt*, Elting E. Morison, ed. (Cambridge, Massachusetts, 1951), p. 32.

[20] Hermann Rauschning, *Hitler Speaks* (London, 1939), pp. 76–77. Dr. Rauschning was the Nazi President of Danzig but was forced to resign in 1934, charged with treachery to the National Socialist party.

[21] Adolf Hitler wrote *Mein Kampf* (My Battle) in 1924 while in prison. It provided a carefully outlined plan for German domination of Europe.

[22] This quote most likely came from Rauschning's book *The Revolution of Destruction*, published in the United States in 1939 as *The Revolution of Nihilism*.

[23] As a part of the American Lend-Lease Plan, large quantities of surplus

military equipment, including fifty overage destroyers, were transferred to Britain through private means in exchange for the rights to establish United States naval and air bases in Newfoundland and the West Indies.

[24] General Hugh Samuel Johnson condemned the German invasion of the small countries and urged support for an extensive program of relief and rehabilitation in Central and Eastern Europe, but did not wish the United States to enter the war. *New York Times* (May 6, 1940), p. 7.

[25] The Embargo Act prevented shipment of arms and munitions to warring nations. Its repeal was "a modified cash and carry plan for future commerce between the United States and the belligerents." *New York Times* (November 3, 1939), p. 1.

[26] At this point in the text, Stevenson struck out the following statement before actual delivery: "I do not think gangsters are content to leave the only rich man alone."

[27] General Robert E. Wood was the national chairman of the America First Committee and organized the Save America Committee. *New York Times* (December 25, 1940), p. 14.

[28] The Maginot Line was the defense system along France's eastern frontier, named for the French Minister of War André Maginot. Although considered impregnable, the whole line became useless when the Germans reversed it by means of the breakthrough of Sedan, which initiated the invasion of France in 1940. Morgenthau, p. 622.

[29] Robert E. Wood, speech delivered to the Chicago Council on Foreign Relations, October 4, 1940, *Vital Speeches* (December 15, 1940), p. 131. On December 14, 1940, Wood stated: "It seems inconceivable to me that Germany at the end of the war, even if aided by its allies, who will be in a worse condition of exhaustion than Germany itself, will attack the United States." *New York Times* (December 14, 1940), p. 10.

[30] As President of the Second Republic of France, Napoleon III, later dictator and then Emperor, also declared himself Emperor of Mexico.

[31] Where Stevenson added Uruguay, he had stricken out before delivery "and a million and a half Italians in the Argentine."

[32] Here about seven lines of Stevenson's original text are lost, ending with the following fragment: "is still another consideration which seems to be imperfectly understood."

[33] Although Walther Funk seemed a very "insignificant" figure when he became Reichsminister of Economics in 1938; he became Hitler's dominant financial adviser. In the 1945 War Trials, he was sentenced to life imprisonment. *Encyclopaedia Britannica*, X, 333.

[34] Members of the "Fifth Column" in the United States were sympathetic to Nazi Germany and sought to control American attitudes as an instrument for changing the power relations between the two nations.

[35] The *New York Times* called Churchill's speech "a slashing attack on the entire foreign policy of the [British] Government." (February 23, 1938), p. 1.

36 In Stevenson's original text, two lines are lost at this point.

37 Colonel Charles A. Lindbergh suggested in a Mutual Broadcasting System radio address, October 13, 1939, that "An embargo should be placed on 'offensive' weapons and munitions but the United States should permit unrestricted sale of purely 'defensive' armaments." *New York Times* (October 14, 1939), p. 10.

38 Brown, p. 36.

39 *Ibid.*, pp. 41–42.

40 Adlai E. Stevenson, *Major Campaign Speeches* (New York, 1953), p. xx.

41 Lord Halifax (Edward Frederick Lindley Wood) was Chamberlain's Foreign Secretary during the Munich agreement, which earned him the unhappy label of "appeaser." He was awarded the title Earl of Halifax for his service as ambassador to the United States and to the allied cause during the war and was a British delegate to the San Francisco Conference. Joseph Paul-Boncour, former Premier of France, French Foreign Minister, and delegate to the League of Nations, headed the French delegation to the San Francisco Conference.

42 Senator Thomas Connally, a delegate to the San Francisco Conference and Chairman of the Senate Foreign Relations Committee, said in his speech to the Senate that: "the fate of the United Nations organization was in [the Senate's] hands, that the new world Charter could not live, breathe, and act without its ratification." *New York Times* (June 29, 1945), p. 1.

43 Stevenson did not include Mrs. Stevenson's verse in the text. Apparently it was never published.

44 Stevenson did not include these stories in his text. The interpreters were so obscure that no record of them can be discovered.

45 The Dunbarton Oaks Conference was sponsored by China, Great Britain, the Soviet Union, and the United States; it was to draw up a blueprint to serve as a basis for the United Nations Charter. Agreement was reached to include France as the fifth Big Power, but no agreement was made on the veto because the Soviet Union refused to bar a member from voting on a question in the Security Council to which that member itself was a party. *Oxford Companion to American History*, p. 257.

46 At this point, Stevenson struck out the following statement before delivery: "Moreover, it should be remembered that under the Yalta formula the five major powers cannot act by themselves since decisions of the Council would have to include the concurring votes of at least two of the nonpermanent members."

47 The Act of Chapultepec was passed at the Inter-American Conference on Problems of War and Peace held at Chapultepec, Mexico, from February 21 to March 3, 1945. The Act outlawed aggression in the Western Hemisphere and incorporated the Pan-American Security System. *United States Department of State Bulletin* (March 4, 1945), p. 339.

48 As quoted by Brown, p. 50.

[49] Adlai E. Stevenson, *Looking Outward: Years of Crisis at the United Nations* (New York, 1963), p. xvi.

[50] This "doctor-patient" metaphor became one of Stevenson's favorites and was used extensively in reference to the Congo crisis during his speeches in 1961.

[51] The Atlantic Charter set forth national policies of the United States and Great Britain with respect to the postwar world, including the concepts of national self-determination for all nations, opposition to aggression, the significance of disarmament, and equal access to trade and raw materials. Morgenthau, p. 611.

[52] The United Nations Declaration was signed in Washington, D.C., and the participating nations "pledged not to make a separate armistice of peace and to employ full military or economic resources against the enemy each is fighting."

[53] The Moscow Declaration, issued by the Foreign Ministers of Great Britain, the Soviet Union, and the United States, endorsed the four-power (including the Chinese) declaration, which called for an international organization and for postwar collaboration among the great allies reminiscent of the 1814 Quadruple Alliance. *Encyclopaedia Britannica*, XXIII, p. 795.

[54] Aristide Briand was eleven times Premier of France and was a winner of the Nobel Peace Prize. He served as Clemenceau's Minister of Education and Religion. Clemenceau's determination urged his country on to victory in World War I, after which he formed his second government as Minister of War and Premier until 1920 when his cabinet fell. *Encyclopaedia Britannica*, V, 896–897.

[55] In his "Perpetual Peace," Immanuel Kant asserts: "The state of peace among men who live side by side is not the state of nature (*status naturalis*), it is rather a state of war." Immanuel Kant, "Perpetual Peace," *Crisis and Continuity in World Politics: Readings in International Relations*, George A. Lanyi and Wilson C. McWilliams, eds. (New York, 1966), p. 11.

[56] Léon Blum was the first Socialist Premier of France during 1936 and 1937 and was the Interim Premier from December 1946 to January 1947. During his earlier premiership, he influenced France profoundly by introducing the forty-hour work-week, nationalizing the Bank of France and the chief war industries, and urging the buildup of national defense against the growing power of the Rome-Berlin Axis. *Encyclopaedia Britannica*, III, 818.

[57] Ernest Bevin, Britain's Foreign Secretary, and Andrei Vishinsky, the Soviet Vice Commissar for Foreign Affairs, clashed heatedly in the Council on February 2, 1946, when Vishinsky charged that British troops in Greece were a threat to peace and Bevin retorted that such a charge was preposterous. On February 6, they reached a compromise when Vishinsky agreed not to press the charge and withdrew his demand that the Council recommend the immediate and unconditional removal of British troops from Greece. Bevin agreed to restrain his demand that the Council issue a formal declara-

534   AN ETHIC FOR SURVIVAL

tion acquitting Great Britain of the Soviet charges. *New York Times* (February 2, 1946), p. 1, and (February 7, 1946), p. 1.

⁵⁸ *New York Times* (March 1, 1946), p. 10.

⁵⁹ Stevenson drew a wavy line from "The world's hope . . ." to "recuperative peace," to add emphasis.

⁶⁰ Stevenson circled from "We must be just . . ." to "than making war."—to remind himself of the importance of these phrases.

⁶¹ Stevenson drew a wavy line on the original draft along this paragraph for emphasis.

⁶² Stevenson encircled from "We have enough faith . . ." to "the future belongs to him who rightly cares."

⁶³ Adlai E. Stevenson, *Friends and Enemies: What I Learned in Russia* (New York, 1958), p. xvii.

⁶⁴ The Third International (Comintern) was founded in Moscow in 1919 and at first represented only the Bolshevik regime in Russia. Under Stalin's control it became wholly totalitarian.

⁶⁵ Stevenson had struck out the "Oder" River and replaced it with the "Elbe."

⁶⁶ The Foreign Ministers Conference, representing the Big Five powers, met twice in 1945 in an unsuccessful attempt to draft peace settlements with the defeated Axis powers. At the 1946 meeting, the Foreign Ministers agreed upon treaties for Finland, Italy, Hungary, Bulgaria, and Rumania, but not for Germany.

⁶⁷ Harry S Truman and Clement Attlee had drawn up the agreement on December 7, 1945, regarding settlements for the bills concerning Lend-Lease, Reciprocal Aid, Surplus War Property and Claims. *Congressional Record* (December 10–21, 1945), p. A/6218. However, the Senate Joint Resolution 138, authorizing the Secretary of the Treasury to carry out the agreement with the United Kingdom, was still being debated during the spring of 1946. *Congressional Record* (April 8–19, 1946), p. 3464M.

⁶⁸ Stevenson encircled nearly three paragraphs for emphasis, beginning with "We can snap out of it," and ending with "a great leap forward toward international understanding."

⁶⁹ Woodrow Wilson's doctoral dissertation, published as *Congressional Government: A Study in American Politics* (Boston, 1896).

⁷⁰ The Congressional Reorganization Act of 1946, Resolution 2177, designed to provide for increased efficiency in the legislative branch of the government, required the registration of lobbyists who attempted to influence the passage of legislation, increased the pay of members of the Senate and the House, and changed the number and types of committees. *Congressional Record* (March 25–April 6, 1946) PA 1889.

⁷¹ From "have tried to say . . ." to "and urgency of war—all of us." was encircled by Stevenson.

⁷² William Benton was with Stevenson during the day on which he died. See his essay "Ambassador of Good Will in Latin America," *As We Knew*

Adlai: The Stevenson Story by Twenty-two Friends, Ed. and Preface by Edward P. Doyle, Foreword by Adlai E. Stevenson III (New York, 1966).

[73] William E. Stevenson, "Two Stevensons of Princeton," *As We Knew Adlai,* p. 15.

[74] Vyacheslav M. Molotov, the Soviet Minister of Foreign Affairs, attacked Bernard Baruch, the United States Representative to the Atomic Energy Commission, accusing him of heading an American school of imperialism, for his proposal to prohibit further making of atomic weapons. *New York Times* (October 30, 1946), p. 1.

[75] The International Refugee Organization was a temporary, specialized agency of the U.N. It was formally established in 1946, to assist refugees and displaced persons remaining in Europe and Asia who could not return to their homelands or refused to do so because of political reasons. See Louise W. Holborn, *The International Refugee Organization: Its History and Work, 1946–1952.*

[76] Senators Arthur Vandenburg and Thomas Connally introduced this resolution, called the Vandenburg-Connally Resolution, on February 24, 1947. Senator Vandenburg's participation in bipartisan foreign policy as a delegate to the United Nations from 1945 to 1947, as adviser to the United States delegation to the Council of Foreign Ministers in London and Paris, and as delegate to the Pan-American Conference at Rio de Janeiro in 1947, gained him considerable praise from Stevenson in his speeches on foreign affairs during the early 1950's.

[77] Major General John H. Hilldring, then Assistant Secretary of State, testified before the Senate Foreign Relations Committee on March 1, 1947. *New York Times* (March 2, 1947), p. 1.

[78] William Shakespeare, *Julius Caesar,* Act III, Scene 2, line 79.

[79] Jacob M. Arvey, "A Gold Nugget in Your Backyard," *As We Knew Adlai,* p. 51.

[80] The white feather as a symbol of cowardice originated from the belief that the white feather in the tail of the gamecock indicates bad breeding, hence cowardice.

[81] The Truman Doctrine provided for $400 million in military and economic aid for Greece and Turkey to stop the spread of communism in the Balkans.

[82] Washington's neutrality proclamation was issued when war was declared between France and England despite the fact that the United States had a treaty of alliance with France.

[83] Kenneth S. Davis, *A Prophet in His Own Country: The Triumphs and Defeats of Adlai E. Stevenson* (Garden City, New York, 1957), p. 291.

[84] Stevenson, *Major Campaign Speeches,* p. xx.

[85] James Bryce, an English historian, statesman, diplomat, and jurist, was chiefly known in the United States for his classic study of American society and politics, *The American Commonwealth.* He apparently gave his lec-

tures "Hindrance to Good Citizenship" at Yale University while ambassador to the United States between 1907 and 1913.

[86] Carl Sandburg was an articulate champion of all classes, regions, and
races of the United States and all that he wrote expressed his belief in the
collective wisdom of the people. *Oxford Companion to American History*,
p. 703.

Sandburg's story, perhaps told here by Stevenson, was not preserved with
the speech.

[87] The Congress of Vienna, held 1814–1815 at the end of the Napoleonic
War, had as its purpose to restore governments and to readjust territories
throughout Europe. The Council of Foreign Ministers, representing the Big
Four powers (now excluding China), had a generally unsuccessful meeting
in 1947.

[88] The only commission so specified by the United Nations Charter, the
Commission on Human Rights, held its first session at Lake Success from
January 27 to February 10, 1947, and produced the Universal Declaration of
Human Rights which was adopted on December 10, 1947. *Yearbook of the
United Nations, 1948–49* (New York, 1950), p. 535.

[89] Henry L. Stimson was Hoover's Secretary of State and Roosevelt's Secretary of War from 1940 to 1945. His article "The Challenge to Americans"
appeared in *Foreign Affairs* Magazine and was quoted in the *New York
Times* (September 21, 1947), p. 34.

[90] Jacob Arvey, p. 55.

[91] See Delbert M. Eubank, "Adlai E. Stevenson, Governor of Illinois, Campaign Promises and Legislative Achievements" (Master's thesis, Southern
Illinois University, 1951).

[92] Transcript of ABC broadcast "Adlai Stevenson Reports," with Prime
Minister Nehru as his guest, November 12, 1961.

[93] Edward Beneš was Premier of Czechoslovakia from 1921 to 1922. In 1935
he was elected President but went into exile after the Munich agreement.
During World War II he headed the provisional government and was
reelected President in 1946. He resigned shortly after the Communist coup
of 1948. Morgenthau, p. 612.

[94] See Morgenthau, p. 309 for details of the "Uniting for Peace" resolution.
Morgenthau relates that the collective security called upon by evoking this
resolution for the Korean War resulted in only sixteen nations sending
forces to aid South Korea, with South Korea and the United States providing 90 per cent of the military forces. Morgenthau, p. 420.

[95] A minor clash between the Chinese and Japanese soldiers at the Marco
Polo Bridge on July 7, 1937 precipitated the Sino-Japanese War. Peiping fell
to the Japanese on July 28 and remained under their control until the end of
World War II. *Encyclopaedia Britannica*, XXI, pp. 478–480.

[96] Secretary of State Dean Acheson, Opening Address, General Assembly
of the United Nations, Lake Success, New York, September 20, 1950,

Representative American Speeches, 1950–51, A. Craig Baird, ed., XXIII (New York, 1951), 26.

[97] Alfred Tennyson's original quote was: "My strength is as the strength of ten,/ Because my heart is pure," from "Sir Galahad," *Tennyson: Poetic and Dramatic Works* (Cambridge, 1898), p. 101.

[98] Stephen A. Mitchell, "Adlai's Amateurs," *As We Knew Adlai,* p. 80.

[99] As quoted by Alden Whitman, *Portrait: Adlai E. Stevenson: Politician, Diplomat, Friend* (New York, 1965), p. 48.

[100] Lillian Ross, *Adlai Stevenson* (Philadelphia, 1965).

[101] James Reston, "Stevenson's Doubts Exceeded His Ambitions as Politician," *New York Times* (April 17, 1952).

[102] As quoted by Whitman, p. 52.

[103] See Walter Johnson, *How We Drafted Adlai* (New York, 1955). Professor Johnson is presently preparing a six-volume edition of Stevenson's papers, to be issued by the University of Chicago Press.

[104] Kings ii, 18–20. Hezekiah's rule, 726–697 B.C., was marked by consistent religious reform and political independence, despite the Assyrian military supremacy. *Jewish Encyclopedia* (1962), pp. 379–381.

[105] William Pitt, Prime Minister of England 1783–1801 and 1804–1806, gave his last public speech on the Lord Mayor's Day, November 9, 1805, in which he said: "I return you many thanks for the honor you have done me, but Europe is not to be saved by any single man. England has saved herself by her exertions and will, as I trust, save Europe by her example." P. W. Wilson, *William Pitt the Younger* (London, 1930), p. 333.

[106] John Randolph, then a member of the House of Representatives, wrote George Hay in 1806: "The old Republican party is already ruined, past redemption." He wrote the remark attributed to him by Stevenson on January 12, 1829, to Dr. Brockenborough, saying: "The country is ruined past redemption, it is ruined in the spirit and character of the people." Hugh Garland, *Life of John Randolph in Roanoke* (New York, 1881), p. 317.

[107] Erasmus believed that where the Reformation had succeeded, the Renaissance had perished. Preserved Smith, *Erasmus: A Study of His Life* (New York, 1923), pp. 1–2.

[108] Heraclitus, in "Fragments Number 44" cited in Bakewell's *Source Book in Ancient Philosophy* (1907), p. 31, stated: "The people ought to fight in defense of the law as they do of their city wall."

[109] The Kellogg-Briand Pact, called also the Pact of Paris, was signed in 1928 by the United States and forty-three other nations, pledging the signatories to renounce war and to seek the settlement of international disputes by peaceful means only. Morgenthau, p. 613.

[110] Stevenson misquotes here Robert Frost's "Stopping by Woods on a Snowy Evening," the last three lines of which read, "But I have promises to keep, / And miles to go before I sleep, / And miles to go before I sleep." In a speech entitled "Why is Robert Frost Our Bard?" that Stevenson gave at a dinner at the Pan-American Union, honoring Frost, March 26,

1962, he remarked: "And if you asked me to name of all poems one poem which enshrines for me the spirit in which as a nation we should confront our troubled future, I would quote you these familiar lines." *Looking Outward*, p. 281.

[111] Stevenson, "Welcoming Address," *Major Campaign Speeches*, pp. 1–5.

[112] Stuart Gerry Brown, *Conscience in Politics: Adlai E. Stevenson in the 1950's* (Syracuse, 1961), p. 11. For studies analyzing the effectiveness of his speaking in the 1952 campaign, see: Malcolm O. Sillars, "An Analysis of Invention in the 1952 Presidential Campaign Addresses of Dwight D. Eisenhower and Adlai E. Stevenson" (Ph.D. dissertation, State University of Iowa, 1956). See also: Raymond Yeager, "A Rhetorical Analysis of the 1952 Presidential Campaign Speeches of Adlai Ewing Stevenson" (Ph.D. dissertation, Ohio State University, 1957).

[113] Stevenson, "Speech of Acceptance," *Major Campaign Speeches*, pp. 9–10.

[114] Stevenson referred perhaps to the statement by some Nebraskan delegates to the Republican Convention in Chicago that half of the French were either agnostics or atheists with the implication that therefore they could not be trusted as allies. *New York Times* (July 31, 1952), p. 1.

[115] Chancellor Adenauer denied that his policy of integrating West Germany into the European Defense Community would bar German reunification. *New York Times* (April 25, 1952), p. 1. While President Truman urged the Senate to add Germany's forces to the Community as a part of the NATO treaty, the British Labor party sought to delay the ratification of the pact for fear that German reunification efforts would cease. *New York Times* (June 13, 1952), p. 1.

[116] In *Major Campaign Speeches*, Stevenson has added approximately two and a half pages which are not included in his original text.

[117] In *Major Campaign Speeches*, Stevenson has added a paragraph not in the original text.

[118] Stevenson has omitted a sentence from the original text in *Major Campaign Speeches*. Several sentences vary between the two texts.

[119] In *Major Campaign Speeches*, Stevenson has omitted a paragraph from the original text he had marked there to show special emphasis.

[120] Stevenson has added two pages of text in *Major Campaign Speeches* not found in the original text.

[121] Stevenson, "The Fundamental Issues," *Major Campaign Speeches*, p. 298.

[122] Stevenson, Introduction, *ibid.*, xxvi.

[123] Barry Bingham, "With Adlai in Asia," *As We Knew Adlai*, p. 191.

[124] As quoted by Bingham, *ibid.*, p. 192.

[125] Perry's signing of the first treaty between Japan and the United States in 1854 made him a recognized authority on the Far East and began the process of modernization for Japan and its development as a world power.

[126] Stevenson apparently intended to include about one-half of his San Francisco speech at this point.

[127] Bingham, "With Adlai in Asia," p. 198.

[128] The other four were: his speech on massive retaliation in September, 1954; his Miami speech on McCarthyism in 1954; his fourth national radio address on the Formosan crisis in 1955; and his speech on the hydrogen bomb before the American Society of Newspaper Editors in 1956. Windes and Robinson, p. 230.

[129] Whitman, p. 115.

[130] These first two paragraphs in the original text were omitted in *What I Think*.

[131] Stevenson has omitted all but the first sentence of this paragraph in *What I Think*.

[132] From "Let me add here . . ." to "I wish I had an hour for Asia," is omitted in *What I Think*. However, in quoting from this speech, Whitman includes the words "I wish I had an hour for Asia."

[133] Stevenson has marked this paragraph with a bracket and "1953" on the right side of the original text.

[134] The three above paragraphs are omitted from *What I think*.

[135] This paragraph is omitted from *What I Think*.

[136] Stevenson, *Call to Greatness* (New York, 1954), pp. xi–xii.

[137] Brown, *Adlai E. Stevenson*, p. 117.

[138] Richard Nixon said in his television speech, March 13, 1954: "Rather than let the Communists nibble us to death all over the world in little wars." *New York Times* (March 14, 1954), p. 44.

[139] The Geneva Conference held by the foreign ministers of France, Great Britain, the Soviet Union, and the United States from January 25 to February 18, 1954, agreed to include Communist China to help preserve peace in the Far East. From April 23 to July 21 the Conference on Far Eastern Affairs was held with representatives of nineteen nations, including Communist China. The partitioning of Vietnam was agreed upon with free elections provided there and the establishment of unified governments in Laos and Cambodia.

[140] Eisenhower's speech was delivered at the Hollywood Bowl in Los Angeles, September 23, 1954 and was printed in part in the *New York Times* (September 24, 1954), p. 14.

[141] The Communist world feared the loss of Iran. Later, on October 25, 1955, the Shah signed into law a measure authorizing Iran to join a military defense pact linking Turkey, Iraq, Pakistan, Britain, and the Baghdad Pact. *New York Times* (October 26, 1955), p. 4.

[142] In the 1954 agreement between Great Britain and Egypt, the former began withdrawing its troops from the Canal Zone, with the last troops leaving in June of 1956.

[143] Trieste had been administered as the Free Territory of Trieste by the United Nations from 1947 to 1954 when it was divided between Italy and Yugoslavia.

[144] On June 18, 1954, Guatemala was invaded by anti-Communist forces organized by Carlos Costello Armas who called upon the army and people

to overthrow the three-and-a-half–year regime of President Jacobo Arbenz, allegedly a pro-Communist. In a State Department White Paper issued August 7, the Arbenz regime was described as "the product of a bold and sustained effort to establish a Communist-controlled state in the Western Hemisphere." *World Almanac and Book of Facts* (1955), p. 108.

[145] The SEATO Alliance was signed September 8, 1954 at Manila by Great Britain, France, Australia, New Zealand, the Philippines, Thailand, Pakistan, and the United States to help meet the Communist challenge in the East. *World Almanac and Book of Facts* (1956), p. 739.

[146] *New York Times* (April 12, 1955), p. 1.

[147] The Japanese Peace Treaty was signed by the United States and forty-eight other nations at San Francisco in 1951. The Soviet Union, Poland, and Czechoslovakia refused to sign. The Treaty accorded full sovereignty to Japan with provision that Japan renounce its claims in Korea, Formosa, and the Antarctic area, and that it would subscribe to the principles of the United Nations. The Allied powers agreed to repatriate Japanese forces.

[148] Napoleon's exact quote was: "In war, moral considerations make up three-quarters of the game, the relative balance of manpower accounting only for the remaining quarter." From *Correspondence of Napoleon I*, XVII, no. 14276, Saint Cloud, August 27, 1808, as quoted in *Bartlett's Familiar Quotations* (1959), p. 360.

[149] In a speech to the American Society of Newspaper Editors in Washington, D.C., on April 23, 1955, Senator George offered similar thoughts on the Formosan crisis: "It is important that we (U.S.) know precisely their (West) thinking on the important problems that have arisen in the Far East and precisely what readjustments, if any, we should be willing to make to meet changing times and changing conditions." *Vital Speeches* (May 15, 1955).

[150] Governor Harriman, address at the Inaugural Dinner of the Joint Defense Appeal, Waldorf-Astoria Hotel, April 3, 1955. *Public Papers of Governor Averell Harriman, 1955* (State of New York, 1956).

[151] As quoted by Whitman, p. 134.

[152] Whitman, p. 135.

[153] Stevenson has omitted this paragraph in *What I Think*.

[154] Stevenson added eight paragraphs in *What I Think* that were not included in the original text.

[155] Wilson's original quote was: "There must be some real ground for the universal unrest and perturbation. It is not to be found in superficial policies or in mere economic blunders. It probably lies deep at the source of the spiritual life of our time." Woodrow Wilson, "The Road Away from Revolution," pp. 3–4. *The Atlantic Monthly* (August 23, 1923).

[156] Wilson's original quote was: "It was due to the systematic denial to the great body of Russians of the rights and privileges which all normal men desire and must have if they are to be contented and within reach of happiness." Woodrow Wilson, "The Road Away from Revolution," p. 5.

157 *Ibid.*, pp. 10–12.

158 See *Encyclopaedia Britannica*, IX, pp. 670–671.

159 Carl Sandburg, "Timesweep," *Honey and Salt* (New York, 1953), pp. 110–111. In *What I Think*, Stevenson cites that the verse is from Sandburg's *Names*, published in 1953. Another of Sandburg's poems is similar: "The people is Everyman, everybody / Everybody is You and Me and all others / What everybody says is what we all say / And what is it we all say?" *The Sandburg Range* (New York, 1957), p. 69.

160 Seymour E. Harris and Arthur Schlesinger, Jr., Introduction in Adlai E. Stevenson, *The New America*, ed. by Seymour E. Harris, John Bartlow Martin, and Arthur Schlesinger, Jr. (New York, 1957), pp. xvii–xviii. See also: Otto F. Bauer, "A Study of the Political Debate between Dwight D. Eisenhower and Adlai E. Stevenson in the Presidential Campaign of 1956" (Ph.D. dissertation, Northwestern University 1959), and Russel R. Windes, Jr., "The Speech-Making of Adlai E. Stevenson in the 1956 Campaign" (Ph.D. dissertation, Northwestern University 1959).

161 Herbert J. Muller, *Adlai Stevenson: A Study in Values* (New York, 1967), p. 117.

162 Schlesinger and Harris, Introduction, *The New America*, p. xvi.

163 Stevenson, "Foreign Policy," *The New America*, p. 30.

164 Mary McGrory, "The Perfectionist and the Press," *As We Knew Adlai*, p. 174.

165 Stevenson, "Middle East," *The New America*, pp. 34–36.

166 Schlesinger and Harris, Introduction, *The New America*, p. xvi.

167 *New York Times* (November 30, 1955), p. 8.

168 *New York Times* (February 24, 1956), p. 1.

169 In his speech to the American Society of Newspaper Editors, Eisenhower said that the "first great step toward global peace must be an honorable armistice in Korea." *New York Times* (April 17, 1953), p. 4.

170 In his speech to the Society on April 21, 1956, Eisenhower called upon Russia to right Stalin's wrongs against other nations and thus earn the West's friendship; he denied defeat in the cold war and defended the Republican foreign policy; and he suggested a citizens' group to give the government advice in handling Soviet-related problems. *New York Times* (April 22, 1956), p. 28.

171 At the Bandung Conference, held April 18–24, 1955 in Bandung, Indonesia, representatives of twenty-four Afro-Asian countries met to discuss: the reluctance of the Western powers to give them support; the increasing tension between the United States and Communist China and the desire of these Afro-Asian countries for opportunities to form peaceful relations between China and themselves and between China and the West; and the continuance of colonialism, especially that of France in Northern Africa. *Encyclopaedia Britannica*, III, 82.

172 This was not an exact quote from Dulles, but a *New York Times* appraisal and paraphrase found in the *Times* of April 4, 1956, p. 2.

[173] Commissioner Thomas E. Murray testified before the Senate Foreign Relations Subcommittee on Disarmament on April 12, 1956, and urged the United States to halt H-Bomb testing and limit their size and number in the weapons stockpile. He stated that there was no reason why more powerful bombs should be developed by the United States. *New York Times* (April 13, 1956), p. 1.

[174] Barbara Ward, "Affection and Always Respect," *As We Knew Adlai*, pp. 220–221.

[175] As quoted by Whitman, p. 180.

[176] Stevenson, *Friends and Enemies*, pp. xii–xiii.

[177] Brown, *Conscience in Politics*, p. 244.

[178] These first two sentences plus "But" are omitted in *Putting First Things First*.

[179] These last two paragraphs are omitted in *Putting First Things First*.

[180] In dedicating my Ph.D. dissertation, I wrote: "To my children, Michelle Ann and Leo Michael, so that they may know that 'The World is now too dangerous for anything but the truth, too small for anything but brotherhood,' as quoted by Adlai E. Stevenson in his A. Powell Davies Memorial Lecture, Constitution Hall, Washington, D.C., January 18, 1959." This theme often reappears in Stevenson's speeches at the U.N.

[181] Stevenson told this same story in several speeches that fall and later in some of his speeches to American audiences while he was at the United Nations.

[182] This sentence has been omitted in *Putting First Things First*.

[183] The original quote is: "That which thy fathers have bequeathed to thee, thou must earn anew if thou wouldst possess it."

[184] This paragraph is omitted in *Putting First Things First*.

[185] The Manchus lived for many centuries in Manchuria, conquering China during the seventeenth century and ruling it for 250 years. The decay of the Manchu Dynasty occurred partially because of the opulence of their life and partially because they gradually absorbed the customs of the Chinese. When the Dynasty was overthrown and it became politically inexpedient to be known as a Manchu, they quietly disappeared into the main mass of the Chinese people. *Encyclopaedia Britannica*, XIV, pp. 766–767.

[186] *Hamlet*, Act III, Scene 2, line 75.

[187] Matthew Arnold, "A Southern Night," quoted by *Hoyt's New Cyclopedia of Practical Quotations* (1940), p. 736.

[188] Stevenson has omitted this sentence in *Putting First Things First*.

[189] Roosevelt built the cottage at Warm Springs, Georgia, after his paralysis in the fall of 1924, viewing it as a curative agent both for himself and other paralytics. See *F.D.R.: His Personal Letters*, ed. by Elliott Roosevelt, Foreword by Eleanor Roosevelt (New York, 1948).

[190] When Senhor José Joaquim da Maia, a Brazilian student in France's University of Montpellier, wrote to Jefferson, then American Minister to France, seeking moral and material support from the United States should

Brazil overthrow its Portuguese yoke, Jefferson's reply was vague and non-committal. Though Maia died before returning to Brazil, his comrades used Jefferson's remarks to support their ambitions to destroy Portuguese rule. Joao Pandia Calogeras, *A History of Brazil*, trans. and ed. by Percy Alvin Marten, Preface by James A. Robertson (Chapel Hill, 1939), p. 45.

[191] Voltaire's quote about the hammer and anvil is not known to me. Long-fellow wrote: "In this world a man must either be anvil or hammer. *Hyperion*, quoted by *Hoyt's New Cyclopedia of Practical Quotations*, p. 101. Goethe wrote: "Thou must . . . be either anvil or hammer," and Spurgeon wrote: "The anvil is not afraid of the hammer." As quoted by the *Home Book of Quotations*, p. 84.

[192] Letter to Edward Carrington from Paris, January 16, 1787, *The Papers of Thomas Jefferson*, Julian P. Boyd, ed., 17 vols. (Princeton, New Jersey, 1950), p. 49. Jefferson also wrote on the same day referring to the decaying European social system: "They have divided their nations into two classes, wolves and sheep." As quoted by the *Home Book of Quotations*, p. 817.

[193] Jefferson wrote to J. W. Eppes from Monticello on June 24, 1813: "The earth belongs to the living, not to the dead." *Writings of Thomas Jefferson*, Andrew Lipscomb, *et al.*, eds. 20 vols. (Washington, D.C. 1905), XIII, 270. In the first draft of the *Declaration of Independence*, Jefferson wrote: "They are endowed by their creator with inherent and inalienable rights." *Ibid.*, XIX, 278.

[194] Alexis de Tocqueville, *Democracy in America*, Phillips Bradley, ed. (New York, 1945), p. 175B. Stevenson added "by their extinction" to "her morality suffered."

[195] Jefferson, Letter to Judge Tyler, 1804, as quoted by *Great Quotations* (1960), p. 366.

[196] Jefferson's original quote apparently was: "It is the manner and spirit of the people which preserve a republic in vigor." *The Jeffersonian Cyclopedia: A Comprehensive Collection of the Views of Thomas Jefferson*, ed. by John P. Foley (New York, 1900), p. 829.

[197] As quoted by Whitman, p. 209.

[198] *New York Times* (July 20, 1960), p. 28.

[199] Stevenson, Statement before the Senate Committee on Foreign Relations, January 18, 1961, unpublished, mimeographed, and released by the United States Mission.

[200] The first two and a half paragraphs are omitted in *Looking Outward*.

[201] *United Nations Charter*, I, 1, iv.

[202] Also see John F. Kennedy, "Inaugural Address," *New York Times* (January 20, 1961), p. 8.

[203] Stevenson, "The New Africa," *Harper's Magazine* (May, 1960), p. 48.

[204] Stevenson, Statement at a press conference at United Nations Headquarters on the adjournment of the Seventeenth General Assembly (December 21, 1962), US/UN 4137, p. 2. For full accounts of the extent of the Congo crisis, see: *Annual Report of the Secretary-General on the Work of*

the Organization (yearly since 1961); *The Congo and the UN,* 3 vols., published for the International Review Service (New York, 1962); *Issues Before the [Fifteenth, Sixteenth, Seventeenth, Eighteenth, Nineteenth,* and *Twentieth] General Assembly,* published yearly for International Conciliation (New York, 1961, 1962, 1963, 1964, 1965, 1966); and *Report of the United Nations Conciliation Commission for the Congo* (March 20, 1961), A/4711, A/4711/Add. 1, and A/4711/Add. 2.

[205] Munongo, Statement to journalists and transmitted to the Secretary-General by his Special Representative in the Congo (February 13, 1961), S/4688/Add. 1, pp. 2–3.

[206] Zorin, Statement in the Security Council, translated from the Russian (February 13, 1961), S/933, p. 3.

[207] The paragraph preceding and up to this point is omitted in *Looking Outward.*

[208] *Looking Outward* omits this paragraph.

[209] Stevenson deleted this paragraph in *Looking Outward* but added two paragraphs not in the US/UN text.

[210] See Michael H. Prosser, "Adlai E. Stevenson's United Nations Audience," *The Central States Speech Journal,* XVI (November, 1965), pp. 270–271.

[211] At this point, *Looking Outward* contains an added sentence which is not in the US/UN text, but omits a paragraph and a half from the US/UN text. This is followed in the book by an addition of two paragraphs not in the US/UN text, and six paragraphs omitted from the US/UN text. The final paragraph of the speech is the same in both *Looking Outward* and the US/UN text.

[212] C. T. Crowe, Deputy Permanent Representative of the United Kingdom, Statement in the Security Council (March 15, 1961), S/PV. 946, p. 12. For other statements by Western representatives see *Ibid.*

[213] Alcott Demming, Director of the Eastern and Southern African Bureau in the Department of State, indicated to me that the speech evoked consternation from Western delegates, anger from the Portuguese with threats of reevaluation of Portuguese-American relations, and suspicion and surprise from the Afro-Asians. Despite the surprise, he suggested that major State Department and United States Mission strategists had been moving toward such a policy of active support for self-determination issues even before the end of the Eisenhower Administration, even though the last vote cast by the Eisenhower Administration in the United Nations had implied the contrary. Interview with me at the Department of State, Washington, D.C., July 26, 1962.

[214] Portugal was an administering member of the Committee for 1961 but failed to send a representative to the meetings. *Yearbook of the United Nations* (1961), p. 709.

[215] Raul Roa, Statement in Committee I, interpreted from the Spanish (April 17, 1961), A/C.1/PV. 1150, pp. 6–50. For a history of the Cuban

crisis, see: United Nations documents A/C.1/PV. 1150, 1151, 1152, 1153, 1154, 1158, 1231, 1232, 1240, 1241; A/C/L. 274, 275, 276, 277; S/5075, 5086, 5095; S/PV. 980, 991, 993, 994, 998, and 999. See also: *Annual Report of the Secretary-General*, 1961, 1962, 1963; *Cuba: Revolution-US-USSR Relations*, I, *Cuba: Invasion, October Crisis*, II, printed for the International Review Service (New York, 1963).

216 Roa, Statement in the Committee I, interpreted from the Spanish (April 17, 1961), A/C.1/PV. 1152, p. 2.

217 Ahmad Shukairy, Statement in Committee I (April 20, 1961), A/C.1/PV. 1157, p. 22. Robert White, Action Officer, United Nations Political and Security Affairs, Department of State, suggested to me that Shukairy's probing questions impressed Stevenson and his immediate advisers as the most eloquent appeal made during the entire debate as well as the most difficult to respond to. Interview with me, Washington, D.C. (July 26, 1962).

218 Muller, pp. 283–284.

219 Kenneth S. Davis, *The Politics of Honor: A Biography of Adlai E. Stevenson* (New York, 1967), p. 458.

220 Muller, p. 282.

221 Davis, *The Politics of Honor, op. cit.*, pp. 458–459.

222 *New York Times* (April 13, 1961), p. 18.

223 Matthew, vii.3.

224 Fulgencio Batista was elected President of Cuba in 1940 but was defeated in 1944 and left the country. After his return, he overthrew the government in 1952 without bloodshed, closed the congress and called for elections in 1954. He was elected President again and on February 24, 1955, declared the 1940 Constitution the law. By 1957, the country was in a state of virtual war led by Castro to oust Batista. He resigned the Presidency and fled on January 1, 1959. *Encyclopaedia Britannica*, VI, pp. 878 A and B.

225 As to Castro's headquarters in July, 1957, the *New York Times* reported: "the location of . . . Castro's . . . headquarters in a Jungle like Sierra Maestra is not known." (July 13, 1957), p. 8.

226 Later, in March 1962, President Frondizi was removed from office by a coup led by General Raul Poggi.

227 José Julian Marti (1853–1895) was considered Cuba's greatest hero and like Simon Bolivar, to whom six Latin-American States owed their freedom from Spain, Marti was a symbol of liberty throughout Latin America.

228 *New York Times* (August 30, 1960), p. 1.

229 President Oswaldo Dorticos, in a speech at the opening of the first Regional Conference of Plantation Workers, Havana. *New York Times* (March 5, 1961), p. 33.

230 *New York Times* (April 16, 1961), p. 1.

231 Dr. Manuel Urrutia and his family received political asylum in the Venezuelan Embassy, April 24, 1961. *New York Times* (April 24, 1961), p.

7. Dr. Emilio Menendez sought political asylum in the Argentine Embassy on November 16, 1960. *New York Times* (November 16, 1960), p. 13.

[232] Kennedy, Address at a White House reception for Latin-American diplomats, March 13, 1961. *New York Times* (March 14, 1961), p. 12.

[233] Secretary of State Dillon charged on September 14, 1960, that the Cuban delegation at the Bogota Conference had extensively insulted other American states. For this, and the Cubans' refusal to sign the Act of Bogota, see: *New York Times* (September 14, 1960), p. 9 and p. 8. For the text of the Act of Bogota, see: *New York Times* (September 12, 1960), p. 16. For John F. Kennedy's plan for an Alliance for Progress, see his State of the Union Address, January 30, 1961, *New York Times* (January 31, 1961), p. 16. By August, it had become a $20 million program of public and private investment in Latin America. *New York Times* (August 8, 1961), p. 1.

[234] The Adlai E. Stevenson Foundation, a part of the Herbert H. Lehman Institute of Ethics, was designed to provide scholarships to outstanding students of the Institute and the Rabbinical School. Opportunities were to be created for holders of these scholarships to meet with students in other traditions in a search for common values, and to invite statesmen and scholars from other countries to live with these students for short periods in an endeavor to develop new insights into contemporary problems. (Registrar, Herbert H. Lehman Institute of Ethics.)

[235] M. N. Das writes: "In such a changing world the question of peace becomes one of paramount importance. Nehru desires to achieve this through the lessening of international tension. He advocates solutions of problems by methods of negotiation establishing growing cooperation among nations in various ways." M. N. Das, *The Political Philosophy of J. Nehru* (New York, 1961), p. 232.

[236] Niccolo da Uzzano writes of Machiavelli: "But since we were living today in such a manner that not much account was taken of just and unjust, he [Machiavelli] would let that matter go and deal only with Florence's advantage." *Machiavelli: The Chief Works and Others*, Allen Gilbert, transl. (Durham, North Carolina, 1965), III, 245.

[237] Stevenson, Statement in Committee I (November 15, 1961), A/C.1/PV. 1195, p. 51. For Stevenson's semiofficial views on disarmament, see "Adlai Stevenson Reports," ABC radio and television transcript, April 29, 1962. For fuller discussions on disarmament, see: *Annual Report of the Secretary-General* (1961 yearly to 1967); *Disarmament: Impact on Underdeveloped Countries, Disarmament: New Proposals Thru 1959*, and *Disarmament: Postwar Decade*, printed for International Review Service (New York, 1960, 1962, and 1963); *Geneva Conference on the Discontinuance of Nuclear Weapon Tests: History and Analysis of Negotiations*, the United States Disarmament Administration, Department of State Publication no. 7258 (Washington, D.C., 1961); *Economic and Social Consequences of Disarmament*, United Nations Sales no. 62 (New York, 1962); and *Issues Before the General Assembly* (1960 yearly to 1967).

[238] US/UN 3816.

[239] Zorin, Statement in Committee I, interpreted from the Russian (November 15, 1961), A/C.1/PV. 1195, pp. 8–10.

[240] Zorin, Statement, pp. 62–65.

[241] Stevenson, Statement, p. 77.

[242] Stevenson has omitted the first page of the US/UN text in *Looking Outward*.

[243] The two paragraphs above are omitted in *Looking Outward*.

[244] The Hague Peace Conferences in 1899 and 1907 were called by the Czar of Russia to establish "a real and lasting peace and, above all, [to limit] the progressive development of existing armaments." The Conference called for 1915 did not meet because of World War I. In the light of history, the Conferences failed because they accepted war as inevitable and merely sought to regulate it as a legal procedure. *Encyclopaedia Britannica*, I, 1113.

[245] The Disarmament Conference of 1932 was attended by the representatives of fifty-nine nations who were unable to agree on whether disarmament should be guided by international control as the French urged, or by qualitative limitation as the British argued. The limited agreement, signed in July, stated that air attacks against civilian populations should be prohibited absolutely and the number of military aircraft limited; heavy artillery and tanks should in principle be limited in size and number; and chemical warfare should be prohibited. *Encyclopaedia Britannica*, VII, p. 485.

[246] Represented by France, Great Britain, Canada, Italy, the United States, Poland, Bulgaria, Czechoslovakia, Rumania, and the U.S.S.R., the General Disarmament Talks began meeting in Geneva in 1960 with no sign of progress. Participants could not agree on a time schedule for disarmament or on provisions for inspection. The break-up of the Paris Summit Conference during the summer essentially ended these negotiations.

[247] The Baruch proposals were first offered in June, 1946, by the United States to the United Nations Atomic Energy Commission to set up an international atomic authority with the power to control and inspect atomic weapons. The U.S.S.R. turned down the proposals with the demand of immediate banning of all atomic weapons.

[248] *New York Times* (September 7, 1961), p. 7.

[249] Joseph Stalin, as quoted by the House Committee on Un-American Activities Report (May 29, 1956), p. 33.

[250] The Treaty of Bresk-Litovsk was signed between Germany and the Ukrainian Republic on February 9, 1918 and with the U.S.S.R. on March 3. Both peace treaties were annulled after the armistice on November 11, 1918. Two days later, the U.S.S.R. declared the Treaty null and void. *Encyclopaedia Britannica*, IV, 156.

[251] *New York Times* (September 27, 1961), p. 14.

[252] *Looking Outward* omits two pages, beginning with "Last spring, as delegates here will recall . . ." and ending with the words "the next step in destroying the machinery of war."

[253] The United Nations Emergency Force was the first peace-keeping armed force employed by the United Nations (in contrast to the forces serving in Korea which were employed to halt aggression) whose function was to create a barrier between the Israeli and Egyptian borders.

[254] Stevenson omits about a page and a half in *Looking Outward*, beginning with "We can begin by drawing lessons . . ." and ending with the words "to avail themselves of the services of rapporteurs."

[255] Garin, Statement in the Security Council (December 18, 1961), S/PV. 987, p. 19.

[256] Jha, Statement, p. 20.

[257] Transcript of the question-and-answer period of Stevenson's press conference at United Nations Headquarters (December 21, 1961), US/UN 3906.

[258] Jha, Statement in the Security Council (December 18, 1961), S/PV. 988, p. 51.

[259] *Ibid.*, p. 56.

[260] US/UN 3906.

[261] US/UN 4045, pp. 1 and 2.

[262] US/UN 4056, p. 3.

[263] US/UN 4069, p. 1.

[264] John F. Kennedy, in an Address to the Nation (October 23, 1962), as quoted by Stevenson, US/UN 4070, p. 1.

[265] Robert and Selma Schiffer, *Looking Outward*, p. 79.

[266] As quoted by Stevenson, US/UN 4071.

[267] Robert and Selma Schiffer, *Looking Outward*, p. 100.

[268] Bertrand Russell quotes Nikita Khrushchev's letter on October 24, 1962, in his book *Unarmed Victory* (New York, 1963), pp. 42–45.

[269] *New York Times* (October 26, 1962), p. 16.

[270] Stevenson, "The Principles of Patriotism: Love of Country," *Looking Outward*, p. 261.

[271] Wilfred Owen, "Strange Meeting," *Collected Poems of W. Owen*, ed. by C. Day Lewis (London, 1963), p. 35.

[272] In Book V of the *City of God*, St. Augustine writes: "Justice being taken away then, what are kingdoms but great robberies? For what are robberies themselves but little kingdoms?" As quoted in *Book of Quotations*, p. 70.

[273] Pope John XXIII, "Mater et Magistra," *Papal Encyclicals*, ed. by Anne Fremantle (New York, 1963), pp. 364–369.

[274] Pope John XXIII, "Pacem in Terris," *ibid.*, p. 421.

[275] A border conflict began between Haiti and the Dominican Republic on April 26, 1963, when Haitian police broke into the Dominican Republic Embassy in Port-au-Prince and seized twenty-two Haitian political refugees who sought asylum there.

[276] John Donne, "Devotions Upon Emergent Occasions," *British Poetry and Prose*, Paul Robert Lieder, Robert Morss Lovett, and Robert Kilburn Root, eds., 2 vols., 3rd ed. (Boston, 1950), I, 488.

277 Stevenson, Statement in the Security Council (July 26, 1963), US/UN 4231.

278 Norman A. Graebner, "Dean G. Acheson," *An Uncertain Tradition: American Secretaries of State in the Twentieth Century* (New York, 1961), pp. 281–282.

279 *Ibid.*, p. 283.

280 Hans J. Morgenthau, "John Foster Dulles," *ibid.*, p. 301.

281 Kenneth S. Davis, *The Politics of Honor*, p. 462.

282 *New York Times* (September 21, 1963), p. 6.

283 On July 31, 1963, the Communist Chinese government denounced the Test-Ban Treaty as "a dirty fraud" and accused the Soviet government of having sold out the people of the Communist Bloc, charging: "It is rotten to the core. China of course cannot be a part to it." As quoted by the *New York Times* (September 1, 1963), p. 1. Kuo Mo-jo, the Deputy Chairman of the Standing Committee of the National People's Congress stated that the U.S.S.R. had betrayed Marxism, Leninism, and proletarian internationalism. *New York Times* (July 27, 1963), p. 1.

284 Mao Tse-tung wrote on November 6, 1938: "Every Communist must grasp the truth. Political power grows out of the barrel of a gun!" From *Problems of War and Security* as quoted in *Quotations from Mao Tse-tung* (Peiping, 1966), p. 33.

285 On September 1, 1963, a Communist Chinese government spokesman denied the Soviet charge that China was willing to sacrifice the lives of 300 million Chinese and half of mankind in behalf of Communist conquest. *New York Times* (September 2, 1963), p. 3.

286 The conference was a forceful attempt to reassert traditional Party principles. The "Regulations Governing PLA Political Work" dealt with military doctrine, organization, political controls, and leadership methods. Alexander George, *Chinese Communist Army in Action* (Hong Kong, 1963), p. 63.

287 William Penn, *Fruits of Solitude* (1693), as quoted in the *New Dictionary of Quotations*, p. 150.

288 Mr. Dooley's original quote was: "A man is old enough to vote whin he can vote, he's old enough to wurruk whin he can wurruk, / And he's old enough to be Prisidint whin he becomes Presidint. / If he ain't, 'twill age him." Finley Peter Dunne, *World of Mr. Dooley*, ed. by Louis Filler (New York, 1962).

289 Zulfikar Ali Bhutto stated in the General Assembly on September 30, 1963: "We see in the test ban treaty a sign and a symbol of the will of the Soviet Union and the Western Powers for peaceful coexistence. President Kennedy and Chairman Khrushchev looked into the abyss and stepped back from it." *New York Times* (October 1, 1963), p. 14.

290 US/UN 4249.

291 Lyndon B. Johnson, Remarks to the Capital Press Club at Washington, D.C. (May 18, 1963).

[292] Muller, *op. cit.*, pp. 300–301.

[293] For texts of the Geneva Accords, see *American Foreign Policy* (*1950 –55*): *Basic Documents*, Department of State publication number 6446, I, 750.

[294] Reprints of the *Special Report of the International Control Commission of Viet-Nam* (June 2, 1962), are available upon request from the Office of Media Services, Department of State.

[295] For the text of the Declaration of the neutrality of Laos and an accompanying protocol signed at Geneva, July 23, 1962, see *Department of State Bulletin* (August 13, 1962), p. 259.

[296] During 1941, when considerable underground activity was promoted by the Allies against the Japanese, Vietnam Communists founded the Vietnamese League of Independence (Viet Nam Doc Lap Dong Minh Hoi) called a coalition of nationalist groups and commonly labeled the Viet Minh. *Encyclopaedia Britannica*, XXIII, p. 146A.

[297] In June of 1962, three factions in Laos signed a pact to end the civil war and form a coalition government containing neutralist, right-wing, and the Communist Pathet Lao. Souvanna Phouma, the neutralist leader, became the Prime Minister. The fourteen-nation Geneva Conference reconvened on July 2 and drew up a neutrality agreement for Laos.

[298] For the text of Khrushchev's New Year's remarks, see *Department of State Bulletin* (February 3, 1964), p. 158.

[299] *New York Times* (July 22, 1954), p. 2.

[300] For text of the statement by Ambassador Charles W. Yost, see US/UN 4391.

[301] Whitman, p. 352.

[302] Muller, p. 307.

[303] Whitman, pp. 252–253.

[304] Brown, *Adlai E. Stevenson*, p. 194.

[305] Dr. Camargo, one of the founders of the United Nations as the Vice-President of Colombia, gave the first of the series of lectures arranged as part of the celebration of the United Nations' twentieth anniversary on January 25, 1965, in the Plenary Session. *New York Times* (January 26, 1965), p. 9.

[306] *New York Times* (August 25, 1961), p. 2.

[307] For background on the United Nations financial crisis see: *Department of State Bulletin* (November 9, 1964), p. 681; (December 7, 1964) p. 826; and (December 21, 1964) p. 891.

[308] *New York Times* (January 19, 1965), p. 10.

[309] *Ibid.*

[310] Davis, *The Politics of Honor*, p. 498.

[311] For Johnson's statements, April 30, May 1 and 2, see *Department of State Bulletin* (May 17, 1965), p. 738.

[312] Whitman, p. 269.

[313] Davis, *The Politics of Honor*, p. 499.

314 Benton, "Ambassador of Good Will in Latin America," pp. 209–210.
315 As quoted by Whitman, p. 270.
316 As quoted by Muller, p. 320.
317 Barbara Ward, "Affection and Always Respect," p. 227.
318 As quoted by Whitman, p. 258.

Bibliography

Selected Published Books, Addresses and Articles by Stevenson*

"Acceptance Speech," *American Public Addresses: 1740–1952*, A. C. Baird, ed. (New York, 1956), pp. 289–293.

"Action by the United Nations," Address, October 22, 1964, *Vital Speeches* (December 1, 1964), pp. 98–101.

"Adlai Stevenson Speaks," ed. and narrated by James Fleming (New York, RCA Records, 1953).

"Address at the Memorial Service for Sir Winston Churchill," *Representative American Speeches, 1964–1965*, Lester Thonssen, ed. (New York, 1965), pp. 103–107.

"Address of the Ambassador to the United Nations, Adlai E. Stevenson, Delivered before a Joint Convention of the Two Houses of the General Court of Massachusetts, April 20, 1965" (Boston, 1965).

"Algeria in the United Nations: Partial Text of the October 4 [1962] Statement by the United States Security Council Representative." *Current History* (January, 1963), p. 51.

"The American Revolution In Our Time," *Progressive* (June, 1960), pp. 26–30. (Adaptation of Stevenson's Founder's Day Address at the University of Virginia.)

"The American Tradition and Its Implications for International Law," *Police* (March–April, 1963), pp. 14–17.

"An American View of the UN," *Intercom* (May–June, 1962), pp. 12–17.

"America's Number One Must [Education]," *National Education Association Proceedings* (1955), pp. 53–59. Also in *Vital Speeches* (August 1, 1955), pp. 1401–1404.

"America's Role" (same as "On Liberty of Conscience"), *Representative American Speeches: 1952–1953*, A. C. Baird, ed. (New York, 1953), pp. 83–91.

"America's Strength," *Instructor* (March, 1959), p. 3.

"America Under Pressure," *Harper's Magazine* (August, 1961), pp. 20–24.

* His numerous addresses and statements included in the *Department of State Bulletin* are not listed here.

"The Art of Coexistence: Our North American Patterns; an Assessment of the American-Canadian Partnership," *Queens Quarterly: A Canadian Review* (Winter, 1956), pp. 578–586.

"Ballots and Bullets," *Look Magazine* (June 2, 1953), pp. 35–38.

"Bipartisan Support for School Construction," *National Education Association Journal* (February, 1956), p. 75.

Call to Greatness (New York, 1954).

"The Centrality of Education: Address Presented at the Honors Day Convocation, University of Illinois, May 1, 1964" (Urbana, Illinois, 1964).

"China and the United Nations: the U.S. Position vs. Admission of Red China to the United Nations," *Yale Political* (Winter, 1964), p. 12.

"Commencement Address," *Representative American Speeches: 1951–1952*, A. C. Baird, ed. (New York, 1952), pp. 172–180.

"Commencement Address: Delivered June 3, 1962, to the Graduating Class of Boston University" (Boston, 1962).

"Congo Question; the Position of the United States," Address, *Vital Speeches* (February 1, 1965), pp. 231–236.

"Cooper Union Address," *Representative American Speeches: 1954–1955* (New York, 1955), pp. 99–108.

"Contributions to Match Our Times," *State Government* (Summer, 1958), p. 172.

"Crime and Politics," *Journal of Criminal Law* (November, 1950), pp. 397–405.

"The Darkest Shadow: Man's Ability to Annihilate Himself," *American Bar Association Journal* (October, 1964), pp. 921–924.

"Disarmament Conference: the United States Position," Address, *Vital Speeches* (June 1, 1965), pp. 482–488.

"Eleanor Roosevelt: Eulogy at a Memorial Service," *Progressive* (January, 1963), pp. 30–32. Also in *Representative American Speeches: 1962–1963*. Lester Thonssen, ed. (New York, 1963), pp. 178–183.

"Extend Our Vision . . . to All Mankind," *Great Reading from Life: Treasury of the Best Stories and Articles Chosen by the Editors* (New York, 1960), pp. 21–35. Also in *American Principles and Issues: The National Purpose*, O. Handlin, ed. (New York, 1961), pp. 289–296. Also in *The National Purpose*, John K. Jessup *et al.*, eds. (New York, 1960), pp. 21–35.

"For Freer U.S. Trade Now and an Atlantic Common Market Tomorrow," Condensation of address before the National Conference of Organizations on International Trade Policy, March 27, 1958, *Freedom and Union* (May, 1958), pp. 4–6.

"For Illinois Schools," *Illinois Education* (October, 1948), p. 37.

Foreword, William Benton, *The Voice of Latin America*, rev. ed. (New York, 1965).

"Four Fears," *Representative American Speeches: 1953-1954*. A. C. Baird, ed. (New York, 1954), pp. 65-74.

Friends and Enemies: What I Learned in Russia (New York, 1959).

"From Containment to Cease-Fire and Peaceful Change," *Toward a Strategy of Peace*, Walter C. Clemens, Jr., ed. (Chicago, 1965), pp. 32-46. Also in *The Quest for Peace*, A. A. Cordier and W. Foote, eds. (New York, 1965), pp. 51-66.

"Full Promise of a Distracted World," Conference on World Tensions, University of Chicago, 1960, *The Promise of World Tensions* (Chicago, 1960), pp. 127-136. Also with same title, Harlan Cleveland, ed. (New York, 1961), pp. 127-136.

"Fundamental Meaning of the United Nations," Address, June 23, 1965, *Vital Speeches* (August 1, 1965), pp. 615-617.

"Fund for the Republic: a Mike Wallace Interview with Adlai E. Stevenson," American Broadcasting Co. (1958), 14 pp.

"Governor Adlai Stevenson Agrees to Run for President" (same as "Speech of Acceptance"), *Treasury of the World's Great Speeches*, H. Peterson, ed. (New York, 1954), pp. 821-826.

"A Governor Looks at Public Welfare," *Public Welfare* (January, 1951), pp. 28-32.

"Grandmother Stevenson, Elder Stateswoman of the P.T.A.," *National Parent-Teacher* (February, 1951), pp. 10-12.

"Hooray for America and Look Out, America!" *National Policies for Education, Health and Social Services*, J. E. Russell, ed. (New York, 1955), pp. 533-539.

"How Illinois Is Advancing in its Educational Affairs," *School and College Management* (October, 1950), p. 26.

"Human Rights," Address, January 28, 1964, *Vital Speeches* (March 15, 1964), pp. 323-326.

"Illinois [excerpts from legislative addresses]," *State Government* (March, 1949), pp. 66-67; (March, 1951) pp. 60-61.

"Improving Education: a Free Peoples' Responsibility," *Improving Education* (San Francisco, 1959), pp. 29-34.

"Interdependence of Nations," Address, June 1, 1965, *Vital Speeches* (July 1, 1965), pp. 548-551.

"Jefferson and Our National Leadership," *Virginia Quarterly Review* (Summer, 1960), pp. 337-349.

"Korea in Perspective," *Foreign Affairs* (April, 1952), pp. 349-360.

"The Kremlin's Challenge," *Background and Foreground: an Anthology of Articles from the New York Times Magazine*, ed. with intro. and notes by Lester Markel (New York, 1960), pp. 59–66.

"Let Us Work While It Is Yet Day," *Contemporary American Speeches*, W. A. Linkrigel, R. R. Allen and R. Johannesen, eds. (Belmont, California, 1965), pp. 286–294.

"Lincoln at Gettysburg: An Address Fourscore and Seven Years Later" (Chicago, 1965).

Looking Outward: Years of Crisis at the United Nations; Speeches and Papers, Robert L. and Selma Schiffer, eds. Preface by John F. Kennedy (New York, 1963).

"Madison Square Garden Address," *Representative American Speeches: 1956–1957*, A. C. Baird, ed. (New York, 1957), pp. 62–73.

Major Campaign Speeches, Intro. by Author (New York, 1953).

"Meet the Press," Radio-Television interview (April 24, 1960); IV, 17, 11 pages; (September 17, 1961) V, 36, 9 pages; (December 22, 1963) VII, 45, 9 pages; (December 13, 1964) VIII, 45, 9 pages; (June 27, 1965) IX, 23, 9 pages.

"Must We Have War?" *Look* (November 16, 1954), pp. 47–48.

"My Faith in Democratic Capitalism," *Fabulous Future: America in 1980, as Seen by David Sarnoff* [and others] Intro. by editors of *Fortune* (New York, 1956). Also in *Fortune* (October, 1955), pp. 126–127+.

"Negotiate Settlements of Issues: Address by the 1952 Democratic Candidate for President at the Chicago Opera House, Chicago, September 15, 1953 (excerpts)," *Documents on American Foreign Relations*, Peter V. Curl, ed. Published for the Council on Foreign Relations (New York, 1954). *The New America*, Seymour Harris, John Bartlow Martin, and Arthur Schlesinger, Jr., eds. (New York, 1957).

"New Dangers and New Opportunities for the Western World," *American Bar Association Journal* (October, 1960), pp. 1103–1107.

"The Next President?" *Economist* (January 9, 1960), pp. 107–108.

"No Peace for Israel," *Look* (August 11, 1953), pp. 38–40.

"The Ordeal of the Twentieth Century . . . Is Far from Over," *A Treasury of Great American Speeches*, C. Hurd, ed. (New York, 1959), pp. 302–304.

"Organized Crime and Law Enforcement," *American Bar Association Journal* (January, 1952), pp. 26–29.

"Partnership of Public and Private Agencies in the Field of Mental Hygiene," *Mental Hygiene* (January, 1952), pp. 1–5.

"Philip Murray," *Symposium*, G. W. Arms and L. G. Locke, eds. (New York, 1954), pp. 205–209.

"The Political Relevance of Moral Principle," *Congressional Quarterly World Report* (January 23, 1959), pp. 131–134. Also in *Contemporary Forum*, E. J. Wrage and B. Baskerville, eds. (New York, 1962), pp. 355–366. Also an adaptation in the *Progressive* (March, 1959), pp. 9–13.

"Portrait of Adlai Stevenson in Conversation with Arnold Michaelis," Recorded by Arnold Michaelis (New Rochelle, New York: Spoken Arts, Inc., 1956).

"Present Imperative: Conviction," *Child Study* (Fall, 1958), pp. 32–33.

"Presidential Elections Campaign: Radio-television Address by the Democratic Presidential Candidate, October 15, 1956 (Excerpts)," *Documents on American Foreign Relations* (1956), pp. 96–98. "November 1, 1956 (Excerpts)," Paul E. Zinner, ed. (1957).

"The Prospects for Democracy," *Challenges to Democracy: The Next Ten Years*, E. Reed, ed., Intro. by Robert M. Hutchins, published for the Center for the Study of Democratic Institutions (New York, 1963).

Putting First Things First: A Democratic View (New York, 1960). Also published in part as an article in *Foreign Affairs* (January, 1960), pp. 191–208.

"Responsibility of the College Graduate," *School and Society* (November 4, 1950), pp. 289–292.

"Reorganization from the State Point of View," *Public Administration Review* (1950), pp. 1–6.

"School's Job in the National Security Program," *American Teacher* (May, 1952), pp. 6–8f.

"Science and Technology in the Political Arena," *Science and Technology: A Symposium* (New York, 1965).

"Science, Disarmament and Peace," Addresses by Stevenson and Gerald Piel, Tenth Annual Roosevelt Day Dinner, Americans for Democratic Action, January 31, 1958 (Washington, D.C., 1958).

"Should the Veto Be Abolished in the United Nations?" *The Town Meeting: Bulletin of America's Town Meeting of the Year*, XII (November 14, 1946).

"Social Welfare in a Changing World," *National Conference of Social Work Proceedings* (1952), pp. 19–28.

"So Many of the Members," *Methodist Women* (June, 1965), p. 16.

"Some Thoughts on Loyalty," *Bulletin of Atomic Scientists* (February, 1953), p. 16f.

"Special Statement Prepared for the NEA Journal by the Democratic Presidential Candidate," *National Education Association Journal* (October, 1956), p. 411.

Speeches, Foreword by John Steinbeck, and brief biography by Debs Meyers and Ralph Martin (New York, 1952).

"Speech of Acceptance," *Representative American Speeches: 1952–1953*, A. C. Baird, ed. (New York, 1953), pp. 66–71.

The Stark Reality of Responsibility: the Welcoming and Acceptance Addresses before the Democratic National Convention, 1952 (Chicago, 1952).

"States, the Federal System, and the People," *State Government* (February, 1950), pp. 24–27.

"The Survival of the Free Society," *Christianity and Crisis* (January 11, 1960), pp. 204–208.

"The Taft-Hartley Act Should Be Repealed," *Commercial and Financial Chronicle* (September 4, 1952), p. 828.

"There Are No Gibraltars," *Contemporary Forum*, E. J. Wrage and B. Baskerville, eds. (New York, 1962), pp. 277–284. Also in *Vital Speeches* (February 15, 1951), pp. 284–288.

"Tributes to John F. Kennedy," *Representative American Speeches: 1963–1964*, Lester Thonssen, ed. (New York, 1964), pp. 30–33.

"United Nations Commemoration Address, June 26, 1965," *UN Monthly Chronicle* (June, 1965), pp. 171–175.

"The United States and the U.S.S.R.," *Challenge to American Youth*, P. Angeles, ed. (Philadelphia, 1963), pp. 184–197.

"Wanted: A Statewide Concept of Higher Education," *Illinois Education* (December, 1951), p. 136+.

"West Builds a Balkan Barrier," *Look* (August 25, 1953), pp. 54–56.

What I Think (New York, 1956).

"Where Is the Money Coming From?" [excerpts from the campaign statement entitled "A Program for the True Economy; Where Is the Money Coming From," with comments by various economists], *Review of Economics and Statistics* (May, 1957), 134 pp.

"World Brotherhood in a Space Age," *Representative American Speeches: 1957–1958*, A. C. Baird, ed. (New York, 1959), pp. 58–63.

"The World I Saw," *Look* (September 22, 1953), pp. 40–46. Also in *Prize Articles: 1954*, The Benjamin Franklin Magazine Awards, administered by the University of Illinois, Llewellyn Miller, ed. (New York, 1954), pp. 115–119.

Selected Published and Unpublished Books, Studies
and Articles on Stevenson

Abel, Elie, *The Missile Crisis* (Philadelphia, 1966).

"Adlai E. Stevenson (special report)," *Congressional Quarterly* (January, 1964), p. 71.

Adlai E. Stevenson—The Man, The Candidate, The Statesman, Bill Scott, narrator (AS–101–61447).

Adlai Ewing Stevenson: February 5, 1900–July 14, 1965, Limited Edition (Chicago, 1965).

"Adlai Stevenson," *Current Biography* (1961), pp. 440–442.

Adlai Stevenson: 1900–1965 of the United Nations, A. Roland, R. Wilson and M. Rahill, eds. (Manila, 1965).

Adlai Stevenson's Public Years, Jill Kneerim, ed. Photographs by Cornell Capa, John Fell Stevenson, Inge Morath. Preface by Walter Lippmann (New York, 1966).

Alsop, S. and C. Bartlett, "Footnote for Historians," *Saturday Evening Post* (January 26, 1963), p. 76.

———, "In Time of Crisis," *Saturday Evening Post* (December 8, 1962), pp. 15–16.

Altman, W. "Adlai Stevenson," *Contemporary Review* (November, 1958), pp. 288–290.

Arvey, J. M. and John Madigan, "The Reluctant Candidate—an Inside Story," *Reporter* (*Fortnightly*) (November 24, 1953), pp. 19–24.

As We Knew Adlai—The Stevenson Story by Twenty-two Friends, Edward P. Doyle, ed., Foreword by Adlai E. Stevenson, III (New York, 1966).

Baird, A. Craig, *et al.*, "Political Speaking in 1952: A Symposium," *Quarterly Journal of Speech*, XXXVIII (October, 1952), pp. 265–300.

Bauer, Otto F., "A Study of the Political Debate between Dwight D. Eisenhower and Adlai E. Stevenson in the Presidential Campaign of 1956." (Ph.D. dissertation, Northwestern University, 1959).

Beatie, William F., "A Readability-Listenability Analysis of Selected Campaign Speeches of Adlai E. Stevenson in the 1952 and 1956 Presidential Campaigns," *Central States Speech Journal*, X (Spring, 1959), pp. 16–18.

Belin, Frederick C., "Address at the dedication of the Adlai E. Stevenson Memorial Stamp, Bloomington, Illinois, October 23, 1965," Information Services General Release 163.

Berkses, R. N., "New Frontier in the U.N.," *Current History*, XIIL (January, 1962), pp. 43-48.

"Biographic Sketch of Adlai E. Stevenson" (mimeographed only, and released by the United States Mission, 1961).

Blankenship, Fanny Jane, "I. A. Richard's Theory of Metaphor Applied to Selected Speeches of Adlai E. Stevenson" (Master's thesis, University of Illinois, 1957).

Bowman, Georgia B., "A Study of the Reporting by Twenty-Seven Metropolitan Newspapers of Selected Speeches of Adlai Stevenson and Dwight Eisenhower in the 1952 Presidential Campaign" (Ph.D. dissertation, State University of Iowa 1957).

Brown, J. M., "Road to the White House," and "Stevenson Speaking," *Through These Men: Some Aspects of Our Passing History* (New York, 1956), pp. 25-36 and 118-140.

Brown, S. G., "Civil Rights and National Leadership: Eisenhower and Stevenson in the 1950's," *Ethics* (January, 1960), pp. 118-134.

——, "Eisenhower and Stevenson in the McCarthy Era: a Study in Leadership," *Ethics* (July, 1959), pp. 233-254.

Brown, Stuart Gerry, *Adlai E. Stevenson—the Conscience of the Country* (Woodbury, New York, 1965).

——, *Conscience in Politics: Adlai E. Stevenson in the 1950's* (Syracuse, New York, 1961).

Busch, Noel Fairchild, *Adlai E. Stevenson of Illinois: a Portrait* (New York, 1952).

Chamberlain, John, "Adlai Stevenson: Twice-Burnt Offering; Behind the Bright Words, An Intellectual Vacuum; He Would Have World Peace and Never Recognize That Its Cost May Be National Survival," *National Review* (June 4, 1960), pp. 357-359.

Coakley, Timothy, "A Comparative Analysis of Adlai E. Stevenson's Use of Humor in the 1952 and 1956 Campaigns" (Master's thesis, Pennsylvania State University, 1963).

Corpe, Mary, "Persuasive Techniques Used by Adlai E. Stevenson in His 1952 Campaign" (Master's thesis, University of Wisconsin, 1954).

Craig, Herbert R., "Distinctive Features of Radio-TV in the 1952 Political Campaign" (Master's thesis, State University of Iowa, 1954).

Craig, Herbert, "A Study of the Issue of Communism in Government in the 1952 Campaign" (Ph.D. dissertation, State University of Iowa 1956).

Crane, John de Murinelly, *Pictorial Biography of Adlai E. Stevenson, Governor of Illinois*, Foreword by John Hersey (New York, 1952).

Crossman, R. H. S., "Adlai Stevenson," *New Statesman and Nation*, XVIL (August 8, 1953), p. 151.

Davis, Kenneth S., *The Politics of Honor: a Biography of Adlai E. Stevenson* (New York, 1967).

Davis, Kenneth Sydney, *A Prophet in His Own Country: the Triumphs and Defeats of Adlai E. Stevenson* (Garden City, New York, 1957).

Dean, Richard L., "Aspects of Persuasive Appeal in Stevenson's Campaign Speeches," *The Speaker*, XXXVIII (December, 1952), pp. 377–415.

Dos Passos, John, "Adlai Stevenson: Patrician with a Mission," *National Review* (October 27, 1956), pp. 11–15; (November 3, 1956) pp. 13–15.

Eaton, Herbert, *Presidential Timber: A History of Nominating Conventions, 1868–1960* (New York, 1960).

"Evening Star," *The New Frontiersman: Profiles of the Men Around Kennedy*, Foreword by William Hill, Intro. by M. B. Schnapper (Washington, D.C., 1961).

Eubank, Delbert M., "Adlai E. Stevenson, Governor of Illinois: Campaign Promises and Legislative Achievements" (Master's thesis, Southern Illinois University, 1951).

Face to Face, Hugh Burnett, ed. (New York, 1965), pp. 70–72.

Faghin, Betty May Rapport, "A Critical Study of Three Addresses of Adlai E. Stevenson in the 1952 Presidential Campaign" (Master's thesis, University of Washington, 1954).

Fowler, Donald Lionel, "Presidential Elections in South Carolina: 1948–1960" (Ph.D. dissertation, University of Kentucky, 1966).

Freeman, Jonathan, "Adlai in Dixie," *Progressive* (February, 1954), pp. 9–11.

Gephardt, Thomas S., "Adlai Stevenson," *American Opinion* (June, 1963), pp. 1–8.

Goodwin, Richard N., *The Sower's Seed—A Tribute to Adlai Stevenson*, Eulogy by Lyndon B. Johnson (New York, 1965).

Graebel, Richard Paul, "Adlai and You and I," A Sermon Preached in the First Presbyterian Church, Springfield, Illinois, September 5, 1965.

———, "Brochure in Tribute to Adlai E. Stevenson containing Communications from Him to Dr. Graebel; Dr. Graebel's Prayer at the Funeral Service at the Washington Cathedral, July 16, 1965, and His 'In Memoriam' Given on Governor's Day, August 19, 1965, at Springfield, Illinois" (Springfield, Illinois, 1965).

Haberman, Frederick W., *et al.*, "The Election of 1952: a Symposium," *Quarterly Journal of Speech*, XXXVIII (December, 1952), pp. 377–415.

Halberstam, David, *The Making of a Quagmire* (New York, 1965).

Hanson, Simon G., "The Failure of the Stevenson Mission," *Inter-American Economic Affairs,* XV (Autumn, 1961), pp. 53–76.

Harris, L. A., "Adlai Stevenson," *The Fine Art of Political Wit* (New York, 1964), pp. 238–254.

Harsch, J. C., "The Long Morning After: The Stevenson Phenomenon," *Reporter (Fortnightly)* (March 3, 1953), pp. 29–32.

Hayman, Le Roy, *American Ambassador to the World: Adlai Stevenson* (New York, 1966).

Heller, Deane, and David Heller, "Adlai Stevenson," *Kennedy Cabinet* (New York, 1961), pp. 32–38.

Hickey, Robert L., "A Subjective Criticism of Stevenson's Speeches," *The Speaker,* XXXV (January, 1953).

Howe, Irving, "Adlai Stevenson: The Last Sad Years," and "Stevenson and the Intellectuals," *Steady Work: Essays in the Politics of Democratic Radicalism,* 1953–1966 (New York, 1966), pp. 218–222 and 206–218.

Ives, Elizabeth and Hildegarde Dolson, *My Brother Adlai* (New York, 1956).

James, Bessie R., and Mary Waterstreet, *Adlai's Almanac: the Wit and Wisdom of Stevenson of Illinois* (New York, 1952).

Johnson, G. W., "Something Old Has Been Added," *Best Articles of 1953: Twenty-five Most Memorable Articles of the Year,* Selected by Rudolph Flesch (New York, 1953).

————, "Reply to Stevenson, Tragedy and Greatness," By H. J. Morgenthau, *New Republic* (August 7, 1965), pp. 17–19; (August 21, 1965) p. 36+.

Johnson, Walter, *How We Drafted Adlai Stevenson* (New York, 1955).

Joyce, J. A., "Stevenson's Last Speech: Passengers on a Little Space Ship." *Contemporary Review* (November, 1965), pp. 239–242.

Kaiser, Alvin R., "Style and Personal Appeal of Adlai E. Stevenson," *Western Speech,* XXXV (May, 1954), pp. 181–185.

Keller, Gordon Wilson, "Adlai Stevenson: the Moral Responsibility of Power," *Humanist* (May/June, 1967), pp. 89–91.

Kempton, M., "Long-Distance Runner," *Speculum* (December 28, 1962), p. 981.

————, "Stevenson: the Saddest Story," *Spectator* (July 23, 1965), p. 100.

Kempton, Murray, "Adlai Stevenson Employed," *Progressive* (April, 1961), pp. 13–15.

Keohane, Robert Owen, "Political Practice in the UN General Assembly" (Ph.D. dissertation, Harvard University 1966).

Kopkind, A., "Man Who Died Twice," *New Statesman* (July 23, 1965), p. 110f.

Kreppranth, Hubert Eugene, "The Elements of Persuasion in the Nationally Broadcast Speeches of Eisenhower and Stevenson During the 1956 Presidential Campaign" (Ph.D. dissertation, University of Wisconsin 1962).

Lasch, Robert, "Illinois: Stevenson's First Year, *Reporter (Fortnightly)* (August 30, 1949), pp. 23–25.

———, "Rhetoric and the Campaign of 1956: Stevenson," *Quarterly Journal of Speech*, XLIII (February, 1957), pp. 34–39.

Levine, I. E., *Spokesman for the Free World:* Adlai E. Stevenson (New York, 1967).

Man of Honor—Man of Peace: The Life and Words of Adlai Stevenson, ed. by the Editors of *Country Beautiful*. Preface by Lyndon B. Johnson, Intro. Stewart L. Udall, Afterword Hubert H. Humphrey (New York, 1965).

Martin, John Bartlow, *Adlai Stevenson* (New York, 1952).

Mathews, Juanita Brown, "Adlai E. Stevenson and Foreign Policy" (Master's thesis, University of Florida, 1954).

McCarthy, E. J., "The Nomination of Adlai E. Stevenson," *Representative American Speeches: 1960–1961*, Lester Thonssen, ed. (New York, 1961).

McCown, T. N., "A Comparison of the Logical Proof Used by Adlai E. Stevenson and Dwight D. Eisenhower in Selected Midwestern Campaign Speeches of 1952" (Master's thesis, University of Oklahoma, 1953).

McGrory, Mary, "Uneasy Politician: Adlai E. Stevenson," *Candidates 1960: Behind the Headlines in the Presidential Race*, Eric Sevareid, ed. and intro. (New York, 1960).

Morgenthau, H. J., "Stevenson, Tragedy and Greatness," *New Republic* (August 7, 1965), pp. 17–19.

Muller, Herbert J., *Adlai Stevenson: A Study in Values* (New York, 1967).

Mumford, Manley, "The Blunt Truth Technique: An Analysis of the Public Relations Approach Used by Adlai Stevenson in the 1952 Presidential Campaign and the Significance of the Technique for Other Public Relations Fields," *Public Relations Journal*, XXII (March, 1954), pp. 8–10.

Murphy, Richard, "Adlai Stevenson: Spokesman," *Today's Speech*, VIII (February, 1960), pp. 3–6.

———, "Stevenson and His Audience," *Today's Speech*, VIII (April, 1960), pp. 12–16.

Murray, Donald, "The Stevenson Campaign at the 1960 Democratic National Convention" (Master's thesis in progress, Brooklyn College of the City University of New York, 1967).

Neuberger, Richard L., "Adlai E. Stevenson: Last Chance," *Progressive*, XXIV (February, 1960), pp. 8–14.

Neustadt, Richard E., *Presidential Power* (New York, 1960).

Norton, Max C., "A Rhetorical Criticism of the Campaign Speeches of Adlai E. Stevenson" (Master's thesis, The College of the Pacific, 1955).

"Presidential Campaign 1960: a Symposium," Part I, *Quarterly Journal of Speech*, XLVI (October, 1960), pp. 243–244.

"Presidential Campaign 1960: A Symposium," Part II, *Quarterly Journal of Speech*, XLVI (December, 1960).

Prosser, Michael H., "Adlai E. Stevenson's Audience in the United Nations," *Central States Speech Journal* (November, 1965), pp. 262–271.

———, "Communication Problems in the United Nations," *Southern Speech Journal* (Winter, 1963), pp. 125–136.

———, "Ethical Proof in the 'Bay of Pigs' Debate in the United Nations," *Today's Speech* (April, 1966), pp. 21–23.

———, "A Rhetorical Analysis of the Speechmaking of Adlai E. Stevenson on Major Issues in the United Nations during the Fifteenth and Sixteenth Sessions of the General Assembly" (Ph.D. dissertation, University of Illinois 1964).

Rabinowitch, E., "Adlai E. Stevenson: 1900–1965," *Bulletin of Atomic Scientists* (September, 1965), p. 2.

Robinson, James, "The Political Speaking of Adlai Stevenson," *Bulletin of the Debating Association of Pennsylvania College* (December, 1956), pp. 11–15.

Roper, Elmo, *You and Your Leaders: Their Actions and Your Reactions* (New York, 1957).

Ross, Lillian, *Adlai Stevenson* (Philadelphia, 1966).

Rovere, R. H., "Adlai and the Intellectuals," *Speculum* (July 29, 1960), p. 172.

Rowse, Arthur Edward, *Slanted News: a Case Study of the Nixon and Stevenson Fund Stories*, Foreword by Erwin D. Conhan (Boston, 1957).

Schlesinger, A. M., and S. E. Harris, "Introduction," *New America*, by Adlai E. Stevenson (New York, 1957).

Schlesinger, Arthur M., Jr., "Stevenson and the American Liberal Dilemma," *Twentieth Century*, CLXIII (January, 1953), pp. 24–29.

———, *A Thousand Days: John F. Kennedy in the White House* (Boston, 1965).

Sevareid, A. E., "The Final Troubled Hours of Adlai Stevenson," *Best Magazine Articles: 1966*, Gerald Walker, ed. (New York, 1966), pp. 291–300.

Severn, Bill, *Adlai Stevenson—Citizen of the World* (New York, 1966).

Sidey, Hugh, *John F. Kennedy, President* (New York, 1964).

Sillars, Malcolm O., "An Analysis of Invention in the 1952 Presidential Campaign Addresses of Dwight D. Eisenhower and Adlai E. Stevenson" (Ph.D. dissertation, State University of Iowa 1956).

——, "The Promises of the Candidates," *The Antioch Review*, XVI (September, 1956), pp. 319–332.

Sorensen, Theodore C., *Kennedy* (New York, 1965).

Stanfield, Paul S., "An Analysis of Propaganda Themes in Speeches Delivered by Dwight D. Eisenhower, Adlai E. Stevenson, and Harry S Truman in the 1952 Campaign" (Master's thesis, University of Oregon 1953).

Steele, J. L., "Two Books by and About Stevenson," *New Republic*, CXXXVII (September 2, 1957), pp. 17–18.

Stelzner, Sara Lathem, "A Quantitative Analysis of Regional and Nationally Broadcast Speeches of Eisenhower and Stevenson in the 1952 Presidential Campaign" (Master's thesis, University of Illinois 1957).

The Stevenson Wit, Bill Adler, ed. (Garden City, New York, 1966).

The Stevenson Wit, Commentary by David Brinkley, RCA Victor Red Seal.

The Stevenson Wit and Wisdom, Paul Steiner, ed. (New York, 1965).

"Stevenson's Biography: Stands on Foreign and Domestic Policy," *Congressional Quarterly World Report*, XVIII (July 1, 1960), pp. 1147–1154.

"Stevenson's Policies, Stands Re-examined," *Congressional Quarterly World Report*, XIV (March 9, 1956), pp. 265–270.

Stone, Irving, *They Also Ran* (New York, 1966).

"The Talk of the Town," *The New Yorker* (December 14, 1963), pp. 47–49.

Votaw, Albert N., "How Liberal Is Adlai Stevenson? Though Liberals May Have Adopted the Former Illinois Governor, His Record Shows Him Preferring Administrative Reform to Social Experiment," *New Leader* (September 12, 1955), pp. 3–4.

Waithman, R., "New Note in American Politics," *Speculum* (September 19, 1952), p. 353.

Wechsler, James A., "The Brothers Alsop and Adlai Stevenson," *Progressive* (March, 1963), pp. 14–18.

——, "The Stevenson I Knew," *Progressive* (September, 1965), pp. 29–31.

White, Theodore, *The Making of the President, 1960* (New York, 1962).

Whitman, Alden and *The New York Times, Portrait: Adlai E. Stevenson: Politician, Diplomat, Friend* (New York, 1965).

Wilson, J. F., "Rhetorical Echoes of a Wilsonian Idea," *Quarterly Journal of Speech*, XLIII (October, 1957), pp. 271–277.

Windes, Russel R., Jr., "Adlai E. Stevenson's Speech Staff in the 1956 Campaign," *Quarterly Journal of Speech*, XLVI (February, 1960), pp. 32–43.

———, "The Speech-Making of Adlai E. Stevenson in the 1956 Campaign" (Ph.D. dissertation, Northwestern University 1959).

———, "A Study of Effective and Ineffective Presidential Campaign Speaking," *Speech Monographs*, XXVIII (March, 1961), pp. 39–50.

Windes, Russel R., Jr. and J. A. Robinson, "Public Address in the Career of Adlai E. Stevenson," *Quarterly Journal of Speech*, XLII (October, 1956), pp. 225–233.

The Wit and Wisdom of Adlai Stevenson, Compiled by Edward Hanna, Henry Hicks, and Ted Koppel (New York, 1965).

Yeager, Raymond, "Presidential Campaign 1960: A Symposium. Part I. Pre-Convention Speaking: Adlai E. Stevenson." *Quarterly Journal of Speech*. XLVI (October, 1960), pp. 243–244.

———, "A Rhetorical Analysis of the 1952 Presidential Campaign Speeches of Adlai Ewing Stevenson" (Ph.D. dissertation, Ohio State University 1957).

INDEX

DATE DUE

GAYLORD			PRINTED IN U.S.A.